SHADOW WARFARE

SHADOW WARFARE

THE HISTORY OF AMERICA'S UNDECLARED WARS

LARRY HANCOCK

with STUART WEXLER

COUNTERPOINT / BERKELEY, CALIFORNIA

Library of Congress Data Is Available

ISBN 978-1-61902-244-7

Cover design by Charles Brock, Faceout Studios
Interior design by Neuwirth & Associates, Inc.

Counterpoint Press
1919 Fifth Street
Berkeley, CA 94710
www.counterpointpress.com

Printed in the United States of America
Distributed by Publishers Group West

10 9 8 7 6 5 4 3 2 1

"If we, the CIA are going to try something like this again, we must be absolutely sure that the people and the Army [in the targeted country] want what we want. If not, you had better give the job to the Marines."

KERMIT ROOSEVELT JR.,
senior officer CIA Middle Eastern Division,
White House debriefing remarks on Iranian
coup/Operation Ajax, 1954

Contents

Introduction

Hot war and Cold War, covert operations and shadow warfare. Some of it public, some of it secret, and some of it very real but ostensibly "deniable."

The "hot" side of the Cold War was always in the news. In the 1950s the Korean conflict saw a large American military contingent deployed as part of a UN force to the Korean peninsula, to block the subjugation of a democratic south by the communist north. American combat personnel made up the vast majority of the 341,000-man UN force, a force coming from some twenty-one nations. And by the time of the final truce, American forces had suffered more than 125,000 dead and wounded in combat. There were reporters on the ground, combat photography in the newsreels, and the veterans returned to write extensively about their experiences in Korea.

Through the 1960s and into the 1970s, the Vietnam conflict was covered as another instance of communist territorial aggression, combat pitting the communist north against the anticommunist south——with the American fear that countries across Southeast Asia could begin falling to communism like dominoes. That combat was the first to be covered on the nightly television news and Americans watched that very hot war for almost a decade. Vietnam escalated to full-scale warfare including Army, Air Force, and naval deployments. The conflict lasted far longer than Korea, involving over half a million American personnel. Combat in and around Vietnam left far more than twice the American dead and wounded than that in Korea. Because the American effort in Vietnam ended in defeat and public embarrassment, it took longer for even individual combat stories to make it into print. Still, at the time, the "hot" side of the Cold War seemed easy enough to understand, win or lose—even if the complex ideological and political agendas in play required some years for a more accurate and penetrating historical analysis.

The "cold" side of the Cold War seemed equally visible, focused on nuclear confrontation with the Soviet Union; immediately following the Second Word War the U.S. Army Air Force prepared contingency plans for an atomic strike on the Soviets and ultimately, with both sides having nuclear arsenals, the strategy of "mutual assured destruction" (MAD) emerged.[1] It would be decades before Americans learned the actual number of atomic weapons involved in the nuclear confrontation. The knowledge of an inventory of over ten thousand atomic warheads in the U.S. stockpile alone would have been staggering. The public was also not generally aware that each year, beginning under President Eisenhower, a special subcommittee of the National Security Council briefed senior government officials on their evaluations of the likelihood of a Soviet preemptive atomic strike on America. On occasion those discussions also turned to the subject of the possible necessity of a preemptive American atomic attack on the Soviets.[2]

During most of the Cold War, secrets—military secrets—were not a bad thing; they were accepted as a fact of life. The country was only a few years out of a bloody world war and military security was engrained in the population. Still, there was lots of popular media coverage of the military. The Strategic Air Command (SAC) was omnipresent during the Cold War era. Books such as *SAC: The Strategic Air Command*, published as early as 1958, gave extensive details on the force including the numbers of both its personnel and its aircraft.[3] The level of SAC operations was indeed tremendous; in a random sample of sixty days in 1955, SAC had some 1,353 planes engaged on "war maneuvers." Every three minutes of every day, seven days a week, both day and night, a SAC aircraft was engaged in a midair refueling or aircraft accident. Accidents and crashes came with that level of preparedness and SAC's airmen suffered ongoing deaths and injuries, especially among bomber and tanker crews.[4]

The North American Air Defense Command[5] was another extremely visible—and comforting—element of the Cold War. Children became used to seeing NORAD track Santa Claus around the world on Christmas Eve; if NORAD could handle that, the American public assumed that the DEW (Distant Early Warning) Line, the Pine Tree Line, the Offshore Line, and eventually BMEWS (Ballistic Missile Early Warning System) and SPASUR (U.S. Naval Space Command Space Surveillance system) could track any incoming enemy aircraft or missiles. All of those organizations, systems, and related weapons were frequently and extensively described in the press, and in a host of constantly updated books.[6] The Air Force was also willing and eager to actively promote its atomic defensive capabilities. In 1957 a *U.S. News & World Report* interview with the Air Defense Command's chief, General Earle Partridge, discussed the use of atomic weapons in air defense—those atomic interceptor missiles would come to include warheads ranging from 1.5-kiloton missiles (launched from F-89 jet interceptors) to the 6.5-kiloton warhead (approximately half the size of the Hiroshima bomb) on high-altitude Bomarc antiaircraft missiles deployed around major American cities.

There certainly were Cold War secrets, matters not necessarily related to weapons development or defensive capabilities—and not shared with the press. SAC's first known nuclear weapons accident was in February 1950, when a B-36 bomber simulating a nuclear attack under artic conditions experienced mechanical problems and severe icing and was forced to ditch off the coast of British Columbia; its Mark IV nuclear bomb was jettisoned from eight thousand feet and reportedly the high explosives triggers detonated with no nuclear explosion. That accident was only the first of that year, with crashes in the Manzano Mountains east of Albuquerque (no damage to the weapons on board; the crash was following takeoff), the forced jettisoning of a nuclear bomb over the St. Lawrence River in Canada, and the crash during takeoff of a B-29 with an atomic weapon on board at an air base outside San Francisco. That aircraft was carrying weapons to be deployed in possible support of the Korean action and the crash not only killed twelve of the twenty crew members but also the following explosion of the bombs' conventional explosive triggers killed another seven people on the ground and produced significant radioactive contamination on the airfield.

In 1958 a fully armed B-47 caught fire on the runway at a SAC base in Morocco and produced a considerable amount of local contamination. In 1957, a nineteen-megaton hydrogen bomb was accidentally dropped in an uninhabited area near Albuquerque; the conventional explosives detonated, producing a twelve-foot-deep crater some twenty-five feet across; some radioactive contamination did result. Later years would see accidents in 1959, 1960, 1961, 1964, 1965, and 1968. As with the previous incidents, some contamination occurred, some bombs were recovered, some were not, and SAC servicemen lost their lives. Almost all these accidents received little or no press at the time and some were only revealed decades later.[7]

The American public also knew little of such military incidents over our and our allies' territory, including the closely held secrets of Air Force reconnaissance, conducted not only in international airspace and waters, but directly over Russia itself. In July 1960, *Time magazine* headlined the return of two Air Force servicemen who had survived after their RB-47 aircraft had been downed by a Russian fighter in international waters, over the Barents Sea, off Murmansk. Only two of the six-man crew survived, spending seven months in Lubyanka prison before being returned to America. The incident was tragic and definitely served to harden public opinion towards the Soviets.

But there was a good deal more to the overall picture of American aircraft around and over Soviet territory than made it into the *Time* article. Behind that single story were literally hundreds of signals of intelligence and reconnaissance missions flown by Air Force and Navy aircraft, not only around the borders of the Soviet Union, but for years, directly over Soviet territory, including major cities and military facilities. As early as 1954 a single RB-47 Stratojet had cruised directly over Murmansk, the largest city and major port in northwestern Russia, at forty thousand feet, on a photo intelligence mission targeting several key Soviet airfields. MIG fighters made a series of attacks against the American aircraft, which responded with fire from its own tail cannon. After surviving attacks by several MIG flights, the Stratojet finally took a hit into its wing and fuselage, causing serious damage and loss of fuel. The RB-47 managed to make its way back across Norway to its home field in England, but sounds of the air battle were heard in northern Finland and the report was even repeated in a U.S. newspaper—the Air Force responded by saying that it had no planes in that area.[8]

In 1956 a SAC aerial intelligence effort, Project Homerun, dramatically escalated flights over the Soviet Union. Some twenty-one RB-47's, supported by twenty-eight tankers, flew 156 missions over a route covering a 3,500-mile stretch of Soviet territory. In the final effort of that year, SAC flew a formation of six bombers over Soviet facilities in eastern Siberia with the Soviets totally unable to intercept them. The RB-47 formation took off from Thule, Greenland, and flew over the North Pole and across Soviet territory, landing at Eielson Air Force Base in Alaska.[9] SAC commander General Curtis LeMay had made a definite point to the Soviets: SAC was unstoppable.[10] [11]

America had Cold War military secrets and it had other secrets as well; it took decades for activities and incidents such as those above to emerge. This book is about another class of secrets that also have been revealed—the covert and clandestine warfare operations that not only occurred during the Cold War but continued after its end, into the current "War on Terror." That part of the Cold War, involving undeclared, covert, deniable warfare—organized by American intelligence officers but carried out by others—has been perhaps best and most bluntly characterized by a well-known military officer who personally participated in activities ranging from Vietnam and Laos to Iran and Nicaragua:

In a tactical sense, that's what the Cold War was about; the two major powers fencing, and taking their lumps, through proxies, with the local people picking up the tab, at least in terms of bloodshed."

—GENERAL RICHARD SECORD[12]

Covert warfare, as explored in this work, is not simply secret military action, "black operations," sabotage, "dirty tricks," or intelligence collection. On occasion it was something of a far greater magnitude, involving the commitment of large-scale American resources to secret military action against another country. Yet even on those occasions, the declared intention was that it had to be deniable—the actual combat was not to be carried out by identifiable American service members. Instead, surrogate fighters would be involved and as far as possible any American funding or involvement would be concealed or at a minimum obscured. The actual combat might be bloody, but the goal was to obtain results without visible American military involvement in the actual fighting.

We will be detailing the operational history of American involvement in shadow warfare, examining how surrogate actions have been authorized and practiced, the types and techniques of deniability (and their effectiveness), and the consequences of successive presidents' uses of the practice. We will also delve into a number of unanticipated consequences of these activities. Of course the practice of covert warfare was certainly not unique to the United States; and other powers including the Soviet Union, China, and Cuba were actively involved in such activities around the globe. In a number of instances, surrogates plus military advisors and even regular military units from America's Cold War opponents were mutually engaged in active combat—with active denial from all parties involved.

United States involvement in covert, surrogate warfare differed in one critical aspect—American deniability was not simply an artifice for foreign relations; it was equally important for domestic consumption. Time after time, the administrations involved chose covert over declared warfare—at times due to a lack of support by Congress and at other times due to a perceived lack of support from the general public. In numerous instances this led to a level of operational dysfunction unique to the American efforts, a problem not encountered in either Moscow or Havana.

We will find that the practice of deniability did work, at least to some extent, in several operations. In many other instances the complex and expensive practice of deniability seemed questionable even at the time—even to the covert operations professionals charged with making it happen.

> *"We're going to mount a secret operation in the Caribbean with tanks?"*
>
> —DAVID PHILLIPS, CIA Plans/Operations Directorate, commenting after his first briefing on what was to become the disastrous landing at the Bay of Pigs

Given that the Cuban exile force landed on the beach, coming off World War II–era landing craft, accompanied by a tank brigade carried in by tank landing craft and supported by parachute landings and both troop and transport aircraft, Phillips's concern can certainly be appreciated. That operation was arguably the least deniable and most disastrous in some forty years of American surrogate warfare. On the other hand, as late as 2001, we still find American CIA officers going into Afghanistan covertly, to organize attacks against Al-Qaeda after America itself had been attacked—yet in 2001, as in all the cold, hot, covert, and clandestine military actions in between, the United States Congress still had not formally declared a state of war.

But there were many other operations, many other surrogates, and for some of them, at the time, the denials generally worked. At least they worked domestically and politically. On other occasions the denials worked far better than the military operations themselves. This book is an exploration of America's conduct of surrogate warfare before, during, and after the Cold War. Readers will be introduced to the details of both the practice and tradecraft of shadow warfare—how to "cover elephants with handkerchiefs," as the covert operations saying goes. Not only operations and practices are explored but also a number of individual participants, both CIA and military—some involved with covert operations over three decades and three continents. But beyond the Cold War, and covert, deniable warfare, we continue by tracing the evolution of the next generation of American military action—a new and very different type of warfare dramatically accelerated by the global war against terror. Today's contemporary military and counterterrorism activities have become much less deniable, instead representing a combination of low-profile military assistance, clandestine operations, and extremely advanced intelligence and communications technologies. The story of the new generation of American military capabilities and contemporary activities conduct is one that actually started long before 2001 and the attacks of 9/11 on New York and Washington, D.C. We will explore that evolution in detail, through the most contemporary global events.

Shadow Warfare presents extensive detail on both the practices and tradecraft of covert operations, over some seventy years around the world. Covert operations in Latin America, Africa, Southwest Asia, Southeast Asia, the Middle East, and the Pacific are examined and profiled. Beyond that, you will find an exploration of the personalities and activities of a number of the individuals involved in those operations. However, the book's overall goal is even more ambitious, addressing both the character and concerns of the senior decision makers who made the determination to go to conventional military action, or to go covert and deniable. We will examine the legal and political context for their decisions as well as the concerns and risks that arose—including a host of unintended consequences and risks not only for the deciders but for the individuals receiving the marching orders. When national security appears to be on the line, it would seem that the most obvious solution would be to turn to conventional military action. The fundamental question would seem to be why American presidents consistently turned to covert solutions.

CHAPTER 1

From Solution to Illusion

The American government operates under a system of checks and balances. The executive, legislative, and judicial branches have their own defined roles and one of the significant responsibilities of Congress is to declare war if circumstances demand that the nation move to active military combat. As commander in chief, the American president directs the conduct of the wars declared by Congress. Given that general understanding, most Americans may not actually realize that the United States has not declared itself to be in a state of war since 1941. The American military fought and died during years of major conventional military action in Asia, ranging from Korea in the early 1950s to Vietnam throughout the 1960s and 1970s. We even call those the Korean and Vietnam "wars." Later there were major American military engagements in the Arabian peninsula, the invasion of Iraq, and years of ongoing combat deployments in Afghanistan. None of that combat occurred with a formal congressional declaration of war. In between those undeclared, conventional wars there were literally dozens of "shadow wars," with their own engagements, combat, and casualties—each directed under the authority of the president as commander in chief and none declared as wars by Congress.

In reality there are a number of alternatives to the formal declaration of war, all of which lead to military action. In profiling "shadow warfare," our first challenge will be to examine how the system really works. We will consider to what extent the checks and balances concept applies to presidential decisions to initiate or approve covert operations and how America enters into military action with its own personnel or with surrogate forces—without congressional declarations of war. In doing so we will pay particular attention to why virtually every president has turned to covert, deniable warfare as a solution for international problems.

More than one president has ordered deniable military operations strictly on his own initiative. More than one president has suffered extreme political and public censure for covert actions. Still, such operations have continued for decades, varying only in frequency and duration. In overt conventional warfare Congress is asked to either declare war or at least pass resolutions endorsing some level of military action. No such legislation is required for presidential directives ordering covert actions; in fact, it was not until the 1970s that Congress passed legislation mandating presidential "findings" that at least would notify select members of Congress that such operations were going to be conducted—or were already in progress. Given the uncertainty of shadow warfare and its huge political risk, we will also address the question of why virtually every president makes the personal decision to choose it as a solution, oftentimes deciding to essentially go it alone.

We must look to the past and to the evolution of warfare itself to understand the development of undeclared warfare and covert operations—concepts generally foreign to the Founding Fathers and to combat in the early years of the American republic. Under the Constitution of 1787, Revolutionary War veteran Alexander Hamilton justified the creation of a unitary executive—the president—in large part on the belief that having a single commander was necessary to protect the United States in an efficient and decisive manner during war and times of emergency.[13] Hamilton, one of General George Washington's chief advisors during the Revolutionary War, argued that, in contrast to a triumvirate or other forms of leadership, a presidency with one "energetic" executive could make the decisive, efficient, and coherent choices required by the exigencies of war. Yet Hamilton's cohort James Madison recognized the need to circumscribe such power through a system of democratic checks and balances, lest war become a justification for tyranny.[14] Therefore under the Constitution, Congress declares war and the president, as commander in chief, "prosecutes" or "directs" the conflict. With the industrialization of warfare and the emergence of totally new forms of weapons, the president's role became further emphasized. New weapons and technology not only changed the nature of combat itself, but posed unique challenges to the decision to engage in warfare.

During World War II, America was extremely fortunate to have the time needed to mobilize and deploy a modernized military force. But post–World War II missile and rocket technology severely limited the reaction time for America's military commanders. The risk of "first strike" nuclear warfare only amplified the dilemma. This threat of instant warfare grew to become a justifiable reason for the creation of intelligence agencies such as the Central Intelligence Agency in 1947 and the National Security Agency in 1952. Those organizations were created with the intent to identify threats *before* they materialized. Weapons innovations also catalyzed the centralization of America's military forces and assets under the "national command authority" of the president and secretary of defense. Only they could give orders to the Joint Chiefs and the Pentagon to move the United States to immediate combat readiness in defense of the nation—and only they could order the launch of atomic strikes.[15]

More than anything, the exigencies of modern warfare placed an even greater premium on Hamilton's original goals of efficiency and decisiveness in command. In a world with no more than fifteen minutes' notification of an impending atomic attack, Hamilton's issue of decisiveness had assumed an overwhelming importance. There is no doubt that compression of decision time in the twentieth century contributed to the shift of discretion to the president, in his role as commander in chief of the American military. Congress has, at times, attempted to reassert its control over military affairs yet the demand for *immediate* response to crises has left the initiative with the president. And, as will be discussed in a later chapter, and demonstrated in the shadow wars profiled throughout this book, while lawmakers tend to complain about a lack of respect by the president for congressional oversight, exemplified by vague or nonexistent notification and guidance about covert operations, the lack of presidential accountability actually has the potential to work in favor politically for members of Congress.

It is significant to note that the United States Congress has not officially declared war since 1941, but that hasn't stopped America from fighting full-scale conventional actions and conducting long-term covert operations. By allowing the president to be left "holding the bag" for military commitments, elected representatives can avoid negative publicity surrounding failed operations. This works both ways, as lawmakers can be blamed for votes in favor of unpopular wars (as in the case of the Vietnam War) or for failing to vote in favor of successful wars (as was the case in the first Iraq War). Avoiding a vote altogether provides political advantages, especially in the case of covert warfare—which by its very nature becomes public only when it fails, sometimes dramatically.

As far back in American history as the early eighteenth-century predations of the Barbary pirates against American commercial ships, the congressional view has held that presidents are free to act in the defense of the nation. Facing ongoing attacks on America's ships and kidnapping of American sailors, Congress considered the need to declare war against the pirates. Alexander Hamilton argued that while a formal congressional declaration of war was required to *initiate* a war, the circumstances in question involved ongoing attacks on American interests. Thus, Hamilton argued, America was *already in a state of war initiated by the pirates*, and a president did not need any formal inspiration from Congress to engage the enemy and defend the country's interests. Congress seems to have accepted that proposition, as no resolution was put forth and President Thomas Jefferson did send the U.S. Navy after the Barbary pirates in North Africa.

The overt military actions since 1941, however, have most often carried the endorsement of some type of congressional joint resolution. Passed by majority votes from both chambers of Congress and signed by the president, the resolutions have the effect of law. But unlike a declaration of war, they are often broadly constructed, providing lawmakers with less detailed accountability for military actions and allowing the president much broader discretion. Still, even with joint resolutions, the court of public opinion indirectly imposes limits on overt wars, as it did with the protests against the "Vietnam War." In a broad sense, the exposure to such popular opinion may have reinforced the temptation to engage in less public military operations, namely covert wars fought via surrogate combatants.

A considerable amount of current media dialogue on covert action and secret warfare appears to take the view that such actions are either fundamentally illegal or at least legally questionable. However, since 1947, all American presidents have taken such action based on provisions in the National Security Act of 1947, which describe and sanction the activities of the Central Intelligence Agency. Based on that act and the U.S. legal code that embodies its provisions, secret warfare actions have been authorized by a succession of presidents over some seven decades. The language of this legislation has been interpreted to mean that the president does not need additional congressional action for such actions. Indeed in the early decades of the Cold War, the interpretation was that the president was not even under any specific legal requirement to inform Congress about such actions in order to ensure maximum operational security and deniability. In some instances presidents did communicate with key congressional leaders; in others they did not. While issues and questions have been raised as to what exactly constitutes covert operations, until this point in time the constitutionality of the National Security Act has not been challenged, much less ruled on by the Supreme Court—leaving it as standing legal justification for presidential covert action.

Even so, it is also clear that individual activities conducted during those operations are still open to arguments of legality. Early in the Cold War years, President Dwight Eisenhower was concerned about defining his parameters as commander in chief. In effect, a five-star general such as Eisenhower was still uncertain of what the president's constitutional and legal options were in regard to both conventional and covert military action. This led Eisenhower to ask the Justice Department to explore the legality of his desire to dispatch the military into potential combat operations, *without* a formal congressional declaration of war, on his own authority as commander in chief. Justice responded with an opinion as to what a president, as commander in chief, can do outside the country without a declaration of war from Congress.

As it happened, a body of legal precedent had recently developed in regard to unilateral presidential behavior in foreign affairs. Several Supreme Court cases related to the issue of executive agreements—agreements between a president and a foreign country that do not require the constitutionally prescribed threshold of ratification by two-thirds of the Senate. Scholar Vikki Gordon noted that these cases "collectively established the president's authority to issue directives involving 'external affairs.'"

In keeping with this established line of thinking, Eisenhower's Justice Department provided him with an opinion about the president's unilateral authority on military commitments. It provided him with several scenarios under which a president could commit military resources to a mission with limited or no congressional approval:

1. In a "state of emergency," the president can commit troops to conventional combat based on a resolution of approval by Congress.

2. If the U.S. military is not personally going into combat or into a live combat zone, the president can approve military assistance to "friendly" governments as a matter of routine international relations. So, while the president cannot just say, "Go ahead, guys! Go get 'em!" he can send troops in for military assistance. And in the case of Indochina, that's what Eisenhower did.

3. Finally, and most relevant to a discussion of the legality of covert warfare, it provided a third allowance: self-defense. The president was seen as justified in commanding the deployed military personnel to defend themselves. Given the multiple ways a president can interpret "self-defense," this becomes an important legal underpinning for the future of covert wars. That general advice provided to Eisenhower by the Justice Department set the context for everything a president can do today. It is, in its simplest form:

If a president wants to send the military into hostilities, Congress needs to pass a resolution that says the president can go ahead and enter combat. If a president wants to act preemptively, in self-defense of the nation or its military personnel, or in providing military assistance to its allies, he can do so without a Congressional resolution.

Following this guidance, Eisenhower and his successors have routinely dispatched American military personnel overseas under the umbrella of "military assistance," in training, advisory, and aid program evaluation roles. In addition, President Eisenhower established a basic practice in deciding between overt and covert warfare. On several occasions, the Eisenhower Administration approached Congress in regard to potential military interventions that it viewed as necessary. In instances when Congress was receptive and passed resolutions to support military deployment (the Taiwan Strait in 1955; the Middle East in 1957), combat resources were openly dispatched. When Congress balked, however, Eisenhower limited the American military role to "non-combat support and logistics assistance" (Indochina in 1954). But when it came to sensitive international or domestic political situations, Eisenhower turned covert, enlisting the operational resources of the Central Intelligence Agency. As initially implemented during the Eisenhower Administration, the context and guidelines for the practice of deniable warfare also became relatively consistent, driven by the language in the National Security Act and the legal code supporting it.[16] In essence, as interpreted by presidents from Harry Truman through Barack Obama, the National Security Act of 1947 said that in regard to covert operations:

1. The U.S. government was not to be officially on record as being in a state of war.

2. No public congressional authorization or declaration was required and all necessary activities were authorized under presidential direction, in the president's role as commander in chief.

3. Covert action was allowed to be preemptive; the nation was not required to wait to be physically attacked. The president would make the decision to turn to covert, deniable warfare in the interests of national security.

Successive presidents applied the same basic practices, and continued to accept the fundamental precept that in self-defense, preemption is a legitimate reason for covert action. It should also be noted that the provisions of the National Security Act and the concept of preemptive action were so well established that multiple presidents, including Dwight Eisenhower, Bill Clinton, and George W. Bush, all initiated projects intended to assassinate targeted individuals including Patrice Lumumba, Osama bin Laden, and Saddam Hussein.

We will see that the president's decision has occasionally been unilateral, but more frequently has been supported by the participation and policy of a highly select body convened to deal with national security issues. Late in 1947, President Truman formalized such a body, describing it as "a channel for collective advice and communication." Truman initially designated the group the National Security Council, which was comprised of the vice president, secretary of state, secretary of defense, and other members as designated by the president.[17] Yet even in Truman's first characterization, he made clear that the council's role was strictly advisory, asserting that the ultimate decision was the president's alone. "With complete freedom to accept, reject, and amend the Council's advice . . . it is the prerogative of the President to determine such policy and enforce it."

In 1948, the Office of Policy Coordination (OPC) was established to conduct both psychological and paramilitary activities. In 1951 the OPC was merged with the CIA, and in 1952 its functions were assumed by the CIA's Directorate of Plans. In 1973, the Directorate of Plans was renamed the Directorate of Operations and as of this writing the organization is designated the National Clandestine Service. Truman's primary objective in setting up the new Cold War–era national security organizations had not been specifically to pursue covert operations, including deniable warfare. But the advent of full-scale warfare in Korea in 1950 proved a huge stimulus for such activities.

The escalation in demand for covert military and psychological warfare operations during the Korean conflict was so significant that CIA Director Walter Bedell Smith asked the National Security Council for direction on the limits of the CIA's scope of operations. The NSC provided no itemized response but based on a growing belief in the importance of psychological conditioning and its impact on warfare, in 1951 President Truman authorized the creation of an additional entity, chartered with focusing on that area—the Psychological Strategy Board (PSB). The PSB's primary function was to assist in the planning and coordination of psychological warfare activities. The PSB initially supported the activities of the Office of Policy Coordination, and its senior members included the deputy secretary of defense, the undersecretary of state, and the director of central intelligence. With the merger of the OPC into the Central Intelligence Agency in 1951, the OPC began to coordinate its work with the CIA.

President Truman also issued a presidential directive (NSC 20/5), which reaffirmed the presidential mandate for covert action and assigned the CIA further authority over guerrilla warfare. According to the State Department's historical studies conducted at the end of the Truman Administration, the CIA was at its peak of independence in terms of covert action: "no group or officer outside of the DCI [director of central intelligence] and the President himself had the authority to order, approve, manage, or curtail operations."[18] At that point in time Congress exercised no control or oversight over covert activities. Such operations were frequently funded from presidential discretionary and military accounts, a practice that would continue in future presidencies. As the Truman Administration ended, the CIA was escalating in independence and authority in the field of covert operations, which would peak during the Eisenhower Administration. The composition and function of the statutory advisory group for both conventional and covert operations (the National Security Council) evolved and morphed under successive presidents. The evolution of the NSC is extensively detailed by historian John Prados in his book *Keepers of the Keys*.[19] Eisenhower continued the NSC much as Truman had created it, by clearly retaining the sole decision-making power Truman had described.

In 1958, after a relatively brief dialogue with select NSC principals and limited questioning of Chairman of the Joint Chiefs of Staff Nathan Twining and Secretary of State John Foster Dulles, President Eisenhower ordered a major American military intervention in Lebanon dubbed Operation Blue Bat. It deployed seventy-seven American warships, four Marine brigades, and a reinforced Army airborne brigade.[20] Prados writes that almost all Eisenhower's decision making had occurred without consulting the National Security Council and that the decision to deploy had taken less than an hour.[21]

During his administration, President Eisenhower did generally use the National Security Council in the capacity of advisors, a practice he inherited from Truman. Eisenhower seems to have relied primarily on NSC board meeting minutes as a topical record, while personally issuing verbal instructions to the CIA director or appropriate military commanders for national security actions. Based on those instructions, the CIA or appropriate military command created specific operational plans to implement the presidential direction. Succeeding Eisenhower, President John F. Kennedy met extensively with NSC members early in his administration but the number of such meetings declined significantly during the following two years. Later Kennedy, more personally comfortable with extended dialogue and give-and-take among a smaller group, assembled the Executive Committee of the National Security Council (EXCOMM). EXCOMM met extensively during the Cuban Missile Crisis. Kennedy formalized the group on October 22, 1962, with National Security Action Memorandum (NSAM) 196.

Presidents from Truman on have generally issued written national security–related guidelines for studies, policy, and actions. To some extent those guidelines define the overall administration—in some respects even the designations the presidents choose to use reflect something of their attitudes towards national security. In line with his formation of the NSC, Truman designated them as "National Security Council intelligence directives," Kennedy as "national security action memorandums," Richard Nixon as "national security decision memorandums," and Jimmy Carter as simply "presidential directives." Ronald Reagan issued both "national security study" and "national security decision" directives. President Obama has issued "Presidential Study" and "Presidential Policy" directives.

Scholar Philip Cooper quoted President Lyndon Johnson's description of his National Security Action Memorandum as being a formal notification to the head of a department or other government agency informing him of a presidential decision in national security affairs, generally requiring follow-up action by the department or agency addressed. Comparing them to another widely used "tool" of unilateral presidential behavior—the executive order—Cooper noted that both presidential security directives and executive orders allow a president to bypass Congress and control the specific behavior of many bureaucratic agencies within the purview of the executive branch, most relevantly the CIA and the military. But while they are similar to executive orders, national security directives "are not defined as such and therefore are not covered by the Federal Register Act." This means not only that they (like executive orders) bypass Congress, but that the "vast majority are classified" from public and congressional review. As time went on, certain congressional figures gained access to these directives, or to "presidential findings" that describe the contours of covert operations. But to presidents who wanted to engage in covert activity with little or no scrutiny from Congress or from the public, national security directives became, according to Cooper, "increasingly attractive tools" for the commander in chief.

Such directives address a broad range of concerns—from national security organizational and operational issues to more specific concerns—and range from classified executive orders to fully classified directives. President Reagan's NSDD-84 dealt with "Safeguarding National Security Information" while NSDD-17 was more operationally oriented, dealing with Cuba and Latin America. Directives also order very specific covert warfare actions—authorizing full-scale covert political action, paramilitary operations, or surrogate warfare operations.

Experts on presidential power, such as William Howell, place national security directives within the broader range of presidential prerogatives that allow the chief executive to exert unilateral power outside the scope of the normal system of checks and balances, such as executive orders and executive agreements. It is worth noting for context as we move forward that Howell is among an increasingly vocal group of scholars who argue that such prerogatives are now ubiquitous for American presidents both in domestic and foreign affairs. Most political scientists recognize that as the central government has become more complex since Franklin Roosevelt's administration, Congress has deferred to the executive branch not only on matters of national security, but in domestic affairs. For the past seven decades, there has been a noticeable increase in the willingness of presidents to use executive orders, executive agreements, and other prerogatives to direct policy in what some historians have referred to as the "imperial presidency." Presidential directives may simply be one manifestation of this growing authority. They may be kept secret for unspecified periods, but to the extent that they do become public, they represent a critical window into covert operations. Formal directives have been issued by presidents for many of the major covert operations that we will explore in detail in the following chapters. Sometimes they are very specific, such as the directive ordering the creation of a specific program of covert action against Cuba during the Kennedy Administration; in other instances they can be as broad as simply referencing the initiation of a new operation by Henry Kissinger during the Nixon Administration, to block communist revolutionary action in Africa.

There have been several instances in which the presidential directives have been even more open-ended, or simply vague—intentionally or not. On at least one occasion, an operation to assassinate a foreign leader (Patrice Lumumba, prime minister of the Republic of Congo) was initiated by CIA Director Allen Dulles based on Eisenhower's general remark that Lumumba had to be eliminated.[22] When President Eisenhower issued a directive to oust the elected but leftist-leaning Árbenz regime in Guatemala, it was with a broad directional statement only. There were no restrictions, funding was open-ended, and the goal was definitive.

One example from the 1970s involves America's covert effort in Angola, which was aimed at preventing the Angola civil war from shifting the Southwest African country in a procommunist direction. According to CIA officer John Stockwell, assigned as chief of the Angola Task Force in 1975, the Angola proxy warfare project was initiated with a very general "presidential finding" issued by President Gerald Ford. Stockwell describes the congressional notification as stating that the effort was "important to the national security of the United States," and noted that it did not even specify the country in question, merely the continent of Africa.[23]

Stockwell's CIA superior informed him that the president had submitted the "finding" to the Senate and that the appropriate committees had been briefed by CIA Director Colby. Stockwell was also told that the Covert Operations Review Committee had allocated $14 million to the effort, with the direction of the Angola Task Force being to "prevent an easy victory by Soviet-backed forces in Angola." Reportedly Secretary of State Henry Kissinger wanted the

Soviet surrogates in Angola stopped but felt that he would not be able to get the funding for a full-scale effort passed by Congress. The compromise was a much less expensive operation, aimed at simply creating a program of paramilitary harassment.[24]

In our examination of covert warfare against Nicaragua, which involved the scandal generally known as the Iran–Contra Affair, we will see that the initial presidential "finding" submitted to Congress discussed only "interdiction" of Nicaraguan arms shipments to El Salvador. The "finding" defined a limited operation quite different from the military activities that actually followed. A study of Nicaraguan operations also reveals that "deniability" in covert operations is not an issue strictly of operational security but more often a matter of dealing with incongruence between official government public position and actual government covert practice. If that sounds a bit conflicted, it is. By the end of the surrogate warfare in Nicaragua, three senior CIA officers would be indicted for giving false testimony to Congress. Charges were also brought against a number of other administration officials and staff. Yet even in such matters, the president has one final option—an option beyond congressional checks and balances—the presidential pardon. On Christmas Eve 1992, President George H.W. Bush issued a presidential pardon for virtually all those who had faced the legal consequences of the Reagan-era Iran–Contra Affair.

As a result of the Iran–Contra scandal, the political conflict over covert warfare took on a legal dimension with limitations imposed by Congress. It also introduced the issue of supporting a covert operation through secret agreements with a publicly identified enemy. In that case the enemy was Iran, which at the time of the Nicaraguan operations openly opposed the United States and held American hostages. The public outrage over the Reagan Administration's dealings with Iran illustrates the extent to which exposure and the weight of public opinion can bring serious political consequences to a presidential decision to choose covert solutions to international problems.

During the Cold War, concerns over public opinion extended not only to domestic but to foreign audiences. America was continuously fighting an image battle, hoping to convince neutral nations to embrace liberal democracy instead of Soviet-style communism. Yet a foundation of Soviet counterpropaganda was to charge that America was expanding its influence overseas to exploit other nations economically. Any overt U.S. military activity played directly into these charges. That was especially true in Latin America, the scene of prior, highly visible American military interventions over almost a century. Yet any shift toward a socialist or communist regime quickly brought congressional calls for presidents to act. Presidents recognized that they had to "thread the needle" between stopping the spread of Soviet influence while not appearing to be the very Yankee imperialists the Soviets were warning the world about. With communism infiltrating Latin America, and anti-American propaganda being spread by the Soviets, it's no wonder Latin America would become the scene of American covert operations for close to four decades.

Shortly after his popular election in 1950, U.S. policy makers began to view Guatemalan President Jacobo Árbenz and his government with considerable concern. By 1952 they were seriously worried that growing communist influence over Árbenz might offer a foothold for Soviet influence within Latin America. Perhaps equally important, Árbenz's agrarian reform polices had begun to damage U.S. business interests in the country, especially those of the United Fruit Company—a business with considerable influence within the U.S. government, all the way up the chain to President Eisenhower. Of course there was really nothing all that new in the consideration of commercial concerns. America began as a commercial republic and one of its earliest foreign military actions (against the Barbary pirates on the coast of North Africa) had been motivated in large part by their impact on America's rapidly growing international trade.

In general, CIA and intelligence community analysis supported the view that the Árbenz regime was falling more under communist influence, a view strongly supported by then–CIA Director Walter Bedell Smith. Internal CIA dialogue began to call for a sanctioned but covert support program to assist the anticommunist elements in the country (the Catholic Church hierarchy, landowners, and business interests, as well as certain university groups and the army) in a move against the Árbenz government. President Truman took the concern seriously and authorized the exploration of options to oust the Árbenz regime. Later he gave approval to launch the first CIA effort against the Guatemalan regime.

President Eisenhower, having just ended one conventional war in Korea, and having promised to reduce the U.S. budget, inherited the initial regime change effort—which he preferred to launching a conventional military effort against Árbenz. In addition, the U.S. maintained a position of noninterference in others nations' political affairs and certainly had no wish to draw new public criticism over American imperialism in Latin America.

Still, Eisenhower was politically sensitive to the ongoing and strident calls for action coming from Congress. In public sessions, the U.S. Congress discussed a resolution proposed by Senator Lyndon Johnson that was intended to serve as "an unmistakable warning that we are determined to keep Communism out of the Western Hemisphere." congressional rhetoric was hotly inflammatory, with Representative Jack Brooks of Texas endorsing the resolution as "so basically American and so basically anti-Communist" that support for it was urgent. The whole situation was a challenge to the Monroe Doctrine of 1823, which held that any European interference with the nations of North or South America would be viewed as an act of aggression and would demand intervention by the United States. Soviet support of communist expansion within Latin America was to be treated as such interference and there could be no question of an aggressive response.[25]

In a study titled "Congress, the CIA, and Guatemala, 1954—Sterilizing a 'Red Infection,'" David Barrett presents the proposition that Congress and the American press were both aware and quite supportive of American intervention in Guatemala. Even operating "deniably," the CIA certainly was acting not only under a presidential directive but in accordance with congressional encouragement and extensive popular support. And none of the congressional resolutions had addressed specific tactics; they adamantly demanded that the administration do whatever it took to "stop the commies."

In that ongoing, passionate political environment, Eisenhower turned to the CIA and launched an even more significant covert operation beginning in 1954, using surrogate troops, "mercenary" air support, intense psychological warfare, and threat of political assassinations. Ultimately the project was even supported with the deployment of an American naval force off Guatemala and the implementation of a naval blockade. This second phase of the secret war against Guatemala was designated PBSUCCESS and it did indeed succeed. PBSUCCESS was lauded by Eisenhower and did a great deal to validate the concept of deniable Cold War surrogate warfare, up to and including regime change in foreign governments.

Early in this chapter we discussed issues of legality and authorization in regard to covert action. But beyond those issues, a host of other concerns arise, including questions of whether or not the risks of collateral damage involved in such shadow warfare are truly justified, whether the concept of deniability actually works, and what other unanticipated consequences may come from such practices. Many countries that were the subjects of American covert intervention during the Cold War suffered horrendous internal political conflict and ongoing civil war in subsequent years, even decades after. In some cases additional bloodshed was brought about by regimes that were put in place or supported by American action, in other instances the same sort of thing happened in countries in which American intervention had failed.

From one perspective, the interventions can to be judged simply in terms of whether or not they accomplished the goals of the presidents who directed them. Often the action is also an attempt to deal with political pressure for assertive national security action, which can be an overriding concern for virtually any president and any administration—whether the pressure is from the president's ideological base or a challenge from the opposing party. The president can decide to act overtly or covertly, but some action must be taken—inaction is simply not acceptable. The decision between overt and covert involves many elements, but presidential personality and character are major factors. A related and pragmatic concern also seems to be whether presidents intend to run for reelection and how soon the next campaign commences. We will find that such political concerns have frequently led presidents (and their key advisors) to decisions that counter the best advice from their military staff, the State Department, or even the intelligence community.

As discussed above, the classic and normative system of checks and balances often fails to apply to covert action. Once the slide down the slippery slope of shadow warfare begins, consideration of "imminent threats," "national security," public opinion, political interests, and, on occasion, even international business interests all play a part in ongoing decisions. But in addition to all of those, presidential "personality" and character are evergreen.

CHAPTER 2

The Personality of Covert Action

Without a doubt, the presidency attracts certain types of individuals, and political scientists have long recognized that personality types orient people to political opportunities both foreign and domestic. For the purposes of the book, we reference the personality typology put forth by political scientist James David Barber, who, in his book *The Presidential Character: Predicting Performance in the White House,* identified four presidential personality types that characterize the presidents whose decisions we explore in this book. Barber found that presidents' levels of assertiveness and internal disposition predictably determine their real-world behavior.

1. *Active-positive:* Adaptive while in office, flexible in their approaches, active-positive personalities create opportunities for presidential action. Examples include Franklin D. Roosevelt, Harry S. Truman, John F. Kennedy, Gerald Ford, Jimmy Carter, George H.W. Bush, and Bill Clinton. By and large these personalities tend to engage in covert action as a means of asserting their energy in foreign affairs. Sometimes this takes the form of risk-taking that can border on recklessness. Yet, generally speaking, active-positive presidents also tend to learn from their mistakes.

2. *Active-negative:* With a tendency toward compulsion in their activity, active-negative personalities are rigid, highly driven, and obsessed with failure or success. Examples include Lyndon Johnson and Richard Nixon. The personalities show a tendency to "double down" on covert actions. That can be advantageous when it is necessary to overcome obstacles. Unfortunately, it is often the nature of covert warfare that dynamic circumstances, outside the control of even the president of the United States, create unanticipated yet major roadblocks to a successful mission. In those instances, active-negative presidents may not simply continue a failed mission; they may well exacerbate what some consider to be the worst, if sometimes unintended, features of covert war—human rights abuses and illegal side ventures.

3. *Passive-positive:* These personalities tend to be "compliant" in their presidential behavior; they may be manipulated by those they trust, and are often reactive rather than proactive. Ronald Reagan is the primary modern example. While Reagan was passionate about the presidency, even in the face of an attempt on his life he delegated a considerable amount of both policy making and management to subordinates, especially in regard to his administration's covert warfare operations.

4. *Passive-negative:* Motivated by a strong sense of duty, passive-negative personalities prefer to set procedures and routines to the usual business of politics, which they often disdain. The only clear-cut passive-negative president is President Dwight Eisenhower, who epitomized someone who serves out of a sense of duty, but who also disdained the accepted give-and-take of politics. Intuition might suggest that any passive president would avoid covert action, for the opposite reasons that an active president pursues it. However, covert action requires less political and public action on the part of a president; covert operations do not have to be "sold" to the public and in

the first three decades of the Cold War, they didn't even need to be "sold" to Congress.

While the sample size is small and must take into account political pressures and institutional arrangements, through understanding of these personality types we can see a pattern emerge. All of these presidential personality types are no more or less likely to pursue covert warfare to begin with. However, some (for example, passive-negatives) are much more inclined to continue operations even when the facts on the ground suggest failure.[26] The president is generally not alone in reaching the decision of commencing covert warfare. There are groups as well as official and unofficial advisors involved in that process. But presidential personality affects to what extent the advice has impact, and in some instances to what extent the president turns over the operation to those same advisors.

All presidents consistently face the challenge of looking strong on national defense and national security. For example, Lyndon Johnson assumed an aggressive position on national security (a position consistent with his voting record in the Senate), while promoting his liberal positions on civil rights. He could not be seen as weak on national security issues if he was to aggressively pursue his liberal policy agendas, including the Voting Rights Act and social programs associated with his election campaign for a "war on poverty." The Johnson Administration's "Great Society" initiative established programs ranging from Medicare and Head Start to the Economic Opportunity and Housing and Urban Development acts. Johnson was well aware that his programs could play to the charges of "bleeding heart liberalism," which were just starting to be promoted by his conservative opposition. To pass his social legislation programs, Johnson had to play a supreme balancing act, one that led him to react aggressively to events such as the reported exchanges of fire between American destroyers and North Vietnamese patrol boats in the Gulf of Tonkin during 1964, and possible communist involvement in the Dominican Republic in 1965. Johnson's personality actually amplified the political pressure to take aggressive foreign policy action. Presidential historians describe Johnson as a man consumed with the notion of outdoing his opponents. Journalist Nicholas Lemann observed that Johnson "wanted to set world records in politics, as a star athlete would in sports." As with many great athletes, this was as much, if not more, about never wanting to lose as it was about wanting to win. Johnson famously bullied and cajoled lawmakers to support his policies on an ongoing basis, to the point that it was labeled "the Johnson treatment."[27] Johnson's tenacity and political skills made it possible for him to pass his Great Society legislation, which fueled an immense desire to demonstrate that he could also win overseas.

On the international scene, Johnson was politically exposed to Republican political pressure on the issue of the Vietnam conflict. He needed to present a strong image for the upcoming presidential election of 1964. When provided with the initial information on the second apparent attack on an American destroyer by the North Vietnamese in the Tonkin Gulf, it appears that Johnson chose military escalation with no discussion. According to Assistant Secretary of State William P. Bundy, even when conflicting information began to appear from pilots and others in command on the scene, Johnson was "in no mood for discussion."[28] And with his political instincts running true, Johnson's action neutralized Vietnam as an issue and significantly bumped his Harris Poll numbers against Barry Goldwater.

Johnson used the congressional Gulf of Tonkin Resolution[29], which allowed American military forces in Southeast Asia to defend themselves against aggression, as authority for all American military combat in Vietnam.[30] In 1965, Johnson again used preliminary remarks made by the newly appointed and inexperienced CIA Director, Admiral William Raborn (who had been on the job for approximately fourteen hours), which seemed to support possible communist involvement in the Dominican coup, to begin a media campaign opposing a purported Cuban/communist revolution in the Dominican Republic.[31] Almost immediately he began referring to the "Johnson Doctrine," which would not allow such takeovers under his watch. Unfortunately for the president, within days the media questioned Johnson about the issue and about the CIA's new (more detailed) information contradicting that the revolt was Cuban/communist inspired or led. The initial CIA lists of purported communists involved in the coup proved to be ill-founded at best. A military history study of the entire Dominican Republic intervention (designated Operation Power Pack) describes the CIA's initial roster of communist involvement as containing so many errors (duplicate names, dead persons, people not in the country or in jail) that it helped fuel a groundswell of domestic and international protest against U.S. intervention.[32]

In spite of a revised CIA position, Johnson continued to argue his stance that there was a communist threat in briefings to Congress, and sent the full 82nd Airborne Division to the Dominican Republic.[33] Senior CIA officer David Phillips, who was immediately assigned to the crisis and was later sent to the island as the new CIA chief of station, wrote that the communists had absolutely nothing to do with the original revolt, but did attempt to involve themselves as the conflict continued. They were actually assisted in that effort by a general spike in anti-American sentiment and antagonism towards the United States due to Johnson's decision to send in the full 82nd Airborne Division. The U.S. had occupied the Dominican Republic from 1916 through 1924, so the arrival of the 82nd to evacuate U.S. citizens appeared to be another U.S. occupation. To Phillips's surprise and dismay, Johnson also sent a large force of FBI agents, relying on FBI Director J. Edgar Hoover's warning that communists might try to take over any new government. One of the first results of the FBI deployment was compromising the CIA's own agents within the local Dominican Communist Party.[34] In addition, to obtain his own intelligence, Johnson dispatched his longtime personal attorney and advisor Abe Fortas to the Dominican Republic to report on the situation. Later, Johnson ordered the State Department to write a white paper defending the intervention. John Prados later summarized the affair when he wrote, "The NSC had tried to warn its boss, but he had not been willing to listen."[35]

In the context of the long-term impact of Johnson's decisions, the Dominican intervention created a credibility issue for America. The U.S. had declared its total neutrality, yet it was obvious to all that it was picking the group that would be placed in power in the Dominican Republic. One historical study asserts that it was the Dominican intervention, not the Vietnam War, that widened the credibility gap that would plague Johnson and future presidents. The study also cites Johnson's and Secretary of Defense Robert McNamara's "over-control and over-management" of Dominican military activities, including overly stringent rules of engagement that "made no sense."[36] Such complaints would routinely surface during both the Johnson and Nixon administrations' military involvement in Southeast Asia.

Lyndon Johnson inherited covert warfare in Southeast Asia from his predecessors, just as President Kennedy inherited an active deniable warfare effort against Cuba, justified and authorized by his predecessor, Dwight D. Eisenhower. For some three years it would challenge Kennedy, with virtually all American covert warfare efforts proving at best ineffectual. As early as December 1960, before Kennedy had taken office, the Eisenhower Administration was still officially in control and had continued to approve plans for a major Cuban operation involving anti-Castro Cuban exiles. The operation was intended to lead to a general revolution inside Cuba, ousting the Castro regime. Eisenhower moved forward with the project even though a Special National Intelligence Estimate from the CIA had described the Castro regime as "firmly in control of Cuba," having consolidated a hold over Cuban society during its first two years in power.[37]

In November 1961, the National Intelligence Estimates Board (a consolidated intelligence community group chaired by the CIA) reported: "The Castro Regime has sufficient popular support and repressive capabilities to cope with any internal threat likely to emerge within the foreseeable future. . . . At the same time, the regime's capabilities for repression are increasing more rapidly than are the potentials for active resistance."[38]

Similar firm negative estimates were issued in March 1962 and June 1963, yet the Kennedy Administration continued covert warfare activities even after the Cuban Missile Crisis. Clearly the brute reality of the political pressure Kennedy would be facing in the 1964 elections forced him to continue actions in regard to the Castro government. A communist Cuba that had shot down U.S. aircraft, and hosted atomic weapons and missiles capable of easily attacking half the continental United States was just ninety miles off our coast. If Johnson felt under political pressure over Vietnam in 1964, Kennedy (having been identified with all things Cuban) would have been under far more pressure over Cuba.

Once again, presidential personality played a role in JFK's decisions. A former athlete raised in a competitive family environment led by his father, Joe, JFK shared a measure of Johnson's will-to-win mentality. But Kennedy's drive had been tempered by the reality of his firsthand combat experiences. He was well aware that complicated foreign policy initiatives often suffered from the "fog of war," the breakdown in communication and understanding that complicates even the best-made plans. There was certainly a pragmatic side to JFK's political personality.[39] His full appreciation of the reality of warfare became clear during his management of the Cuban Missile Crisis, and would surface again in a practical and secret approach to resolving the Cuban situation—an approach in full play at the time of his assassination.

President Kennedy couldn't ignore Cuba. It was too close, too visible, too much an ongoing concern. He had little choice other than to remain "engaged," even if the CIA had failed to deliver on its promises at the Bay of Pigs in the spring of 1961. For the next two years the Kennedy Administration launched an ongoing series of covert warfare operations against Fidel Castro. The U.S. military was also directed to prepare contingency plans for full-scale military intervention in Cuba, and large-scale military exercises were started, with Cuba as the probable future target. Yet what we have learned in the years since 1963 is that President Kennedy was considering an attempt to break out of his political box by covertly exploring an extremely high risk—a creative alternative to both covert and overt military action. He was pursuing the possibility of negotiations with Fidel Castro and the potential of an agreement that would end the American trade embargo on Cuba, while forcing the exit of the Soviets from a "neutral" Cuba. The details of that outreach, beginning early in 1963 and ending with Kennedy's murder, are now well documented. A New York attorney named James Donovan was involved in the effort to gain the release of American citizens remaining in a Cuban prison. At the end of January 1962, as Donovan was departing Cuba, Rene Vallejo (Castro's personal physician and confidant) privately broached the possibility of reestablishing diplomatic relations with the U.S. Donovan was invited back to Cuba on a private visit with his wife for extended conversations with Castro himself.[40]

Upon his return to New York, Donovan informed his State Department contact, who in turn sent a confidential memo to Secretary of State Dean Rusk and communication to CIA Director John McCone. Word of Castro's outreach was passed to President Kennedy, who maintained that no conditions should be set that Castro could not fulfill and that more "flexibility" was in order. Donovan did return to Cuba in April, and when back in the U.S., was debriefed by the CIA. McCone himself wrote Kennedy that Castro knew that relations with the U.S. were necessary and that Castro wanted relations developed. President Kennedy met privately with McCone and expressed great interest in opening up a dialogue. McCone responded that he would be sending Donovan back to Cuba at the end of April. Following that visit McCone characterized Castro's tone as mild, frank, and conciliatory. He also said that Vallejo had told Donovan that Castro realized a viable Cuba (and Cuban economy) required a rapprochement with the U.S. Castro did not know how to proceed, so it had been impossible to discuss the subject with Donovan.

In May 1963, for apparently the first time, discussion at a covert operations overview meeting (by the oversight group Special Group Augmented) included remarks by National Security Advisor McGeorge Bundy, to the effect that they were facing the prospect that it might be impossible to get rid of Castro. Defense Secretary Robert

McNamara then remarked that it might be necessary to "buy off Castro," ending the American embargo in exchange for Castro breaking his ties to the Soviet Union.[41] Senior members of the CIA and state and administration officials were aware of what seemed a credible and serious outreach by Fidel Castro towards normalizing relations with the U.S. Associated memoranda indicate that there was also a high sensitivity to the political danger associated with such a dialogue. Senate subcommittee inquiries were seen as a particular risk because the leaders of such committees were viewed as potentially seeking political advantage by surfacing information that might reflect adversely on the administration or the president. Faced with a political backlash and CIA opposition, the president (who clearly did want to pursue a dialogue) seems to have tabled the matter, although records of a Special Group oversight meeting of June 6 show that the group discussed "various possibilities of establishing channels of communication to Castro," and while it was characterized as a "useful endeavor," no actions were taken.[42]

This impasse began to change dramatically and rapidly in September 1963. Individuals who had close personal contact with Castro, as well as Cuban contacts at the United Nations, established a "back-channel" conduit between JFK's and Castro's representatives and dialogue between JFK and Castro was proposed. The back-channel approach was endorsed by Averell Harriman, Undersecretary of state for political affairs. Due to a variety of opposition to such contacts, it was clear that they would have to be kept secret and informal. Opposition by the CIA was anticipated, as Harriman confirmed when he said, "Unfortunately, the CIA is still in charge of Cuba."[43]

By November 1963, it had become clear that Castro remained highly interested in secret and private accommodations. Castro himself was to be present at the talks and no one else would be involved (Castro had specifically mentioned Che Guevara, the well-known and favored communist revolutionary, who had associated himself with the Cuban Revolution). A U.S. official would meet directly with Castro, and in consideration of security the Cubans would pick up the delegate in Mexico, using a private plane. The individual would be flown to Castro's private retreat near Varadero Beach, where Castro would speak to him personally. These offers caused quite a stir among those working on the Cuban issue; Kennedy was interested but wanted to establish an agenda before an official dialogue. On November 5, the Special Group endorsed a Castro contact working through back-channel contacts at the UN. On November 18, 1963, President Kennedy delivered an address in language suggesting that if Cuba were to drop its Soviet relationship and stop Latin American subversion "everything is possible." His speechwriter has stated the language was specifically intended to signal Kennedy's interest in normalizing the relationship. But Kennedy went further, passing his personal interest on to Castro through yet another back-channel: a French journalist, Jean Daniel, who was scheduled to visit Cuba and meet with Fidel. Kennedy had told the journalist that the Cuban embargo could be lifted if Castro would stop his support for leftist subversion in Latin America, and invited him back to talk after his return from Cuba. On November 22, the journalist was in Cuba and both he and Castro later commented that they felt that Kennedy was in the process of building bridges to Cuba. But that conversation had taken place on the morning of November 22, and after 12:30 Dallas time, there would be no more Kennedy initiatives for coexistence with anyone.

President Kennedy's approach to the Cuban stalemate reflects a man who wanted to "win" in a given political environment—even when it required risks—as well as someone who had a keen sense of pragmatism. This two-track approach to Cuba—covert warfare coupled with covert outreach—may also explain the ongoing debate over Kennedy's intentions in Vietnam. Historians disagree widely over whether Kennedy wanted to expand the war, as his successor, Lyndon Johnson, did or whether he would have limited American involvement to the point of withdrawal. JFK's secret approach to Castro illustrates that in foreign policy as a whole, Kennedy kept his options open and that he did not appear to share Johnson's "win-at-all-costs" attitude.

In the case of Harry Truman, personality trumped political considerations. The pragmatism and arguably the courage of Truman is exemplified by his willingness to suffer massive public criticism over his decision to do "nothing" about the communist takeover of China in the late 1940s, even as the CIA was secretly sponsoring extensive clandestine warfare against the communist regime. Presidential personality and attitude may be seen to play an even stronger role in covert warfare—where the president's autonomy is even more pronounced. President Reagan, not only a former actor but a noted extrovert, was extremely visible in calling attention to the need for humanitarian aid in those areas where his administration was conducting particularly brutal covert warfare. He even publicly declared himself to be a member of the opposition party in Nicaragua, wearing an I'M A CONTRA TOO pin while the United States secretly plotted the overthrow of the Sandinista regime in that nation.

Viewed by Barber as having a passive-negative personality, President Eisenhower was a career military officer conditioned by decades of involvement with military rules, regulations, and protocols. He was not of a nature to go tilting after the windmills of either public or congressional opinion. Eisenhower would have preferred to intervene on the side of the French against the insurgencies in Indochina. In 1954, French forces were under heavy siege by the Viet Minh insurgents at Dien Bien Phu in Vietnam. A victory for the rebel army was viewed as a potential knockout blow to the French military in its struggles with the insurgency in Indochina. U.S. Secretary of State John Foster Dulles remained publicly adamant that American intervention was neither imminent nor even under consideration. At the same time, an American military mission was secretly working with the French, studying the possibility of a massive B-29 bombing mission to relieve the siege at Dien Bien Phu. Some ninety-eight bombers would have staged out of Clark Air Base in the Philippines, crossing the airspace of Thailand and Laos to attack forces besieging the critical French base. However, the final conclusion of the mission was that the radars of the B-29s could not support the precision bombing required, and that the mission would fail if it relied on conventional weapons.[44] During the same period, reports from French diplomats suggested that the subject of atomic weapons was floated in discussions over military options. In the end, Eisenhower proved unwilling to take the risk of any major American involvement in Indochina. His decision was that the risk far outweighed the potential reward.

When the president's interest is to get reelected, anything that risks positive public opinion or reaction could conflict with that interest. President Kennedy's exploration of a risky solution to the ongoing Cuban problem illustrates the tug–of-war between alternative options that can become solutions, and political considerations. Due to the political risks, the decision can be a highly personal matter. The choice between overt and covert military action does rest solely on the president. Some seek advice; some don't. Both Truman and Eisenhower were relatively consistent about seeking formal advice on national security decisions, as was President Kennedy. Kennedy's pragmatism and experiences with the Executive Committee of the National Security Council during the Cuban Missile Crisis seem to have amplified his inclination to solicit a wide range of advice. Other presidents were more comfortable keeping to their own counsel, or limiting their consultation to only a few people.

Historian John Prados writes that Kennedy changed the relationship of the presidency with the National Security Council staff, essentially making it a more personal dialogue with a smaller group of principals. It was simply in Kennedy's character to prefer an extended, freewheeling dialogue with his key advisors—a much livelier environment than the structured meetings held for Eisenhower. In turn, the change was largely based on his own personality. Johnson, on the other hand, changed the basic relationship between himself and the NSC principals. "Johnson called the shots on who would attend unfettered by the exigencies of the National Security Act."[45] With the exception of Secretary of Defense McNamara, Lyndon Johnson had a great deal of disdain for many of the "Harvard whiz kids" he inherited as advisors after Kennedy's death. While supremely confident in his own abilities, paradoxically Johnson was plagued with self-doubt amplified by his insecurities of being the son of a poor farmer living in a world of political elites.

Johnson also micromanaged attendees of NSC meetings, defying parameters set up in the National Security Act. His consultations included many officials who had historically joined such meetings, such as the secretary of defense and the national security advisor, but privately Johnson also sought counsel from members of the White House staff, trusted personal friends, and individual political pundits including influential media personalities. While this ad hoc and very personal approach set a precedent, not all future presidents were eager to limit the amount of dialogue or feedback being provided by the full National Security Council. Kennedy had welcomed a multitude of opinions in his meetings; Johnson had not. As Prados described it, Johnson created a "cabal" to run the government and "undesired voices" went unheard.[46] Successive presidents would shift between these two poles, largely based on their own personalities and character.

Over time and with successive presidents, that formal National Security Council advisory structure established by President Truman evolved into a matter of personal chemistry, involving one or two preeminently trusted advisors—which was particularly visible during the Nixon and Reagan administrations. Some presidents went far outside the official structure, seeking out political and business advisors beyond the individuals formally involved in their administrations. In fact, in our review of some of the earliest operations, such individuals became a major influence not only in decisions to "go covert," but as participants in the actual operations.

As the process for national security decision making evolved, so did the structure for implementing the decisions—not only as orders and directives but in the form of an extended government structure for executing and managing covert action. As we move to that in the next chapter, we will find that presidential personality also emerges as a key element in the actual conduct of those activities. Some presidents were very much hands-on, some turned to micromanagement, others were inclined to leave decisions to the professionals, and in some instances "distance" from covert warfare came to be desired by the commander in chief.

CHAPTER 3

Evolution of a Covert Warfare Infrastructure

During 1963, President Kennedy retained personal approval over specific missions to attack Cuban targets. President Johnson became notorious for personally taking control over missions in Laos and against North Vietnam. But more often than not, once the decision is made to implement covert warfare, the level of involvement of the president, and even his advisors, generally diminishes. The details, execution, and management of the covert projects become the responsibility of the appropriate group within the CIA, normally the Plans Directorate (later designated the Operations Directorate). Of course it makes sense for the president to hand off a project to the professionals, but in some instances it has also provided a useful level of separation, a type of "distance." We will examine instances in which operations ended in scandals, with the president adamant that he was not aware of the details involved. On occasion that is certainly conceivable, but it can also serve to isolate the president from legal action. Presidents also hold the power to pardon those individuals who might actually receive criminal sentences. In 1992, President George H.W. Bush pardoned six individuals convicted of illegal actions relating to the Iran–Contra scandal during the Reagan Administration.

At the beginning of the Cold War, during the Truman Administration in 1948, coordination of covert practices became the responsibility of Truman's newly created Office of Policy Coordination (OPC). In 1951, President Truman folded the Office of Policy Coordination—initially chartered with covert and clandestine activities—into the Central Intelligence Agency. Most of the Central Intelligence Agency's early secret activities were focused on economic, political, and psychological operations targeting the expansion of international communism. Because of the nature of these complex activities, it was desirable and necessary to coordinate various departments and groups. One practical advantage of conducting such operations through a clandestine agency was the use of "unvouchered" executive branch funds, which shielded covert operations from public accounting by the Office of Management and Budget and from routine congressional budgetary oversight.[47] This practice, which began early on and before the legislation that required advising Congress on covert operations, was thought to enhance security and add a measure of political insulation to the president's covert actions.[48]

During the Eisenhower Administration, covert and deniable military activities escalated significantly. Given his personality and his career in the military, Ike took the initiative to ensure that CIA operations were coordinated with the State Department, the secretary of defense, and the branches of the armed services. The National Security Council issued Directive 5412 in March 1954, and while it affirmed the CIA's lead role in covert operations, it also stated that the CIA director was responsible for ensuring that operations were "planned and conducted in a manner consistent with U.S. foreign and military policies"—a policy not always practiced in successive administrations.[49]

The Operations Coordinating Board (OCB) was designated as the mechanism to channel the required coordination. Advance notice of all operations was to be given to both the departments of state and defense—another practice that would not be consistently or even effectively practiced beyond the Eisenhower era. The Operations Coordinating Board would be succeeded by different groups, with different designations by the various presidents; however, the concept that a covert operations oversight and coordination group should exist was a key practice, with much to recommend it. In December 1955, under Directive NSC 5412/2, the Operations Coordinating Board became known as the Special Group (or Special Group 5412), with the responsibility to "review and approve covert action programs initiated by the CIA."[50] In 1961, following the CIA's disaster at the Bay of Pigs in Cuba, and with advice from General Maxwell Taylor, President Kennedy (in coordination with the issuance of presidential national security directives NSAM 55, 56, and 57) began a series of activities to move covert and deniable warfare from CIA to military control. Kennedy also ordered a more proactive role for the Special Group.[51] The Special Group was to become involved not only with interdepartmental coordination but also with the review and planning of covert operations proposals. The Special Group also formalized criteria, addressing risk and probability of success, potential for exposure, political sensitivity, and cost. Per President Kennedy's direction, actions relating to Cuban covert operations also involved Attorney General Robert Kennedy and General Maxwell Taylor, who in those meetings were referred to—along with the rest of the group—as the Special Group Augmented (SGA).[52] President Kennedy also created an additional Special Group (Counter-Insurgency) with NSAM 124.

Under President Johnson the Special Group was redesignated the 303 Committee, although its composition, functions, and responsibility were the same. National Security Advisor McGeorge Bundy served as chairman. Special oversight groups approved 163 covert actions under President Kennedy and 142 under President Johnson. Those actions constituted about 14 percent of CIA covert operations—with the balance being considered too low cost, low risk, or low profile to consider by the 303 Committee—and therefore they were left in the hands of the CIA alone.

The Nixon Administration had its turn to rename the oversight group, calling it the 40 Committee. President Nixon's own approach to national security decisions and the use of an advisory council was considerably different from previous Cold War presidents. For example, in regard to deniable operations against Chile, President

Nixon not only made the decision to bypass the 40 Committee but also ordered the CIA to act without informing the secretaries of state and defense. The CIA was ordered to block the election of Salvador Allende as president in Chile, even if that necessitated a military coup. Only after that effort failed, and Allende was elected, did Nixon involve the 40 Committee as part of a massive effort to instigate opposition and oust Allende.[53]

In succeeding administrations, the covert actions oversight group would be restructured and renamed according to each individual president's style and comfort levels: the Operations Advisory Group (Ford), the NSC Special Coordination Committee (Carter), and the National Security Planning Group (Reagan). Under Reagan the group included the vice president, secretary of defense, secretary of state, assistant for national security affairs, and director of the CIA.[54]

John Prados writes that President Nixon knew exactly what national security arrangement he wanted for his administration, "a strong National Security Advisor with an expert staff to function as a 'little State Department.'" At a meeting to review Secretary of State Henry Kissinger's proposal for the new structure, Nixon told the group he had already approved it.[55] Clearly the new model was going to be Nixon and Kissinger making decisions (Kissinger was given the title assistant to the president for national security affairs.) To a large extent Nixon relied on Kissinger to make things happen.

From that point on the NSC principals' comments would become a matter of written record but would be considered "observations" rather than "recommendations" to the president. Essentially they would be on record but not directly accountable. To a large extent this reduced their active participation in any decision-making process—not even on record as having made concrete recommendations. It was a far cry from what Truman had intended in the initial creation of a National Security Council. It was also a good deal different than the manner in which Eisenhower had interacted with the group or Kennedy had involved EXCOMM in a decision-making process. Decisions would become more unilateral (or, more accurately, bilateral) under Nixon/Kissinger and, as under Eisenhower, deniable operations would dramatically escalate—both around the globe and especially in Latin America.

The NSC function (and even more so any "special group" type oversight) had become so diluted by the Reagan years that ultimately deniable warfare in Nicaragua was conducted completely outside the CIA and all its established covert action processes. It was organized by National Security Council personnel, and funded from sources outside the American government. Reagan's deniable warfare decisions would be made in sole consultation with National Security Advisor John Poindexter, and the scope of Reagan Administration covert warfare would once again escalate dramatically across both Latin America and Southwest Asia.

Senior CIA clandestine officer David Phillips (future chief of CIA Western Hemisphere Operations) was designated to lead the initial Nixon-ordered effort against Salvador Allende in Chile and later wrote:

> *The effort to thwart Allende's inauguration by whatever means, had not gone to the 40 Committee. This was disturbing: a covert action scheme to be launched directly by a President and his intimates—in this case Kissinger and Haig—without being on the agenda of the 40 Committee and at least wafted by the Secretary of State and Secretary of Defense.*[56]

By the end of the Reagan Administration, such level of presidential autonomy had become relatively standard practice. In our examination of actual deniable operations over several decades, we will find that as of the Reagan era, the broad NSC advisory role that Truman had conceived had been all but abandoned, along with the highly structured control over covert operations conceived by General Taylor under President Kennedy. Unfortunately we have no remarks from the late David Phillips on another significant first in clandestine affairs, which occurred during the Reagan era. Given Phillips's own legendary reputation within the CIA for his fieldwork in propaganda and creative use of disinformation, it would have been interesting to hear his thoughts on President Reagan's signing of the national security decision directive. That particular directive related to a massive State Department disinformation campaign targeting Libya, utilizing both "foreign placements" of articles in the international media *and* background news placements in the American domestic press.[57] Not providing information to the American press was nothing new; neither was denial of American involvement in overseas operations—but running structured disinformation campaigns targeting the American media was something relatively new.

In our discussions of the media and deniable operations, we will find considerable voluntary cooperation by the American press through the early years of the Cold War. That supportive relationship began to weaken during the warfare in Southeast Asia in the late 1960s under Johnson and then Nixon. Reagan's order of a domestic propaganda effort seems to reflect the perception of a less cooperative, more skeptical American press in the years immediately following Watergate and the mid-1970s congressional investigations of the Central Intelligence Agency.

Deniability had long been a key in dealing with the American press in regard to overseas covert operations, but the Libyan project and its element of authorized domestic disinformation programs (with intentionally leaked information that Libya was on a collision course with the U.S. and that another military operation against Muammar Gadhafi was pending) were early examples that Reagan was willing to go far outside the traditional covert practices in pursuit of his goals. And, unfortunately for those driving the operation, the press began to sense a pattern of false information leaks—which worsened when one of the real documents related to the program leaked. Reagan's national security advisor, Robert McFarlane, became involved in a confrontation with *The Washington Post,* denouncing its story on the real project. Within days he was forced to assure everyone that Reagan had "no plan to conspire or mislead the American press" while at the same time stating, "Deception was a tool that the government can use."[58] It would be only a month until a transport plane carrying supplies to the Contras—in an effort not authorized by Congress—would crash in Nicaragua. The topic of disinformation would escalate dramatically for the Reagan Administration.

The president makes the call—overt or covert. Early in the Cold War, during both the Truman and Eisenhower administrations, the director of the CIA and the secretary of state had a major influence on such decisions. In both the Johnson and Kennedy administrations the secretary of defense had significant influence, and in the administrations that followed, the president's national security advisor became significant in the decision making. In the beginning the decision process had been relatively straightforward and the national security principals were very much involved. With a process in place and covert warfare a defined alternative option to conventional military action, Eisenhower's personal reliance on covert action laid the foundation for the development of an intricate American covert warfare infrastructure:

> *Research into Eisenhower's previously classified papers highlighted for me in a new and different way the pivotal role played by covert operations, dirty tricks, and counterinsurgency. . . . He worked largely undercover. America's most popular hero was America's most covert President. Eisenhower participated in his own cover-up. His Presidency involved a thorough and ambitious crusade marked by covert operations that depended on secrecy for its success.*[59]

A former CIA officer of the period offers a pragmatic insight into the relationship of President Eisenhower and the unique combination of two highly placed brothers—Secretary of State John Foster Dulles and CIA Director Allen Dulles. They were Eisenhower's dual options.

> *We didn't realize in the early winter months of 1953 as the administration took shape, just how cozy the Dulles brothers' arrangement for handling all American business abroad would be. It*

came to mean very quickly that when a situation would not yield to normal diplomatic pressure, Allen's boys were expected to step in and take care of the matter.[60]

The quantity of covert operations, the extent of surrogate warfare, and the growth of what amounted to a "covert operations complex" during the Eisenhower Administration would not be seen again until three decades later, during the Reagan Administration. But by that point we will find that matters become considerably more delicate and complicated, far beyond the reach and power of the Central Intelligence Agency. The trend away from total CIA dominance began under President Kennedy but it accelerated dramatically during the mid-1970s. Numerous media revelations had raised public concern about the American intelligence communities' (seen somewhat simplistically as the CIA) involvement in covert operations, both overseas and at home. In January 1975, the Senate established a study committee on intelligence operations (commonly known as the Church Committee, after Senator Frank Church, who drove the study). The House also formed an intelligence inquiry, the Select Committee on Intelligence, which initially was headed by Congressman Lucien Nedzi, shortly replaced by Congressman Otis Pike.

While the Church Committee focused on the most sensational (and historical) charges against the CIA—including domestic spying and foreign assassinations—the Pike Committee focused on systematic and relevant questions about the Agency's effectiveness as well as the cost of its intelligence activities. It's fair to say that both committees experienced a combative relationship in regard to collecting information from the CIA; in particular, the Agency stonewalled the Pike Committee in its efforts to secure any measurable view as to the size, nature, or allocation of intelligence spending within the federal budget. The Pike Committee followed hearings with a detailed examination of the role of the National Security Council and the 40 Committee, the major decision-making bodies in covert action approval. The key question for the committee was whether the CIA was a "rogue elephant" or under strict control of the president and the executive branch. The Pike Committee concluded that covert actions "were irregularly approved, sloppily implemented, and, at times, had been forced on a reluctant CIA by the President and his national security advisers."[61]

The Pike Committee's assessment was based on the first two decades of covert warfare operations, a period in which the Central Intelligence Agency was generally dominant and in which operations were under the intense scrutiny of its security and financial accounting divisions. We can only speculate what their view would have been a few years later during the Reagan Administration, as surrogate warfare came to be increasingly "privatized" and "outsourced" during the 1980s, first in Afghanistan, and later in the second phase of the secret war against Nicaragua. Over time, as the very existence of the Pike Committee would illustrate, Congress had begun to insert itself into the conduct of both clandestine and covert operations. Yet it is clear, as the Pike Committee report itself suggests, that the presidency was and remains the key to understanding when and why America becomes involved in covert warfare in the first place. The president's assessment of political reality, his personality, and his relationship with individuals within his own administration would become the dominant factors in the decision to go covert. All presidents take an oath to "preserve, protect, and defend" the Constitution of the United States. The political reality is that the public looks to the president to preserve, protect, and defend American citizens and to secure the nation from attack. Presidents are generally applauded for doing "whatever it takes" to defend against what are perceived as imminent threats—at least initially. Presidents may suffer the consequences of their decisions at a later date, but it is a simple political reality that no president dares go up for reelection while appearing to be weak on issues of national security.

Modern American presidents have consistently exercised the option to order covert warfare and covert action. In most instances they have informed Congress of their decisions in advance, yet in some instances they have acted totally unilaterally. Time after time this has produced major discord between presidents and Congress, and serious political concerns for the administrations involved. There is some reason to speculate that as early as the Kennedy Administration, President Kennedy sensed that covert warfare was not worth the consequences and considered other courses of action. No doubt such a decision would have exposed him to great political risk—being seen as "soft" regarding national security, which has always been one of the key political exposures for any president.

The strategy of "preemptive defense," the tactics of shadow warfare, the deaths of civilians, the issues of legal authority and oversight, the question of whether counterinsurgency ever really works, and the concern over ideological radicalization are all a part of contemporary dialogue in regard to dealing with radical religious terrorism and the jihadi insurgencies of the twenty-first century. Yet with some seventy years of perspective, we find that many of those elements are not all that new. Preemption and covert warfare have been more common than most may realize—so common that we have seen them as almost constant. President Roosevelt attempted to preempt further Japanese territorial expansion through the use of covert action in China. President Truman turned to covert support of the Republic of China in a series of operations that he hoped would either blunt or stall territorial expansion by communist China. By the Eisenhower era, with the Cold War in full swing, Eisenhower turned to perhaps the greatest range and number of preemptive actions ever conducted to halt or push back against the new ideological threat of expanding communist regimes. Kennedy initially followed the Eisenhower lead, although he quickly began to turn to a more pragmatic range of options. His successor turned from low-intensity covert warfare to full-scale conventional military combat in Southeast Asia.

The reality is that no president would or could afford to be seen as weak on national security. National security and the economy have always been the two most fundamental areas of political exposure for any administration, giving the opposition leverage both in Congress and with the popular vote. "Losing China" hurt the Democrats during the Truman Administration; the "missile gap" that really wasn't helped put JFK into office. Of course it's not all politics; during the Cold War the country as a whole feared communist expansion, and any move to confront it or even push it back generally received strong support. No president really concerned himself with losing political leverage because of a move against communists and communist influence, whether in Guatemala, Cuba, the Congo, Nicaragua, or Afghanistan. Preemption was generally viewed as strength, a show of will, a good thing. When Eisenhower ordered the CIA to overthrow the elected government of Guatemala, he was acting covertly in total consistency with public remarks being made on the floor of Congress—where senators were calling on the administration to do "whatever it takes" to push back against the communists.

It was only when the preemptive intervention—either covert or conventional—went terribly sour in Vietnam, Laos, Nicaragua, Iraq, and Afghanistan that Congress and the public turned against the warfare and the president who was continuing it. Of course the other constant that we will follow across the decades is that Congress generally has been happy to let the president undergo the actual risks of preemptive action. The fact that there have been no formal declarations of war by Congress since the Second World War has left the president to make the decisions about when to exercise preemption in the interest of national security. While that is perhaps understandable as a matter of politics—leaving an opening for one party or the other to take issue if things do go badly—it also smacks of hypocrisy. In the chapters that follow we will detail a number of instances in which well-briefed members of Congress chose to leave administrations "hanging in the wind" as popular opinions shifted—large-scale covert action in Laos being one of the more obvious examples.

Historians have written at length on the relationship between Congress and the president in covert action, the apparent lack of oversight, and the clear limits of legislation requiring that Congress be advised in a timely fashion. Yet, as perhaps best explored in *Power and Constraint: The Accountable Presidency After 9/11*, by Jack

Goldsmith, the rules that have been in play since the 1970s seem to be exactly what members of Congress desire. The existing relationship gives them a variety of political options, without their having to go on record as actually approving or disapproving any presidential action. If this view seems a bit jaded, consider the fact that Congress failed to formally declare war even after a series of direct, obviously coordinated attacks not only on American citizens and military personnel overseas in 1998 but directly on the continental United States in 2001.[62] In setting out to write this book, we hoped to determine whether or not the president's use of covert and clandestine action has changed during the decades. What we found was that every president has consistently considered shadow warfare as an option when national security is in question. And when the decision is made in favor of covert action, preemption is not an issue.

We also found that certain contemporary issues are not really all that new, including the preparation and use of "kill lists" in covert action. If the president deems that an individual or group of individuals constitute a national security threat, the authority of commander in chief has been used to order action. One major change that did occur, triggered by public and congressional inquiries into President Nixon's covert activities in Southeast Asia, was the passage of legislation in 1974 that mandated certain constraints under which Congress has to be advised about such presidential decisions. The various presidents have complied with that legislation, although often on their own terms. Perhaps the most unique instance was President Reagan's position that he had not only issued findings "after the fact" but that in one instance the finding had been "mental." We will discuss those particular incidents in our exploration of covert operations during the Reagan Administration. Still, following 9/11, when circumstances demand urgent action, such requirements are far from the president's first concern. Legal limitations on both notification and spending simply fade into the background, at least for the time being. After 9/11, CIA Director George Tenet went to President George W. Bush with a plan for moving against Al-Qaeda and Osama bin Laden in Afghanistan. He emphasized that the plan would be very expensive, very expensive indeed. It would approach at least $1 billion. Bush's reply was succinct, and represents the response of virtually any president in regard to an imminent national security situation. The president's response required no speech, no diatribe, and only three words: "Whatever it takes."[63] Most writers who turn to the study of covert warfare conduct begun with a focus on the creation of the post–WWII intelligence organizations, with emphasis on the point that individuals who joined covert operations felt they had volunteered for nothing less than a continuation of total world war, with the Soviets simply replacing the Third Reich. Much is also written of National Security Council Document 68 (NSC 68), issued by the NSC and authorized by President Truman in 1950. The language contained in NSC 68 was strident, declaring that "the Soviet Union is animated by a new, fanatic faith, antithetical to our own, and seeks to impose its absolute authority over the rest of the world."[64]

It is tempting to visualize deniable warfare as a practice forced on America by the national security concerns and politics of the Cold War. If the Soviets, as Truman feared, could win control over governments and peoples even in regions where neither Soviet forces nor Soviet officials were present, then clearly America had to turn to tactics other than massive conventional force with uniformed formations. Of course if we followed that line of thought literally, we might anticipate that when the Cold War concluded, so would covert action and surrogate warfare. Certainly that did not happen. A more realistic view recognizes the fact that the concept of deniable warfare ranges far back in human history. In relatively recent times, prior to WWII, we find one particular project, the creation of an American Volunteer Group in China, which established a great deal of the logistics, banking, and covert practices that became standard practice in following decades. It also produced a number of individuals who would gain access to the ears of both Presidents Truman and Eisenhower—men who would heavily influence covert action during the 1950s and early 1960s. When representatives for the Chinese central government began to approach President Roosevelt and key figures in his administration with the idea of a covert American intervention against the Japanese, it was emphasized that the whole thing could be done "without any direct participation of the United States Government." No direct American financing would be required, no uniformed American military personnel would be involved, and any U.S. military weaponry required could be handled totally through third-party sales. Overall it would be a "commercial venture," but one allowing America to achieve a major strategic military objective. And most importantly, "it could be safely carried out by the Roosevelt administration, guaranteeing *no political ruckus* would emerge from the shadowy activity."[65]

Decades later, General Richard Secord would cite the China operation as being virtually identical to the privatization of the proxy warfare against Nicaragua, which ended in the Iran–Contra scandal. Secord argued that the operation had established a precedent by which presidents could avoid congressional bans on American support of foreign military operations. In putting forth his argument, Secord also stated that the pre-WWII initiative made the Contra project look like "a small-scale operation."[66] Since we will cover both operations in depth, you will be able to evaluate that judgment for yourself. We begin our journey into the actual practice of deniable warfare not with the traditional Cold War starting point, rather with a strategic, covert operation that began when China was not an expansionist enemy but a friend and ally.

CHAPTER 4

Armies of Opportunity

The decision to respond to China's call for help in 1940 was President Roosevelt's. At that point in time there was no American national security infrastructure as developed during the Cold War, no security council, no coordination board, no covert oversight group, and no operational organization such as the CIA to execute presidential decisions. Even the famed Office of Strategic Services (OSS), which conducted covert and clandestine operations during the Second World War, would not be formed until 1942. Roosevelt's decision was catalyzed through the efforts of his own trusted advisors and put into action by a small group of Americans already involved with military aviation in China. The process was orchestrated and supported by Dr. T.V. Soong, brother-in-law of Chiang Kai-shek, head of the Chinese National government and leader of its armed forces. The friendly government of China was fighting not only the Japanese but various independent warlords and its own internal communist insurgency. Soong was financially involved with both the Bank of China and a variety of Chinese trade activities with the U.S. (primarily conducted through the Universal Trading Corporation).

Soong's position as one of the wealthiest men in the world resulted in a close personal relationship with both Treasury Secretary Henry Morgenthau and Navy Secretary Frank Knox, which enabled Soong to convince both men that covert American involvement in China would serve America's interests. At the time, Japan had already attacked a flagged American Navy ship, killing three U.S. sailors, and wounding forty-three others—including five civilians.

The 1937 Japanese sinking of the USS *Panay*, involved in evacuation of Americans upon the approach of the Japanese army in Nanking, China, drew a Japanese apology and indemnity. Despite this, constant newsreel coverage of ongoing Japanese atrocities in China placed American public sympathy directly on the side of China. In the broader geopolitical perspective, there is little doubt that President Roosevelt viewed both Germany and Japan as fundamental, strategic threats to the United States. And now, through the research of Alan Armstrong, and the newly revealed material in his book *Preemptive Strike: The Secret Plan That Would Have Prevented the Attack on Pearl Harbor*, we know that President Roosevelt had begun looking for some option that would both aid the Chinese and slow the pace of Japanese territorial expansion in Asia. As early as 1940, and continuing up to the attack on Pearl Harbor, Hawaii, in December 1941, Roosevelt was personally involved in a covert project that would have enabled the Chinese to bomb targeted Japanese military and transport facilities. Roosevelt privately expressed the hope that such bombing might at least delay an imminent Japanese threat to the British in Singapore.[67]

While American opinion was generally sympathetic to the Chinese, Roosevelt faced a strong isolationist mood in the country. He had become involved in an active and heated public opinion battle with Charles Lindbergh and his Committee to Defend America (America First) as well as a number of isolationist congressman and senators. It was debated as to whether America should intervene in foreign affairs at all. America was officially neutral in the Sino–Japanese conflict (not an uncommon position in most of the deniable warfare that we will discuss) and strong U.S. neutrality laws were in place to limit America's involvement in any overseas conflict. Pragmatically, Roosevelt was involved in trying to equip and sustain the British in their efforts against the Germans—well aware that the U.S. military was anything but ready to go head-to-head with any major military power in either Europe or the Pacific. Even in 1941 the U.S. was ranked fourteenth in terms of international military strength; in 1939 the Army had been ranked nineteenth in global ground forces, ahead of Bulgaria and just behind Portugal. The Army Air Corps had rated higher at fourth or fifth but only because there were relatively few international air forces. In 1939 the Army Air Corps had only twenty-six thousand personnel and some twelve hundred bombers and fighters, many of them obsolete.[68]

The situation would only become more challenging with Roosevelt's decision to lend some of America's better aircraft to Britain and allow British recruitment of some of America's most experienced civilian pilots. The shortage of experienced pilots and aircraft was a major issue in rearmament during 1940–41—especially with significant numbers of pilots going through Canada to serve with the British, and with continuing aircraft shipments to the British. In addition to its Army and Army Air Force deficits, America was in no position to directly engage the Japanese in the Pacific; the U.S. could field only three advanced aircraft carriers in the Pacific to match the eight in the Japanese Pacific fleet.

All things considered, any strategic military move against the Japanese called for American deniability and enough diplomatic cunning to avoid formal military engagement with Japan. The good news was that the Chinese government was very much willing to agree to those terms and meet whatever conditions were necessary—especially when it came to securing American air resources.

Two men wielded special influence within the Roosevelt Administration—Treasury Secretary Henry Morgenthau and Navy Secretary Frank Knox; they were members of what Secretary of War Henry Stimson's wife called the Plus Four, FDR's inner circle within his Cabinet. The "Plus Four" included Stimson, Morgenthau, and Knox, as well as Secretary of State Cordell Hull. The opinions and recommendations of the Plus Four carried special weight with the president.[69] In the fall of 1940, both Knox and Morgenthau became highly supportive of Soong's ideas. Joining them in their enthusiastic support was Thomas Corcoran, a speechwriter for President Roosevelt. Eventually Morgenthau's private papers would expose a good number of details about the subsequent plan to establish a "Special Air Unit," which would operate bombers from eastern China to attack Tokyo and other Japanese cities.[70]

We summarized political science presidential expert James David Barber's presidential personality profile, which describes Roosevelt as "active-positive," being both an adaptive and a flexible leader. So when Knox and Morgenthau presented this Special Air Unit option to President Roosevelt, it is hardly surprising that he considered it. The same man who was willing to engage in bold experiments to "fight" the Great Depression would, of course, be open to innovative measures when it came to foreign affairs. But public opinion was strongly on the side of isolationists, with formal measures such as the Neutrality Act circumscribing any kind of overt effort to aid China or Britain. All signs were pointing to the choice of covert action.

A Special Air Unit did indeed come into existence thanks to secret oral directives from Roosevelt. The unit became known publicly as the American Volunteer Group. The choice of names was very much intentional, as it added a cachet of American support to the effort without officially sanctioning the military action as an act of the American government. Its first element, a fighter group (AVG-1), would later become even better known as the Flying Tigers, who would play a pivotal role in air operations in China and after Pearl Harbor. The group's commander, Claire Chennault, rejoined the Army Air Force as a major general commanding the 14th Air Force after the outbreak of war with Japan. But the second element of the unit (AVG-2), the strategic bomber group anticipated by President Roosevelt, was delayed by struggles in gaining aircraft allocations. The Army Air Force and the British were not at all happy about losing aircraft construction to go to China.

As late as September 1941, Chennault was deeply involved in plans for the transport of Lockheed Hudson bombers to China, along with recruiting and transporting the crews needed to man them.[71] But within three months, world events and the Japanese attacks at Pearl Harbor and in the Philippines had superseded those plans. While the Flying Tigers and the American Volunteer Group would become popular heroes, the deeper story of Roosevelt's efforts to get bombers to China as a strategic move against Japan remained largely untold, until *Preemptive Strike* was published in 2006. It is notable that even in 1940, the anticipated strategic bombing plan against Japan had initially focused on the highly capable B-17 four-engine bombers and the use of incendiary bombs against the wood and paper building construction found in Japan.[72]

This pre-WWII effort presents us with many of the most fundamental "practices" of covert action. The techniques that evolved to create deniability for the Special Air Unit would lay the foundation for covert operations in the entire postwar period. In terms of deniability, the fundamental concept was to put a "guerrilla air force" into China. The aircraft would have been U.S.-built, but commercially purchased by China through Chinese companies, and paid for with Chinese funds. The maintenance and support personnel would have been employees of those same Chinese companies. Pilots and flight crews would have been experienced American former military personnel with a cover story. They were to have "resigned" from the service and would participate only as private citizens. If necessary they could be referred to as "soldiers of fortune." We will find that this approach becomes an accepted practice for moving uniformed personnel into deniable programs. The use of these basic components—commercial front companies and the claim of citizen volunteers working for foreign interests—would become standard operating procedure in a great many covert operations in future decades, along with a public stance of neutrality.

The idea was that America would remain officially neutral, no active-duty military would be involved, and no American tax money would be used in China. The simplest part would be the financing. Covert support of a "friendly" government offers a great many options for the obfuscation of funding. Fundamentally, the U.S. simply had to encourage the Export-Import Bank to guarantee loans to China's Hong Kong and Shanghai Banking Corporation. In turn, that Chinese bank would issue loans to Chinese companies, which would then pay independent businesses to purchase aircraft, engines, and related equipment, operate the necessary facilities, and employ American air unit personnel.

Universal Trading Corporation (T.V. Soong's company) would be designated to buy aircraft and aircraft engines for the project; it also served as the business representative of China Defense Supplies, Inc. While sounding like a private Chinese business, China Defense Supplies was simply a shell company organized by Tommy Corcoran (who served as outside legal counsel). Corcoran was known as a well-connected lawyer and lobbyist in Washington, D.C. In *Peddling Influence: Thomas "Tommy the Cork" Corcoran and the Birth of Modern Lobbying*, Corcoran's biographer David McKean describes him as Roosevelt's most trusted advisor and personal companion, acting as Roosevelt's emissary in Washington circles. In fact, Corcoran's influence may have an occasion equaled that, of the highly influential "Plus Four."

Tommy Corcoran's brother David served as president of China Defense Supplies, while Roosevelt's elderly uncle Frederic Delano acted as its "honorary counselor." China Defense Supplies' offices were in the Chinese Embassy in Washington, D.C. Money for the company's purchases came directly from bank credits guaranteed by the American government.[73]

With financing handled, the next stage in the project became heavily influenced by aviation-oriented American business connections already in place in China, specifically those of William Pawley. He served as sales agent for Curtiss-Wright aircraft in China in 1927, before striking out on his own to become president of Nacional Cubana de Aviación Curtiss in Cuba, and then president of Intercontinent Corporation in New York. That position took him to China, where he first managed the China National Aviation Corporation and then went into partnership (using Intercontinent as a holding company) with the Chinese government to create Central Aircraft Manufacturing Company (CAMCO). CAMCO purchased aircraft for the Chinese government, and operated a series of aircraft assembly, maintenance, and repair facilities.

Pawley's own aggressiveness, which we will return to in exploring other covert warfare activities, led him to insert himself into virtually any aviation activities in China. When he learned that China Defense Supplies had made a purchase of some one hundred P-40 fighters from Curtiss-Wright, he demanded a 10 percent payment on the $4.5 million deal. In fact, Pawley went directly to Chennault and threatened to obtain a legal injunction against the sale.

Henry Morgenthau pushed back (and threatened government confiscation of the P-40 fighters). Pawley agreed to take a $250,000 payment, a bit over 5 percent—a fairly average percentage for such things—but with the agreement that CAMCO would assemble, service, and test fly the actual aircraft destined for Burma and China. On the basis of that agreement, Americans who were recruited for service in the new Special Air Unit would serve first in Burma and later in China as employees of Pawley's CAMCO.

The primary elements of deniability for the China Special Air Unit included the purchasing of aircraft and supplies through a shell company (China Defense Supplies) organized by Roosevelt Administration insiders, and initial financing through secured loan guarantees provided to an offshore bank (in this case in China) rather than directly with American funds.

Later, circumstances would allow the Roosevelt Administration to actually extend a $100 million loan to China from the U.S.[74] In what we will come to see as typical in such operations, financial transactions were intentionally clouded though the use of "layered" companies such as Universal Trading Corporation (used for actual purchases) and through field operations conducted with existing "in-country" businesses, primarily CAMCO (which was itself a Chinese subsidiary of Intercontinent, a U.S. corporation). This sort of financing is something that works most easily in operations involving covert support for friendly regimes. Loans and loan guarantees can be made to legal solvent governments, which then redirect them to the covert operation. Financing becomes a lot more difficult—and a lot more expensive—with operations against hostile governments, especially when the funding is for regime change.[75]

With regard to recruiting combat personnel, Roosevelt directly authorized the Special Air Unit representatives to contact both American Army and Navy pilots, and assurances were given that individuals could resign their commissions, take private jobs overseas, and later return to their prior military positions with equivalent or possibly even higher ranks. The individuals serving in China would be acting strictly as private citizens employed by a private company in a foreign country, in this case CAMCO. As the project evolved, personal documents from the Plus Four participants and other principals refer to hush-hush meetings and note that arrangements involving serving military personnel as well as any releases of discretionary funds had to be conducted orally with no paper records of any sort.[76] In a precedent that would be followed during a number of successive administrations, President Roosevelt issued a secret, oral executive order directing covert assistance in the formation of the new air unit without consultation with or notification of Congress.[77]

Another theme that will become common to covert programs is intervening press coverage. Despite all efforts at secrecy and deniability there was active U.S. and Chinese press coverage of the creation and deployment of the Special Air Unit, beginning with the purchase of aircraft from American companies and continuing through the Americans' joining the AVG in China. The Japanese could hardly have been unaware of the operation. As early as July 9, 1941, United Press carried a dispatch about mechanics arriving in San Francisco from New York, on their way to Rangoon, Burma—en route to service in China. A *New York Times* article at the end of October of that year discussed and illustrated the potential bombing of Japan from a number of points, including Chungking, China, and Hong Kong. And perhaps most amazingly, on Saturday, November 15, 1941, General George C. Marshall was reported to have secretly briefed several major newspapers and magazines about American plans for an offensive air war against Japan from the Philippines and China. Given that the briefing was held only days before AVG-2 (the bomber group) was to depart San Francisco, this might have been an effort to satisfy the press for the time being; it also might have been an attempt to leak information that would give the Japanese pause. Whatever the intent, Marshall later personally confirmed the briefing.[78]

It is actually not unusual for covert operations to receive significant press coverage. In this particular instance, some of that coverage might have been intentional, a bluff to convince the Japanese to cease widely anticipated military advances beyond China. In later instances, if even small-scale military activities are often picked up by the press, it becomes a question of whether they can be managed to preserve deniability. The volunteer group operation is a seminal illustration of covert warfare, introducing several of the basic legal, financial, and business arrangements required for covert, surrogate warfare. It also introduced several of the individuals and even businesses that we will see repeatedly in other clandestine operations through the 1960s. As we noted in the first chapter, the president is the final decider on a commitment to deniable warfare, but in virtually all instances someone had the ear of the president in such decisions.

William Pawley and Tommy Corcoran were powers in clandestine activities during the years of Roosevelt's presidency and affairs in China, however they eventually rose to positions of influence with senior people in the Central Intelligence Agency and within Washington, D.C., circles of power well beyond Roosevelt. In 1945, President Truman appointed Pawley ambassador to Peru, and then ambassador to Brazil in 1948. Pawley became close to President Eisenhower and senior CIA officers, including Allen Dulles and J.C. King. Pawley's seminal position in regard to American covert operations is also demonstrated by the fact that in 1954 President Eisenhower appointed him to a top-secret five-member panel chartered to review and evaluate all aspects of American intelligence—including the CIA and all groups involved in such activities. The panel was directed to present its findings via personal reports to the president.[79]

William Pawley was vetted as a security cleared source for the CIA, a common status for U.S. businessmen operating overseas or with international contacts. However, Pawley is especially interesting because of the influence he had with Eisenhower in regard to the Cuban Revolution, where he acted as an informal U.S. emissary to Cuban President Fulgencio Batista. Pawley was also a source of constant, aggressive anticommunist remarks to both senior policy makers and the media.[80] In that context Pawley's major long-term involvement would be in having the ear of presidents and senior CIA figures, often pressing for covert action. However, we will examine in detail one instance when he did personally participate in a very high-risk mission into Cuba during the Kennedy Administration.

Tommy Corcoran, the second recurring character in America's early covert operations, was widely regarded as a master lobbyist and Washington insider, who became close with Presidents Roosevelt and Eisenhower. As a representative for the United Fruit Company in Latin America, Corcoran was in a position to pass numerous political insights to senior CIA officers like J.C. King and directly to the president.[81] It appears that several of those insights related to political events in one of United Fruit's major operating areas—Guatemala.[82, 83]

As already noted, it appears that in many instances, presidents' decisions have been as much influenced by their most trusted advisors as by the official intelligence community. This fact was highlighted by comments made by E. Howard Hunt, a figure most known for his role in the Watergate scandal as well as for being a CIA figure in U.S. covert operations against Guatemala. Hunt had been CIA station chief in Mexico City in 1950, and was later assigned as a political officer to the Guatemala project, a mission of regime change to oust Árbenz, the popularly elected left-leaning president. In public remarks made some years later, Hunt described personally having made a serious effort to get Washington to take note of a potential communist takeover of the government in Guatemala. His concern had been in regard to national security. His statements show that he was frustrated and upset when he later learned that Eisenhower's decision to address issues in Guatemala was not based on intelligence but on the business interests of Thomas Corcoran of the United Fruit Company, who apparently had persuaded Eisenhower and other senior officials.

As Hunt put it:

> *Hey, you know, I'm working for the United States of America, I'm not a hireling for United Fruit. . . . but I went ahead with my assigned tasks in any case, and if United Fruit benefited from that, that was part of the set game. If somebody had said, "Well, we can't go in for the right reasons, but Thomas Corcoran is working on Eisenhower and we think that Eisenhower will give the go-ahead, so just stand by," I would have stood by and done exactly what I had done before, but liking it a hell of a lot less.*[84]

Claire Chennault remained involved in commercial ventures in China following the end of WWII. Many of those involved flying air transport support for the Nationalist Chinese government's ongoing efforts against revolutionary forces and the People's Liberation Army. While the war had ended, fighting between the Chinese factions continued across a broad range of fronts. At that point, the Nationalist government retained significant military forces in the south of China, particularly in the Yunnan and Kwangtung provinces. Chennault's wartime services and his personal commitments inside China allowed him to form strong personal bonds with both Chiang Kai-shek and his American-educated wife, Soong May-ling (known simply as Madame Chiang in the U.S.). Chennault was reportedly one of the few Americans to gain a position of trust at the highest levels of the Nationalist leadership.

In 1949, Chennault went to Washington, D.C. with a plea for a major covert American operation to support the Nationalist Chinese/Republic of China forces in developing a final stronghold in southern China and to aid ROC guerrilla forces in ongoing combat with the People's Liberation Army across the country. At that point the Nationalists had not yet been totally defeated and still had significant military positioned in the south, in the Yunnan and Kwangtung provinces.

Chennault was essentially rejected by the State Department, so he turned to his two partners in his private airline in China, Tommy Corcoran and Whiting Willauer, who formed Civil Air Transport

(CAT) with Chennault in 1946. Corcoran made the right Washington introductions for Chennault—especially to his friends inside the CIA, where there was considerable interest in the potential for using CAT to engage in deniable CIA operations. Previously CAT had largely lived off contracts for the transport of troops and supplies for the Nationalist army, so its crews and support personnel were already quite experienced in supporting military and paramilitary missions. While discussions were under way in Washington, the Nationalist forces on the mainland collapsed and retreated out of China and into the frontier regions of Burma and Vietnam. What was left of the Nationalist military forces and leadership moved offshore to Taiwan. In the U.S. the "fall" of China to the communists became a major political controversy, with aggressive claims that communists inside the U.S. government had undermined support for the Nationalists.

In spite of Chiang Kai-shek's ambivalence towards the U.S. and widespread American concern over corruption in the Nationalist government, the U.S. actually provided some $2.2 million worth of aid and military equipment to the Nationalists in the years immediately following World War II.[85] Later, following the Nationalist retreat from the mainland to Taiwan, President Truman issued secret orders that resulted in covert support for full-scale warfare from Taiwan against the mainland from 1950 on. The CIA leaders in that effort were veterans of the World War II Office of Strategic Services, and the second in command, Desmond FitzGerald, would go on to become one of the key names in future CIA deniable warfare projects, rising to major prominence during the 1960s secret war against Castro in Cuba. FitzGerald sent Nationalist Chinese military personnel to Fort Benning, Georgia, for training (a decade later he would be sending Cuban exiles there) and the CIA established a commercial business cover on Taiwan. The base supported extensive training and assistance. Officially named Western Enterprises, it was often referred to as Western Auto by its personnel.

The Nationalist government in exile had made it clear that it intended to continue its battles and to return to the mainland.

Large-scale guerrilla operations were indeed staged from Taiwan. In the spring of 1950 a force of some thirty thousand Nationalists managed to isolate the Chinese port city of Canton and the CIA estimated that more than half a million men loyal to the Nationalist cause were still in arms on the mainland (the Chinese communist leader Mao Tse-tung described them as "bandits").[86] The CIA also supported offshore paramilitary operations. In one incident, a Norwegian freighter was en route to China with humanitarian aid from India as well as medical supplies and materials for three field hospitals. An operation designated TP-Stole was directed to stop the ship, in any way necessary. The CIA feared that the supplies could be transferred to Chinese support of the North Korean military invasion of South Korea. Arrangements were made to sabotage the ship in Hong Kong if it stopped there, but in the end, CIA officers in gunboats operated by the Nationalist Chinese directed (from concealment) the interception of the ship and the removal of its cargo.[87, 88]

Chennault and his Civil Air Transport business associate Whiting Willauer found that their private airline had evolved into a desirable property for covert support operations in Southeast Asia, but CAT was in financial straits. There would be no military business from the new communist leadership and as Chennault and CAT were closely identified with the Nationalists and Chang Kai-shek, there would also be no domestic air business for the company.

The CIA immediately saw great potential in CAT for use in covert military operations and quickly arranged to contract its services. The first CAT mission for the CIA was flown in October 1949, and by November, Corcoran (acting as legal counsel for CAT) had signed a formal agreement for its use by the CIA.[89] In the end, CAT required ever more subsidization and essentially became one of the first CIA "proprietary" companies: an ostensibly private company with major investment from the U.S. government that was on priority call for U.S. projects from the CIA, the U.S. military, and other government agencies. This was accomplished by forming a holding company, the American Airdale Corporation, a Delaware-registered corporation. Airdale operated a subsidiary named CAT Inc., which owned 40 percent of

Civil Air Transport. CAT contracted for a large number of operations, beginning with the "Booklift" operation during the Korean conflict. This was a secret agreement between the U.S. military and CAT, which moved military supplies all across Southeast Asia, and later with the French government, for support of its efforts against the Viet Minh.[90] CAT, in a variety of incarnations, would go on to serve CIA covert operations around the world, not just in Southeast Asia. We will find it in and around covert projects from Latin America to Africa. Willauer's name will be found in documents pertaining to air support for the first major CIA regime change operation in Guatemala. In 1957, in an effort to make its activities and associated companies more obscure (and CAT less visible), the CIA restructured American Airdale into a new holding company: Pacific Corporation.[91]

President Roosevelt had taken a gamble; the concept of using air strikes out of China to shock and divert the Japanese was tactically sound. The success of the surprise American bombing mission, the Tokyo raid of April 1942, led by Lieutenant Colonel James Doolittle, demonstrated that. There was already conflict between Japanese military factions, and air attacks would have shattered the domestic propaganda line of Japanese invulnerability. The combination of B-17 bombers and firebombing tactics would likely have made a major impression even if only the first surprise missions out of China had succeeded.

Certainly such raids, using American aircraft—even if legally owned by the Chinese and flown by contract air crews—would have made it clear that America was not going to be locked out of the Pacific. General Marshall's press conference of November 15, 1941, had aggressively asserted that position, with its description of American air war against the Japanese home islands from China or the Philippines. Of course the Japanese already had made their own preemptive decision. Planning and training for the attacks on the American Navy base at Pearl Harbor, Hawaii, had been under way beginning in July 1941. In a matter of historical irony, the crew members of the AVG-2, the bomber component of the American Volunteer Group, were scheduled to depart from San Francisco, on their way to China, at the end of November 1941. Whether Marshall's amazing press conference was simply the lead to the AVG effort or, given increasing warnings about a pending Japanese military initiative somewhere in the Pacific, to a last-ditch effort to make them reconsider, Roosevelt's covert China gambit was simply too late.

CHAPTER 5

Fighting Communist China . . . Deniably

America's "shadow" operations in pre–World War II China were fil-tered through "business as usual" corporate and banking institutions that conducted day-to-day business activities while serving as platforms to field deniable personnel and equip surrogate forces. The relative ease in which these relationships formed was due largely to the confidential invitation from the Nationalists in China—a friendly government and soon-to-be ally in actively opposing the Japanese military advances in the region. Once the Cold War became a reality, America didn't always need an invitation. In his book *The Craft of Intelligence: America's Legendary Spy Master on the Fundamentals of Intelligence Gathering for a Free World*, former CIA Director Allen Dulles discussed the Truman Doctrine, which was issued in 1947 to counter the Soviet expansionist threat to Greece and Turkey. The doctrine asserted that when "free institutions and national integrity" were threatened by communist subversion, and when those nations requested American support, it would be U.S. policy to extend it. Later, that doctrine would be extended to the Middle East by President Eisenhower and referred to as the Eisenhower Doctrine. As the years passed, various presidents issued doctrinal statements that covered geographic areas around the globe. In 1965, Lyndon Johnson began speaking of a doctrine that directly involved the Dominican Republic, but could have been interpreted as applying to entire Caribbean, or possibly all of Latin America. In his 1980 State of the Union address, President Carter declared the Persian Gulf as a vital area of American interest and stated that the U.S. would oppose any power attempting to control it.

But Dulles also noted that, on occasion, leaders of foreign governments might come into place legally and even democratically, through "the usual processes of government." If it was determined that those leaders held the intention of creating a communist state, America was justified in working with anticommunist factions within those countries to overthrow and replace those governments as a preemptive action. There was no need for any government in power to issue an invitation for America to become involved; preemptive action was considered to be justified and required for national security.[92] We will examine a number of such uninvited interventions that eventually became known as regime change, as American covert operations took place in a much more conflicted environment. Even if America would be dealing with combatants eager for its support, geography would mean that America would sometimes have to provide that support by operating in and around governments opposed to the intervention. This alone was enough to convince presidents of the decision to act covertly while maintaining an official position of strict neutrality.

Following the end of World War II, the U.S. took a hands-off position on the Chinese civil war between the Nationalist government of China—later named the Republic of China (ROC)—and the communist insurgency being carried out by the Chinese People's Liberation Army. Covertly the Truman Administration had made a major financial and military mission commitment to the Republic of China. After giving way to the communists on the mainland and retreating offshore to Taiwan, the Nationalists became actively engaged in large-scale guerrilla operations at several points across the mainland. In addition, Truman supported Republic of China efforts against the communists. Later, with China's 1950 intervention in the Korean conflict, support for the Taiwan government and its guerrilla operations on the mainland significantly increased. In the larger picture, during the 1950s America would engage in a range of covert and military assistance projects, all designed to blunt communist territorial expansion, from the Taiwan Straits, across Indochina, even to Tibet and the Indian border.

In 1950, President Truman ordered the U.S. Navy's 7th Fleet into position in the Taiwan Strait to block any assault from the mainland against the Republic of China on Taiwan. On multiple occasions, the U.S. would assert its intent to defend the Taiwanese government from any aggression launched by communist China. Preservation of the Republic of China became standard American policy, with the United States military established as a buffer against attacks from communist China. By 1951, following China's intervention in the Korean combat, the Joint Chiefs took the position that Taiwan was critical to guerrilla operations in China and that active military assistance and—if required—actual American military intervention would be justified to preserve Taiwan as an operational asset in the fight against North Korea as well as to preserve its function in covert operations against China throughout Southeast Asia.[93] Covertly, the U.S. prepared to do far more than assert a defensive position in the Straits of Taiwan.

Early in 1951, President Truman had already begun a more proactive response, signing a national security directive (NSC-101) that authorized support of aggressive and deniable operations against communist China, and another order (NSC-118) that focused on disrupting Chinese supply lines into Korea.[94] A $300 million budget was allocated for covert operations and the CIA established a "proprietary" Pittsburgh-based import–export company called Western Enterprises, Inc. (WEI). WEI was to be used specifically as a front or cover for moving supplies and advisors that would support the Republic of China. CIA personnel were active in Taipei on Taiwan and conducted special military training for airborne and seaborne operations.[95]

Western Enterprises' new head, Raymond Peers, could not have been more experienced in paramilitary operations. He had personally headed the famed Office of Strategic Services Detachment 101 in Burma during WWII, famed for its success in organizing and directing native forces against the Japanese. The unit was exceptionally effective in organizing large-scale tribal resistance against the Japanese in Burma. Peers at the helm of WEI quickly turned to CAT to support aggressive airborne operations (the ROC already had a 1,500-man parachute regiment) and CAT made a series of airdrops, flying covertly out of American military bases and across mainland China, ranging as far as the Amdo region of Tibet.[96] In addition, the U.S. covertly approached a variety of anticommunist Chinese groups not affiliated with the ROC, training them in Japan and at a highly secret training facility on the island of Saipan. The Saipan operation was "covered" by the military designation Naval Technical Training Unit.[97] Arms for some two hundred thousand guerrillas were allocated to autonomous anticommunist forces not affiliated with the Taiwanese regime, and a number of its fighters were inserted into China via CAT flights from South Korea.

Initially one of the practical problems involved with support for Taiwan was the lack of available weapons. The U.S. military was in short stock itself, so the CIA purchased WWII-era weapons from Europe—particularly German weapons. Samuel Cummings, who recently had been hired by the CIA as a small-arms specialist (in weapons identification) in the Office of Scientific Intelligence, was sent off urgently to Europe. Working undercover as a film industry purchasing agent, Cummings was quite successful on his trip, and weapons soon began flowing to the ROC from Europe. At least some portion of that weaponry may have been diverted to a reserve for future CIA needs.[98]

At first glance, Cummings's use of a film industry cover might seem a bit odd. It does, however, give us an insight into use of commercial business covers in CIA activities. Shortly after the CIA was formed, officers in charge of deniable operations realized they would need a supply of "clean" or "sterile" weapons. Such weapons are normally foreign made and do not contain serial numbers that can be traced back to U.S. manufacturers. While details are obscure, it is known that a Hollywood promoter named Leo Lippe, who had no previous involvement in the arms business, presented a convincing business proposition and managed to convince both the State Department and the CIA that he could be successful—resulting in government support for two new Lippe companies, Western Arms and Winfield Arms Corporation.

Sam Cummings became yet another of the seminal figures we will encounter often as we explore the first two decades of CIA deniable warfare. And, as with others, he would remain both a commercial asset and an intelligence source even upon his departure from formal Agency employment. Initially, Cummings left the CIA to work in sales for Lippe's Western Arms.[99] Yet it would not be long before Cummings formed his first company, Interarmco (later to be changed to Interarms).

In addition to denying its extensive and constantly escalating covert military support of Taiwan against communist China, the U.S. denied accusations that it was providing military support to Republic of China forces inside Burma—when in fact it was most definitely involved in providing them with weapons and military supplies. Burma had been concerned about the presence of Republic of China–backed combatants that had moved into the Shan States area, a region bordering Thailand and Laos to its east and southern China in the north, in early 1950.[100] That army was loyal to Taiwan and the Republic of China, not to the country from which it was operating; it was organized for what was hoped would be a significant diversionary offensive into China's Yunnan province.

As time passed, Burma's problems with the foreign ROC-affiliated military groups continued to grow. Not only did the ROC collect its own taxes in regions it controlled but eventually it began to join cause with Burmese rebel groups, adding to security concerns and undermining central government control. In fact, the Burmese government was so alarmed that the Burmese army had begun a series of military containment operations against the Nationalist Chinese forces by the end of 1950.

The U.S. was faced with growing international concerns over its apparent entanglement with the ROC armies in Burma. In particular, neutral countries such as India were sympathetic to the Burmese and threatened to take the issue to the United Nations. In the first decade following the Second World War, the U.S. was quite sensitive to charges of imperialism and intervention, especially as many of its staunchest allies remained colonial powers. With the developing Western and Soviet political blocs challenging each other for influence with the neutral and emerging nations, a UN floor debate on the subject would have been a major propaganda victory for the Soviets. All of which raises the question: How in the world was the U.S. able to conduct covert operations inside Burma in the first place, without official sanction or support from the Burmese government?

Surrogate warfare is a simple concept, centuries old in practice. Often when a nation is heavily engaged in large-scale warfare, its force may become stretched thin. At that point a diversion or even a flanking action against its enemy seems highly desirable. Or it may be that a nation or group wishes to frustrate an enemy nation without entering into combat that may escalate into full-scale war. In either instance, if a third-party force—either hostile to a common enemy or already engaged in some sort of insurgency or combat—presents itself, the option of surrogates appears.

America benefited from the surrogate strategy at its birth, when France, engaged in global warfare with the British Empire, took the opportunity to openly support the American rebels as a desirable diversion for significant numbers of royal army and naval forces. During the American Civil War, the Confederacy received a limited amount of clandestine and nonmilitary support from the British; it had hoped for recognition and active British military support against the American national government. In contrast, during 1951, America was actively and covertly supporting an independent army inside Burma. The covert support by an officially neutral U.S. for military operations inside neutral Burma placed the American State Department in a position of doubling down on denial. Officially, America was not militarily supporting Nationalist military action against the communist regime on the Chinese mainland. And it was most certainly not supporting a rogue ROC army inside Burma. In reality, the United States was doing both.

The key to covertly supplying forces inside a neutral country—that does not want or appreciate any such activity inside its territory—is to operate through a cooperative border nation. In 1951, Thailand, which had evolved strong connections to both the U.S. military and the CIA, was that border nation. In the 1960s, when the U.S. needed to support deniable armies in Laos, it would once again turn to Thailand, Laos's neighbor to the south. Indeed, American military and CIA connections to Thailand—and in particular to key Thai police and military figures—would become key enablers to deniable warfare in Southeast Asia for two decades to come. Those connections would also provide channels and entanglements resulting in a massive escalation in drug smuggling out of the Golden Triangle border regions. One of Asia's two main opium-producing areas (the other being Afghanistan), the Golden Triangle overlaps the mountains of four Southeast Asian countries: Myanmar (formerly Burma), Vietnam, Laos, and Thailand. During WWII, the American Office of Strategic Services had been extremely active in occupied Europe and in Southeast Asia, China, Indochina, and Burma. OSS Detachment 101 proved exceptionally effective in organizing, arming, and directing Kachin tribal fighters against the Japanese forces occupying Burma. With less than a thousand personnel, the 101st supported an army of more than ten thousand Kachins; it was the first American unit to organize and employee a major guerrilla army deep within enemy territory. In addition, the unit developed between 70 and 90 percent of all combat intelligence used in the northern Burma campaign.[101]

A considerable number of the CIA clandestine warfare officers whose names will emerge repeatedly throughout this book served in World War II OSS units, especially those units in the China–Burma–India theater. Some, such as Howard Hunt, would become well-known to the American public. These officers included Paul Helliwell, who had served as chief of the Far Eastern Division of the OSS within the War Department, and John Singlaub, who had served with the OSS behind the lines in France, working with French resistance fighters, and also served in combat in Korea. He went on to become a founding member of the CIA and to head CIA operations in Manchuria.

Certain of these individuals, in particular Colonel Helliwell and Lieutenant Colonel Willis Bird, remained in Southeast Asia at the end of the Second World War. These former OSS officers established extensive business and social contacts in Bangkok. Their contacts included former wartime comrades in the Free Thai Movement who had become senior Thai military officials. The mutual connections and activities of the OSS veterans remaining in Thailand proved quite helpful in facilitating the CIA's activities within Thailand, both in supporting the covert operation with the ROC forces in Burma and later in various activities in both Laos and Vietnam.

In *The Secret Army*, Richard Gibson relates that in early 1950, a group of these former military officers formed an anticommunist, pro-America committee (the Narasuan Committee), which reached out to the local CIA station through Willis Bird. Bird's major Thai counterpart was Thai National Police Chief Phao Sriyanond. As a result of the influence of the Narasuan Committee and the personal relationships it formed with key Thai security leaders, an agreement was reached to send a team of CIA personnel to Thailand. The initial agreement was to train and arm approximately 350 Thai police, who would be used as a special counterinsurgency unit targeting communist rebels. The contact and agreement were done largely without the knowledge of the Thai prime minister or the American ambassador in Bangkok.[102]

In contrast to other military assistance programs we will encounter, the CIA played a major role in both training and supplying the Thai National Police. Some three hundred CIA personnel were involved in the training and advisory effort intended to develop a more skilled and capable counterinsurgency and internal security force. The Truman Administration's support for the new Thai military assistance was ensured by the recommendations of a Joint State–Defense Mutual Defense Assistance Program Survey Mission to Southeast Asia—a mission that had been dispatched in the summer of 1950, following the beginning of the Korean conflict in

June. Members of the mission were actually in Bangkok at the time the first CIA personnel were arriving to respond to the request of Willis Bird and the Thai anticommunist Narasuan Committee.

Major General Graves Erskine was the leader of the mission. Later his career would lead him to command the Pentagon Office of Special Operations for the Joint Chiefs of Staff. The group also included Glenn Craig of the Economic Cooperation Administration. In its report to the president, the mission recommended that Thailand receive substantial military assistance, largely to ensure that it could serve as a credible military buffer against infiltration of communist rebels from China. It was hoped that the Thai counterinsurgency effort be complemented by the ROC forces in the Shan States of Burma. Of course, while American strategists saw even a modest military buffer against the communist Chinese as a good thing, the Burmese central government remained worried that any ROC activity on its borders might simply invite intervention by the Chinese People's Liberation Army.

In contrast to official American military assistance missions around the world, CIA police training and support group personnel in Thailand operated under what we have come to recognize as a business or commercial cover, in this instance that of the Overseas Southeast Asia Supply Company (SEA Supply). Commercial covers would be used repeatedly in the region. SEA Supply itself was a true commercial entity, incorporated in Miami, Florida. OSS Far Eastern Branch alumnus and former CIA employee Paul Helliwell, who acted as Thailand's honorary general consul in Miami, reportedly served as legal counsel and advisor to SEA.

Such independent commercial companies conduct their own business while remaining available to take contracts for covert CIA activities, or to simply have their offices, addresses, and business identities used as covers for CIA officers in the field. In some instances the companies make sufficient money to be independent from a financial perspective, but in other cases they need ongoing contracts for CIA business to keep them functioning. Such businesses are typically owned and operated by either retired military officers or security-cleared and trusted individuals. One of the issues in such operations is that while serving its own financial interests, an independent company may engage in dubious business practices or even in illegal activities. In any event, such companies have far more leeway for independent business activity than companies established and managed solely by the CIA. Such companies are known as proprietaries, with some level of operational and financial oversight by CIA employees.

Compartmentalization is the key to the maintenance of secrecy. Using commercial business as covers or fronts became so common and so effective that in many instances company personnel had little idea of the complex financial and banking activities that separated legitimate business from Agency business. At times one part of the company would handle the conventional business arrangements with foreign police, military, and government officers, unaware that another component of the same company was arranging clandestine shipments of arms and equipment to these same officials. The separation of duties also offered the opportunity for CIA clients within the military or government to take financial advantage of the compartmentalized relationship situation. In reality it often became difficult to separate Agency from client business, or "sanctioned" transactions and shipments of CIA surrogates—especially those of senior police or military officers—from the personal business of those same police, military, and government officers.

The evolution of covert commercial and legal operations (involving independent businessmen, lawyers, and bankers who are not actually employees of the CIA) has been just as fundamental to deniable warfare as has the evolution of covert paramilitary operations. Companies such as Overseas Southeast Asia Supply served as independent cover or front companies, while companies such as Civil Air Transport eventually became almost totally funded through CIA contracts, assuming the role of true CIA proprietary companies under actual Agency oversight. Both types of commercial fronts were used to shield the employment of personnel and the conduct of covert operational activities.[103] It might be imagined that arms transfers, even under the umbrella of front companies, are difficult to obscure in a deniable operation; after all, shipments of rifles and ammunition leave a paper trail. But when these transfers are arranged with the help of American "clients" such as the Thai National Police or the Thai military, the shipments become much more deniable. Import and export paperwork for such apparent government weapons transfers is easily arranged, since all parties act in accordance with the cover story.

According to Sam Cummings, a major figure in the international arms business for decades, weapons transactions offer the CIA the opportunity to further solidify personal relationships with foreign heads of state, government ministers, or military officers. The client state representatives simply agree to exorbitant prices for the weapons and then pocket the difference, with bills of sale and related paperwork adjusted according to an unstated agreement. Issues of local, client-state military, or political graft are of no legal concern to weapons venders such as Cummings's Interarms Corporation—or to the CIA itself, which is focused on its primary missions and operations.[104]

With deniable arms transfers in place, the next step is often more demanding; it involves the logistics for actually putting weapons and supplies in the hands of surrogate fighters. This can be challenging since the sales and shipments ostensibly are destined for a foreign, national government entity. In Thailand, SEA Supply assumed a major role in helping organize and arm special military units within the Thai National Police. The units were equipped with mortars, machine guns, rifles, and communications equipment from WWII stocks from Okinawa. Eventually SEA Supply added tanks, artillery, and aircraft to the select police units. With SEA Supply handling both shipment and distribution, not only was the CIA's position with the Thai police strengthened but the relationship also allowed the Thai police to skim materials and make money for themselves on weapons deals for transshipment to the ROC forces operating from the Burmese frontier. Given the positive American–Thai relationship, with presidential endorsement for the CIA military assistance program to the Thai police, and with SEA Supply organized to provide cover for covert shipments of materials and employment of CIA trainers and advisors, all the pieces were in place for what came to be known as Operation Paper—the American effort to support an ROC invasion of China's Yunnan province.

The U.S. had been receiving requests for money and weapons support from ROC commander General Li Mi and his representatives for some time. But when China began sending volunteers into the Korean conflict on the side of the North Koreans in November 1950, President Truman became receptive to the idea of a diversionary action against China. The initial advance of the North Koreans—and the constant threat that the Chinese would intervene in support—put immense pressure on the White House. It seemed that anything that might divert the Chinese communist military could only be a good thing, and General Li Mi's offer was one of the few options on the table. Still, senior officers of the CIA expressed doubts over the value of such an effort. Director Walter Smith and Far East Division Chief Desmond FitzGerald reportedly felt it would have little impact on deployment of the Chinese military. Despite the CIA's doubts, President Truman ordered that support be given to Li Mi's forces, using the logistics relationship with the Thai police as a type of cover. As previously noted, weapons were covertly provided to the ROC forces, rerouted from shipments officially recorded as going to the Thai police units being trained and supplied by the CIA.[105]

Weapons were shipped into Thailand by sea, using cargo carriers of the Republic of China–owned Taiwan Shipping Company and by CAT air transport. Ship manifests showed the cargo to be sugar and foodstuffs, while in reality it consisted of rifles, machine guns, mortars, radio equipment, and ammunition. At least four CAT planeloads of similar material were shipped in and transported by Thai police vehicles to the border for transfer to the ROC forces in Burma. Two Americans, using the ranks of major and captain, accompanied the Thai police with the shipments; they referred to themselves as CAT employees. We don't have their names or any further detail, as any extant documents relating to their dispatch are unavailable; what we do know is largely from local newspaper reports out of Burma at the time. The two Americans continued on with the ROC forces in their incursion into Yunnan province, using radio communications to coordinate further CAT airdrops of supplies.

It is unlikely that the Americans were aware that the weapons shipments followed a route and exchange process already well used by certain elements of the Thai police and Li Mi's forces. In addition, Li Mi had been raising money to sustain his forces by providing armed escort for the long-established opium shipments coming out of the border area into Thailand. The Thai police–Li Mi drug connection itself was well-known inside certain circles within Thailand even at the time. An American diplomat working in Thailand during the period described the Thai National Police chief as "the principal opium dealer in Thailand."[106] The surrogate armies chosen to open a new military front in southern China would receive American-supplied arms and advisors; those armies were already sustaining themselves largely through drug trading and they would continue to do so long after American support had come and gone. It would be the combination of the ROC–Golden Triangle–Thai military connections and significantly improved transportation options that would provide the first major surge in drug shipments from the Golden Triangle outside Thailand and Vietnam—to both Europe and the Americas. It would be a pattern that would extend over the following decades from Central America to Afghanistan.

The fact that the U.S. was equipping the ROC force became a rather open international secret. In April 1951, Burma protested to the American ambassador in Bangkok that stocks of arms, ammunition, and medical supplies were being transported from Taiwan to Thailand and, with U.S. involvement, being transported from Thailand to ROC forces inside Burma. By May, Burma was once again threatening to raise the issue at the United Nations.

And in May, Republic of China forces moved into China's Yunnan province, supported by some eleven CAT airdrops, including three thousand rifles and 160,000 rounds of ammunition. By June the communist Chinese People's Liberation Army had counterattacked, and shortly afterward Li Mi's forces were in general retreat back into Burma. Back inside the Burmese border, the two Americans were flown back to Bangkok by Thai police helicopter, and departed from there to Japan. In January 1952 Peking and Moscow raised the issue of the incursion at a UN general meeting in Paris. For its part, the U.S. officially denied any support being given to ROC troops in Burma or elsewhere. The American ambassador responded that the U.S. had been unable to find any evidence of U.S. citizens being involved with Li Mi's activities.[107] This had to be the American position since the U.S. was officially neutral and certainly could not be viewed as having American servicemen in the field with Republic of China forces invading China, which could potentially be portrayed by the Chinese as an act of war.

Although the first Yunnan effort was obviously a failure, Taiwan would independently continue its support for ROC forces in Burma, including ongoing air supply missions. Another Yunnan incursion was launched as late as 1957. Eventually Burma would actually invite Chinese People's Liberation Army forces into its border areas to help suppress and drive the ROC-affiliated forces out of Burma. That would only force the Republic of China–affiliated groups away from Burma and deeper into the Laotian border area of the Golden Triangle—eventually reducing access through Thailand by Taiwan and leading them into an even greater dependence on the drug trade.

Operation Paper had ended up as a fiasco, as the CIA itself predicted. It had not actually had any significant impact on the People's Liberation Army inside China, much less the situation on the ground in Korea. In early fall 1951, the CIA began to discontinue supplying Li Mi's army and the Defense Department began to cut financial subsidies, making its last payments in April 1952, at a time when direct military engagements between Burmese forces and Li Mi's troops had dramatically escalated.

Apart from some newspaper coverage in Taiwan, the whole affair had been largely absent from American press coverage; the American press itself was largely focused on Korea. In February 1952, *The*

New York Times carried a report that witnesses inside Burma had reported seeing Li Mi's troops with brand-new American weapons. The secret offensives against China, the actual American-backed invasion of Yunnan out of Burma, and the much larger-scale military support for ROC guerrilla operations on the mainland had all remained secret, at least from the American public.

American financial and weapons support for ROC forces in Burma had, however, helped expand and cement certain commercial relationships between Thai officials and Li Mi's forces. Those relationships would continue long after Li Mi himself was succeeded by others. A large and well-American-armed ROC force in the Shan States of Burma sustained itself not only by taking control of Burmese territory and by taxing the locals but also by organizing and massively escalating the opium trade into Thailand. In March 1952, a *London Sunday Observer* article datelined Bangkok described the process by which the ROC in Burma provided opium to the Thai police, who themselves facilitated arms shipments into the Burmese border area. The article named Willis Bird (former OSS officer and member of the original Thai Narasuan Committee outreach to the CIA), his company, and other Americans as "key middlemen" in the "arms-for-drugs" connection. The article also quoted U.S. Embassy sources in Thailand as admitting that "it cannot be denied we are in (the) opium trade" due to American involvement in supporting Li Mi's forces in Burma.[108]

One of the primary by-products of Operation Paper was that it added a new level of logistics to what was a centuries-old opium trade out of the Shan States of Burma. Caravan routes down through Burma and into Thailand were used for the trade, with the opium being carried by pack animals. Merchants were left to make their own individual deals and arrangements with Thai middlemen. With the arrival of the ROC forces, and their focus on fund-raising via the opium trade, shipments became consolidated, and high-level deals between ROC leaders and senior Thai officials dramatically increased the efficiency and volume of the Shan States drug trade.[109]

In addition, the potential for illicit air shipments increased as Operation Paper ended and Taiwanese aircraft took over the long-term supply chores for various ROC units in Burma. In order to support the initial Yunnan operation, CAT began a series of flights into relatively unimproved airfields in the Burmese border region. Supplies for Li Mi's troops were dropped in by parachute from CAT missions transiting either through Thailand or through Saigon or Da Nang in Indochina. As the U.S. had backed off Operation Paper, CAT permission to fly into the area was terminated during the fall of 1951.

However, by early 1952, an airfield was improved to support actual landings and takeoffs and Taiwan refused to give up on its armies in Burma. A small Taiwanese airline (Fu Hsing) began sending in flights using a U.S. Catalina PBY aircraft. From 1952 to 1953, Fu Hsing Catalina aircraft made some thirty flights into the Burmese border area. Some thirty tons of supplies were reportedly carried in by the aircraft, in low-altitude night flights across Vietnam, Thailand, and Laos. Exactly what might have been transported out of the region on the return flights is not a matter of record but it seems unlikely that aircraft going in with thirty tons of supplies came back totally empty.

While ROC transport flights into the area tapered off, light aircraft began to come into the remote camps, taking out drugs and delivering gold and weapons in payment. In 1955, a small Thai Airways plane crashed on takeoff from a primitive airstrip on the Laotian side of the border (ROC-affiliated groups easily operated across the borders in the Golden Triangle area); the Thai pilot was killed while resisting arrest and drugs worth some $150,000 at the time were taken into custody by Laotian police.[110]

Although Operation Paper was over in a matter of months, American entanglement in the Golden Triangle drug trade had just begun. And in terms of international relationships, U.S. military involvement with a surrogate army in Burma, and the constant, official American deniability statements, had strongly alienated the Burmese government.

Taiwan would continue to support its allied forces on the frontiers of Burma, Laos, and Thailand, without direct U.S. involvement but on more than one occasion siphoning off American military assistance supplies including weapons and ammunition intended for use on Taiwan, and rerouting them to ROC units in the Golden Triangle region. As American materials continued to show up along the borders, it continually raised suspicions of American complicity. Eventually those same Republic of China forces in the Golden Triangle would reemerge in Laos at the end of the decade.

But the effort to contain Chinese communism went far beyond the Burmese border and beyond the hot war on the Korean peninsula. In Washington's view those were just the first stages in a Chinese push that could cost the West all of Indochina and eventually the entire Pacific Rim. If China could not be stopped, America might find itself back on a battle line at Hawaii, as it did in 1941. That would be intolerable. It would also be the strategic concern that would continue to focus American attention on Indochina.

CHAPTER 6

Regime Change

Both Presidents Truman and Eisenhower expected the CIA to be on guard against the growth of communist influence, to identify such threats, and to generate proposals to counter them. This was standard operating practice and would continue until the end of the Cold War. In looking for potential threats in Latin America, the CIA came to the view that the popularly elected liberal, socialist-leaning leader in Guatemala, President Jacobo Guzman Árbenz, was becoming a focal point for Soviet bloc penetration of the Americas. That attitude was initially supported by Truman Administration CIA Director Walter Bedell Smith. Smith and the CIA began lobbying for a sanctioned covert support program to assist anticommunist elements in Guatemala, identified by the CIA as the Catholic Church hierarchy, landowners, and business interests, as well as certain university groups and the army.

But this was not Indochina, where America had established military assistance relationships in place, with access to existing forces such as those of the Republic of China on Taiwan. There was no organized insurgency against Árbenz, no rebel force engaged with his regime. Covertly and deniably deposing a democratically elected government in Guatemala was going to be new challenge for both the Eisenhower Administration and the CIA. It would prove quite a learning experience for both, setting a precedent and developing a brand-new band of shadow warriors.

From America's perspective, the Guatemalan regime change effort would eventually be viewed as amazingly successful. It was relatively bloodless at the time, despite the fact that new regimes in Guatemala in later years produced a legacy of violence and death squad murders. Most importantly, its final success during the Eisenhower Administration was a major influence on President Eisenhower, encouraging an increasing tendency to turn to the CIA and deniable operations as a solution for international challenges to his administration.

Eisenhower would go on to establish an American practice of preemption; there was to be no hesitation in responding to threatened or actual communist expansion anywhere around the globe. Publicly the position was that if any anticommunist regime felt threatened and asked for help, the United States was going to provide it with assistance. Of course in certain situations, as in French Indochina, American military assistance was going to be limited, ranging from financial support to very low-profile involvement of American aircraft and service personnel. And military assistance to friendly albeit endangered governments was certainly not the only response. As noted by CIA Director Allen Dulles, the U.S. didn't really have to wait to be invited. It was accepted that communist-leaning leaders and governments might unfortunately come into place legally and even democratically, through "the usual processes of government." In such instances America was perfectly justified in working with anticommunist factions to overthrow and replace those governments. Years later Henry Kissinger, a man with the ear of more than one president in the positions of national security advisor and then secretary of state, would state such a viewpoint even more succinctly, in regard to covert American regime change in Chile, in 1970: "I don't see why we need to stand by and watch a country go Communist due to the irresponsibility of its own people."[111]

And just as no invitation was required, it was also not necessary for the U.S. to announce its activities; it might well maintain an international position of strict neutrality while moving into active covert political or even paramilitary operations. Preemption—either overt or covert—would not just be the stance of the Eisenhower

Administration. National security, and whatever it would require, would remain the first concern of every successive administration both during and beyond the Cold War. Failure to deal with emerging threats would also represent a major area of administration criticism from whichever political party was not in power.

The 1950 popular presidential election in Guatemala of Jacobo Guzman Árbenz generated American concern that he might be easily influenced by communist factions. Additionally, his agrarian reform policies were perceived as being especially threatening to the United Fruit Company and other American business interests within the country. Much has been written about United Fruit's ability to influence congressmen and other figures in Washington, D.C. There is little doubt that United Fruit had a mutually supportive relationship with the CIA, even allowing its operatives to use the company as a commercial cover.[112] While United Fruit's Washington connections were indeed considerable, it may well have been most important that one of its employees, Tommy Corcoran, had direct access to policy makers in Washington, D.C. Corcoran had been active during the Roosevelt Administration, with the American Volunteer Group in China prior to the Second World War.

Among his many later activities, Corcoran also served as legal counsel for United Fruit and had the ear of President Eisenhower. Corcoran was also close to CIA officer J.C. King, whose jurisdiction was the Western Hemisphere Division.[113] With extensive business connections inside Guatemala, Corcoran was able to serve as an important source of information on both political factions within the country, as well as the emerging reform measures of the Árbenz regime. There is no doubt that Corcoran was a source of information for both the CIA and the president in regard to commercial and political affairs in Guatemala, and his concerns over a growing communist influence are well documented.[114, 115] As we noted in an earlier chapter, even CIA officers believed it had been Corcoran, rather than the Agency, who had convinced Eisenhower to order a revitalized covert action operation against Guatemala.[116]

Other U.S. government factions, especially the State Department, were at first more cautious about taking any action against Guatemala, offering the view that it would be seen as an overreaction on America's part, which would indicate U.S. weakness in Latin America. State likened U.S. intervention to "the spectacle of the elephant shaking with alarm before the mouse."[117] As an alternative, the State Department would have preferred a moderate policy of persuasion and cooperative assistance that would have included defense assistance pacts with the neighboring states of El Salvador, Nicaragua, and Honduras. The approach was of the classic "carrot and stick" form, offering American developmental cooperation with Guatemala to discourage it from moving too far towards the Soviet bloc, while at the same time building buffer zones around it through military assistance to its neighbors.

Both the initial Truman Administration Guatemala covert action project of 1952—known as PBFORTUNE—and its successor, PBSUCCESS, were heavily influenced by President Somoza of Nicaragua. In April 1952, during a visit to Washington, Somoza proposed that, if provided with arms and support, he and Guatemalan exile Carlos Castillo Armas could overthrow the Árbenz government. Armas had been a part of the Guatemalan military establishment, serving on the general staff and receiving training at Fort Leavenworth, Kansas. He was fervent supporter of the conservative factions in Guatemala and an aggressive anticommunist. President Truman reportedly asked CIA Director Walter Bedell Smith to investigate the potential of covert action, and Smith dispatched a high-level officer to explore the possibility. As we will see, virtually all American covert operations require one or more third-party nations as willing or at least amenable partners, and there would be volunteers to support the Guatemala project—with Nicaragua being a major asset.

The State Department's proposed "neutrality" position was accepted as the public American posture towards Guatemala; but behind that public position, work began on a plan to oust the Árbenz regime. The covert action project was given the CIA cryptonym PBFORTUNE.[118] A CIA officer was directed to contact Guatemalan dissidents about armed action against the Árbenz regime.

Based on his report, the CIA initially supplied Armas, the CIA's surrogate rebel leader, with arms and $225,000 in funding. It was also agreed that the friendly and openly anticommunist leaders of Nicaragua and Honduras be encouraged to covertly assist in providing bases and perhaps even aircraft that could be used in air support for Armas. The State Department ultimately concurred with a program of covert action and the operation began to move forward.

A CIA historical study of the early weeks of the Guatemala project in its first PBFORTUNE incarnation reveals that one of the contemplated tactics—initially proposed by Somoza—was assassination. Months before the actual project approval, CIA Directorate of Plans officers compiled a hit list. They worked with an existing Guatemalan army list of communists and with information from the CIA Directorate of Intelligence. Their first effort produced what was described as a list of "top flight Communists whom the new government would desire to eliminate immediately in event of a successful anti-Communist coup."[119] Project discussions had included a proposal from a CIA officer for first spreading rumors that the communists were dissatisfied with Árbenz, then killing him in a fashion that would be "laid to the commies" and used to create massive army defections to the Armas forces.

In late November 1952, an Árbenz opposition leader reportedly confirmed that Armas had special "K" groups whose mission was to kill all leading political and military leaders, and that the hit list with the locations of the homes and offices of all targets had already been drawn up. The project officers asked headquarters to review the eliminations list and also a list of some sixteen additional communists/sympathizers who should be locked up after a successful coup. The compilation and review of target lists—sometimes referred to as blacklists given their high level of secrecy—continued to be a part of the PBSUCCESS project, which replaced PBFORTUNE. Some nine months later Armas forwarded CIA headquarters a "disposal" list that called for the "execution through executive action" of some fifty-eight "category 1" Guatemalans and the imprisonment or exile of another seventy-four designated as "category 2."[120]

In December 1952, a project officer related that Castillo Armas planned to make maximum use of the K groups. Another CIA source provided the information that Nicaraguan, Honduran, and Salvadoran soldiers (operating in civilian dress) were designated to infiltrate Guatemala and assassinate unnamed communist leaders.[121] A CIA Western Hemisphere memo of 1953 also suggested assassinating key military officers if they refused to convert to the rebel cause; and that fall, another CIA plan of action included a reference to "neutralizing" key military leaders.

At the same time, CIA headquarters was advised that as of September 1952, General Rafael Trujillo of the Dominican Republic had agreed to aid Armas in return for the murder of four Santo Domingans residing in Guatemala. Armas had agreed, but stipulated that the murders were not to be carried out during the military coup due to security reasons. The CIA history notes that Armas was independently planning similar eliminations and had already organized and was training special squads for that purpose. The history noted no headquarters response to the compilation of the lists and to Armas's elimination squads.[122] That is consistent with what we will generally see in regard to assassination as a political tactic in covert operations: surrogates propose it; they receive intelligence assistance and even target lists, but there is never any record beyond that point. This practice provides its; own form of CIA deniability.

One of the first challenges was to get considerable quantities of weapons and military supplies staged inside and around the borders of Guatemala, and to do so in the face of a variety of U.S. neutrality laws, customs regulations, and diplomatic hurdles—all without exposing the entire project to either the media or other interested parties. And the first lesson learned was that problems with logistics could in themselves be fatal to even the most diligently organized operation.

Much of the following exploration of the logistics effort is taken from the detailed research and writing of Canadian researcher Gary Murr, including the review of some fourteen thousand newly released government documents relating to clandestine operations in

Guatemala and Cuba—specifically focusing on weapons, ammunition, and logistics as well as the activities of Sam Cummings of Interarmco/Interarms. Murr's document sources will be cited independently of his manuscript, *The Forgotten.*

> The obvious starting point for sourcing deniable weapons was to gather together enough "foreign arms and ammunition" in a secure location, one with easy access to international shipping. Guatemala project documents disclose the cryptonym for that effort—a source designated as COATHANGER.[123] A series of memoranda from 1952 discuss shipments involving COATHANGER, including how the material would be packaged and handled in preparation for shipping; the crates were to each weigh less than 200 pounds to permit hand carry and treated for a minim [sic] of six months storage in a tropical climate. It was also noted that some of the containers might still be in their "original Spanish crates."[124] Further study of the documents strongly suggests that the materials associated with COATHANGER were held at the Army's Raritan Arsenal [in Raritan, New Jersey]. Using Raritan as a collection point for materials for clandestine operations made perfect sense given the nature and location of that facility. Located adjacent to the Raritan River and some 20 miles southwest of New York City, Raritan Arsenal had been one of the major supply points for weapons going overseas during WWII (it would continue in service until 1963).
>
> The initial shipment destined for the Guatemala operation involved some 60,000 pounds of material, which would have required multiple covert flights if air transport was used. The alternative was "to have a Company boat guided by the Coast Guard to a secret place not far from [redacted] where the material could be loaded by our own people, but where there would be the risk of the vessel's crew knowing that arms and equipment are being obtained in the United States by means at least winked at by the authorities."[125]
>
> If a CIA boat were to be used, the material was to be picked up at the dock in Free Trade Zone, New York City, and taken to

Puerto Cabezas, Nicaragua. Further memoranda discuss using a ship coming from DTROBALO, a major CIA facility at Robalo, Panama, which would pick up the consigned "hardware" and carry it on to Puerto Cabezas and Castillo Armas. The ship itself was referred to as being of the "Nicaraguan Line" and the CIA field head of the Guatemalan project would receive the shipment, supervise its unloading and storage, and take care of its distribution.

Plans were for the supplies to begin moving in September, 1952 . . . with a small shipment of 172 boxes weighing only 28,212 pounds would be airlifted and the rest, involving some 124,493 pounds of cargo, would go by boat. The shipments were truly huge, especially in regard to the size of the small Armas force. No more than two hundred fighters were being supplied with 750,000 rounds of rifle and pistol ammunition as well as 600 rounds of both high explosive (HE) and armor piercing (AP) anti-tank artillery. In addition they were shipped 2,200 hand grenades. Beyond the initial shipments, it was planned to send an additional 917,000 rounds of ammunition through the port of New Orleans on the motor ship *Leon*. Associated documents reflect that at least $250,000 was being provided to Armas and the rebel effort. Clearly a major covert warfare operation was being anticipated.[126]

Early in October 1952, with PBFORTUNE operations finally underway, the son of Nicaraguan leader General Somoza happened to be in a meeting in Panama with the Assistant Secretary of State for Inter-American Affairs. During casual conversation the son inquired whether or not the "machinery" promised his father "was on the way." This seems to have produced considerable discussion among those present and sent Secretary of State Dean Acheson directly to President Truman. Apparently Acheson, who had grudgingly accepted the project in the first place, made a convincing case that the operation had been compromised and was coming [sic] a diplomatic risk. Within days the PBFORTUNE was suspended.[127] That sort of disconnect between the State Department and the CIA would become far too common, as would leaks of planned operations. We will find that compromised operational security become an ongoing issue in Latin American covert operations. To many CIA officers it simply seemed to be a cultural risk.

The mixed emotions at the State Department seem to have faded as concern about a communist foothold in Guatemala continued to escalate. By the fall of 1953, U.S. policy makers were increasingly frustrated as Árbenz seemed to be moving even closer to the communists, legalizing the Guatemalan Communist Party and suppressing anticommunist opposition. Perhaps equally important, he had further infuriated American business interests and had begun expropriating more United Fruit Company holdings as part of his agrarian reform initiatives.

In public session the U.S. Congress had discussed a resolution proposed by Senator Lyndon Johnson that was intended to serve as an "an unmistakable warning that we are determined to keep communism out of the Western Hemisphere." Congressional rhetoric was inflammatory, with Representative Jack Brooks of Texas endorsing the resolution as "so basically American and so basically anti-Communist" that support for it was urgent, in light of the fact that "a Communist-dominated government in Guatemala is only 700 miles from Texas—only 960 miles, or a few hours' bomber time, from the refiners, the chemical plants, and the homes of my own Second District in Texas. The Monroe Doctrine—1823—is still a vital, living force. But it needs restatement in light of modern conditions," said Brooks. Fellow Texan Martin Dies agreed: "The Soviet government . . . has challenged the Monroe Doctrine. To that challenge there can be but one response."[128]

Behind the scenes, senators were closely in touch with the senior officers of the CIA, encouraging them to take an aggressive stance against the communists in Guatemala. Senator Alexander Wiley of Wisconsin had encouraged Allen Dulles to go public in announcing shipments of Soviet client state weapons to Guatemala as "part of the master plan of world communism." Senator George Smathers of Florida consistently used similar language, warning that "the Politburo of Guatemala" was "taking orders from Moscow" and that the arrival of a cargo ship with armaments "was concrete evidence of Soviet intervention."[129]

While these dialogues occurred, the CIA determined that Guatemala had purchased a shipment of military equipment from an Eastern Bloc country. The shipment was coming by cargo ship from a Soviet client state. Allen Dulles promoted the idea that with these weapons, Árbenz could "roll down and seize the Panama Canal."[130] Later, CIA officers working in support of the coup operation managed to bribe a Guatemalan military officer, who confirmed that the shipment, brought in by the ship Alfhem, had carried a mix of virtually unusable Czech weapons including heavy cannon designed for railcar mounting, antitank guns, and a large quantity of vintage WWII German and British weapons—most of which were rusted and nonworking. The shipment itself was in reality not so much Soviet intervention as Czech profit-taking. The determination of the actual content of the shipment via the bribe occurred after PBSUCCESS paramilitary CIA officer William "Rip" Robertson had tried (unsuccessfully) to attack the train carrying the shipment from its port of arrival.[131]

In a study titled "Congress, the CIA, and Guatemala, 1954—Sterilizing a 'Red Infection'," David Barrett presents the proposition that Congress and the American press were aware and supportive of American intervention in Guatemala. The CIA certainly was not operating without extended moral support from the American government. And while none of the resolutions addressed tactics, Congress was clearly expressing its desire to do "whatever it took to stop the commies"—without doubt the consensus attitude of the earliest days of the Cold War.[132] Gradually, over the course of several months, the CIA Guatemala operation reemerged—with most of the same players, the same plans, and much the same logistics. Only the name had changed—to PBSUCCESS.

During the interim between PBFORTUNE and PBSUCCESS, the assembled weapons shipments went into holding, transported by the motor ship SS *Leon* (as planned) and deposited at a CIA facility, Punta Robalo, in the Panama Canal Zone. The *Leon* was not a CIA ship, but rather a vessel owned and operated by none other than United Fruit. Working with supportive American companies became routine, and CIA Western Hemisphere head J.C. King established regular communications with a number of corporate leaders. In a practice that would seem at least to have annoyed the CIA security division, King also began briefing those leaders in advance about pending operations. Documents reveal that King conducted a number of confidential meetings shortly before the actual start of the secret military effort against the Árbenz government in Guatemala. Those meetings included the directors of that several major American companies, that had major financial investments in Guatemala and whose businesses involved significant imports and shipping out of Guatemala. The list of companies being briefed included W.R. Grace and Company, Standard Oil of New Jersey, American Coffee Corporation, and others unnamed in the documents. The briefings are described in notes as an "approach to heads of American companies for covert action."[133] Such corporate briefings seem to have become somewhat the standard, at least within King's Western Hemisphere region. We find similar executive corporate briefings occurring prior to the Bay of Pigs landings in Cuba.

In anticipation of renewed effort on the Guatemala project, the CIA had already begun construction on a new pier at Punta Robalo, Panama. It would allow them to handle larger vessels while avoiding being seen at U.S. Navy piers in the Canal Zone. The CIA also began working with Armas for his purchase of a landing craft–type vessel (LCI) that could be used to transport weapons and supplies on "caching runs" from Punta Robalo to invasion staging points. In addition, plans were made for test flights to prove in aerial supply operations out of the Canal Zone. It appears from CIA operational memos that the air supply practice runs were successful. However, the LCI craft purchased for the effort ultimately proved to be unsatisfactory. On one trip, problems with the ship required that it be rescued by a U.S. Navy ship. The Navy was not impressed with an independent CIA shipping operation and registered its view of the CIA's maritime competency with senior figures in Washington. That particular maritime supply approach was abandoned, although the CIA would return to the sea in later projects.

Instead of continuing the use of its own ship, the CIA turned to what would become a more standard practice: using standard shipping companies with appropriate commercial cover and licenses. In order to accomplish that and to enable further shipments out of the Raritan Arsenal, it turned once again to its former employee, now the head of Interarmco: Sam Cummings.[134] That approach would prove more successful and probably continued over an extended period. During the covert CIA Indonesian coup effort later in the decade, one crate of weapons with INTERARMCO stenciled on it would be recovered from the Indonesian rebels. Cummings would vehemently deny being involved, and maintained that his company was being unknowingly used as a cover for weapons shipments.[135] Given Cummings's extended history with the CIA, his claim to being used as a cover seems quite justified. However, it would be hard to credit that it was unknowingly.

With a $3 million working budget, the new PBSUCCESS project was going forward with a vengeance. Actual field operations would begin with psychological warfare but if that did not succeed over a period of eight months, the military option was to go into play. With final approval from President Eisenhower, the CIA significantly accelerated its support for the Armas insurgents, from financial and logistic activities to training and propaganda. In the previously mentioned briefing meetings with selected corporate leaders, J.C. King and CIA Deputy Director General Charles Cabell had been quite explicit: "General Cabell stated we not only have a full green light to go ahead, but a bayonet prodding our back to get going."[136]

Ultimately, PBSUCCESS had come to involve effective coordination with a supportive State Department; its official objective was "to remove covertly, and without bloodshed if possible, the menace of the present communist-controlled government of Guatemala."[137] However, even in the project outline, the "roll up" of communists and collaborators to follow after a successful coup was discussed.

At the national policy level, the project was viewed (or at least documented) as to be conducted without bloodshed, possibly with the simple imprisonment or deportation of Guatemalan communists as its final result. As we will repeatedly see, the high-level documents authorizing neat, surgical covert operations—with minimal casualties and collateral damage—rarely resemble the reality of field operations. When such neatly defined projects are turned over to the operations personnel who have to make them work, the mission becomes the driving factor and the tactics chosen are simply the tactics that will do the job. These early covert warfare operations began to build a cadre of shadow warriors who developed their own tactics and techniques, as well as their own codes of conduct in regard to accomplishing their missions.

CHAPTER 7

Shadow Warriors

Guatemala and the PBSUCCESS project brought together a group of CIA shadow warriors whom we will be following in operations through some three decades. Their success brought them commendations directly from President Eisenhower and secret awards from the top levels of the CIA. On occasion that same CIA leadership would face congressional inquiries based on certain of the individuals' activities—it would even get to the point of senior officers committing perjury to obfuscate and cover up actions of this same set of clandestine operations officers. The techniques, tactics, and even attitudes this group first demonstrated in Guatemala would have an impact on covert operations from Latin America, across Southeast Asia, and even into Africa. They developed confidence that CIA leaders would support them even in the face of protests from American ambassadors.

As we proceed we will find that that opposing views between the CIA and the State Department were not all that unusual; there are numerous examples of such disagreement over the need for and implementation of covert action. During the Eisenhower and Kennedy administrations CIA positions led presidents to issue directives for covert, deniable interventions, as in Guatemala—often with initial State Department opposition. In those instances where State's arguments initially carried the day with the president, the next stage was often an enhanced program of economic aid, coupled with enhanced military assistance activities, as in Laos. Interestingly, we will find that in later administrations, State Department figures and secretaries of state would be the ones pushing for more aggressive actions, while the CIA issued warnings that the operations State was pushing for were not going to be successful.

In instances in which the State Department's political and economic initiatives stalled, concurrent military advisory programs carried the potential for establishing influential contacts with anticommunist military leaders. If necessary, those personal contacts could then be used to stimulate coup attempts. We will explore examples of such unsuccessful efforts in Indonesia, and ultimately inconclusive success in Laos. Later, during the decades of the 1970s and 1980s, American-backed military coups would become much more successful at ousting suspect regimes across Latin America. By that time, many members of the PBSUCCESS team would be back at work supporting replacement regimes with new military assistance efforts. In fact, one of them—David Sánchez Morales—would become a major counterinsurgency advisor, working for the Joint Chiefs of Staff across the continent of South America.

The names of those assigned to the Guatemala project are still officially redacted from the available PBSUCCESS documents. In succeeding years, however, autobiographies and CIA historical studies of the Agency have revealed considerable detail. As an example, in David Phillips's autobiography of his CIA career, *The Night Watch*, he described the PBSUCCESS command structure in descending rank order: at the helm, Allen Dulles (director), followed by Richard Bissell, Frank Wisner (head of the Directorate of Plans), Tracy Barnes (project chief), and J.C. King (director, Western Hemisphere). These individuals will become familiar as we delve into the highly secret CIA operations against Fidel Castro and Cuba during the Kennedy Administration.

David Phillips wrote about being personally recruited for the PBSUCCESS project by Tracy Barnes, described by Phillips in his autobiography as a "super grade" GS18 officer in the Directorate of Plans. Phillips was recruited to head the propaganda activities of the new Guatemala project. He had entered the CIA as a contract employee after being a professional actor and Latin American newspaper operator. Contract employees are sometimes brought into the CIA for specific projects and are often used in fieldwork to provide special deniability, often already having jobs or roles that provide a type of built-in cover. Phillips was assigned to psychological and propaganda operations in PBSUCCESS and his work proved to be seminal in the overall operation, helping to save what had become a small-scale military invasion that stalled out, even in the face of limited military opposition. Phillips's propaganda and psychological work was considered so outstanding that he quickly established a reputation as a psychological and propaganda prodigy within the Agency.[138]

Tracy Barnes had been one of the first employees of the newly formed Central Intelligence Agency, later widely viewed and described as one of the "old boys," the core "cadre" of the organization.[139] During the Second World War, Barnes had served in the Office of Strategic Services and was quite close to and personally endorsed by Allen Dulles—whom Barnes had assisted with some of Dulles's European Office of Strategic Services projects. Following the war and before joining the CIA, he served as a special assistant to the undersecretary of the Army, and as deputy director of the Psychological Strategy Board during the Korean War. In 1953, Barnes had been appointed special assistant for paramilitary psychological operations, a unit generally referred to as the "PP," with a staff that contained both psychological and paramilitary personnel. There is a general consensus that Barnes's fast track within the agency was heavily influenced both personally by Dulles and by the perceived success of the Guatemala project, but even at the start of that project, Barnes was already a super-grade officer, reporting to former OSS officer Frank Wisner, who in turn reported to Richard Bissell.

Richard Bissell had also served in the OSS during WWII and had extensive social and political connections with a group of Washington journalists, politicians, and government officials that became known as the Georgetown Set. Bissell had been appointed as administrator for the Marshall Plan in Germany and went on to head the Economic Cooperation Administration. After that he had worked for the Ford Foundation before Wisner persuaded him to join the CIA. He eventually replaced Wisner as deputy director. Tracy Barnes served as the senior officer in charge of the Guatemala project and his staff included Albert Haney and Haney's protégé Henry Hecksher. Hecksher had come into the agency from Army Intelligence and after service in the OSS. He initially served as acting chief of the Berlin CIA station under State Department cover. Known for his aggressiveness and anticommunist passions, Hecksher in 1953 had cabled for permission to issue arms and weapons to the East Berliners during their abortive revolt against the Soviets. In Guatemala, Hecksher posed as a German coffee buyer, reportedly wearing lederhosen in support of his chosen image. In reality he was busy recruiting intelligence sources and assets, including army officers. Hecksher also took CIA contract employees into the field inside Guatemala.

Paramilitary operations and training for the project were conducted by William "Rip" Robertson and David Morales. Generally speaking, the CIA operations directorate neither needs nor can afford to maintain a large pool of experienced military personnel. In later operations we will frequently encounter American military officers who were detached from their regular assignments for specific service with the CIA. Such individuals were commonly referred to as detailees since they were detailed for covert Agency service on a project basis. Individuals who performed well would often find themselves routinely moving back and forth between normal duty assignments and CIA projects. Robertson had been in the Marines during WWII, earning two Silver Stars at Saipan, and came into the Agency as a paramilitary officer. He displayed a tendency towards independent action and disregard for orders during the Guatemalan project. Robertson dispatched aircraft to bomb a British commercial vessel, the *Springfjord*, suspected of carrying a weapons shipment. That was not only against direct CIA orders but reportedly at the command of Nicaragua's General Anastasio Somoza. That affair left

Robertson in the bad graces of certain senior officers, especially J.C. King.[140] It was later determined that the *Springfjord* had been carrying only coffee and cotton. After PBSUCCESS, Robertson left the CIA for several years, moving and working in Nicaragua, where he had personal ties to the Nicaraguan dictator, giving him a certain leverage on local business activities. During his service in Guatemala, David Morales was assigned as an operations officer on the Paramilitary Psychological staff. Following the success of the project, he became an intelligence officer assigned to CIA foreign intelligence and served under State Department covers in several Latin American assignments, including Cuba. Over the next decade, Morales would rise in rank from Army corporal to the government personnel equivalent of lieutenant colonel. The obituaries of Morales and Robertson make mention of their military service but none of their years of employment and work with the CIA. In fact, Morales's employment by the CIA is still officially denied. Both men represent the prototypical Agency "shadow warrior."

The activities of the individuals selected for PBSUCCESS provide us with considerable detail on the CIA's covert warfare practices in its earliest operations. Initial military resources for the project consisted of a mix of some 170 Guatemalan exiles; personnel made available from Nicaraguan President Anastasio Somoza and Rafael Trujillo, the ruler of the Dominican Republic; and American "soldiers of fortune"—more accurately described as CIA paramilitary contract employees. Beyond that, possibly the most important resource was a "guerrilla air force" of planes, pilots, and service personnel. The air element was critical in projecting the image of a much stronger and better-equipped rebellion than actually existed. And the "rebel" air unit was organized by Whiting Willauer, formerly the senior manager of Civil Air Transport, the CIA-affiliated company utilized across all secret front operations against communist China.[141] Most of the PBSUCCESS force operated out of Honduras and comprised a dozen aircraft, including three bombers, fighters, and fighter bombers. Two of the fighter aircraft had been loaned by President Somoza and conducted a number of the more effective air strikes. And, as in a number of other air operations we will describe, the identity of the pilots flying the guerrilla air force planes posed a major problem for overall deniability—it would have been hard to explain why the planes supposedly being flown by the rebel air force were Chinese.

With personnel, air support, and weapons in place, the next major step was training and tactical preparation. David Morales was deeply involved in the Guatemala project's training efforts just as he would later be in preparations for training select exile intelligence units for insertion and landing in Cuba. And although the CIA's historical study notes that "assassination was not mentioned specifically in the overall plan," it went on to point out that the project chief "requested a special paper on the liquidation of personnel on 5 January 1954." This paper was to be utilized to brief the training chief for PBSUCCESS before he left to begin training Armas's forces in Honduras in January 1954. The next day, another cable requested twenty silencers for. 22-caliber rifles—strongly suggesting that Armas's people were indeed going to be prepared for assassinations. Documents also show that the chief discussed the training plan, which included "Armas's request for PBSUCCESS to train the 'assassins with a senior project officer.'" The training of the assassination specialists was discussed with Armas again in February of 1954.[142]

Regardless of any official position in Washington, PBSUCCESS CIA field staff were involved with the subject of assassination and in preparing surrogate personnel to carry out political eliminations. This conclusion is corroborated by the preparation of an actual CIA "assassination manual" drafted early in 1952 in support of the Guatemalan project. Titled *A Study of Assassinations* and containing background on the employment and justification of—as well as planning of—assassinations, the document provides an in-depth study of techniques and commentary on devices and strategies ranging from bare hands to, "accidents" and the use of drugs, "edged" weapons, various firearms, and explosives. In addition, some twenty-plus known political assassinations were listed and outlined. The document has the appearance of a training guide in that it contains detailed instructions and advice in regard to various assassination techniques.[143] Decades later, in an ironic twist, a CIA contract officer would prepare a similar, albeit less detailed assassination manual for President Reagan's secret war against Nicaragua—the same country that had played the key third-party support role in PBSUCCESS.

As far as official documents go, the idea of assassination teams (K groups) apparently originated with Armas. But as early as 1952, the Guatemala project head routinely included two assassination specialists in his training plans. In early 1954, the plans for sabotage teams also included the creation of a K group trained to perform assassinations—focusing on local communists and communist properties rather than attacks directly on the Guatemalan army. A chart depicting Armas's organization (Calligeris, a cryptonym for Armas) showed a K group and the chart being distributed in paramilitary training packages in the spring of 1954. A June briefing also mentioned that the sabotage teams would assassinate known communists once the invasion operations were under way.

Years later, a CIA internal study of assassination related to PBSUCCESS asserted that none of its related assassination training or plans were actually implemented; specifically the study stated that "no covert action plan involving assassinations of Guatemalans was ever approved or implemented." It also noted that no CIA headquarters replies of any sort were located in regard to certain assassination proposals, and pointed out that no evidence had been found that individuals from the early PBFORTUNE target list had actually been killed either before or in the final coup.

Although not generally discussed in regard to most of the historical treatments of PBSUCCESS—and certainly not mentioned in David Phillips's autobiography—it appears that assassination, or at least the threat of it, was also a significant weapon in psychological warfare. In one instance, "mourning" cards were mailed to top communist leaders, mentioning purges and executions of communists around the world and hinting at the "forthcoming doom" of the addressees. Death-threat letters were also sent to top Guatemalan communists. These actions, part of the "Nerve War Against Individuals," included sending wooden coffins, hangman's nooses, and phony bombs to the targeted individuals. Beyond that the targets were treated to slogans such as "Here Lives a Spy" and "You have only 5 days" posted on their houses.[144] The rebel leaders pushed to go beyond threats, pressuring for the "violent disposal" of senior communist leaders. In one instance PBSUCCESS headquarters pushed back against endorsing immediate murders while giving mixed messages, including remarking that the idea was not a good one for the present time, since it might touch off violent reprisals. The responses noted that a CIA field officer might wish "to study the suggestion for utility now or in the future." The CIA's own historical study of PBSUCCESS notes that the field officers continued to seek headquarters support for assassinations and for Armas's K group plans, but no record of any documented endorsement from high-level personnel at either the State Department or the White House exists. In March 1954, a meeting at PBSUCCESS headquarters was held to consider the murder of fifteen to twenty of the top Guatemalan leaders by "Trujillo's trained pistoleros." The record indicates that the idea was endorsed by the CIA Director of Plans Operations Richard Bissell, with concurrence from the State Department representative. Another attendee stated that "such elimination was part of the plan and could be done," objecting only to murders at that particular time. Another unnamed attendee was very much in favor of the assassinations, stating that "knocking off" the leaders might make it possible for the army to immediately take control.[145]

It is important to note that in virtually none of this planning and discussion was it assumed that CIA employees themselves would be conducting assassinations. Such actions would be done in a totally deniable fashion, by working with Agency surrogate fighters, members of the rebel forces (paramilitary trainees), or individuals provided by other anticommunist governments. Generally speaking, the murders would be restricted to those "irrevocably implicated in Communist doctrine and policy," "out-and-out proven Communist leaders," or "those few individuals in key government and military positions of tactical importance whose removal for psychological, organizational, or other reasons is mandatory for the success of military action." The CIA project chief seems to have consistently emphasized to Armas that any assassinations should take place only during the actual invasion and coup attacks.[146]

The records reveal that the CIA field officers engaged in ongoing discussion of assassinations, including disposal of specific individuals, and a constant dialogue about whether they could wait for the military action or would indeed have to move beforehand to ensure success of the coup. On occasion specific proposals were passed to headquarters for approval. The historical study found no replies either approving or denying requests. We will continue to observe that such directions appear always to have been given verbally and not committed to paper in any fashion. The Guatemala operation teaches us a great deal about how the Agency became entangled in the subject of political assassination as a part of regime change. Initially the idea came from its surrogates, the Armas faction. The reality is that rebels, especially those with intense political views, often feel that literally eliminating their opponents is the fast and sure road to a quick victory. In a number of the operations we will cover, rebel leaders broached the idea of assassination to their U.S. contacts; it is a constant we find from Latin America to Southeast Asia and on to Afghanistan. The only question arising is to what extent the American personnel respond to the idea of assassination. As we discussed in the preceding chapter, there certainly was intense pressure from both the president and the American Congress in regard to success in Guatemala. It must be acknowledged that intense pressure for success at any cost was coming from the very top of the American government. And that pressure was felt within the PBSUCCESS team. In June 1954, a senior project officer traveled to Washington and submitted a proposal for "specific sabotage and possibly political assassinations" as an alternative to the paramilitary action program.

At that time the proposal was rejected "for the immediate future" but a CIA headquarters directive was given to generate a more specific plan, including individual targets, timing, and statements of purpose and advantage for each target. The situation seems to have been that the team might debate the effectiveness and timing of political assassination but there simply was no fundamental objection to its use as a tactic in covert action. It is also clear that to the extent it was approved, it would have been carried out by deniable surrogates and not by CIA officers or personnel. This pragmatic CIA view of the use of assassination is illustrated by the fact that when the team chief returned from the Washington meeting, he reported to the PBSUCCESS staff that the consensus in Washington had been that "Arbenz must go; how, does not matter."[147] Armas's forces did engage in minor combat, but almost all of it was quite remote from the Guatemalan capital. Árbenz showed no sign of becoming personally involved in military action to repel the attacks. On June 16, 1954, CIA-backed armed Guatemalan exiles entered remote border areas from Honduras, advancing tentatively and having difficulty overcoming even the resistance from local police forces and citizens. As David Phillips described it, the "invasion" consisted of "several trucks crossing the border without opposition . . . Carlos Armas out front in a battered station wagon." The rebel forces were divided into four groups, entering at five separate points on the border to give the image of a massive effort, yet numbering less than five hundred men in total. That approach was also consciously selected in order to prevent the effort from being aborted due to the destruction of the entire force. Some ten saboteurs were sent to blow up selected bridges and cut telegraph lines. A conscious effort was also made to avoid engagement with the Guatemalan army. The "invasion" was actually more of a psychological device than a serious military effort to match the much larger regular Guatemalan military forces. Armas's forces moved quite slowly and in their first battle, 122 rebels were crushed by some thirty-three Guatemalan soldiers. Only twenty-eight of Armas's troops escaped being killed or captured. In another attack on a heavily defended port city, the local police chief used local dock workers to oppose them and the majority of the rebels were killed or captured, with the few remaining fleeing back to Honduras. Inside three days, two of the four rebel groups had been neutralized. Amazingly, at that point Árbenz reportedly ordered his military to allow the remaining Armas forces to advance, apparently due to a concern that if they appeared totally defeated, the American military would intervene. Such a fear was not without some cause.

In early June, the U.S. Navy had implemented—with both ships and submarines—the centuries-old blockade practice of stopping and boarding commercial vessels headed for Guatemala, supposedly in search of weapons shipments from the Soviet bloc. The naval operation, designated Operation Hardrock Baker, was directed to use force in its blockade even if foreign ships would be damaged. The naval blockade included the boarding of foreign flagged transports in international waters as well as suspect vessels destined for Guatemala. The blockade, arguably illegal under international law, might well have produced incidents with foreign powers—including America's own allies—had it continued for any extended period. In fact, the Dutch government lodged a formal protest after one of its flagged vessels was boarded at San Juan, Puerto Rico.[148] During the naval blockade even British and French ships were challenged, stopped, and inspected. There is no record that any weapons were found during the boarding. Even more aggressively, a force of five amphibious assault ships and an antisubmarine (helicopter-equipped) aircraft carrier were deployed off the Guatemalan coast. The landing assault ships were backed with a full battalion-level Marine landing force. Reportedly rumors were rampant within Guatemala that the Marines would support Armas. Árbenz felt the fear of U.S. forces would encourage his army commanders to strike a deal with the rebels.

Prior to Armas's incursion, CIA-sponsored CAT pilots had already been flying leaflet drops over Guatemala City and other towns, calling for widespread defections from the Árbenz regime, especially by the regular military forces. In conjunction with Armas's border crossing, fighters and B-26 bombers began strafing and bombing selected targets. The news of insurgent troops in-country, combined with the aerial attacks, seems to have seriously frightened President

Árbenz. He was certainly not an aggressive leader and he engaged in a series of obviously panicked actions, first suspending civil liberties and then ordering an electrical blackout—with no imminent danger other than ongoing CIA psychological efforts including radio broadcasts and leaflet drops.

His failure to dispatch troops, much less to lead them, against the modest Armas forces further undermined the confidence of the regular army. The CIA's guerrilla air force did make limited strafing and bombing attacks but nothing that seriously affected the Guatemalan military. However, one stroke of David Phillips's psychological warfare campaign seems to have been exceptionally effective: He ordered the bombing of the parade ground of the largest military base in the capital city, while broadcasting false messages of a major air attack. He followed that with "news" reports that two rebel columns were rapidly converging on the capital. Within twenty-four hours, Árbenz broadcast a resignation speech, and fled to the Mexican Embassy with several hundred supporters. Shortly afterward he departed the country. Armas and his troops were flown directly from their remote location to a landing field outside the Guatemalan capital, and entered with a victory parade.

Despite all the training, the preparation of K teams, and the plans for assassination to soften the Árbenz regime, in the end the CIA believed that the success of the Guatemalan project was brought about by a combination of an extremely successful radio propaganda–psychological warfare effort, highly visible aerial action conducted by mercenary pilots using WWII-era aircraft, and Árbenz's personal fear of an actual U.S. military intervention to support the exiles. Phillips's technique of broadcasting what were positioned as official government denials of rebel success convinced much of the population that the government was experiencing major defeats.

An alternative argument can be made that it was not the limited progress of Armas's small units or Phillips's psychological warfare that panicked Árbenz. The unauthorized but dramatic air attack on a neutral ship seems to have been interpreted by Árbenz as a sign that the U.S. would stop at nothing to oust him. The actions of a major U.S. Naval force off his coast, complete with Marines and landing craft, may also have been a significant factor in his final decision to call it quits and simply flee.

Following the successful 1954 coup against Árbenz in Guatemala, members of the CIA project team (with the exception of Robertson) were personally introduced to President Eisenhower, who commended them for their work. Morales and Phillips both received highly prestigious CIA awards. In his recommendation for full-time employment, J.C. King, director of Western Hemisphere operations wrote that Phillips "developed and sustained a completely notional situation without parallel in psychological warfare . . . he personally created and directed a psychological weapon which has no equal."

Realistically speaking, the lack of bloodshed during the Guatemala coup may well have been largely due to the quick resignation of Árbenz and his immediate departure from the country—along with most of his supporters—which occurred well before Armas moved any of his forces into the capital. After the coup and in following years, political assassination did become a major fact of Guatemalan life. Armas assumed dictatorial power and even David Phillips was forced to write that under Armas's rule, government security officials organized "death squads" and eliminated any real opposition to the dictatorship. Studies conducted by human rights groups suggest that during the next four decades (1954 to 1994) more than 140,000 Guatemalans were either killed or "disappeared."[149]

CHAPTER 8

The Tibet Project

The Tibet Project was one of American's earliest long-term covert operations and lasted in one form or another for almost two decades (1956 to 1974). Strategically it was yet another effort to hinder Chinese communist territorial expansion. The operation's goal was to connect with, supply, and support armed resistance groups opposing the Chinese political annexation of Tibet. The project involved a number of extremely challenging elements, including locating, recruiting, and secretly training Tibetan volunteers, and brought about one of the most highly creative, heroic and deniable supply operations ever conducted by the United States.

During the Second World War, the American Army Air Force had waged a monumental effort to supply China in its struggle against the Japanese. That effort had involved flying transport aircraft through and over the Tibetan Plateau, which contains some of the highest mountains in the world, including the mighty Himalayas. The plateau, known as "the roof of the world," is a vast area of some 970,000 square miles, feeding rivers extending from the Yangtze and Mekong in the east to the Ganges and Indus in the west. The Tibetan Plateau's uplands and mountains are generally above thirteen thousand to fifteen thousand feet. Navigating through its mountain passes in good weather is dangerous enough. Dramatic and highly changeable weather conditions, including icing, updrafts, and downdrafts of over one hundred miles per hour, made transport additionally hazardous. The 10th Air Force and later the Air Transport Command delivered thousands of tons of supplies from India to China, building an "air bridge" to support China's struggle against the invading Japanese. The effort was later described by the air crews as flying over "the hump." In doing so they suffered the loss of over five hundred aircraft and thirteen hundred crew members, leaving an "aluminum trail" though the mountains.[150]

Flying over the hump into and through Tibet, supported by both the full resources of the Army Air Force and the use of large, modern air bases in British India, was a challenge in the Second World War. Launching a covert air operation and secretly overflying the airspace of neutral and newly independent Asian nations, such as India, was a challenge of an even greater magnitude. Conducting air operations in Tibet would start with supply flights of some two thousand miles, staged out of Thailand and into small, isolated airstrips in Pakistan, and later India. It involved locating and conducting missions into isolated regions of the Tibetan Plateau, at altitudes where supply airdrops had never been done. Tibet was very possibly the worst arena for the relatively new CIA operations group to develop, test, and hone its long-distance covert action skills—but because of the decision to respond against continued Chinese territorial expansion, the choice of battleground would not be up to the Agency.

Under the leadership of Mao Tse-tung, the communist Chinese People's Liberation Army (PLA) consolidated its hold over the Chinese mainland, forcing the Nationalists offshore and beyond its southern borders. The PLA moved through southern China, establishing firm control over the Yunnan province; and units moved on towards Tibet. Although China had constantly affirmed its authority over Tibet (which China claimed to have inherited from the Chang dynasty), Tibet had existed in a relatively nebulous international status for some time, maintaining a position of autonomy. Communist China paid no heed to Tibet's position of independence or to international calls for China to recognize Tibet as an autonomous region. It also ignored India's 1947 recognition of Tibet as an independent nation during the Asian Relations Conference in New Deli, India.[151] Following the communist regime's ascension to power in China, delegates from Tibet were sent to Beijing, where they reportedly received considerable instruction and direction from the new Chinese leadership. The delegates from Tibet said that while in Beijing they had received "wonderful lessons from the Communist Chinese and from Comrade Mao Tse Tung but the Tibetans would be very happy if the Chinese now withdrew and allowed Tibetans to put these lessons into operation all by themselves. . . . The Chinese answer was to imprison the delegates."[152]

By spring 1950, the Chinese had begun to solidify their claims through force, as the People's Liberation Army invaded the Amdo region of Tibet and was prepared to move on through Kham, across the Yangtze River, and on to the capital of Lhasa. As of May 1950, the small Tibetan garrisons in the Kham region of eastern Tibet were outnumbered ten to one by People's Liberation Army forces just across the Yangtze. In October, with North Korea's invasion of the south diverting the attention of the world and becoming America's preeminent military focus, China dispatched some ten thousand troops to "peacefully seize Tibet." The local Tibetan forces were overwhelmed, and on October 19, the regional commissioner-general handed over the Kham region to China.[153]

China immediately required Tibet to send representatives to Beijing to negotiate an agreement. In reality there was no negotiation; upon arrival, the Tibetan delegates were given a Chinese written document known as the "Seventeen Point Agreement for the Peaceful Liberation of Tibet" and ordered to sign it. There was no discussion of terms, just a prewritten document, which the delegates had no authority to sign, but they did so after being denied requests to communicate with their central government (led by the fourteenth Dalai Lama) in Lhasa. The Tibetan delegates succumbed to ongoing pressure and threats by the Chinese, who would continue their advance into central Tibet.[154] When the installation of the Seventeen Point Agreement was communicated by radio, the National Assembly of Tibet in Lhasa and the Dalai Lama had little choice but to accept, and did so via radio message. The exchange had effectively confirmed Chinese sovereignty over Tibet.

President Truman had faced direct combat between American troops and the Chinese People's Liberation Army when China intervened in the Korean conflict in 1950. About two hundred thousand Chinese attacked the American and UN forces. Even larger forces were positioned behind the first waves. By 1951, the Chinese had three full field armies in Korea, with some seven hundred thousand men. In the face of that extreme Chinese military provocation, and with thousands of American casualties, Truman made the decision not to use atomic weapons and not to directly attack Chinese staging areas, support facilities, or airfields. Still, over the next two years of the Korean conflict, extended and vulnerable supply lines and the lack of an effective field air defense hampered the Chinese and North Koreans—which led to an eventual stalemate that Dwight Eisenhower campaigned to conclude. Given the American engagement in Korea, there was little thought towards immediately opposing Chinese entry into Tibet with military action.

Neither Lhasa nor the Dalai Lama openly opposed the communist regime in Beijing, and China began road-building to develop Tibet commercially and to allow massive and rapid movement of PLA forces into eastern Tibet. Initially the Chinese made efforts to cultivate the religious leader of Tibet, the Dalai Lama, and to establish positive business relationships with the Tibetan aristocracy. China was well aware that taking full military control of the vast Tibetan Plateau would require an extensive network of roads and airfields and such construction would take time (approximately three years). In the interim the Chinese did not tread too heavily over the religious observations and practices of the Tibetans, although during a visit by the Dalai Lama to Beijing in 1954, Chairman Mao took time to offer some striking and unwanted advice about the evils of religion.[155]

In 1955, with their new logistics infrastructure in place, the Chinese took the gloves off, moving to full-scale cultural integration activities: introducing atheist doctrine into Tibetan schools, collecting firearms from the population, and implementing a rigid Chinese-style agricultural collectivization system. As 1955 came to a close, it was clear that a series of Tibetan armed uprisings were developing across the country. In one series of engagement, tribal forces temporarily blocked the massive Chinese road-building effort. The result was several thousand dead Chinese soldiers and the capture of several People's Liberation Army garrisons.

The PLA responded by sending large four-engine Tupolev Tu-4 bombers against the rebels. Even operating the proven and rugged Tupolev aircraft in the Tibetan Plateau was difficult, and several were lost. Undaunted, the Chinese continued air attacks, and the bombings killed thousands of Tibetans.[156] The PLA was going to show no mercy in pacifying Tibet. In counterstrikes against the rebellion, a grand Tibetan monastery with five thousand monks was razed to the ground. The severity of the Chinese response demonstrated that the PLA was willing and now quite able to continue large-scale military operations across Tibet.

President Eisenhower had been elected on a platform of bringing the Korean conflict to an end, reducing the budget, and in general, returning America to a peacetime footing. So, while eager to push back against further communist territorial expansion, he was not eager to send American servicemen to conventional combat in Asia. That attitude was reflected in America's tentative steps to enter Tibet. Newly available State Department documents confirm that there were confidential contacts between American representatives and the Dalai Lama as early as 1951, but it was not until 1956 that any move was made to actively—even if covertly—intervene in the Chinese annexation of Tibet. The decision appears to have been prompted both by the growing size of the Tibetan resistance and the perception that it might indeed constitute an effective surrogate force that could give China pause in terms of further expanding its border annexations. In addition, Eisenhower's frustration over the recent failure of the American effort to support the French against a communist insurgency in Vietnam (ending in 1954) may have moved him to support a new initiative blocking communist territorial aggression. In 1956, with oversight by the covert operations screening committee (the 303 Committee), a plan was accepted to launch a covert Tibet Project, which would include not only political action and propaganda but paramilitary and intelligence operations.[157] The CIA would be tasked with the Tibet Project, specifically the personnel within the CIA's Directorate of Plans.[158]

In planning for shadow warfare in Tibet, the CIA had to face the fact that it was operating beyond the scope of any of its previous covert military activities. Given the size and geographic challenges of the Tibetan Plateau, even locating and contacting the Tibetan resistance groups that had formed was going to be challenging. Before any progress could be made, a great deal of intelligence needed to be collected. In the beginning the CIA had absolutely no human intelligence out of Tibet, no reconnaissance of the region, and very little idea where potential rebel groups were actually located. The CIA was going to have to go hunting for the insurgency. And what it was going to need first was a local base of operations and an air corridor that would lead from American bases in the Pacific, from Okinawa and Clark Field in the Philippines, across Southeast Asia, and ultimately to a working staging area adjacent to Tibet. As of 1956, that need was certainly not going to be met by India, which was the perfect location across the hump of the Tibetan Plateau for a wartime missions launching point. India was recently independent and protective of its neutrality and territorial rights. The initial solution, which made possible high-risk missions into Tibet, was the new nation of Pakistan—an avidly anticommunist, fundamentally religious nation with an active military assistance agreement with the United States (Mutual Defense Assistance Agreement) signed in 1954. An American military assistance unit was stationed at Pakistan army headquarters in Rawalpindi. Hundreds of Pakistani officers had already been sent to the U.S. for training, and a number of strong personal relationships had already been built.[159]

Following the actual commitment to American covert action in 1956, the pressing need was for intelligence collection, and if possible the location and exfiltration of rebel leaders—bringing them out for extended discussions, planning, and communications training to support operations once they were inserted back into Tibet. The Tibet Project was going to be fostering deniable warfare—with Tibetan rebel surrogates—in a region that was claimed by a major foreign power, one that had fielded its own armies against American troops in Korea only a few years before. The Tibetan Plateau was an active combat area for the People's Liberation Army, a target defined in covert operations terminology as militarily "denied."

A standard practice in deniable warfare—if at all possible—is to avoid having identifiable personnel on the ground, especially if there is an active military defense or combat in progress. Only your surrogates should be in the actual combat zones. If American personnel had been captured inside Tibet, especially in association with any Tibetan rebels, the Chinese would have considered it extremely provocative and turned it into a major international incident. In addition, the individuals captured would have likely been treated as spies. The project was going to have to locate Tibetans who could give insight into what was going on with the insurgency inside Tibet, where fighting was actually occurring. In such a large region, rebels would have to be trained in communications, and prepared to go back onto the plateau and coordinate or possibly lead rebel combat—all at a very great distance from any individuals who could be associated with the United States.

In early 1957, the CIA began its move to develop a picture of what active resistance was going on inside Tibet. Officers were to locate Tibetan candidates who could be taken into training and put back into the country for intelligence collection. The candidates were often refugees who had fled Tibet earlier, into India, Pakistan, or other neighboring states such as Nepal or Mustang. Moving cautiously, CIA officers inside Pakistan located and contacted a handful of individuals who were willing to go into Tibet to search for active rebel groups. As a military assistance partner, Pakistan was supportive but extremely cautious, because the Chinese intervention in the Korean conflict had made everyone quite sensitive about doing anything the Chinese might interpret as aggressive against its territories.

With Pakistan's permission, the first Tibetan trainee candidates were secretly flown out of Pakistan for training. The CIA was given secret access by the Pakistani military to an unused airstrip at Kurmitola, outside Dacca in East Pakistan. The actual covert aerial mission was carried out by the special U.S. Air Force 322nd Troop Carrier Squadron, operating out of Kadena Air Base in Okinawa. After a three-day stay in Kadena, Japan, for medical examinations, the Tibetan volunteers were flown to the highly clandestine training facility on the island of Saipan. In 1950, the CIA had established a secure and secret facility on Saipan to be used for training agents, paramilitary operatives, and resistance fighters from across Asia. The base was operated under military cover as the Naval Technical Training Unit. By the time the Tibetans arrived, the base had already been used for training Chinese Nationalists and other anticommunist factions for guerrilla war on the Chinese mainland, as well as South Koreans for covert operations in North Korea. In later years it would also provide covert operations training for both Laotians and South Vietnamese. Given the remoteness of the island location and the security in place, it was decades before anyone realized the true nature of the installation on Saipan.

Initial operations inside Tibet itself involved a continual state of what can best be described as "fits and starts." Generally the initial Saipan trainees had to be sent into Tibet on "blind drops," landing with little or no assistance waiting on the ground for them; and in some cases, guidance might come only from extended family connections or rumors about the location of rebel groups. The volunteers sent in-country had no source of income and even if they made it into the planned location, they had to depend on family members for money or were at the mercy of the locals. In a significant number of instances, individuals and entire teams were quickly reported to the PLA or local militia and either arrested or killed in action.

Before the CIA's volunteers could arrive to offer support, matters in eastern Tibet were especially difficult. The insurgent groups inside Tibet were extremely limited in weaponry, far outclassed by the comparatively modern Chinese weaponry, modern communications, and airpower. The rebels themselves had no radios, communications equipment, or experience in the operation of such devices. The only hope of communicating with them in anything approaching real time was to train radio operators and get them into the country with active rebel groups. However, the losses of virtually all the initial "black entry" agents illustrated the fact that even communications would be a major challenge.

The People's Liberation Army had sent some 150,000 additional troops in via the new roads, and those forces had quickly overwhelmed Tibetan resistance in the region. The largest such rebel force, the National Volunteer Defense Army (NVDA), was originally understood to number some fifteen hundred fighters and to represent a major opportunity for covert support to the U.S. But before the resistance on the ground could be contacted by the U.S., it had been totally rerouted by a PLA campaign and forced out of the east to regroup in central Tibet.

The limited resources on the ground, coupled with the fact that atmospheric conditions and the mountains themselves significantly hampered radio communications between locations on the plateau and the CIA facility in Pakistan, added to the operational difficulties. The agents had to be parachuted in with mobile radios and none of the insurgent groups were operating fixed base radio stations. The rapidly moving PLA forces ensured that fixed positions would be quickly overrun. Lack of reliable communications with a few surviving trainees left the CIA in a quandary. The CIA decided to continue supply drops to groups identified by its few in-country Tibetan volunteers, but deep concerns about deniability led the CIA to turn to outdated wrifles such as British Lee-Enfield rifles. Such rifles might obscure American involvement, but they were far short of the modern automatic and heavy weapons the Chinese military was using.

Early supply drops were made using the Civil Air Transport (CAT) air crews staging out of East Pakistan and there was some encouragement because the NVDA did manage to regroup and continue attacks on the Chinese. Given the disparity in weapons, those attacks turned out to be heroic but suicidal. Still, Tibetan recruits continued to be identified and trained, and by 1958 a new facility was established for more realistic training than on Saipan. The new training center was in Colorado, a location chosen by the CIA because its geographic terrain mimicked the relevant regions of Tibet. However, other than an accelerated training program, neither major opportunities nor momentum developed for the Tibet Project during 1958. Things would change dramatically the following year.

The major challenge had been in finding insurgent groups in such a large area before they were wiped out by the Chinese army. However, in 1959, three years into America's involvement in Tibet, two major events would deepen the American commitment to Tibet. The first was the implementation of new unwanted Chinese practices, including a push for an even broader agrarian reform along collectivist principles within Tibet. This dramatically increased resistance against the Chinese across the region and brought approximately seven thousand new recruits into the Tibetan NVDA resistance force.

The second event was the Chinese increasingly moving to negate the cultural and political influence of the political/religious leader of Tibet, the Dalai Lama. The Dalai Lama's spiritual position and unique position in Tibet's culture had made him a rallying point for opposition to the Chinese. A series of moves against religious centers in the country and against large numbers of Tibetan monks led to fear that the Chinese might seize or somehow isolate the Dalai Lama in protective custody, severing his personal contacts inside Tibet. Ultimately those fears, and ongoing Chinese plans to suppress native Tibetan religious practices, forced the Dalai Lama to flee the country and declare open resistance to the Chinese from exile in India.

At the four hundredth meeting of the National Security Council on March 26, 1959, Director of Central Intelligence Allen Dulles discussed developments in Tibet during his briefing on significant world developments. The relevant portion of the memorandum of discussion of that date by S. Everett Gleason reads as follows:

The Director of Central Intelligence said that he would report first on the situation in Tibet as it had developed up to this hour. Beginning on March 10 at Lhasa there had occurred a series of events which led to the flight from Lhasa of the Dalai Lama whom the Chinese Communists were about to kidnap and carry off to Peiping. When the people of Lhasa became aware of these plans, thousands of Tibetans flocked to the city and took the Dalai Lama into protective custody. Disorders followed in Lhasa. A Chinese Communist strongpoint was captured. The Lama supported the rebel activity. Peiping at first tried a policy of leniency but subsequently was obliged to take strong measures. The rebels had abandoned Lhasa on March 24.

While these events do not constitute any real threat to Peiping's control of the main towns of Tibet, the Chinese Communists will certainly be obliged to face guerrilla operations by rebellious Tibetans. The situation will also be awkward because the Chinese Communists wish to avoid drastic action in Tibet lest such action offend India.[160]

As matters evolved, CIA Director Allen Dulles was shown to have seriously underestimated how willing China would be to use increased military force not only within Tibet but across the border and into Indian territory. In the meantime the CIA continued its covert operations, selecting and training even more agents and teams at the new, secret facility in Colorado. The hope was that an expanded training cadre, increased insertion of security, and ongoing supply missions could be used to accelerate the newly stimulated resistance groups inside Tibet. Such hopes were preempted by the ease with which the Chinese army was able to move its formations throughout Tibet using the new road networks it had established. The Chinese encountered little effective military opposition and became increasingly aggressive. Even Dulles had to report at an April NSC meeting that the Chinese were making good use of their pool of Korean War veterans to make a "very effective military showing."[161]

In frustration, the U.S. military proposed options for disrupting Chinese movements; the proposals ranged from using American aircraft in attacks to destroy road access to Tibet, to the dispatch of parachute teams against key points on the roads. Even the thought of dropping in Republic of China combat teams from Taiwan was broached. In the end, only one such operation—code-named ST WHALE—was approved. President Eisenhower also approved U-2 flights for the necessary reconnaissance and CIA air assets were used to drop a team of deniable Taiwan trainees in for road sabotage. The drop was made, but the team was quickly captured. The Chinese then attempted to convince the team's radio operator to call in more such missions, setting the stage for ambushes. They were apparently unable to "turn" the radioman and no further sabotage missions were attempted.[162]

As 1960 began, the Tibet Task Force CIA and military personnel continued their best efforts at training guerrillas, inserting them by air and supplying them inside Tibet. With a growing level of local resistance inside Tibet, there were at least hopes for more success against the Chinese. And although it had taken some years, the CIA had developed access to an increasingly capable covert air supply system, one capable of significant supply drops into Tibet. That new resource would be very valuable to covert warfare operations throughout the late 1950s and into the 1960s and its development was key to American shadow warfare in both decades.

Early in this chapter we discussed the demanding nature of covert air operations involving not just reconnaissance but parachute drops of both people and supplies onto the Tibetan Plateau—especially considering the extremely high concerns over deniability. As it happened, the infrastructure for such air operations had already begun to evolve earlier in the Far East, first as part of the effort to support clandestine operations against North Korea during that conflict, and later, as part of the massive clandestine military support effort for the Republic of China in intelligence and guerrilla operations against mainland communist China.

Even before the Chinese entry into the Korean conflict in late 1950, it had become clear that North Korea was receiving support from the Chinese and a highly classified U.S. project was developed to secure human intelligence from inside North Korea. That was to be accomplished by conducting twenty "dark of the moon" agent parachute drop missions. The drops were made in total darkness on new-moon cycles over a month's time. A special unit of the American 5th Air Force—led by Captain Harry "Heinie" Aderholt—participated in several missions, one in which he observed and reported very large formations of Chinese troops moving into Korea from Manchuria. Aderholt made his report to the 5th Air Force, saying that "the whole god dammed Chinese Army is coming across the Yalu, moving south."[163] No action was taken and two days later the Chinese push had the entire UN force in retreat.[164]

During the Korean War, the Air Force and the CIA began to actively collaborate in the creation of a major American covert air war capability. The units involved were to be highly classified, designated as the Air Resupply and Communications Service (ARCS). The first wing of ARCS, the 581st, was established at Mountain Home Air Force Base in Idaho and then deployed to Clark Air Force Base in the Philippines, flying missions into Korea. However, plans to create wings to deploy around the globe faded with the Korean armistice. In 1953, the 581st wing moved to Kadena Air Base on the island of Okinawa.

With the Korean conflict over and the Eisenhower strategic emphasis on massive nuclear deterrence and military budget reductions, the concept of a global unconventional air command was shelved. In 1956, the overall Air Resupply and Communications Service wings were formally disbanded. However, with the Tibet Project and other CIA activities still active in the Far East, the Kadena-based resupply and communications unit was actually retained in place and renamed the 322nd Troop Carrier Squadron. A relatively small special detachment of the overall unit was tasked with carrying out the most sensitive missions, and its aircraft was provided by the CIA. That unit's three planes were pieced together with a host of different parts, and their tail numbers were removable (and often changed multiple times during actual missions). The unit's missions for the CIA, which were highly classified, took them through neutral airspace, into a number of countries. The missions required filing false flight plans with various air traffic control facilities, and the planes flew on "circuitous" routes, which masked both their origins and destinations.[165] It was the sort of covert operations "tradecraft" developed specifically to disguise or at least obfuscate American support of both "friendly" surrogates in neutral nations and insurgents in unfriendly ones.

Meanwhile, Aderholt had taken an assignment with the CIA, detailed to assist in the training of a highly select group of pilots as well as CIA case officers who would be used in covert air and air supply missions. The training ranged from airborne jump training at Fort Benning, Georgia, to tactics and techniques of special air operations at Camp Perry (known within the CIA as the Farm) as well as infiltration and supply exercises across some three hundred miles of mountains in Virginia.[166]

That assignment would take Aderholt back to the same Air Force unit that had continued to support unconventional and paramilitary projects for the CIA—the 1007th Air Intelligence Service Squadron—and would expose Aderholt to some of the most senior CIA officers, including Richard Bissell. On his assignments to the CIA, Aderholt's performance evaluations were signed by deputy plans directors Richard Bissell and Richard Helms. In 1959, as part of a major escalation in the Tibetan operations, Aderholt was dispatched to Okinawa to take command of the air unit (Detachment 2, 1045th Operational Evaluation and Training Group) supporting Tibetan operations.

Upon arrival, Aderholt dramatically upgraded the Tibetan air support operations and established a much improved support facility at Takhli, Thailand. As noted earlier, the secret Tibet supply corridor was a lengthy one, moving materials from the huge U.S. base at Kadena, Japan, onto a transfer base in Thailand and covertly out of there onto the secret East Pakistan base, from which the final flights into Tibet departed. Aderholt's Operational Evaluation and Training Group detachment at Kadena also flew CIA proprietary

CAT air crews into and out of Thailand to the staging field in East Pakistan, and provided logistics support for them.

Beyond the creation of an effective covert air corridor from Japan into East Pakistan, the Tibet Project also resolved a number of operational issues. High-altitude flights were not just an aircraft issue in terms of what the aircraft could actually carry, but were also an issue for the parachute drops themselves. To solve that challenge, the CIA turned to a very special breed of professionals that it had first used in Korea: "smokejumpers" from Montana and the mountain West. Their experience parachuting into American forest fires had led them to develop a high degree of expertise in steerable chutes and rough-terrain jumping—exactly the expertise required for covertly delivering both agents and cargo into Tibet.[167]

The air crews flying from East Pakistan into Tibet flew "stripped" Air Force B-17s, painted black, with specially muffled exhausts. The planes originally had been prepared to provide CIA support for the Republic of China missions over mainland China. In the interest of maximum personnel deniability, the aircraft and Tibetan insertion teams were actually flown out of Okinawa by the covert operations' 322nd Troop Carrier Squadron, through Thailand, and into the staging area in East Pakistan. The actual flight crews going into Tibet were transported separately over the same route. In East Pakistan the Air Force crew was replaced by the deniable flight crews. On the first airdrop mission into Tibet, Polish pilots, on loan from the CIA in Europe, were used. The Poles may have found it a bit of a relief, as their normal assignment was conducting airborne intelligence penetrations into Soviet territory.[168]

All of the Tibet flights operating out of Pakistan in the early years of the Tibet Project had to transit Indian airspace without permission. If even a "sanitized" B-17 bomber with all identification removed had gone down and been recovered in India or Tibet, the sponsorship of the mission would have been obvious, regardless of the nationality of the flight crew. It seems unlikely that any idea of a routine commercial cover would have helped either; Tibetan guerrillas were unlikely to have been able to organize a business contract with Civil Air Transport in Taiwan. Fortunately for the Tibet Project team, none of its aircraft went down—an amazing feat given the hazards of flying over Tibet. Other CIA operations would not be nearly as fortunate. In fact, during the same period as the early Tibet Project, operations just like this one occurred in another area of Asia—Indonesia.

While the CIA was launching the Tibetan operation and using CAT resources there, it was also using CAT as a commercial cover for its air operations in support of an American-sponsored resistance movement in Indonesia. The Indonesian project was an early example of creating regime change via a coup attempt by rebellious Indonesian army officers and units. In an operation designated Archipelago, CIA officers covertly attempted to recruit coup participants while conducting training for the Indonesian national police. Archipelago was carried out largely under the supervision of senior CIA officer Desmond FitzGerald, who also was to assume authority for the Tibet operation, being described as the primary "cheerleader" for that effort. In September 1957, an NSC meeting had given direction for the CIA to "support non-communist forces in the outer Indonesian islands, while continuing attempts to produce action by Non-communist elements on Java."[169]

Ultimately the Indonesian military coup group received American supplies delivered both by submarine from Subic Bay in the Philippines and by CAT aircraft. CAT personnel in the operation included Americans, Nationalist Chinese, and Filipinos. Both transport aircraft and an actual attack force of some fifteen B-26 fighter bombers were put into operation.[170] Archipelago was an ambitious operation, and a highly deniable one. It further illustrated the Eisenhower Administration's distrust of neutral regimes, even while itself maintaining a public posture of neutrality.

As in the case of almost all the operations we will review, the Indonesian government did not take long to understand, and publicly protest, American involvement with its rogue military. President Eisenhower himself responded with a statement that the U.S. was totally neutral in the internal Indonesian struggle. However, in qualification,

Eisenhower added, "Now on the other hand, every rebellion that I have ever heard of has its soldiers of fortune."[171] Eisenhower simply may have been trying to set some context for future deniability, but it proved not only ineffective but quite embarrassing as well.

In May 1958, one of the B-26 aircraft attacking Indonesian territory was brought down after bombing a crowded village marketplace. The pilot was an American, Allen Pope. Pope had flown in Korea and in Indochina for CAT. John Foster Dulles and the U.S. State Department reaffirmed that Pope must have been acting independently, since there was absolutely no American interference going on with the revolution in Indonesia. However, the Indonesians found that Pope had, despite mandatory strip searches and aircraft sanitation procedures, carried both CAT and Air Force identification papers, including a contract for the air operation and a base exchange ID for Clark Air Force Base.

The net result of that single incident was the total cancellation of the Archipelago operation, making it one of the shortest such operations on record. Following the media attention given to the American and CIA embarrassment in Indonesia it would become unlikely that any future American military aircraft downed in action would be attributed to anything other than an American covert operation. Yet, as we will see, such things tend to repeat themselves, and decades later a similar incident would expose a U.S. secret war against Nicaragua.

The Tibetan resistance, having grown in numbers, continued to attempt combat against the People's Liberation Army, which was a massive, aggressive, and tough force. The Tibetans were continually defeated by the Chinese. Still, the CIA had finally established ongoing contact with active insurgent forces inside Tibet and had developed the capacity not only for communications with them but for a serious air supply capability. At that crucial point the whole Tibet Project effort went into hiatus due to an incident thousands of miles away in the heart of Russia. In May of 1960, an American U-2 high-altitude reconnaissance aircraft was shot down by the Soviets near Kusulino, in the Ural region of Russia—after overflying and photographing Soviet ICBM launch sites and plutonium production facilities. Suddenly the subject of American aircraft flying on spy missions over other countries became an international worry. While America initially tried to deny any spying, claiming an off-course weather aircraft, the Soviets' introduction of the pilots' full confessions at the United Nations proved a tremendous embarrassment for the Eisenhower Administration. America was portrayed as an out-of-control military power, and a number of countries suddenly became tentative about their secret activities that supported the CIA. In response, President Eisenhower issued a directive ordering that all covert aerial missions over communist bloc countries immediately cease. International diplomatic and domestic political concerns caused Eisenhower to immediately suspend all such flights until the November 1960 American election. And during the period of May to November a significant number of Tibet Project volunteers operating on the ground inside Tibet were crushed by the Chinese army.

Still, that was not the end of the Tibet Project. It would take almost a year for it to resume, but in early 1961, under the Kennedy Administration, the newly organized Special Group oversight committee for covert projects recommended the continuation of the Tibet Project. At that point it was estimated that over the preceding years it had actually managed to make ongoing contact with some two thousand combatants inside Tibet, eight hundred of whom had been armed by airdrops. Given the relatively small size of the operational groups, the decision was made that their best use was going to be as road and border watch teams to report on potential Chinese army buildups and movements.[172] In short, the project's focus had shifted from creating a viable Tibetan insurgency to utilizing the groups established for intelligence collection on the possibility of further Chinese territorial expansion.

President Kennedy accepted the concept of a Tibetan covert operation, including the further expansion of armed groups of Tibetan refugees. He also endorsed the idea of creating a secret base and staging area for them in the small independent Tibetan border state of Mustang. However, Kennedy was also quite concerned about the

American political relationship with India. Under the Eisenhower administration, with a decided hostility towards neutrality in the Cold War, the Indian relationship had been cool at the very best. Kennedy moved towards a new outreach towards India. And that outreach quickly produced results—largely because Indian neutrality would become much less of a concern as India itself was invaded by the People's Liberation Army in October 1962.

The communist Chinese People's Liberation Army had taken an assertive stance in regard to areas along the Tibetan border with India, which it claimed for China; the same areas were claimed by India as its own lands. In 1958 the PLA had arrested Indian police in Ladakh. The following year, after the Dalai Lama's flight into Indian exile, India had sent patrols into its North East Frontier Agency (NEFA). The Indian patrols were attacked by Chinese forces, and nine Indians were killed by the Chinese military. CIA Director Dulles advised the NSC that the PLA's success in Tibet had led to a new assertiveness in the Indian border areas and that they were strengthening their presence, even constructing secret roads into areas that were unknown to India.[173]

During 1962, the Indian military had increased its own presence inside areas that it claimed along the border. Then on October 20, 1962, the PLA advanced down the Himalaya frontier in strength, crushing Indian border outposts. Massively outnumbered, the Indian forces were able to offer little resistance as the Chinese army advanced. With its border forces soundly defeated and uncertain about when and where the Chinese would stop, India dramatically changed its attitude and approached the U.S. government for military assistance. President Kennedy approved the request, and soon the U.S. Air Force was openly flying eight missions into India a week from Europe; short-range American transports ferried the weapons to the front lines. In spite of the aid, an Indian counterattack failed and within days the entire Indian battle line on its North East Frontier had collapsed.[174] With its border forces soundly defeated and uncertain about when and where the Chinese would stop, India dramatically changed its attitude and approached the U.S. government for military assistance.

As American and Indian military collaboration continued, India found the concept of a Tibetan guerrilla force attractive—with the potential for harassing PLA supply lines at best, and at least the capability for advanced reconnaissance and road watch operations. From that point on, India became an active, if covert, partner in supporting Tibetan resistance forces. The CIA continued its independent efforts to develop a viable paramilitary resistance inside Tibet, and to control the Tibetan force in Mustang. The Indians organized and directed a tactical guerrilla force including Tibetan recruits. That force, designated Establishment 22 (and using an Indian cover as the "12th Gurkha Rifles"), was to be kept secret from the Indian public and also from the Indian military. India would demonstrate that it too could conduct covert paramilitary projects.[175] And during a highly emotional, secret review of the Tibetan force, Indian Prime Minister Jawaharlal Nehru would assure the Tibetan force that India backed it and he "vowed that they would return to an independent country."[176] In retrospect, Nehru's remarks seem eerily similar to the words of President John F. Kennedy in 1963, addressed to the American-organized Cuban exile Brigade 2506 in Miami, after their release by Fidel Castro.

With Indian and American support, Tibetan units trained and deployed in a limited fashion; in doing so they engaged in only a handful of actual combat operations throughout the 1960s. Radio teams provided some level of intelligence from remote positions, but in spite of the new sponsorship, from 1964 the substantive armed resistance in Tibet was done. India would continue its support by integrating Tibetan elements into its special forces—forces that were used in battle to support India's move into East Pakistan. By 1971, with the Nixon Administration's focus on improving relationships with China, the longtime support for the Tibet Project was history.

In 1964, the CIA prepared an "eyes only" review of the Tibet Project for Special Group review. That review gives us an accurate idea of the actual American activities and their costs.[177] The combined costs to that point were $1,735,000, including $500,000 to support Tibetan guerrillas, $400,000 for the training site in Colorado, and

$185,000 for deniable air operations. In today's dollars, America spent approximately $13 million on the Tibetan shadow war in 1964 alone. Yet another review in that same year, by the newly renamed 303 Committee, clearly states that the costs outweighed the benefits. Despite eight years of "political action, propaganda, paramilitary, and intelligence operations . . . aimed toward lessening the influence and capabilities of the Chinese regime" the report lamented that "there are no apparent signs that the Tibetan people are capitalizing upon this internal chaos to seek further autonomy." It added that "Chinese security has shown no signs of deterioration and its control over Tibet, both political and military, remains as pervasive as ever. Tibetan leadership has been purged, leaving the Chinese in direct control of the local administration, and a large number of underground assets have been uncovered and neutralized."[178]

Such memoranda, not generally available for the operations we will be exploring, give us some of the few detailed insights we have into the dialogue and discussions that occurred during the actual oversight of covert warfare operations under both the Eisenhower and Kennedy administrations. Of course, remarks such as "no radio teams remaining" fail to express the fact that after over ten years of recruitment, infiltration, extensive training, and highly risky aerial insertion operations, all the volunteers had been killed, captured, or otherwise removed from action. A simple statement, "Because of the diplomatic sensitivity occasioned by the presence of the Tibetan force . . . it has been enjoined from offensive action which might invite Chinese . . . retaliation," fails to express the fact that even with the advent of direct support from India, years of training and equipping a force large enough to conduct actual sabotage or modest attacks on a Chinese infrastructure within Tibet had accomplished little more than producing a small army that was being sustained in place, essentially as armed refugees, with all the potential problems such a group might produce.

The Tibet Project began under the Eisenhower Administration, continued on through the Kennedy and Johnson presidencies, and ultimately faded only in the 1970s under Richard Nixon. Its efforts produced few military results inside Tibet and quite obviously had no significant impact at all upon the Chinese incorporation of that nation. Perhaps its most significant result was the creation of Tibetan exile military units, and the availability of Tibetan exiles for use by the nation of India. India deployed some three thousand Tibetan special forces in its military efforts against East Pakistan in 1971, in battles that led to the creation of Bangladesh. In Tibet, as well as elsewhere, America's surrogate armies often did not simply vanish once the United States ceased to support them. Operation Paper ROC combatants from Burma ended up fighting in both Laos and Cambodia. The CIA-trained Tibetans would fight for India. In later chapters we will follow CIA-trained Cuban exiles in battles across Africa and Latin America. America's surrogate combatants would fight back and forth across the African borders of the Congo (modern-day Zaire) and Angola for decades. And eventually, surrogate Islamist volunteers from the Afghanistan insurgency against the Russians would end up fighting and conducting terror attacks against their former sponsors, including the United States, into the twenty-first century.[179]

CHAPTER 9

Face-off in Indochina

Both Presidents Truman and Eisenhower felt strongly that a firm re-sponse to communist territorial expansion was a matter of American national security. Therefore there was to be no hesitation in responding to perceived threats around the globe. The appearance of a constantly escalating communist threat led to the view that neutral nations represented a series of potential dominoes—the fall of one to communism could easily lead to the rapid loss of a series of governments in an entire region. Indochina was seen as an area of major exposure to communist advance, especially given the emergent nationalist movements that followed the Second World War. The entire region lying between India and China had long been subject to cultural influence from both countries, but in the 1800s French colonial efforts had created an artificial political unit of Indochina (the Indochinese Union) out of the ancient nations of Laos, Cambodia, and Vietnam. That union was shattered by the Japanese seizure of Indochina during the Second World War, in particular the occupation of Vietnam and Laos.

In World War II, well before any artificial North–South division in Vietnam, the U.S. Army's Office of Strategic Services (OSS) had been active throughout the entire region. In 1944, Vietnamese independence movement leader Ho Chi Minh offered American military officers access to his Viet Minh guerrilla network and aid in recovering

Allied pilots shot down in combat operations against Japanese forces. He also explored obtaining a visa to travel to the United States, most likely to plead his nationalist cause against French colonialism. At the same time Ho Chi Minh went so far as to meet with General Claire Chennault, commander of the U.S. 14th Air Force. Later, in 1945, an OSS team (code-named Deer) parachuted into Ho's camp, finding him extremely ill, and treated him for a variety of diseases, very possibly saving his life.[180] With the Japanese defeat and departure, Ho Chi Minh immediately declared Vietnam an independent nation. France responded by recognizing Vietnam as a "free state" but only within the French Union. It dispatched French troops and almost immediately, ongoing military clashes began.

During World War II, President Roosevelt had taken a position against a return to French colonial dominance in Indochina following the ouster and defeat of the Japanese. While his successor has been characterized as sharing the same "adaptive, active-positive" personality type as Roosevelt, President Truman lacked Roosevelt's international experience—which itself had been reinforced by Roosevelt's serving as commander in chief of America's military for longer than any president in American history. Following the Allied victory, France immediately moved to reassert its former status across Indochina, and Truman faced the choices of opposing a major ally or moving towards a new American position regarding nationalist states and neutrality in the region.

In the immediate postwar period, as supreme leader Joseph Stalin aggressively asserted Soviet influence in Europe and the Soviets began to build a communist bloc in Eastern Europe, the American State Department viewed a strong alliance with France as an overriding goal in international affairs. Indochina was initially a secondary concern to Europe—and remained so until the completely unanticipated establishment of a communist Chinese regime ruling mainland China. Influenced by State Department concerns, Truman moved to a compromise position. In October 1945 he issued a public statement that the U.S. would remain officially neutral towards affairs in Indochina. However, it would not oppose France's assertion of its former colonial rule. He also confirmed that there was no thought that America would question France's sovereignty in the region.[181]

France itself struggled mightily in its attempts to reassert its control, facing ongoing opposition from a variety of military forces in both Laos and Vietnam, including Ho Chi Minh's increasingly communist-oriented Viet Minh insurgency. The French agreed to grant Laos a degree of autonomy as an "associated state" within the global French Union. The French government then entered into an agreement with a Vietnamese political faction that officially confirmed Vietnam's independence—yet gave France full control over Vietnam's defense, diplomacy, and finances. The agreement also called for the development of a national anticommunist army. That move effectively left the Vietnamese nationalist opposition (and its communist element) with few options. As the widely recognized "nationalist voice" of Vietnam, Ho Chi Minh made a final international appeal for support against France, declaring that he would take an independent Vietnam neutral in the Cold War.[182] The United States viewed that as a potential loss in the face-off between the international power blocs led by America and Russia.[183] Ho Chi Minh's appeal was ignored by the Eisenhower Administration, which gave no response at all and offered no intercession with the French for increased Vietnamese autonomy, or any sign that it would recognize Vietnam as a fully independent nation. That was consistent with the American fear that any officially neutral regime would be immediately subverted by aggressive communist political elements.

With a total lack of American response to his outreach, Ho Chi Minh turned to Russia and China for political recognition, which they quickly granted in early 1950. As far as the Western powers were concerned, that simply confirmed their worst fears. Any overall victory for a nationalist insurgency in Vietnam was viewed to be a loss to ongoing communist territorial expansion. And with insurgencies still active in neighboring Laos, it seemed quite possible that Indochina and especially Laos and Vietnam could become the tipping point for communist regime takeovers stretching from China to the borders of India. At that point the American position on Vietnam moved almost immediately away from neutrality and to active military support of the French. In 1950, President Truman met with the National Security Council in regard to acting against apparent communist expansion in Southeast Asia, and it was agreed that "military assistance" to the French would be the most practical response. Immediately $10 million in American aid was allocated for that purpose, with the money to be taken from congressional appropriations that had been made for countries in the "general area" of China.[184]

By the end of that same year, some $100 million was committed to the French counterinsurgency effort. America also began sending transport and B-26 attack bombers and WWII–era fighters to the French forces in Indochina. During the next two years, leading into the Eisenhower Administration, some twelve shiploads of materials would be sent to the French each month; the two-hundredth shipload would arrive in July 1953. Shipments included some 777 armored fighting vehicles, thirteen thousand transport vehicles, 228 aircraft, and 253 naval vessels. The following year the French received $170 million in American aid, and historian John Prados estimates that by 1954 the U.S. was financially covering between one-third and one-half of the entire French military effort in Indochina.[185] And that effort, even with American funding, did not go at all well; the Vietnamese insurgency simply grew stronger year by year.

By 1954, with the French military effort in dire straits, the existence of major U.S. financial and military support was certainly no secret. It would have been virtually impossible to conceal the volume of shipments and transfer of military stocks in any event. The establishment of an American military mission with American service personnel actually in-country was also no particular surprise. Given the amount of American aid, it would only be expected that the U.S. would want some level of field oversight for its investment. Still, committing American military personnel overseas always raised the question of whether to do it openly or covertly. That question became especially critical with the possibility that the personnel might move beyond advisory or administrative duties and become involved in support of actual military operations.

As the French effort to oppose Ho Chi Minh's communist insurgents proceeded and continued to falter, demands grew for more air transport, and specifically for more combat air power. The French themselves did not have the wherewithal for either and Britain, their WWII ally, was in no position financially or militarily to provide any aid. The French could turn only to the U.S, requesting more B-26 bombers and some four hundred American military personnel. The American response, extended through the U.S Joint Chiefs of Staff, was quite similar to something we have seen before—that the French might organize a volunteer air unit comprised of personnel from various anticommunist nations and groups.[186] But the French needed help and they needed it quickly. The National Security Council responded by authorizing the transfer of two hundred mechanics from NATO service in Europe to Vietnam. That action was to be strictly secret, with assurances from the French that under no circumstances would the personnel be exposed to combat or potential capture. Those assurances were given. Later, as the numbers of American support personnel increased, some of them were exposed to insurgent attack, some were wounded, and at least five would be reported captured by the Viet Minh.

Eisenhower felt that sending technicians such as aircraft mechanics should not require special congressional authorization; after all, such personnel were already deployed in Korea, Taiwan, and Iran. A top secret airlift (Operation Revere) used three Globemaster transports out of Japan and another dozen out of Clark Air Base in the Philippines. In addition to personnel, twenty-one separate flights ferried in more than seven hundred tons of supplies to the French.[187] Eisenhower's first response to the French military failure in Vietnam had been to double down on military assistance, not only with money but with aircraft and support personnel. His next choices were going to be considerably more difficult. Any further military commitment was going to have to go far beyond that—and then word came that a major French military force had become encircled and was under siege in a remote area known as Dien Bien Phu.

The French were facing a disastrous defeat in the spring of 1954 and President Eisenhower was facing the fact that the only way out might well be full American military intervention. At a minimum that would require massive naval and air strikes in support of the trapped French outpost at Dien Bien Phu. In preparation for just such an effort, an American naval carrier group including the carriers *Wasp* and *Essex* (with some 134 aircraft) was secretly ordered to proceed within air operations distance of Vietnam. Special equipment that would enable radio communication with French forward air control was secretly loaded onto the vessels—it would be needed for any tactical bombing around the besieged French force.

Eisenhower then directed the Justice Department to assess just what legal requirements would be necessary for conventional military combat intervention. The response was that the president, as commander in chief, had the authority to send forces outside the United States without a formal declaration of war, but that a Congressional resolution would be required to actually commit the forces to combat.[188] President Eisenhower listened to the legal advice from Justice and to all his advisors, and took a firm and politically sensitive position.[189] Publicly John Foster Dulles continued to declare the administration's view that Indochina was of "transcendent importance," and he personally raised the concept of the domino theory. In public remarks reported by *The New York Times* on April 17, 1954, Vice President Nixon declared that if the French were defeated all of Indochina would become communist-dominated within a month: "It is hoped that the United States will not have to send troops there but if this government cannot avoid it, the Administration must face up to the situation and dispatch forces." Eisenhower himself began to privately discuss sending in two squadrons of aircraft carriers, and the American military secretly began to evaluate not only major naval air action, including attacks on Chinese airfields (if China chose to intervene), but extensive aerial bombardment, using a massive attack by up to ninety-eight B-29 bombers flying out of Clark Air Base in the Philippines.

In all that dialogue and all that planning, Eisenhower had begun to establish a series of ground rules for committing to overt American military action, even if kept as low-profile as possible. He had authorized ongoing and increased covert logistics support for the French. U.S. Air Force Globemaster transports had ferried French paratroops from France to Vietnam. American transport aircraft operating out of Clark Air Base had carried out a major supply effort: some eighteen hundred flights with a total of over ten thousand passengers and seventy-six hundred tons of freight had been moved into Vietnam.[190] That sort of activity had not remained unknown to the press, which had observed and reported on it; what they missed was the fact that some 450-plus American military personnel had actually gone in-country in Vietnam supporting the air effort. They also missed reporting that a secret Navy task force had flown well over two thousand "training" and reconnaissance flights (sorties in military terminology) over Vietnam, the Gulf of Tonkin, and even southern China. In the end, all supply flights, all the planning and the secret reconnaissance missions were for naught as an encircled and desperate Dien Bien Phu fell from French control—followed shortly by the rest of the country. At that point the dialogue, international outreach, and political jockeying by the Eisenhower Administration became moot.

President Eisenhower strongly considered direct American military intervention to support the French. He had examined his legal options and directed an intense round of political outreach to potential international allies and to Congress. Eisenhower's conditions were fourfold: 1) There would have to be a public request for intervention from one or more states in the area, 2) There would have to be some indication of multination support for an allied military response, 3) Congress would have to be informed, and 4) Congress would have to pass a resolution approving the intervention. And Eisenhower gave John Foster Dulles the mission to fulfill those conditions.[191]

Secretary of State John Foster Dulles had gone to the press, to Congress, and to America's staunch British and French allies. In the end he failed to gain what Eisenhower needed. The British simply didn't see matters in the same light as Dulles; he was reportedly very upset when British Prime Minister Anthony Eden rejected a proposal for a Southeast Regional Anticommunist Coalition to support the French. And the French, with apparently the most to gain, seemed to constantly vacillate. The French even declined to consider moving some sort of face-saving political agreement to be reached at yet another Geneva conference. On the American home front, Dulles was also quite upset with the fact that several key Republican senators had failed to line up behind military intervention. Dulles was not sparing in his comments, remarking to confidants that he simply could not understand Congress's attitude: "We must not give in to the Communists and we must keep our allies. That is a tough job. Why those people on the Hill cannot understand that and back us up is more than I can understand!"[192]

With ambivalent allies and a Congress relatively unenthusiastic about overt American military action in Indochina, Eisenhower's only other option would have been to take the issue directly to the American public.[193] Given Eisenhower's election pledge to maintain peace and reduce the federal budget, such a move would certainly have been politically questionable. Allen Dulles was less than enthusiastic about any such effort, although his lack of enthusiasm may have more ideological than political. In remarks to Vice President Richard Nixon, he expressed the view that "one cannot explain everything to our own people, as it also explains things to the enemy."[194] In the end Eisenhower held back when the international consensus and political support he had sought did not emerge. His caution would not be a precedent consistently followed by his successors—many of whom appear to have possessed personalities more predisposed to proceeding strictly on their own initiative. Eisenhower was personally quite depressed at both the failure of the French effort in Indochina and the partition of Vietnam at the subsequent Geneva Accords of July 1954.

The United States flatly refused to acknowledge or sign the accords, which called for an International Control Commission, a *temporary* dividing line between the south and Ho Chi Minh's communist regime in the North, and plans for a free election for a unified government to occur no later than July 1956. The president wrote of being exasperated and frustrated by being forced to watch a communist victory without being able to send combat troops. Eisenhower was a general, a major figure in the Allied effort in the Second World War. His first thought had been of U.S. military and Allied intervention in Indochina. Yet the only part of that initiative that had actually come to be had been a low-profile but quite expensive military assistance program for the failed French counterinsurgency effort.

We will find that from 1954 on, Eisenhower began to rely less on John Foster Dulles and the possibility of united Western alliance military action in the Cold War. Instead he began to turn more and more towards John's brother Allen—towards covert alternatives to be organized and orchestrated by the CIA. John Foster Dulles and the State Department had failed him in Indochina, but Allen and the CIA had brought the Eisenhower Administration key regime-change victories, first the covert political action of Operation Ajax in Iran in 1953, and then the armed coup against the Árbenz regime in Guatemala with PBSUCCESS. Those successes not only established the credentials and capability of the CIA but would continue to drive Eisenhower's future thinking.

The Guatemalan operation not only established a model for future covert warfare, it also produced a lasting impact within the culture of the CIA's Covert Action Directorate. Eisenhower clearly wanted the CIA to be proactive in resisting communist efforts to take control in any country. Guatemala was just one example. The CIA was expected to pose a response to communist efforts to subvert or take control in any country—a preemptive practice that has no official designation but that was referred to within the CIA as "forward leaning." That term and the worldview it represents continued to be applied within the CIA for decades. It was commonly used in the CIA's Far Eastern Division during the tenure of Desmond FitzGerald in the 1950s and is still in current use; most recently it appeared in a 2011 message of congratulations concerning justice being done in regard to Osama bin Laden.[195, 196] CIA officers who are felt to be "forward leaning" are praised for their willingness to be aggressive and take risks.

There was indeed considerable opportunity to be forward leaning during the Eisenhower Administration. A "Soviet beachhead" in Latin America had been intolerable to Eisenhower, and that issue had been resolved. In Southeast Asia, the possibility of yet another gain of political influence by the communists was emerging. Eisenhower mistrusted neutrality in the Cold War, whether it was in Indonesia, India, Egypt, or Laos. During his administration Laos had become a politically fragmented, unstable nation in a part of the world where neutrality had become common. It was also a region where new communist regimes were emerging. While there were no imminent indications of a communist takeover in Laos, the views of the period held that communists would be able to take advantage of neutral regimes.

While America had moved into overt but low-profile military assistance in Vietnam, it had also begun taking initial steps of the same nature in Laos, but with a far more covert element and a much more active involvement by the CIA. American entry into Laotian politics had first come in the form of a 1950 developmental aid mission to the country. Following in the spirit of the Geneva Accords of 1954, and the defeat of the French in Vietnam, the United States moved to enhance the Laotian aid mission. In 1955 it established the U.S. Operations Mission (USOM) in the Laotian capital, Vientiane, where the mission established a Program Evaluation Office. Ostensibly the Program Evaluation Office (PEO) existed to facilitate and evaluate aid going into Laos. However, the office was also used as a type of cover to send in what amounted to a military assistance mission with reserve and retired American military personnel, serving not in uniform but in civilian clothes.

The PEO handled military aid to the neutral Laotian army, an army increasingly funded by the U.S. It served covertly as a vehicle to organize and direct military activity against any communist or other rebel groups that challenged the central government. In those early years, the CIA was very much involved in general aid activities in those areas of Laos that were not already under communist Pathet Lao control. Major humanitarian aid efforts began in the summer of 1955, when a major rice failure put thousands of Laotians at risk of famine. Many of the endangered areas were in remote and mountainous regions, and America began air-dropping food. The U.S Agency for International Development contracted for some two hundred food relief missions flown by Civil Air Transport (CAT), operating out of the Udorn airfield in northeastern Thailand. By 1957, CAT would operate on a full-time basis in Laos under an ongoing contract with the U.S. Embassy. Working through the American Embassy in Laos, the CIA was able to call for Civil Air Transport missions to drop supplies and even courier personnel to remote locations. Demand for those types of air missions escalated over time and CAT continued to fly for the embassy, performing work for a number of American government–affiliated agencies as well as the CIA.

America's "forward leaning" in the highly contentious and fragmented Laotian neutralist government meant identifying anticommunist or at least pro-American individuals and political parties, and ensuring that American international aid resources were directed towards those parties. That approach was certainly not one developed specifically for Laos; it was general practice in CIA stations around the world. Indeed, CIA station chiefs in friendly and neutral countries were often evaluated primarily on their skills in such techniques of "political action." Political action, involving covert contacts and selective assistance to military and government officials, did carry its own risks. Playing favorites with financial and military assistance tended to expose State Department personnel in embarrassing situations—just one more area of potential conflict between agencies—especially dicey given that the CIA stations and personnel were operating under State Department diplomatic assignments used as an employment cover for their covert activities.

Laos in the mid- to late 1950s provides us with a dramatic illustration of how points of conflict arose between the State Department and the CIA. Conflicting agendas between the two American entities would evolve for well over a decade, as CIA covert activities in Laos developed into full-scale, barely deniable warfare. In 1958, democratic elections in Laos were intended to reintegrate several competing factions (nationalists, socialists, communists, and various tribal leaders) into a functioning government. An effort was also made to integrate competing armed units—including the Laotian communist military groups (the Pathet Lao)—into a single national army, the Royal Lao Armed Forces. That effort was the first of dozens of such attempts made though the 1950s and 1960s, all doomed to failure but sustaining the "possibility," or more realistically the illusion, of a working, neutral Lao state. The U.S. ambassador to Laos, Horace Smith, actively promoted such Laotian neutrality as, at minimum, a barrier to losing the entire country to the communists. In turn, the Eisenhower Administration first cut back overall development aid, and then turned to dramatically increasing military aid to the central government when open combat with the communist Pathet Lao began to occur. The CIA station proceeded with its own agenda, rather openly courting both anticommunist and nationalist leaders.

In the early American days in Laos, circa 1958, PBSUCCESS team veteran Henry Hecksher was assigned as CIA chief of station in Vientiane. As previously noted, Hecksher carried the reputation of being an aggressive and unapologetic "Cold Warrior." Working at the CIA's Berlin Station he had asked for permission to arm the East Berlin rioters in 1953. Such a move would indeed have been "forward leaning," but highly risky in one of the Cold War's most contentious flashpoints—his request had been denied. While in Laos, Hecksher engaged in ongoing opposition to the State Department and the ambassador's neutrality agenda; sensing that neutrality views were carrying the day, he cabled back to his CIA superiors, asking, "Is HQ still in friendly hands."[197] Indeed, Hecksher was so adamant in his anticommunist aggressiveness, and became so diametrically opposed to the American ambassador in Laos, that CIA Director Dulles was requested to remove him.

But Hecksher had gained a good deal of status from his work in the CIA "regime change" activity in Guatemala and his views were far more in line with Dulles's own firm anticommunist stance than with Ambassador Smith's goal of a neutral Laos. Dulles refused the ambassador's request, allowing Hecksher to complete his tour and then leaving him in the region, assigning him to a certain special, unspecified role in "cross border" operations out of Thailand. Thailand, once again firmly in control of a pro-American military leadership, would prove to be a key supporter and a key military base for U.S. warfare in Southeast Asia through the coming decade of the 1960s. It would serve as a launching point for overt combat missions in Vietnam, and covert operations in Laos and Cambodia.

Dramatic changes in Thailand had occurred in 1957; the head of the Thai police had lost his position and gone into exile. As part of those changes, the SEA Supply, which had continued to be the main channel for American military support to the Thai police, had lost much of its leverage within Thailand and was forced to close its doors and cease operations there. The Nationalist Chinese drug and supply network from Burma through Thailand also had gone out of business and the Thai overland routes to the Burmese Shan States had, for the time, closed down as well. Yet another CIA-associated company, this one a full-fledged CIA proprietary, would step up to take an even larger role in covert military logistics support throughout Southeast Asia. As previously discussed, one the first new roles for CAT had been support of the Tibetan covert military operation.

As the anticommunist combat in Laos escalated, Taiwan began to dramatically strengthen and reinvigorate its affiliated forces remaining in the area of the Burmese–Laotian frontier. These were the same Nationalist Chinese units that had been forced north from Burma into the panhandle area of Laos on the Mekong River. Taiwan had begun pressuring those forces to conduct new raids into China's Yunnan province. Late in 1957, some three divisions had once again moved, reportedly without much enthusiasm, across the Chinese border into Yunnan—they were quickly driven back by local Chinese militia forces.

But Taiwan remained insistent and the following year it began its own small-scale aerial supply of the border forces. Additional raids were made across the Chinese border. And in 1959, a major aerial supply effort was initiated, and regular Republic of China troops were sent to the border area from Taiwan.[198] Officially the U.S. had no role in any of Taiwan's military efforts—yet the Nationalist Chinese forces clearly had easy access across the Laotian border and into northwestern Laos. And the Laotian army chief made no efforts against Taiwanese-backed forces moving into Laos. Beyond that, in late summer 1959, senior Laotian military officers became involved in discussions of inviting Nationalist Chinese troops into Laos. Talks were even held concerning the possibility of their joining the coalition central government battles against communist-aligned insurgent military units.[199] In the end, the talks were overtaken by events within Laos, and in 1960, U.S.-backed Laotian political factions staged a coup that fractured the volatile political foundation of Laotian neutrality and increasingly pitted those factions and the central government Royal Laotian Army against the Pathet Lao communist units.[200]

After the coup, the American-backed parties following defense minister and Lao army commander Phoumi Nosavan once again contemplated the use of both Taiwan's border forces and Nationalist Chinese forces as potential military assets in the fight against the Pathet Lao. Nationalist units were allowed to move into Laos, and permission for flights inside the country was also given by the Laotian government to Nationalist Chinese aircraft. The planes were registered as belonging to China Airlines but were officially "leased" to the Laotian international airline (Veha Akhat). On its own, Taiwan began diverting American military aid from its own defense and began sending it on to its border forces in Burma and Laos. ROC military transports flew into Laos, refueling in Bangkok, Thailand. As usual, the American diplomatic position was that it knew nothing about any such activities. While it is likely the State Department did indeed have some knowledge and may have quietly objected, it is also quite possible that CIA officers such as Hecksher and the CIA/military assistance personnel on Taiwan may have known a good bit more about Nationalist Chinese activities inside Laos.

Ultimately, international diplomatic protests about Taiwanese involvement in Laos put an end to the Nationalist Chinese military option. Phoumi would be left to rely on the Royal Lao Army, and some help from his American friends. With their "forward-leaning" history, both the CIA and the Americans working in Laos (whose official role was simply as an extension of the American military assistance mission to Thailand) were in a position to take advantage of and provide increasing military support to Phoumi. The central Lao government began receiving increased military backing covertly from both the U.S. and Thailand—there simply would be no need for the Nationalist Chinese–affiliated units or Taiwanese involvement. The increasingly independent Nationalist surrogate forces would be left to sustain themselves as they had been doing since their retreat from China, by taking advantage of the drug resources of the Golden Triangle. They would find substantial opportunities to grow that business during the 1960s, as the U.S. military arrived in force in Southeast Asia.

In regard to American military involvement in Laos, President Eisenhower authorized the dispatch of some 107 Green Berets to Laos in summer 1959, in a covert operation designated Hotfoot. The Special Forces personnel were flown into Bangkok, Thailand, and on into Laos by Air America; they wore civilian clothes and operated as employees of the Programs Evaluation Office, the overt administrative program that nominally monitored all American aid programs in Laos. By 1961, American support for the central government of Laos had become far more open and the military assistance program was renamed White Star. One of the officers involved in the White Star operation was reportedly none other than Rip Robertson, like Henry Hecksher a veteran of the CIA's Guatemalan regime-change operation. White Star continued until the 1962 Geneva peace conference. That conference, with agreement by both Russia and the United States, produced a declaration of neutrality for Laos, with a new, neutral central Lao government to be a power-sharing coalition between the three major factions in the country.

In the early 1960s, matters in Laos became far more complex, with an ongoing desire for neutrality during the both Kennedy and Johnson administrations—and a continuing concern over direct combat not only with North Vietnamese forces but with the possibility of Chinese military intervention. America would continue its military support for the ostensibly neutral central government and escalated its aid and development efforts, which became tightly integrated with the establishment of indigenous anticommunist military forces. The majority of the CIA's involvement in Laotian "civic action programs" was in the southern region of the country, down the panhandle adjacent to South Vietnam. The CIA actively encouraged economic development for the lowland Lao people in the Mekong Valley as well as the indigenous hill tribes of the Bolovens Plateau. The Agency became involved with pig-breeding centers, new types of livestock, and vocational schools that offered training in skills ranging from carpentry and brick-making to auto repair. By 1964, the U.S. had begun a "village cluster project" for rural development; the project included the formation of village militias. Unlike the fundamentally unsuccessful Vietnamese "hamlet" program, the Laotian village cluster project flourished, and military advisors were added to the program.

One aspect of Laotian activity that changed considerably during that period was the number of missions flown with helicopters. Initially both commercial and military two-engine transports went into Laos, and missions to remote sites involved both cargo and personnel airdrops. Over the years, single-engine aircraft capable of, and short takeoffs and landings were introduced, but several types of helicopters also became routinely operated, especially in support of military missions. By the end of 1960, the CIA had arranged for the transfer of Marine helicopters to Air America, and a group of Marine Corps helicopter pilots was officially discharged on Okinawa. They followed the helicopters to new jobs in Laos. The shift in air operations occurred incrementally and over several years. At the time it seemed imminently practical; ultimately it would become a fundamental enabler backbone for covert military operations in Laos.

While matters in Laos appeared to have stabilized somewhat in the early 1960s, Vietnam had seen an increase in covert military action—largely based in what turned out to be the partition of the country. The Geneva agreement signed by the French in 1954 had called for regrouping opposing factions into different north–south zones, in anticipation of nationwide elections that would establish a unified government. Given Vietnam's long history as an independent state, that was clearly an artificial construct rather than any sort of border natural to the Vietnamese. The Eisenhower Administration, with its deeply held conviction that communists would take control in any such government after such an election, refused to support the agreement. The years of French military failures and the fervor of Ho Chi Minh's fighters had convinced Eisenhower that a communist takeover would be virtually inevitable if no preemptive action was taken. In opposition to the Geneva Accords, Eisenhower directed the CIA to begin covert political action, providing financial support to anticommunist factions, particularly in the south of the country. The U.S. also began referring to the southern zone as South Vietnam, in an effort to isolate it from communist influence in the north. The U.S. and France also moved to begin relocation of some million or more Catholics, as well as others who feared communist rule. The goal of all those efforts was the creation of a massively anticommunist political bastion in the south.

The CIA had already established a station in Vientiane, Laos, and in June 1954, CIA teams were dispatched to Vietnam—a month before the formal signing of the Geneva Accords. In the south, a team commanded by Air Force Colonel Edward Lansdale operated under cover of the Saigon Military Mission. But more covert personnel were also sent north, to Hanoi and Haiphong. Covert action in the north was headed by OSS veteran Lucian Conein, a veteran of OSS work with the French Resistance during the Second World War, afterward serving in Indochina. The Geneva agreement had stipulated some three hundred days for regional regrouping, including alternative movement of anticommunist Vietnamese from the north to the south, and communist factions from south to north. That window, and the movements of the general population, provided a window of opportunity for Conein and his team.

Conein's focus was entirely different than Lansdale's; he was to put "stay behind" teams in place. Such teams consisted of individuals who would remain in an area taken over by enemy forces, positioned and supplied to conduct sabotage and guerrilla military action. The concept for such teams was well established by that point; the CIA had organized such teams in Western Europe in advance of an anticipated Soviet push to the west. Teams were in place in Germany and in Italy. In addition, an effort had been made to insert paramilitary teams in contested and denied Soviet satellites in Eastern Europe. Ultimately that effort was recognized to have been a horrific failure, with team after team "rolled up," captured, tortured, and/or pressured to broadcast misleading radio reports. The radio broadcasts drew in yet more personnel to traps in which they were seized, then either imprisoned or executed. One retired senior American Army officer who had been assigned to the CIA operation summarized his experience in the following brief remarks: "I went down to the airfield each time an agent team was about to be inserted into a target country . . . to do a final check of their equipment and to wish them luck. . . . At the time, none of those I was responsible for made contact after being inserted."[201]

As we will see, the CIA's Eastern European experience would prove a terribly accurate indicator of what was going to happen to those volunteers sent into North Vietnam. Conein's "stay behind" efforts were made in an area of Vietnam that was increasingly denied, day by day. In addition, his orders were aggressive—his teams were not only to generate political unrest but to conduct sabotage operations. To that end his personnel recruited anticommunist volunteers and sent them to Saipan for paramilitary training, following the same regimen as the Koreans, Chinese, and Tibetans who had preceded them.

Once trained, some of the two hundred men were inserted into the stream of communist sympathizers who were moving out of the south and into the northern zone. Other personnel were infiltrated by the U.S. Navy. A "black" (totally covert and deniable) supply effort by CAT aircraft and boats from Navy Task Force 98, designated to support the CIA's covert operations, took in over eight tons of supplies for the anticipated northern guerrilla action network. The supplies included explosives, pistols, rifles, radios, and ammunition.[202] Sabotage focused on the northern transportation network, oil for trains was laced with acid, and explosives were concealed in coal. Actual results of the effort were limited; most of the teams were arrested, charged, and put into anti-American show trials.[203]

In the south, Lansdale's CIA team focused on political action, propaganda, and political warfare. They organized a variety of "dirty trick" propaganda and political action activities, planting rumors that Chinese troops had been violating Vietnamese villages in the north and spreading word that local soothsayers were predicting doom under communism. In a significant success, Lansdale personally gained the favor of a Catholic anticommunist leader named Ngo Dinh Diem, providing covert American aid and financial support for Diem's campaign. The CIA also funded bribes of more than $3 million to the leaders of rival groups for their support of a Diem regime. With Lansdale's advice in political maneuvering, Diem became secure enough to declare that the south was rejecting the Geneva-mandated referendum, declaring itself an independent state.

After taking office, President Kennedy requested an in-depth review of the Vietnam situation and, in January 1961, invited Edward Lansdale to attend a National Security Council meeting. At that point Lansdale held the rank of general and had accumulated years of experience with Vietnam. Lansdale had also just returned from a two-week fact-finding tour of the region. The meeting was being held as a review of a "Basic Counterinsurgency Plan for Vietnam" submitted by the U.S. Embassy in Saigon. Kennedy was impressed with Lansdale's comments on the plan, which Lansdale supported. The possibility of shaping foreign affairs while avoiding overt warfare appealed to both Kennedy and Lansdale. General Lansdale's enthusiasm for bold covert operations gained Kennedy's personal support first in Vietnam, and later for operations against Cuba.

Kennedy approved low-profile counterinsurgency operations in the south, as well as covert action in both the north and south regions of Vietnam. In the south, U.S. military operations involved the dispatch of Air Force resources from the 4400th Combat Crew Training Squadron at Hurlburt Field, Florida. That particular unit was selected because its personnel were experienced with and still flying WWII-era fighter bombers and transport aircraft. Aircraft to be sent to South Vietnam were painted dull gray, carried few markings, and would be routinely flown not only in a training role but also in strike missions against the Viet Cong insurgents. The first American unit was designated Detachment 2 Alpha and deployed to Bien Hoa, South Vietnam. The overall operation was designated Farm Gate; personnel were given an official military assignment to the Philippines as a deployment cover and used Philippines armed forces postal addresses for all their mail.

The unit's overt mission was training pilots in the South Vietnamese Air Force (Republic of Vietnam/VNAF) and flights always carried a Republic of Vietnam passenger. The American pilots wore no name, rank, or unit designations on their flight suits and initially were instructed not to log their individual missions. During missions the pilots "sanitized" themselves by removing all identifiable personal materials (referred to as pocket litter) from their persons. In reality their missions were "fire support" for South Vietnamese infantry forces engaging the communist Viet Cong insurgents and the Americans coordinated their air strikes with directions from fire controllers with the Vietnamese troops. This was full-scale combat against Viet Cong ground forces, who were themselves equipped with a variety of weapons including antiaircraft guns. The American unit was quite successful in its support role. At that time, in 1961–62, combat was truly localized in the south and the Americans, including a young Air Force captain named Richard Secord, were in a well-defined and limited combat support role.[204]

It would initially be the CIA and not the American military that was tasked with a major new effort against North Vietnam. On May 11, 1961, Kennedy issued a national security action memorandum

(NSAM 52) authorizing a series of covert military actions to prevent the fall of the Diem government. Specifically, the CIA was chartered with organizing deniable warfare against North Vietnam. Approval for those activities was to come from the new Special Group (Counterinsurgency) with operational oversight from the 303 Committee. The CIA found North Vietnam to be an exceptionally difficult target for "black entry" infiltration. There was no organized or even developing resistance in the north, a key issue and one that had proved exceptionally helpful to Office of Strategic Services operations in France during the Second World War. The people staying in the north were by and large supportive of the communist leadership and celebrated their successful ejection of the French. Locals in North Vietnam were also very observant and routinely reported unknown persons or any sort of abnormal activity; a sighting of a parachute, a suspicious boat, or the appearance of strangers not known to the locals was quickly reported. Even the noise of a low-flying aircraft, or relatives of local families who suddenly appeared—all routinely triggered reports to government authorities.

Additionally, the new communist government in the north was extremely control oriented; it exercised very tight regulation over individual movement throughout the country, especially near the coast and borders. To make matters even more challenging, there was little or no noncommunist commercial traffic across the borders or into port; the use of business covers for infiltration was generally not an option. In the end almost all the individuals and teams sent into the north by the CIA faced having to operate independently, isolated from contacts with the locals that would result in their exposure. Based on the initial experiences of Conein's teams and the lack of success in the few missions attempted against the north back in 1957, the CIA's Far East Division had held no illusions about black operations in North Vietnam. A 1959 memorandum on the subject described such operations as a "complete waste of time"; in even stronger terms it commented that in regard to the agents being sent north, "we might as well shoot them."[205] Yet agents would continue to be sent north for years to come. As we will continue to note, field experience and recommendations often seem to have had little impact on high-level national security decision-making.

The Kennedy Administration covert action initiative began with a relatively small American presence in South Vietnam and began by extending programs already in existence. The U.S. had begun operating a small military mission (Saigon Military Mission) circa 1961, and a CIA station was also in place in Saigon—with a very small North Vietnam Operations Branch. Clandestine cover for actual missions into the north was provided within an existing South Vietnamese unit, the 1st Observation Group. The group had been created in 1956, to operate behind enemy lines in the event of an invasion from the north. The unit (a section of the South Vietnamese Presidential Liaison Office) was already outside the normal South Vietnamese army chain of command and reported directly to President Diem. A handful of limited missions were run into the north as early as 1956–57 for the purposes of supporting small anticommunist networks rumored to be in operation; without exception such networks turned out to be nonexistent.[206]

Saigon CIA Chief of Station William Colby directed the initial covert operations into the north—designated Project Tiger—from 1961 to 1963. Actually, the first agent had been sent in across the demilitarized zone between the north and south during late 1960; he was never heard from again.[207] In 1961, to provide further compartmentalization and layered cover, the 1st Observation Group was moved under the Presidential Survey Office's new Special Topographical Exploitation Service. At the same time, the CIA created the Combined Studies Group to house its activities for the northern operations.[208] In further pursuit of secrecy and compartmentalization, the actual agents and agent teams would be inserted into the north by yet another CIA proprietary airline, Vietnamese Air Transport (VIAT), registered in Delaware and manned with Nationalist Chinese flight crews. Given the challenges in the north, the initial idea of organizing insurgent groups turned out to be wishful thinking, and by 1962 the teams were charged with simple sabotage and harassment. Eventually Colby would characterize Tiger as only a "modest effort" with the goal of establishing resistance guerrilla operations.[209] To the personnel involved it was something more than "modest."

Four- to six-man indigenous Vietnamese teams were inserted "totally black" by Vietnamese Air Transport airdrops beginning in 1961 and extending through 1963. That meant they carried no false identification and had no resistance elements to receive them. Most were dropped into relatively isolated areas and faced operating totally independent of any local support. In addition to airdrops, teams were also inserted by slow boats, specially designed and built to resemble local fishing junks but especially configured for infiltration and sabotage teams. Some thirty teams and several "singleton" individual agents were inserted with teams going in by air and by sea. At the end of three years, four teams and one individual agent were thought to be free and operational. The rest had been killed, captured, or, worse yet, forced ("doubled") to send back radio transmissions requesting follow-on agent and supply drops. The North Vietnamese success in coercing false transmissions from CIA team radio operators resulted in the loss of a string of teams and essentially gutted the entire operation. The first radio-equipped agent had been captured after two months, and the first air-dropped team (Castor) captured and turned after four days, the next (Echo) caught and its radio operator doubled immediately. Team Dido lasted one week in the field and others suffered the same fate. In addition, one supply plane was shot down, junks were captured, and in the end the only notable sabotage success was a frogman attack on two gunboats in June 1962.[210] The total losses for Colby and the modest Tiger effort were brutal: 26 men lost in 1961, 68 in 1962, and no less than 123 in 1963.[211, 212]

Colby and the CIA did openly express their concerns about the situation. Colby had personally acknowledged being "well aware that black entry operations against the Soviet Union and Eastern Europe were found to be unfruitful," and in June he wrote the CIA director of operations that "no intelligence of value has been or likely will be obtained from such operations."[213] Still, in spite of those views, Colby neither suspended nor canceled any of the ongoing black entry or maritime sabotage missions, and continued to send in as many teams as could be trained. When Colby met with Defense Secretary Robert McNamara later in 1963, there is no indication that he reported suspicions that the majority of the Tiger teams had been compromised or that there were serious concerns of security issues within the South Vietnamese side of the program. That concern was later confirmed—but only well after the end of fighting in Vietnam. Only then was it revealed that infiltration team activities had been routinely reported on by informants within the South Vietnamese military forces.

The Kennedy Administration had become less than confident with the CIA's competence in paramilitary operations following the disaster at the Bay of Pigs. By June 1961, Kennedy had already issued three NSAMs (numbers 55, 56, and 57), which directed a major responsibility switch of covert warfare projects from the CIA to the Pentagon. In particular, NSAM 55 removed prior exclusive CIA authority for planning and executing deniable warfare operations. The overall change in role and authority was designated Switchback. As part of this change in direction, Kennedy also directed General Lansdale to participate in a study that would generate recommendations for the Joint Chiefs of Staff at the Pentagon, assigning it a new level of responsibility for covert operations. By October 1961, the planned shift of covert paramilitary activities from the CIA to the Army began as Switchback began to be implemented. The transition would take some time to accomplish.

Of course General Lansdale's proposals for covert operations were always ambitious, whether in regard to action against North Vietnam or, later, secret warfare against Cuba. They included not only sabotage but also psychological warfare psy ops operations and the organization of resistance movements—all against highly denied territory. Without a doubt Lansdale set a high level of administration expectations. Such expectations would strain not only the limited CIA staff detailed to support the covert action mission against North Vietnam but also the new army officers who were to take over responsibility for the effort.

In a broader sense, as far as the Army was concerned, its new responsibilities were not limited strictly to missions against North Vietnam. Switchback was a shift in global responsibility and required a new command structure under control of the Joint Chiefs of Staff. In February 1962, the Joint Chiefs began implementing the new Office of Special Assistant for Counterinsurgency and Special Activities (SACSA). That office and its staff were established inside the Office of Special Operations of the Joint Chiefs of Staff, and its first head was Major General Victor Krulak of the Marine Corps. SACSA would play a role around the world during the 1960s and 1970s.

Even after Colby personally reiterated to Kennedy that there was no reason to think that military-led denied-entry operations in North Vietnam would prove any more productive than the CIA's earlier failures in Eastern Europe, neither President Kennedy nor Defense Secretary McNamara was convinced. To McNamara, the former CEO of General Motors, the issue was simply a matter of scale. The problem could be solved by increasing the commitment of resources. He felt the CIA had been running a minimalist effort but the military had the assets, skills, and overall clout to make it work. His view appears to have been that the CIA played at clandestine warfare, but the military were the true professionals, and it was time to hand it off to the first string. President Kennedy's new national security directives suggest that he was fully willing to allow the military to prove that it could take on covert missions beyond the CIA's capabilities.

The end result of all the dialogue was the development of Operational Plan 34A (OPLAN 34A), which outlined a significant escalation of covert warfare in Southeast Asia. As written, OPLAN 34A plan was comprehensive and aggressive. More would be better; the military would carry the day by applying more resources, more organization, and tighter control. Whether or not President Kennedy would have accepted the plan remains a standing question. President Johnson approved it on November 26, 1963, four days after President Kennedy's assassination. In a less-than-encouraging indication of political realities, the senior policy review process for the plan ended in the elimination of all language about creating resistance movements, and the removal of other ambitious elements. Concerns were raised that if the U.S. was too combative in North Vietnam, the north would escalate its activities in the south; there was even a fear of triggering some level of Chinese intervention.[214]

Beyond the surge of caution, the proposed start date of early February 1964 began to slip as reality further asserted itself. On January 24, 1964, Military Assistance Command in Saigon issued orders to set up a new group: the Studies and Observations Group, generally known as SOG. Unfortunately in its planning (and in its expectations), Washington—from McNamara to the Joint Chiefs—seems to have taken little practical note of the fact that the military was going to have to build its own covert operations team in Saigon, and find the staff to run it. That would be a real challenge given that the Army had not wholeheartedly responded to Kennedy's earlier push towards unconventional warfare and that it would take time—and encouragement—to build an even a basic special operations infrastructure. Those difficulties are described in detail in books such as Richard Shultz's *The Secret War against Hanoi* and Robert Gillespie's *Black Ops, Vietnam: The Operational History of MACVSOG*.[215]

The bottom line was that the military personnel assigned to the new command had to start from scratch. The CIA station had its own mission in South Vietnam, and the task of "going north" had been taken from them and placed under control of the American military. CIA support for missions against the north became relatively limited—and in the eyes of the military officers newly assigned to the mission, more than a bit lukewarm. "It was all a guess and by golly, step by step type of operation," observed Colonel Clyde Russell, the first of some five chiefs of Military Assistance Command, Vietnam Studies and Observations Group (MACVSOG). He elaborated that he and the other officers assigned simply had no experience in "denied area" operations, and that it should have been obvious that it would take time for them to learn how to operate in that sort of environment.[216, 217] Russell was assigned thirteen CIA officers to support MACVSOG in 1964, and the number was cut to nine the following year, consisting primarily of psychological operations officers. The CIA clandestine operations people were rapidly being assigned to new CIA projects in the south.[218]

In the face of that reality, the end result for operations against the north—aside from some dramatic improvements in air insertion and supply—was a continuation of the CIA's preceding three years of failed efforts. MACVSOG continued to use the same personnel that it inherited from the CIA effort, and then sent new teams in after them. Not surprisingly, time after time, teams were captured or doubled by the North Vietnamese. And after some two years, in 1966, the missions to the north were redirected and refocused primarily to a road watch function in an effort to monitor what was happening on the feeder routes to the Ho Chi Minh supply trail down the Laotian border. Even those road watch teams came under heavy pressure, and the challenge became one of simply getting teams in and then successfully getting them out. The concern about getting them out might sound intuitive, but it seems not to have been—since in the end, not a single one of some five hundred long-term agents placed in the north ever successfully made it out alive![219]

Wrestling with that level of failure is a challenge in itself. It would be simple to blame it all on the confidence placed in Secretary McNamara, and his assurances that the military could put deniable pressure on the north—on its own territory. In that view the CIA and later the military were simply following orders. Yet Colby had already begun Tiger on his own before being ordered to escalate efforts against the north. And after being challenged to be more aggressive, the CIA simply increased the magnitude of its agent insertion effort, totally ignoring previous internal studies that showed that those efforts were a waste of time—and people. Whether it was inertia or lack of options, there was still no change in tactics. William Colby's later comment might be the simplest answer: "We went back to our World War II experience of dropping people in by parachute and things like that."[220]

Yet Colby had made it quite clear after the first two years of escalation that it wasn't working. He sent that message to the president; he personally reiterated it to Secretary of Defense McNamara. But at that time it was McNamara who had Kennedy's ear, not the CIA (the CIA disaster at the Bay of Pigs had ensured that). And as for McNamara, the harsh truth is that he simply had no experience and no knowledge of the history or practice of clandestine warfare. Colby related that McNamara took the position that only the military had the "critical mass," the "horsepower" to go to the north effectively.[221]

After Kennedy's murder, McNamara bonded with President Johnson, who continually turned to him for advice—often following McNamara rather than either the Pentagon or the CIA. McNamara's can-do attitude and assertiveness fit Johnson's own personality—yet in turn Johnson's caution and McNamara's compliance continually undermined the actual implementation of the aggressive portions of new plans. Covert warfare, like the overall Vietnam War, became a game of "graduated response," with caution driving each stage. And in 1968, as part of continually changing strategies and political realities, Johnson canceled all operations against the north as an element of opening peace negotiations with North Vietnam.

Historian and security studies specialist Richard Shultz Jr. expresses the opinion that President Kennedy might well have been intuitively correct in his early thoughts that aggressive clandestine operations could have made Hanoi feel insecure, that the approach was "strategically sensible" and might have forced the north to diminish its own covert military support of the Viet Cong insurgency in South Vietnam. Yet the CIA couldn't make it happen and it would be years before the military could assemble that capability, which then never came to be truly tested. As we will consistently see, across numerous covert operations, timing appears to be a key factor in the success of denied-entry covert warfare. If the opponent is given time to stamp out resistance movements, to put in place a totalitarian security system, it can effectively make black entry a virtual impossibility. No amount of covert resources or volunteers seems to make a difference, and as we will see, micromanagement of operations isn't all that helpful, either.

CHAPTER 10

Covert to Overt in Laos

Both the initial American military mission and CIA activities in Laos could best be described as efforts at "regime stabilization." The mission was to support the central government and prevent a takeover by communist factions such as the Pathet Lao. Optimistically, the American goal was to put an anticommunist regime in the Laotian capital of Vientiane. Given the geography of the country and the numerous tribal groups, power in the capital largely defined the nation. But after some initial political success, simply maintaining a neutral central government became the priority and challenge. The country was simply too factionalized, too distrustful of foreign intervention, and too heavily influenced by the regional armed communist elements who had been key in the combat that ousted the French. But in the middle of the 1960s, the tenuous agreements among the various factions would significantly weaken, a variety of military coups occurred, and the Pathet Lao continually received increasing support from North Vietnam. Most important, right across the eastern Laotian border, in the latter half of the decade, the Viet Cong insurgency continued in Vietnam but the overall military situation was rapidly devolving into a full-scale north–south war, with massive military escalation by both North Vietnam and America.

The expanding military mission in Laos involved not only aiding the Laotian army and indigenous forces in opposing the Pathet Lao, but new efforts to interdict what became known as the Ho Chi Minh Trail from North Vietnam into the south. At first the route was simply a series of foot trails running down the Laotian side of the Vietnamese border, used by North Vietnam to infiltrate supplies and by a limited number of both political and military cadres. Later those foot trails evolved into a multi-road transportation corridor down the length of the Laotian border, carrying North Vietnamese troop formations, truck convoys, and even tanks to the south. To a great extent, the escalation of American military activity in Laos became not simply a matter of the Pathet Lao insurgency; it was about opposing the expansion of the North Vietnamese supply corridor, which ran down the eastern Laotian border with Vietnam. Increasingly, both the Military Assistance Command and the CIA shifted their attentions—first to intelligence collection ("road watch"), then to sabotage and eventually towards large-scale interdiction of the corridor. To do that, and to do it covertly, the CIA needed local fighters.

The CIA conducted its focused Laotian paramilitary activities with a variety of surrogate Laotian indigenous tribal groups, generally referred to as irregulars. However, the American military mission in Laos was also active, with American military and special operations advisors working with Royal Lao Armed Forces (FAR) against communist and other antigovernment factions around the country—including mutinous army units. Early Royal Lao Army activities involving the U.S. military were conducted with American service personnel sent into Laos in Operations Hotfoot and White Star.[222] The Eisenhower Administration sent 107 Green Berets under White Star in 1959, flown from Fort Bragg under contract by Air America. The Green Berets were assigned in mobile training teams to each of the twelve battalions of the Royal Lao Army; they wore civilian clothes and operated under PEO cover. The Green Berets were nominally assigned as advisors and trainers, but they were also prepared to lead in combat if the situation demanded it; they would act in that role more frequently as combat expanded. The first White Star commander was Lieutenant Colonel Arthur "Bull" Simons. Simons's efforts in Laos also involved recruiting Laotian tribesmen on the Bolovens Plateau for early guerrilla and intelligence-collection operations against the Ho Chi Minh Trail, already being used for North Vietnamese infiltration into South Vietnam.

By 1960 Bill Lair, one of the CIA's legendary Southeast Asian paramilitary officers, was operating in Laos. He and the Thais brought some ninety-nine Border Patrol Police (PARU) advisors into the country to work with Hmong tribal irregulars in northeastern Laos. The CIA's goal was to create a guerrrilla force that could collect intelligence and pressure both Pathet Lao and North Vietnamese Army units in the early stages of establishing a western defense buffer zone for the trail.[223] Although the Border Patrol Police technically served under the Thai National Police umbrella, it had a great deal of autonomy and enjoyed sponsorship by the Thai royal family. The Border Police also had strong ties to the Royal Thai Army, and many of its commanders were former Thai army officers. In contrast to the drug-related activities of certain senior Thai National Police leaders, the leadership of the patrol had remained largely independent and the unit had proved effective in both counterinsurgency and counter-smuggling operations. As we noted earlier, in 1956 leaders of the Thai National Police lost in an effort to increase their power over the Thai government and in doing so lost considerable political influence within the country. In contrast, the Border Patrol Police continued their activities against both rebels and smuggling in the Thai border regions. Working in support of the patrol, Bill Lair had gained a reputation for being both low-key and effective. In doing so he had established tight personal bonds with the Thai military and intelligence services. Those bonds would become increasingly important as the CIA turned to Thailand for covert support for Laos, including numbers of Thai scouts, advisors, and combat volunteers.

As events in Laos moved through the early 1960s, Laotian military activity came to involve a mix of participants that made operational coordination increasingly challenging. There were large irregular forces, organized and directed by the CIA. Often the irregular forces acted autonomously, yet they were formally classified as being under general central government–Royal Lao Army command.

U.S. military assistance advisors were working with the Royal Lao Army, with Thai military advisors, and CIA military case officers. Both regular and irregular Royal Army forces became increasingly involved in large-scale conventional actions against combined Pathet Lao and North Vietnamese regular army units. And both supply and combat air support for operations came from the U.S. Air Force, the U.S. Navy, the Royal Laotian Air Force, and Air America.

Air America's contract work led it into a broad variety of transportation missions ranging from routine supply flights to missions for combat support as well as search and rescue activities for downed Air America or U.S. military pilots. By the end of 1966, Air Force officer Richard Secord had returned to Southeast Asia. He had been a Kennedy-era Operation Farm Gate pilot in the early days of covert air support for South Vietnamese troops. Upon his return he was detailed to support ongoing air activities in Vietnam. But after a short stint in that position, he was moved into another covert CIA detail assignment: running what was evolving into a full-scale air war over Laos. His chief of ground operations was CIA officer Tom Clines, reassigned from his service in the JM WAVE Cuba secret war operations. Covert air activity in Laos grew to involve some twenty helicopters and a limited number of propeller-driven attack aircraft. They were also allowed to call on air strikes from the USAF 7th and 13th Air Force at Udorn, Thailand.[224] In addition, a variety of shorter-range air transports for supplies and personnel were operated by Air America.[225]

In northeastern Laos, the Hmong hill tribes lived in the region of the Plain of Jars to the west of North Vietnam. The Hmong were commonly referred to by the Laotians as the Meo people. They were of Chinese descent, extremely independent, and fiercely anticommunist and anti-Vietnamese. The Hmong had supported the French in their struggle against the communist Viet Minh insurgents, and also opposed the communist Pathet Lao. As early as 1957–1958 the Hmong were conducting harassment activities against communist fighters in northern Laos. During a series of Laotian coups and counter-coups in the early 1960s, antigovernment forces and the Pathet Lao both moved significant combat forces into Hmong-populated areas of the Plain of Jars region, part of the general Meo homeland. The Hmong were demonstrably more aggressive fighters than the Lao central government forces and were used to fighting in and for their homeland. That immediately drew American attention, and the CIA supplied some two thousand rifles to them in late 1960.[226] Early on it had become clear to CIA military officers such as Lair that the Hmong in the Meo homeland were facing a territorial threat not only from communist Pathet Lao but increasingly from North Vietnamese Army units. One of the long-term CIA challenges in working with the Hmong was that they, as well as many of the other Laotian ethnic tribal peoples, existed in a relatively tenuous political relationship with the central government in the capital of Vientiane. The ever-changing politics in the Laotian capital often left the Hmong with no strong central government support—even when Hmong tribal leaders were designated as area military commanders in the Royal Lao Army.

On the other hand, the Hmong were very amenable to American training and the CIA was able to set up specific centers in the Meo homeland. CIA officers assisted in recruiting with the full and enthusiastic support of the preeminent Hmong tribal chief Vang Pao. A large number of individual Hmong tribal groups were under his umbrella of influence. Small units could be trained, equipped, and dispatched into the contested areas—with only general direction by a very limited number of CIA military field officers. Acting independently, the Hmong were quite successful in providing information on the Pathet Lao and performing a variety of harassment activities that prevented communist territorial seizure or consolidation. In fact they become so successful that in February 1962, President Kennedy approved a plan to significantly enlarge the Hmong combat forces. That authorization approved training and support for up to eleven thousand Hmong irregulars. In addition they were to be equipped with 75-millimeter recoilless rifles. Also, based on the Hmong success, authorization was given to recruit additional tribal irregulars in both the far north and the southern panhandle. In the south, the

Kha tribes were armed, and their operations would be supported by U.S. Special Forces; coordination would come from the regional CIA base at Pakse, Laos.

The resiliency and willingness to fight displayed by the Hmong was definitely not reflected in the rest of the Lao central government forces. During early 1963, the Royal Lao Army began to yield territory everywhere, to the point that virtually the entire Laotian–Vietnamese border became denied to the government. That situation allowed the North Vietnamese to perform a dramatic expansion of the Ho Chi Minh Trail, eventually building it into a multi-road corridor. In its earliest days the Ho Chi Minh Trail had primarily served to move advisors, troops, and political cadres to the south, in support of the communist Viet Cong insurgency in South Vietnam. An estimated four thousand men moved down it in 1961, fifty-three hundred in 1962, and forty-seven hundred in 1963. The actual numbers could have been double that, but it was still primarily a route for infiltrators.

In June 1963, President Kennedy issued NSAM 249, directing that the Hmong be provided with artillery howitzers, heavy mortars, some aircraft, and additional funding. In addition, he gave conditional approval to NSAM 256. That directive called for U.S. military aerial reconnaissance in Laos, as well as action to pressure the Royal Lao Air Force for aggressive air and ground attacks. It was intended to buy time for the establishment of operational but covert U.S. military air support out of Thailand.[227] By the end of summer 1963, the Hmong units were being redirected from simple guerrilla activity onto larger formations and actual military campaigns. The CIA was also preparing for a major escalation in the type and quantity of covert air support, including heavy-lift military helicopters to move in the heavy weapons authorized by NSAM 249. The CIA had been given the mission, authority, and budget to organize a surrogate Laotian military force far beyond the size of anything it had previously undertaken in shadow warfare.[228] In one effort a thousand Hmong assaulted Pathet Lao forces near the Plain of Jars for over five days. As time progressed, the budget for maintaining the tribes in the Plain of Jars as a viable force grew to approximately $300 million a year. In support of the overall effort, the the U.S. Agency for International Development (USAID) mission to Laos also played an aggressive role in supporting the tribes. The CIA organized a truly massive support mission to the Hmong, air-dropping some three hundred tons of rice a month into the Plain of Jars region, as well as a range of other supplies ranging from kettles to cement.

By 1964, with massive North Vietnamese Army (NVA) efforts at road-building, and conversion primarily to trucks for transportation, the Ho Chi Minh corridor was estimated to be carrying some twenty to thirty tons of supplies each day, and over nine thousand NVA regular army troops had moved down the corridor and into South Vietnam.[229] That left the U.S. with only one immediate military option to throw against the corridor, the CIA and its irregular forces. Those forces were in positions from which they might at least provide reconnaissance and harassment in portions of the trail while at the same time continuing to prevent the Pathet Lao from rolling across their homeland and into central Laos.

In May 1964, with approval by President Johnson, the CIA began Operation Hardnose, deploying twenty radio-equipped road-watch teams to collect intelligence on the Ho Chi Minh Trail. The teams themselves were composed of native irregulars, trained by the Thai PARU teams that Lair had brought into Laos. The Thais had also fielded first four, and later ten of their own six-man road-watch/trail-watch intelligence teams, under White Star. In addition, Thai pilots in Operation Mill Pond flew covert air missions in southern Laos, using fighter bombers identical to those flown by the Royal Lao Air Force.[230] President Johnson also approved Operation Barrel Roll, the first covert U.S. military air strikes against the trail inside Laos in 1964.

By 1965 the trail had developed into a complex network of roads capable of supporting extensive heavy truck traffic. The amount of supplies moved equaled the total of the previous five years, and some seven NVA infantry regiments and twenty battalions came down from the north. Literally hundreds of trucks were moving each direction each week. In Laos the CIA had become increasingly involved with efforts against the trail. In March 1965, concurrent with the first major round of American air strikes against North Vietnam (Operation Rolling Thunder), Johnson approved escalated attacks on the trail, with Barrel Roll strikes continuing in the north and a wave of air strikes designated Operation Steel Tiger going against the trail in the southern panhandle of Laos. The American Military Assistance Command, Vietnam (MACV) was granted control over covert strikes in the southern panhandle across the border from Vietnam. Given the official U.S. position on Laotian neutrality, all such operations from South Vietnam were highly secret—and arguably beyond the scope of the Tonkin Gulf Resolution, the only congressional legislation authorizing defensive activities for American forces in South Vietnam.

"Bull" Simons had been relocated from Laos to South Vietnam, to organize and direct covert American cross-border operations against the trail. The first such U.S.-led cross-border effort out of South Vietnam, Operation Shining Brass, began in 1965. The missions were carried out by a mix of American Green Berets and South Vietnamese Special Forces. The covert Special Forces action involved both road watch and military traffic monitoring activities as well as limited sabotage and placement of mines. The units also conducted bomb damage assessment and produced intelligence for air strikes. The teams did exchange fire with both North Vietnamese Army and Pathet Lao troops, but combat was largely in self-defense given their primary intelligence role. The covert cross-border operations against the trail in Laos continued, renamed Prairie Fire in 1968, and in 1971 designated as Phu Dung as the Vietnamization program of the Nixon Administration became the American strategy.

As full-scale conventional warfare escalated in Vietnam, so did the demand for irregular forces in Laos—and that led to significant growth at tribal chief Vang Pao's primary base of operations, Long Tieng. Long Tieng was to remain Vang Pao's main military base throughout the Laotian warfare. It was given the radio designation of Sky, becoming the logistics hub for Hmong support. C-130 four-engine aircraft would drop pallets full of supplies and smaller Air America transports would distribute them to a host of remote operations bases designated Lima sites. Military supplies destined for the Hmong were concealed within routine military assistance shipments to Thailand or the Royal Laotian military, and Air America performed challenging and dangerous distribution missions under contract to USAID. On the other side of the mountain from Long Tieng, USAID ran a large operations center. It was all very efficient; supply flights came in from Udorn Air Base in Thailand every day and Air America carried them out from Long Tieng for distribution, dropping rice, foodstuffs, and supplies to Hmong villages. Air America missions also carried combat personnel, advisors, and military supplies out from Long Tieng into Lima sites and also into live combat operations. It should also be noted that all the Laotian activity occurred with presidential, NSC, and congressional oversight.[231]

The matter of Laotian oversight only became controversial at a later date, as American military involvement in "neutral" Laos became politically controversial. The CIA had briefed key legislators on its appropriations subcommittees as well as the senior congressional leadership. For example, Senator Stuart Symington was routinely briefed on the warfare in Laos by senior CIA officers, including Chief of Station Ted Shackley. Shackley even personally introduced Symington to Vang Pao during a trip Vang Pao made to the United States. Symington himself invited Shackley to secretly brief the Senate Armed Services Committee. Later, during an inspection trip to Southeast Asia, Richard Secord personally gave Symington a tour of Vang Pao's headquarters at Long Tieng. But Congress was never given a request for a resolution approving covert operations in Laos. It never approved a budget for the Laotian secret war. Just as with the secret war against Cuba, approval was via the "small CIA subcommittees of the armed forces committees."[232] That budgetary process provides a very effective type of domestic cover for deniable warfare and special operations. At least it does so as long as Congress is willing to accept those budgets and not insert restrictions relating to monies being used for specific purposes.

The initial success story of the CIA's Laotian irregular forces had been an attractive one for senior American political figures during the early phases of Laotian covert combat; the Hmong routinely pushed back Pathet Lao incursions and even performed successfully against hardened North Vietnamese Army forces on occasion. They were fighting for the Meo homeland, they were aggressive, they were definitely anticommunist—in short, from 1962 on into 1966 they were undeniably successful, a textbook example of a working counterinsurgency. The same success characterized CIA work with the Lao and tribal irregulars in the south during the 1962–1965 time frame. The CIA had conducted a very impressive aid and civic action effort; the "village cluster" program had been effective beyond expectations and its associated militias had performed well against the Pathet Lao. The region was secure enough that at the CIA support base in Pakse, American personnel could bring their wives and families. When David Morales arrived from JM WAVE in Miami (under USAID cover) to assume his duty as chief of base at Pakse, he brought his entire family including young children. But, as with the Meo homeland, in reality Pakse would remain at the mercy of the North Vietnamese. If and when the North Vietnamese determined to apply enough force to guarantee the security of their Laotian supply corridor, both the Plain of Jars and Pakse would be overrun.

The year 1966 saw the beginning of dramatic changes in Laotian surrogate warfare and those changes were in direct response to full-scale North Vietnamese and American military engagement in Vietnam. As noted, traffic on the trail didn't just escalate in 1965. The trail itself was worked into a full-scale military supply operation, bringing in regular forces and heavy equipment. The effort not only involved construction and logistics units but was supported by major North Vietnamese Army groups—units equipped with everything from artillery and tanks to antiaircraft guns. What had begun as a buffer around the trail would become a military security zone run by the North Vietnamese Army. To expand and support that security zone, regular North Vietnamese Army units joined the

Pathet Lao in a series of ongoing pushes across both the Plain of Jars and the Bolovens Plateau.

Those attacks were a sign that things were changing dramatically in Laos; during 1966 and 1967 the force balance in Laos altered significantly. In 1964 the Royal Lao military numbered fifty thousand men plus some twenty-three thousand CIA irregulars; they faced twenty thousand Pathet Lao and around eleven thousand North Vietnamese regulars. By 1968 the Lao government forces would be facing an opposing force of over one hundred thousand, including some thirty thousand regular North Vietnamese infantry. And as the North Vietnamese sent in larger and larger units, the irregulars began "bleeding" the indigenous group's manpower. With the maximum U.S. support available, and the most aggressive recruiting practices, Vang Pao managed to reach a maximum strength of some forty-thousand potential combatants. Of that number, about twenty-five thousand were used in local defense activities and the rest were assigned to special guerrilla units, for mobile use. The Hmong force ultimately peaked and from that point on Vang Pao faced an increasing shortage of manpower, even as he increasingly turned to teenagers during the following three years.[233] They were simply no match for the well-equipped and combat-ready formations being continuously sent in by the North Vietnamese Army.

Full-scale, large-formation, positional warfare came to Laos in 1966. Major attacks on a remote Lima logistics site brought U.S. AC-130 gunships into support of the Hmong and by the end of the year, U.S. aircraft had been shot down in combat. Starting in 1966, Americans serving in Laos were given "hostile fire" pay. During the course of that year the U.S. Air Force conducted over seven thousand missions over Laos, the majority of them combat strikes in support of the irregulars or attacks on the enlarged Ho Chi Minh supply corridor. And that year Air America, under contract to the CIA, moved some six thousand tons of supplies a month in support of indigenous forces.[234]

The overall picture in the southern Laotian panhandle was generally similar but without the more massive combat seen in the Plain of Jars. Upon his 1966 assignment as chief of station in Laos, former JM WAVE Station Chief Ted Shackley almost immediately canceled many of the village programs. He retargeted available resources and irregular Laotian fighters towards efforts against the Ho Chi Minh Trail. In 1967, CIA irregulars in the south were tasked with a helicopter-inserted attack against a position on the improved corridor. The one-hundred-man force, attacking without air support, was quickly counterattacked and overrun; only fifteen men returned from the mission. The North Vietnamese Army and its Pathet Lao surrogates continued to respond aggressively to any perceived threat to their major supply corridor. They completed a purging operation they had begun in 1966, clearing out locals to neutralize the possibility of guerrilla support.[235] Within a short period of time, the North Vietnamese Army had expanded its buffer defense to the west of the corridor, generally overrunning the CIA's expanded village cluster region.[236]

Shackley's aggressiveness was not limited strictly to the Plain of Jars or the plateau region in the panhandle. He pushed the concept of taking the war to the North Vietnamese by placing combat forces on the North Vietnamese border in north-central Laos. With American Embassy agreement, Lao army forces and irregulars were sent to expand the Nam Bac garrison. A number of embassy staff disagreed with the action, as did the "old man" of Laotian covert operations, Bill Lair. Lair told Shackley that the logistics were impossible and that Nam Bac would only serve as an immediate target for the North Vietnamese Army. Given their aggressiveness in the buffer zones, a base only forty-five miles from their border would be intolerable to them. In the end, with widespread embassy staff opposition, but with the U.S. ambassador's support, several thousand FAR and a limited number of irregulars were deployed to Nam Bac. The garrison was supplied with howitzers, and supported with Lao and U.S. Air Force air strikes as well as both large-scale supply drops from Udorn and individual Air America supply missions. However, in less than a month the garrison had been totally routed by the North Vietnamese. No more than a third of over three thousand Lao troops were ever heard from again; many of the Laotian troops had never been in combat before, while the North Vietnamese formations consisted of battle-hardened regulars.[237]

From 1968 through 1971, the CIA's Laotian irregulars would be supplemented by more covert American military activity. That included a dramatically increased aerial logistics effort and U.S bombing campaign. Hmong formations would be assigned roles in conventional military operations, both with the Royal Lao Army and on their own. American B-52 carpet-bombing strikes would become common in Laos. When Vang Pao's base at Long Tieng was besieged—as it would be on multiple occasions—both Vang Pao and the U.S. Embassy requested B-52 strikes. Massive air attacks were seen as the only option to save his positions from full-scale assault, involving not only massive artillery and infantry fire, but also ground attack by both Vietnamese infantry and tanks. And from 1968 on, Air America would increasingly be called on to operate under fire, both in transport and supply missions. They would also be tasked with more and more rescue missions for downed American flyers or for special operations personnel in imminent danger of being overrun. In addition, Air America would be called on for rescue and relocation of entire Hmong villages, as their homeland essentially was being occupied by North Vietnamese forces. Both American military and Air America casualties in Laos would escalate significantly as they became directly involved in the fighting.[238]

Of course, with the increased level of combat, at some point any serious notion of deniability was going to go out the window. As with the tanks at the Bay of Pigs in Cuba, it's hard to conceal heavy-weapon-class warfare. In some of the B-52 strikes in Laos, the noise of the bombing could be heard across the border at towns in Thailand. However, the American war effort in Laos did largely stay out of the domestic U.S. press. To some extent that was because the cover of military assistance to the central Lao government and the developmental aid programs effectively masked the creation of surrogate indigenous armies. Given all the attention focused on events in Vietnam and the escalating military effort there, the press had its hands full simply trying to keep up with shifts in Vietnamese politics, the various strategies for dealing with the north, and the change from guerrilla warfare to full-scale combat. Simply reporting on American troops, the Johnson Administration, and the power shifts in Saigon was a full-time job.

Of course, the Lao tribal armies were no secret within certain congressional circles, and neither was the news that Hmong losses were so severe that the special guerrilla Units (SGUs) were being augmented with contract mercenaries from Thailand. As the Hmong were driven totally off the Plain of Jars, and as the core of their territory, including Long Tieng, came under attack, the whole indigenous army strategy began looking more questionable to people in Washington. To some it was no real surprise. One early U.S. ambassador in Laos had gone on record stating that ultimately the indigenous army strategy could be very dangerous to tribes such as the Hmong, especially if they ended up being sacrificed in a political compromise. Ambassador William Sullivan also expressed his reservations to National Security Advisor McGeorge Bundy as early as May 1965: "It would be immensely cruel and counterproductive to develop such a movement and then bargain it away as part of a political counter."[239] In 1968, a CIA headquarters memorandum was both blunt and accurate in its long-term assessment of the proxy armies: "The guerrilla operation in the north [of Laos] has survived only on the sufferance of the North Vietnamese. It will continue only as long as the enemy calculates that the harm done to him is not worth the effort to stop it."[240]

During 1969 it became increasingly clear that the North Vietnamese sufferance was ending. One full North Vietnamese Army regiment plus two additional battalions had moved to put increased pressure on the Hmong's core positions. In response the CIA encouraged an operation to push back onto the Plain of Jars. But that effort, optimistically named Off Balance, accomplished little against the new North Vietnamese Army formations—by that point well equipped with heavy weapons and tanks. A second effort that year, About Face, was given literally all the manpower available—even ethnic Lao battalions from the south were brought in by Air America for support. Some ten battalions plus the Hmong irregulars were supported with over 130 U.S. Air Force air strikes a day, plus 90 more from Lao fighter bombers operating with American forward air controllers. At first About Face enjoyed some surprise and success—but it also generated enough "noise" that congressional attention to Laos began to rise. Senator John Cooper began hearings on U.S. involvement in Laos and an amendment was introduced aimed at restricting the use of the American military in Southeast Asia was introduced.

Perhaps more importantly, following publication of a series of articles about Laos in *The New York Times*, Senator Symington called a secret committee hearing. It seemed the senator, after earlier having been in Laos visiting Vang Pao, was now "outraged" over news of a secret war in Laos and prepared to accuse "high government officials" of withholding information from Congress.[241] Secretary of State Kissinger's response to media leaks on the B-52 missions in Laos was simply that the appropriate Senate committees had indeed been briefed. The formal Nixon Administration response was equally understated; the State Department made a public announcement to the press that combat in Laos had been extremely limited, so limited that there had been no American military casualties—only twenty-five "contractors" and one dependent. The press quickly researched and revealed a number of additional American personnel losses and the Nixon Administration was shortly forced into admitting that 200 Americans had died and 193 were missing.

Separately, the CIA responded that it had briefed as many as sixty-seven congressmen on Laos, beginning as early as 1963. They also noted that CIA Chief of Station Theodore Shackley had personally briefed Senator Symington both in Washington, D.C., and inside Laos. Given the general American dissatisfaction with just about everything going on in Southeast Asia as of 1969, it appears that just as decisions on deniability can be driven by political considerations, decisions on congressional exposure of deniable operations can be equally political. In the end, Symington's own committee was forced to admit that it had failed to proactively inquire into military activities in Laos.[242]

The scope of American involvement in Laos was further revealed when press touring the USAID office on the other side of the hill from Long Tieng simply walked over that hill. They quickly noted the military aspect of the operations at the base. An immense amount of air operations were obviously in process—the press counted about a dozen transports on the ground, along with ten light planes, a dozen or more unmarked T-28 fighter bombers, and several helicopters. Air traffic was so dense that a flight control program was obviously in place, with aircraft holding slots in a landing and takeoff pattern.[243] The revelations about Long Tieng, the B-52 strikes, and the American casualties in Laos created a chasm of skepticism between the media and the Nixon Administration. Perhaps more importantly, it produced a hugely embarrassing situation in regard to Congress's knowledge about Laotian operations. That embarrassment became one of the key elements in setting much of Congress against not only the Nixon Administration but also the CIA. From the Agency's viewpoint that was definitely unfair but it was a political reality and it marked the first stage of a political battle over clandestine activities that would continue during much of the 1970s.

By the beginning of 1970, some twelve thousand new North Vietnamese Army troops had entered Laos; the Hmong were being forced into classic perimeter defense of their territory. While still fighting exceptionally well, they simply faced overwhelming odds and were pushed into a "fighting retreat." William Sullivan, the American ambassador in Vientiane, continued requests for B-52 missions to block the North Vietnamese drive and after a two-week wait air strikes began in February 1970. By March, the Hmong were evacuating families from the Meo homeland and Long Tieng was only preserved with a combination of B-52 attacks and irregular troops ferried up from the Laotian panhandle.

The situation was brutally clear: at the end of 1970, it was estimated that there were some sixty-seven thousand North Vietnamese Army troops in Laos, while the Hmong had fewer than five thousand men remaining for combat. During the course of the year they would take huge casualties, with one thousand killed and an additional fifteen hundred wounded—a 50 percent casualty rate. With many of the Hmong having already fled from their villages, they were almost totally dependent on American supply and support. In the face of that, President Nixon and Secretary of State Kissinger, with 303 Committee approval and oversight, directed the continuation of major Hmong harassing attacks against the Ho Chi Minh corridor in the north; and irregular forces in the panhandle were ordered into the same type of effort. As time had passed and the situation in Vietnam had worsened, American support for the Hmong had evolved far beyond their use as a willing buffer against local communist forces' expansion in Laos. The CIA proxy armies in Laos had come to be a military resource for the White House, and a card to be played in the ongoing negotiations with North Vietnam. As the 2006 comprehensive historical work by The Center for the Study of Intelligence notes, "The plight of the Hmong could perhaps not be ignored . . . but it would not be the operative factor in Washington's policy decisions."[244]

With the regular Laotian army no longer playing any significant role, ongoing combat fell strictly to the CIA irregulars. In early 1971, four battalions of irregulars (eleven hundred men) were moved by helicopter in an operation to cut the North Vietnamese supply corridor in the Laotian panhandle. They were supported with B-52 attacks and a major South Vietnamese effort across the Laotian border (Operation Lam Son 719). Two of the irregular battalions had already been repulsed by the time the South Vietnamese effort launched. The North Vietnamese fielded some thirty-six thousand men and stalled the operation. Eventually both the Laotians and the South Vietnamese were forced into fighting retreats. The force imbalance had simply become too great for the corridor to be cut, and Washington was well aware that the North Vietnamese could take all the Bolovens Plateau and Pakse base at will.[245]

Beyond those new moves against the North Vietnamese Army's main supply line into South Vietnam, Nixon and Kissinger pushed to send irregular guerrilla units into North Vietnam on sabotage missions. Their purpose was strictly political, in support of negotiations with Hanoi; a CIA briefing on those "Commando Raider" operations concisely described the goal as that of simple harassment of the North Vietnamese: "to prick the political and military sensitivities within their own borders."[246] The Commando Raider operations did successfully blow up one pipeline, and resulted in attacks on one North Vietnamese divisional army headquarters as well as a limited number of other targets. However, the ground infiltrations were extremely lengthy, and in the end only twelve of some twenty-two missions had successfully conducted attacks. The Commando Raider effort had cost $3 million and resulted in twenty-nine casualties. Official evaluations describe the effort as producing "meager" results with little reason to expect anything more. The penetration project was canceled in May 1971. As some observers had feared, the remaining Hmong military capability had ended up being little more than a sacrificial element in the final American political negotiations with the North Vietnamese.

The endgame for the irregular forces in Laos began in 1972. As had often been predicted, when the North Vietnamese Army determined it was necessary, it had the ability to overrun the Hmong anytime it chose.[247] In the end a concentrated attack literally blasted the Hmong out of the Plain of Jars. Heavy casualties were taken and Long Tieng came under heavy artillery bombardment as well as tank attack once again. And when the North Vietnamese Army moved to cross the north–south Demilitarized Zone in Vietnam and invade the south, there were few resources left for Laos—and few resources for the U.S. inside Laos other than the Hmong. Kissinger once again pushed Nixon, and a White House directive ordered Vang Pao to attack yet again—and Vang Pao responded, throwing virtually everything he had left against the Plain of Jars. Yet no real support plans had been laid, U.S. airpower was virtually all being directed against North Vietnam, and even when air support arrived for the push, after days of bad weather, there was little chance that it could be sustained.[248]

In the southern Laotian panhandle, during the early 1970s it had become more common for CIA case officers to actually participate in combat operations, not simply direct them. Road-watch missions against the Ho Chi Minh corridor had evolved towards sabotage and interdiction attacks. In general, special military operations in the south resembled the historic Office of Strategic Services–type of directed irregular warfare.[249] Still, the North Vietnamese attacks of 1970 had led the CIA to equip the southern irregulars with heavy weapons and they had begun to use them in more conventional combat, defending against North Vietnamese Army thrusts.[250] But the thrusts succeeded nonetheless and by the end of 1972, the North Vietnamese had captured major towns in the Mekong Valley; Pakse Base itself was open to attack.

From the American perspective, it all came to an end in February 1973, with a formal cease-fire agreement for Laos. As a part of that agreement, the Hmong forces were to be fully merged with the regular Laotian military. The practical result was that in May, Vang Pao left Long Tieng, and the Hmong came under the oversight of a central government that had little real use for them—even with the CIA funding their integration into the Laotian army. Beyond that, it seems that a number of political factions had a great many scores to settle and the Hmong had very few friends in the capital of Vientiane. The Hmong had 250,000 refugees outside their homeland, twelve thousand war widows, sixteen thousand orphans, and two thousand disabled veterans. In 1975, following the final massive North Vietnamese move into South Vietnam, Vang Pao was asked to resign; he in turn went to the United States, pleading for help in evacuating those of his people who were the most at risk. The State Department agreed, but only for a few hundred persons.[251] Communist forces surrounded Long Tieng, American aircraft evacuated no more than five hundred people, and then Long Tieng was taken. In the end some twenty-four hundred Hmong had been airlifted to Thailand; eventually something like eight thousand made it by themselves across the border as refugees. Ted Shackley, head of the CIA's Far Eastern Division at the time, rejected further pleas to help resettle Hmong refugees to the U.S., and simply left the matter as a problem for the Thais.[252] Ultimately, some thirty-thousand people ended up in Thai refugee camps, and eventually another fifty-five thousand Laotians were resettled in the U.S.[253]

It would be unfair not to record that no thought had ever been given to the risks being taken by the surrogate Laotian fighters. As combat dramatically escalated in the 1965–1966 period, there had been dialogue that it might be necessary to relocate the Hmong if the communist response was overwhelming. There are memoranda discussing resettlement possibilities, but of course the whole issue for the Hmong was fighting to stay in their own homeland. Doug Blaufarb, who had been chief of station during the buildup of the Lao indigenous forces before being replaced by Ted Shackley, probably captured the context most accurately in his remarks about the failure to fully consider the full consequences of the American strategy: "[The] foresight which might have suggested that, regardless of the extent of U.S. aid, Meo forces could not be equalized with those of North Vietnam, did not exist."[254]

Decades after the end of combat in Laos, Ted Shackley spoke harshly about the U.S. abandoning its "partners," stating that it had been incumbent to have a "contingency plan" but that the U.S. had never had a contingency plan for defeat. He had no problems with the use of indigenous armies, laying the blame strictly on the failure of Washington to support them. As a counter, Shackley's biographer cites others who served with him in Laos as having a different view, describing Shackley as a great organizer but also as a man enthusiastically "chasing delusions of a victory which was not possible."[255]

CHAPTER 11

Against the Castro Regime

Following the overthrow of the military dictatorship of Fulgencio Batista, the new regime of Fidel Castro remained a bit of a mystery to the United States, but only for a time. CIA Director Allen Dulles produced memoranda with uncomplimentary remarks on Castro's character, and Deputy Director Charles Cabell told a Senate subcommittee that neither the Cuban Communist Party nor the CIA considered Castro a communist. Richard Nixon felt Castro to be either naive about communism or a closet communist. President Eisenhower's response to it all was simple: "We'll check on it in a year."[256] But during the course of 1959, Castro began to implement widespread land reform and, worse yet, nationalization of foreign-owned Cuban businesses. Both practices were virtually guaranteed to trigger calls for regime change in Washington.

In the case of Cuba, the State Department actually seems to have led the charge for intervention: in November, Secretary of State Christian Herter completed a proposal that he immediately dispatched to President Eisenhower. It recommended doing nothing to support Castro, encouraging opposition to him inside Cuba and the pursuit of a "reformed" Cuban government.[257] Eisenhower endorsed Herter's strategy: there would be no yearlong evaluation period for the Castro regime. By December 1959, CIA Western Hemisphere Chief J.C. King had sent Director Dulles a memorandum recommending, among other things, the "elimination of Fidel Castro," in order to "accelerate" the fall of the regime. Director Dulles endorsed the concept, simply substituting the phrase "remove from Cuba" for the reference to "elimination."[258] By January 1960 the 5412 covert action oversight group had conditionally approved the start of a paramilitary operation, and within days, J.C. King had begun organizing a Cuban task force. A top-secret paper was drafted with the title "A Program of Covert Action against the Castro Regime." The program's goal was replacing Castro with a government "more acceptable to the U.S. in such a manner to avoid any appearance of U.S. intervention."[259] With final approval by President Eisenhower, the Cuba covert warfare project began in March 1960. The secret war against Cuba was under way long before Castro's 1961 declaration of Cuba as a socialist country and of himself as a Marxist-Leninist.[260]

A select group of CIA officers was brought into a new project organized at CIA headquarters. Although controlled from Washington, D.C., the project would eventually lead to the creation of one of the largest CIA stations in existence: a totally domestic station in Miami designated JM WAVE. The station was created to service the secret war against Cuba, and expanded dramatically during 1960. It would remain a huge, domestic covert operational base for years, only to fade away with the shift of American attention to Vietnam in the mid-1960s. As far as personnel were concerned, the initial Cuba project team involved several senior officers from the Guatemala regime-change operation. Richard Bissell was overall project chief, with Tracy Barnes his project manager. Henry Hecksher also joined the Cuba project, working at multiple locations including Washington, D.C., and the main CIA surrogate army training camp in Guatemala.[261]

The initial Eisenhower-era Cuban secret war plan, as drafted by CIA officer Jacob "Jake" Esterline in January 1960, was a basic "resistance"-oriented operation. It called for exfiltrating a select group of Cubans off the island of Cuba, training them, and putting them back on the island in the Trinidad region in an operation to be named Pluto.[262] The group would then be covertly supported in its guerrilla military activities, with the intent of igniting a major anti-Castro revolutionary effort—similar to the one that ousted Batista. The plan was conceived as practical in that a Trinidad insertion would give the newly trained personnel easy access to the Escambray Mountains, where an active anti-Castro network was already in existence. Initially the staffing for the entire Cuba Task Force (WH/4) was set at approximately forty people, with eighteen in Washington, twenty at the Havana station, and two in eastern Cuba.

But as time passed, something dramatic happened to the original, low-profile Operation Pluto plan—apparently with little notice by President Eisenhower. Decades later Jake Esterline told reporter and author Don Bohning that the original plan approved by Eisenhower on March 17, 1960, never had a chance to develop. The Cuba project's senior officer, well known to us from PBSUCCESS in Guatemala, moved towards a much more elaborate operation. According to Esterline the initial resistance effort turned into something entirely different under Bissell's leadership. "It was taken away by Bissell's decision to go for more, much more, and create an invasion force."[263] The Bissell-led project was not only going to grow into a full-scale conventional military operation, it was also going to have a significant propaganda/psychological operations element, headed by David Phillips, and a political action effort with Cuban exiles in Miami, organized by Howard Hunt.

Along with those Guatemala veterans, David Morales was brought into the project to train special groups of exiles for intelligence and special political action activities inside Cuba intended to neutralize Castro's communist supporters. Both Phillips and Morales had recently been in Cuba. Morales operated under a State Department cover and attached to the U.S. Embassy. Phillips was a CIA contract employee who went undercover, was given an alias, and worked under a public relations business cover. Morales's cover was blown when authorities discovered his name on a Batista secret police credentials list. Then Phillips blew his cover when his activities with anti-Castro activists became known to Cuban intelligence. In his biography, *The Night Watch*, Phillips described that upon being recruited into the new Cuba project, his immediate question was, "What's the plan?" The reply: "The Guatemala scenario."[264]

By the last month of the Eisenhower Administration, the basic components of Bissell's Cuba project had come to include the formation of a Cuban exile organization; a major propaganda effort; creation of a clandestine intelligence and action apparatus inside Cuba; and development of a paramilitary force to be introduced into Cuba to organize, train, and lead resistance groups. A briefing paper presented in August to Eisenhower and the Joint Chiefs stated that the paramilitary force was to consist of five hundred trainees and thirty-seven radio operators "available to use as infiltration teams or as an invasion force." The paper also noted that any successful large-scale paramilitary operations would be "dependent upon widespread guerrilla resistance throughout the area."[265] Along with those elements, the operation also included a highly compartmentalized effort to assassinate Fidel Castro himself. The direction for that action remains unclear, even after extensive investigation. Certainly J.C. King had recommended it to Allen Dulles; whether or not Dulles discussed it with Eisenhower is unknown. Given that Dulles had already attempted to carry out the murder of one foreign leader, Patrice Lumumba, at Eisenhower's direction he may simply have assumed that assassination was an acceptable tactic. What is certain is that Cuba project head Richard Bissell actually initiated the effort and that Western Hemisphere head J.C. King was aware of it. As far as recorded testimony indicates, Bissell and Tracy Barnes decided that the best approach would be to contact criminal elements inside Cuba to bring off the murder. That way it could be portrayed as a revenge killing for Castro's expulsion of the former Havana gambling casino owners, ending a massively profitable business for organized crime.

The story of this particular assassination track is long, convoluted, and covered in other works. It was intensely investigated during 1975–1976 by the United States Senate Select Committee to Study Governmental Operations with Respect to Intelligence Activities (more commonly referred to as the Church Committee after its chair, Senator Frank Church). Bissell himself gave varying testimony on the origins of the effort but several senior CIA officers knew about it at the time. In 1997, Jake Esterline told Don Bohning him that in the fall of 1960 he had received a mysterious request for a large amount of money. He refused to issue the funds and eventually J.C. King obtained Bissell's agreement to inform Esterline that the money was for the Castro assassination project using the "Mafia." At that point Esterline approved the request, issuing $200,000 for the effort.[266]

The origins of the Mafia plan as well as several CIA Castro assassination efforts remain mysterious, decades after the fact. Equally mysterious is how the limited guerrilla project that President Eisenhower initially approved developed into a full-fledged maritime invasion at the Bay of Pigs. Following the disaster by the Cuban exile Brigade 2506 in the Bay of Pigs landing, both the CIA's own inspector general and a presidential panel could find no specific date or set of orders changing the original small-scale Pluto guerrilla insertion operation into something different. However, they did find that by November 1960 a cable from Washington directed a reduction in the guerrilla teams' training to sixty men, and the formation of the rest into an amphibious and airborne assault force. Although the details of the shift in the operations plan are unclear, there is no doubt as to what the ultimate project became. Bissell himself wrote of "a metamorphosis shifting to reliance on an invasion force of some 1,500 men."[267]

It appears that between Eisenhower's initial approval of Pluto and the transition between the Eisenhower and Kennedy administrations, the Cuba project had morphed into something much more grandiose—and risky—than initially conceived. Colonel Jack Hawkins had been detailed from the Marines to support the CIA Cuba project, and he headed the paramilitary preparations of

Brigade 2506. Late in 1960 he was directed to revise his plans in accordance with the new strategy. Hawkins responded with a January 4, 1961, memorandum on "Policy Decisions Required for Conduct of Strike Operations against Government of Cuba," warning that the incoming President, John Kennedy, would need to concur with launching the operation before March 1. This was for a variety of reasons, the most important being that Castro's security and military defense efforts were gaining momentum—the first trained Cuban jet pilots were expected to be available to Castro's air force by early spring. Again, even at this late date, exactly what briefings and cautions were given to the new president remains unclear, as does the extent to which President Eisenhower understood the changes in the operation. President Kennedy would later comment that he was surprised that in his transition meeting with Eisenhower, the outgoing president spent much more time talking about the dangers in Laos than in Cuban matters, which Kennedy had assumed would be a national security priority.

By 1961 the overall Cuba project had seen its personnel roster balloon to nearly six hundred CIA personnel. The CIA station in Miami would come to have a huge "shadow" staff of Cuban exiles. The station was ultimately estimated to have had two hundred case officers, who in turn handled four to ten Cuban exile "principal agents." In turn, each principal agent handled another ten to thirty exiles, creating a CIA reach that extended to thousands of exiles. But the station's reach went beyond Miami exiles. Every foreign CIA station had at least one officer assigned to Cuban affairs, collecting intelligence on Cuban activities and foreign contacts to be reported to JM WAVE. The watch on Castro's Cuba and its activities was global.[268]

As the Cuba project mushroomed, a much more formal military element was added, involving several military and paramilitary personnel including Guatemala veteran Rip Robertson and Grayston Lynch. What had begun as a low-profile guerrilla training and insertion project had morphed into a "go for broke," single, large-scale military action—an action that would include a daylight military invasion of Cuba using a fleet of boats, WWII-era landing ships and landing craft, tanks, and heavy weapons units landed on the beachhead. It was a far cry from the original plan described by Esterline, and from Eisenhower's demand that the project require "avoiding any appearance of U.S. intervention."

It is hard to see how the new plan for a beachhead landing of a fully equipped exile brigade could be perceived inside Cuba as anything other than an American invasion. Propaganda psychological warfare specialist David Phillips described the change in strategy as "madness." He further stated, "What had been conceived as a classic guerrilla warfare operation with individual fighters carrying their own weapons had been converted only a few days before D-Day into an amphibious landing of tanks on Cuban beaches." Phillips's comment is incorrect in regard to timing; as we noted, the shift in focus from guerrilla tactics to an amphibious invasion had happened considerably earlier, certainly by November 1960. As noted earlier, Phillips simply could not conceive of mounting a secret operation in the Caribbean with tanks.[269]

As the American Cuba project itself evolved, Fidel Castro had become increasingly ruthless and effective in taking internal security measures. In September of 1960 he organized Committees for the Defense of the Revolution (based on the highly successfully Soviet model) and instituted neighborhood spy networks against "counterrevolutionaries." There had been numerous executions of suspected counterrevolutionaries and even of individuals whose class associations made their loyalties suspect to an increasingly radical regime. A great number of professionals, including teachers, had either been jailed or had fled the island. By the end of 1960, non-regime-approved opposition newspapers had been closed, and radio and television stations were under strict state control. As a finishing touch in consolidating power, by 1961 Castro had either jailed or executed a good number of his own revolutionary comrades.

An extensive and highly effective Cuban counterintelligence program, modeled on similar programs that had been extremely successful in Eastern European nations behind the Iron Curtain, put the

CIA station in Havana under heavy pressure. The U.S. Embassy had to be closed and the CIA infiltration program encountered a great many problems. A very active and aggressive resistance by anti-Castro groups had developed on the island, supported by the Cuban community in the United States as well as an increasing number of Cuban exiles. This movement had developed independently, as Castro's communist leanings had become public and as anticommunist elements of the Batista revolutionary movements began to realize that they had been politically outflanked by Castro. However, the resistance was fragmented both by ideology and by competition for financial and third-party support. The resistance was also thwarted by the fact that Castro continued to jail tens of thousands of suspected opponents. Thousands would still be in prison by the time of the Bay of Pigs landing.

By March 1961, the largest on-island group, UNIDAD, was preparing for local uprisings, a rebellion within the Cuban navy, and a coup of some military officers. But UNIDAD advised the CIA that it was not yet ready to support any major military actions and had communicated that message to its network inside Cuba. In his memoir *Reflections of a Cold Warrior: From Yalta to the Bay of Pigs*, Bissell included UNIDAD's concerns over the effectiveness of Castro's repressive moves and the lack of effectiveness of anti-Castro propaganda.[270] Castro was arming and training at an increasing rate, and trained Cuban jet pilots were quickly coming on board. Castro's efforts were quickly turning the island into an effective police state. In the months leading up to the Bay of Pigs landing, an ongoing stream of Miami newspaper reports suggested that the U.S. was heavily involved in covert action against Cuba. And early in 1961, in the final months before the Bay of Pigs landing, an alert Cuban security apparatus reportedly picked up twenty-three of thirty-five CIA personnel inserted onto the island, capturing many of them within a day of insertion.[271] We lack detailed records on those insertions, but if the numbers are even close it should have been an early warning sign of what was to come in the planned landing operation.

Colonel Hawkins continually placed particular emphasis on the amount of air support required for a successful landing of Brigade 2506, including the amount of aircraft and number of missions. He specifically stated that if policy considerations did not permit an aggressive tactical air campaign, the project should be abandoned. Yet following the landing fiasco, the Kennedy-appointed inquiry (the Taylor Commission) determined that while Esterline did forward Hawkins's memo to Bissell, there was no evidence that it had ever gone beyond Bissell's office, and it was not presented to either the president or his national security advisor.[272]

Don Bohning eventually conducted an extensive series of interviews with Hawkins and Esterline, showing them Cuba project documents that were only made available in 1990. Bohning's interviews reveal an ongoing disconnect between the demands of deniability and the metamorphosis of a PBSUCCESS-style campaign into a full-fledged seaborne invasion. And Richard Bissell was clearly at the center of that disconnect. Hawkins felt that Bissell had made his own military decisions in regard to dramatically increasing the side of the landing force, adding a parachute battalion and even a tank platoon—changes not recommended by either Hawkins or Esterline. In fact, Colonel Hawkins had specifically warned that the use of parachute troops and tanks would unquestionably brand the invasion as a U.S. undertaking. Bissell remained firm in his decisions, and there was no further discussion of the point.[273]

Esterline eventually learned that it was Bissell who had banned him from high-level Washington meetings and came to the conclusion that Bissell was giving the president assurances and commitments on deniability that were not being shared with his force commanders. Esterline also concluded that at some point, possibly even before the transition to the final Bay of Pigs landing site, Bissell had given a commitment to President Kennedy that the operation would indeed be low-key and would use absolutely minimal air power—an agreement not communicated to Esterline or Hawkins. Bohning notes that there is reason to think that a private agreement was indeed made; he points out that Secret Service logs show that in the first three months of 1961, Bissell had some thirteen off-the-record personal meetings with President Kennedy. Hawkins also remarked that not once did Bissell pass on any feedback or direction from the presidential meetings to him or Esterline.[274] These Bissell–Kennedy meetings remain tantalizingly mysterious as does the possibility of other influences on Bissell, but Bohning's interviews clearly suggest a major disconnect between the White House and the operations element of the Cuba project at that point, with Richard Bissell in the middle of it. Another element that remains mysterious is the extent to which Bissell might have expected either the Mafia plan or another little-known attempt involving a sniper attack on Castro at his seaside retreat to succeed; eliminating the Cuban leader would have significantly altered the Cuban military response to the Brigade 2506 landing.

It is also worth noting that none of this planning and dialogue involved the Cuban exiles themselves; nor was any of it shared with them, even with their senior officers. Manuel Artime had been one of the Cuban exiles meeting with Senator Kennedy as early as the Democratic Convention in July 1960, and his prominence resulted in his becoming the senior exile political leader involved in the landing at the Bay of Pigs. Artime was captured during the landing and spent almost twenty months in a Cuban prison along with other members of Brigade 2506. However, Artime and a fellow exile officer named Rafael Quintero would reemerge in 1963 as principal figures in the final Kennedy Administration secret warfare initiative against Castro. Quintero had also been involved with the Bay of Pigs operation, having been inserted into Cuba in advance of the landings. After the failure of the landing, he managed to remain undercover for several weeks before making his way back to Florida. Reportedly he participated in a number of interim missions and went into a holding mode following the Bay of Pigs landing fiasco.[275]

Both Hawkins and Esterline did make one final, last-minute effort to express their objections, after working furiously to prepare a new plan and relocating the landing site from the Trinidad region to the Bay of Pigs. The two military officers had concluded that while they might seize the beachhead, it would be virtually impossible to extend the force beyond the beachhead operations, and that such an operation could not achieve the goals of the project. The following day both officers drove to Bissell's home and for three hours gave him a detailed account as to why the invasion plan was not adequate to ensure complete destruction of Castro's air force and said that if *any* of Castro's fighters and bombers survived the first attack they could defeat the brigade. The brigade air support was very limited, and flying over such distances it could not "loiter" to maintain constant air cover over the beaches until a landing strip had been secured and planes could actually be refueled, resupplied, and operated locally from a secure beachhead. In particular, Hawkins and Esterline were concerned that the brigade air support was not even under their operational control. Any surviving Cuban planes would make beachhead operations of the brigade's B-26 bombers suicidal.

Both officers then stated they would resign if the Trinidad invasion was not canceled. Bissell responded by saying that that was impossible, but made a firm promise that he would gain Kennedy's authorization for more aircraft and more strikes. Esterline told Bohning that Bissell "solemnly pledged to Hawkins and I that he would ensure we would get the total number of planes, he would go to the President and explain why it simply had to be."[276] Within two days of that pledge, Bissell actually did the complete opposite, committing to Kennedy that he would cut the attacking B-26 force in half.

Bissell was aware that both officers had expressed their concern that if any of Castro's air force survived the prelanding first strike, the effort was likely doomed and would result in significant casualties to the Cuban exile brigade. And post-strike intelligence had confirmed that only something like half of the Cuban fighters and bombers were taken out in the first B-26 attack; that news made no apparent impact on Bissell's decisions. Hawkins and Esterline had a firm grasp of the reality of the situation and continually worked at making that clear. But, based on their interviews with Bohning, no trace of that ever passed beyond Bissell.[277] In addition to the fact that the permitted air strikes had left significant Cuban aircraft operational, there were a number of other last-minute operational failures. A diversionary landing in Oriente Province—which might have diverted Castro and his forces—aborted after encountering heavy seas and reportedly seeing Cuban soldiers in the beach area. Another diversion off the coast at Pinar del Río failed to draw any significant Cuban force response. Clearly, even before the assault brigade approached the beaches, the signs were not good and it appears that President Kennedy was given little in the way of operational status reports.

It took decades and the ongoing release of key documents before Esterline and Hawkins reached the conclusions they later shared with Bohning. At the time of the invasion they had no idea of the situation, no suspicion that Bissell had gone his own way, made his own agreements, and in the end possibly bet the lives of the brigade on a successful landing. What Esterline found "most unacceptable" was that even while the brigade was going in, Kennedy offered Bissell and Cabell an opportunity to talk with him about additional air support and "they elected not to." In fact, at that point Bissell did not even personally communicate with the task force officers at headquarters. Instead Bissell sent Cabell to deliver the bad news that the absolutely necessary air strikes were not going to occur and to greet the firestorm the news generated.[278]

The Bay of Pigs fiasco produced passionate reactions among a great number of the CIA staff. Hawkins called the decisions on the air strikes "an act of criminal negligence." Jake Esterline, in a tremendous show of courage, took personal leave and went to Miami to meet with families of brigade members, by then either dead or in Cuban prisons. In the emotionally charged meetings he could only say that he had tried to call it off. That it was not his fault. That they had all "been screwed by Kennedy" and that he had "been made to send the men off to slaughter." At the time, Esterline had no idea that both Bissell and Cabell had declined a last-minute invitation from President Kennedy to present the case for more air support, another strike, and to state flat-out that without it the invasion was doomed.

Others, further from the Washington scene—and not knowing of Hawkins's and Esterline's efforts—assumed that the plan had been fully communicated, that their commanders had no outstanding concerns, and that the Bay of Pigs invasion had been fully endorsed at all levels. The failure at the Bay of Pigs immediately sent all those involved, as well as the general public, looking for someone to blame. Since it clearly was not the result of any failure on the part of the exiles—who had obviously fought heroically on the beaches—that meant it must have been weakness in the American will to support them. Speculation actually began that the Kennedy Administration, and specifically President Kennedy, simply had not wished to follow through on Eisenhower's Cuban initiative—that he had signed off on the operation to let events take their course. Brigade 2506 was well trained, well armed, and highly motivated; it had been organized, trained, and based in Guatemala, and it clearly was going into action in some fashion, even if independently. There was even speculation that it might have tried to take matters in its own hands, launching its own autonomous military operations against Cuba or taking over a Central American government for its own anticommunist, anti-Castro purposes.

In 1998, Grayston Lynch, who along with William "Rip" Robertson had been the only American military officer to personally participate in the brigade landings, wrote a book: *Decision for Disaster: Betrayal at the Bay of Pigs*. Lynch and Robertson had come into the project when it had already morphed into a full-scale sea-based invasion, complete with tanks, trucks, heavy weapons groups, and a variety of military landing craft. In the book, Lynch provides a unique insight into what he believed the brigade was capable of—if it had been wholeheartedly supported, regardless of the foolish issue of deniability. The problem is that Lynch's view is totally at odds with the final assessment made by Hawkins and Esterline, the one that compelled them to call for a cancellation of the invasion. His remarks also illustrate how totally divorced the landing operations were from the different levels of the CIA chain of command. Lynch went in with the exile landing force believing in a plan involving a level of air support that Bissell had taken off the table in talks with Kennedy weeks before the operation launched.

A commitment to extensive air support was a vital factor in Lynch's beliefs. If the brigade B-26s could have operated unopposed for two to three weeks, not only sealing off the beachhead but going on to seriously damage much of Castro's military force and even prevent landing of Soviet support, then "the majority of the Cuban citizens must, in the end, lose." The brigade would have been built up on the beachhead to a force of some fifteen thousand (with recruits from the local area, and volunteers flown in from Miami). Castro would have been faced with a force he could not dislodge, and one that totally ruled the sky above Cuba. With open support from the U.S. and other countries, the provisional government would result in Castro's regime simply "throwing in the towel."[279]

There is no doubt about Lynch's conviction; but there is also no doubt that he was unaware of the situation that had evolved at command levels above him, even as the brigade ships neared Cuba. Military concerns were simply not making it beyond the Cuba task force leader, and were definitely not being shared with the president. And it is now clear that the size and scale of the air support Lynch envisioned had never truly been part of the agreement between Bissell and Kennedy. But there was no way for Lynch to know that, just as there had been no way for Esterline and Hawkins to understand the true situation as the brigade went ashore.

The only conclusion they could all draw was that they had been betrayed by the president of the United States. The words Lynch uses for President Kennedy go beyond "criminal negligence" and "screwed." He states explicitly that it was a lack of courage and leadership—and implies something even worse, that it was a conscious effort to dispose of the troublesome exiles by "dumping them into Cuba." However, it was CIA Director Dulles who had pointed out to Kennedy that just as with the brigade in Guatemala, he could not simply cancel the brigade landing, as it would represent a huge "disposal problem." If the plan had aborted at that point, the full brigade would have to be brought back from Guatemala, infuriated, bitter, and suspecting treachery by the American government guaranteeing its support. Certainly its members would not have given up their struggle and efforts against Castro. It could well become a domestic security and political nightmare. At that point it appears that Kennedy simply concurred with Dulles and introduced the choice of selecting a lower-profile invasion site than the Trinidad area.[280]

Lynch concludes his book with a chapter on "Rewriting History," in which he argues that the Kennedy Administration "feared exposure more than they feared defeat," and that Kennedy himself made the "decision to sign the death warrant of the Cuban Brigade." With the publication of Bohning's 2006 book and the inside information from Esterline and Hawkins, it has become clear that matters were not as black and white as Lynch had still believed in 1998. But in the months and years immediately following the failed landing, the CIA officers involved directly with the brigade felt they had been betrayed, that the new American president lacked courage, could not be trusted, and had in some sense already committed treason in allowing a communist regime to take full power ninety miles off American shores. The incident had also seriously damaged the president's image in the minds of many officers within the Agency, especially within the Directorate of Plans. Conversely, it had seriously undermined President Kennedy's confidence and trust in the CIA. With the creation of the brigade and the massive military operations not only at the Bay of Pigs but in a number of related naval deployments and diversionary activities, the CIA had moved from covert operations to the deployment of what were undeniably American surrogate military operations. Eisenhower had launched a covert warfare project and Kennedy had inherited a public military disaster.

The Cuba project as initiated by the Eisenhower Administration had died at the Bay of Pigs. But Cuba was still ninety miles away, receiving a growing array of Soviet military hardware. No American president could doubt or ignore that a communist beachhead now did exist in the Western Hemisphere. In the months following the disaster, JM WAVE in Miami covertly continued intelligence collection on all things dealing with Cuba and the Castro regime as well as infiltration, exfiltration, and limited sabotage operations against Cuba. The CIA also continued active contact with Cuban exile groups such as Directorio Revolucionario Estudiantil, or the Cuban Student Directorate (DRE), and Junta Revolucionaria Cubana, Cuban Revolutionary Unity (JURE). During 1962, high-risk and aggressive Cuban exile attacks against Cuba, and Russian targets around the island, drew considerable media attention. DRE boat raiders shelled a Havana hotel in August 1962, and a newly formed exile paramilitary group named Alpha 66 emerged to begin its own raider boat missions. Its attacks were targeted on Russian ships and camps and received extensive media coverage, especially by *Life* magazine.

In Washington, the question was not whether to continue the regime-change effort against the Castro regime, but rather how to make it work. President Kennedy had become doubtful of the CIA's ability to engage in large-scale covert operations partially because of its failure at the Bay of Pigs but also because of its similar failure in aggressive covert operations against North Vietnam. After taking office, Kennedy had requested an in-depth review of the Vietnam situation, and in January 1961 he had invited General Lansdale—with years of experience in Vietnam and just back from a two-week fact-finding tour—to attend a National Security Council meeting. The meeting was being held as a review of a "Basic Counterinsurgency Plan for Vietnam" submitted by the U.S. Embassy in Saigon. Kennedy was impressed with Lansdale's comments on the plan (which Lansdale supported) and felt Lansdale to be "in synch" with his own views. General Lansdale had impressed Kennedy during the evaluation of covert operations in Vietnam with his thoughts about an integrated military–interagency approach to large-scale paramilitary operations. President Kennedy appointed Lansdale to lead a reinvigorated effort against the Castro regime, designated by Lansdale as Mongoose. In that new effort the CIA would be relegated to a support role, its officers would be under intense scrutiny, and their span of tactical control would be seriously limited. Overall strategy, mission selection, and final approval would come from Washington. CIA personnel were not happy with their new role, more than a little skeptical about Lansdale's offbeat psychological warfare ideas, and infuriated with his micromanagement.

In that they had company. The State Department's representative on the new interagency team wrote that "the entire operation was pathetic and I ruefully longed for a way to turn it off." Arthur Schlesinger, a Kennedy White House special assistant, remarked in one interview about the Mongoose effort (which lasted only nine months) that the CIA simply disliked it as much as everyone else.[281] By February 2, 1962, Lansdale had submitted a firm timetable and a thirty-nine-page action plan, in six sections. Phase I started on March 1 and Phase VI, scheduled for October, dealt with the establishment of a new government in Cuba. Something dramatic did happen in October 1962, but it certainly was not the appearance of a new regime in Havana; it was the public disclosure of Russian intermediate-range nuclear missiles inside Cuba.

The Cuban Missile Crisis is a story unto itself, a high-risk gambit by Soviet Premier Nikita Khrushchev to counter what had become a dramatic American advantage in strategic military power. The United States had effectively put Russia at risk with the Strategic Air Command during the Eisenhower Administration, the addition of a seaborne force of atomic submarines with Polaris intercontinental ballistic missiles, and the advent of the first full squadrons of American intercontinental ballistic missiles emplaced in belowground silos rather than on exposed surface launchpads. Atlas intercontinental ballistic missiles had moved the United States into a position in which the Soviets truly feared an American-launched preemptive atomic attack. The Soviets could counter only with relatively short-range, surface-launched missiles and their ICBMs were not positioned in belowground silos but mounted on surface launchpads, fully exposed to an American first strike. America was also at the peak of its Cold War air defense capabilities, more than ready to counter the propeller-driven force of long-range Soviet bombers. The American advantage was indeed so strong that President Kennedy had actually been briefed that the window for an American first strike on the Soviets truly existed.

Khrushchev's response was to attempt to checkmate any such temptation to American preemption as well as to blunt the use of U.S. military superiority as leverage in international affairs. What made the Russian initiative so risky was that the effort included not only emplacing intermediate-range ballistic missiles (IRBMs) in Cuba but also moving in atomic warheads and supporting the entire effort with fully equipped Soviet army units—themselves provided with tactical short-range atomic missiles to defend against American naval landings. That Soviet move effectively placed most of the U.S. east of the Mississippi River within range of an atomic strike from Cuba. When the existence of the missiles was detected and publicly announced on October 22, 1962, by President Kennedy, both the Soviets and Castro claimed it was merely a move to protect Cuba against further American aggression. In reality it had been a gambit in the face of the massive American military advantage, and when exposed, Khrushchev had little choice but to withdraw the forces—with nothing more than an assurance from President Kennedy that there would be no American invasion of Cuba if the missiles and forces were removed.

The extreme tension created by the missile crisis and the non-invasion agreement involved in the removal of the Soviet missiles led to the termination of the Mongoose project. What it did not lead to was the end of intense American concern over the obviously aggressive Castro regime only ninety miles from its shores. Unarmed American reconnaissance aircraft had been shot down over Cuba, and Castro remained obstinate. He refused to honor the Soviet agreement and adamantly rejected United Nations calls for inspections to determine that all the Soviet missiles had indeed been removed. The issue of the Castro regime remained a major national security and political concern for the Kennedy Administration. The secret war against Cuba was going to continue; the question was, once again, how to carry it out. And this time, it would have to be even more deniable, given the agreement with the Soviets. JM WAVE operations continued out of the CIA's Miami station, agents and exiles were brought out of Cuba, intelligence missions were run, and planning began for some level of highly controlled sabotage aimed at regime destabilization. The Special Group Augmented, led by Robert Kennedy and Maxwell Taylor, intensely reviewed proposals for a new round of covert military operations, and President Kennedy held the authority to personally approve individual missions. In January 1963, a National Security Council memorandum addressed reorganization of the clandestine effort against Cuba, noting that future activities would have to consider the "no invasion" pledge while still attempting to put pressure on the Castro regime. That would lead to a somewhat schizophrenic approach, focused more on economic pressure and Cuban internal political opportunities than on military action. Sabotage of clearly defined economic targets would be part of the program—if it could be done without too much press visibility. The obviously conflicted approach led CIA operations officers into catch-22 situations; certainly Cuban facilities such as oil refineries and power stations could be attacked in destabilization efforts, but if the mission had a really significant target, such as the power station serving Havana, it would be hard to deny after all the lights in the city went out.

The period following the end of Mongoose was one of fits and starts. However, it also marked the beginning of a major crackdown on exile military action against Cuba by raiders operating out of American waters. Much of JM WAVE's intelligence work in the months following the missile crisis was directed towards identifying and aborting Cuban exile raids out of Florida and Louisiana. President Kennedy ordered a federal crackdown on the exiles and the FBI began its own initiative to block exile arms purchases and group missions against Cuba. The crackdown seriously frustrated the more aggressive exile military groups, adding to their ire following the failure of the administration to intervene militarily in Cuba during the missile crisis.

The Kennedy Administration did have every intention of restarting secret warfare against the Castro regime, but the new effort would have to be one of ultra-deniability. It would need Cuban exile surrogates but they would have to be totally disassociated from American support. They would also have to operate from bases well removed from the continental United States. The next phase of the secret war would have to give the appearance of total autonomy for the Cuban forces involved.

CHAPTER 12

Autonomous and Deniable

The concept of waging covert warfare against Cuba with a select group of autonomous Cuban exiles was very much in line with Robert Kennedy's ongoing concern that the CIA had not been taking full advantage of the exiles' potential. Robert Kennedy had been critical of what he felt was CIA overcontrol of its own exile assets, and was constantly being told by his personal exile friends that they could do the job on their own if they simply had American financial and logistics support. The Special Group decision was made that select exile leaders and groups would be supported, but only if they moved their operations offshore and publicly broke any connection to the U.S. government. That new approach would come to be described as the autonomous group strategy, a precursor to the outsourcing of surrogate military activity that would follow during the a Nixon and Reagan administrations.

The thrust of the autonomous group approach was the creation of relatively small, but extremely well-equipped, Cuban exile military groups, whose missions would primarily be of a naval nature. In concept the new effort sounded much more like the guerrilla operations the CIA had favored in times past and much less like the full-scale military operations of Cuban Brigade 2506. It once again involved supplying and supporting a regular military force, but these groups would be much smaller than the brigade that had landed at the Bay of Pigs. And this time the effort was to be truly deniable. The Kennedy Administration was willing to trade control for deniability and aggressiveness and would provide the money; the CIA was to support the autonomous group effort with logistics, intelligence, and training, but this time it would not be in charge of the actual military operations.

For this new effort, logistics was going to mean providing money, contacts, and introductions to CIA assets, including vetted CIA companies and weapons vendors. The groups would operate on their own—once they were located in Caribbean countries—supplied and provided with the ships and transportation capabilities to conduct military operations against Cuba. In the context of autonomous action, the primary CIA officers assigned to work with the autonomous groups functioned more as advisors and coordinators than in the more rigid role that was standard practice for JM WAVE. Henry Hecksher played the lead role with autonomous group liaison functions in Washington, D.C. He also provided political and media advice for the main group, headed by Manuel Artime. Carl Jenkins, a paramilitary specialist, assisted in arranging training, and coordinating contacts and support for the Artime effort. Jenkins had also been with the Cuba project since the early days, before the Bay of Pigs, reportedly involved in training and in organizing advance missions into Cuba. CIA files detail his role with the Artime project, and a civilian-era résumé lists his background as a paramilitary, survival, evasion, and escape instructor for the CIA in 1952–1953. During the 1950s he had trained Thai and Nationalist Chinese and worked in maritime infiltration for various Southeast Asian projects, including Indonesia.

The process of moving towards support for only approved, autonomous groups had actually begun early in 1963. Once the new Cuba project leader, Desmond FitzGerald, was appointed in January, one of his first acts was to go to Miami and bring all the relevant agencies (Coast Guard, Air Force, Navy, Immigration, police, FBI, and so on.) into an orchestrated effort to block exile group staging of missions from the U.S. Of course that was a challenge, because in the beginning it meant the individuals and groups on the approved list would have to be given special treatment until they could move their operations offshore. It also meant that special permissions had to be given to the ongoing "official" Kennedy Administration–approved infiltration, intelligence collection, and sabotage missions still being run out of the JM WAVE station in Miami. Needless to say, this contributed to a good bit of confusion among all parties, and a great deal of tension within the Cuban exile community.[282]

The autonomous group strategy evolved over five months in 1963, following the release of the brigade prisoners who had been held in Cuba since the Bay of Pigs landing. Robert Kennedy had been very much involved in that effort—which had solidified his personal relationships with a number of exile leaders including Manuel Artime. The prisoners began coming back to America in the winter of 1962–1963, and initial talks with selected exiles in regard to autonomous action began early in 1963.

President Kennedy and his wife had welcomed the full contingent of brigade prisoners back from Cuba with a ceremony held in the Orange Bowl in Miami, Florida. Prior to that, Manuel Artime and other brigade leaders recently released from captivity in Cuba had been in Washington, D.C., meeting with Robert Kennedy and offering their thanks for his efforts in gaining their release. Artime had personally met with the president as well, and it appears that in succeeding months Robert Kennedy and Artime continued personal communication. While in Washington, Artime met with CIA officer Henry Heckscher, followed by an extended meeting with Desmond FitzGerald, newly assigned to the relaunched but still clandestine Cuba project, which had assumed yet another iteration, now designated the Special Affairs Staff (SAS). Artime also made trips to Central America in March and May, soliciting aid for a new anti-Castro effort. The March trip took him to avowedly anticommunist regimes in Nicaragua, Costa Rica, Honduras, and Venezuela, asking for financial aid as well as access to bases that could be used for efforts against Castro.

During the FitzGerald meeting Artime criticized the CIA for "overcontrolling" the Cuban exiles, essentially micromanaging all their activities against Castro, totally controlling their funds, and having the final say in any and all of their activities. Such a view was very consistent with the remarks previously expressed by Robert Kennedy, and FitzGerald admitted that there might be some substance to that criticism.[283] He then presented Artime with the concept of a more "cooperative" relationship—one in which the CIA would furnish advice and funds as well as assist in logistics and making arms available. The caveats were that more than one group might be involved and they would all have to operate and be based outside the United States.[284]

Artime was successful in reaching agreements for operating facilities in Nicaragua and Costa Rica, both countries with regimes having close ties to the U.S. By the end of July, Artime was deeply involved in the initial stages of personnel selection, and the creation of draft purchasing lists for supplies, weapons, and equipment, including a variety of naval vessels. The project was in play and the CIA program of support for the autonomous group operation was designated AMWORLD. The CIA had reserved the right to give Artime and his officers advice and if necessary raise issues, but there was one caveat: "the stipulations . . . were designed to obtain one single purpose; namely, to make sure that 'no one can say you and your group are being run by Americans.'"[285]

Artime was also informed by FitzGerald that he would be equipped with weapons and military equipment by way of clandestine transfer to Artime through the Nicaraguan government. Purchases would be financed with money from the U.S. government, not the CIA itself. FitzGerald had moved to the point of putting the American position in quite simple terms: "We'll give you [Artime] the money and they get the arms."[286]

The CIA was serious about giving Artime the money. FitzGerald described setting up a Swiss bank account for Artime, which would provide funds for operating expenses as well as for reimbursements to third parties for the purchase of supplies and equipment. Over time some $7 million was directed towards Artime's accounts.[287] Working accounts were opened in both the name of Artime and a personal friend, Sixto Mesa, who had been secretary of finance for Artime's own counterrevolutionary group Movimiento de Recuperación Revolucionaria, the Movement to Recover the Revolution (MRR); the accounts were to be maintained at an amount of $25,000 each. Two and perhaps three Swiss accounts were used because Artime had also established a small base of operations inside the United States. The American operations were needed for recruiting, "letter drops," and the purchase of materials only available domestically. In the interest of deniability and compartmentalization it was standard practice to maintain separate accounts and funds for separate operations. Money from the Swiss accounts was to be transferred using a financial "cutout" (a third-party institution through which funds are passed to obfuscate the transactions) through the First National Bank of Miami, "with which HQS [headquarters] Monetary Branch maintains special relations."[288]

As a corollary to the autonomous group initiative and with the aim of establishing a very high-level cover for moving the secret warfare against Castro offshore, it was going to be necessary to publicly demonstrate that America had gone out of the business of supporting aggression against Cuba. By extension, that meant the regular JM WAVE intelligence effort in Florida was redirected to monitor those exile groups that were not trusted as part of the new autonomous group initiative—activist groups never associated with the CIA and with histories of launching their independent raids against Cuba, groups such as Alpha 66 and its spin-off, Comandos L. If groups such as Alpha 66, DRE, and Comandos L had been allowed to continue operating from ports or airstrips inside the U.S., it would have given the obvious public impression that the Kennedy Administration had not been serious in its promise regarding Cuba.

The simple fact was that the individual exile groups existed because they either had different political agendas or those involved in them did not personally trust each other. All efforts to coordinate even those groups supported by the CIA had been challenging at best, and by 1963 several of the more activist groups had little use for the CIA or the government in general, preferring to be left to their own devices. As matters progressed, even the groups invited into autonomous operations proved unable to work with each other, and Artime's group evolved as the single entity receiving serious financial support. The situation between the various groups had become so tense that at one point, Artime was given permission by his CIA advisor to have his boat groups fire on other exile groups they encountered during operations.

During 1963, new American sabotage missions were planned and reviewed by the Special Group. But since those sorts of missions required presidential approval, the net result was that approved JM WAVE missions became extremely tightly focused operations, planned in great detail and relatively small in number. In April, FitzGerald proposed three sabotage targets—a railroad bridge, some petroleum refineries, and a major molasses storage tank. The attacks were selected to "meet the president's desire for some noise level" while focusing on targets that would not cause excessive collateral damage or casualties. They could be carried out fairly quickly, in a matter of weeks. President Kennedy was not terribly impressed by the overall proposal, comparing it to what the communists were doing in their effort to overthrow the Laotian government. Discussion continued and by late April, the thinking seemed to be that refineries and power plants would be the best economic targets.

As 1963 progressed, with limited Cuban operations out of JM WAVE in Miami and the autonomous group strategy slowly jelling inside the Special Group, the Miami station staff became increasingly frustrated at their lack of success in getting plans and proposals accepted by the president. It would not be until June 1963 that President Kennedy approved a general outline plan for "sabotage and harassment" targeting power plants, fuel production, and storage and manufacturing facilities—all in an effort to destabilize the Castro regime economically. FitzGerald committed to beginning actual sabotage operations in July that year; it didn't happen. Virtually no sabotage activities were carried out during the first six months of 1963, and it would not be until October 24 that the president signed off on thirteen specific missions to start in November, involving a power plant, a refinery, and a sugar mill, among other targets. Even for the "not-sabotage missions"—the placing of supply and arms caches, infiltration and exfiltration of intelligence personnel—detailed plans had to be prepared, and approval obtained from the Special Group. In testimony and in remarks, the JM WAVE station chief, Theodore Shackley, would later complain about how painful it was to get approval for even the most routine maritime operations.[289]

The perspective of the Special Group seems to have been that at least a minimal level of sabotage attacks would complement both the developing offshore autonomous group and a new covert intelligence effort intended to locate military and civil leaders in Cuba who could be persuaded to join in a coup against Castro. The coup project was given the crypt AMTRUNK and was universally opposed by old-time JM WAVE personnel who had been around since before the Bay of Pigs, such as Shackley and Morales. They viewed the coup project as unrealistic, given Castro's immense power and the efficiency of his counterintelligence operations. CIA documents on AMTRUNK through 1965 reveal that this pessimistic view was well-founded. Virtually all the individuals contacted inside Cuba responded that they would never participate unless Castro was first eliminated. Even worse, virtually all the coup assets inside Cuba, the individuals (designated by CIA crypts beginning with AMWHIP) recruited to make contacts with those government and military figures who might support a coup, were later revealed to have been "turned" by Castro intelligence very early in the effort. In retrospect, it appears the AMTRUNK project was generally as ineffective as Shackley and Morales had presumed.

The existence, goals, and process for the other new CIA project—support for Artime with AMWORLD—were communicated on a restricted level in June 1963 with an extremely small number of CIA staff involved.[290] The primary CIA officers assigned to work with Artime functioned more as advisors and coordinators than in the more rigid role that had previously been standard practice for JM WAVE.

In an effort to establish maximum deniability, the support effort inside the CIA was to be so compartmentalized that there would be a special staff, isolated from the JM WAVE station, and a great number of support activities and meetings were conducted far away from the Miami area and JM WAVE. When they finally heard about the project, JM WAVE senior officers were equally negative about AMWORLD. Shackley was especially outspoken with his own opinion: "The whole operation was set up as a result of Artime's discussion with the Kennedys; I was asked my opinion of it and I said it was a lousy idea . . . the whole thing was an exercise in futility."[291]

The autonomous group effort was ready to launch, with a focus largely on Artime and his group. Robert Kennedy and the Special Group viewed it as innovative and with real potential, especially if the foundations could be laid via AMTRUNK for a coup effort inside Cuba. Virtually all the CIA officers involved were much less sanguine, not just those in Miami but even the senior CIA officers assigned to Artime. Only time would tell which view was going to be more accurate.

The fundamental public relations challenge of Artime's operation—and of the recruiting of his new exile army—was that he personally had to conduct a false public effort soliciting funds and denying American support while at the same time taking advantage of extraordinarily covert CIA financial and logistics involvement. The goal was to create a new, very well-equipped, primarily maritime, strike force to stage highly visible missions against Cuba. There would be limited covert air capability for insertion and support to resistance forces inside Cuba. And it was to occur in parallel with CIA efforts to recruit disaffected Cuban leadership, who would join in a coup at the appropriate time. The hope was that the overall effort would eventually evolve into a major revolution that would be viewed as totally independent of American sponsorship. At least that was the plan.

There were two principal Cuban leaders involved with the new autonomous group effort: Manuel Artime and Rafael Quintero. While in college in Cuba Artime had joined the 26th of July Revolutionary

Movement against Batista and battled along with Castro's forces in the Sierra Maestra. Following the revolution he was appointed by Fidel Castro as an administrator in one of the new agrarian reform cooperatives, but he quickly became disenchanted with what he felt were Castro's plans to "communize" Cuba. After publishing an inflammatory letter about his declarations in a Havana daily newspaper, Artime managed to escape from Cuba to Miami with the assistance of the CIA.

In September 1963, Artime's military case officer wrote a report documenting the military operations, which Artime felt would be vital to the success of the autonomous group project. Artime's thoughts were actually quite similar to the activities discussed for use in the PBSUCCESS regime-change effort in Guatemala. In one section ("Commandos") he discussed the use of abductions and assassinations targeting Castro G-2 intelligence informants, agents, officers, and foreign communists. Such activities would be used to "raise the morale" of people inside Cuba.[292]

Rafael Quintero was also well respected, both within the CIA community and by senior members of the Kennedy Administration. Following his return from Cuba after escaping capture during the Bay of Pigs landings, Quintero had drafted plans for a new covert operations initiative and presented them to Special Group leaders Robert Kennedy and Maxwell Taylor, who in turn offered the plans to CIA Deputy Director of Plans Richard Helms. Helms was favorably impressed and forwarded the plans on to the president's military representatives.[293] Quintero was second in command of Artime's new organization and accompanied him to the most secret meetings. These included meetings in Europe with an extremely classified and compartmentalized CIA asset within the Castro regime senior leadership, Rolando Cubela. He (code-name AMLASH) was being separately courted by Desmond FitzGerald as an adjunct to his Special Affairs Staff effort. FitzGerald saw Cubela not only as a possible coup participant but potentially for something even more important. Cubela was solicited for yet another assassination attempt against Fidel Castro. During their discussions, Cubela made it clear to both

Artime and Quintero that a coup in Cuba was virtually impossible without first assassinating Castro. They even discussed the specifics of staging a raid when Castro was in residence at Varadero Beach, capturing or killing him and "freezing" the Cuban militia in place with news of his death.[294]

A summary report of the meeting noted that the AMWORLD military case officer had specifically focused on discussions of developing contacts within Cuba that were capable of "eliminating Fidel Castro and seizing and holding Havana, at least for an appreciable time that would be sufficient to justify recognition."[295] If FitzGerald's plans had jelled, there would have been an important linkage between the AMTRUNK coup project, Cubela's participation in eliminating Fidel Castro, and immediate military support by what would be perceived as a totally autonomous Artime force—with no linkages to either the CIA or the much-mistrusted American government.

It is interesting to note that Carl Jenkins, assigned as military advisor to the Artime effort, has also surfaced as associated with a still-little-known and apparently highly secret CIA project designated as Pathfinder. Several National Photographic Interpretation Center (NPIC) employees have described their photographic and mapping work on that project—which apparently involved a planned pre–Bay of Pigs attack on Fidel Castro at his Varadero Beach retreat (a beach vacation spot).[296] Such high-level technical support is especially significant given the fact that NPIC was extremely classified—personnel working there actually used CIA employment as their commercial cover! NPIC did produce satellite and other advanced photographic intelligence; it had provided the studies and maps used by President Kennedy during the Cuban Missile Crisis. Any Castro assassination project supported by NPIC had to have approval from the highest levels of the CIA.

Further research has turned up little more on Pathfinder other than a related January 1961 file that refers to Frank (Fiorini) Sturgis. Sturgis had a prior history with proposals to assassinate Castro. He had helped supply Castro's forces during the revolution against Batista, and later had been in the field during the revolt. He was awarded with a variety of command positions in the new regime, taking charge of a parachute unit at one point. While still in Cuba and in his Cuban military position, Sturgis had approached the CIA with an offer to assassinate Castro in 1959; he was well acquainted with Castro and his senior Cuban military cadre. Extremely disaffected with Castro's move towards communism, Sturgis left Cuba and became actively engaged in anti-Castro activities in Florida. He had also became an informant for the CIA by 1961. Later, after his arrest with Howard Hunt's Cuban exile burglary team at the Watergate Hotel in 1972, his name would become quite familiar to the general American public.

Two additional documents provide further insight into the mysterious Pathfinder assassination mission. One contains an interview with a former JM WAVE case officer (whose name is deleted in the document) who confirmed his personal knowledge of the mission. He mentioned the name Felix in regard to the operation, which was aborted due to boat and infiltration problems during the insertion. Cuban exile and later CIA employee Felix Rodriguez would write his own biography entitled *Shadow Warrior: The CIA Hero of a Hundred Unknown Battles,* telling how he volunteered for an assignment to shoot Fidel Castro. Rodriguez discussed that the plan was to insert him into Cuba at Varadero Beach, carrying a rifle specially presighted (with its telescopic sight adjusted for the estimated distance of the shot) for the attack. He described several failures upon being taken into Cuba, which prevented the mission from being carried out.[297] For reference, Felix Rodriguez is listed as being carried into Cuba by Alberto Fernandez and the private CIA infiltration ship *Tejana*, which had suffered a number of engine problems during its final missions into Cuba in the months immediately before the Bay of Pigs landings.[298]

In 1963, Felix Rodriguez was personally recruited by Artime and Quintero while in U.S. Army training at Fort Benning, Georgia. Artime was given recruiting access to some of the most experienced and aggressive Cuban exiles, many of whom were in military training with the U.S. Army at Fort Benning, or with the U.S. Air Force at Sheppard Base in Texas. In a process reminiscent of the pre-WWII

American Volunteer Group recruiting, Artime was allowed to visit military bases, and trainees were even given leave to meet with his group and participate in the early stages of planning. In turn, Artime agreed to hide his connection to the CIA and the U.S. government, insisting to the recruits that he had no official American support. The cover story was that he was being secretly funded and supported by the Somoza regime in Nicaragua, as well as by unspecified European backers. In truth he was indeed receiving political support from Somoza, but Artime's money was coming from the U.S.

Rodriguez took Artime's offer and joined the effort upon completion of his training, after having taken an added course in radio operations to prepare for a role as a communications specialist with Artime's group. He joined them at their new base in Central America in October 1963. Quintero and Rodriguez would become perennial shadow warriors, both first for the CIA and later independently.

Both the Pathfinder project and the AMTRUNK efforts to bring about Castro's elimination as part of a coup illustrate how targeted killing easily becomes associated with covert warfare. In Cuba, as in Guatemala, it was seen as a quick and perhaps necessary means with which to bring about regime change. It is also seen as routinely necessary by the surrogate fighters who become involved in covert warfare projects. Both Artime and his military aide Quintero had proposed targeted kidnappings and assassinations as basic to their plans, submitted to the highest levels in Washington. Quintero viewed them as necessary tactics and tools to ensure that Castro's communist supporters would be eliminated and pose no threat to a new regime to be put in place after the coup. Blacklists of communist regime supporters were created for Guatemala, and appear to have existed for use following a successful brigade landing in Cuba. In later operations, surrogate target lists would grow to include thousands of individuals in South Vietnam during the Phoenix Project of the late 1960s, and tens of thousands across Latin America during the 1980s Condor era—which will be discussed in detail in a following chapter.

The fact that Artime was covertly given access to American military bases and personnel—at the same time officially denying connection to the American government—proved confusing to many parties. Elements of the U.S. military community were more than a little interested in finding out exactly what was going on with their trainees. One report from the 112th Military Intelligence Group describes a trip by Artime to Fort Benning. The report states that Artime was obviously recruiting for a revolutionary camp in Nicaragua. He was quoted as telling recruits that the U.S. government was not going to do anything for Cuba and that he had obtained aid and instructors from Europe. One of the recruiters working with Artime stated that Cuba would not gain its liberty with U.S. assistance and the U.S. government was not going to do anything for Cuba, which needed to look for help from another country. In fact he felt that the U.S. had decided to coexist with Cuba. The good news for the exiles was that a Latin American country was buying planes from England for Artime and had promised its support for his military operations. The report also notes rumors that the Somoza government was very involved and the group would have bases in Nicaragua—Artime and other leading Cuban exiles had recently had meetings with Somoza and had gained his personal support.[299] To that extent, the report demonstrates that the autonomous group cover seemed to be working, at least with the American military.

Additional information from the 112th relates that on November 18, 1963, communications from the Army Intelligence section at Fort Holabird in Baltimore—home of the Army Intelligence School and Counter Intelligence Records Facility—had requested that a trainee be allowed to travel to Washington, D.C., for a meeting the following day. The request had come from the exiled officer who had been second in command at the Bay of Pigs, and the trainee (who had been the intelligence officer with exile Brigade 2506) was required for a meeting with Robert Kennedy. It was confirmed that Attorney General Kennedy was indeed holding meetings with the Cuban exiles, and on November 17, he met with Artime and several of his key officers and personnel. Additional meetings were scheduled in Washington for November 21 and 22, 1963. Military intelligence personnel following the reports would likely have concluded that the story that Artime was giving at least some of his recruits was a cover for an operation actually supported at the highest levels of the Kennedy Administration. No doubt the true situation was also obvious to recruits such as the trainee described as traveling to Washington for meetings.

Overall the AMWORLD cover story was a credible one, certainly the best that could be constructed under the circumstances. Artime himself seems to have been generally keeping to the script—although Felix Rodriguez would later write that when approached by Artime and Quintero at Fort Benning, he was told that the effort was being personally sponsored by John and Robert Kennedy.[300] Numerous AMWORLD memoranda from Hecksher and Jenkins deal with maintaining the cover story and discuss measures, including ongoing advice to Artime, on how to maintain it—especially in the press. That was certainly challenging given that Artime had to be a highly visible Cuban exile leader, soliciting independent support for his campaign. He had to appeal to the media, to anticommunist groups, and to appropriate corporate interests, and he had to make the appeals in a call to action for an autonomous crusade against Castro. It involved the Kennedy Administration in actively supporting secret warfare against Cuba while exposing itself publicly to charges of doing nothing about the Cuban communist threat. Both Presidents Truman and Eisenhower might well have appreciated the irony of JFK's position.

Covert operations often sound clean and well defined when we read about them in the minutes of the various executive planning and oversight groups. They also seem reasoned and structured when described in special presidential national security directives or in classified presidential "findings" to Congress. But the day-to-day activities sometimes tell quite a different story. The CIA staff assigned to AMWORLD support for Artime was quite small, in contrast to Cuban operations out of the JM WAVE station in Miami. It included Hecksher's own secretary, Mrs. "Bobbie" Hernandez; her husband, Raul Hernandez; Carl Jenkins; and Richard "Dick" Beal, a career logistics employee, as well as Beal's secretary. Other individuals involved included Karl Rohrer, the CIA staff member who handled AMWORLD matters in Miami, and Dr. Cesar Baro.[301]

In the fall of 1963, Henry Hecksher was advising Artime on political correctness and media relations. Carl Jenkins was setting up various types of paramilitary training for Artime and Quintero, and CIA officer Raul Hernandez was handling the day-to-day logistics and supply side of the Artime operation. But Raul Hernandez also had other peripheral duties. They included working directly with Artime, assisting him as required. Some of Artime's needs and some of the calls for help Hernandez received are quite interesting—they illustrate the pitfalls of deniable activities. One example began with a call Hernandez received from Artime, just arriving from a trip to Central America. It seemed that Artime was actually being held in custody at the Miami airport, where customs had seized his briefcase.

Artime had been taken into custody because it had been obvious that the material he was carrying included confidential government documents. Among other things, the materials included sketches of various sabotage devices, a letter from the Nicaraguan president in regard to secret meetings, a notebook with HQS AMWORLD phone numbers, and what amounted to a weapons shopping list complete with related purchasing and inventory information. In the end, the matter was resolved and Artime was released. Clearing the matter with customs and obtaining his release required a considerable amount of communication and persuasion. The airport incident provides insight into the reality of many covert operations and illustrates the extent to which the personal element introduces real-world consequences quite different than those that enter into the discussions in planning and oversight meetings at headquarters in Washington, D.C.[302] In this instance, the people at headquarters may have been especially irritated, since Artime had been provided with and trained in the use of a very special briefcase for exactly the documents that had been seized.

The briefcase was a sophisticated, professionally constructed concealment device. Unfortunately for Artime and everyone else, he had neglected to activate the concealment functions. The CIA report on the incident notes that Artime needed to be forcefully prompted on concealment, especially since another similar incident had very recently happened with one of his people.[303] Fortunately, for our purposes, the customs people did take and record a comprehensive list of materials and correspondence, and that list gives us a number of clues to the extremely clandestine supply chain that had been established for the project. Among the suppliers noted were Interarmco and Atlantic Chesapeake Corporation. The information from the customs seizure gives us quite a detailed view into CIA practices in deniable weapons and materials purchasing. As we have already seen, the use of "cutouts" in covert supply activities was standard practice and Artime was referred to Dr. Jorge Casteleiro, who acted as an intermediary with various weapons suppliers. Transactions were also made through third parties in Costa Rica and Nicaragua. One of the complications would be that both those nations were telling Artime that they wanted an exclusive relationship with him and his project.

Unlike the operations we have previously examined, from the beginning it was clear that Artime's military actions were going to be largely naval in nature. He was going to need some serious maritime assets. His activities would require at least one relatively large "mother ship," somewhat like those the CIA had been using to facilitate its own maritime missions into Cuba. There would also be a need for a variety of smaller transport/landing craft as well as actual attack boats of the "swift" type, light naval craft fitted for exceptional speed. Those small, very fast, and well-armed craft had been in use both by JM WAVE against Cuba, and in covert sabotage attacks against North Vietnam. The AMWORLD staff was going to have to assist Artime in covertly putting together a modest naval operation, while leaving no paper trail to the United States. The goal was to have all his activities pointing to his ostensible third-party backers, Costa Rica and Nicaragua. Setting up the covert naval group and equipping it with weapons, communications, and supplies would turn into a task taking the better part of a full year.

To kick off supplying the project, in June 1963, JM WAVE staff assessed various options and proposed the Colombia-registered *Olga Patricia* light cargo ship (LCS)—which could either be purchased through a dummy corporation for $150,000 or leased on a monthly basis at a rate of $5,500.[304] The *Olga Patricia* had originally been built for the U.S. Army in 1947, then acquired by the U.S. Navy, serving initially in the South Pacific; in the summer of 1963 it was sitting in Biscayne Bay Harbor off Miami.

Artime turned his side of the purchasing and supply activity over to his newly designated secretary of finance, Manuel Gutierrez. Raul Hernandez advised Gutierrez that the purchase of the *Olga Patricia* could be facilitated by contacting the "Ads & Cargo Corp." Apparently Ads & Cargo of Miami was yet another CIA proprietary, possibly for leases and charters of temporary-use assets.[305] The purchase of the ship, and other maritime resources, was to be conducted through a newly established Artime front, a Panamanian company named Maritima BAM.

Another transport vessel was identified, apparently for charter rather than purchase.[306] The *Joanne* was berthed in Baltimore; it was ideal for hauling and/or barge-towing activity for large military cargo. A Cuban exile crew had to be recruited as the ship would be an "operational" vessel, used to carry not only military supplies but combat personnel.[307] On the *Joanne*'s first operational mission it carried the "black nine" resistance team as well as several electrical generators, two radio sets, and fourteen silenced pistols with some fourteen hundred rounds of ammunition. The ship's destination was Artime's new base at Tortuguero, Costa Rica.[308]

Artime was going to be receiving large-scale quantities of military equipment, and those would need to go into isolated bases that lacked the necessary port facilities for receiving such shipments. That requirement meant that barges and landing craft were going to be needed. Finding a barge would be relatively easy: JM WAVE had a list of known suppliers in Florida. Using cutouts, Artime's people were also referred to a "vetted" marine supplier in Tampa who would lease an appropriate barge. For the marine landing craft (LCM), things were a bit more complicated; they would need to be purchased through a military cutout. That was accomplished by using Artime's Costa Rican contacts to purchase two LCMs for the sum of $120,000. The transaction was made through the

Cooper-MacDonald National Marine Bank in Baltimore and the vessels were to be delivered to the Nicaraguan National Guard.[309] Then there were the smaller transport craft and attack boats. For those the CIA turned to the U.S. military, and four vessels were supplied. Of the four, one came from the Navy and the other three from the Air Force—two smaller craft transferred from a location in Miami and the other a surplus craft transferred from Port Canaveral in Florida.[310] While Artime's new navy was being put into place, arrangements also proceeded to obtain the quantity of weapons and ammunitions that would be needed.

AMWORLD documents make it clear that in the case of weapons for Artime, the CIA once again turned to one of its standard sources of the period, Sam Cummings and Interarms/Interarmco (International Armament Corporation).[311] By November of 1963, a comprehensive list of desired military weapons had been sent to Cummings, ranging from rifles to four-barrel cannons. There were some problems in that Interarmco did not have all the items on the list, in particular certain Czech and Russian weapons that had been included. Artime's own personnel appear to have actually gone to Europe to work though those issues. As a result it was accepted that half of the shipment (referred to by the reference Folies Bergère) could be available the first week in January and the remainder in March.

By mid-December some $80,000 had already been sent to Interarmco and accepted in payment for the first shipment.[312] The balance of the purchase, some $240,000 worth, was due upon delivery. A total sum of $326,262.82 was to go into Interarmco's bank, the Banque Genevoise de Commerce et de Credit, 2 Rue Diday, Geneva, Switzerland.[313] Logistically, one of Artime's new ships was designated to receive the shipment from Interarmco in Baltimore and to carry the weapons on to the new base in Nicaragua.

In early 1964, the initial Artime maritime operation was in place at Monkey Point in Nicaragua. A paramilitary camp had been set up at Puerto Cabezas and also in Costa Rica, where Artimc's people were sharing the use of a private airstrip with the brother of the owner. The brother was running his own air operation, which involved whiskey smuggling. At the time that seemed of little concern but would ultimately produce some major headaches for Artime. In addition, a refueling base had been established in the Dominican Republic and overall some three hundred men were involved in operations. Those operations included the use of a pair of 250-foot "mother ships," two swift attack boats, one C-47 transport aircraft, and two Cessna light aircraft.

But by the time Artime was becoming capable of actual combat operations, the key premise of the autonomous group concept had already been compromised. As early as July 1963, the *Miami News* carried an article by Hal Hendrix with the title "Backstage with Bobby," focusing on RFK's role in working with select Cuban exiles to stage new military actions against Cuba. Two days later Hendrix interviewed Artime, focusing on his move out of the U.S. to begin operations from Central America. Artime stayed on script with the approved story line, talking about support from wealthy Latin American citizens, political parties, and governments. He denied any support from RFK or the U.S. Regardless of the denials, the newspaper stories had definitely established the image of a relationship between Artime and the Kennedy Administration, and other reporters continued to aggressively pursue that story. The exposure was significant enough that it was discussed in Special Group meetings and viewed as an extremely serious matter. Yet other than continuing denial, little could be done after the fact.

The appearance and timing of Hendrix's stories are especially hard to understand, given that there is much to suggest that Hendrix himself had been a vetted and trusted contact for JM WAVE—and in particular for Station Chief Shackley. William Pawley is reported to have introduced the managing editor of the *Miami Herald* to Shackley, pointing out that Shackley had provided Hendrix information for some of his key articles.[314] Reportedly Hendrix was connected to both Ted Shackley and David Phillips, and it is noteworthy that neither CIA officer thought highly of the new Central American autonomous initiative. It seems at least feasible that the lead for Hendrix's rather negative RFK article might have been leaked to Hendrix from his CIA friends—possibly with the hope that the visibility might forestall any further effort on the project.[315] In any event, with new attention on Artime and possible high-level Washington support, the media had been given a new story line to pursue.

Over a period of some two years, Artime's active military operation involved the staging of fourteen missions, with four of them being at least partially successful.[316] In May 1964, an attack team struck at the Pilón sugar mill in Oriente province. It was a significant success, destroying warehouses and up to seventy tons of sugar—worth $1 million in desperately needed revenue for Cuba. Yet that success seems to have brought no great gains to Artime's overall effort—even if it compared favorably to other surrogate combat operations in Tibet or against North Vietnam. What was abundantly clear was that Artime's effort was extremely costly in terms of U.S. funding. During 1964 Artime was receiving $225,000 each month to cover his expenses. In September 1964, one of Artime's attack boats had engaged what they thought was the pride of the Cuban commercial fleet. In reality, they had attacked the Spanish freighter *Sierra Maestra*, which was off the Cuban coast and carrying in a cargo of commercial supplies. The captain, first mate, and engineer were killed in the attack. Several other crew members were injured, and the ship itself was heavily damaged. There was an international diplomatic explosion, and Artime was ordered to stand down. By November, there were further news stories in Miami papers about scandals in Artime's Central American camps, including reports that Costa Rica was investigating Cuban exile participation in smuggling inside its borders. That was followed by a December article stating that Costa Rica was expelling the exiles. The story was not accurate but it became one of a stream, maintaining a negative media focus on Artime and his operations.

It had been both too little and too much: too little military success and far too much expense and publicity. By early 1965, the State Department was increasingly unhappy. As for President Johnson, he had never been focused on Cuba; and following his brother's death, Robert Kennedy retained little political influence inside the Johnson

Administration. In February, the 303 Committee recommended that Artime's group be cut off and that financial support cease. That message was communicated to Artime and also to the governments that had been supporting him.

The secret war against Cuba had started during the Eisenhower Administration, evolved through multiple phases under President Kennedy, and eventually simply faded away under President Johnson. It had involved major conventional military action of an undeniable sort, a series of assassination efforts against Fidel Castro extending over at least four years, the operation of a huge domestic CIA operations base in Miami, and ultimately an extreme attempt at deniability compromised at its very beginning by media coverage very probably leaked from within the Miami station itself. It was perhaps the most intense regime-change effort ever undertaken by the United States—and ultimately a total failure.

The CIA had been removed from its preeminent position in covert operations due to the failure at the Bay of Pigs, and responsibility had been shifted to Mongoose, a multiagency effort micromanaged by the Special Group. Mongoose lasted only a few months, ended by the nonintervention agreement produced by the Cuban Missile Crisis of 1962. The final phase of the secret war had been an exercise in ultimate deniability; its failure suggested that deniability had become an exercise in wishful thinking. Still, we will find the practices of deniability continuing for decades, generally with little more success. In the end, perhaps the most significant product of the entire effort had been the emergence of a body of extremely well-trained and experienced Cuban exile fighters. Those individuals continued their own private struggles against the Castro regime across Latin America during the better part of two decades. Many of them volunteered to fight communism in Vietnam. Others joined a new effort to oppose a new communist initiative in Africa. There they would oppose forces personally dispatched by Fidel Castro and led by the second most prominent revolutionary figure in Cuba, Che Guevara.

CHAPTER 13

Holding the Line in the Congo

Cold War–era presidents were extremely sensitive to the establish-ment of communist-leaning regimes, especially in countries that were seen as being the key to entire regions falling under the influence of the Soviet/Eastern bloc. The loss of one nation could lead to adjacent governments being infiltrated and lost to the Eastern bloc, one after the other—the "domino theory" in action. Guatemala had been seen as a key regime in Central America, Laos in Southeast Asia. In Africa the view was that the Belgian Congo, with its huge mineral resources in its Katanga province, was a pivotal state in a region of some dozen countries struggling with the transition from colonialism to self-rule. The emergence of active African nationalist movements and a growing push for early independence from colonial rule were seen as creating not only a volatile environment but one ripe for socialist and communist agitation.

Crises and civil war have been all too common in the Congo in modern times. Internal conflicts have surfaced, with ethnic, regional, and tribal rivalries escalating in the 1950s, followed by calls for independence and an ongoing series of riots and protests at the end of that decade. Belgium began to lose control over sections of the country in 1959, and retained central authority only with promises of more Congolese participation in government, and ultimately independence. That promise led to an immense surge of political activism, almost all based on tribal factions—some fifty political parties were officially registered. The surge in anticolonial activism forced Belgium to dramatically advance the date when the Congo would be granted independence, and elections were held in May 1960.

In the election results, local parties largely related to tribal affiliations carried the day in each of the provinces, with the highly pivotal provinces of Katanga and Oriental being carried by the parties of Moise Tshombe and Patrice Lumumba, respectively. On a national basis Lumumba won a quarter of the total seats and managed to organize a coalition that put his chosen president in control of what was fundamentally a Lumumba regime in the new Democratic Republic of the Congo. Yet from a military point of view, the result of the elections was essentially the establishment of a series of semiautonomous ethnic and tribal strongholds, each with their own fighters. Up to that point, the military affairs of the Belgian Congo had been those of the Belgians and the congolese army; however, issues with the Congolese army (ANC), which had never had its own officer corps (all the officers in the force had been Belgian), were going to produce a far more complex situation with a number of additional parties fielding their own military forces.

Within a month of the Congo's June 1960 independence, a mutiny within the Congolese army led to widespread violence and the apparent breakdown of civil government in many areas of the country. In response, Belgium dispatched its own troops into the Congo on a stability and civil protection mission. Belgium felt compelled to protect its many citizens living in the Congo. However, the intervention was viewed by the Congolese as gross external interference with their new independence, if not a less-than-subtle effort to reestablish colonial rule.

To make matters worse, in July 1960, the province of Katanga declared its independence as a separate State of Katanga, under a regime led by Moise Tshombe. In August, a second eastern mining province, diamond-rich Kasai-Occidental, also declared itself to be an independent nation, South Kasai. Belgium had invested heavily in the mining infrastructure of the region, especially in Katanga, and

Tshombe retained the support of Belgian business interests, a large Belgian military detachment, and a well-trained force referred to as the Katanga Gendarmerie. Not all of the ethnic and tribal factions of Katanga were satisfied by a Tshombe regime and a number of them immediately began their own secession movements. Tshombe's response was to turn to foreign military assistance, using the wealth of the province and money from Belgian supports to bring in mercenaries from Belgium, Rhodesia, and South Africa—one of the best known of the units being Major Mike Hoare's "4 Commando" unit from South Africa. Both South Kasai and Katanga continued to defy the authority of the central Congolese government. Within months of its independence the central government had effectively lost control over the southeastern section of the Congo.

The Lumumba regime quickly appealed to the United Nations for help in evicting the Belgian military forces inside its territory. It also appealed to the United States and a number of other countries, including Russia, for military aid to allow it to reassert its authority over the Katanga and South Kasai territories. The American Embassy in the Congo cabled Washington that the Belgian military issue was simply being used to inflame the situation and that it feared that Lumumba would eagerly work with anyone who would support the central government's efforts to assert national authority and control. The U.S. made no response to Lumumba's request, and available correspondence reveals that the political establishment in Washington clearly viewed Lumumba himself in an extremely negative light, largely due to his vocally expressed views on anticolonialism and pan-African nationalism. The events that followed were politically complex, including the involvement of UN forces in a Congo peacekeeping mission, based on a Security Council resolution that called for Belgium to remove its troops and for UN assistance to the Congolese army. There was ongoing disagreement between the UN leadership and Lumumba about the exact nature of that mission and any combat roles by UN troops, especially their use against Katanga. With the UN hesitating, Lumumba turned to the Soviet offer of assistance.

As the U.S. Embassy had warned, Lumumba had been willing to turn to anyone for help, and with the lack of any immediate response from the U.S., he had turned to Russia. Russian aircraft quickly began to airlift central government troops into a bloody assault on Kasai. The acceptance of Russian military assistance reaffirmed the drumbeat of messages that Eisenhower was getting from Ambassador Clare Timberlake at the U.S. Embassy in the Congo, the State Department, and CIA Director Allen Dulles.[317] In remarks to the National Security Council, later reported by the Senate Select Committee on Intelligence, Dulles was quoted as advising that "in Lumumba, we were faced with a person who was a Castro or worse." Dulles went on to describe Lumumba's personal background, as "harrowing." Further, he stated, "It is safe to go on the assumption that Lumumba has been bought by the Communists."

State Department officials characterized Lumumba as "messianic," not rational, in fact "irrational and almost psychotic."[318] By August, the National Security Council had reached the position that the U.S. should be prepared "at any time to take appropriate military action to prevent or defeat Soviet military intervention in the Congo."[319] The final straw for President Eisenhower appears to have been the Soviet agreement to provide airplanes, weapons, and military advisors to assist Lumumba in dealing with the secession of Kasai and Katanga, the Congo's richest provinces.

Russia's involvement with the Congo's central government and its developing relationship with Lumumba was troubling; the perception in Washington—that Lumumba was essentially offering the Congo and commercial access to its vast mineral resources for sale to the highest bidder—escalated that concern. Finally, the rise of successful regional forces inside the Congo, some of them vocally declaring their communist agenda, had magnified the perceived immediacy of the threat. An ongoing series of dispatches from U.S. Ambassador Timberlake positioned the situation in the Congo as a classic Cold War confrontation. His bottom-line assessment was that "Congo [is] experiencing [a] classic communist effort [to] takeover government . . . there may be little time to take action to avoid another Cuba."[320] The ongoing warnings deeply worried President Eisenhower. When added to Eisenhower's own deep concern over Soviet expansion, Timberlake's assessments moved the president to express the view that Lumumba must be "eliminated." Based on Eisenhower's remarks, CIA Director Allen Dulles initiated an operation to assassinate Patrice Lumumba.

Documents made available to the National Archives only in the late 1990s show that President Eisenhower addressed the subject of the Congo and Lumumba at a National Security Council meeting on August 18, 1960. No direct quotations were allowed for notes taken in Eisenhower's NSC meetings, so the actual dialogue was not recorded. However, in a meeting of the Senate Committee on Intelligence (the Church Committee) in 1975, NSC meeting note-taker Robert Johnson related that in the 1960 meeting Eisenhower had turned to Allen Dulles and said something to the effect that "Lumumba should be eliminated." In later testimony Johnson was a bit more cautions, saying simply that he could not recall the exact words but that he felt they were an order that Lumumba be killed.[321]

Whatever Eisenhower specifically intended, we know that Allen Dulles definitely interpreted the remark as a direction for the CIA to kill Lumumba, because Sidney Gottlieb of the CIA's technical services division was dispatched to the Congo with a vial of poison. He was to hand over the poison to CIA contacts who had been sent from Europe to arrange for using it on Lumumba. This proved to be quite a surprise to the CIA station chief in the Congo, since, as standard Agency practice, the language even in secure field communications had been intentionally vague. On August 26, 1960, CIA Director Dulles had cabled the Congo: "In high quarters here, it is the clear-cut conclusion that if [Lumumba] continues to hold high office, the inevitable result will at best be chaos and at worst pave the way to Communist takeover. . . . [H]is removal must be an urgent and prime objective." The station chief, Larry Devlin, later testified that he was amazed when Gottlieb showed up with poison, as he had interpreted Dulles's cable in terms of political action, not murder.[322]

Due to confusion between different CIA case officers, the two assets from Europe were separately sent to the Congo, apparently with no knowledge of each other and only vague instructions on how to contact Gottlieb to receive the poison. Both registered at the Hotel le Regina in the capital of Leopoldville. One man had initially been recruited by the Agency for work in Europe, specifically "spotting agent candidates," in particular criminals with connections including drug smuggling and burglary, which would have been used to support activities relating to foreign intelligence collection.

The other asset was an experienced criminal already active in drug smuggling, who was expected to have contacts that could be used in "sensitive operations" ranging from burglary to assassination. Neither man had any contacts or experience in the Congo. Objectively the whole poison effort seems to have been about as well organized as a pickup basketball game. With both the European men staying at the same hotel, one actually tried to recruit the other for the Lumumba poison delivery. But because they had no knowledge of one another's CIA affiliations, the offer was refused. One man simply gave up on the job, engaged in some local moneymaking activities, and left the Congo on less than good terms with the Agency. The other appears simply to have returned to Europe.[323]

The total lack of coordination in regard to the CIA assets dispatched to the Congo prevented Gottlieb from actually handing over the poison for use. Confusion reigned, but not strictly in the ranks of the CIA and its assets. As the CIA was organizing, or attempting to organize its executive action against Lumumba, factions oriented towards the West moved against Lumumba. After much political jockeying and dramatic shifts within the ranks of the central Congo government, a military coup in September 1960 removed Lumumba from power. The military coup, the ouster of Lumumba, and the extent of his popular support—especially in the eastern Congo—intensified the Congo drama occurring during the transition between the outgoing Eisenhower Administration and the incoming Kennedy Administration. The September military coup had placed the head of the army, Joseph Mobutu, in a position of supreme power in the

Congo government. That move was strongly endorsed by the United States, as Mobutu was seen as Western-leaning; that perception was confirmed with his order that all Soviet advisors were to immediately leave the Congo.

In January 1961, Lumumba was taken into custody by the Mobutu government. He escaped and was making his way through Kasai to friendly forces in the east when he was captured by Mobutu forces but handed over to his secessionist political enemies. While in custody Lumumba was brutally murdered and the Congo moved into even more bitter regional factionalism. In regard to the CIA's efforts to eliminate him, the House Select Committee on Assassinations eventually concluded only that the CIA was not "directly" involved with his death.

Despite strong Russian objections the UN continued its military mission in support of the central government. Initially UN officers in the Congo focused on facilitating negotiations between the various factions, with the primary intent of bringing Moise Tshombe and Katanga back from secession in order to create a stable national government. Despite his official agreement on various terms, Tshombe retained both Katanga's Belgian military support and his various military commands.

The United Nations force in the Congo moved to carry out its mission, facing the fact that Tshombe and Katanga were showing no real signs of complying with a pledge to reunite Katanga into a unified government. Tshombe continued to rely on Belgian financial and military support as well as his mercenary forces; he even managed to patch together a small air force, which proved relatively effective in attacks on Congolese army forces. UN peacekeepers began to move more aggressively to disarm Katanga troops and arrest foreign mercenaries. While the United States had been encouraged by the new direction of the Congo's central government, the general political fallout of the military coup and Lumumba's murder had resulted in four major independent regimes across the breadth of the Congo, with the central government in control of no more than half its territory as 1961 progressed. Perhaps more worrisome, one of the new independent regions was led by Antoine Gizenga. The region under Gizenga's government covered the entire northeast of the country and Gizenga was being actively supported by the Soviets, Fidel Castro's Cuba, and a number of left-wing nations across Africa.

While a faction of the U.S. Senate was inclined to support Tshombe, whom they considered a staunch anticommunist, as well as the Katanga secession, the new Kennedy Administration took a firm stance in support of the elected Congolese central government. Other than its failed attempt to assassinate Patrice Lumumba in the final months of the Eisenhower Administration, the CIA had not been a driving force in regard to early U.S. involvement in the Congo. That involvement had been quite "overt" and in the form of routine military assistance. With a newly elected president coming into office, in the early months of 1961 activities in the Congo fell primarily under direction of the American ambassador to the Congo, Clare Timberlake.

Ambassador Timberlake's own initiative can be seen in his action in March 1961. With UN peacekeeping forces in the Congo under extreme military pressure and with an explosion of rebellion and secession attempts against the Congolese central government, Ambassador Timberlake had personally directed the Navy to bring a small regional contingency force of five vessels, including two destroyers and two landing ships, into Congolese waters. Timberlake apparently gave the orders without consulting the Defense Department, the State Department, the national security advisor, the secretary of defense, or President Kennedy himself.

President Kennedy only learned of the Navy's deployment from press coverage and expressed thoughts on the incident to Secretary of State Dean Rusk and Defense Secretary Robert McNamara. His remarks included a desire to have the opportunity to review such deployments in the future.[324] The Kennedy Administration had initially taken a less politically combative view of the Congo than Ambassador Timberlake, focusing on reconciling the various factions, supporting the elected central government, and building up the central government's Congolese National Army (ANC) as an effective force.

In December 1961, in a four-month campaign, the Congolese army retook control of the secessionist region of South Kasai for the central Congolese government. Next, as the result of a series of further UN military actions, Tshombe fled into northern Rhodesia while Katangese forces began to engage units of the UN in combat. The fighting went badly for both Congolese army forces and for the UN force. A company of Irish peacekeepers was taken captive and held for a prisoner exchange. Another Irish unit was ambushed and killed by tribesmen in northern Katanga. In order to obtain the release of the Irish prisoners, the UN was forced into an embarrassing cease-fire with Tshombe, and the push to reclaim the Congo's southeastern region stalled.

In order to ensure the survival of the Congolese central government, the offensive against Katanga would have to be relaunched. In a low-profile move, the Kennedy Administration went beyond covert support to lay the groundwork for renewed UN operations against Katanga, including the preemption of any opposition by the Katanga air force. Kennedy indicated that if necessary the United States Air Force might directly intervene to eliminate Katanga air assets as a threat. The UN mission itself was wholeheartedly ready to move again, and in the fall of 1961 began actively preparing plans for a major push against Katanga—this time with significant air support of its own. In that advance, the UN was supported not just by transport aircraft but by a combination of jet fighters and fighter bombers from the Swedish air force and the Ethiopian air force, as well as Canberra bombers from the Indian air force. The American air force also made itself available for any and all required transportation and logistics support.

Tshombe continued to hold steadfastly to a vision of Katangan independence and his forces continued to impede UN efforts whenever possible during 1962. In December 1962 they went so far as to shoot down a UN helicopter, killing everyone on the aircraft. That was the last straw for the UN commanders, and their forces began a rapid movement into Katanga. The new UN air arm destroyed all the Katangan aircraft as well as the airfields and runways from which they had operated. By January 1963 Katanga was subdued and the UN forces began their withdrawals from the Congo.

By early 1963, a level of calm if not full stability had returned to much of the Congo. The U.S. felt that the establishment of an anti-communist leadership in control of the central government and the overall loss of Soviet influence in the Congo had been a significant strategic victory for the Western bloc. That spring, President Kennedy met with Congolese leader Joseph Mobutu at the White House, congratulating him on standing up to communist expansion. Kennedy's praise for Mobutu was effusive: "General, if it hadn't been for you, the whole thing would have collapsed and the Communists would have taken over."[325] Unfortunately Kennedy was only seeing the calm before the storm. Following the withdrawal of UN forces, any sense of stability in the Congo proved to be strictly temporary. It would vanish by the end of 1963.

A significant number of the populace, especially in the east, was still outraged by Lumumba's murder; they blamed it on the central government and foreigners working with it. They also viewed the UN's activities in the Congo as a foreign invasion. There remained a wellspring of anticolonial hatred, and Westerners of any stripe became targets of new rebel movements. By the spring of 1964, the central Congo government was once again facing a dramatically escalating rebellion and rapid territorial advances by a variety of rebel factions. The most violent and fanatic fighters belonged to a group calling themselves Simbas, "lions" in the Congo's dominant Swahili language. A number of regional and tribal political figures also raised their own armies and effectively assumed the roles of tribal warlords.

Several of those armies would prove dangerous; the Simbas quickly showed signs of being able to defeat the Congolese army in combat and to scare it into retreat on a number of occasions. The Simbas managed to gain broad popular support, but their reliance on witch doctors, native magic, and certain drugs turned them into fierce fighters with little fear and no self-control; their treatment of captives was so brutal that they terrified opposing native forces.

With their ability to panic local populations and units of the Congolese army, the Simbas rapidly evolved into a threat very capable of bringing down the central government.

With the departure of the UN forces, the central government in Leopoldville had continued to rely on the ANC, which itself continued to be less than reliable in combat. In much of the country central government control was nominal and in combat the morale and performance of the ANC was desperately lacking. Perhaps equally important, it lost tactical advantage after the departure of the UN, as the central government had historically operated with only limited air transport capability and had no air units capable of effective ground support for its troops, much less tactical attacks on enemy concentrations or strong points.

That situation was to change dramatically during 1963 as the Congo's central government began to benefit from a very professional, experienced, and aggressive air capability, courtesy of a group of Cuban exile pilots, mechanics, and support staff organized and sent to the Congo by the CIA. That volunteer group effort was covert and extremely low profile. Given the general lack of documents relating to the formation of the Cuban air group, we are fortunate to have new and detailed research in a book by Frank Villafaña, *Cold War in the Congo: The Confrontation of Cuban Military Forces, 1960–1967*. With his very recent research we can finally relate a great deal more about the details of the Cuban force's recruitment and deployment. Unfortunately, we still know little about the detailed dialogue and decisions that led to the establishment of covert American military support for the Congolese army, including who influenced the decision making and how the directives were officially issued.[326] We know what happened, but we don't have the paper trail or even the oral history to determine exactly who proposed the action, or who gave the orders.

What is certain is that in mid-1962, in Miami, a Cuban veteran of the Bay of Pigs, Roberto Medell, was approached by the CIA and asked to help recruit and organize a group for military air action in the Congo. Cover for the group was to be a commercial one; its employees would work for the Caribbean Marine Aero Corporation (Caramar), a Florida corporation with an address at Miami International Airport. Personnel would be issued visas by the Congolese Consulate in New York. The recruiting was done in a rented office in a building just outside the Miami airport and it was all done by word of mouth among anti-Castro fighters. The air unit program would eventually continue over some five years, from 1962 to 1967, beginning under the Kennedy Administration and continuing under President Johnson.[327]

It appears that the group's pilots flew under commercial contract with the Congolese government, a relationship reminiscent of the American Volunteer Group in China. The CIA worked with the U.S. ambassador to the Congo and the State Department in facilitating and handling logistics, but the basic employment arrangement was a third-party commercial affair, offering the U.S. full deniability. Ostensibly the Cubans were hired as trainers for a new Congolese air force, flying AT-6 "Texan" trainers. They were retained for six-month tours and the first six men arrived in Kinshasa in late 1962. The pilots were designated as the Cuban Volunteer Group, but were referred to in Swahili as Makasi, "strong and powerful," by Congolese army personnel. They began by flying unarmed aircraft—not on training missions but rather on intimidation flights over rebel positions.[328] A cable from the U.S. ambassador discusses the need to keep the contract arrangement in place through at least 1965. The cable was transmitted to the State Department, the CIA, and the White House, and mentions the need to keep the relationship confidential.[329]

By the fall of 1963, in the face of the aggressive and expanding rebellion—especially the Simbas—the American military assistance group in the Congo also approved arming some half dozen aircraft; the CIA provided machine guns and air-to-ground rockets. The Makasi began regular attack missions against the rebels, both independently and in support of ANC forces. Their missions would continue for the duration of the Congo combat.[330] In October 1963, covert air resources in the Congo included twelve T-28 fighters and seven B-26 bombers, plus a small number of transport aircraft. At that point there were some twenty Cuban exile pilots flying, as well as a number of Cuban exile maintenance crews.

Given that not just the Congolese but the general international community was very sensitive to foreign interference in the Congo—and given that Western nations had effectively maneuvered politically with the Congo's central government, getting the Russians expelled from the country—it was highly desirable that the Cuban group appear to be strictly a commercial enterprise, contracted by the Congo government—and not a sign of American intervention in the Congo. In the interest of maintaining deniability, a new cover firm had been created for further recruiting. Anstalt Wigmo was registered in Lichtenstein; Wigmo was an acronym for Western International Ground Maintenance Organization.[331] The goal was to have all the connections to the Cuban exile volunteers appear to be on a commercial basis, on a par with the Congolese government's move to bring in foreign mercenary forces to fight the Simbas.

While the Cuban exile air group was covert, the U.S. also moved overtly, with further military assistance. It had opened the United States Military Mission, Congo (COMISH), under Colonel Frank Williams. The military mission was public and the U.S. supplied six T-28 fighters, six helicopters, and ten C-54 twin-engine transports as part of COMISH's effort to strengthen the Congolese army and enable it to advance against the various secessionist factions.[332]

The Congo's central government was receiving American military assistance, both overtly and covertly. In addition, it was determined to employ foreign professional combatants—mercenaries against the expanding insurgency. Mike Hoare returned to lead another commando unit in the Congo, this time fighting for the central government. The United States tacitly agreed to the Congo's employment of mercenary troops, "providing they were neither Belgian nor American."[333]

It did take time for the new central government initiatives in adding foreign combatants and air support to help in rallying the Congolese army. In the interim the Simbas continued their advances and by July 1964, the rebellion in the Congo had virtually consumed the country. The Simbas gained control over major cities, including Stanleyville in Orientale province during August 1964. The Simba capture of Stanleyville, which had a population of over thirty thousand and a significant European community, left some sixteen hundred foreigners hostage in the city. The Simbas openly accepted military aid from both the Soviets and the Chinese, and several of their factions and leaders presented themselves as communists. After seizing Stanleyville, Simba leaders declared a "People's Republic of the Congo." It was an especially dangerous situation because the rebels had been repeatedly hurt by Makasi air strikes, which they blamed on the United States, inflaming their hatred for Europeans and now especially for Americans. In their view, American support of the Congo's central government was simply another foreign move at colonial domination and further convinced them that all Americans and Europeans were deadly enemies. The Simbas continued to torture and murder Europeans. All European captives were treated as enemies and hostages.

The Simba leaders had also learned that American military officers from COMISH had been seen in the field, apparently working with ANC forces. The new combination of the Cuban Commando ANC group strikes; and the organization and initial action of Hoare's 5 Commando ANC, who had been hired to help the ANC fight the general insurgency; and a more aggressive ANC; had begun to push the Simbas, inflaming their anger. On August 21, the Simba commander ordered that all Americans were to be arrested and "judged without mercy," a virtual death sentence.[334] As combat and Simba losses continued, the Makasi air strikes became a focal point in the fighting. Following a successful Makasi air attack on October 1, a radio intercept recorded that the Simba commander in Stanleyville had been ordered to kill one European or American for every Congolese killed in an air strike.[335]

In response to the dire threat to the European hostages (but only after extensive political and diplomatic dialogue), the U.S. and Belgium hurriedly and clandestinely assembled a complex airborne rescue operation, with the overall designation of Dragon (there were

Red Dragon and Black Dragon components). With approval by President Johnson, planning for the Dragon operation began on November 1964, and mission forces were on the ground in the Congo before the end of the month. The overall Dragon mission involved several military elements—some conventional and some deniable—including a special CIA ground force led by Rip Robertson. Its full story is complex, spectacular, and heroic. It was the first rapid-response international hostage rescue mission since the Second World War.

Focused initially on a large group of European hostages held by the Simbas in Stanleyville, it managed to rescue several thousand hostages—men, women, and children who were under threat of immediate slaughter. Some forty-seven hostages had already been killed, and another thirty were brutally murdered as Belgian paratroopers jumped into the city from American Air Force transports. The Makasi air unit of Cuban exiles provided highly targeted strikes and ongoing air cover for the Belgian forces. Military studies note the fact that Makasi air support was a key element of the Dragon rescue operations.[336] Not only did attacks by the volunteer air group provide continual close air support for the Dragon ground forces, but on a number of occasions they prevented the massacre of groups of hostages. In several instances the close air support allowed relief forces to advance just in time to save other groups.

In addition to the overt but low-profile U.S. Air Force support of Dragon, a special covert unit of Cuban exile ground troops was also deployed to the Congo; the unit was led by Rip Robertson, a veteran of CIA covert warfare in Guatemala, Laos, and Cuba. He handpicked a small but highly skilled Cuban exile combat group. Their mission would be to move along with the Dragon force and rescue American diplomatic personnel, in addition to as many other Americans as possible. The unit consisted of eighteen heavily armed Cubans, led personally by Robertson and operating under extreme deniability. Robertson's team moved quickly and effectively to rescue both Americans and Europeans. In the combat, five Cuban exiles were killed, and the group rescued several European missionaries who had been in the Congo for years. They were literally rescued in the midst of Simba preparations to execute them.

The Congolese army and Mike Hoare's 5 Commando ANC mercenary units also carried out extensive combat and military advances in support of Dragon. Their combat actions not only rescued a large number of European hostages and saved other foreigners from being killed, but also resulted in massive combat and losses for the Simba rebels. It has been estimated that as many as ten thousand rebels may have been killed in the separate central government military operations against the Simbas in support of Dragon. By early 1965, the central government advances had fully reclaimed half of the Congo territory that had fallen to Simba rebels during 1964. Frequently, the central government advances were ensured only through the aerial reconnaissance and aggressive close air support given by the Cuban volunteer air group.[337]

By May 1965, Hoare's command units and the ANC had progressed to the point of being able to close off the rebel supply corridor running into the northeastern region of the Congo from Sudan. That route had allowed truckloads of supplies to be brought into the rebels. The route was reportedly guarded by a Cuban army detachment dispatched by Fidel Castro, a unit that had formerly been in Algeria.[338] Much has been written about Hoare and his 4/5 Commando mercenaries—both his initial combat for Katanga and later his work for the central government of the Congo. Hoare's personnel were a mix of nationalities (Belgians, some Spanish, a handful of French and Italians) but at least half the total force was South African and Rhodesian. Air support for the commandos was with the Cuban volunteer air group through CIA paramilitary personnel. The U.S. was quite sensitive to the subject of mercenaries in the Congo and was much involved with the public relations management of media attention directed towards the subject.[339]

After successfully closing down the cross-border ground supply routes for the rebels, the ANC and Hoare's forces were in position to launch a major military operation against their remaining supply routes, which extended across Lake Tanganyika. Hoare's attention also turned to reports that supplies and rebel infiltrators were coming across Lake Tanganyika from Tanzania, and that the rebels had new advisors from the Cuban army. Hoare's force had resources for operating on the lake: tugs, barges, and even six PT boats. It also had considerable Makasi air support, including six armed T-28s and a flight of B-26 bombers to soften up targets. With those resources, Hoare launched a new initiative designated Operation Banzi.[340]

As the operation proceeded, in June 1965 Cuban military combatants were confirmed in the fighting. That would bring additional covert American support, with a new Cuban exile team being brought into the Congo. Castro viewed African independence movements as fertile ground for spreading the communist revolutionary message. The European colonial history in Africa was seen as being of particular value in establishing a common cause with anti-Western political movements.

The third group of Cuban exiles to go to the Congo would be nothing less than a naval force for the "Great Lakes" of the Congo. The Cuban exile maritime volunteers were recruited by the CIA in late summer 1965, and they came from a unit that we have discussed in detail: the highly secret Artime autonomous group effort begun in 1963. Some sixteen exiles were interviewed and recruited in Miami, told that they would play a vital role in stopping the communist overthrow of yet another country.[341] Told that when they returned they would have full American support for further efforts against Castro, they would later be bitterly disappointed when the promise was broken. As one Cuban veteran expressed it, "We were told . . . 'when this mission is completed, you will have our unconditional help in the fight against the Castro regime' . . . when we returned from Congo, our leaders were told by the same CIA operatives that they were no longer in a position to help. The rug was pulled out from under us."[342]

While in the Congo, the exile maritime unit had the chance to directly face one of their most hated enemies in the form of some 180 Cuban army combatants operating in the area of Lake Tanganyika. The Cuban military volunteers had been sent by Fidel Castro to act as advisors and eventually as leaders to groups of Simba rebels.

Their goal was to support the ongoing secession of Katanga province, in a broader strategy that would have led to an independent Katanga allied with Tanzania. Strategically such an alliance was intended to serve as a launchpad for the additional communist overthrow of Angola. Upon arriving in the Lake Region of the Congo, the Cuban army contingent immediately began to experience their own problems, including missing weapons parts, the wrong caliber ammunition for Soviet weapons provided to the rebels, and totally inexperienced recruits. On June 19, 1965, Makasi aircraft located and strafed the Cuban camp. The Makasi aircraft also had begun patrolling the lake, which represented the main supply conduit for the rebels, during the day. By September the exile maritime unit was on the lake with their very familiar CIA-armed swift boats.[343]

The Cuban advisors managed to organize several ambushes and one serious attack on a Congo army camp. Otherwise their efforts were generally ineffective. In their most serious initial assault, they were totally repelled, with five Cuban army troops killed and the Cubans unable to recover all the bodies. A diary recovered from one of the dead Cubans (kept against all orders) revealed that Che Guevara was personally leading the Cuban unit.[344] In the end, the force led by Guevara was defeated, not only militarily but by having their overall mission undercut by Congolese political maneuvering that ended the Katanga secession. The agreement also removed the communist leadership that had been driving the Katanga secession. With that, the Organization of African Unity (OAU), formed in 1963 and dedicated to defending the sovereignty, territorial integrity, and independence of nations across Africa, ceased its support for the rebels and joined in a general call for all foreign troops to leave the Congo.[345]

Fidel Castro ordered Guevara and his contingent out of the Congo in November 1965. The covert Cuban exile ground team departed by the end of that year, the maritime unit by the end of 1966, and the Cuban air group in 1967. The CIA had brought just over one hundred Cuban exiles into the Congo, beginning with the first elements of the air group in 1962. Castro had sent an army contingent of more than two hundred troops in 1965, only after the Simbas had been effectively and thoroughly beaten throughout most of the country. Once again, timing proved to be the key factor in which side would win in the covert intervention.

In 1967, acting Congo leader Mobutu banned all political parties in the Congo from 1969 to 1974, Mobutu and the Congo enjoyed extremely good relations with the Nixon Administration, and the Congo made considerable economic gains. Mobuto himself focused on emphasizing the country's independence and its African heritage. The Congo was renamed Zaire in 1971, Mobutu changed his own name to Mobutu Sese Seko in 1972, and issued an order that baptizing a child with a European name would bring a five-year jail sentence. He also began comprehensive nationalization programs, including that of the economically critical mining industry.

Mobutu's most significant future move was his decision to align himself and Zaire with rebel factions that would become involved in a new civil war, next door in Angola. In July 1964, Mobutu announced that Chinese military advisors were to come to Zaire—expressly to train rebel forces for the civil war in Angola.[346] However, after flirting with Chinese support, Mobutu and his forces would become actively involved with the CIA in covert activities to sway the Angolan civil war towards the victory of those rebels favored by the United States. It would be a strange interlude in covert operations, with different factions opposing the Angolan central government, and this time the U.S. and Congo/Zaire would pick one faction, while other groups would be supported by the Chinese and Soviets, and yet others by South Africa. And in the Angolan conflict, Fidel Castro and Cuba would involve themselves again, this time not with small advisory groups but with fully and heavily armed brigades. While U.S. covert action with the Cuban exile groups in the Congo was seen as a bright spot for the CIA's covert action efforts during the 1960s, Angola would be quite a different story in a later decade.

CHAPTER 14

Unanticipated Consequences

In the twenty years following the Second World War, the decisions to engage in shadow warfare were grounded in America's ideological confrontation with, and preemption of, global communist expansion. While America was not itself directly attacked in any of the instances we have reviewed, the prevailing fear of communist domination produced a level of broad bipartisan support for such actions that was almost unrivaled in American political history. For all three presidents of those years—Truman, Eisenhower, and Kennedy—there was never a question that action needed to be taken to stop the communists; the only real issue was what actions could be taken short of open combat, which could possibly lead to a new world war against the Soviet Union and the entire Eastern Bloc. Deniability became the theme of America's covert warfare, despite ongoing exposures—some as undeniable as the Bay of Pigs landing. As years passed and the number of operations mounted, the problems associated with shadow warfare became a bit more obvious.

The pitfalls and unanticipated consequences of covert warfare were not nearly as clear in the initial decades, under the Truman and Eisenhower administrations, as they would become by the end of the 1960s. From a purely monetary standpoint, with the significant expenses required to pursue deniability, covert warfare became exceptionally expensive—albeit with the true costs buried in either presidential discretionary budgets or within overall Department of Defense appropriations.

Indeed, it became increasingly difficult even for Congress to determine the real expenditures involved in covert action, or for that matter even what the CIA as an organization was actually spending, and from the earliest days of the Agency cost overruns became a fact of life. In 1953, a political covert action effort, designated Operation Ajax, produced a coup against the Iranian regime of Prime Minister Mohammad Mossadegh. The CIA had initially estimated it to cost $100,00 to $200,000. In reality, the final bill for the operation was somewhere between $10 million to $20 million, plus another $45 million in American aid for the new Iranian regime.

In reviewing the Tibet Project, which lasted for over two decades, we noted that in 1964 alone the project had consumed over $13 million in contemporary dollars. However, given the lack of released documents on most operations, it is still virtually impossible to estimate the expense of many of them. In most instances the public was either unaware or only marginally aware of the covert operations themselves, and completely unaware of their costs. Deniability and the practice of intentionally obscure budgeting practices (justified for operational security) kept costs from becoming a domestic or congressional political issue, and, in turn, made it a good deal less politically painful for presidents to move to covert options. In later years we will find that even when Congress became concerned enough to intervene and conduct its own inquiries, congressional committees would become frustrated in attempts to determine actual CIA spending—including its true overall budget.

Each of the early post–WWII presidents pursued deniability for certain national security activities, from Truman's covert action against communist China, to Kennedy's operations against Cuba and North Vietnam. However, given the relative frequency with which President Eisenhower turned to deniable covert action, it seems clear that he was exceptionally supportive of the practice and confident that deniability could be maintained. Perhaps his attitude was best captured in his private remarks. During a lunch with two businessmen, while talking about the crisis in Indochina, Ike brought up the fact that the U.S. was considering sending two aircraft carriers to provide bombing support for the French at Dien Ben Phu in Vietnam. But he noted that if he was forced to take such an action, it would have to be done covertly. "Of course, if we did," he said, "we'd have to deny it forever."[347]

Despite a few embarrassing incidents such as the capture of a CIA pilot supporting a military coup in Indonesia, few of the Eisenhower covert actions had been exposed, and even those had generated little domestic response. Certainly none of the covert warfare operations had produced international drama comparable to the incident in which the Soviets shot down an American U-2 reconnaissance aircraft flying over the heart of the Soviet Union in May 1960. Domestically, the Cold War dialectic was in full play and it would be hard to call out any single covert action under Eisenhower that was not fully endorsed by the State Department or the highest levels of his senior staff. It might even be said that with John Foster Dulles in charge and with his "fierce partisanship" with anyone dedicated to fighting communism, deniable warfare had sometimes started in the State Department. Reportedly, it was John Dulles who pushed his brother Allen into action on Laos in 1958.[348]

It is perhaps surprising that given his willingness to engage in shadow warfare, Eisenhower seems only to have grasped the potential risks associated with what he termed the "military–industrial complex. Remarks from that speech clearly expressed his concern about the emergence of that new power center:

> *This conjunction of an immense military establishment and a large arms industry is new in the American experience. The total influence—economic, political, even spiritual—is felt in every city, every State house, every office of the Federal government. We recognize the imperative need for this development. Yet we must not fail to comprehend its grave implications. Our toil, resources and livelihood are all involved; so is the very structure of our society. In the councils of government, we must guard against the acquisition*

> *of unwarranted influence, whether sought or unsought, by the military–industrial complex. The potential for the disastrous rise of misplaced power exists and will persist.*[349]

Given Eisenhower's high-profile warning from 1961, it is clear that he appreciated the potential for the emerging Cold War–era defense industry to influence both the military command structure and Congress—with its own potential for driving strategic government decisions and policies. What he seems not to have considered was how fast a new national intelligence complex had also developed and the equally grave implication that it too could have its own effect on influencing government policy.

The rate at which the national intelligence complex had developed was quite dramatic. In 1952 the Office of Policy Coordination had been combined with the CIA Office of Special Operations. As of that year the consolidated entity had some six thousand personnel in forty-seven field stations. Over half of its employees were overseas contract personnel, with the majority being in the Far East Division. The majority of its growth had been in paramilitary personnel and its budget was in excess of $82 million. Given the Korean conflict, the preeminence of a clandestine operations division (60 percent of the total CIA personnel and 74 percent of its budget) is not too surprising. What is more striking is the relative size of the covert action branch during the years following the Korean combat. Under Allen Dulles, the CIA's covert operations function (Directorate of Plans) remained the largest component of the Agency, with a thousand more employees being added under the Eisenhower Administration. The branch consumed the majority of the Agency's budget, some 54 percent. It also massively expanded its reach in Africa, more than doubling the number of its field stations there.

During the Kennedy Administration, the relative strength of the CIA covert action operations branch continued, with personnel increasing in the Western Hemisphere Division by at least 40 percent between 1961 and 1965.[350] Historian John Prados points out that the frequency of authorized tactical missions was also escalating dramatically, largely in support of the secret war against Cuba—as well as missions in Laos and against North Vietnam. Some 163 actions were approved between January 1961 and November 1963, compared to 104 in the eight years of the Eisenhower Administration. And that reflects only activities reviewed by the Special Group, which considered only actions of a certain scale and cost; the 163 noted were estimated to have been less than 20 percent of the total conducted.[351]

The new infrastructure developed to support the covert warfare missions had also grown significantly. Throughout the CIA there were some one thousand personnel in other groups whose activities supported such missions. The Agency was supporting and coordinating the use of an extensive series of proprietary, cover, and contract businesses. Even before its explosive growth during the Southeast Asian combat, CAT/Air America had employed six thousand people. As combat escalated in Laos and Vietnam, that number jumped to twenty thousand. The company owned or operated approximately 167 aircraft. Another CIA affiliate company, Southern Air Transport, was much smaller but still large enough to operate four-engine transports and jet aircraft. One of its contracts with the Air Force, solely for interisland passenger service in the Far East, equaled almost $4 million. The overall effort was so massive that in 1963, the CIA created an Executive Committee for Air Proprietary Operations (EXCOMAIR), just to administer and conduct financial oversight of its investments in air capabilities.

By the middle of the 1960s, the Directorate of Plans was comparable to the entire Department of State, using 60 percent of the CIA budget and with some eighteen hundred covert action officers, not to mention another forty-two hundred in espionage and counterespionage. And the action directorate had also been given easy access to military services support via the Office of Special Operations (OSO), an element of the Joint Chiefs of Staff. Following the Bay of Pigs, the OSO was disbanded and its staff reassigned. However, in line with the Kennedy Administration preference for an expanded military role in special operations, most of the OSO functions, including covert military coordination with the CIA, were transferred to the new Joint Chiefs office of Special Assistant for Counterinsurgency and Special Activities; SACSA and its assets would become an important part of the covert action story in Vietnam.

President Eisenhower had been gravely concerned that the economic clout of the military–industrial complex would lend it political reach and influence into every state house and every office of the federal government. The emerging national security complex had its own political clout—we have seen information being provided to major corporations, as those same corporations provided covers and even logistics support for Agency operations. But the CIA itself had a type of clout that the presidents may well not have fully appreciated—media reach and media influence.

During the 1950s and early 1960s, covert activities were assisted by a newly developed asset, one that the Agency had assiduously developed: major print media access. The ability to influence the media's perception of events was not only desirable for maintaining deniability but also of value for the psychological side of the CIA's operations. Initial media access by the Agency largely had been a matter of personal networking with influential reporters and columnists. One example of such high-level networking can be seen in the CIA's relationship with Joseph Alsop. He was a highly influential media voice, especially during the 1950s and 1960s; his column ran for decades in the *New York Herald Tribune*. He was an outspoken advocate of communist containment and of America's involvement in Vietnam. Alsop became a close personal friend of early OPC figures Frank Wisner and CIA Deputy Director for Plans Richard Bissell. Alsop had known Bissell since childhood and both men shared the same high level of concern over the Soviet threat. In later years Alsop proudly admitted performing intelligence collection for the CIA and otherwise supporting its efforts; he described it as "the right thing to do," "my duty as a citizen." Alsop felt that it was a fundamental patriotic duty for the media to work with the CIA in national security matters.[352]

A good number of reporters and columnists shared Alsop's view and were eager to do their part in the CIA's Cold War efforts. Others were cultivated by Agency officers and essentially traded information, serving as useful sources and in turn profiting from scoops and awards from privileged information provided to them. In some instances simply being hours ahead of the pack could produce Pulitzer Prizes. Washington, D.C., media figure Bob Woodward described his personal relationship with CIA Director William Casey as "a partnership over secrets."[353] By the early 1970s, what had been standard CIA media practice was beginning to come under scrutiny from the public and within the media itself. In 1973, the CIA was forced to respond to a series of questions from the newspaper industry in regard to Agency relationships with the press. Initially the CIA admitted that it had an "active relationship" with "some three dozen" reporters.

In 1976, pressed for further elaboration during congressional inquiry, the Agency admitted that the number was more along the lines of fifty journalists. Later estimates would move that figure to an estimated four hundred reporters and journalists who had been used as CIA sources or channels during the 1950s and early 1960s—the so-called "golden age" of covert operations.[354] Under normal circumstances the sort of media access and partnership described above could only be seen as highly desirable from a national security standpoint; keeping deniable operations from being exposed by the press could only be a positive thing in terms of the overall mission and the White House's strategic agendas. However, there is good reason to speculate that on occasion, when key CIA officers' views differed from the White House strategy, the media card may have been played in an entirely unanticipated manner.

One example of that risk can be seen with an operation we reviewed in a previous chapter, the Artime autonomous group project. As we noted there, the key to the entire strategy, initiated by Robert Kennedy and the Special Group Augmented, was that the U.S. would covertly fund a totally deniable Cuban exile operation from locations throughout Latin America. The operation would present itself as totally independent from the U.S. and the CIA. Artime was cautioned to separate himself from the Kennedys, and to present an entirely separate group of offshore sources for his funding and support. Any press coverage putting him together with Robert Kennedy was seen as the kiss of death for the operation. We also noted that senior JM WAVE officers such as Ted Shackley and David Morales were openly dismissive of the project and privately outspoken in their views about Robert Kennedy's plan as being ill conceived. Station chief Shackley was convinced that the new autonomous group initiative was simply wasting his time: "[I]t was not going to work . . . it was an exercise in futility . . . the thing was a poor effort . . . a waste of time."[355] That may well have been one reason why the management of the project was compartmentalized with a separate AMWORLD CIA group, with its senior officers working out of headquarters in Washington and with highly compartmentalized communications within the Agency.

Yet CIA documents reveal that by the end of the second week of July 1963, a major problem had already surfaced, specifically the issue of media exposure. That exposure raised "the question of disappointingly premature publicity concerning our autonomous operations with Artime."[356] The issue was the topic of concern and discussion at a meeting of the National Security Council's Standing Group. The concern was very real and exacerbated because of the accuracy of certain of the articles, one of which was titled "Backstage with Bobby."[357] The article had discussed Robert Kennedy's involvement with Artime, and also mentioned an understanding with Nicaragua's General Somoza, a relationship still very much under negotiation. The story was followed only days later by Hendrix's personal interview with Artime; the article stated Artime's denial of American support, but it restated the speculation that Robert Kennedy was personally involved with Artime and his efforts.

Certainly the articles were a serious issue; publicity would be the one thing that could kill the new, ultra-deniable project at its very beginning. But another significant concern, apparently not surfaced during the Special Group Augmented conversation, was that Hal Hendrix was one of the CIA's most trusted media outlets. We have discussed this incident previously, but further detail is in order given that it seems to reveal a serious effort at obstruction of Kennedy Administration policy.

Since he was running a highly deniable covert operation in one of American's major cities, media access was definitely one of Station Chief Shackley's concerns. Given that anything about Cuba was a major subject of interest in Miami, that seems only reasonable. In April 1962, Shackley reported that he had established a new and successful press relationship with a local media person, stating that the individual would be useful to JM WAVE as a press outlet, especially in regard to "select propaganda items."[358] Documents also reveal that the station had developed a string of media outlets, in an operation designated AMCARBON.

Years later, one of the first AMCARBON reporters would relate that the editor of his paper had actually been directed towards Shackley as a source—compromising Shackley's CIA identity in the process—by none other than William Pawley. He felt that Shackley could be very helpful, since he had fed information about missiles in Cuba to reporter Hal Hendrix. Inside information about Cuban matters had apparently given Hendrix a series of scoops, winning him a Pulitzer Prize.[359] Early leaks about missiles in Cuba, including information passed to one prominent senator who would never name his source, had also been a major political problem for President Kennedy.

Hendrix has also been described as a close personal friend of CIA propaganda specialist David Phillips. A former CIA officer who worked at the JM WAVE station described meeting Phillips in the company of Hendrix during the time he himself had had been living with Hendrix's daughter.[360] The suspicion that Hendrix CIA sources was also well established with his media peers. Scripps Howard News Service writer Seth Kantor wrote that it was well known that if you wanted the scoop on matters relating to anything Cuban, the man with the inside connections was Hendrix. Hendrix was known as "the spook" within the Scripps Howard organization.

If there had been any doubt that Hendrix was close to Shackley, events years later in Chile resolved that issue. Hendrix had worked on a story about cooperation between ITT (International Telephone & Telegraph) and the CIA in organizing a potential coup against Chilean President Salvador Allende. As part of that inquiry, Hendrix had discussed the CIA's activities against Allende with Henry Hecksher, the CIA chief of station in Chile. Hecksher had been very involved in contacts with military officers who were plotting a coup against Allende.[361]

Ultimately individuals supported and armed by covert CIA field officers would assassinate Allende's military chief.[362] That assassination, among others, led to congressional inquiries into CIA activities during the 1970s. During the congressional investigation of CIA activities in Chile, Shackley personally intervened to ensure that Hendrix would say the correct thing—that he would deny to the congressional committee that he had discussed the CIA move against Allende with Hecksher.[363]

Hendrix's stories about Soviet missiles in Cuba, and later about the Artime AMWORLD project, certainly had posed a variety of problems for President Kennedy and his administration's activities. If those leaks had come from CIA officers at the station, it would have been more than an abuse of CIA media access. It would have been something far more serious than simply objecting to administration orders and policies. Rather, it would have been an example of active interference in American foreign policy.[364]

Of course there is no absolute proof of that, but it does illustrate the possibility that on occasion CIA officers such as Shackley might have inserted themselves into areas of policy. In confirmation of that speculation, Don Bohning has written that Hendrix's "Backstage with Bobby" might well have come from CIA sources—specifically from Ted Shackley. It is a serious thing to find indications that highly secret information was intentionally leaked to known CIA media outlets by officers who wished to expose Special Group projects that they considered ill conceived—or even to raise issues that would undermine administration policy. It would be a far greater concern if CIA officers had been involved in an operation with media outlets that, when reported, could have essentially brought down a presidency.

In the winter of 1962, Soviet equipment was still coming out of Cuba in accordance with the Cuban Missile Crisis agreement with the Soviets. At that time a rumor began circulating within Cuban exile circles in Miami. There were already a number of reports and protests that the Russians were cheating on their agreement, hiding missiles in caves and playing a waiting game. Castro's total refusal to allow any UN inspection lent credence to such talk. But the new rumor was much more specific. According to certain anti-Castro insurgents still active on the island, two Soviet officers had contacted them and wanted to defect. In return they offered to reveal details of how the Soviets were cheating on the missile agreement. The officers would provide specifics on hidden rockets and even atomic warheads. Word of their defection had been smuggled out of Cuba through an exile letter chain running through Mexico City and Spain.[365]

It appears that the primary source for the original Soviet officer story came from Cuban exile group Alpha 66 members, in particular Eduardo Perez aka Eddie Bayo. Alpha 66's success in attacks on Soviet targets in Cuba lent some credibility to it having contacts that might provide such intelligence. Those missions had received extensive photojournalism coverage in *Life* magazine. During a variety of meetings in Miami that included reporter Hal Hendrix, the story was essentially shopped to certain conservative political figures. The point man in that political outreach was anti-Castro advocate John Martino.

Arrested in Havana in 1959, Martino had been recently released from prison in Cuba. Martino's release and its coverage in Miami newspapers had given him considerable local visibility as a Cuban exile champion. His story had also served as a focal point for new newspaper stories about Castro's abuses—his imprisonment of innocent people, torture, and executions. Martino served as a firsthand witness to much of that and began working with a conservative ghostwriter, Nathaniel Weyl. He had previously produced *Red Star Over Cuba* and would pen the book on Martino's Cuban experiences, *I Was Castro's Prisoner.* At the time, Weyl was also working on a book with William Pawley.

It appears that Martino's contacts with political conservatives resulted in word of the purported Russian defectors reaching all the way to Senator James Eastland, the highly active anticommunist chair of the Senate Internal Security Subcommittee. Eastland in turn passed the word on to William Pawley, well-known for his ongoing support of anti-Castro activities. Pawley had also been outspoken in media criticism of the Kennedy Administration for being too soft on Castro. Pawley's inquires convinced him that the matter should be aggressively pursued. Obviously, if the Soviets could be extracted from Cuba and put before Eastland's committee, the political damage to the Kennedy Administration would be immense. Demands for military action against Cuba would be extensive. Kennedy's chances for reelection in 1964 likely would become minimal if it was demonstrated that the Russians had fooled him, leaving missiles behind in Cuba—stored or even secretly emplaced.

Given Pawley's high-level national security connections, he felt comfortable taking the matter of the purported Russian defectors both to JM WAVE Station Chief Shackley and to Marshall Carter, deputy director of the CIA. After discussions with Shackley and Carter, Pawley committed himself and his own private yacht to a Cuban mission to bring out the Russian personnel. John Martino also joined the mission and appears to have brought in a number of Alpha 66 personnel, including Eddie Bayo. However, the exiles agreed to participate only if *Life* magazine was brought in to provide coverage of the mission. Such media was a total violation of CIA operational security rules, and nothing of that nature had ever been allowed in any of the missions supported out of the Miami station.

After a complex series of discussions, JM WAVE Chief Shackley and Deputy Director Carter did commit operational CIA personnel from the Miami station to the TILT operation. JM WAVE was represented on the mission by none other than Rip Robertson. Released CIA documents include his after-action mission report on TILT, using Robertson's pseudonym Irving Cadick.[366] A CIA officer who could speak some Russian was also assigned to the mission so that he could do a quick debriefing of the Soviet officers. A considerable number of automatic weapons were provided to the party and it was even agreed that at least two of the exiles could stay behind in Cuba, ostensibly to join rebel groups operating on the island. The navigator and boat guide for the mission was Rolando Eugenio Martinez. Along with Robertson, Martinez was a virtual legend among Cuban exiles based on the number of high-risk missions he had guided into Cuba. Later he would become well-known because of his participation in the Watergate burglary.

One of the more exceptional things about the TILT mission is the extent to which standard CIA security rules were violated. J.C. King accepted an agreement that allowed *Life* magazine to send a news photographer to record the operation. There was also personal communication about the mission with George P. Hunt, *Life* managing editor—with no indication that Hunt had any special security clearance for CIA or for JM WAVE operations. A promise was made that *Life* simply would not mention the CIA in any form in coverage of the operation. Essentially the agreement handed the Russian defector story directly to *Life* magazine—and to Senator Eastland's Internal Affairs subcommittee.

The TILT mission finally came to fruition in June 1963. It was a complex effort, supervised by JM WAVE's chief operations officer, David Morales, involving Pawley's yacht, an aircraft used to ferry in personnel for a rendezvous off Cuba, and the shadowing of the entire operation with search radar coverage by one of the Agency's two highly secret and specially equipped mother ships, the *Leda*.[367] A full shipload of heavily armed and supplied fighters, including Bayo himself, was sent in towards the beach; the boat never returned and from that point on no further contact was ever made with the team.[368] No reports ever came out of Cuba on Bayo or his team members; seemingly, if they had been killed or captured it would have been headline news within Cuba. Pawley himself later speculated that the craft might have been lost at sea not long after launch. Yet an after-action report from a CIA operations office on Pawley's yacht describes a smooth launch, with no problems with the seas. It states that a radio check was conducted with the team's boat some twenty minutes after departure.[369]

William Turner has written that "[i]n 1995 ex-Cuban security chief General Fabian Escalante told me that Bayo's boat was found swamped near Baracoa, but there were no signs of its occupants."[370] In addition, interviews with Bayo's wife revealed that she was aware of the mission but that her husband had given her no indication that he would not be returning shortly; she felt sure that if he had intended to go into Cuba for an extended stay he would have told her.[371] The author's current belief is that Bayo's boat may have foundered at some point, being overloaded with both weapons and people.

Aside from its apparent security violations, perhaps the most interesting thing about the TILT mission is that as far as currently available documents indicate, there seems to be no record that it was discussed within the Special Group or the Special Group Augmented. There is no confirmation that Robert Kennedy or the president was aware of the mission or that it had any sort of official clearance other than that of Pawley's longtime personal friend, Western Hemisphere Chief J.C. King. There is also no sign it was coordinated in advance with the new Cuban Special Affairs Staff (SAS) under Desmond FitzGerald. One document, from July 26, 1963, indicates that the SAS chief was copied on TILT information, but only after the fact; the copy includes a full background review on how the project came about and all reference documents are dated post-mission.[372]

That lack of administration approval is especially striking given the level of Robert Kennedy's involvement in Cuban operations, the firing of former Mongoose Project CIA team leader William Harvey for authorizing boat missions into Cuba without RFK or Special Group permission, and Shackley's own comments about even minor missions requiring authorization. It is even harder to understand given the operational participation of a former U.S. ambassador who had served as part of a unique presidential team evaluating U.S. national security in respect to all of America's intelligence services. Pawley had gone into Cuban waters with a boatload of heavily armed Cuban exiles and CIA paramilitary officers. His possible capture or death at the hands of Cuban forces would have had international consequences.

It seems virtually impossible for the senior CIA officers involved with TILT not to have appreciated the political consequences of bringing out a pair of Russian missile officers and handing them over to a Senate subcommittee whose chair was notoriously critical of Kennedy Administration actions in Cuba. While that was occurring, *Life* magazine could well have been running national stories on the entire affair, complete with extensive photographic coverage. The missile crisis and autonomous group press stories became some of the first signs that intentional leaks from within the Agency could create difficulties for presidential policies and politics. The TILT affair is one of the few known instances in which an entire covert operation might have been conducted with the knowledge that a successful result could effectively unseat a sitting president.

The evolution of a massive covert intelligence and operations complex did not go without question, even within the CIA itself. In 1962 the Agency's legal counsel prepared a statement for the record stating that there was no "statutory authorization" for covert operations but there was also no explicit prohibition. The 1947 law creating the CIA had contained no reference to paramilitary operations, and the reference to "other duties and functions" had been specifically in terms of intelligence activities, not military operations. Specifically the legal opinion noted that it would be stretching that section too far to include a Guatemala or a Cuba even though intelligence and counterintelligence are essential to such activities. Its overall assessment on covert warfare was even more succinct: the executive branch, under the direction of the president, was acting without specific statutory authorization, and the CIA was simply the agent being directed to conduct such actions.

Beyond the question of legal authorization, the only argument that CIA counsel could make towards congressional approval for covert action was that Congress appropriated money for the CIA knowing that some of it would be spent for clandestine activities. But even with those approvals, Congress had no specific knowledge of any covert action beyond those communicated to specific committees and senior congressional leaders. In expressing its doubts about the legal basis for the new covert warfare complex, the CIA essentially kicked the ball back to the president; it was doing as ordered and the legality of the matter was the president's issue.

But issues of the legality of covert operations seem quite tame when compared to the reality and unanticipated consequences of certain Agency activities. As a mild example, one of the functions of Staff D of the Directorate of Plans/Operations was to obtain information related to foreign communications. In real-world terms that often meant stealing code books, cryptographic lists, and related materials from foreign governments. Staff D hired professional safecrackers and burglars, true criminal professionals. We encountered a couple of its European employees in the Lumumba poisoning fiasco in the Congo. Domestically, its employees were well-known to the FBI. Their travel had to be reported to the Bureau, possibly in the event of other suspicious burglaries that might suggest they were engaging in private activities on the trips.[373]

Involvement with burglars and safecrackers is one thing—even if your employees are professional criminals. Involvement with organized crime in the United States would escalate the issue of illegality exponentially. And that is exactly what happened to the CIA in the earliest days of the secret war against Cuba. Based on extensive congressional inquiry we now know that in the early days of the first Cuba project, the CIA's office of security facilitated an approach to a Las Vegas gambling figure, John Roselli, who had been deeply involved with the casino business in Havana before the Castro revolution.

The CIA felt that someone like Roselli, with connections to a host of former Havana figures, could provide them with contacts to be used to assassinate Fidel Castro. In their initial approach to Roselli, CIA liaison officers suggested a typical mob-style shooting contract on Castro, nice and simple. Roselli rebuffed them, and in the end it was agreed he would organize an effort to poison Castro. The next step was a meeting in Miami to work out the logistics and meet the individuals Roselli would recruit for the job. Roselli brought to the meeting two individuals who would support the effort, and the deal was done. Unfortunately for the CIA, it would learn later that the two men in question were in reality Sam Giancana, and Santo Trafficante Jr., major organized crime syndicate godfathers from Chicago and Florida.

The FBI became aware of the CIA's association with two of its major organized crime targets and ultimately raised the issue directly with Attorney General Robert Kennedy. Kennedy was extremely upset with the news and ordered that no such activities should be undertaken in the future. Based on available records it appears he was not told that the project had actually been restarted as part of the new Mongoose project. The full extent of the CIA involvement in assassinations and Mafia contacts was known to only a handful of senior CIA officers, who sometimes seem to have attempted to shield it even from one another. We will return to additional consequences of the association with criminal figures, in particular drug smugglers, in later chapters; however, it's safe to say that this sort of consequence was something never anticipated by President Truman when he signed the National Security Act in 1947.

By the early 1960s, a certain level of national concern was growing over the possibility that the CIA had become so autonomous that it was actually beginning to interfere with national policy. Political events in Southeast Asia during the Kennedy Administration had raised the question of whether CIA personnel might sometimes be working at odds with administration policy or in a manner inconsistent with the other government departments—in particular the State Department. Even the media had raised the issue of whether or not CIA activities might be compromising State Department activity and administration policy in Vietnam.

Arthur Krock, writing for *The New York Times,* had raised the issue that the Agency was involved in an "Intra-Administration War" in Vietnam.[374] Krock said that there were good sources reporting from Vietnam that at least twice the CIA had flatly refused to carry out instructions from American ambassador to Vietnam Henry Cabot Lodge. Beyond that, in one instance the CIA had "frustrated a plan of action that Mr. Lodge brought from Washington because the agency disagreed with it." Krock's article referred to the situation as "disorderly government," and maintained that the president had already tolerated the situation for too long. The article concluded by noting that there was no way to absolutely verify the details of the situation, but that it certainly appeared that certain CIA officers were inserting themselves into policy matters normally the business of the State Department and the president.

It is certainly not difficult to find instances of policy disagreement and conflict between CIA field officers and U.S. ambassadors or State Department personnel. Such disagreements even occurred under the Eisenhower Administration. In Latin America, the initial Guatemala covert operation had come to a screeching halt over State Department objections about not being properly briefed—even when state was in agreement with the concept of an operation against Guatemala.

Later, in Laos, CIA officer John Hasey, who adamantly advocated support for a particular Laotian strongman, was booted out of the country—"transferred at request" in more politically correct language—at the initiative of Assistant Secretary of State Averell Harriman. The transfer occurred only after strong objections from regional CIA officers Desmond FitzGerald and William Colby. In fact, FitzGerald had specifically directed Hasey to cultivate the individual in question. When chided for being out of sync with the State Department, Hasey reportedly said, "I don't give a damn what they say!"[375] Hasey's actual boss at the time was none other than Henry Heckshеr, whose independent attitudes we noted earlier. Later the U.S. ambassador to Laos asked that Heckshеr be removed from his position, only to have Allen Dulles flatly refuse the State Department request.

Clearly the State Department sometimes felt that CIA personnel were acting on their own agendas. For an ambassador to Laos to request that the CIA chief of station in Laos be removed for acting against official policy and to have the director of the CIA refuse the ambassador's request is quite a dramatic turn of events. By the end of 1963, former President Harry Truman, who had signed the

National Security Act of 1947, was also beginning to question the conduct of the CIA. Truman had reached the conclusion that the operational side of the CIA had developed in a manner that he and his associates had not anticipated, and he was not happy about it. Changes needed to be made. At the end of 1963 the national press carried a public letter from Truman; the letter called for limiting the CIA's role strictly to intelligence collection and analysis.[376] While Truman was clearly concerned about the operational roles that had evolved within the CIA, there were also issues with the independence of the Agency as a whole: "For some time I have been disturbed by the way CIA has been diverted from its original assignment. It has become an operational and at times a policy-making arm of the Government. This has led to trouble and may have compounded our difficulties in several explosive areas."

Truman's concerns were specifically about the issue of "peacetime cloak and dagger operations" that added an air of "sinister and mysterious foreign intrigue" to America's international image. He felt strongly that the CIA's covert actions might be seen as a "subverting influence in the affairs of other nations," enabling the country's enemies to score propaganda victories, painting the U.S. as imperialist and willing to exploit other nations for its own capitalist interests. Truman seemed to fear that the CIA had actually become an operational arm of government, appearing at times to actually be taking policy making upon itself. And certainly the CIA and the overall national security complex had grown tremendously, with expenditure far beyond anything originally anticipated, yet intentionally obscured by "black budgeting," supposedly for operational security but so convoluted that even Congress would not be able to follow the money. There is evidence that the CIA had acquired sufficient media reach and power that its officers could personally obstruct presidential policy and perhaps even politically endanger presidential administrations. With the basic legality of covert operations still in question, the CIA had even become involved with major Mafia godfathers in foreign assassination programs. Certainly there were more than enough issues in play to justify Truman's second thoughts. And as of 1963, a further consequence of the intelligence community's mysterious and somewhat sinister behavior was emerging—even private citizens with "shadow warfare" connections were becoming afraid of what might be going on in the shadows.

Garrett Underhill was such an individual, close enough to shadow warfare activities to gain insights into many of the CIA's secret operations in the early 1960s. Underhill was a Harvard graduate who had made a career in the field of military weapons. Prior to the Second World War, from 1938 to 1942, he had worked for David Cort at *Life* magazine as a specialist on weaponry and military affairs. Cort had lobbied to keep him out of the draft during WWII, describing Underhill as the world's number-one expert on military weaponry and key to *Life*'s accurate coverage of the war. Cort also described Underhill as being key to the magazine's military intelligence collection and making a serious contribution in lobbying for rearmament prior to the war.

In spite of that plea, Underhill was called to serve in army intelligence for two and a half years, working as a technical and weapons evaluation specialist. He received a War Department citation for superior work and was released in May 1946.[377] Reportedly Underhill's military views had a significant impact on *Life*'s coverage of the war and on publisher Henry Luce's views of both World War II and Korea.[378]

Following the war, Underhill worked as an analyst and contributor for a number of national publications and information bureaus, including *Esquire*, *The Washington Post*, *Collier's*, and *Fortune*. He also served as a consultant to an army coordinating group. In the 1950s Underhill became personally associated with none other than Samuel Cummings, familiar to us for his beginnings in the CIA; his involvement in many of the earliest covert warfare operations, from Burma to Guatemala; and his 1963 involvement in arming the Artime operation. During the 1950s, Underhill had occasional contact with the CIA, once reporting an individual who had come to him with photos of Russian weapons while he was working for *Collier's*. In 1957, the CIA Office of Security requested security background checks on Underhill. The CIA study also confirmed that Underhill had been associated with Cummings on Interarmco, remarking it as a significant possible exposure for the Agency because of his and the company's services for the Agency.[379]

In 1963, Garrett Underhill worked for the Washington, D.C., bureau of *Fortune* magazine in the areas of military, defense, and intelligence under Charles Murphy. A close friend, Asher Brynes of the *New Republic,* reported that one of Underhill's main interests in 1963 was the Russian missiles that had been placed in Cuba. Underhill felt that the Kennedy Administration story was not the full truth and that there was still an outstanding mystery in regard to the missiles.[380] We can only speculate on what sources Underhill may have approached in pursuit of that interest, and wonder if he crossed the paths of those involved with the TILT operation.

The day following President Kennedy's assassination, Garrett Underhill showed up at the house of friends in New York City; they were packing to leave for a trip overseas but he had time to discuss what he had learned about a "clique" within the CIA—a clique dealing with weapons and gun-running and making money for itself. The individuals involved had Asian connections. He also mentioned narcotics dealing, as it was his understanding that individuals in the clique were manipulating regional politics to serve their own ends. Underhill was frightened that those individuals had been involved with JFK's murder; he felt that JFK had become aware of their dealings and was about to move against them in some fashion.[381] At the time, his friends, the Fitzsimmonses, were totally baffled by Underhill's remarks. Later, Robert Fitzsimmons remarked that the reason they had not taken Underhill seriously was that "we couldn't believe that the CIA could contain a corrupt element every bit as ruthless—and much more efficient—than the Mafia."

In May 1964, Underhill was found dead in his apartment. His apartment door was unlocked, and he was found in bed, killed by a single shot behind his left ear. The weapon used was one of his personal pistols. The pistol was found under the left side of his body. The police investigation was minimal and the coroner reported the death as a suicide. His friends pointed out several issues with that verdict; they felt his death to be suspicious.

Underhill's emotions may have been exaggerated by a recent marital problem. However, his core fear seems to have come from dialogues and inquiries involving missiles still in Cuba and news of a new round of covert weapons activities in progress with his friend Sam Cummings—most likely the weapons destined for the Artime project. Underhill had been talking to people who were clearly saying some very bad things about certain individuals working in and alongside CIA covert operations.

The bottom line is that as early as 1963 Garrett Underhill, most definitely someone in a position to hear insider information and very possibly knowledgeable of *Life*'s participation in the TILT mission, came to fear that a "dark side" of covert operations existed. He was expressing the same fears and concerns about rogue CIA activities, including murder and drugs, that we will see emerge more and more frequently during the late 1960s and 1970s. And he was afraid that a clique of CIA officers and their associates might even have become powerful enough to kill an American president and get away with it. Underhill was not the only individual to have such suspicions or to express such fears. Polls in later years would show that a majority of the American public believed there had been some element of conspiracy at work in President Kennedy's assassination. Ultimately two well-known CIA officers, David Phillips and Howard Hunt, would state that American intelligence officers had indeed been involved in the Kennedy assassination, with Hunt specifically naming David Morales.

CHAPTER 15

Congressional Intervention

At President Johnson's request, in 1964 Congress passed legislation authorizing additional military assistance for Southeast Asian mutual defense pact partners.[382] The resolution was passed after two incidents in the Gulf of Tonkin in which it appeared that North Vietnamese boats had attacked American destroyers in international waters. One of the main goals of the legislation was to ensure that American forces had the authority to adequately defend themselves. We discussed issues relating to what came to be known as the Gulf of Tonkin Resolution early in this book, in regard to presidential character and personalities. Regardless of any issues about the destroyer attacks or Johnson's decision it is certainly unlikely that the majority of Congress would have assumed that single resolution would be used by Presidents Johnson and Nixon as the sole legal justification for almost a decade of full-scale conventional warfare in South Vietnam against North Vietnam, as well as massive covert warfare actions in both Laos and Cambodia.

The Tonkin Gulf Resolution authorized the president "to take all necessary steps, including the use of armed force, to assist any member or protocol state of the Southeast Asia Collective Defense Treaty requesting assistance in defense of its freedom." Neither Laos nor Cambodia had officially requested such an action, and the United States itself maintained a position of neutrality in regard to the affairs of both nations. As we have seen, in its own declared position and the official positions of both Laos and Cambodia, the U.S. was faced with the reality of major North Vietnamese supply routes running through neutral countries into South Vietnam. As combat escalated, the Laotian route also began to be used to move large, well-equipped regular North Vietnamese Army formations into the south. Yet despite that obvious fact and despite years of covert warfare in both Laos and Cambodia, neither President Johnson nor President Nixon requested further resolutions from Congress, much less declarations of war. In retrospect it appears that Congress had simply allowed itself to be removed from both the overt and covert warfare decision-making process.

Beginning in 1967 and increasingly in 1968, the combat in Southeast Asia had become a major American domestic political issue. Calls for repeal of the Tonkin Gulf Resolution, which was being characterized as a "blank check," had begun. Even within Congress there were second thoughts about the passage of the original resolution. A Senate Foreign Relations Committee inquiry surfaced more information about the original incidents in the Tonkin Gulf, including early indications in ships' messages that the critical North Vietnamese second attack had not actually occurred. The justification for the resolution came under even stronger criticism as more details emerged. In 1971, journalist Eugene Windchy's book-length study of the Tonkin Gulf incidents made a strong case for the Johnson Administration having suppressed evidence that no second North Vietnamese attack had actually been made in the Gulf of Tonkin, and raised serious questions about the facts presented to justify Johnson's request for a congressional resolution.[383]

The Nixon Administration initially opposed repeal of the Tonkin Gulf Resolution. Nixon wished to preserve his overt military options, while at the same time dramatically escalating the scale of covert military engagement in both Laos and Cambodia. Under continued pressure, Nixon then maintained that even if the resolution were repealed, the president, as commander in chief, had full authority to take any actions necessary to protect deployed American troops. Given the administration's shift to a policy of "Vietnamization"—handing off actual ground combat to South Vietnamese forces—and beginning troop withdrawals, Nixon's altered position allowed continued American military involvement, even after the Tonkin Gulf Resolution was repealed by Congress in 1971. Congress continued to reassert its role of approving American military action and in the early 1970s it was supported by widespread public concern on that issue.

Initially, the Nixon Administration had given the appearance of accepting the call for congressional approval of covert actions. Early in 1970, Nixon signed a directive that changed the name of the covert action approvals group to the 40 Committee (the existing 303 Committee had been named in press reports) and added the attorney general to membership in the group, which included Assistant to the President for National Security Affairs Henry Kissinger, Secretary of Defense Melvin Laird, CIA Director Richard Helms, United States Army Chief General William Westmoreland, and other administration principals. The exact reason for that move is not known but it seems to reflect Nixon's well-known political sensitivities, and essentially did add an element of legal review to the approvals process. Nixon's directives made it clear that the CIA's director was to bear responsibility for coordination, control, and conduct of covert operations, but needed to obtain 40 Committee approval for all major and "politically sensitive" covert operations.

While such moves appeared to be positive, the problem that quickly emerged (only one of a number of Nixon Administration trust issues), was that not all major operations were brought to the 40 Committee, and within months, Nixon began ordering a series of CIA operations against Chilean President Salvador Allende. That operation was not taken to the 40 Committee or through any type of oversight or congressional approvals process.[384] Concern over the lack of congressional oversight in the Southeast Asian conflict, combined with new issues of Nixon Administration mistrust, led to a number of related congressional inquiries and investigations. The net outcome of it all was an ongoing push to establish effective congressional oversight over both intelligence agency activities and covert military action. In an effort to formalize and force a process of congressional consultation in regard to presidential commitments to military action, Congress passed the War Powers Resolution of 1973. That legislation mandated presidential consultation with Congress in regard to any decision that would place regular American military forces into actual or even imminent hostilities.[385] President Nixon attempted to veto the measure but it was passed by both houses of Congress over his objection. In addition to that measure, which primarily addressed the overt deployment of the military, members of Congress proposed legislation that would have added additional oversight and approval to the types of covert actions initially authorized by the National Security Act of 1947. The legal code associated with that act established the legal parameters of authorization and oversight of covert warfare.[386] The new effort towards congressional intervention in the covert warfare process involved a series of bills introduced between 1974 and 1980. Senator Harold Hughes, who joined in introduction of the legislation, asserted that additional legal requirements were needed to ensure that military, intelligence, or national security personnel could not conduct operations without full knowledge of the president. He had become especially sensitive to that issue while serving as a member of the Senate Armed Services Committee, which investigated Air Force and Navy air actions against Laos and Cambodia. The committee had found evidence that orders and post-action reports had been falsified to conceal the fact that the combat was being conducted against neutral nations rather than in South Vietnam. Reportedly the orders and approval for concealment had come directly from the White House, although not necessarily from the president. We will revisit Senator Hughes's concerns over full presidential knowledge of covert operations in our later discussion of President Reagan and Nicaragua.

The 1974 Hughes–Ryan Amendment to the Foreign Assistance Act of 1961 required that the president report all covert operations of the CIA to one or more congressional committees within a set time limit. The president was also required to certify that each funded operation was critical to national security. Acknowledging the process by which earlier actions were either hidden in the CIA's own unvouchered funds or simply authorized by Department of Defense committee or subcommittee budget requests, the Hughes–Ryan Amendment prohibited appropriated monies to be used for covert operations without a specific finding being submitted by the president to the appropriate congressional committee. Initially six committees were designated. Two more were added at a later date, leaving a total of some two hundred legislators and staff required to be briefed prior to any clandestine operation. By the mid-1970s, with the Ford Administration in charge, Congress had not only assumed a new level of legal oversight over covert operations but had oversight with some financial teeth—tied to actual funding of such operations. At least for a time, if Congress chose to do so, it had the tools in place to actually involve itself in the president's decisions to engage in covert warfare. During the Reagan Administration we will see that initially, in regard to new covert warfare projects in both Africa and Central America, Congress did assert itself and constrain presidential action—up to the point when the administration moved the whole practice of covert warfare outside the box that Congress had established.

As we saw in the Congo, the rise of nationalism and a general push for an end to colonial control raised a real fear that newly independent regimes would be easily influenced and taken under control of the communist bloc. That was not a new worldview, as it emerged immediately after the Second World War, triggering American's first covert actions in Asia and Latin America. The situation in Africa was especially difficult for the United States (as it had been in Indochina for the French), since colonial powers such as Belgium and Portugal were members of the North Atlantic Treaty Organization (NATO) and blocking Soviet expansion in Europe had been a bedrock American strategic priority since the beginning of the Cold War. Historically, America's policy-level approach to Africa had been grounded in the Eisenhower Administration's overriding strategic commitment to the European powers in regard to Cold War confrontation with the Soviets. There was also the issue of Eisenhower's own personal caution in regard to the wave of nationalism and anticolonialist movements sweeping the globe following the end of the Second World War. Eisenhower described the advent of the African independence movements as a "destructive hurricane." And his assistant secretary of state warned, "Premature independence and irresponsible nationalism may present grave dangers to dependent peoples."[387]

Despite Eisenhower's concerns, it would actually be John Kennedy and his administration that faced the challenge of openly taking a policy position on independence movements across Africa. As early as 1956, while still a senator, Kennedy had had taken a radically different position on how the U.S. should act (if a Democratic administration were in office) in regard to African independence movements: "We shall no longer abstain in the UN from voting on colonial issues, we shall no longer trade our vote on other such issues for other supposed gains. We shall no longer seek to prevent subjugated peoples from being heard."[388] By 1961, an escalating wave of nationalist fervor, violence, and extreme responses by the Portuguese military had moved colonialism in Angola (along with the Congo) upward on the list of Kennedy Administration geopolitical issues. Angola was not as high up on the list as Cuba, Laos, and Vietnam, but it was significant enough to bring the new president into direct conflict with Portugal's seventy-two-year-old leader, António Salazar. Salazar had declared that "no quarter" would be given to agitators in Portugal's extremely profitable African colony.

Yet despite his own personal sympathies, and his dramatically different view of colonialism and nationalism in Africa, Kennedy was forced to face the basic fact that Portugal was not only a member of NATO but a militarily vital part of that strategic alliance. U.S. air bases in the Portuguese Azores islands were considered absolutely vital to the American Air Force, enabling the Strategic Air Command to project American nuclear power across both Europe and the Middle East. The Lajes complex of air bases in the Azores were key to military air supply routes across the Atlantic and had been a critical asset in enabling American military intervention in Lebanon in 1958, the reinforcement of Berlin in 1961, and U.S. engagement in the Congo in 1960–61. The Joint Chiefs insisted that the bases were indispensable, pointing out that the Lajes base complex was a vital element of the American early-warning system and that its antisubmarine capabilities were also critical—indeed they would play a key role in 1962, monitoring Russian submarines moving towards Cuba at the time of the Cuban Missile Crisis. The military value of the Portuguese-controlled Azores bases simply could not be ignored.

In turn, Prime Minister Salazar, made it clear that any U.S. move to endorse a transition to independence in its colony of Angola—especially if it meant voting in favor of such a proposal at the UN—would be regarded as a dramatic change in American policy and would jeopardize Americans' welcome in the Azores. In response to Salazar, Kennedy turned to the U.S. military assistance mission to Portugal, and the option for imposition of conditions on American weaponry and supplies being provided to the Portuguese government. Perhaps all equipment purchased from the U.S. could be required to be used solely within NATO and not in any fashion applied to combat in Angola. The use of American military materials, supplied to Portugal as a NATO member but used by the Portuguese against Angolan rebels, had been noted by a number of foreign observers. NBC News had threatened to air a special on the subject, including the Portuguese use of American-supplied napalm in Angola.[389]

American John Marcum, who had visited National Front for the Liberation of Angola (FNLA) insurgent camps, had watched Portuguese planes bomb and strafe villages. He copied information from 750-pound napalm bomb cases, which carried stickers reading, "Property of U.S Air Force."[390] Ultimately the Kennedy initiative to restrict the use of American-supplied weaponry was undermined by the terms of the Eisenhower Administration's military assistance agreement with Portugal. The agreement stipulated that there would be no "prior consent" usage approval related to the arms sales. Actually invoking such a threat could provide grounds for Portugal to cancel its treaties with the U.S., including the Azores lease.

As an alternative, in 1961 the National Security Council, under personal pressure from Robert Kennedy, authorized a very small covert funding to Holden Roberto, an Angolan anticolonial leader.[391] As would often be the case, covertly giving financial support of any sort to insurgents leads them to use it to their own political advantage, immediately claiming strong American backing. It did not take long for word of the payments to come to Portuguese attention, further exacerbating Portuguese views about American meddling. After a series of continuing diplomatic exchanges, President Kennedy was forced to face the fact that Portugal was in position to stonewall the Angolan issue based on the strategic value of the U.S. presence in the Azores.

In response to an ongoing list of Portuguese complaints in regard to the United States meddling in its affairs, Washington was forced to respond that "Our efforts . . . are not designed to force Portugal to leave Africa but to encourage measures which we are convinced are necessary to enable her to stay and complete work which she has begun."[392] Sensing the American dilemma, Portugal further hardened its position by not only refusing to support the U.S. during the Cuban Missile Crisis but by allowing the Azores lease to expire with no renewal. They would only allow its use to continue on a day-to-day basis. In the end, by the fall of 1962, the Kennedy Administration was forced to accept the status quo in Angola, making no further moves to support international calls for Portugal to give independence to Angola. America's use of the air bases in the Azores would again become a major issue in 1973, following American support for Israel in that country's Yom Kippur War of that year. Only Portugal, the Netherlands, and Germany had supported the U.S. resupply operation to Israel, and air shipments had been dependent upon the Lajes base. With the importance of the Azores bases once again highlighted, Portugal waged a major diplomatic campaign with the U.S. for more and better weapons, and the end to any objections to the weapons being used in Africa, especially in Angola.

In general, the policies of the Nixon Administration and of Nixon's National Security Advisor Henry Kissinger[393] were much more in line with the earliest Cold War anticommunist dialectic than with the more pragmatic worldview of the Kennedy Administration—especially in regard to the threat of communism taking over African independence movements. Kissinger tended to be very nervous about African nationalism, and particularly any insurgencies tainted by support from communist or even neutral nations. In line with that view, Kissinger was very supportive of providing arms to Portugal for use in Angola, to counter Soviet shipments to insurgents battling for independence from Portuguese colonial rule. When his staff argued the negative effects of such a move on overall African relations, Kissinger chided them for being "too sensitive."

While Kissinger may not have been concerned about African sensitivities, he was quite aware that after its Southeast Asian experience, Congress was indeed sensitive about American covert action. Convincing Congress to provide yet more arms to Portugal, to quell insurgencies in Angola, proved to be a tough sell. But as we will see, Kissinger was not one to be easily boxed in by Congress; he immediately began to pursue other options ranging from presidential action to third-party weapons transactions—it would not be the first time he would turn to traditional CIA practices as an option, even without the CIA itself being involved. We have no idea where that particular effort might have led because the following year, 1974, a new Portuguese government came into power; Salazar was out and the new regime proved eager to work out a quick colonial exit plan for Angola.[394]

In April 1974, Secretary of State Kissinger directed a comprehensive review of "Military Assistance and Arms Policy in Black Africa" by the NSC Interdepartmental Group for Africa. The report was to be submitted in May for presidential review.[395] Among the points to be addressed in the study was military assistance and its potential effects on African insurgencies—as well as a review of congressional limitations on all levels and types of military aid. As produced, the report made no special mention of Angola. More specifically it made no mention of the fact that certain insurgent groups inside Angola had already been receiving covert American support, or the fact that

Zaire (previously the Congo) was actively training and supporting rebel forces fighting against the colonial regime in Angola.[396]

Either the NSC study group did not have all the facts, or perhaps security prevented the facts from going into an official report. In any event, such apparent gaps once again illustrate the difficulty in tracing the chronology of covert military involvement in Angola. At the point when the formal Black Africa policy report went to President Nixon, both the State Department and the CIA should have been quite aware that Zaire was training and supporting selected Angolan independence groups—in particular the FNLA forces of Holden Roberto. As noted earlier, Roberto had received token U.S. monies over a decade earlier, during the Kennedy Administration. But in the summer of 1974, the CIA began a new round of payments to Roberto and the FNLA insurgency, without approval of the 40 Committee, and with a public American policy of neutrality in effect.[397] It would be one of several instances in which the Nixon Administration bypassed its own covert action oversight committee.

The Portuguese regime change dramatically accelerated events in Angola and in January 1975, the Alvor Agreement granted and established a timetable for Angolan independence; in addition it provided for power sharing among the regional insurgencies and factions inside the country. Unfortunately, in a pattern quite similar to earlier events in the Congo, each faction immediately dedicated itself to enlarging its own territorial control to try to strengthen its position in claiming a leadership role in a new national government. The immediate result, as in the Congo, was that the bloody anticolonial fighting, which had been going on for over a decade, escalated into full-scale combat among the Angolans themselves.

Although there were numerous factions and tribal forces, essentially three major groups entered into civil warfare in Angola—each backed by foreign support that positioned them as surrogates in the ongoing Cold War between the Eastern and Western blocs. The People's Movement for the Liberation of Angola (MPLA) and the National Union for the Total Independence of Angola (UNITA) both claimed socialist principles, yet the MPLA openly appealed for foreign support from Marxist-Leninist–oriented regimes including Cuba and the Soviet Union, while UNITA declared itself aggressively anticommunist, ultimately accepting support from not only the United States but also South Africa, generally regarded with outright hostility by many African nations due to its aggressive apartheid racial policies. The MPLA was primarily an urban faction, with its power base in the country's capital of Luanda. Its control of Luanda provided it with a claim to represent a national government.

A third major faction, the National Front for the Liberation of Angola (FNLA), also took an anticommunist position, receiving overt support from neighboring Zaire and covert support from the United States using military assistance to Zaire. This was used as a cover to channel money, weapons, and other support to the FNLA, which established bases inside Zaire while actively engaging in combat against the MPLA inside Angola. The FNLA as well as UNITA were basically rural movements; both faced the fact that in addition to controlling major territory, ultimately they would have to seize control of the capital to assert a claim to being a national government. Ultimately Zaire and the United States would come to the aid of the FNLA in that effort, while UNITA would be supported by the United States and independently by South Africa. In turn the MPLA would defend its position and control of the capital with Soviet military aid and eventually a major deployment of Cuban army brigades dispatched by Fidel Castro.

Virtually all sources are in agreement that, at the highest levels of American government, it was Secretary of State Kissinger who began applying pressure for significant U.S. involvement in Angola. It was also Kissinger who eventually forced the CIA into a 1975 full-scale paramilitary operation to oust the MPLA from the capital in Luanda and establish an anticommunist national government. His position appears to have been based in both a general need to preserve American "great nation" status—maintaining the superpower confrontation with the Soviets across Africa—and an equal need to demonstrate "will and determination" following the fall of South Vietnam. Kissinger was outspoken on the need to maintain America's image: "Look, a great country that cannot give military aid in these revolutionary situations is going to become irrelevant."[398] And he was clearly concerned that aggressive action was needed to counter the American defeat by communist powers in Vietnam: "In addition to our substantive interest in the outcome [in Angola] playing an active role would demonstrate that events in Southeast Asia have not lessened our determination to protect our interests . . . at a time of great uncertainty over our will and determination."[399]

Clearly Kissinger was going to be pushing towards covert intervention in Angola, but months before that would occur he personally obtained approval from the 40 Committee to go ahead and send $265,000 to Holden Roberto, the leader of the FNLA movement. The money was supposed to give Roberto leverage in securing a position in any central government power-sharing agreement. Roberto took it to mean something else entirely and, just as he had years earlier with small payments from Robert Kennedy, began to claim full American support. President Ford was briefed on the evolving Angolan situation—the inability of the insurgent factions to compromise on a joint central government and the escalation in clashes between their members—in an NSC meeting of June 27, 1975. The discussion included three major American options in Angola: a) neutrality, b) diplomacy, and c) "active support."[400]

It was noted that failure to act assertively could lead to loss of confidence by President Mobutu in neighboring Zaire. There was little doubt that Mobutu wanted to have a major influence with any new Angolan regime, for political reasons and to ensure support in opposing tribal factions within Angola routinely making incursions into the border regions of Zaire. Mobutu was also continuing his own ongoing requests to the U.S. for more and newer aircraft and weapons, and consistently playing China and other potential sponsors as leverage in dialogues with U.S. representatives. Discussion of active support has been redacted from the NSC meeting record but the result of dialogue was Ford's directive to the CIA to produce an operations proposal.

The full decision-making process for going covert in Angola is not revealed in currently available U.S. government materials. As with the Congo and other African interventions, the State Department is still holding documents that might shed more light on matters. In fact, certain articles directly relevant to this study have been removed from the State Department's history site, to "ensure accuracy and clarity," and are now temporarily unavailable.[401] Certainly the decision for a covert solution would have reflected concern over congressional opposition as well as international opposition to any overt meddling in the emergence of a new African nation. One clue, as we detail below, may be in the fact that the presidential finding provided to Congress did not even specify Angola as the target of a new African covert operation—that may reflect that Kissinger was indeed more sensitive to Congress than to the Africans.

What we do know is that a CIA memorandum stated that it was understood that Secretary Kissinger favored a $14 million commitment to an Angola project, with an emphasis on material support to the anticommunist factions. The memo also noted that Assistant Secretary of State for African Affairs Nathaniel Davis opposed any covert action program in Angola. The description of Davis's position and the strength of his opposition to covert action appear to have been quite accurate given that when Kissinger rejected his proposal for a diplomatic initiative, Davis resigned.[402] Davis certainly has not been the only person to question Kissinger's "Cold War" view of the civil war in Angola. In his study of the Angolan war, investigative reporter and journalist Jonathan Kwitny writes that "one really has to question the sanity of someone who looks at an ancient tribal dispute over control of distant coffee fields and sees in it a Soviet threat to the security of the United States."[403]

Under pressure from Kissinger, CIA Director William Colby promised a covert operations plan by early July 1975, but had not delivered one as of the 40 Committee meeting on July 13. Kissinger then gave Colby forty-eight hours to produce an operation. On July 17, President Ford approved Operation IA-FEATURE for Angola.[404] By June 27, 1975, the first planeload of American arms was on its way towards Zaire, where it would be transported by

Zairian aircraft to the U.S.-backed rebels inside Angola. Given the requirements of the new agreement with Congress for set rules of engagement in covert warfare, President Ford did indeed submit a "findings" statement in support of the operation. His compliance seems to have been less than wholehearted, as the statement itself made no specific mention of Angola or gave any detail, simply referring to the need for a new national security action in Africa. CIA Director Colby did, in accordance with the Hughes–Ryan oversight legislation, notify the Senate Foreign Relations Committee, the House Armed Services Committee, the Special Subcommittee on Intelligence, Emerging Threats and Capabilities of the House Armed Services Committee, and the Defense Subcommittee of the House Appropriations Committee.[405]

In a broad sense, much of the covert warfare operation in Angola appears quite reminiscent of the early years of deniable warfare in Laos—before full-scale war in Vietnam altered it into something much more conventional. The general U.S. goal in Angola was to avoid a communist-dominated central government. U.S. military aid to Angola would be going to its preferred anticommunist factions—primarily Roberto's FNLA, which operated in the north of the country and out of bases in Zaire—as well as to a third, smaller anti-MPLA group primarily located in the south of Angola, UNITA, led by Jonas Savimbi. Most of the military aid would go covertly into Angola via Zaire, in much the same manner—although again on a much smaller scale—that military aid to American surrogates in Laos had gone in though Thailand. Zaire had previously been heavily involved in training and supporting the FNLA just as Thai advisors had worked with tribal groups in Laos. And significant numbers of Zairian military would actively engage in combat in Angola, just as Thai volunteers had increasingly been involved in combat in Laos. Ultimately the U.S.-supported rebel groups in Angola would simply be outgunned and numerically overwhelmed by a far superior Cuban/MPLA force, much as massive intervention by the North Vietnamese Army had overwhelmed U.S. tribal surrogates in Laos.

Angola clearly demonstrates the same escalating cycle of military action that we saw in Laos, although in Angola, the cycle was extremely compressed and involved a considerable number of third-party country sponsors, with the list changing every few months over a two-year period. Initially the three major Angolan political factions were all represented in the Angolan capital of Luanda, even though the city was politically a solid stronghold of the MPLA. That began to change when Zairian transport aircraft began arriving with uniformed FNLA troops as early as October 1974. The first round of the new civil war began shortly after the initial American monetary payment to the FNLA; that payment was officially authorized by the 40 Committee in January 1975. On January 26, 1975, FNLA troops in Luanda attacked the government radio station and kidnapped its assistant director—who was an MPLA member. From February 3 through March 1975, Roberto's FNLA fighters attacked MPLA headquarters and several other MPLA installations in the capital. Portuguese efforts at a cease-fire failed and in April, the FNLA began assaults on the MPLA around Luanda and in other Angolan cities.[406]

It appears that the potential for American support had encouraged Roberto (and apparently his Zairian backer, Mobutu) to act aggressively. In addition to attacks by FNLA fighters already in Luanda, Roberto sent a motorized column directly towards Luanda and in one incident, FNLA fighters murdered some fifty unarmed MPLA activists. The FNLA attacks and appearance of general civil warfare stimulated a significant increase in Soviet supply to the MPLA both by air and ship. It also moved the MPLA to formally request military support from Havana. The first Cuban advisers reportedly arrived in Angola during the spring of 1975. Most importantly the MPLA had maintained its control of Luanda and its ability to represent itself as the official government of the new country—all well before the CIA's operation IA-FEATURE was in play.[407] Fortunately for our study of deniable warfare in action, we do have a unique firsthand view into the CIA activities of the IA-FEATURE project, from inception to defeat. That insight is directly from the CIA's own Angola task force leader, John Stockwell.[408] The following description of activities on the ground in the Angolan covert operation is based on Stockwell's own commentary, unless otherwise noted.

In the summer of 1975, the CIA's Angolan task force logistics team was pulled together, staffed with personnel formerly contracted as paramilitary officers in Southeast Asia, and given orders to get weapons and military supplies into Angola as quickly as possible. Stockwell provides full lists of the weapons shipped in during the two-year (1975 to 1977) conflict; a partial inventory includes 622 crew-severed mortars, rockets, and machine guns; 4,210 antitank rockets, and 20,860 rifles (primarily of obsolete WWII vintage). For reference, the total of insurgent FNLA and UNITA fighters did not exceed ten thousand. What the U.S.-backed groups did not get were heavy weapons such as artillery or armored vehicles, which would have been of American manufacture and much less deniable. It was the sort of issue that always concerned the United States but never seems to have bothered the Soviets, Chinese, or Cubans. This left the American surrogate factions at a major disadvantage since field rocket launchers provided by the Soviets to the MPLA offered a range several miles over the mortars provided by the U.S. The range differential allowed FNLA and UNITA positions to be bombarded while these groups were unable to respond. The U.S. had nothing in inventory corresponding to the Soviet rocket launchers and it took some time to find foreign weapons that offered something comparable. As events proved, that single weapons discrepancy was decisive in a number of combat engagements inside Angola.

As IA-FEATURE became fully operational in the summer of 1975, it began by taking advantage of the low-profile military aid program to Zaire, covert only in the sense that Zaire was using the supplies to support the FNLA inside Angola. There was to be absolutely no use of CIA officers or American military personnel inside Angola and most certainly not in any combat context. The 40 Committee issued directives that specifically forbade putting CIA personnel in Angola. The American military aid program was to be conducted in isolation, through Zaire, with no coordination with other powers involving themselves in Angola. In reality, events turned out a bit differently. In general, covert operations in Angola followed a pattern very similar to other projects we have explored. The goal was to supply and support surrogate forces inside Angola, working though a cooperative third party neighbor, Zaire. CIA officers would handle logistics and provide directions, while shipments and transfers would be covered under the long-term military assistance agreements with Zaire, and the surrogates would be totally deniable. Zaire might be seen to be interfering in its neighbor's affairs but the United States and the CIA would be invisible players.

CIA paramilitary officers and field support personnel were flown into Zaire and a new support base was set up in Kinshasa, Zaire. During 1975, eighty-three CIA officers were dispatched to stations in Zaire and South Africa to work air and ground transport as well as logistics and propaganda activities. Unknown to the 40 Committee or even CIA headquarters, making the mission work required American personnel actually going into Angola to work that end of the supply chain. As we have seen many times before, people in the field do what is necessary to actually get the job done, but they do not necessarily share all they are doing with headquarters. Initially three supply flights by Air Force C-141 Starlifters carried small arms and supplies from a CIA storage facility near San Antonio, Texas, directly to Kinshasa. A large inventory of twelve M-113 tracked amphibious vehicles, sixty trucks, twenty trailers, five thousand M-16 rifles, forty thousand rifles of other types, a million rounds of ammunition, and additional rockets, mortars, and recoilless rifles were transported by the U.S. Navy transport *Challenger*, sailing out of Charleston, South Carolina. The Navy billed the CIA $500,000 for use of the ship. By the end of August 1975, President Ford had authorized over $24 million for the Angola operations.

Under President Mobutu's orders, the Zairian Army hauled or flew materials into FNLA bases in Angola, enough arms for two full infantry battalions as well as additional armored cars. Additional U.S. C-130 transport aircraft sales to Zaire were expedited to ensure sufficient aircraft for the supply operations. All in all, transportation had become simpler, dramatically larger in capacity, and much less deniable than covert operations of earlier years. The U.S. Air Force and Navy were playing much more obvious roles in support of covert operations. There was no recourse to complex "deniable" transport such as seen with the Artime project or even with the commercial (if CIA-affiliated) air carriers used in Laos. Direct American involvement with the factions in Angola might be officially denied but it was quite visible to everyone in the region. Well, perhaps not to everyone. Although the initiative behind the Angola project had come from Secretary Kissinger and the State Department, care was taken for the CIA chief in Zaire to brief the U.S. consul general in Luanda, Angola, that there was military assistance, approved at the highest levels in Washington, for preferred factions in Angola. But the consul was assured that there would be no direct involvement by the CIA in that country. He was told that both the FNLA and UNITA were being funded, but there was to be no direct provision of materials to their groups, and any arms provided would be a matter of Zaire selling its own weapons directly to the Angolan groups.

With the initial supply chain in operation and in anticipation of the November 1975 independence target, a U.S.-supported force of fifteen hundred FNLA Zairian commandos and Portuguese mercenaries advanced across open plains against Luanda. They were supported by four artillery pieces, manned by South African artillerymen. As the units advanced, they were first bracketed and then utterly smashed by massive 122-millimeter rocket fire from the MPLA forces. Some two thousand rockets, roughly one hundred salvos of twenty rockets apiece, brutally overmatched the limited artillery support available to the advancing force. The rocket fire stopped and then utterly routed the advance. That engagement was the first in which Cuban advisors had actively joined and fought with the MPLA.[409] Over the weeks that followed, a slow, highly methodical advance by Cuban/MPLA forces drove the FNLA units back to the Zaire border.

As noted above, and in direct contradiction to the consul's briefing, CIA paramilitary officers were already supervising the shipments going into Angola from Zaire and as matters progressed, they would also go into the field in Angola itself. In operational terms, it simply would have been impossible for such a major supply effort to occur without some intelligence from the field and without at least some paramilitary people on the ground in contact with insurgent group leaders. Stockwell himself was the first officer to go into Angola, but by the fall of 1975 CIA communications personnel, paramilitary trainers, and case officers were working inside the country. Having absolutely no case officers working in-country would have harkened back to the days of the failed autonomous Cuban groups program. So, as generally happens, the professionals assigned to the mission did what they needed to—and reported only what they had to. Advisors placed inside Angola were designated as "intelligence gatherers"; officers as high as retired army colonels were placed under contract and sent into Angola. An infantry training team was dispatched to Kinshasa in Zaire, and then rerouted to an FNLA camp inside Angola. Personnel wore utility uniforms and on occasion even referred to themselves as mercenaries.[410] And when CIA Director Colby later wrote in his book *Honorable Men: My Life in the CIA* that "no CIA officers were permitted to engage in combat or train there [in Angola]," that was officially true; apparently it was even true in terms of the Angola team reports being filed with headquarters. As we have learned, the CIA Operations field staff were perfectly capable of practicing deniability not only with the State Department, but up their own chain of command.

Stockwell describes the fact that even at CIA headquarters level, the chief of the African Division allowed no verbatim transcripts to be taken of group meetings. He wrote all official memoranda and documents himself and circulated "blind" memoranda among the group, without using headings or addresses. Those reports were not designated as official numbered CIA documents, and as such, they stayed out of the regular filing system, going into "soft files," which technically had no official or legal existence.[411] Stockwell treats that routine as simply as a matter of assumed practice. No one regarded it as lying per se, just as a standard security practice, even when they were reading or writing reports that were contradictory to reality.

He refers to such practices as "several levels of untruth functioning simultaneously"[412]—a strikingly accurate description, and certainly something not unique to the CIA Angolan operation.

As the U.S.-backed rebels had prepared for their first assault on the Angolan capital, South Africa had also been preparing for a covert intervention in the Angolan civil war. In October 1975 it launched its own combat operation into southern Angola, in support of UNITA. In a surprise move, a South African assault unit with fifty armored cars and some one thousand troops with artillery and logistics vehicle trains moved to join with UNITA forces in the south. UNITA was under such military pressure that it was willing to accept help from anyone, even the black African nemesis of South Africa. Some two thousand additional South African troops were providing logistics support from their side of the border, flying transports, and operating fuel trucks. The combined force rolled through opposing MPLA units and began a successful march north up the coast as well as in the interior. As the November 1975 date for formal Angolan independence approached, the MPLA retained control of the capital of Luanda and three provinces. Various rebel groups occupied the rest of the country. Still, once in the capital the MPLA was in position to declare itself the official independent government of Angola.

The major South African military movement, although ostensibly conducted covertly and with total deniability, quickly became obvious to everyone, including all the African states. And since South Africa had intervened on the side of one of the U.S.-backed groups, the international community and in particular the African nations assumed that the U.S. was supporting them. Any military intervention in Africa pairing American and South African support was emotionally and politically a kiss of death for U.S. diplomatic relations in Africa. In reality the U.S. was not officially backing the South African intervention; indeed, all available documents show no sign on any presidential level that American encouragement was being given. South Africa was acting in its own interests, securing its borders but also protecting its major investment in a massive hydroelectric dam project, which it had funded but which was physically located within Angolan territory. However, within the CIA's African Division and the IA-FEATURE project team, connections to South Africa were a bit more complex.

Stockwell describes meetings between members of the South African Bureau for State Security (generally referred to as BOSS) and CIA officers, including the CIA Africa Division chief. The meetings were held in both Pretoria, South Africa, and in Washington, D.C. The CIA chief of station in Pretoria was ordered to brief BOSS on IA-FEATURE, and ongoing intelligence reports on Angola were relayed to Pretoria for updates to be given to BOSS. On at least one occasion, two South African C-130 aircraft were used to transship a load of U.S. arms, transferred from a CIA C-141 transport. So, without the need for official memos or direction, coordination with the South Africans "just happened." It also just happened that when extra ammunition was needed for South African howitzers being used in Angola, the CIA chief of station in Pretoria arranged for it to appear.[413]

The cooperation could have become even more obvious. When the FNLA and UNITA began to run short of fuel, the CIA division chief proposed having a tanker ship bring in a fuel shipment through a South African port. His proposal quickly encountered opposition from within his own working group. In addition, the position of the American ambassador to South Africa was that shipments of fuel or weapons to or through South Africa would be illegal. The CIA chief ordered a search of the relevant legal guidelines. He then returned to the group, telling them that there was no such law—it was simply a presidential directive from the time of the Kennedy Administration, intended to support Kennedy-era outreach to the new African nations. According to the CIA team chief, "times have changed." Eager to proceed, he was forced to pause only by opposition from Edward Mulcahy, deputy assistant secretary of state for African affairs at the State Department. Mulcahy's response clearly suggested that there would still be one problem: "If you do ship any arms to South Africa, I will resign in protest."[414] The subject received no further discussion in IA-FEATURE team meetings. Coordination with the South Africans continued but no shipments were made into South Africa. The subject of active cooperation would surface again in 1976 as the entire IA-FEATURE project moved through disaster to impending defeat.

In the fall of 1975, Cuba had begun a major military supply effort into Angola, in support of the central MPLA government. In response to the South African intervention it dramatically increased that aid, with virtually no African objection to Cuba's involvement. The Cuban government ships *Vietnam Heroico*, *La Plata*, and *Coral Island* left for Angola in November, carrying materials and additional advisors. The Cubans themselves were very sensitive to accusations of being invaders, especially with the buildup occurring shortly before the date set for Angolan independence. The date had actually been moved forward by the Portuguese from the initial Alvor Agreement date of January 1975. The Cubans took great pains to quickly move their arriving forces to select MPLA camps.[415] The boat shipments were supplemented with an "air bridge" (Operation Carlota) to take fully equipped Cuban army combat brigades into Angola. The twenty-eight hundred troops already there were joined by another ten thousand.[416] Their combat units were fully equipped with tanks, armored cars, helicopters, and trucks. The MPLA forces also continued to receive massively increased Soviet supplies, including deadly medium-range rocket batteries. These units had begun to engage and blunt the South African/UNITA columns by the end of the year.

The Soviets also sent in some seven shiploads of equipment, estimated at $225 million. That compared to CIA funding of some $25 million. One hundred Soviet supply flights had gone to the MPLA; the CIA had sent nine to the FNLA and UNITA factions it was supporting. And the MPLA held the moral high ground, having not only been initially attacked by the FNLA but also having been engaged by the South African military. Unless the U.S. was to massively escalate the type of weapons it was adding or commit some sort of covert air support, there was little hope for the insurgent groups it was sponsoring. Yet while the Cubans and Soviets were open in their involvement, both declaring themselves committed to opposing American aggression against emerging African nations, both the U.S. and South Africans had gone the route of deniability; ostensibly there were not even any American advisors in the field.

During 1976 the IA-FEATURE team struggled on against increasingly heavy odds. Their efforts ranged from sending in much more sophisticated weaponry to putting American advisors actively in the field. Use of various mercenary forces was also considered. Virtually all the African CIA station chiefs involved pushed for stronger cooperation with the South Africans. The Kinshasa station was especially active in that regard and sent officers to Pretoria for discussions. Even Henry Kissinger seems to have been quite open to stronger involvement with South Africa in fielding deniable units via mercenary operations.[417] In China, during conversations with Vice Premier Deng Xiaoping, Kissinger discussed the Angolan situation, stating, "We are prepared to push South Africa as soon as an alternative military force can be created."[418] Although different mercenary groups were approached, no viable force ever emerged and by spring 1976, South Africa was removing itself from the Angolan equation.

The rest of the 1970s Angolan civil war story is fragmented but relatively straightforward. During the winter of 1975–1976, the Cuban/MPLA forces rolled over all their opponents, employing tactics and equipment that were simply unstoppable. Initially a well-organized Cuban attack stopped a South African column dead, at the Battle of Ebo. The South Africans halted their advance and the Cubans were given time for a heavy artillery regiment to arrive. Then four additional Cuban ships arrived with full units of motorized infantry.[419] The South Africans, faced now by large and very well-equipped Cuban forces, were left with the choice of either a major move into full-scale warfare or managing a quick, relatively quiet exit from Angola. Seeing no major American military escalation, they simply disengaged and withdrew back behind their own border and were out of the picture by the end of February 1976.

During 1976, a Defense Intelligence Agency report noted forty-four

Soviet flights into Angola plus nine Soviet ships making deliveries into Angola in 1975–1976, with equipment and supplies transshipped though the Republic of the Congo. The report's assumption was that much of the material delivered to the Marxist-Leninist regime of the Republic of the Congo was going to the MPLA in Angola, with short-haul transports and small ships carrying the materials on to MPLA bases near Luanda.[420] The report also noted the arrival of an estimated seventy-five hundred Cuban personnel during 1975. Clearly the American intelligence community was running behind events in the field. The DIA report also notably lacked any mention of or comment on the FNLA military advance into Angola and its attacks on the MPLA. Instead the report simply noted that the increase in Soviet support would "threaten vital lines of communication and gain access to a wealth of natural resources but would also establish a base for Soviet subversion, which would present a clear danger to the remaining white minority regimes in southern Africa. Use of Angolan facilities would enhance Moscow's strategic position and project a Soviet presence into the South Atlantic."

While the IA-FEATURE team was facing an imploding military situation and struggling with alternatives including further involving the South Africans, the Organization of African Unity was incensed by the South African incursion. It voted forty-two to four to recognize the MPLA in Luanda as the official government of Angola. Then things went from bad to worse. The CIA and IA-FEATURE had been caught cheating on Congress.

The president, the secretary of state, and CIA had been playing by the new congressional oversight rules in regard to the IA-FEATURE project, but only to a limited extent. A vague presidential finding had been issued, select committees and subcommittees were briefed that something was going to happen in Africa, and Director Colby continued to brief congressmen. Yet his briefings were using the same official characterization that had been given to the American consul general in Luanda: no American arms were being delivered directly to Angola. The U.S. simply replenished Mobutu's arsenal in Zaire as he sold weapons to the insurgents in Angola. No Americans were on the ground in Angola, and there was certainly no mention of contact or coordination with the South Africans. Those briefings were a bit shy of reality and problems would emerge from the fact that one of the briefings had been given to Senator Dick Clark, chairman of the Subcommittee on African Affairs of the Senate Foreign Relations Committee.

Very possibly Congress as a whole would have remained uninvolved—if Senator Clark had not personally set off on an extensive 1975 fact-finding tour in Africa. Clark's visits were not a comfortable thing for the CIA; many at headquarters remained bitter over the manner in which Congress had treated them in regard to Laos. The CIA Angola team went so far as to brief both Mobutu and Roberto on how to talk with the senator, specifying that he had already been briefed on the Angolan project and that it did not need to be a topic of conversation. Congress may still not have fully trusted the CIA, and by that point the CIA did not wholeheartedly trust Congress. During his trip Clark was reportedly treated with "absolute defiance" by both State Department and CIA personnel. Upon his return, State Department insiders observed that Secretary Kissinger had little appreciation for "junior" senators who "utterly fail to appreciate the nuances of balance-of-power considerations."[421]

The "junior" senator had come back from his trip skeptical that he was being told the full story about the Angola operation, but he simply didn't have any solid proof that would crack the operation's political cover story. Matters became more complicated when, in November, Clark's questions to the State Department about aid to Mobutu produced a response that Mobutu was not using aid from the U.S. to support the insurgents in Angola. Clearly not everyone was working off the same script. In December 1975, CIA Director Colby again assured the House Intelligence Committee that there were no Americans in Angola. Separately in December, the Senate Foreign Relations Committee received totally conflicting answers from the State Department and CIA officers in regard to arms going directly into Angola. The end result was ongoing mistrust, and Senators Alan Cranston and Dick Clark introduced an amendment that forbade any fiscal year 1976 funds to be spent in Angola for any purpose other than the basic collection of intelligence.

Despite congressional disapproval, both the CIA and Secretary Kissinger continued to pursue support for the FNLA and UNITA for much of 1976. The Agency was given access to funds from the existing 1975 budget and five more Air Force Starlifters were sent off with cargo to Kinshasa, Zaire; some twenty-two transshipment flights carried the supplies on into Angola. As late as February 1976, when the FNLA had totally ceased to be an effective fighting force, Secretary Kissinger sent a cable to the American State Department representative in Kinshasa to be passed on to UNITA. The message was that America would continue to support them as long as they demonstrated they could effectively resist the MPLA. That communication sounds strangely like the final messages from Kissinger to Vang Pao in Laos, urging him to resist the Pathet Lao and the NVA at all costs.

In Angola the civil war simply continued. UNITA continued its struggle as a guerrilla movement in the south of Angola, the MPLA continued to receive massive Cuban support, and Zaire found itself invaded by rebels staging out of Angola. Zaire managed to repel them but only with French assistance and a bit of American support. Eventually the Reagan Administration would be faced with yet another challenge in Angola, as general civil war returned to the country. But by the spring of 1976 Project IA-FEATURE was effectively done. The CIA was once again frustrated, congressional oversight was in vogue, and at least for a time covert warfare would be under the legislative microscope. Secretary Kissinger was left extremely unhappy with Congress and its meddling. At one point, very early in 1976, when the Angola team was looking for anything that might turn the tide, they had proposed sending American advisors actively into Angola—actually they had already started doing that, but things were getting to the point where they felt they needed official concurrence. Edward Mulcahy, deputy assistant secretary of state for African affairs at the State Department, had taken the written proposals to Kissinger. He returned to a team meeting with a very concerned CIA Angola working group only to tell them that

Kissinger had not really approved or disapproved the action. He had read the paper and then just grunted. Not a clear pro grunt or a con grunt, just a grunt. After considerable discussion of the meaning of such a response, the group decided it would be safest not to proceed with the advisors. As Mulcahy would comment later, "It was a strange way to run a war."[422] Actually covert warfare was about to get a lot stranger, and the secret warriors were going to be moving far outside the models and patterns we have studied up to this point, even into the shadows and eventually totally outside the box Congress had attempted to establish. To follow that story, we will travel back from Africa to Latin America.

CHAPTER 16

Maintaining Anticommunist Regimes

Holding actions. The first years of the Cold War had seen American conventional and covert military activity as largely a story of holding actions, attempts to block communist territorial expansion and ongoing efforts to remove and replace regimes that were seen to be leftist or communist-leaning. In pursuit of deniability, those operations involved different types of surrogates: opposition political or military factions, insurgents, rebels, and exiles. In most of the operations the United States worked though supportive third parties, neighboring countries, or at least regional allies, who provided bases and various types of logistics support as well as personnel covers. There had been exceptions: nominally neutral regimes such as Laos and the Democratic Republic of the Congo, where both military assistance and covert actions were used to help maintain the central government against communist insurgencies. During the Johnson and Nixon administrations, regime change efforts continued, but counterinsurgency activities with anticommunist allies became increasingly common. Given some dramatic early successes in Latin America, counterinsurgency began to evolve rapidly, acquiring a covert element and expanding to the first experiments with full-scale political warfare against communist insurgencies.

In following that new trend in shadow warfare we will focus on a number of interventions where counterinsurgency was the major focus, where America's uniformed military and its shadow warriors became involved with defending allied governments not from communist aggression or territorial expansion but rather from internal revolutionary and popular reform movements. Given the official American commitments to the governments involved, and formal military assistance programs supporting those commitments, those activities held less need for the classic practices of deniability. However, much of the support for friendly military, special security, and police units will be seen to be more "shadowy" than might be expected. It also involved a growing need to maintain a certain level of distance, especially legal distance, from the increasingly questionable practices of certain allied nations.

The term Southern Cone refers to the southernmost geographic region of South America, which most often is considered to include Argentina, Chile, Peru, Bolivia, Uruguay, and Paraguay—with the addition of southern and southeastern regions of Brazil. In general, the Southern Cone countries had been relatively prosperous, with considerable natural resources and an active business community. Culturally conservative, the region did have a general problem with income inequality, and land reform remained a controversial issue. During the 1960s and early 1970s popular reform movements had begun to develop in certain of the countries, but the United States was not bashful about moving against the establishment of what it had perceived would be leftist-leaning regimes—socialist and reformist governments that would only serve as entry points for communist influence. Initially American covert involvement in those instances largely consisted of political action, the distribution of large sums of money to antireform factions, active media and propaganda activities, and diplomatic support for factions—particularly military groups—that were willing to oust any populist regimes that might be elected into power. American diplomatic recognition, financial support, and military assistance agreements with new and declaredly anticommunist governments quickly followed, even if the regimes had come into power in military coups against elected governments.

As early as 1964, President Johnson had ordered aggressive U.S. support for an impending coup, which in a memorandum was referred to as "the democratic rebellion" of the Brazilian military against the reformist government of João Goulart in Brazil. Johnson's remarks to Secretary of State George Ball on the subject were entirely consistent with his preference for projecting strength through immediate and aggressive action. LBJ said, "I think we ought to take every step we can, be prepared to do everything that we need to do . . . I'd get right on top of it and stick my neck out a little."[423]

The U.S. ambassador in Brazil strongly urged coup support, declaring that failure to back the military could lead to a failure as great as the loss of China to the communists.[424] The ambassador recommended activities ranging from CIA political action and psychological warfare support for the military forces and their supporters to the use of American submarines to clandestinely deliver arms at select sites; the weapons would of course need to be of "non-U.S. origin." The U.S. proceeded to organize a naval task group, including several Navy tankers with petroleum supplies, and assembled an airlift of some 110 tons of ammunition out of the CIA's New Jersey depot stores. As those preparations were getting under way, the coup quickly succeeded with relatively minor military action and the American naval and air contingency plans never became operational. The military government established through the coup was led by General Castelo Branco, whose military maintained its control over the Brazilian government until 1985.

In the early 1970s it appeared that Chile might be the next pivot point for popular reform in the Southern Cone. Salvador Allende was making a strong bid for the presidency of that democratic nation and his platform was definitely socialist-oriented. An elected socialist regime in Chile was anathema to the Nixon Administration, much as an elected socialist regime in Guatemala had been during the Eisenhower era. President Nixon, in a strictly unilateral decision, ordered the CIA into a political action operation of campaign donations, propaganda, and bribery to forestall Allende's election. In issuing the order Nixon had sought neither comment nor approval from his designated covert operations committee (the 40 Committee), and he personally committed a discretionary budget of $10 million.[425]

The CIA officer selected to lead the CIA's Chilean task force was David Phillips, veteran of successful regime change in Guatemala and unsuccessful attempts to oust the Castro regime. At the time of his assignment to the Chilean task force, he had been serving as CIA chief of station in Brazil. While working on the Chile project, Phillips and his team became aware of a pending military coup being orchestrated by a cabal led by Chilean army General Roberto Viaus. If successful, the coup would have prevented Allende from taking office. CIA field officers Bruce McMasters and Tony Sforza were part of the CIA field team in Chile; Sforza had been deep undercover in Cuba in earlier days and afterward ran the counterintelligence effort at JM WAVE. Sforza and McMasters established contact with the coup members and supplied them with three machine guns.[426] One of the first individuals to be eliminated in the coup was Allende's well-respected military chief, General Rene Schneider.

General Schneider was indeed assassinated by members of the military group that the CIA had been in contact with, and three members of the coup group were later convicted of Schneider's murder. CIA records confirm that the three men had been contacted by CIA field officers, but since CIA paramilitary operations were not legally sanctioned for Chile, the men were represented to have simply been intelligence collection agents. Because General Schneider was killed with handguns, the CIA was able to further distance itself from the actual assassination—since it had offered different types of weapons to the military cabal. Officially the CIA took the position that its field officers had actually discouraged the coup plotters and "disengaged" with the military cabal before the actual assassination. Since such disengagement would have meant cutting off the CIA's major source of intelligence of the pending coup, such a claim is difficult to accept at face value. It is also questionable whether the team would have withdrawn from supporting a coup that would have immediately accomplished its mission. The elimination of General

Schneider removed Allende's primary support within the Chilean military and following Allende's election to the Chilean presidency, a military cabal eventually did move against the elected president, putting siege to the presidential residence. Allende refused to accept exile and instead committed suicide. Within a year, a regime backed by the military and strongly supported by the United States was in control of the country.

While support for military coups in the Southern Cone started under President Johnson, it escalated significantly under President Nixon, moving on from Chile to Argentina. President Ford would inherit several of the resulting regime relationships and a number of the humanitarian issues resulting from Nixon-era support of emerging Latin American military dictatorships. Certainly the return to a Cold War worldview in the Nixon Administration had a great deal to do with such matters, as did Secretary Kissinger's view that any faction that was anticommunist was intrinsically positive for the U.S. in the ongoing contest with the Soviets. As secretary of state, Kissinger was one of the preeminent voices within the Nixon Administration calling for maximum support for a new military government in Argentina, regardless of the bloodletting that some feared the generals would perform to consolidate their power.

Kissinger was cautioned by William Rogers, his top deputy on Latin America, that in supporting the Argentinean military, the United States would have to expect not only repression of civilians but also "a good deal of blood."[427] In response, Kissinger made it quite clear that he simply wanted the generals in charge. It was important to encourage them and not to stand in their way, or look over their shoulders in regard to popular or humanitarian concerns: "I do want to encourage them. I don't want to give them the sense that they're being harassed by the United States."[428]

Released documents show that there was a Nixon Administration political sensitivity to supporting the Argentinean military junta (a ruling group seizing power through force rather than political process) but that it was primarily one of Secretary Kissinger not wishing to have to battle Congress over humanitarian and ethical issues involved with supporting the Argentinean generals. The Argentinean military contacts were continually cautioned that it would be a long-term issue in Congress. In other words, the American Congress might object to too much bloodshed but that would take time; the generals needed to act to be firmly in power before that became an issue. Kissinger's pragmatic view of the matter comes across in a quote taken from a diplomatic dialogue between Kissinger and a representative of the junta:

> *Look, our basic attitude is that we would like you to succeed. I have an old-fashioned view that friends ought to be supported. What is not understood in the United States is that you have a civil war. We read about human rights problems but not the context. The quicker you succeed the better. . . . The human rights problem is a growing one. Your Ambassador can apprise you. We want a stable situation. We won't cause you unnecessary difficulties. If you can finish before Congress gets back, the better. Whatever freedoms you could restore would help.*[429]

Unfortunately, this dialogue appears to have convinced the Argentinean representative that the U.S. position was that the junta should act aggressively and quickly, with any humanitarian issues being secondary. Within Argentina there were widespread media reports of mass arrests, massacres of prisoners, and other acts of military/police terror. However, Ambassador Robert Hill reported that the military junta was surprised that Hill was raising humanitarian issues with them. According to Hill,

> *The Foreign Minister [Cesar Guzzetti] said that GOA [government of Argentina] had been somewhat surprised by indications of such strong concern on the part of the USG [United States government] in human rights situation in Argentina. When he had seen Secy of State Kissinger in Santiago, the latter had said he "hoped the Argentine govt could get the terrorist problem under control as quickly as possible." Guzzetti said that he had reported*

this to President Videla and to the cabinet, and that their impression had been that the USG's overriding concern was not human rights but rather that GOA "get it over quickly."[430]

Clearly the military junta had taken Kissinger's remarks to mean that if they acted quickly and aggressively to seize power, American congressional concerns over their methods would be a moot point.

In regard to Deputy William Rogers's original remarks to Secretary Kissinger, Kissinger simply stated that he understood the concerns, but that clearly, supporting the military government would be in the best interest of the United States and that money should not be an issue. Shortly thereafter, the International Monetary Fund, headquartered in and strongly supported by the United States, gave a line of credit in the amount of $127 million to the new military junta. In regard to Rogers's concern over "a great deal of blood" and succeeding quickly, documents now available include a secret internal Argentinean military communication in Buenos Aires. The cable indicates that as of mid-1978, an Argentinean secret police battalion had counted at least twenty-two thousand Argentinean citizens killed or "disappeared" in the political security activities under the junta.[431]

Through a combination of their own internal politics and active American support for military coups, the countries of the Southern Cone did indeed come to represent a true bastion for anticommunism by the latter half of the 1970s. Because of their strong anticommunist stances those governments were considered friendly and pro-American; they received active military and security support from the United States, both overtly and covertly.

Military assistance and advisory groups (MAAGs) are actually the principal contact point between the Department of Defense (secretary of defense) and individual foreign armed forces.[432] Active U.S. military missions operated in Moscow from 1943 to 1945 and in all NATO countries in Europe from 1947 to 1964. We've previously touched on the activities of military assistance groups, initially in regard to the Republic of China, Thailand, and the

Congo. Following the Second World War, it took about a decade for Europeans to return to weapons manufacturing and begin to sell abroad.[433] During that first decade, one of the MAAG's major actives was arranging the grant of weapons and weapons systems to European countries to enable them to rearm to face the Soviets. Most of the weapons were WWII surplus and were donated rather than sold. As early as September 1950, President Truman dispatched a MAAG to Indochina to assist the French in their battles with the nationalist insurgency. Through the 1950s MAAG activities were largely centered on establishing modern, well-organized conventional armed forces for friendly governments. Training was conducted to prepare mobile infantry and light armored groups. The general orientation was preparation for conventional warfare, ensuring that American allies could at least initially defend themselves from armed invasion by conventional Soviet, Chinese, or other communist bloc forces.

Through the 1950s and 1960s, the largest and most active MAAG units were in Taiwan, Thailand, Laos, and South Vietnam. Military Assistance Command, Vietnam (MACV) eventually ran the U.S. ground war in Vietnam.[434] The Vietnamese MAAG assumed a preeminent position in Southeast Asia. Previously the Taiwanese MAAG, serving the Republic of China from 1951 to 1978, had held that position. MAAG Laos had been established in 1961, replacing the Programs Evaluation Office and succeeded by the Requirements Office, which served as a cover for CIA military and proxy army activities in an officially neutral Laos. MAAG Cambodia ended operations in November 1963 upon the Cambodian government's cancellation of all American aid. By the mid-1960s there were advisory groups in Thailand, Laos, Cambodia, Korea, Japan, and the Philippines in Southeast Asia; as well as in Argentina, Bolivia, Brazil, Chile, Colombia, Costa Rica, Cuba, Dominican Republic, Ecuador, El Salvador, Guatemala, Honduras, Nicaragua, Panama, Paraguay, Peru, Uruguay, and Venezuela in Latin America. Beginning in the 1960s, the United States began to ship much larger quantities of weapons, including newer arms, to Southeast Asia and Latin America.

Historically military assistance had been very public, even if occasionally low profile due to cultural concerns. We noted that in the early days of South Vietnam, military assistance pilot training was used as a cover for actual combat air support of the South Vietnamese army against communist insurgents. Events in the Congo had demonstrated that the open involvement of American MAAG officers with Congolese army units in the field had produced a firestorm within the Simba insurgency. But in most countries standard American military assistance activities were limited to training, supply, and logistics efforts; any joint military field activities were viewed as training exercises and certainly involved no American personnel in active combat. That orientation began to change dramatically during the 1970s, as threats from within became the primary challenge in maintaining friendly regimes. But as the focus began to shift from preparation of friendly nations for defense against communist invasion to counterinsurgency operations against internal rebellions, covert activity began to assume a more significant role. In that role, CIA operations personnel and military Special Forces teams would be new players.

The Eisenhower-era success in bringing about regime change in Guatemala with the PBSUCCESS operation had been a major factor in establishing both the concept of covert operations and the image of the CIA. Some years later, a spectacular counterinsurgency success in Bolivia helped create the same image for the CIA's entry into regime preservation activities. The operation was a joint effort among the CIA, the American military, and the MAAG program in Bolivia. The result was the targeted capture and subsequent killing of legendary communist revolutionary Che Guevara. Officially, American military assistance programs were and are not supposed to involve the U.S. military in combat operations. Supporting a friendly regime with training and equipment is one thing, but fighting along with its troops to suppress populist movements is not viewed as a positive thing for international relations. Yet as we have repeatedly seen, putting experienced American paramilitary personnel into field operations can often make a major difference. The question becomes how to maintain some degree of distance between the assistance program and its personnel while still directly supporting actual field combat operations. Che Guevara had gone to Bolivia with the goal of stimulating a populist insurgency movement. In helping the Bolivians stop him, the CIA turned to assets that by now are quite familiar to us. It would be experienced Cuban exile paramilitary officers who would join with MAAG personnel and the Bolivian military to eliminate Guevara.

By late 1963, Felix Rodriguez had completed U.S. Army training at Fort Benning and had moved on to participate in the covert Artime autonomous exile project, spending two years in Nicaragua. After the Artime group folded, Rodriguez began to participate in field missions for the CIA, taking orders from JM WAVE officer Tom Clines. Rodriguez himself points out that that was totally deniable, with not being a CIA employee. He describes his missions into Latin America as being with only an oral understanding: no contract, no papers, but paid as a "principal agent."[435] Following a short assignment, which took him to Caracas, Venezuela, for three months with two other Americans, Rodriguez joined two other Cuban exiles, whom he had first met in Army training at Fort Benning. The three men moved on to a military advisory assignment in Bolivia. Rodriguez makes the point that since none of them were American citizens, they were free to engage in actual combat operations. That was important because an edict against U.S. personnel engaging in such activities had been issued by the American ambassador to Bolivia.[436] Rodriguez used a commercial cover in the Bolivian operation, representing himself as a Cuban businessman. In reality, he joined an ongoing military assistance operation in which a U.S. Green Beret Special Forces major was training Bolivian army rangers. The Cuban exiles and a CIA field officer operated with the personal endorsement of the Bolivian president and the chief of the Bolivian armed forces. They were issued military identification and Rodriguez used the pseudonym Felix Ramos, with the assigned rank of captain. He worked not only with the Bolivian army 2nd Ranger Battalion but also with Bolivian intelligence officers.

This sort of arrangement, placing CIA-approved, non-U.S. citizens into field combat operations, created a form of legal distance if not total deniability. The individuals were not officially employed by the CIA, they were not even citizens, and in most cases they were selected for cultural and physical characteristics that allowed them to blend into the regions where they operated. To some extent this replaced the "volunteer/mercenary" model we saw in earlier decades, with American servicemen detached to volunteer for overseas contract work. We will follow that practice across Latin America and into Southwest Asia, particularly Afghanistan. The basic agreement for the Bolivian military group support activities was an extension of the Foreign Assistance Act of 1961. In the spring of 1967, the U.S. and Bolivia agreed that in light of a perceived internal threat to the security of Bolivia by communist insurgents, a U.S. military assistance group would provide aid and training to establish a counterinsurgency, rapid-reaction force within the Bolivian military.[437]

By late spring 1967, the U.S. had definitive intelligence that Guevara was in Bolivia with a small group of rebels. In June, the military training mission, which would involve Rodriguez, went into Bolivia. Based on CIA documents, it is now clear that Rodriguez and another CIA Cuban operative, Gustavo Villoldo, were sent to Bolivia specifically to assist in the capture of Guevara and the destruction of his group. The unit included a CIA paramilitary case officer ("Jim"), Rodriguez, Villoldo, Mario Osiris Riveron, and two other agents who performed communications duties. One of Rodriguez's major contributions was intelligence assistance to the Bolivians, helping to pinpoint the probable location and movements of Guevara's group.[438] After Guevara's capture by the Bolivian army unit, Rodriguez and Villoldo were flown into the field and participated in an attempted interrogation of Guevara. According to Rodriguez, he passed on a message from the Bolivian military command to the Bolivian army unit to execute Guevara in a manner that would make it look like he had died in combat.[439] The Johnson Administration was quite pleased with the outcome of the Bolivian "advisor" team's work. In an update to Johnson, Walt Rostow (special assistant for national security affairs in the Johnson Administration) confirmed that Guevara was indeed dead. Rostow thought that it was "stupid" that the Bolivian military had ordered Guevara executed in the field but felt that the operation showed the "soundness of our preventative medicine strategy."[440] Rostow's remark can be seen as a strong endorsement for preemptive action in counterinsurgency but it also raises a number of issues dealing with the conduct of undeclared warfare that continue in today's counterterrorism operations around the globe.

With such dramatic success in Bolivia, Rodriguez's skills and techniques were in most definitely in demand. In 1968, following a request by the president of Ecuador, Rodriguez and his Cuban teammate were sent to train an elite intelligence unit in counterterrorism and counterinsurgency. This time they traveled undercover as U.S. military officers. Training of Ecuadorian officers in interrogation skills and the use of advanced communications equipment was also conducted in the U.S.[441] After Ecuador, Rodriguez went on to Peru with his CIA leader from the Bolivian team. Their assignment was to teach both intelligence and patrol fundamentals to a Peruvian paratroop unit. The mission was a combined project among U.S. Special Forces, CIA paramilitary/intelligence officers, and the Peruvian military.[442] A model for a new, much lower-profile and legally distanced form of surrogate warfare was becoming established across the Southern Cone. In this model, the armed forces, security forces, and police of officially friendly nations would replace the types of surrogates we dealt with in covert regime-change operations. CIA officers would not be giving the orders; they would simply be providing intelligence, technology, and training. American servicemen would not be active in the field; they would serve as trainers and at most as advisors. Advice, money, and support—in some ways it is perhaps most like the autonomous group concept, but with the alliance being publicly announced and endorsed.

Certainly American military and CIA operations personnel had worked together previously; we have seen examples from Laos to the Congo. The willing and open cooperation of American military advisors and CIA field intelligence had always been potent. If anything it had been minimized by the demands of strict deniability in covert operations. In official cooperation supporting friendly governments it began to evolve into something much more ambitious—something that would call for a much higher degree of intelligence collection and analysis, a practice that would become referred to as infrastructure warfare. Perhaps it would be more accurate to call it political warfare. The fundamental point is that not just combatants—fighters, armed groups—were designated as targets, but political leaders, organizers, couriers—essentially anyone acting against the allied regime—could be classified as part of the insurgent infrastructure. Conceptually the lower-level political supporters and activists would be identified, detained, or captured, and interrogations would expose mid- and senior levels of the political action leadership.

Full-scale political warfare actually came to its full potential in Southern Cone counterinsurgency efforts, in the pan-national cooperative effort Operation Condor. Condor would raise the practice of counterinsurgency to something immensely potent, and something almost unimaginably bloody, with tens of thousands of civilian casualties. But eventual "success" in the Southern Cone nations did not spring full-blown. Instead it developed from a political warfare project first put into practice in South Vietnam. To follow the intricacies and violence of Condor, to grasp the consequences of successful full-scale infrastructure warfare, we first have to explore Condor's predecessor, Phoenix. The concept of political targeting was not totally new to the CIA; it harkens back to the "blacklists" and the intelligence function that we detailed in Guatemala, first in PBFORTUNE and then in PBSUCCESS. It also takes us back to certain of the CIA's preparations under the JMARC operation, the first phase of the secret war against Cuba. Under JMARC, David Morales prepared key groups of Cuban exiles not only for intelligence work but to essentially become the intelligence arm of a free Cuba, capable of eliminating the communist cadre and political structure established by Fidel Castro.

Acting as the counterintelligence officer for JMARC, Morales had selected and arranged for extensive and special training for thirty-nine Cuban exiles, designated as AMOTs. A small number of those individuals were infiltrated into Cuba in advance of the Bay of Pigs assaults. The rest went along with the invasion force. The AMOTs received special training because they were intended to form the backbone of the new political regime in Cuba, also serving as the new Cuban intelligence service. Perhaps most importantly, a JMARC document, which reviews Morales's counterintelligence program, notes that special training was provided by a Chilean ex-police officer and that during the "action phase" of the operation, the group's primary objective would be to "identify and contain rabid 'Castroites,' Cuban communists, members of the Cuban security services." They would also develop blacklists pertinent to that objective.[443] None of the lists survive, but based on what we saw in Guatemala, where Morales served as training officer, we would expect to find lists of Castro political cadres, individuals designated as communists or communist-leaning, and individuals who could pose a threat to a new regime. Rumors of the highly secret covert political warfare operation associated with the Bay of Pigs effort, said to have been described internally as Operation 40, circulated in Miami for some time.

Final confirmation of both the existence of Operation 40 and its congruence with the Cuban personnel trained and prepared by David Morales surfaced as late as 1998. Grayston Lynch was one of only two CIA officers accompanying Cuban Brigade 2506 during the landing at the Bay of Pigs. In his own book on the operation, he wrote that the ship *Lake Charles* had transported the men of Operation 40 to the Cuba landing area. He noted that the men had trained in Florida, apart from the regular brigade members, and were to act as a military government after the overthrow of Castro's regime. Their task would be to administer first the beachhead and following that all of the "liberated" areas in Cuba as the anti-Castro forces advanced.[444]

As we have seen, quite different circumstances led to a lack of actual implementation of planned "political warfare" in either Guatemala or Cuba. But the situation was far different in South Vietnam. The CIA was supporting an officially declared ally, South Vietnam, in a desperate battle against a communist Viet Cong political insurgency. A new type of warfare was deemed to be necessary, one against the political infrastructure of the overall Viet Cong movement. If the political leadership of the Viet Cong could be eliminated, the movement would collapse. It was going to be infrastructure warfare on a grand scale—and it would receive its own name: Phoenix.

The deep roots of the Phoenix counterinsurgency program can be found in the early rural pacification effort in Vietnam. Pacification was supported by the U.S. with its Office of Civil Operations (OCO), and operated with a budget from the CIA. Following William Colby's arrival in Saigon, the CIA had moved into expanded control over OCO activities and exercised considerable influence through its operation of the Revolutionary Development Cadre Center. The center trained and fielded a variety of teams including counterterror and armed propaganda units. The counterterror teams were later renamed provincial reconnaissance units (PRU) and given the responsibility for intelligence collection as well as anti-terror activities.[445] The Vietnamese had their own commander with the regional development center but he was seconded by a senior CIA representative, a shadow warrior from Guatemala, Laos, Cuba, and the Congo: Rip Robertson.

Provincial reconnaissance unit trainees, CIA field officers, and American Special Forces would become key elements in the Phoenix operation. Beginning in 1966, six different regions in Vietnam were designated for PRU activities, and regional CIA officers were assigned to coordination roles. The Agency increased its personnel to some seven hundred officers and began increased field activity. A dramatic increase in provincial interrogation centers was another necessary element in the planning for Phoenix and the initial six to eight centers ultimately multiplied to forty-four. The growth in interrogation centers was accompanied by equal growth in the number and staffing of the provincial reconnaissance units. The PRU force grew to include an estimated five thousand troops, essentially created and funded by the CIA. These units were initially supervised by CIA field officers, although eventually American Special Forces would assume a major role in their operations.[446]

The final step to a full-scale counterinsurgency program was targeting members of the Viet Cong infrastructure, and that was to be done by focusing on the Viet Cong political hierarchy, reported to be widespread throughout rural villages. That political hierarchy, known as the Viet Cong Infrastructure (VCI), was supposed to became the priority target in the provisional reconnaissance units' infrastructure warfare. The formal name given to this overall infrastructure attack was intelligence coordination and exploitation (ICEX). Intelligence was the key to ICEX. If the VCI could be identified, it could be dealt with, and dealing with it would ensure the success of pacification.

The plan was for the PRUs to evolve from a relatively specific counterterrorism operation into a force that could be used in an attack on the political structure of the entire Viet Cong insurgency. That political attack would be heavily supported by the Vietnamese Special Branch Police and operationally based on the use of informants, interrogation, and spies. That intelligence collection would be followed by arrests and military actions, including sweeps, ambushes, and conventional assaults. Given that the initial struggle in South Vietnam was seen as that of an anticommunist nation facing a local communist insurgency, the ICEX seemed the ideal solution. It would maximize the value of American intelligence skills while keeping the military response in the hands of the South Vietnamese police and special security forces. Perhaps best of all, it would conceivably hold down the growing numbers of regular American military on the ground and in combat sweeps. It would be a counterinsurgency solution rather than an escalation of conventional field warfare against Viet Cong forces.

The ICEX concept was approved by President Johnson. It was then presented to the South Vietnamese police director, who did not approve of it—most likely due to internal South Vietnamese political jousting. The police director was a strong political supporter of Vice

President Nguyen Cao Ky. Ky was actively competing for power with President Nguyen Van Thieu. Following the police director's obstruction, the U.S. went directly to South Vietnamese President Thieu, who gave his approval and mandated Saigon's participation in the new project effective December 1967. American personnel in the I Corps area of Vietnam were the ones who came up with a more usable name for the ICEX operation—they referred to the program simply as Phoenix.[447]

Phoenix was undoubtedly a CIA program. The Agency provided key staff in Saigon, including the central intelligence staff. It supplied many of the field officers at both the provincial and regional levels who worked with the provincial reconnaissance units, and it paid for their training center. The PRUs were funded by the CIA to the tune of some $7 million a year. The Special Branch of the National Police, which would be in charge of detentions and interrogations, was funded and advised by the CIA, as was its central intelligence operation. The numerous interrogation centers used by the Special Branch were paid for by the Agency, and CIA officers were assigned oversight over an estimated 90 percent of those centers.

Still, the Special Branch ran its own intelligence operation, producing its own target lists while the Interior Ministry ran the prisons where captured VCI were housed. In concept, the CIA was coordinating the intelligence work; and its field officers would coordinate sweeps, ambushes, detentions, arrests, and any required combat operations. Police security forces would make arrests, take detainees, and proceed with interrogation and legal actions. If major combat sweeps or attacks were necessary, the PRU was to conduct them, with advice from American military officers and guidance from CIA field personnel. On numerous occasions, American Special Forces, including both Navy SEALS and Army Green Berets, were called to back up PRU operations. The Americans were officially attached in advisory and coordination roles but more and more frequently became involved in combat themselves.[448]

Of course counterinsurgency activities in Vietnam had been a part of overall American support for the South Vietnamese regime since the earliest days of the Kennedy Administration. General Victor Krulak of SASCA had been part of the presidential task force evaluating American options in the early 1960s.[449] Krulak had been a major proponent of the pacification program as well as search-and-destroy missions targeting the Viet Cong Infrastructure.[450] By the time ICEX (Phoenix) was proposed, General William DuPuy was the fourth commander of SACSA. Dupuy had previously commanded the Army 1st Infantry Division in South Vietnam and was also a firm proponent of search-and-destroy missions. He was later reassigned to the Pentagon and became head of SACSA in 1967. Acting in that position, he gave full support to the ICEX concept and actively committed Special Forces to the Phoenix operations, as requested by the CIA and the PRUs.[451]

The CIA was keen to ensure that political warfare was seen as a Vietnamese activity. The targets were Vietnamese citizens. Their arrest or detention was a matter of Vietnamese law, and their interrogation and imprisonment was carried out by their own countrymen. The concept of distance in American involvement was seen as extremely important. On paper it appeared to be a model system—organized, coordinated with a clear chain of command and defined responsibilities at all levels. In reality, field operations were very much dependent on the personalities and characters of the local American and Vietnamese personnel involved.

From its inception, the Phoenix program began to run into significant operational issues. Initially many detainees were simply released due to lack of holding and interrogation facilities; even prison space was limited. The court system was also not prepared to handle a VCI infrastructure campaign. In his review of the Phoenix program, the South Vietnamese justice minister confirmed that the province security committees had been authorized to sentence suspected VCI to up to two years without legally accusing them or convicting them of specific crimes, due to difficulties in assembling solid legal cases. Complaints of false arrests, detentions by the American military, and torture inside the interrogation centers soon became widespread.[452]

Even the commander of the Vietnamese Special Branch—the unit in charge of interrogations—was concerned that the program could be counterproductive. He was concerned with the rise in false accusations, arbitrary detentions, and unjustified arrests.[453] In 1969 a CIA internal review expressed displeasure with the quality of the PRUs and complained that so many of the "supposed VCI" were being killed rather than captured—and that little intelligence was being produced.[454] As an illustration, one PRU raid in Region II, in the northern half of the country, killed seven Viet Cong suspects and captured eight. But the prisoners were not exploited for intelligence and five were simply shot in the head. And for record-keeping purposes, the executions counted as "neutralizations."

That CIA's own internal complaint about too much killing and too little intelligence appears especially striking in light of a 1969 news story in the *Washington Post* (apparently planted by the Agency itself) that some 8,104 VCI cadre had been "neutralized" in 1968 and that the goal for 1969 was 33,000. Reportedly Region II was the most active in combat deaths. That region was also an active combat area for MACV special operations from Vietnam against the Ho Chi Minh Trail. David Morales had come over from Pakse Base in Laos to work in Region II of South Vietnam. Morales's exact position is not specified in his available personnel records but it appears to have been a senior one. Morales has been identified in photographs with Colonel Nguyen Van Dai of the South Vietnamese National Police and with Colonel William Graves, the senior American advisor to the Vietnamese field police circa 1970. And in 1970, Felix Rodriguez had been assigned to Vietnam, to work as an advisor to the PRUs in the Saigon region. He used civilian cover but operated as an Army employee, with the equivalent rank of major.[455]

Intelligence collection for Phoenix consistently proved problematic. It seems that given the advisory role of American military and paramilitary officers and the enthusiasm of the actual South Vietnamese forces, the sacrifice of intelligence collection in the interest of direct military action became common practice. In the murky world of who was really on whose side, the pragmatic approach was to simply identify known "VC" and go after them with combat sweeps or ambushes. Some good intelligence work was done, especially in the Saigon region. In one raid, Felix Rodriguez came up with twenty-three VC suspects. Professional interrogation produced a list of one hundred additional VCI members. A helicopter raid based on the information led to the roundup of twenty-eight more people, producing yet more names.

But by 1971, developing the details of the size and nature of the Viet Cong insurgency was proving somewhat discouraging; data showed that rather than being destroyed, the Viet Cong Infrastructure was actually growing over time. In fact the VCI actually appeared to have grown dramatically since the initiation of Phoenix, and extrapolation calculations estimated close to a million-person network throughout South Vietnam. That was something that Ted Shackley, formerly of head of JM WAVE and by 1968 CIA chief of station in Vietnam, would not want to report, and Washington would not want to hear.[456]

One serious risk of moving into organized political warfare is the probability that it will be used by senior leaders within the regime to gain political advantage. Because Phoenix's senior Vietnamese official was the National Police director, a supporter of Vice President Nguyen Cao Ky, who was competing for power against President Van Thieu, the infrastructure warfare never ran cohesively, with all players on one side politically. Instead of focusing strictly on the VCI, on occasion, the National Police reportedly turned their efforts against certain elements of Van Thieu's political support for the program.[457] In addition to more senior Vietnamese officials targeting individuals for their own political purposes, in many cases the targeting was left to local officials, who simply used it as a tool to carry out their own personal agendas, from settling old personal or village grudges to conducting blackmail to obtaining land and businesses by having individuals arrested or otherwise eliminated.

Since the CIA occupied the primary position in the overall Phoenix program, it faced a bit of an internal conflict. On one hand, in its intelligence role it needed well-placed spies and informants within the

VCI. That meant either converting existing Viet Cong leaders into informants or planting spies inside the leadership. On the other hand, Phoenix was set up to identify and neutralize Viet Cong leaders—the sorts of individuals who were key to the operation of the VCI network. The goal would have been to leave the desired informants and spies in place while eliminating the true VCI leaders—but the identity of key informants was a precious intelligence secret. Sharing it with the Phoenix teams could easily compromise the sources; not sharing meant having them appear on Phoenix targeting lists, and being captured or killed.

The reality of the matter was that the CIA most frequently turned to one of two actions: either keeping its own informants and sources off Phoenix target lists or actually recruiting VCI off the Phoenix lists for its own purposes. Given that CIA headquarters staff could either "take over" individuals for their own purposes or suppress information to ensure their key sources were not identified in the Phoenix effort, one military officer commented, "One of the first things you learn about intelligence gathering is that the CIA can absorb any agent it wants."[458] This was a fundamental problem for Phoenix but it's a problem we will encounter in other arenas as well—especially when the CIA mission crosses the missions of other U.S. agencies.[459] The bottom line is that given the CIA's priority of intelligence collection, other agencies' priorities, including prosecuting weapons and drug smugglers, become secondary. To achieve its mission, the CIA has and will override law enforcement priorities—a risk we will explore in detail in later chapters. The net result was that there were constant complaints about the level of real VCI intelligence produced by the interrogation centers, since the interrogators were largely untrained National Police Officers. Numerous CIA officers reported witnessing prisoners held in terrible conditions along with the routine use of torture. Following a routine inspection of a Region II center, one officer reported, "All [the interrogation center officers] had the ability to do was to beat the shit out of those people."[460]

It was no secret to the CIA regional officers that torture was a common interrogation center practice; many of them have been quite open about it and others simply decried the fact that Phoenix was a waste of time from an intelligence standpoint and never produced anything useful. Knowledge of the interrogation center practices went all the way to the top in Saigon, to CIA Chief Ted Shackley. He went on record with his own comments about such problems,

> *What can you do . . . it's their institution . . . we saw it as counterproductive . . . you can't torture people and get information . . . you could see the marks on the prisoners and the instruments . . . you agonized over it . . . you didn't want to be associated with it . . . the publicity was so damaging . . . what do you do . . . withdraw support . . . that's what we were stuck with.*[461]

And it was not only within Phoenix that choosing to work at a distance led to such incidents. CIA officer John Stockwell, a former Marine officer with experience as a CIA chief of station, was assigned to a provincial position in Vietnam. He quickly discovered that one of his chief assets was using a CIA safe house to pursue his personal activities as a practicing sadist, dumping bodies into a canal at dawn. Stockwell went to his CIA supervisor and was told that the personal activities of Vietnamese officials were their own business. It was not part of Stockwell's mission to interfere; the man was important and needed for the mission and if Stockwell "didn't have the stomach for the job he could be reassigned," but only with great risk to his career. Stockwell closed the safe house and passed on word of his disapproval of such activities. His final observation was that his staff simply learned not to tell him about such things, allowing him to remain distant from them and enabling him not to have such things on his conscience.[462]

Aside from moral and ethical concerns, one very basic failure of Phoenix was that it simply did not damage the VCI on the scale that had been anticipated. There were areas where it drew Viet Cong attention and concern, particularly in the region around Saigon. In other regions such as the highlands, results were considerably less. And the "damage" reported in the "neutralization" numbers was more in terms of cadre deaths than defections or conversions. It seems fair to say that the intelligence effort represented by Phoenix was more productive in terms of combat counterinsurgency than political pacification. And that was the upside; the downside was the significant number of Vietnamese who were turned against the central government by the methods of the PRUs and the interrogation practices of the National Police.

The pitfalls of Phoenix would range far beyond Vietnam itself, leading to harsh political criticism from the international community, the American media, and the U.S. Congress. Even Phoenix's most active proponent and defender, William Colby, could only fall back on the "distance defense"—Phoenix was never designed to produce killings in noncombat situations. That was never part of the program; if it happened, then individual members, subordinates, and other people in the program had done it on their own, without official orders or direction. When challenged on how many innocent people had ended up on the Phoenix blacklists, he could only say that he was never "highly satisfied" with the accuracy of U.S. intelligence on the VCI.[463]

Phoenix obviously had its problems, as did many of the counterinsurgency tactics and techniques first used in South Vietnam and even in Laos. But it did have its successes, especially in the centralization and computerization of intelligence. Phoenix demonstrated that an intelligence picture of even a very complex insurgency could be created. With the proper communications, members of that network could be tracked, monitored, and often even pressured into becoming informants. Phoenix also allowed successful targeting of raids and kidnap missions. In fact it was so successful that military units were tempted to simply assault and kill Viet Cong leaders rather than capture them for intelligence purposes.

And Phoenix retained its champions within the counterinsurgency community, advocates who simply felt that it had come too late to make any difference in South Vietnam. Its champions felt that its abuses had simply added to an already exploding opposition to the central government rather than shattering that opposition when it was still possible to have done so. Certainly by the time it had all come together, during 1970–1971, the failure of successive South Vietnamese governments, widespread internal political and religious conflicts, and general distrust of the Saigon government would have put any counterinsurgency program in jeopardy.

Officers within both the CIA and the military felt that the Phoenix concept—the concept of targeted infrastructure warfare—could be quite successful under the right circumstances and with regimes that were unified enough to effectively pursue it. We will explore the concept's effectiveness in another incarnation, that of Operation Condor. Condor would demonstrate the impact of a truly effective infrastructure warfare program. It would also produce a degree of brutality and numbers of civilian casualties that would make the Phoenix experience pale in comparison.

CHAPTER 17

Targeted Infrastructure Warfare in the Southern Cone

Popular unrest became an increasing fact of life in the nations of the Southern Cone in the final years of the 1960s. The unrest had roots in a variety of causes but economic stress had been preeminent. Most of the countries involved had begun to encounter economic stagnation, saturation of domestic markets, and growing inflation. With such stresses, much of the cooperation previously seen between the working populace and the industrial classes faded, and establishment political factions turned to more authoritarian positions, placing their trust in conservative political parties and their military establishments.[464] As the economic situation worsened, the insurgent movements themselves became more radical and much more violent. The result was a dramatic escalation in militancy across the Southern Cone.

In Brazil, foreign diplomats became kidnap targets, held as hostages for the release of political prisoners. The American ambassador to Brazil had been kidnapped in 1969 (and released); and in 1970, the German, Swiss, and Japanese consuls in São Paulo were all kidnapped and then released in prisoner exchanges. The individuals involved in the kidnappings described their movement as socialist and themselves as engaged in a popular revolution against elitist, military-powered, and inherently antidemocratic autocracies. By the early 1970s, even in as small a country as Uruguay, there were some five thousand members of the Tupamaros Movement of National Liberation organized into urban cells.[465] Across the Southern Cone, revolutionary tactics ranged from massive, million-plus-person street demonstrations to actual acts of terror. In Uruguay, American security advisor Dan Mitrione, who had been accused of teaching torture as part of a course on interrogation techniques, was kidnapped. As in Southeast Asia, USAID was often used as a cover for counterinsurgency and counter-guerilla trainers and advisors. In addition, the FBI was indeed involved in several countries, working with police and public safety groups. Mitrione was an FBI agent assigned to the State Department's International Cooperation Administration. He had worked in Brazil, and was indeed teaching advanced counterinsurgency techniques in Uruguay. After being released by his kidnappers and spending time back in the U.S., he returned to Uruguay. During his second tour he worked with national Office of Public Safety as a USAID employee. While in that job he was murdered by Uruguayan revolutionaries.

In Chile, the Movement of the Revolutionary Left (MIR) began the armed phase of its insurgency in anticipation of the military coup against Salvador Allende—first trying to split the Chilean armed forces in an effort to forestall the coup. If successful, the effort would have led to civil war, but in the end military loyalties superseded other concerns and the army took virtual control of the country. Personnel who might have supported the elected Allende government were purged and the new government, led by Augusto Pinochet, began a brutal suppression of opposition.[466]

Under Allende, Chile had actually been a safe haven for a relatively large number of young internationalist revolutionaries from across Latin America. With the Pinochet military newly in charge and targeting anyone and everyone of that stripe, a great number of them fled to adjacent countries, to Argentina or Peru. As more and more countries came under military rule, Argentina served as a refuge for revolutionaries from Bolivia, Uruguay, Paraguay, Brazil, and finally Chile. Historian John Dinges describes this process in detail in his book *The Condor Years: How Pinochet and His Allies*

Brought Terrorism to Three Continents, demonstrating the manner in which an international revolutionary infrastructure established itself across the Southern Cone countries. Groups such as the Tupamaros from Uruguay; the National Liberation Army from Bolivia; the Argentine People's Revolutionary Army and its political arm, the Workers' Revolutionary Party; and MIR from Chile began to meet and plan operations together.

The Chilean military coup had defined the playing field. Either the revolutionaries would be able to organize successful combat against the military governments or they would face extermination. By 1973, the groups had organized to the point of forming a formal pan-national alliance for funding, training, and intelligence collection. The new alliance named itself the Revolutionary Coordinating Junta (JCR).[467] It was something entirely new, a multinational insurgency, seen by its members as a common revolutionary movement. In turn the Southern Cone governments viewed it as an international terror alliance.

With increasing internal class conflicts and worsening economies, by the mid-1970s virtually all the nations of the Southern Cone had come under control of conservative military regimes. The military and security organizations held a widespread distrust of all reformist or populist movements as being the dupes of communist revolutionaries, and justified their own actions as defending the established anticommunist regimes. In turn, the American administrations of the period shared that anticommunist worldview and pledged support for the conservative regimes, ensuring that opposing movements stayed out of power—or were removed if they had managed to win democratic elections.

It became increasingly clear that voluntary economic and political reform was simply not going to happen. The established militaries and conservative governments of the Southern Cone region had come to view any call for reform as a threat, and anyone unwilling to disavow reform as a potential revolutionary—not just groups and parties but even individuals were being treated as traitors and subversives. Fear led the military governments to visualize an enemy of grand proportions; such an enemy demanded a broad response. In the past, counterterrorism had been conducted against revolutionary military units, such as Che Guevara's group in Bolivia. In the nations of the Southern Cone, it was going to be targeted against a much broader range of individuals. Moderates and reformists were not going to be exempted. They were going to be associated with the truly militant network, the Revolutionary Coordinating Junta, which would by 1974 proclaim its own state of political warfare against the established regimes:

> *We are united in the realization that the strategy of revolutionary war is the only viable strategy in Latin America. . . . The Continental character of the struggle is determined fundamentally by the presence of the common enemy. North American imperialism is carrying out an international strategy to stop socialist revolution in Latin America. It is no accident that fascist regimes have been imposed in countries where a mass movement in ascendancy has threatened the stability of oligarchic power. The international strategy requires a continental strategy by the revolutionaries.*[468]

Objectively it seems hard to wholeheartedly argue against the view that American foreign policy was preventing socialist revolution in Latin America. We have the examples of the Johnson Administration's coup support activities in Brazil and the Nixon Administration's ongoing efforts to prevent an elected president (Allende) from taking power and later to encourage his removal. We have the aggressive counterinsurgency efforts by the U.S. military assistance missions in Ecuador and Peru—missions that had expanded into almost every Southern Cone country as the 1970s began. Certainly there seems to be a consistent pattern of American support for aggressively anticommunist (translated to antisocialist and antireformist) governments in Latin America. During the Nixon Administration, this foreign policy position was even more clearly stated with Secretary Kissinger's now-famous position statement: "I don't see why we need to stand by and watch a country go communist due to the irresponsibility of its own people."[469]

Of course, in later years administration figures became a bit less forthright in their positions, especially in remarks given to Congress. CIA Director Richard Helms denied, in a sworn statement, that the CIA had tried to overthrow the government of Chile. Four years later he was indicted for perjury on that statement, pled no contest, and was pronounced guilty. And as historian John Prados points out, in his own memoirs Henry Kissinger vigorously complained about people not being willing to follow orders—orders that Kissinger himself officially refused to admit to Congress had been given.[470] But our concern here is the practice and pitfalls of shadow warfare. To pursue that subject, it is necessary to trace what actually came about in the Southern Cone during the early years of the 1970s, a period that ended with the ultimate appearance of pan-national, infrastructure warfare. U.S. policy and clandestine actions would indeed prevent the loss of a single Southern Cone country to communism. The humanitarian consequences of that victory would be enormous.

The existence of a regional revolutionary infrastructure in the Southern Cone was no myth; the Revolutionary Coordinating Junta had amassed a significant war chest from hostage payments, on the order of $20 million. In Chile, MIR offered the other groups an operational weapons factory, capable of producing semiautomatic submachine guns as well as light mortars, hand grenades, and grenade launchers. Millions were spent on airplanes and trucks and in creating a logistics and courier network that could move people, money, and weapons into a number of countries. At the end of 1973, the Revolutionary Coordinating Junta began a campaign of high-profile kidnapping in Argentina, beginning with the general manager of the Argentine branch of the Exxon oil and gas corporation. After negotiations and on the threat of murder, the kidnappers received $14.2 million for his release. Similar kidnappings brought $3 million from Firestone and $3.2 million from Swissair.

By 1974 the Junta would be prepared to take the military offensive. Some eighty fighters seized a tank garrison in Buenos Aires province, killed the commander, and captured his second in command, withdrawing after a seven-hour battle. Tactically it was a failure, as no weapons or ammunition were seized. As propaganda it was a huge success for the revolutionaries.[471] It was further leveraged for media announcements of the four-country front, and to declare an offensive against the Argentinean army. The gauntlet had been thrown down, the challenge given. The revolutionary network was in place: it had money, it had will, and it had fighters and a rapidly expanding infrastructure. It had declared political war.

There was an answer to that sort of challenge—one already tested, even if not ultimately successful, in Vietnam. The answer would be infrastructure warfare. In Vietnam it had been Phoenix. In the Southern Cone it would be Condor. It had taken years for the Phoenix operation to fully come together in Vietnam; its roots were in earlier and less ambitious programs. The same can be said for Condor, which evolved from several years of contacts, training, and advisory work by Central Intelligence Agency officers during the early 1970s. Many of those individuals moved to Latin American assignments directly from the Phoenix experience in Vietnam. Indeed, several of them are familiar names from earlier shadow warfare ranging from Guatemala to the secret war against Cuba and beyond to Southeast Asia.

Tony Sforza was one of the first Vietnam alumni to return for assignment in Latin America. He was assigned to the CIA's 1970 effort against Salvador Allende in Chile. Sforza had played a key field role, working with the military cabal plotting against both Allende and his military supporters. Director Helms cabled Chief of Station Henry Hecksher to "sponsor a military move . . . using all available assets and strategies . . . every hour counts . . . all other considerations are secondary . . . contact the military and let them know the USG [United States government] wants a military solution . . . and we will support them now and later."[472] That effort was conducted by Sforza, using cover as a Colombian businessman, and Bruce McMasters, using cover as an American businessman representing the Ford and Rockefeller foundations. To enable a coup, Allende's military chief, General Schneider, had to be "removed." Initially Sforza and McMasters pursued a kidnap effort and agreed to deliver "paralyzing gas" to the plotters. They also committed $250,000 in financial support to the coup. CIA estimates of a successful military coup actually gave it marginal chances (one in twenty) of success but ever-increasing pressure to act against Allende was applied directly by President Nixon.[473] In turn, CIA headquarters continued to press Hecksher and his in-country team: "Review all your present and possibly new activities to include propaganda, black operations, surfacing of intelligence or disinformation, personal contacts, or anything else your information can conjure which will permit you to press forward toward our [deleted] objective in a secure manner."[474] In the end, there were officially no further CIA contacts with the military, and General Schneider was murdered. The act occurred "at a distance," with no direct involvement of CIA officers or use of provided weapons. Later, when the assassination was investigated by a Senate committee, the CIA officers were essentially presented as acting in a rogue fashion. Documents now available suggest that, instead, the CIA was being pushed by the White House to foster virtually any action that would have blocked the elected Allende government from taking office.[475]

David Morales came back from his Laos and Vietnam assignments to move into a very special position in 1971. Morales traveled constantly across Latin America, in particular the Southern Cone region, through 1975. Acclaimed for his intelligence and political warfare training skills in the Guatemala and Cuba projects, Morales was a specialist in both covert intelligence collection and paramilitary operations. He had moved from being head of operations at JM WAVE to become CIA chief of station at Pakse in southern Laos. In Laos he had worked under USAID cover. Following that assignment he worked under Department of Defense cover in Vietnam, reportedly as a "training" advisor for Phoenix field operations.

Morales's exact role in Latin America is unclear but we know that he worked first in Peru under USAID cover, as a counterinsurgency advisor to the Peruvian National Police.[476] Following that he assumed military cover, to be specific as a counterinsurgency advisor to the U.S. Joint Chiefs of Staff, working in countries across Latin America with a focus on the Southern Cone. Morales's position as a Joint Chiefs of Staff consultant may have been a cover, but it carried considerable prestige. Morales's lifelong friend Reuben Carbajal describes being invited to visit Morales in Washington, D.C., and touring the Pentagon with him. Morales had a parking space designated for senior staff officers there (the parking spaces were primarily for generals). During the visit Morales introduced Carbajal to CIA Western Hemisphere Chief Ted Shackley.

Given the Joint Chiefs' previously discussed role in worldwide special operations, and the known involvement of Special Forces officers as trainers and advisors in Latin America, Morales may well have served in a key liaison role between the Joint Chiefs and the CIA in covert training and advisory missions. Unfortunately little remains to document Morales's specific Latin American work rather than a final résumé describing his assignments. In his CIA-approved résumé, prepared for his separation, Morales states,

> *From 1971–1975 I served as a counterinsurgency advisor for Latin American matters to the Joint Chiefs of Staff in Washington, D.C. During this period I traveled extensively throughout Latin American countries, primarily Argentina, Panama, Paraguay, and Uruguay. In all these assignments I worked directly with senior officials of the government of the country to which I was assigned. In all cases my responsibility was one of insuring that U.S. Government policies were understood, and insofar as possible, coordinated, supported, and carried out.*[477]

Considering that David Morales was the single-known senior CIA/military officer in contact with all the Southern Cone military groups, acting as a representative of the Joint Chiefs of Staff during the period leading up to as well as the actual formation of the Condor pact, we can only speculate on his personal impact. Given Morales's documented extreme anticommunism, his longtime involvement with blacklisting and infrastructure warfare, and his personal aggressiveness, his advice would certainly have had an impact on the offices he was advising. It would also be difficult to imagine that his training included a heavy emphasis on issues of operational restraint. And as we review the ultimate consequences of the Condor program in the remainder of this chapter, it is very likely that with the rise of death squads, the torture of tens of thousands of civilians, an equal number kidnapped and "disappeared," and a combined death toll in the hundreds of thousands, neither the CIA nor the Joint Chiefs might have been happy to fully acknowledge Morales's final remarks that his responsibility had been to ensure that U.S. policies were coordinated, supported, and carried out by the nations he was advising.

In 1972 another longtime counterinsurgency professional, Felix Rodriguez, moved from supporting Phoenix field operations in the Saigon region of Vietnam to a new post in Argentina. He describes being personally requested by the commanding general of the Argentine army, whom he had briefed on intelligence and counterinsurgency operations in Vietnam. Rodriguez was working with and for Tomas Sanchez de Bustamante, commander of the 1st Army and the federal police, the second most powerful military figure in Argentina at that time. As a CIA employee, he worked under commercial cover in Argentina, specializing as an advisor in counterterrorism and "low-intensity" warfare. He stayed in that position until 1973.[478]

During their Latin American activities, both Morales and Rodriguez would have been working under the CIA Western Hemisphere chief, and as of 1972 that was none other than Ted Shackley. While Morales and the other Vietnam alumni who moved into Latin American work might have seen Phoenix in action in the field, Ted Shackley would have had the broader, headquarters view. Among other duties, Shackley had overseen CIA activities in support of the Phoenix project. He had arrived in Saigon from Laos in 1968, in the earliest days of Phoenix development. While the overall infrastructure warfare program had been administratively assigned to CORDS (civil operations and revolutionary development support) the CIA provided the financing for most of its key elements, as well as staff personnel in Saigon and field officers in the provinces. When

Shackley took over from William Colby as chief of Saigon station in 1968, he had to become familiar with both the operational and political issues relating to Phoenix operations. In fact Shackley became personally notorious for coopting Phoenix intelligence assets for CIA control and use. Many of Shackley's Vietnam personnel, including David Morales, Felix Rodriguez, Tony Sforza, and Rudy Enders (all JM WAVE Cuba project alumni) worked either in or around Phoenix in Vietnam and went on to serve in Latin America. Shackley and his people had the opportunity to know Phoenix from the inside out, while maintaining at least some distance from its pitfalls.

As we saw with Phoenix, the foundation of political warfare lies in the collection and organization of intelligence. In South Vietnam the Viet Cong insurgency was operating within one set of borders, even if actively supplied from North Vietnam. In Condor, the challenge was going to be uniting the intelligence collection and operations of several participating countries. It would involve a type of multi-regime trust and united action, which were both new and quite striking. Indeed, it would involve a level of domestic intelligence collection and analysis that had existed in none of the member countries prior to 1973. Before that time they had worried about their neighbors, focusing intelligence collection on conventional military action. The new direction would be on internal rather than external threats. Even Manual Contreras, the head of DINA (the Chilean Directorate of National Intelligence), is on record as having nothing beyond a standard military-type intelligence system prior to receiving training from CIA officers.[479] All in all, there would be unity and common support for Condor among all the participating intelligence and security groups that had simply been absent from Phoenix in South Vietnam.

Details of the training given DINA and the other intelligence services remain somewhat mysterious. The CIA has not been forthcoming with documents that would shed light on the process. Given the eventual consequences of the training and resultant congressional inquiries, that is not surprising. At this point in time we can provide only the following context in terms of both process and people. It is clear that the individual countries requested CIA intelligence training and assistance. Contreras has described travel to the U.S. in 1974, meeting with various agencies including the CIA. The CIA did provide training, although not acknowledging it was done on-site in Chile. However, following Contreras's visit to the U.S., DINA opened a new operational center, and he has stated that some eight CIA personnel went to Chile to conduct training sessions. Documents acknowledge training being provided to DINA, although they stress that the topics were strictly limited to the "fundamentals of intelligence organization and management." Of course, as we have seen previously, the content and conduct of any such training would depend largely on the experience, views, and orientation of the individuals involved with or overseeing the training. The person in charge of overseeing a response to training requests such as that of DINA would have been the chief of Latin American and Caribbean operations, David Phillips. Phillips's previous assignments are familiar by now, from PBSUCCESS in Guatemala and the initial Cuba secret war project (JMARC), through his various Latin American assignments, first as chief of station in the Dominican Republic during the U.S. intervention there, and then chief of station in Brazil, only to be pulled to lead the first American effort against Salvador Allende.

David Phillips's activities in Chile were a matter of considerable concern to Congressional committees in the mid-1970's and testimony was offered connecting him to reported assassination efforts related to the CIA Chilean project. While the committee could reach no conclusive indictment, in November of 2013 well-known Cuban exile activist Antonio Veciana issued a written statement confirming information disclosed by House Select Committee investigator Gaeton Fonzi. Veciana stated that beginning in Cuba in 1960, he had been in contact with CIA officer David Phillips, who used the alias of Maurice Bishop. Phillips had himself acknowledged being in contact with Cuban revolutionaries planning an attack on Castro while he served undercover in Cuba. Based on Veciana's known activities it appears that Phillips became involved with him while the group was organizing an ultimately abortive bazooka attack on Castro in April, 1961.

The relationship between the two men continued for some 13

years, Phillips assisted Veciana in organizing the Alpha 66 paramilitary group, which staged repeated attacks against Russian targets inside Cuba during 1962–63—in direct opposition to Kennedy Administration directives to the CIA. In 1968, while under INS restriction to the Miami area, Veciana obtained a job with a USAID agency in Bolivia, apparently through Phillips's intervention. While working for the International Investment Development Bank, Veciana participated in organizing further assassination efforts against Fidel Castro, with the final attack aborting during 1971 in Santiago, Chile. Veciana's disclosure of Maurice Bishop as David Phillips raises a great number of issues related to Phillips's activities, including the extent to which they were actually CIA sanctioned, and at what level they were known within the Agency—considering that the CIA itself firmly denied the relationship and Phillips's involvement with Veciana during the congressional inquiries. The full story of David Phillips in Latin America remains to be revealed, including his role during the formative years of what became the Condor project.

As Condor was being established, Phillips's activities involved organizing CIA training of the various Southern Cone countries' intelligence and security services. In his autobiography, Phillips describes a personal tour of Latin American countries in 1974, when he received a personal request from the president of one such country (which he refers to only by a fictitious name) for training and advisory assistance. In relating the story, Phillips notes that the president had "gratefully accepted training and technical assistance" in working against "extremists" trying to overthrow his government—extremists with foreign support.[480] We have come to know all these CIA shadow warriors as being fiercely anticommunist, willing to bring all possible U.S. resources behind covert political, psychological, or paramilitary efforts against communist insurgencies. They all carried the same Cold War worldview and all have been seen to be "forward-leaning," willing to act on their own initiative to carry out their missions. It was an attitude and force of character that may well have been influential in further shaping the intelligence and security leaders in the nations of the Condor operation.

American involvement with the Southern Cone multicountry infrastructure warfare operation—Condor—appears to have evolved through three discrete phases. Its initial phase involved personnel from a number of different U.S. government agencies, including military trainers and advisors, CIA intelligence officers, FBI officers within the various nations, and U.S. State Department personnel from country ambassadorial level to senior staff in Washington, D.C. In Condor's formative phase, special operations and intelligence personnel were sent to train and advise various military/intelligence units. Training was also given to police and security forces. As the intelligence services of each country began to focus on political warfare it became clear that they were dealing with an insurgency supported by a multicountry infrastructure: the Revolutionary Coordinating Junta. The junta had built a large-scale, pan-national logistics network and established political support overseas, primarily in Europe but to some extent within the United States. Perhaps most important, it had successfully used kidnapping hostage payments to build a huge financial war chest. Condor would have to be built to operate against the full breadth of the junta's financial, operational, and political network.

The second phase of Condor's development involved the establishment of a working multination system for indexing and sharing political intelligence as well as the implementation of, and a technical/communications network for, access to information for rapid response by the military and security forces of each nation. That first step in that project began in early 1974 with meetings by the security forces of Argentina, Chile, Paraguay, Bolivia, and Uruguay. The meetings were in Buenos Aires and the goal was "coordinated action against subversive targets." The meeting was reported by the CIA, which noted that the effort was not yet "very effective." The Agency continued its observations of an increasing series of organizational meetings.[481]

To become effective, the new group needed to formally organize, but it also needed support. To gain that support, DINA chief Contreras traveled to Washington, D.C., a number of times during 1975. He met with the Lieutenant General Vernon A. Walters, deputy director of the CIA; with a State Department representative; and even with U.S. congressmen. Following his last visit, Contreras flew directly to a Caracas, Venezuela, meeting with the head of Venezuelan security (DSIP) and laying out plans for a multinational project. Venezuela was of high interest to Chile since many of its exiles and opponents had sought refuge there, and Contreras wanted to act against them. By the end of 1975, representatives from all the Condor countries were meeting in Santiago, Chile, in the First Inter-American Working Meeting on National Intelligence. The participating parties established the new working agreement, naming it Condor in respect for the host nation: the condor is considered the national symbol of Chile but also of Argentina, Bolivia, Colombia, Ecuador, and Peru. The key to Condor would be the establishment of a central data bank, containing intelligence from all countries and remotely accessible by all the intelligence services. It was also important for Condor to gain information from the United States. FBI agent Robert Scherrer has described his provision of extensive American intelligence as acting as a Condor liaison in Buenos Aires.

But to make Condor truly effective, the nations involved needed critical technical assets that they could not provide for themselves. Their first need was computers and computer data storage. The second was a communications network. According to Condor participants, both were provided by the United States. The CIA provided the computers and the necessary systems training as well as the communications equipment. Communications were via telex units provided to each country. The systems were equipped with code encryption and became the core of the information exchange process. Beyond that, the United States provided unrestricted access to its long-distance military radio network with the central transmitter in Panama. The network had been originally installed to support military assistance advisory groups in each country as well as to allow military students at the School of the Americas in Panama to communicate back home while in training.[482]

Clearly the United States, through several of its agencies, was enabling the Condor intelligence system, not only with technology and training, but also with the positive advice and encouragement of intensely anticommunist personnel. It was also providing data, and no doubt collected new data for its own use from the system. At the same time, virtually all American participants expressed an ongoing concern for the security practices of the Condor nations: wide-scale torture of any and all suspected regime opponents and their sympathizers, brutal security practices, extensive domestic political executions, and a broad variety of basic humanitarian violations. In one sense the CIA and the other agencies maintained a strict distance from those practices; certainly no Americans were officially allowed to participate. Yet whether or not individual advisors or trainers might have done so at their own initiative remains problematic.

Two results of the second phase are clear. First, the coordination and aggressiveness of the individual security services worked dramatically. In the summer of 1975, the capture of Revolutionary Coordinating Junta representatives in Paraguay had produced an intelligence bonanza of notebooks and contact lists with names, locations, pseudonyms. Harsh interrogation had also developed names of political supporters across Latin America, Europe, and the United States. The information was shared across the Southern Cone countries and with the U.S. through the legal legate (FBI intelligence officer Scherrer) in Buenos Aires, Argentina. The second result was that the success of Condor and of the individual nations' practices had created a tremendous sense of confidence and emboldened them to pursue their targets far beyond the Southern Cone. Contreras himself told a CIA officer that Chile and DINA were prepared to "go to Australia if necessary to get our enemies."

In the third phase of Condor, its reach extended far beyond the borders of the Southern Cone. The Condor network actively pursued political assassination in both Europe and America. And by that point in time, the definition of "enemies" had expanded to include not just the Revolutionary Development Cadre infrastructure, but any of their political supporters, liberals, or virtually anyone unsupportive of or unsympathetic to the existing governments of the Condor nations. Later, in the 1980s, that classification would be equally extended to any humanitarian or religious groups expressing opposition to the brutality of the regimes. Phase three of Condor, its involvement in foreign assassinations, is explored in great depth by John Dinges in *The Condor Years*. Basically the Condor group had been so successful in tracing and eliminating insurgents within the region of the Southern Cone that it felt capable of pursuing its suspected enemies anywhere on the globe—and executing them there. It certainly was not an activity in which the United States was involved, nor one that it sanctioned. At that point the Condor personnel were sufficiently confident to go their own way. In fact, there might well have been some risk in attempting to stop them.

U.S. intelligence connections were sufficient to produce warnings of the new overseas assassination efforts and even to monitor certain of the activities leading up to foreign assassinations. But a decision was made at the highest levels of the American government, by Secretary Kissinger, to essentially ignore that intelligence—including warnings from within his own State Department. The result was that no American warning was provided to Condor-targeted individuals in either Europe or the United States before actual murders occurred. Indeed Kissinger went further than that, ultimately directing aides not to even attempt to caution the Southern Cone countries planning acts of assassination.

U.S. intelligence had been following the extension of Condor and its plans to send assassination teams abroad. On August 30, 1976, a cable from Assistant Secretary of State for Inter-American Affairs Harry Shlaudeman had put matters directly on the table for Secretary Kissinger. Concerned about the potential diplomatic damage from known American allies conducting assassinations in foreign countries, Shlaudeman wrote the following in an Operation Condor memorandum: "What we are trying to head off is a series of international murders that could do serious damage to the international status and reputations of the countries involved."[483] Kissinger had initially responded, directing that individual Condor-country American ambassadors express to the military leaders of those countries a "deep American concern" over the possibility that they might be involved in plans to assassinate subversives, politicians, or prominent figures "both within the national borders of certain Southern Cone countries and abroad." In essence Kissinger had handed off the ball and the responsibility to the in-country ambassadors, exactly the people who might themselves be placed at some risk just by delivering the message.[484]

And at least two of those ambassadors felt they would indeed be personally placed at risk by simply conveying the caution. Instead of acting on Kissinger's directions they literally declined to deliver the message. In Montevideo, Uruguay, the U.S. ambassador responded that his life would be in danger if he delivered such a message to Uruguayan generals. The Chilean ambassador had protested that any such message to a general in the ruling junta would be taken as a personal insult and could also hurt the American diplomatic relationship with Chile. Both ambassadors requested further orders before proceeding. And for some two weeks they were given no reply.

At that point Kissinger ordered that no further action be taken in regard to protesting Condor-nation assassination plans, effectively rescinding the effort at preemption. No mention was made of warning individuals who would be likely targets of such plans even though certain of the targeted individuals had sought refuge in the United States.[485] Only days later, a massive car bomb blast in Washington, D.C., killed former Chilean Foreign Minister Orlando Letelier and his American assistant. Following the murders, a member of the CIA staff in Chile did meet with Contreras, expressing U.S. "concerns" over Letelier's murder. No other diplomatic or military assistance responses were made in regard to Chile or the Condor project.[486]

It should be noted that Harry Shlaudeman had produced the finding that a cooperative Condor foreign assassination project was in progress. On July 20, 1976, representatives from the State Department and the CIA sat down in a meeting and performed an objective and accurate evaluation of the evolution of Condor into an assassination mechanism. Documents from this and related meetings are heavily redacted but indicate that the CIA actually had managed to develop a list of potential Condor targets, including foreign citizens in both Paris and Lisbon.[487]

Later the CIA would uncover other Condor targets, Americans

who had been known to express humanitarian concerns over events in the Southern Cone nations. These targets included Democratic congressman and future New York City mayor Ed Koch. Koch himself was personally warned of the plot by then–CIA Director George H.W. Bush; however, historian John Dinges relates that an extensive search of all available records fails to reveal any dialogue or protest with Chile over the incident. His study suggests that in the end, the success of the Southern Cone nations in destroying a perceived communist threat simply outweighed all other considerations. So, unlike Phoenix, Condor had triumphed, at least in the short run.

In one sense, the infrastructure warfare in the Southern Cone had been dramatically successful. The Southern Cone revolutionary movement had been violently defeated—not just defeated but totally shattered. The effort had also encouraged an escalation of outright political warfare even beyond the Southern Cone: the rise of private "death squads" would terrorize reform movements across both Central and South America for another decade. The bitter fruit of the Condor victories, including the explosive growth of Latin American government paramilitary groups and their associated death squads, is covered extensively in *Our Own Backyard: The United States in Central America 1977–1992* by William M. LeoGrande. Both Dinges's and LeoGrande's works are highly recommended to readers who wish to pursue the story of American foreign policy in the region. It is not an encouraging story; nor is it one for anyone without a strong stomach. We will return only to limited portions of it in the following chapter, as we explore yet another major change in American surrogate warfare.

That change was brought about in an ongoing battle among President Reagan, his chief advisors, and Congress. Initially the CIA would be caught in the middle of that battle. Ultimately it was to be left largely behind as Reagan chose to return to classic "surrogate" warfare with insurgents and rebels acting to unseat communist regimes. But in that return to regime change, the Reagan Administration would eventually go completely "outside the box" and beyond the CIA itself, in authorizing, controlling, and funding undeclared warfare in both Nicaragua and Afghanistan.

CHAPTER 18

Pushing Back

The Carter Administration witnessed a number of incidents that become important to our study of trends in shadow warfare. However, during much of his administration, Carter's attention was focused on a number of domestic economic problems, including spiking energy prices, and his own personal interest in global human rights. It was only in the final year of his single term that the 1979 seizure of the American Embassy in Tehran, Iran, and the taking of American hostages, and later the Soviet invasion of Afghanistan, led him into tentative steps that would turn into full-scale covert operations in both Afghanistan and Nicaragua during the administration of his successor, President Ronald Reagan. Carter's first reaction in each case was a return to the "holding the line" strategy of previous decades. Reagan's would be quite different: surrounded by assertive advisors, his administration sought not just to blunt perceived communist expansion, but to push it back. For President Carter, the year 1979 was exceptionally difficult. Aside from events in Iran, he first faced the ouster of a friendly regime in Nicaragua that had been an American standby for decades. That was in July. By December he was dealing with an even more dramatic international challenge. Afghanistan had already been taken over by a communist regime, but in December 1979, the Soviets invaded and occupied the country. Carter would respond, launching covert operations against the Soviets, but first he had to address Central America.

It all begin with a longtime American ally and the fear that it might suddenly go communist just as Cuba had, joining with Cuba to push its revolution across Central America. Nicaragua had long been considered a geographically strategic country in Central America, not just during the Cold War but for well over a century. When six thousand U.S. Marines were dispatched to crush a 1927 revolution against an American-supported regime, it was a continuation of armed intervention dating back to 1848. Several of the very earliest American military incursions had been provoked by the private affairs of American citizens. In 1853 a contingent of U.S. Marines landed in Nicaragua to settle a commercial dispute involving railroad and shipping tycoon Cornelius Vanderbilt and his investments. The business dispute was resolved on Vanderbilt's terms.

A year later, a personal insult to an American diplomat led to a U.S. gunboat shelling a Nicaraguan port, pounding it to the ground. A Marine party was then dispatched to the shore to burn the remains. Marines would be sent into Nicaragua to assert American will on some eleven different occasions.[488] And the U.S. was not at all bashful about its actions or its right to assert its interests. As American Undersecretary of State Robert Olds described matters in 1927, "Until now, Central America has always understood that governments which we recognize and support stay in power, while those which we do not recognize and support fall. Nicaragua has become a test case. It is difficult to see how we can afford to be defeated."

A Marine peacekeeping force was kept in Nicaragua for some years, withdrawing only in 1933 after organizing and training an internal security force, the National Guard. Anastasio Somoza García, at the time foreign secretary of the country, used his contacts with the Americans to become commander of the country's National Guard and leveraged that power base to move into the presidency. He established a regime that ruled the country for some forty-two years. Given its strong relationship with the United States, the Somoza family regime became a linchpin of American regional power in Central America. Its rule was acknowledged to be less than benign, but its role was considered vital. Franklin Roosevelt continued the American tradition of openness about the relationship in his anecdotally reported remarks about Somoza: "He's a son of a bitch, but he's our son of a bitch."

Indeed the Somoza family was not just loyal to the U.S. but aggressively willing to play a role as a critical surrogate in American covert warfare for some two decades, from regime change in Guatemala in the 1950s to the basing and training of Cuban exiles for the landings in Cuba in the early 1960s. A minor Nicaraguan insurgent movement, the Sandinista National Liberation Front, did eventually develop during the early 1960s, and like all such movements in Latin America, it received Cuban encouragement and limited support. Best estimates placed its size at no more than fifty persons and it lacked the resources to maintain even a fixed base of operation.

It would not be until 1970 that serious signs of a liberal opposition became noticeable, with the first incident in which the Catholic Church joined in support of protesting student groups, declaring opposition to long-standing corruption in the Somoza government and in particular civil rights abuses by the Nicaraguan National Guard.[489] The U.S. took note of the trend but for practical purposes it remained entirely tied to the Somoza regime. As of 1970 the only real point of discussion in the American relationship with Nicaragua was how the U.S. should handle an increased training role with the Nicaraguan National Guard, which held the responsibility for police duties, security functions, and conventional military operations. The question was whether increased support should go through the American Military Group (MILGP) and its Military Assistance Program (MAP), whether USAID should become involved instead, and who would hire and pay the new police trainers. The general agreement was that it was an opportune time to focus on the issue, as a new commander, Francisco Somoza, a cousin to the president, had been appointed to the National Guard in Managua.[490]

A comprehensive U.S. State Department assessment of the government of Nicaragua in 1970 envisioned no immediate political concerns for the current ruler, Anastasio Somoza Debayle, other than that of term limits on his presidency and how Somoza might address that issue. American concerns were more with the stagnation of the country's economy. The assessment did take note of the limited student demonstrations and labor union protests but projected that any major political protest movement would be a number of years away.[491] The first signs of popular opposition to Somoza followed a series of floods and a major earthquake in the capital. Those natural disasters set the stage for a significant change in Nicaraguan affairs. The Somoza family was generally believed to have engaged in massive profiteering from the natural disasters, including the sale of relief supplies. The National Guard drew public ire for its action in dynamiting and clearing buildings following the earthquake, rather than conducting searches for survivors.[492] The resultant outcry galvanized what had been a small opposition movement into something that quickly became a major liberal opposition to the Somoza regime and the conservative political factions in the country.

The Nicaraguan congress had dissolved in August 1971, effectively leaving Somoza as the sole power in the government. A new government was supposed to be established through Constituent Assembly elections in 1972. The only real alternative to having Somoza remain alone in power appeared to be likelihood that the election would bring into control of the assembly a conservative party headed by Dr. Fernando Agüero. That would have laid the foundation for Agüero and his Partido Conservador Tradicional (PCT) to launch a successful presidential campaign in 1974, replacing Somoza with Agüero—assuming that Somoza would have been willing to exit the political field. However, even Agüero doubted that Somoza was likely to go quietly or to reach an accommodation with the PCT.[493]

Agüero and his party conducted an aggressive campaign but instead of sweeping the seats in the Constituent Assembly as they had anticipated, the 1972 elections delivered a resounding victory for a series of liberal candidates. That effectively spoiled chances for a conservative-controlled governmental transition via the anticipated open election of Agüero in 1974. Yet even the massive liberal successes in the election seem not to have led the American State Department to forecast any imminent problems for the Somoza regime. The U.S. State Department anticipated no imminent threat to U.S. interests in the country; nor did it seem to anticipate any long-term issues for Nicaraguan relationships in the face of an expanding reformist movement.[494] And at no time did the increasing liberal and insurgent pressure on Somoza seem to soften American support for the Somoza regime.

Within Nicaragua, political moves, countermoves, and insurgency continued throughout the decade with no definitive result other than the increasing autocracy of the regime and its escalating use of kidnapping and murder to silence popular opposition. Blatant violence by the regime led to international protests and in 1977 the Carter Administration cut off aid to Nicaragua due to human rights violations. In January 1978 Pedro Joaquín Chamorro Cardenal, the publisher of a leftist newspaper in the capital of Managua, and a highly visible critic of the regime, was murdered. His death was immediately seen as yet another abuse by Somoza. Riots and a general strike followed, shutting down some 80 percent of businesses not only in the capital but also in large provincial capitals. The Organization of American States attempted to broker a democratic power-sharing arrangement but Somoza showed no real interest. In early 1979, U.S. intelligence estimates continued to state that, given the strength of the National Guard, Somoza would quite successfully crush any moves against his regime. However by June 1979, insurgent forces controlled the majority of the country outside Managua, and the much-hated National Guard was proving no match for the military fervor of the rebels. In July the capital of Managua fell, and by the middle of the month the Somoza regime was history and both he and his National Guard commander were in exile in Miami, Florida.[495]

Given that Nicaragua had long been viewed as a strategic choke point in Central America, there was some concern in Washington that a revolutionary government in its capital of Managua would aggressively begin to support insurgencies in adjacent countries. That fear held that the Sandinistas could be viewed as a potential exporter of the Cuban Revolution, encouraged to action by Fidel Castro. The Carter Administration assessed that scenario and concluded that although some Nicaraguans certainly did endorse other revolutions and had shipped some supplies and weapons to neighboring El Salvador, there was no convincing case for thinking Nicaragua had become another Cuba, "aiding, abetting, or supporting acts of violence or terrorism in other countries." President Carter allowed the certification of a general Central American aid package that included Nicaragua.

The litmus test for true Sandinista intentions, the first sign that they would become active in spreading revolution, was viewed to be El Salvador. The fear was that El Salvador's relatively liberal regime would not be able to maintain power if Nicaragua initiated a serious effort to support the relatively weak leftist insurgency already existing inside El Salvador. The first American response to the potential of Nicaraguan involvement in what had up to that point been a very modest Salvadorian insurgency was an escalation of "friendly forces" assistance to the government of El Salvador.

President Carter appointed a new ambassador, Robert White, with some twenty-five years' experience in Latin America, known for his strong advocacy for human rights. White's views of what El Salvador needed were somewhat in contrast to those of the Pentagon, which had directed its Southern Command (SOCOM) to immediately begin developing a major counterinsurgency program involving U.S. advisor teams and equipment such as helicopters. Southern Command proceeded with its plan; some three hundred Salvadorian army officers went to Panama for military and human rights training. While El Salvador's central government was not rabidly anticommunist at that point in time, it did contain an element that held that view—which was even stronger in portions of its military. In October 1980, a team of U.S. Army logistics advisors was sent in country for "training," and in November an Army team went into El Salvador to assess equipment needs. The same month, a five-man Army Operational and Planning Assistance Team (OPAT) was also sent to help the Salvadorian army organize counterinsurgency operations to protect the annual coffee harvest (Operation Golden Harvest).[496]

Any hopes for what had optimistically been described as a "clean counterinsurgency," not involving excessive government brutality, quickly fell prey to the well-organized and extremely aggressive ultra-right, fanatically anticommunist military element within the Salvadorian army. Although one coup attempt against the moderate government failed, the army itself was then internally purged of its moderate officers, and by late 1980 a militant national organization of both military and paramilitary forces had developed. By the end of 1980 more than eight thousand people had been killed and the central government was effectively in control of the anticommunist network.

Yet El Salvador still harbored an active if small insurgency, despite the increasing terror tactics and the emergence of right-wing death squads. The American concern was that any insurgency left the country exposed to intervention by Nicaragua. Nicaragua had indeed given some cause for such concern, even to Ambassador White and President Carter. American intelligence confirmed that Cuban arms shipments were moving through Nicaragua and into El Salvador by late fall of 1980. Even White concurred that, in a break with earlier practice, Nicaragua had become active in arming the Salvadorian insurgency. As Carter's term was ending, Washington's concerns about Nicaragua and El Salvador were escalating.

In January 1981, the National Security Council concurred with a new CIA report that significant amounts of military material were going into El Salvador. The Agency presented aerial photographs of supply flights staging out of Nicaragua. Based on that information President Carter suspended all aid to Nicaragua. Within weeks the insurgency in El Salvador launched a military offensive. That military move was a total failure, very possibly because of death squad murders that had gutted popular movements within the cities. Still, the State Department, the Pentagon, and the National Security Council all proposed a substantial increase in the ongoing military assistance mission in El Salvador, and on January 14, 1981, Carter approved almost $6 million in "lethal" (versus humanitarian) aid. In order to expedite the shipment, Carter invoked emergency provisions in the Foreign Assistance Act and directed the aid be sent without congressional approval. Carter's action would set the stage for a series of future independent presidential actions that would occur throughout the Reagan Administration. Carter left office having upped the ante against what initially did appear to be the intent of the new Nicaraguan regime (the Sandinista regime) to export popular revolution. It was not the only challenge he faced at the end of his presidency: he also faced actual Soviet aggression in Afghanistan and upped the ante there as well.

In 1978, a faction of the Afghan People's Democratic Party (PDPA), known as the Khalq, had launched a successful coup, installing a Marxist regime in Kabul. The Khalq included a number of army officers who had trained in the Soviet Union and who had become extremely radical politically, especially in the context of Afghan tradition and religion. At the time, the coup was first suspected to be Soviet influenced but it was most likely in response to the Afghan president's move to purge the army of leftist elements. U.S. Secretary of State Cyrus Vance and the State Department ultimately reported that "we had no evidence of Soviet complicity in the coup."[497]

The Khalq and the PDPA immediately instituted a series of radical reforms, all of which flew directly in the face of the country's Muslim religious tradition and practices. Perhaps the most inflammatory was an edict mandating that girls must be taught to read. Those actions quickly generated a growing backlash with the Afghan Muslim populace, against not only the PDPA but also its perceived ideological sponsor, the Soviet Union. Actually, the presumed sponsorship seemed rather obvious in that the new Afghan regime had invited in hundreds of Soviet "advisors" to assist in organizing everything from coeducational schools and factories to secret police networks.[498]

Among the groups taking up arms against the new communist central government were a number of Islamist factions, all calling for holy war, a jihad. In mid-March 1979, the antigovernment fury consumed Herat, an Afghan city close to the Iranian border. Some five thousand people were killed, including dozens of Soviet advisors and their families.[499] The new regime's response was to send bomber raids into Herat, killing up to an estimated twenty thousand people in Herat alone. With that level of brutality, a countrywide rebellion was soon in progress, and Kabul was pleading for aid from the Soviets. Soviet regimes to that point in time had never been known for temperate responses to revolts against their own proxy regimes. It seemed obvious that the Soviets would become more deeply involved. The only question was the extent to which they would respond.

Yet in this case the Soviets were faced with a very unsatisfactory leadership in Kabul, one that was not truly their puppet. Notably, it ignored Soviet advice to temper its aggressive Marxist social agenda; it appeared both unpredictable and extreme.[500] The reality was that the existing leadership of the communist regime in the Afghan capital of Kabul was in the process of making the Soviets look like a very bad neighbor to the rest of the nations in the region—in particular the ones with Muslim majorities and very traditional ruling regimes. The American response to all this was a bit conflicted. The State Department did not necessarily see the new regime in Afghanistan as being part of a structured Soviet move into the Persian Gulf. In contrast, President Carter's national security advisor, Zbigniew Brzezinski, took a very different geopolitical view. In his worldview the Soviets were laying the groundwork for political control of the entire Gulf region—a potential body blow to the strategic balance of world power. Brzezinski's adamantly stated views had already begun to sway President Carter towards covert action to block Soviet moves in the region.

The initial Carter Administration discussion of a response against the regime change in Kabul had begun many months before the Soviets themselves moved. In March 1979, the National Security Council's special group for covert action—under Carter designated as the Special Coordinating Committee—had revisited even earlier discussions of covert action in Afghanistan. In reality the CIA had very limited contacts inside the country and little understanding of the various insurgent groups. There was no possibility of quick regime change in Kabul, where the Russians were already deeply involved.

In July 1979, President Carter approved a program of strictly nonlethal aid to a series of Afghan insurgent groups. The program was relatively inexpensive, only half a million dollars, and included not only relief supplies but communications and medical supplies as well as a variety of propaganda and psychological warfare activities. Carter's initially cautious moves in the uncertainty of Afghanistan would be similar to President Obama's first responses to the 2012 insurgency against the Assad regime in Syria.

Two points from the very first Carter aid outreach to Afghanistan were to become increasingly significant over the long term. First, the aid included actual cash to be distributed directly to rebel groups, and that cash was going solely through Pakistan and its own intelligence service, Inter-Services Intelligence (ISI). The use of the Pakistan intelligence service as a go-between would be seminal to future events. Of course in the earliest days there was little alternative. Up to that time the only American interest in and information about groups inside Afghanistan had been through Drug Enforcement Agency personnel who had been totally focused on ongoing drug smuggling out of Afghan poppy fields and through Pakistan.

Even in the earliest stages of the Afghan revolt against the communists in Kabul, it should have been obvious that American covert involvement might carry a high risk of entanglement with factions involved in drug smuggling.[501] On the other hand, it was less obvious then that Pakistan's leadership and its intelligence service were primarily interested in maintaining a Muslim religious barrier in Afghanistan, a barrier against Soviet communism that would allow Pakistan's military forces to remain focused on its eastern border with India. Of course the Carter-era initial aid was relatively quite limited, both in terms of weapons and money. If it had stayed at that level, the relationship with Pakistan might not have produced its ultimate consequences. But then the other shoe dropped and the Soviets moved massive military forces across the borders of the Soviet bloc in late December 1979.

The Soviets moved to occupy and directly control Afghanistan, sending planeloads of Soviet airborne troops directly into the Kabul airport. The Soviet 40th Army and its tanks moved across the Afghan border and a large group of paratroops and paramilitary forces deployed to isolate and eliminate the existing uncontrollable PDPA leaders. The Soviets were going to install Afghan regime leadership they could trust, and support it with major Soviet military might. Within the American leadership, the immediate temptation to compare the Soviet move to Vietnam and to anticipate it as a potential "morass" for the Russians was virtually overwhelming.

Brzezinski did not present the occupation of Afghanistan to President Carter as simply a characteristic Soviet response to popular revolt against a Soviet-backed regime, the sort of response seen repeatedly in Eastern Europe. Instead he interpreted the move as the first action in a bold Soviet geopolitical strategy to expand control throughout the Persian Gulf region and its vital oil resources. He proposed to Carter that it represented an American tactical opportunity to bleed the Russians as America had been bled in Southeast Asia. In Brzezinski's view, the U.S. had lost a major battle in Southeast Asia and the emboldened Soviets were moving to take the advantage in the Middle Eastern oil fields. Brzezinski would prove very influential with Carter and his influence would eventually lead to accelerated spending in Afghan covert warfare. Ultimately Brzezinski's worldview would be taken up and reasserted in the new Reagan Administration by Secretary of State Alexander Haig and CIA Director William Casey.

In the interim, even if Carter had not totally bought into Brzezinski's scenario, given the scale of the Soviet military move, he could not disregard the political implications of having the United States ignore the Soviet occupation, widely touted in the conservative American press as simply the first step in a major strategic thrust into the Arabian Gulf oil region. The result was a public statement of the "Carter Doctrine," declaring the region was of vital interest to the United States, the expansion of the U.S. military complex at Diego Garcia in the Indian Ocean, and the focusing of new Rapid Deployment Joint Task Force (RDJTF) on the Middle East and Central Asia. By 1983, the RDJTF had evolved into a separate unified command designated CENTCOM, with its commander reporting directly to the secretary of defense.

President Carter also signed a new finding for Congress, directing the CIA to send in more military aid to the Afghan insurgency. The focus of the initial mission was simply to make the Soviet occupation costly. Groups to be supported would be those with the greatest potential for carrying the war to the Soviet forces. Yet even with that direction, the first shipment of weapons was to be the classic and deniable bolt-action, single-shot WWII-era Lee-Enfield rifle, supplies of which were obtained from Greece and India and shipped into Pakistan for distribution.

From Carter's perspective, the initial move to deniable support may very well have seemed no more than a blocking action, on the same order of his initial approval of covert action to block Nicaragua from supplying arms to Salvadorian rebels. With a longer view and in a tactical sense, his move to surrogate warfare in Afghanistan seems not all that different from Eisenhower's decision to engage in limited tactical actions against China on its southern border in Yunnan or Tibet. The initial Carter Administration findings for covert action in both countries, as submitted to Congress, were tightly focused. In Central America the goal was simply to interdict and stop weapons that were believed to be coming from Cuba and transiting Nicaragua to the El Salvadorian rebels. In Afghanistan the goal was to blunt the advance of the Soviets beyond their border state "zones of influence." Such an immediate tactical response does appear to have been the Carter Administration goal, as expressed in a confidential letter from Brzezinski written immediately after the Soviets had moved into Kabul: "Our ultimate goal is the withdrawal of Soviet troops from Afghanistan. . . . Even if this is not attainable, we should make Soviet involvement as costly as possible."[502] That initial Carter-era Afghan covert mission statement is an important benchmark in tracing the dramatic changes that would soon occur in surrogate warfare under the Reagan Administration.

The mission of the Reagan Administration, in both Central America and Afghanistan, was going to be considerably different over the long run, even if it did begin on somewhat of a similar note. The CIA officer assigned to lead the Afghanistan mission described his assignment succinctly: "Just go out there and kill the Soviets, and take care of the Pakistanis and make them do whatever you need them to do."[503] The CIA officer first assigned to the Nicaragua project described his only plan as going to Nicaragua and killing Cubans.

Zbigniew Brzezinski appears to have been an extremely influential voice in President Carter's decisions in regard to Afghanistan. Under the new Reagan Administration, Secretary of State Haig and CIA Director Casey would consistently push Reagan towards an assertive and broad-based initiative against the Soviet–Cuban "evil empire." They viewed it as critical to America's national security not only that the communists be stopped from going beyond Afghanistan or Nicaragua, but also that the movement literally be pushed back and that both countries be recovered for the Western bloc.

A finding issued by President Carter in 1979 and reauthorized by President Reagan in 1981 authorized provision of weapons to the Afghan insurgents—generally referred to as mujahedin—but specifically stated that the CIA itself was not to attempt direct control of any military actions. It was forbidden from acting "unilaterally." And it was directed to consult with Pakistan on all supply activities. America was going to move supplies into Pakistan, but it would be the Pakistanis who would distribute them. The Reagan Administration's orders to the CIA for Afghanistan would be to use the Pakistanis and "make them do whatever you need them to do." It would lead to covert warfare practices unlike anything we have seen before, inserting a third party between the U.S. and the surrogate fighters and ultimately allowing third parties to take operational control of the surrogates. Initially, United States money provided the funding, but that was the extent of the American involvement.

The approach seemed like standard surrogate warfare in one sense. However, it ignored the very fundamental cultural and religious differences of the region. The Pakistanis held inherent credibility and control with certain Afghan rebel groups due to their shared Muslim religion. Those same groups would have little more than disdain for the interference of religious infidels in their affairs. As we will see, the long-term American money going through Pakistan would have little to do with the longer-term American geopolitical agenda and everything to do with Pakistan's view of its own security concerns and priorities.

The Afghan effort would become extremely costly for America, just as it would be for the Soviets. Estimates of the actual Afghan rebel fighters even in the early years ranged from twenty to thirty thousand individuals in combat and literally hundreds of thousands more cycling though farming, moving back and forth to relatives in Pakistan, or engaging in their traditional activity of smuggling.[504] Consultation with Pakistan and its military intelligence agency also took on a radically different form. CIA officers were not permitted by the Pakistanis to make any direct contact with the mujahedin. Pakistani intelligence would channel all weapons and all payments itself; in doing so it obviously had the ability to select groups and leaders that matched its own preferences and goals. The effect was fundamental: aid and support was channeled by the Pakistani ISI almost entirely to extremely fundamentalist religious groups of fighters. Of course such groups viewed CIA officers as infidels—much in the same light as the Russian invaders they were fighting. The ISI-organized training camps conducted weapons and tactical training, handled all the transportation (the U.S. would supply hundreds of trucks), and even sent commando teams with the mujahedin on attacks against the Afghan government and Soviet targets. The money was American, but the surrogate fighters were loyal to the Pakistani ISI. As time passed, they would become increasingly hostile to later attempts by CIA field officers to insert themselves into the process, even to collect intelligence.

During the Reagan years those sorts of issues were either not apparent or, if raised, considered not to be an immediate problem.

The goals were to ship in as many weapons as possible (advanced weapons such as grenade launchers, mortars, and machine guns would increasingly come from China) and to kill as many Soviets and damage as much expensive Soviet equipment as possible. Ideologically the whole enterprise was a bit conflicted, with increased contact with Chinese intelligence and dramatically expanding purchases—buying weapons from the Chinese communists to kill Soviet communists.[505] And it all grew increasingly expensive. Supplying the Afghan mujahedin cost the U.S. some $30 million in 1981, and the cost had escalated to $200 million by 1984.

But it was successful, tactically speaking. By the end of 1981 the rebels were conducting some five hundred attacks a month, and the Soviets had lost over four thousand personnel and some five hundred vehicles. By 1984 the Soviets held no territory safe from attacks, and longer-range Chinese rockets allowed more deadly attacks. The ISI itself had sent its personnel into Afghanistan, disguised as rebel fighters, staging attacks on the Soviet air base at Bagram and destroying some twenty-two Soviet aircraft.[506] Clearly the Soviets had indeed stepped into the sort of bloodletting the U.S. had taken in South Vietnam. And all it was taking to make them suffer was money. Even better, not all of it was American money. The Reagan Administration had negotiated an agreement with the Saudi royal family to match American funding.

From its beginning, the Soviet occupation of Afghanistan had carried far more significance for both the Pakistanis and Saudis than for the U.S. To the Carter Administration it seemed a tactical opportunity to block Soviet political influence from expanding into the Gulf. To the Reagan Administration it seemed like just another opportunity to aggressively push back at the Soviets—at best it could cause them the same sort of losses and international embarrassment as had the American defeat in Southeast Asia. In either case it was just one more front in the geopolitical maneuvering between the West and East power blocs.

To the conservative Muslim religious-based governments of Pakistan and Saudi Arabia, Soviet influence in Afghanistan was seen as a much more fundamental threat, not a matter of politics but one fundamentally of religious belief. A Soviet regime in Afghanistan would signify that communist atheism was expanding, along with Marxist social beliefs. That had happened in Kabul with the PDPA, which had attempted to overturn hundreds of years of tradition. It was a deeply felt threat. Turning back the Soviets and their Afghan communist regime was not just territorial; it was a religious struggle against unbelievers. Fundamentally, the Pakistanis and, later, other Muslim nations would view it as a Muslim religious challenge, a jihad in which non-Muslims really had no place.

That co-religious attitude ultimately would bring not only the Saudis but also a host of fundamentalist Muslims into the battle against the Soviets. In the beginning it was those concerns about communist expansion that fueled Saudi bonding with the Reagan Administration and brought in Saudi money to the Afghan effort. During the Reagan era, William Casey was able to increase the official Saudi government contribution to a level that actually matched U.S. congressional funding. More importantly, and with profound long-term consequences, nongovernment contributions and very large-scale financial support from "charitable" elements within Saudi Arabia began to surge. At the time it was all thought to be good, government or nongovernment. Later it would be viewed as a disaster: the bond would bring Saudi money into the secret war in Central America as well. As time passed, it would not be just money from the Saudi government going to Afghanistan, but huge "charitable" donations from fundamentalist Saudi princes, wealthy families, and religious leaders and schools.[507]

The lessons of that Saudi involvement would become clear—and painful—only with time. Circa 1984 the participation of third-party outsiders, such as Pakistan and Saudi Arabia, in American surrogate warfare against the Soviet bloc was seen as highly desirable. It was going to be a common crusade against the "evil empire" with the potential of achieving a goal from decades earlier: "roll back." It was an intoxicating prospect—as long as no one spent too much time pondering the underlying cultural issues and the potential long-term consequences. Afghanistan and ongoing Soviet losses were indeed intoxicating. In fact the effort was so successful and so strongly supported by Congress, especially through Congressman Charlie Wilson's personal involvement as its champion, that the CIA's primary immediate challenge was simply dealing with the increasingly massive amounts of appropriations that Wilson was driving its way. Frequently Wilson's efforts would double or even quadruple the CIA's actual requests. And more and more Pentagon money was rerouted to Afghanistan. In 1983, a $20 million CIA allocation had been supplemented with $39 million in Pentagon money, rerouted through Wilson's ongoing pressure.[508]

However, Afghanistan was far from being the only area of Reagan Administration covert action. By the beginning of 1985, some fifty American covert operations were under way, on three continents. Covert activity had escalated some 500 percent beyond that of the Carter Administration, reaching levels equaling or exceeding those conducted under the Eisenhower Administration. And CIA staffing had increased by one-third, with some eight hundred of the officers released during the Carter years being brought back, the majority of them as contract employees.[509] Yet while covert warfare against the Soviets appeared to be a striking administration success, pushback efforts in Central America had been a far different story, with numerous missteps, limited military success, a good deal of bad public relations, and substantial domestic and congressional concerns.

The overall Reagan-era covert effort was being promoted and driven by CIA Director William Casey. Casey was so personally and directly involved in Reagan-era shadow warfare that historian John Prados has used the term "Casey's War" in writing about efforts against the Soviets in Afghanistan. Given the strength of Casey's personality, the moral certainty of his private views, and the raw enthusiasm he brought to his activities, we are tempted to designate both Nicaragua and Afghanistan as "Casey's Crusades." Clearly Casey's ideological views and his Cold War enthusiasm accurately reflected those of President Reagan, yet certain facets of Casey's character, in particular his strong religious beliefs, were to become a key element in the Reagan Administration's dramatic new approaches to financing and conducting shadow warfare not just in Afghanistan but all the way around the globe in Nicaragua.

The other major figure in the Reagan Administration was Secretary of State Alexander Haig. Haig had served as a military aide on Henry Kissinger's national security staff beginning in 1969. It seems fair to say that Haig carried the Nixon/Kissinger Cold War worldview of confronting the Soviets into the Reagan era. In fact that link in worldview can be seen in Kissinger's personal support of Haig, and Haig's rapid rise to become Kissinger's deputy then his rapid promotion from colonel to four-star general—a career record virtually unequaled in the American military. Reagan's appointment of Haig illustrates that the Reagan Administration was resetting American priorities to the familiar Cold War scenario, focusing on the Soviet bloc as the major national security issue for the U.S. The Reagan Administration worldview would bring a much more aggressive approach to international issues in Latin America as well as other regions. President Carter's measured responses to events in El Salvador and Nicaragua became a thing of the past. From its earliest days the Reagan Administration approached Nicaragua with the view that it was nothing less than a Cuban (and hence Soviet) surrogate, willing and able to export communist revolution throughout Central America.

With a view towards confronting the expansion of communist-bloc influence, Haig pushed for tackling the El Salvador issue head-on, with military action against not only Nicaragua but also Cuba. He lobbied the NSC for blockades and even for military action against the supply line leading from Cuba to El Salvador. The rest of the NSC was far less sanguine about such high-profile acts and was more inclined towards an aggressive counterinsurgency effort inside El Salvador. The Pentagon had already sent several military survey teams into the country and reported back that El Salvador had become so violently polarized that any commitment would require a long-term effort.

Exactly that commitment was made in an NSC meeting of January 27, 1981. During Reagan's first month in office, $25 million in new military aid was authorized, more than the allocation for all the rest of Latin America and the Caribbean that year. Twenty million was to be sent immediately under the same emergency provision President Carter had used, with no congressional approval. Reagan also approved up to fifty-six military advisors to be assigned to mobile training teams to train special rapid-response battalions.

President Reagan also submitted a covert-action finding to Congress, informing them that he had authorized CIA operations including both political action and paramilitary combat to interdict and sever supply routes to El Salvador from Nicaragua and Honduras. Some $19.5 million was allocated to the CIA projects.[510] Reagan had begun a massive commitment to surrogate warfare in Central America; exactly how deniable it was all going to be would be another matter. And deniability was especially important because domestic polls showed that while 30 percent of the public endorsed the Reagan initiative, 38 percent did not, and with new post-Vietnam-era legislation now in place, Congress's attitude towards covert action oversight seemed far more assertive than during the clandestine warfare in Southeast Asia a decade earlier. President Reagan had provided a finding to Congress. However, Congress had not responded with an enabling resolution supporting presidential action.

In addition, a national security directive[511] authorized building a Nicaraguan rebel army of up to fifteen hundred (it would grow to something on the order of five thousand by 1983) under a start-up budget of $19 million. Language in the directive focused on "interdiction" but with room for broad interpretation. American paramilitary action to eliminate a Cuban supply structure was specified.[512] In organizing its new surrogate army, the CIA encountered certain of the same problems the JM WAVE team had two decades earlier. There were a number of insurgent political figures competing for leadership, most of them currently residing in Miami. Political leaders from the anti-Sandinista coalition Nicaraguan Democratic Forces (FDN), organized by the CIA, made only one group trip to the military camps in

Honduras.[513] The contrast between the expatriate political leadership and the field commanders was dramatic. There were several military commanders available, but the majority of them had been with the National Guard, an organization almost as universally hated by the general Nicaraguan public as Batista-era security forces had been by the Cuban public. More liberal anti-Sandinista personalities were aggressively rejected by hard-line anticommunist Nicaraguan exile factions just as the more populist Cuban leaders had been by hard-line anticommunist Cuban exile factions.

Beginning in mid-1981 the CIA had been sending large amounts of money to the exile political leadership in Miami, and exile training camps would again be established in Florida. In the spring of 1981, there were media tours and stories in both *The New York Times* and *The Washington Post* about the camps, including the use of Green Berets and former Vietnam veterans as trainers. By 1982 an estimated eight hundred to twelve hundred volunteers were reported in training inside the United States.[514] Public perception of the anti-Sandinista military forces, ultimately referred to as Contras, suffered from the fact that most of their larger columns were led by former National Guard leaders, members of the especially despised "Rattlesnake Battalion." they had been brutal and violent, and their sponsorship by the U.S. could not but help generate a humanitarian outcry. It didn't help at all that one of the most media-eager Contra field commanders, who used the nom de plume Commander Suicide, continuously bragged about the murders and atrocities that his two-thousand-man force was committing.[515]

What began as accelerated military assistance to El Salvador under President Carter quickly developed into a major Reagan Administration secret warfare effort against Nicaragua. In reviewing the initial planning for action against Nicaragua, it all sounds amazingly similar to the previous secret war against Cuba. Eventually the Nicaraguan secret war would even see the return of JM WAVE–type maritime attacks and CIA "mother ships," and a budget of $21 million in 1983 and $24 million in 1984, with access to a great deal more direct U.S. military support. However, Congress, still in a more active oversight mode, attempted to build constraints into the new covert operations.

As early as December 1982, a rider had been attached to the appropriations bill funding the CIA operations. The language in the legislation, known as the Boland Amendment, seemed strong and was positioned as assertive control. In reality it simply denied money for "the purpose of overthrowing the government of Nicaragua or for provoking a military exchange between Nicaragua and Honduras." The funding bill itself set a cap of $24 million for fiscal 1983.[516] In a practical sense, that left a lot of maneuvering room for military support. As to the Reagan Administration's view of the action, one comment from an NSC memorandum of July 1983 asserted that "State does not believe the Boland Amendment constrains covert U.S. activities in Nicaragua to a serious degree."[517]

Under the Reagan Nicaragua initiative, the CIA was given extensive direct access to both the regular military and to Special Forces. Under the umbrella of preexisting military assistance agreements with Honduras, and in line with Honduran concerns about the new leftist regime in Nicaragua, some two hundred additional American military personnel were deployed to support covert operations from that country; the team included fifty Air Force personnel operating large-scale radar surveillance of Nicaraguan airspace. Some 100-plus Green Berets and 150 CIA personnel, along with a large CIA contingent supporting ground logistics, were operating out of Honduras by 1983.

During 1983, Contra forces conducted a large-scale offensive in the north of Nicaragua, attacking towns and villages with the goal of consolidating a liberated zone where a "provisional government" could be established. Their tactics had already alienated much of the population in the area and they received no general support. Counterattacks by the Sandinista Popular Army drove them back across the Honduran border to their staging areas. At that point, the U.S. intelligence community produced a national intelligence estimate quite similar to those repeatedly generated during the secret war against Cuba. That estimate, leaked to the *Washington Post*, concluded that "there are no circumstances under which a force of U.S.-backed rebels can achieve a military or political victory over the leftist Sandinista government."[518] In the fall of 1983, Contra/FDN forces possibly numbering as high as twenty thousand mounted yet another similar effort (Operation Dark Moon) and again proved unable to take and hold Nicaraguan territory.[519] As we saw with CIA indigenous forces in Laos, if the ground troops couldn't do the job by themselves, the standard response was to bring in heavier but very covert fire power—both air and naval.

The first call in Nicaragua was for attack aircraft. To obtain them the CIA turned to Investair Leasing, which used a nonexistent corporate address at Dulles International Airport. Three military O-2A push-pull propeller aircraft were obtained through Investair. The aircraft had simply been declared military surplus, removed from the Air Force inventory, and then transferred to a special Joint Chiefs project designated Elephant Herd. The project was a multiagency operation that cleared a variety of materials of military inventory, transferring them to the CIA. The Elephant Herd project had been authorized by President Reagan in June 1983, and was specifically used to provide a cover for transferring military assets covertly to the CIA for use in the Nicaraguan secret war. The CIA then transferred the aircraft to Investair, using it as a commercial cover.

Elephant Herd also provided a means for Reagan and the CIA to work around the $24 million budget cap set by Congress for Nicaraguan "aid." The Pentagon could simply declare material surplus, assign it zero monetary value, and hand it over to the CIA—exactly what happened with the two O-2A aircraft. It has been estimated that some $12 million worth of material was transferred through cover of the Elephant Herd process.[520] Two similar O-2A aircraft, known to be from a New York air guard unit, were declared surplus and sold directly to El Salvador. Following the sales, all the aircraft went to Summit Aviation in Delaware to be equipped with rocket pods. Other similar aircraft were sold directly by the manufacturer through a California company named Armairco and its East Coast branch, Shenandoah Airleasing.[521] Nothing was really new in all this, of course—the practices remain the same, the companies and names change, and incidents occur. Eventually the truth emerges, but for real-time operational purposes it works—until it doesn't.

To be more specific, it works and remains deniable until one or more of the aircraft is involved in an accident or is brought down someplace where it and its pilot should not be. In the Nicaragua secret war that happened first in El Salvador. A night reconnaissance mission returned only to crash-land, killing one CIA employee and three CIA contract employees. The following month a CIA helicopter went down in an aerial attack against a Nicaraguan military installation, killing two American "freelancers." American military involvement was further exposed by a series of accidents involving personnel in Honduras. One incident killed a helicopter pilot who strayed over Nicaraguan airspace; two SEALS also died in accidents, and four other Americans were killed and six injured, including Green Beret special operations personnel.

Given the lack of any real Contra military success, by the end of 1983 the CIA had also turned to recruiting experienced paramilitary volunteers from across El Salvador, Honduras, Chile, Argentina, Ecuador, and Bolivia. These fighters were known to the CIA from its Condor-era contacts, were extremely well trained, and were far more effective than the Contra forces. Personnel in this new force were described as "unilaterally controlled Latino assets" (UCLA) and their missions were to target ports, refineries, oil pipelines, boats, and bridges in very fundamental economic warfare. It was a similar strategy to what had been conceived two decades before against Cuba, but never carried out by the Kennedy Administration due to concerns over lack of deniability and potential international ramifications.

While the Contras were positioned as the ones responsible for carrying out the attacks, the techniques and equipment being used—such as specialized high-speed attack boats with mortars and machine guns, mother ships with helicopter pads, frogman raids, and bombing and rocket attacks from aircraft and helicopters—were not likely to fool either the international press or Congress in the long run. Eventually BBC journalists would air two extended documentaries on the UCLA, including interviews with one of the attack team leaders.[522] Later, in 1984, an equally negative media impact was produced by the discovery and publication of yet another CIA-provided training manual to the Contras, with sections on the selective use of violence and assassination, the practice of hiring professional criminals for certain activities, and the possibility of creating martyrs though the death of the Contras' own personnel. Publicity generated by the manual would ultimately become a last straw for Congress.

Yet with all the military logistics support, money, and persistent supportive speeches from President Reagan and his White House team, after some two years the Contra combat against the Sandinista regime had produced virtually no significant military impact. Hostilities had started with Contra forces blowing up two major bridges within Nicaragua, but beyond that it had become largely a matter of raids and sniping attacks on Sandinista security patrols and outposts—as well as attacks on villages, crops, and warehouses in the north of the country. There had been some fracturing of the Sandinista internal political infrastructure itself but that was primarily based on factional issues and the results of ongoing American economic pressure against the Nicaraguan regime.

In conjunction with the use of unilateral surrogate forces, in October 1983, President Reagan approved a national security directive allowing American personnel to conduct "harassment" military actions including attacks on infrastructure targets, such as bridges, ports, refineries, and oil pipelines. CIA helicopters also began to provide "suppression fire" against defensive weapons installations as cover for both UCLA and Contra attacks. The new directive took matters far beyond the initial presidential finding to Congress, which had made no mention of involving actual American forces. By 1984 it seems fair to say that a full-scale secret war was in progress against the government of Nicaragua. Combat had escalated far beyond "interdiction" of supplies to the insurgency in El Salvador. And in terms of CIA surrogate warfare, about the only things lacking were substantial numbers of American military advisors or CIA paramilitary officers on the ground—and the sort of full-scale military air support seen in Laos.

The overall combat escalation had begun to involve a number of maritime attacks, launched from swift-class boats and supported by larger "mother ships," just as we saw in the early 1960s in the secret war against Cuba. However, this time the naval warfare was going to include something brand new. It would be a major escalation with international ramifications. The United States was going to covertly mine major Nicaraguan harbors on both the Atlantic and Pacific coasts. The CIA dispatched boat teams that used special equipment to place canister mines developed in conjunction with the U.S. Naval Weapons Center in approaches to major Nicaraguan ports. The action was publicly attributed to Contra forces. The Contra radio propaganda outlet was then ordered to broadcast international warnings. During the first week of April 1984, some dozen commercial vessels from six different countries were damaged by the mines, seamen were injured, and two Nicaraguans were killed. When the Soviet Union—one of whose ships had been damaged and crew injured—protested, the Reagan Administration denied all involvement, once again distancing itself by pointing towards the Contras.

Within days newspaper reports revealed the fact that the United States had been directly involved with placing the mines. The Reagan Administration was forced to fall back on the legal defense of the mines being a "legitimate means of interrupting the flow of arms destined for infiltration . . . or to disrupt the flow of military and other materials essential to the attackers' overall aggressive effort."[523] Neither the international community nor even the administration's most adamant political supporters were going to accept that justification, and the secret war against Nicaragua had just become very public. Clearly the Contras were not acting alone and were receiving lethal American support.

The harbor-mining action produced a firestorm. Domestically, popular opinion was overwhelmingly against it. Internationally, even America's European allies were outraged. France offered a minesweeper to Nicaragua. When Congress queried the administration, CIA Director Casey responded with the stock CIA response about it being an independent action by the Contras. Feeding the Senate Intelligence Committee the standard Agency cover story was a very bad idea. The committee's chairman, Barry Goldwater, responded angrily to CIA Director Casey. Goldwater also went on record stating that the move was a flagrant violation of international law, declaring it an actual act of war with no conceivable explanation. Daniel Moynihan, the vice chairman of the committee, resigned in protest.

In context, it has to be acknowledged that according to numerous sources, neither Director Casey nor the CIA head of the Contra project, Dewey Clarridge (who had come up with the idea for the harbor mining), had much confidence in and little personal respect for Congress or its oversight.[524] Clarridge had already been active in trying to frustrate Intelligence Committee oversight. In an action reminiscent of those we first encountered with congressional oversight in Angola, Clarridge had ordered the CIA station chief in Panama not to speak with Senator Patrick Leahy during a committee fact-finding mission. When Leahy tried to cable CIA headquarters, the chief of station refused to communicate, only relenting when Leahy threatened to call Washington using an open line, which would have made the communication open to interception, violating all standard CIA security practices.[525] Oliver North, who worked with both Casey and Clarridge during Contra operations, commented that both men had a lot in common, "including an unmistakable lack of affection for Congress." However, Clarridge was somewhat unique in not making any effort to conceal his attitude during congressional appearances.[526]

Director Casey grudgingly apologized to members of the congressional oversight committee, acknowledging that they had not been kept fully briefed. Moynihan reclaimed his seat, and the White House eventually approved a compromise to provide more information to the oversight committee, with details beyond those in the presidential finding.[527] In April 1984, the Senate overwhelmingly passed legislation opposing the use of federal monies for mining Nicaraguan harbors. This was reported by the media as a "rebuke" to President Reagan.[528] However, Congress did not pass any additional resolutions constraining administration military action; nor did it cease major annual budget allocations for "humanitarian" aid, which continued to go through the same FDN contacts being used to supply the Contra fighting forces. And later that same year, two Americans were killed in a helicopter crash in Nicaragua; the helicopter had been providing support for air attacks on a Sandinista military school.

Once again publicity forced Congress to take a stand. Senator Moynihan called it a "crisis of confidence" with the Reagan Administration. Senator Joe Biden described the continuing secret warfare in Nicaragua as a "charade," where a presidential finding for covert action was being manipulated into operations far behind its stated intents and purposes.[529] Still, the best Congress was able to manage was a moratorium on support for action against the Nicaraguan government. The moratorium was specifically directed towards forbidding direct or indirect support for military actions by any U.S. "intelligence agency." Of course that raised the possibility that military action might be taken by some part of the government that was not designated an intelligence agency. Congress had assumed that the administration would continue to operate under the general practices defined by the National Security Act of 1947. That would prove to be a false assumption.

Through the end of the Carter Administration and in the earliest years of the Reagan era, covert action had continued under the guidelines of the National Security Act of 1947. Within accepted legal guidelines covert operations was assigned to the Central Intelligence Agency. Covert actions had been performed with certain relatively standard practices, not only in Nicaragua but across the globe. CIA Director Casey, with the president's support and direct access to the National Security Council, had been following the rules. However, congressional funding strictures had placed a type of box around future activities against the Sandinista regime in Nicaragua. America was to be providing only humanitarian aid to the Contra rebels, and the CIA's role was to be limited to intelligence work. Those strictures did not satisfy the Reagan Administration and they most definitely did not satisfy Director Casey.

The Reagan Administration wanted to push the Sandinistas out of power in Nicaragua just as badly as it wanted the Russians out of Afghanistan. Both activities were going to require lots of money and some very creative operational activities outside the CIA. Covert action was on the verge of going out of the box, to outsiders, for both funding and operations. Some of the outsiders would be overseas; others would be much closer.

CHAPTER 19

The Outsiders

A series of dramatic missteps—including the mining of Nicaraguan harbors—had led Congress to pass legislation that constrained the CIA's covert Nicaraguan operations and restricted Contra aid to nonlethal, humanitarian efforts. Congress had attempted to essentially build a legislative and funding box around lethal American activities in Central America. What they appear not to have appreciated at the time was the degree to which President Reagan, his advisors, and a number of individuals within certain government agencies were committed to ousting the Sandinista regime. Congress might have pulled the CIA off military operations and was certainly demanding increased oversight in Central America, but the administration was fully prepared to turn to other options and other resources. William Casey had demonstrated he could bring in more Saudi money for Afghanistan and he was already bringing in covert donations of weapons for the Contras from Israel; he would demonstrate that he could do much more.

Casey was very adept at tapping nontraditional sources not just for money but for a great many other resources, including people. As we have seen, the U.S. military has routinely been involved in support of CIA covert operations just as the CIA routinely supports military clandestine actions. The military most definitely has its own covert operations specialists. Many of the CIA's paramilitary case officers and managers come and go from military careers, detached for CIA duty as required. William Casey and the Reagan Administration would demonstrate just how easy it would be to bring such resources into covert activities. In doing so they would turn not just to people within the active military but to officially retired individuals, some acting simply as volunteers sharing a similar anticommunist passion, as well as others who would work "for a percentage." The Reagan Administration would also set the stage for many new trends in covert operations, among them privatization.

Historically presidents prior to Reagan had conducted major covert warfare projects with the full support and involvement of the National Security Council. On certain occasions, as with Nixon and Chile, a president has chosen to act strictly on his own, going directly to the CIA with a directive to run an operation. In the second phase of the war against Nicaragua, the White House significantly modified the accepted NSC consultative relationship. Robert McFarlane, Reagan's national security advisor (with much advice and counsel from CIA Director Casey) actually ran the second phase of the Contra operation through the National Security Council itself—or more specifically, through NSC staff. The staff member at the center of the activity was Lieutenant Colonel Oliver North. North was the NSC deputy director for political and military affairs; his chain of command to the White House would be through McFarlane, later succeeded by Admiral John Poindexter. Ultimately the NSC–North effort would result in what became known as the Iran–Contra scandal. Iran–Contra would bring about denials and recriminations in regard to who knew what, who authorized what, how much President Reagan personally knew, and of course who was really to blame for a variety of things—not to mention the obvious administration rejection of congressional oversight for covert operations.

Oliver North would demonstrate that a national security staff officer could indeed run a covert warfare operation in Nicaragua, without the CIA and without congressional funding. Beginning in the summer of 1984 and continuing into the fall of 1986 he would do so largely on his own, with a limited number of aides, liaison personnel, and some key partners outside the United Stated government. With the power of a national security staff position, Oliver North could make a lot of requests without necessarily getting challenges or questions. "Implicit" authority has an impact within the national security hierarchy, even with the Department of Defense or the CIA. Implied White House support can be helpful as well. Implicit (or simply verbal) authorization seems to have carried over to a number of agencies, particularly to Customs and DEA, which by all accounts, for at least a time, adopted a hands-off attitude towards certain commercial and private shipments coming and going from airfields and even major airports in Florida. When challenged, their initial response seems to have been that they routinely followed certain practices for the CIA and assumed that ongoing covert flights going south had the same Agency sanction. Law enforcement agencies also turned away from issues involving violations of neutrality law. In Florida, things began to look a great deal like the early 1960s, with planes coming and going as heads were being turned the other way. Apparently a number of people were working under the impression that it was all standard authorized CIA business.

Yet Oliver North faced some very basic operating challenges, including a lack of funding from Congress and the inability to fall back on established CIA proprietary companies and logistics. CIA Director Casey had already begun to pursue options for him to deal with both issues, including going outside the U.S. for weapons and financial support. Early on in the Contra campaign against Nicaragua, Casey had arranged for the donation of considerable quantities of deniable Soviet weapons from the Israelis. North described how Casey organized Operation Tipped Kettle, using the Pentagon to coordinate the transport of hundreds of tons of Israeli-captured Soviet weapons to Department of Defense warehouses. Then the CIA shipped volumes of weapons from those warehouses to the Contras and other proxy forces. All quite familiar practice and all actually carried out under the supervision of an Air Force officer with extensive experience in covert operations, Richard Secord.[530]

CIA Director Casey clearly had begun thinking about how the Contra military could be sustained with the withdrawal of CIA operational support and particularly without funding from congress for lethal aid.[531] Documents suggest he began following that line of action well before the arrival of the actual congressional deadline on spending. A CIA memorandum of March 1984 anticipated the cessation of congressional funding and laid out specifics of how it could be replaced. In the memo the CIA director specifically proposed and endorsed the idea of seeking "alternative" funding to avoid congressional constraints. The memo even specified certain sources—also removed from the document—addressed procurement alternatives, and suggested setting up private foundations to solicit domestic contributions to the effort. Casey's memo went directly to McFarlane, Oliver North's supervisor. The memo itself is clear evidence that Casey was going to be taking a leading role in guiding the effort to organize an administration end run around Congress's removal of the CIA from the project.[532] It was Casey himself who would suggest Richard Secord as a resource for North's efforts: "He's got the right experience for this sort of thing. He knows the right people, he gets things done, and he keeps his mouth shut. Why don't you call him?"[533]

Without a doubt, Secord did have the right background, including extensive military sales and purchasing expertise. He had headed the American military mission to Iran from 1975 to 1978 and later served at the Pentagon, directing U.S. military sales worldwide. Secord and his friend Albert Hakim worked together in support of an alternative Iranian hostage rescue mission. Secord had then been appointed deputy assistant secretary of defense for Near East, Africa, and South Asia, and was clearly on his way to a third star when former CIA and Naval Intelligence officer Edwin Wilson became involved in a scandal over sales of explosives and the contracting of other services (including assassination) to Libya.

Wilson charged that Secord had privately profited from certain arms sales and shipments to Egypt, and another Wilson associate claimed that Secord had taken kickbacks for sales to Iran in the

1970s. Secord was put on indefinite leave during an investigation but was fully cleared by the Department of Defense. Secord personally filed and was awarded damages relating to the charges, but the incident blighted his career. He became bitter over the whole affair, taking early retirement from the Air Force and opening a consulting firm. He did continue certain of his Pentagon relationships, acting as a consultant on intelligence support activity and remaining a member of the Pentagon's Special Operations Policy Group (a panel focused on the doctrine of low-intensity warfare).[534]

While Secord's military career had been damaged by his association with former CIA officers, his contacts and networking within the worlds of intelligence, military, and international weapons sales would become fundamental to the second phase of the secret war against Nicaragua. If Casey and North's new project was going to operate outside the legislative and funding box established by Congress—and be shielded from routine covert operation oversight—it was going to have to locate a host of new resources outside the normal clandestine intelligence infrastructure. Those resources would include individuals with purchasing, logistics, and paramilitary experience and connections. But those individuals could not be inside the system; nor could they be active-duty military or CIA personnel. We will explore how they did access such resources in considerable detail, as their activities illustrate new practices in establishing both distance and deniability in covert action. They also represented the first in a long series of privatization moves, which would lead to the widespread use of security and intelligence contractors in coming decades—a trend that would turn out to be equally high risk.

We've spent considerable time discussing the practices used to support deniability in sanctioned covert operations. Deniability was especially important in operations involving regime change. Earlier we noted that President Truman felt that being perceived as a "symbol of sinister and mysterious foreign intrigue" had become a real problem for the CIA and presented a serious propaganda opportunity for America's communist adversaries—and that was in 1963. Deniability is also a serious issue when military actions may possibly provoke significant intervention from third parties. We noted that as a serious concern in operations ranging from Tibet to Laos.

With friendly nations, including with military assistance and counterinsurgency programs, maintaining distance was desirable. In such activities it was not really possible to escape the fact that American military personnel and other agencies ranging from the CIA to the FBI were working with the friendly nations. Yet from South Vietnam across Latin America, we examined friendly regimes being actively supported by the U.S. that moved into what amounted to widespread political warfare. We saw counterinsurgency escalated to the point of producing tens of thousands of casualties, in some instances knowingly aided and abetted by paramilitary death squads. When supporting such allied regimes, the maintenance of distance became imperative. The U.S. might be training and advising the regimes' militaries, it might even be providing communications and computing resources for multination efforts, but legally, any associated murders or atrocities were being committed by our allies' own police, security forces, or anticommunist paramilitary organizations. Official U.S. military assistance training and advice did and still does include messages on democracy, human rights, and respect for basic civilian freedoms and legal process. Unfortunately, those elements often slide far down on the priority lists for trainees who return to become embroiled in bitter political and civil warfare. It is a sad but cold truth that eventually human rights groups would conclusively connect a significant number of U.S.-trained Latin American military officers to large-scale political murder and ultimately to death squad activities.[535]

Distance would also become a major concern in the secret war against Nicaragua. At first it had been important in disassociating the U.S. from certain of the more brutal Contra military actions. But in the second phase, with congressional limitations in place, distance had to be created between the authorized humanitarian aid (nonlethal) and the very lethal aid and activities being organized by Oliver North. Given that Contra military activities and combat inside

Nicaragua would certainly be covered by the media, it would have to look as if it were being done without any actual American government support. In a way it was a return to the Kennedy Administration concept of autonomous exile groups, but this time it would even have to be kept secret from the full National Security Council, from the covert action oversight group, from Congress, and ultimately, according to eventual testimony, even from President Reagan.

The first step in establishing that level of distance was to turn to personal and financial resources outside the system. As we review the individuals who became involved in the outside Contra support efforts, we will encounter not only people with official military and CIA experience, but individuals who had served as CIA assets (not employees) in the secret war against Cuba and similar covert operations. Participants ranged from those who had worked for CIA proprietary companies to a wide variety of eager civilian volunteers. It would be a highly unusual mix of people and practices but it would also be an environment that would have driven experienced CIA security and financial personnel straight out of their minds.

In contrast to earlier CIA-run operations we have studied, the North phase of the Nicaraguan war had very limited operational security and relatively little financial oversight. In terms of limited control, it would be exceeded only by efforts against the Soviets in Afghanistan. Since the Nicaraguan lethal activities were not being funded by Congress and not controlled though the CIA financial system, the effort was always desperately in need of money and would turn to a number of new and sometimes questionable sources. Worse yet, as in the Artime autonomous group operation we examined earlier, money that was raised was often just dropped into an operational account for FDN/Contra leaders. The actual use of the money was at their discretion.

Small grocery stores and similar businesses in Miami and Costa Rica were used as Contra purchasing and supply fronts. They literally handled tens of millions of dollars in both humanitarian and lethal aid—with little detailed accounting and no independent financial control. Purchasing was done using a series of "cutouts" involving financial transactions through offshore banks, but not the same banks or accounts used in similar CIA activities. Eventually the Government Accounting Office (GAO) would estimate that some $4 million had gone missing from authorized Contra humanitarian aid alone. In a memorandum to Oliver North, his chief Contra liaison reported that one of the main Contra leaders was selling American dollars on the black market for a 37 percent profit. Other contra leaders and Honduran generals floated money from bank to bank in Miami, the Caymans, and the Antilles, generating marked-up purchase orders and raking in substantial skimmed profits off arms sales. A number of those same banks eventually would be investigated separately for the concealment and laundering of money from drug shipments into the Caribbean and the U.S.[536]

These sorts of issues left the individuals involved with the Contra effort particularly exposed to becoming entangled in a great number of other bad things. General Secord had seen his Air Force career ruined simply by being associated with one former CIA officer, Ed Wilson. Many of those involved in the second phase of the Nicaraguan secret war, dubbed the Enterprise by Secord and North, would learn exactly how much worse such personal entanglements could become. Distance did eventually protect President Reagan from the scandals that eventually developed—at least in a legal sense; it would not serve others nearly as well.

In arms and weapons acquisition the Enterprise's activities did resemble standard CIA operating practice. In fact it looked so much like CIA practice that there is little doubt that many of the individuals involved in the field would have assumed the CIA was still running the show. Only those involved with the financial payments might have realized something different might be going on, especially once they learned that money was being carried by couriers associated with the NSC. The other fundamental difference was that it was all being done under contract with independent agents.

Following his retirement from the Air Force, Richard Secord had leveraged his extensive experience in military procurement to join an international trading business. The firm's leading company, Stanford

Technology Trading Group International, specialized in security systems and did business around the world. In approaching Secord for support, North made it clear that the arrangement would be on a commissioned sales basis and that it would involve international weapons deals and transfers. Secord's business services for North would be those of an agent, allowing Secord and his business partner to operate as a contractor to the North project, earning a commercial profit on transactions. As an example, the profit margin on the weapons sales orchestrated by Secord and his associates appears to have been on the order of 38 percent.[537]

In terms of public fund-raising—for humanitarian/nonlethal aid—the Enterprise was highly visible. Much of that success was due to the personal participation of President Reagan and the frequent use of his name and endorsement in fund-raising appeals. Money was raised through three different sources: private donations, foundation fund-raising, and public donation campaigns by smaller groups, including the Contra central council (the FDN) itself. In reality, the Contra council humanitarian aid fund-raising served as a type of cover for more significant and highly secret efforts to bring in major amounts of money for the Contra effort. Reportedly such humanitarian campaigns brought in less than one thousand dollars, as compared to the millions of dollars that would be raised for lethal Contra aid from foreign governments and anticommunist domestic donors. Private and public donations for humanitarian aid served as a valuable cover for secret donations and since all the funds were channeled directly to Contra leaders, they were able to use them with few restrictions. We also will see that the sanctioned U.S. government humanitarian aid provided a type of cover for lethal support activities as well, not only in purchasing but in transportation and distribution.

Perhaps the most visible and significant individual, aside from President Reagan, involved in bringing in both private money and volunteers for Contra activities in Nicaragua was retired Army Major General John Singlaub. He had his own personal history of military special operations, including service with the Office of

Strategic Services in Europe and China. He had been China desk officer for the CIA in 1949, CIA deputy chief in South Korea during the Korean War, and later commander of the Joint Unconventional Warfare Task Force (JUWTF) during the Vietnam War. Singlaub maintained an extensive range of social contacts to conservative, ultraconservative, and activist anticommunist associates through his involvement with both the World Anti-Communist League (WACL) and the United States Council for World Freedom (USCWF).

Oliver North wrote sparingly about General Singlaub's fund-raising activities and connections. He referred to him simply as a volunteer, and discussed Singlaub's assistance in regard to a single $5 million arms purchase. It appears that Singlaub's involvement was strictly voluntary, without a commission being involved. North did note in his writing that the prices Singlaub had obtained for the deal were better than other deals that Secord was negotiating. However, he seems to have been hesitant to use Singlaub's contacts any further, perhaps because Secord advised North that the Singlaub-assisted purchase had produced a high level of "noise" within the international weapons community.

There is extensive evidence that Singlaub was a key player in the public Reagan Administration effort to rouse popular political and monetary support for the Contras. In 1981, Singhlaub had organized a meeting for the purpose of creating an American chapter of the World Anti-Communist League. The American chapter, the United States Council for World Freedom, filed for incorporation in 1981. Its vice president had formerly served as the head of the Defense Intelligence Agency; other officers included the former Marine commander in Vietnam and retired Air Force and Army colonels.[538] The United States Council for World Freedom advocated and aggressively pursued—primarily in Latin America—a level of unconventional warfare beyond what Congress appeared eager to publicly support. Therefore, World Freedom was formed with the assistance of a $20,000 loan from Taiwan and it came to include a host of prominent figures. The Contra effort against the Sandinistas in Nicaragua offered an ideal opportunity for its members and their money.

Singlaub was in a perfect position to learn more about the renewed effort going on under North and to communicate it throughout his own social network. He began doing so in 1984 at the league conference in San Diego. That meeting received messages of endorsement from a host of staunch anticommunist figures, ranging from military dictators and Operation Condor leaders such as former Paraguayan President Alfredo Stroessner to President Reagan himself.

During the league meeting, the organization committed itself to becoming an "operational" player in the struggle against communism, directly supplying materials and support to "liberation forces" in the field. Within a few months the first DC-3 load of supplies from the league arrived at a Contra base camp in Honduras. It would be followed by more such shipments in the following months.[539] By 1986, the league had become even more active as Singlaub himself had received requests from the White House to organize a new private fund-raising initiative after Congress moved to shut U.S. government funding for Contra military operations. The push for donations may also have been helped a bit by the fact that the United States Council for World Freedom had received a highly desirable tax-exempt status. The Los Angeles office of the IRS had initially denied an exemption but after appeal it was approved by IRS headquarters in Washington.[540] Wealthy conservative donors lined up for the cause and North does note that Singlaub brought in a $10 million donation from the government of Taiwan.[541] Singlaub also opened his own offshore bank account to facilitate moving private donations to the FDN.

But for really serious funding, and particularly the money routed to lethal aid efforts, highly secret foreign contributions provided the vast bulk of the money. Robert McFarlane would eventually estimate contributions from Saudi Arabia at some $31 million, with another $10 million coming from the Kingdom of Brunei. The money went into a Swiss bank account set up by Secord's business partner Albert Hakim. Ultimately, in a highly creative if possibly illegal move, North would find yet another source for substantial secret funding.

The Reagan Administration had reached an agreement to facilitate the release of American hostages held in Iran by secretly arranging weapons sales to the Iranians. The Iranians were desperate for weapons, being themselves in a conventional war with Iraq, which had been going on since 1980. The first sale of weapons to Iran actually came from Israel and later shipments were from American military stocks. Oliver North was assigned to the logistics of the agreement and turned to Secord to help facilitate the first weapons transfer. The Israelis paid North a $1 million fee for his services, and reportedly the bulk of that payment was rerouted by Secord to North's Contra support project. North felt that such secret weapons sales could provide an ongoing flow of money not only for the Contras but for other covert projects, circumventing the need for congressional funding—as well as any need to advise Congress about the activities being conducted with money from the sales.

President Reagan had authorized the Iranian arms sale and North took the concept of such secret weapons sales as a new way to fund clandestine actions to his then-NSC boss, Admiral John Poindexter. Poindexter was apparently quite impressed with the concept and personally approved it. Reportedly CIA Director Casey was quite "enthusiastic" about the idea. Before the whole matter turned into the scandal known as Iran–Contra, some $16 million in profit was taken from arms transfers, with almost $4 million going to the Contras.[542] If the concept had actually taken hold, it could conceivably have led to the establishment of a totally autonomous secret warfare infrastructure, controlled only by the White House. It would have given the president the ability to conduct worldwide covert operations completely independent of Congress, allowing the administration to carry out its geopolitical agenda with complete autonomy. Largely due to events in Nicaragua and the scandal that became Iran–Contra, it never actually got to that stage.

With money available, the next agenda item for North was to get supplies of weapons and ammunition flowing to Contra field forces. International weapons businessman Raymond Martin and his RM Equipment sent at least $2 million worth of mostly Spanish-sourced rifles, ammunition, and hand grenades to the Contras through Honduras. In the main, however, the primary logistics of Contra arms support were carried out by a group of companies and associates linked to Richard Secord. In a broad sense, Oliver North had been recruited to act as a high-level manager for the White House, taking direction from National Security Advisor McFarlane and advice from CIA Director Casey. He in turn had outsourced much of the operational work to Richard Secord, Secord's business partner finance specialist Albert Hakim, and their private companies such as Stanford Technology Trading Group International. That company would come to handle a good deal of the military purchasing and shipment logistics for the lethal side of the Enterprise.

In addition to his own companies, Secord would use fictitious American and Canadian business fronts, referred to as notional businesses in CIA terminology, to buy weapons in Spain and Portugal, and planes and boats in Belgium, Canada, and the United States. Secord also reached out to retired Air Force Colonel Richard Gadd, who was already operating a private business providing covert transportation facilities to the Pentagon. Secord brought him into the Enterprise for aircraft purchase and leasing. Other Enterprise-associated missions such as Seaspray, Yellow Fruit, and Delta Force, reporting to Intelligence Support Activity, would carry arms and supply shipments, and a front company in rural Pennsylvania would be used to pay the crews operating the boats and planes.

The Enterprise also piggybacked shipment of its nonlethal supplies by sending them through the State Department's Nicaraguan Humanitarian Assistance Office (NHAO). NHAO contracted with AirMach planes to ship supplies into El Salvador. After unloading the humanitarian aid, the AirMach planes would be reloaded with lethal Enterprise cargoes for transport to Contra bases in Honduras. That left the Enterprise footing only the air supply bill for the short runs to the Contras.[543] Many of the pilots, cargo handlers, and maintenance crews involved had worked for Air America in Southeast Asia. The Enterprise also purchased and leased aircraft from the former CIA proprietary Southern Air Transport, which had gone independent in 1973 but still did a good deal of work for the CIA and its associated company, Corporate Air Services.[544]

A final point to note about Enterprise lethal aid shipments is one that we profiled in international arms dealing far back in the first decade of Cold War deniable warfare. It was one thing for Oliver North to outsource weapons supplies to commercial arms vendors such as GeoMilTech, RM Equipment, or the Secord companies, but to actually ship the purchases via regular international commercial carriers (by either ship or air transport), the transactions needed to involve weapons sales to recognized governments, and be supported by legal end-user certificates. Such certificates may only be issued by legally recognized governments. With such certificates and the proper paperwork, shipments are perfectly legal and can go through regular ports of entry with no customs issues.

Certificates being used in the Contra supply transactions came from the governments of Guatemala and El Salvador. With approval from the president of Guatemala, North and his boss McFarlane arranged for Guatemalan certificates to cover some $8 million in purchases. The documents were signed by a Guatemalan military officer and transmitted through a fictional company (Trans-World Arms of Montreal, Canada), which in turn allowed purchases to be made through international arms broker DefexPortugal. Other fully legal, government certificate–based purchases were transferred via Energy Resource International of Vienna, Virginia (itself another nonexistent "notional" company), which conveniently used addresses matching the actual office addresses of Secord's Stanford Technology Trading Group International and Richard Gadd's American National Management Corp.

Richard Secord had also brought a variety of CIA alumni into his efforts. Those individuals brought experience and expertise—and certain types of risks—to Enterprise operations. Secord brought in retired CIA officer Tom Clines for his expertise in purchasing deniable weapons.[545] Clines had worked with under Ted Shackley at JM WAVE in Laos, and then at the Chile desk in Washington during the Nixon-era covert operations against Chile. Clines was known as being some of a CIA "cowboy." He had suggested using former Cuban exile assets for assassinations in Chile. Clines did work as an Enterprise purchasing agent for Secord, operating out of Lisbon, Portugal. But he also brought valuable expertise in operating a string of complex foreign bank accounts; he had acquired that expertise in the Chilean operations, assisting with the massive economic warfare program that had targeted the Allende regime.[546]

In addition to bringing Clines on board for purchasing, Secord brought in Rafael Quintero to work directly with the Contra base camps in Honduras. Quintero had also participated in the secret war against Cuba. He had been second in command to Artime in the autonomous group efforts and had an excellent reputation for both fearlessness and intelligence. Reportedly Quintero had continued work as a CIA contract employee, becoming involved with a variety of companies in Mexico and Central America that were used as fronts for CIA activities against Cuba. After leaving the Agency in 1971, Quintero continued to do occasional work for his former JM WAVE associates, in various businesses. In 1976, Quintero had been approached by former CIA officer Ed Wilson for help in getting a loan out of Miami for a start-up freight-forwarding business. Wilson, another former Plans/Operations Directorate officer who had worked at JM WAVE, had left the Agency, only to go on to work for Naval Intelligence and in a variety of his own "security"-related activities, including some that would involve highly questionable work in Libya.

Quintero responded by personally loaning Wilson $10,000. Two months later, Wilson was back with another proposal that involved an assassination project. Thinking that it was a CIA-sanctioned activity, Quintero agreed to listen to the proposal and he and an experienced Cuban exile demolitions man flew to London to get more details. In those discussions it became clear that it was a private job, actually one involving Russians as well as Wilson's Americans in the Gadhafi assassination projects—at which point Quintero adamantly refused. After returning to Miami, Quintero sought counsel from his old CIA friend Carl Jenkins, who encouraged him to separate himself from Wilson, which Quintero did. His experience with Wilson is just one indication of how difficult it had become to determine which old CIA colleagues were no longer working for the Agency, and which operations were officially sanctioned. Old ties could surface opportunities, but they could also bring along considerable risk.

In 1985 Quintero was to serve as the Enterprise point man on the ground, working in El Salvador, Costa Rica, Honduras, and Guatemala and arranging shipping clearances with government authorities and military departments.[547] He also provided advice in regard to Contra military activities. As an employee of Secord, Quintero was paid a $4,000 a month salary, which was also intended to cover his travel and operating expenses. The assignment effectively led to a situation in which a private individual with no official American government employment, security clearance, or supervision was conducting high-level contacts with foreign governments and military agencies. Quintero also played a role in providing field intelligence, which was used to plan and set up a network of small distribution airfields (forward air bases) in Costa Rica, Honduras, and El Salvador. Oliver North had persuaded Secord to take on the task of developing the same sort of covert air operation that the CIA would have put into place if Congress had not removed it from Contra military operations. North continued to involve Secord in more and more tasks, including the Iranian hostage/weapons project.[548]

Yet another of the JM WAVE alumni to appear in Contra operations was Felix Rodriguez. Like Quintero, Rodriguez had been briefly entangled with Ed Wilson before joining the Enterprise effort. Rodriguez writes about becoming involved in a security advisory job in Lebanon while still officially a CIA employee. Rodriguez flew with Wilson to Lebanon, accompanying a planeload of weapons destined for Christian militias in that country. Rodriguez describes "hoaxing" his CIA case officer while still officially a CIA employee, in order to go overseas on the job. That remark supports the point that CIA assets were free to pursue their own activities while in between sanctioned projects and missions. In writing about his career, Felix Rodriguez portrays himself as a valuable addition to the Enterprise operations, for his far-ranging activities in Latin America had introduced him to military figures in countries throughout the region. Rodriguez had officially retired from the Agency in 1976. However, Ted Shackley had arranged that he be allowed a public retirement (extremely rare for operations field personnel), freeing Rodriguez to acknowledge his Agency service. The upshot was that Rodriguez was free to list his CIA employment as an impressive element of his résumé.

After retirement, Rodriguez had also become personally involved with some of the earliest private support for opposition to the Sandinista regime in Nicaragua. The Cuban exiles in Miami had long been supporters of the anticommunist Somoza government. While still in power, Somoza had traveled to Miami, meeting personally with Cuban exile leaders. Rodriguez describes his own 1981 travel to Honduras, Costa Rica, El Salvador, and Guatemala in efforts to encourage and assist the Contra movement. In 1982 he was privately involved in the multinational government efforts against insurgents in Honduras, El Salvador, and Guatemala. He conceived and implemented the use of a "tactical task force" for use in those efforts, and air operations were supported by Cuban exile pilots.[549]

Rodriguez submitted his concept to high-level CIA officers and to Don Gregg (Vice President Bush's national security advisor) and it was circulated to Robert McFarlane at the NSC. McFarlane did forward it to Oliver North but Rodriguez writes that he had no direct response from North. Instead, Gregg personally introduced him to North. At that point in time the CIA was still running the Contra project, with congressional funding, and Rodriguez took a military advisory position in El Salvador, serving as the technical advisor to a Salvadorian quick-reaction counterinsurgency helicopter squadron. During 1984 and 1985 he flew some one hundred combat missions with the air group.

By 1985–1986 both Quintero and Rodriguez would become Enterprise employees, facilitating logistics and shipping and coordinating Secord's air assets for supply drops throughout Nicaragua. Rodriguez had also been helpful in negotiating clandestine use of the base at Ilopango in El Salvador, and acted as liaison to key Salvadorian military and political figures. Operations at Ilopango were also assisted by the commander of the U.S. military mission to El Salvador. In contrast, the CIA chief of station refused any involvement, declaring the whole activity to be in violation of Congress's Boland Amendment.[550] Secord also used Rodriguez to obtain additional El Salvadorian end-user certificates made out in the name of Lake Resources. Those certificates were for missiles to be used somewhere outside the Contra war. That made perfectly good sense because North and the Enterprise had need for deniable rockets and missiles far beyond Nicaragua.[551]

Since he still had his regular job with the Salvadorian air unit, Rodriguez brought in another Cuban exile activist, Luis Posada, to run day-to-day activities at Ilopango for the Enterprise. Posada, using the pseudonym Ramon Medina, took full-time charge of Enterprise activities at the base, including air shipping and transfer operations. Following his involvement in the early CIA operations against Cuba, Posada had engaged in a long history of anti-Castro activities. During the mid-1970s he had become associated with Frank Castro and CORU (Coordination of United Revolutionary Organizations) and later with Jorge Mas Canosa of CANF (Cuban American National Foundation).[552] After its formation in 1976, CORU claimed credit for some fifty anti-Castro terror bombings over the next ten months, in locations ranging from Miami and New York City to Venezuela, Panama, and Argentina.

After the CIA's Cuba project had been closed down, Posada and several of the other exiles had carried on their struggle against Castro throughout the 1970s. House Select Committee on Assassinations investigator Gaeton Fonzi found evidence that Posada had been involved in an assassination attempt on Fidel Castro in Chile in 1971. Reportedly Posada had provided forged identity and travel-related papers for the individuals involved in the plot as well as cover jobs with Venezuelan television.

Venezuela and Chile had both proved to be very friendly environments for the Cuban exiles, with assurances that both the Venezuelan national police (DSIP) and the Chilean security service (DINA) were supportive of the Cuban exile cause and were willing to provide support and assistance. On occasion the exiles were asked to show their support for their host governments' anticommunist efforts by doing favors, such as cooperating in foreign assassinations.[553] Posada worked for the Venezuelan internal security service, served as advisor to the army, and eventually became chief of security for the national police. After a major change in the government took certain of his Venezuelan supporters out of power, Posada left that position to form his own private security company.

CIA officer David Phillips would later admit that Posada was indeed one of his operatives and that Posada had worked closely with him in his Chilean activities.[554] Following his role in the CIA Chile project, Phillips had become chief of station in Caracas, Venezuela. Ultimately Posada was charged with and convicted of the 1976 terror bombing of a Cuban airliner that killed seventy-six people. He spent nine years in a Venezuelan prison, only to escape in 1985 and then to appear in Honduras working for Felix Rodriguez and the North–Secord Enterprise. Felix Rodriguez and Posada both claimed that Posada had been framed in the airliner bombing. That assertion is countered by the fact that two of Posada's security agency employees had indeed been onboard the aircraft and had deplaned at the final stop before the explosion occurred. Arrested in Trinidad, they admitted planting bombs on the aircraft and stated that the mission had been organized by Posada and Orlando Bosch, another activist member of Frank Castro's CORU group. It is also known that Bosch visited Posada in Venezuela immediately prior to the terror attack on the airliner.

In moving covert operations from the CIA to North's network of contractors and volunteers, the Reagan Administration had essentially privatized the project. The Enterprise simply did not have the benefit—or the burden—of many of the support and oversight functions developed for the national intelligence infrastructure. As a consequence the Enterprise did not have the accounting and audit mechanisms of the CIA's purchasing, transportation, or logistics systems. It had none of the Agency's personnel screening and records services and perhaps most importantly it had no involvement with the CIA's Office of Security. In his biography, Oliver North writes of complaining to his NSC bosses that he simply could not replicate all of what the CIA had been doing before Congress pulled it out of the secret war. Turning to outsourcing and contractors had allowed him to distribute money as well as to purchase and distribute lethal aid to the Contras. But outsourcing and volunteers did not give North access to professional CIA financial oversight or related administrative staff support. And, in retrospect, it seems quite unlikely that CIA administrative officers would have been happy with most of the accounting and security practices of the Enterprise. It is also unlikely they would have been happy with a number of its field personnel, including Luis Posada. That raises an interesting point that we will return to in the following chapter. In between operational activities, CIA assets were sometimes on their own for periods of time. During those periods they became accessible to individuals with whom they had worked, whom they trusted, and whom they might well assume to be working on officially sanctioned, although clandestine, projects. Felix Rodriguez's recruitment of Posada would not be the only example of entanglement with questionable personnel who would dirty the Enterprise's record during the eventual Iran–Contra investigation.

Rodriguez himself became less than enthusiastic about Enterprise operations. He claimed that little Enterprise money was spent on aircraft outfitting or maintenance and that Secord not only routinely billed two to three times the actual shipping costs, but also sold weapons and ammunition at hugely inflated prices.[555] In turn Secord writes that Rodriguez's claims about Secord's prices were actually based on information from a competitor, Ron Martin Associates (RMA), which was manipulating Rodriguez in an effort to take away Contra sales from Secord. Secord felt that by 1986 Rodriguez had become the biggest detractor and critic of Enterprise air operations, while being paid $3,000 a month for his government and military liaison work in El Salvador.[556] Ultimately Rodriguez would portray Secord as running the Enterprise to maximize his own profit, and would complain to Donald Gregg that the Contras were being "ripped off."[557] The Enterprise made use of seasoned veterans of both CIA and military covert operations, many of whom had worked with one another previously. The lack of formal structure produced incidents such as Secord and Singlaub's competition for weapons sales, and Felix Rodriguez being suspected by Secord of undermining Enterprise operations and serving the interests of a weapons competitor. The privatization of covert warfare was clearly not without its own special problems.

Another unique element of the Enterprise phase of the Nicaraguan effort was the extent to which private volunteers joined in field operations. Of course in many covert operations under CIA direction, volunteers had participated. When brought to the press's attention they were simply denied by being labeled soldiers of fortune or mercenaries. However, those volunteers were generally either associated with CIA proprietary companies such as Air America, professional mercenary forces such as Mike Hoare's commandos in the Congo, or experienced volunteers such as the UCLA (Unilaterally Controlled Latino Assets) personnel used in the first phase of Nicaraguan combat operations. Most often such personnel were under some level of either direction or at least coordination from proprietary companies or CIA field officers. By 1985, with congressional restrictions in place and with the CIA officially out of field operations, a new wave of volunteers appeared along both the northern and southern borders of Nicaragua, either in Contra base camps in Honduras or at the residences of American ranchers in Costa Rica who were known to be supporting the Contras.

Reagan Administration efforts to popularize American opposition to the Sandinistas had certainly contributed to the wave of private volunteers, as did the promotion of anticommunist combat in publications such as *Eagle* and *Soldier of Fortune*. *Soldier of Fortune* sent some of its own staff to Contra camps for training activities and promoted articles about volunteers going into combat with the Contras in the jungles of Nicaragua. The magazine also started an El Salvador–Nicaragua Defense Fund to support Contra operations.

Private American paramilitary groups joined in the volunteer effort, with the most active being the Civilian Military Assistance group headed by Tom Posey, who had started his own effort to collect money and send volunteers to the Contras as early as 1983. Posey described his volunteers as "missionary-mercenaries," reporting that three of them were in Contra camps by January 1984. By 1985 Posey claimed donations of $5 million and the dispatching of fifty men a month as Contra trainers and military advisors. Posey, who provided security at Singlaub's World Anti-Communist League conferences, and Singlaub both reached out to other paramilitary groups, ranging from the Recondo Military Training School in Dolomite, Alabama, to the Cuban exile Brigade 2506 in Miami.

The practical result of this volunteer recruiting effort was that a good number of individuals began to show up along Nicaraguan borders, many of them armed, many of them acting clandestinely, and none of them clearly reporting to anyone or under any sort of control or oversight. Some of them did indeed perform important functions, as trainers for the Contras, providing medical assistance, and serving as mechanics and pilots. Others merged their own agendas (both political and financial) with the overall Contra support effort being conducted by the Enterprise. That would result in an even more complex cast of characters, and it significantly upped the chances that at least some of those involved would be doing things that would come back to haunt the CIA, Oliver North, and the Reagan Administration.

The Reagan Administration's hope was that the Enterprise effort was simply a sustaining one. It believed that the Sandinistas would further reveal their communist agendas and sponsorships, Congress would come to its senses, and the CIA would resume an ultimately successful covert action leading to regime change in Nicaragua. Instead, both "distance" and "deniability" were compromised in one fell swoop with the crash of an Enterprise aircraft inside Nicaragua. A single crew member, Eugene Hasenfus, survived that crash and made a public statement that the plane and its mission were part of a covert CIA operation; his capture and statements generated a firestorm of publicity. Actually Hasenfus was wrong about the plane. As we noted earlier, many of those involved in the Enterprise simply assumed it was a CIA effort, using routine covers. Hasenfus was a long-term Air America veteran, and by that point in the 1980s a lot of people were becoming a bit unclear about just who was employing them, and who was sanctioning their missions.

Matters were made worse by the fact that the plane itself had been used in a drug sting against the Sandinistas in 1984, so clearly it did have a U.S. government history. Investigation would also turn up the fact that Secord and the Enterprise were using the same transit airfields used in official humanitarian aid flights to the Contras. Aircraft records also revealed that the plane had been used for Contra supply flights under the cover of Southern Air Transport, a company widely known to do work for the CIA.

The exposure of ongoing covert activities against Nicaragua was only the first step in a series of revelations that ultimately brought public issues such as the arms–hostages deal with Iran and the movement of Iranian weapons sales money into Contra secret warfare. Eventually fourteen people were indicted under various charges including actual violations and obstruction of justice due to efforts to conceal related activities. The list included major figures such as National Security Advisor Robert McFarlane, Secretary of Defense Caspar Weinberger, and Oliver North, as well as various other individuals including acting CIA officers. Eventually three CIA officers would be indicted for providing false testimony in regard to their knowledge of Enterprise air activities.[558] Several individuals were convicted, some of convictions were overturned on appeals, and ultimately President H.W. Bush issued six pardons for those remaining. We will address details of the legal exposure of the CIA officers in a following chapter.

Iran–Contra evolved into a national scandal and produced a massive congressional inquiry. In the meantime, the Contras continued their efforts, the U.S. maintained its diplomatic pressure on Nicaragua, and not much else changed. Ironically, to the total surprise of the Reagan Administration, free elections in Nicaragua would remove many of Sandinista leaders from political power. The Sandinista regime then began to gradually unravel due to a combination of factors, including domestic charges of corruption against some of its leadership. In the end, it would be the Sandinistas who voluntarily determined their own fate, not the military success of a Contra army or any form of American covert warfare. The Reagan Administration effort against Nicaragua failed, yet regime change ultimately did occur. Its parallel effort in Afghanistan succeeded dramatically, the Soviets were forced to withdraw, and regime change in Afghanistan succeeded—with far different long-term consequences.

In an operational sense, deniable warfare have almost always involved reliance on regional third-party nations for access and support. And on occasion those nations have made use of American surrogate fighters for their own purposes. India had actually deployed a force of Tibetan fighters along with the Indian army in the Bangladesh conflict. In the Congo, Mobutu made use of surrogate fighters and his own troops in political struggles within neighboring Angola. One Laotian regime had been interested for a time in using Republic of China–armed units from early shadow warfare in Burma. And numerous Latin American nations eagerly used the services of Cuban exile fighters originally involved in the American secret war against Cuba. Yet no nation had actively made use of such surrogate fighters in opposition to America or its interests.

In Afghanistan in the 1980s, America's relationships with Pakistan and Saudi Arabia—which at first were viewed as quite desirable—would ultimately produce dramatically negative side effects. Shadow warfare in Afghanistan did indeed bloody and embarrass the Soviet Union but it also produced a generation of well-trained, battle-hardened, fanatically fundamentalist religious fighters who would conduct attacks against all three of their original sponsors: Saudi Arabia, Pakistan, and the United States.

In the first phase of covert action in Afghanistan, any differences in national agendas among the three partners were largely concealed by their mutual enthusiasm for opposing the Soviet move into

Afghanistan. As CIA Director Casey escalated American participation, and Congressman Wilson turned on the funding floodgate, it seemed a simple matter of supporting Afghan "freedom fighters" in blocking the Soviets and their puppet government from "securing" the country—fundamentally a strategy of denial.[559] That overall strategy worked well. What was generally ignored at the time, at least among senior American decision makers, was that both Pakistani and Saudi leaders were very much focused on establishing a fundamentalist Muslim religious context for the blocking action.

The leader of Pakistan, Mohammed Zia ul-Haq, made no secret of the fact that he considered Islam the "organizing principle" of Pakistan, just as Judaism was that of Israel. Pakistan had been created around Islam and would fail if it did not maintain itself on that basis. To that end he had personally pushed for the creation of hundreds of religious schools (madrassas) along the Afghan border. The schools were specifically intended to embed a very rigid concept of Islam in young men and to establish a shield of thousands of Islamic fighters willing to accept martyrdom to defend Pakistan from any challenge from its west. It would be Zia, and his claim for total control of surrogate warfare against the Soviets, that would shape the initial American surrogate involvement in Afghanistan. And within the Reagan Administration, nobody was balking at giving Zia free rein. Remarks from George Schultz, secretary of state under Reagan, indicate American dependence on Zia: "We must remember that without Zia's support, the Afghan resistance, key to making the Soviets pay a heavy price for their Afghan adventure, is effectively dead."[560]

It would be Zia who would take total control over all CIA weapons and supplies going into Afghanistan, Zia who would forbid direct contact between CIA officers and Afghan commanders, and Zia who would consistently route the majority of weapons and materials to Muslim Brotherhood–linked fundamentalist rebel leaders rather than the more traditionalist royalist and tribal groups. Zia mandated that all training would be conducted by Pakistani military intelligence officers (ISI). Even when more advanced weapons began to be supplied, American trainers would train Pakistani Intelligence, which in turn would pass on the training. And it would be Pakistani advisors and assault teams to operate inside Afghanistan, not CIA paramilitary officers. By 1987, Pakistani ISI-supported teams were actually crossing into Central Asia and conducting attacks inside the Soviet Union. In one instance a team sent a wave of some thirty incendiary and high-explosive rockets into a Soviet factory complex. Regardless of any thoughts the U.S. might have had on the subject, the ISI itself was more than a little interested in bringing about Islamic destabilization along the Soviet southern border nations, all with significant Muslim populations.

As for the Saudis, they were especially eager to have their aid going to the "correct" jihadi factions inside Afghanistan. They approached the problem pragmatically: Saudi intelligence invited Afghan insurgent leaders to Mecca for the annual pilgrimage. While there they were heavily socialized, networked, and courted by fundamentalist religious leaders. They were also given money from wealthy Saudi donors. And one of the key figures in that networking process was a wealthy young Saudi fundamentalist named Osama bin Laden. To ensure donations went to the appropriate factions, bin Laden personally traveled to Pakistan to meet with Afghan commanders.[561] Later, the International Islamic University in Islamabad, Pakistan, would become a focal point through which donations could be routed via Abdullah Azzam, a Muslim Brotherhood scholar and fund-raiser who had relocated there. Azzam became quite close to bin Laden and used him as his own bridge into Saudi Arabia, for recruits and for donations.[562]

While Casey and other Reagan national security officials celebrated the ongoing damage being done to the Soviets, it would be Pakistan that would initially mold the Afghan resistance into a Pakistani-linked Islamic proxy force rather than a more nationalist Afghan movement. And while the U.S. failed to acknowledge the reality of what the Pakistanis were doing, certain of the early Afghani factions, nationalists, monarchists, and Muslims (but not necessarily jihadi fundamentalists) began to route complaints to the U.S.

through independent international channels (diplomats, the media, and businessmen) outside control of the Pakistani ISI. Despite the growing number of complaints that those groups not favored by Pakistan were being shut out or left to be picked off in the fighting, senior CIA officers preferred not to meddle in a campaign that was becoming increasingly successful against the Soviets. At the same time, the Pakistanis themselves failed to realize that to some extent their own effort was in the process of being hijacked by jihadi fundamentalist involvement coming out of Saudi Arabia.[563]

It would be unfair to say that the CIA was satisfied with being totally held out of Afghan field operations. It had pushed for more involvement and in the spring of 1985 President Reagan signed off on NSDD-166, titled "U.S. Policy, Programs, and Strategy in Afghanistan." Under that order the CIA began an effort to establish more direct contact with guerrilla forces, largely to provide them with improved intelligence and secure communications. In addition to shipment of Stinger missiles and other controlled weapons, such as high-tech night-vision sniper rifles, the support being routed to the Afghans was far beyond anything deployed in any surrogate warfare up to that point in time. In practice the U.S. was giving the rebels the tools for full-scale conventional warfare against the Soviets. Eventually efforts would even be made to deliver captured Soviet tanks into eastern Afghanistan.

To accomplish all this, the CIA needed feet on the ground, and given Zia's original constraints, it had to hide that effort from the Pakistanis. The new assets were primarily volunteers using the covers of journalists and photographers. Most were Europeans, willing and eager to travel on their own, who operated independently. Eager for action, some were even inserted with secure communications equipment. They provided a channel for sending back field observations and also reporting on Pakistani activities within Afghanistan.

One of the initial themes in those reports was the ongoing string of complaints about Pakistani selectivity in distribution of materials. It was something that had previously been either ignored or downplayed. But at that point it was becoming clear to some in the CIA that total reliance on Pakistan had not necessarily been all good. Yet other CIA personnel considered the new agents—referred to as the unilaterals—as unsophisticated, certainly more enthusiastic than professional.[564] Indeed there would be officers within the Agency still supporting the Pakistani relationship even after the events of 9/11.

At the same time it was deploying unilaterals, the U.S. began supplying a variety of materials, and conducted Pakistani ISI officer training that allowed the ISI to train its own new round of Afghan insurgents. That training focused on the handling of plastic explosives, the construction of sophisticated bombs with electronic detonators, and the use of night-vision-equipped long-range sniper equipment. Afghanistan began to see car (and camel) bombings and sniper attacks, initially targeting Soviet military—particularly officers.

As events proceeded, the Pakistani-favored groups turned to both political and religious targets, including professors at Kabul University, movie theaters, and cultural events.[565] Terrorism in Afghanistan was becoming both an issue and a question, at least to some of those within the CIA Afghan team. And, once again, the mission began to override what was permitted to go into CIA internal reports and memoranda. At CIA headquarters, the head of the Afghan task force addressed legal concerns over memos about sniper rifles by describing them as "individual defensive devices." As we saw in Angola, at some point actual field operations can be conducted with only verbal directions, and reports to headquarters become self-censored to avoid raising issues and questions.

After headquarters expressed certain concerns over guerrilla terror activities seen coming into play, the head of the CIA's Afghanistan task force sent memos to his field officers directing them not to communicate "anything more on that subject ever again."[566] Yet while the Agency was wrestling with the concerns and complaints coming via the unilaterals and filtering its own communications, at its senior levels it totally failed to grasp that certain events were in the process of polarizing and fragmenting the overall Afghan campaign.

By 1986, a huge complex of camps and training facilities had been developed on the Pakistani side of the Afghan border. Upwards of eighteen thousand new trainees were being processed each year, and of that number, some six to seven thousand were committed Muslim jihadists, increasingly "salted" with Arab volunteers from Palestine, Algeria, Tunisia, Egypt, and Saudi Arabia. The Pakistani military commander is reported to have increasingly arranged for training of the jihadi fighters to be conducted independently and out of even direct ISI control. And advanced training had begun to focus on explosives work, urban sabotage, car bombs, and land mines, as well as sniper weapons and antiaircraft weapons.

Beyond actual military training, a much larger jihadi infrastructure had evolved, financed initially by the Saudi government but increasingly by wealthy Saudi donors and by the fundamentalist religious schools and charities encouraged by the Saudi kingdom. Millions of dollars poured into Pakistan outside of either Pakistani ISI or American control or oversight. And by 1986 a new group named the Islamic Salvation Foundation had been organized in Peshawar, Pakistan. Its mission was recruitment of volunteers for the Afghan struggle. It was establishing centers along the border and eventually would open a major complex in eastern Afghanistan, in a remote cavern system that would eventually come to worldwide attention as Tora Bora.

The wealthy Saudi, Osama bin Laden, was personally financing the new group. Bin Laden was effectively creating his own small army, offering $300 to any Arab willing to fight in Afghanistan and recruiting around the world, including inside the United States.[567] He was constantly at work on infrastructure construction for his favored Afghan commanders, and in his spare time he built his own personal fortress in the area, the "Lion's Den." At the time, the U.S. had no conceptual problems with any of his efforts, since the CIA had itself explored the thought of an "Arab Legion" for Afghanistan—Bin Laden had simply moved to do that on his own.

But by 1987 the CIA unilaterals in Afghanistan had begun to report complaints from Afghan fighters that they were being not only harassed but displaced by thousands of Arab volunteers. The volunteers were fundamentalist Wahhabi believers who accused them of ignorance of the Koran and began desecrating Afghan graves. Curses had been exchanged, firefights had erupted, and the rebel groups were beginning to fragment over the issue of religion. In retrospect the seeds for the future division of Afghanistan—between a jihadi-supported Taliban and its nationalist opponents—were being planted through the Pakistani and Saudi creation of a fundamentalist religious force, with a great number of its volunteers coming from outside of Afghanistan itself. That movement intended to establish an Afghan religious state where sharia, the enforcement of the moral and religious codes of Islam as public law, would be the dominant force. In the U.S., reports from the field simply circulated through and among the various agencies and teams involved, to no particular result. During the next two to three years upwards of $25 million a month of private Saudi and other Arab money flowed into jihadi militaries in and around the Pakistani border regions. Fundamentalist Pakistani ISI officers had virtually gutted the secular, leftist, and royalist Afghan factions, which had initially risen to oppose the Soviets. The active rebel forces were Islamists, with an obvious religious agenda. They had gotten extremely proficient, they were extremely well armed and trained, and Soviet casualties were escalating.

It appears that excitement about the bloodletting the Soviets were taking simply overrode any longer-term U.S. concerns. And indeed the Soviets were taking a bloodbath. The American Stinger missiles had blunted their close air support advantage and the Afghan proxy regime increasingly found itself forced back inside a few key urban defensive centers. By the end of 1986, the new Russian leader, Mikhail Gorbachev, was asking his military how long they were going to have to remain in Afghanistan and talking about a two-year time limit. In 1989, the Soviets would agree to a UN-mediated withdrawal and the Afghan Marxist regime would be left to its own devices. In one sense the U.S. and the CIA had achieved their most dramatic proxy victory since Guatemala in 1954, and this time it had been directly against the Soviet military itself.

In the years that followed, the CIA would remain at least marginally involved in Afghanistan, largely in a political action role, supporting the ongoing insurgent effort to totally oust the Marxist regime in Kabul by funneling in money, trucks, and hundreds of Toyota pickups. The pickups would become standard field equipment for both the mujahedin and Afghan smugglers. Things would get even more difficult for CIA officers and even unilaterals inside the country. In one incident a CIA agent team that crossed over into Afghanistan encountered a roadblock manned by Arab Islamic fighters. Their Afghan escort was accosted, a shouting match ensued, and the Saudi jihadi fighters declared that the Americans were "infidels with no business in Afghanistan." The Americans took shelter behind their jeep and it was only after an extensive dialogue, led by their Muslim interpreter, that the Saudi fighters reluctantly agreed to let the Americans leave without being executed on the spot.[568] It would seem that the signs should have been quite obvious, but through 1989 the CIA continued to send millions of dollars in weapons, supplies, and humanitarian aid into exactly the same border regions that the Arab jihadi fighters and their ISI fundamentalist sponsors had come to control.

By 1992, the Soviet Union had officially dissolved and in that year the CIA's directive for Afghan covert operations was canceled. CIA involvement did not, at least for the time, entirely end. President George H.W. Bush allocated special funds for a new CIA mission in Afghanistan, but the effort was minimal. In contrast, Pakistan continued to pour major funding into its own proxy factions. The rebellion against the Soviets had indeed succeeded but it had left a country fragmented. With Pakistan remaining the major power and money broker, a new force began to take over large sections of the country. That force became known as the Taliban. It brought order, security, and a very strict enforcement of fundamentalist religious law. Ultimately the Taliban, with sufficient funds to bribe numerous local tribal commanders and warlords, would install itself as the new central government in Kabul.[569]

Opposition to the Taliban remained. Its territorial expansion in the north of the country was blocked by a number of armed tribal groups and its fundamentalist religious rule and self-declared authority was opposed in areas throughout the country. The opposition groups would become referred to as the United Front, although Pakistan and the ISI officers supporting the Taliban would attempt to diminish its scope by referring to it strictly as the Northern Alliance.[570] The fighting inside Afghanistan never totally ceased, even after the ascendency of the Taliban. The continued fighting led to a continued and increasing demand for money to sustain the parties involved. With no central government, the world's largest poppy group, and a dramatically improved cross-border road complex—and hundreds of Toyota pickups provided as part of the earlier supply effort—the situation was ideal for an explosion in the age-old narcotics traffic out of the country. By 1992, literally hundreds of tons of heroin were moving out through Pakistani ports or over long overland routes though the newly autonomous Russian republics.

The commercial and social connections needed to facilitate the trade had been in existence for years and it was widely rumored that district and regional Pakistani military officers were involved in providing security and transportation for drug shipments. The Pakistani military administrator for the Khyber Pakhtunkhwa province in northwestern Pakistan had supervised the overall clandestine and training support effort. He was largely responsible for developing the Afghan mujahedin; in turn he had a personal reputation for being involved with the Afghan drug trade and was listed by Interpol as a known narcotics trafficker.[571, 572]

But something other than drugs was also going on inside Afghanistan. A new set of training camps, funded by both Pakistan and Osama bin Laden, had been set up for jihadi fighters. Some of them would join in to support the Taliban in local combat. But in addition to Arab volunteers, Pakistan was sending volunteers from Kashmir, India, into the camps. Those trainees would go back home to India to produce a constant stream of terror attacks, destabilizing Pakistan's relations with India. In time the products of the Afghan training camps would move on to feed insurgencies around the globe.[573]

CHAPTER 20

Risky Business

We have now reviewed several decades of deniable warfare—covert interventions using surrogate fighters around the globe, much of it in high-risk, denied territories, virtually all of it in conjunction with third-party nations—with operations increasingly involving surrogates with their own independent agendas. Earlier we paused to examine certain unanticipated consequences of the undeclared warfare in the decades immediately following the Second World War. If anything, concerns and issues only escalated in the following decades. There is no question that the decision to go covert carries many types of risks, for the president, the administration, those personnel directly involved—as well as the nation. Overall it seems that presidents appear to view operational success or failure strictly in terms of the primary mission; broader judgments are left to subsequent administrations or to political scientists and historians. Discussion of peripheral consequences and collateral damage is simply avoided when possible, or if not possible, dealt with in the political arena.

Kennedy Administration National Security Advisor McGeorge Bundy is on record saying that prior to his murder, President Kennedy was in the process of concluding that covert warfare was a tempting but ultimately bad choice. Kennedy seemed to be leaning towards a mix of pragmatic diplomacy, limited counterinsurgency support for friendly nations, and highly surgical military operations. Based on his own experience with CIA operations, President Kennedy had certainly come to appreciate certain risks associated with shadow warfare. Still, with his limited time in office even Kennedy may not have realized the full scope of the risks that had developed in conjunction with the practice of deniable actions. With the history we now have at hand, even a general review quickly demonstrates that those risks include legal exposure of the covert action personnel themselves. Just as special legal codes and statutes protect the American military from the consequences of acts that would be illegal under normal civil code, there are certain protections for CIA personnel. Still, shadow warfare is a risky business for a number of reasons and legal exposure and entanglement can add their own element of risk. Legalizing illegal action has been challenging and more than a little conflicted over the decades.

In the years immediately following the Second World War, there was a universal feeling that the United States was involved in a life-or-death struggle with the Soviet Union and communist ideology in general. Under that premise there was no choice but to do whatever was necessary to prevail. Neither conventional laws nor morals would be allowed to preempt actions. For such reasons, clandestine personnel are ordered and expected to perform a number of activities that are illegal. That fact was acknowledged early on in the Cold War and addressed in both presidential orders and the National Security Act of 1947. We have detailed interventions where CIA officers, military personnel, military support groups, contractors, and even technical staff were placed in combat zones and exposed to hostile action. Beyond physical risk, even their support activities routinely required that they violate a variety of U.S. neutrality laws and customs regulations. Even CIA logistics activities required that personnel associate with and on occasion make use of smugglers, assassins, and other criminals, exposing them to personal legal entanglement.

In the broader picture, having CIA personnel involved in normally illegal activities is not unique to Plans/Operations Directorate employees engaged in covert warfare. For example, individuals in the CIA's Office of Security as well as the Office of Technical Services were assigned to tasks including the use of nonlethal (but highly illegal) chemicals and drugs in interrogation, kidnapping, and assassinations. The CIA Technical Services Group also performed its work in conjunction with various military projects that were largely centered on the biological warfare program housed at the Edgewood Chemical Biological Center (ECBC) at Fort Detrick, Maryland. The CIA's Chemical Division was headed by Dr. Sidney Gottlieb of CIA Technical Services and it utilized the staff of Fort Detrick's Special Operations Division (SOD) both for the production of lethal and nonlethal toxins and work on developing delivery systems.

In 1950 the Agency established an informal agreement with the Special Operations Division to pursue a variety of designated projects including lethal chemicals. Initial funding for the lethal chemicals project (designated Project MKNAOMI) was on the order of $500,000 annually and reached a high of $675,000 by the mid-1960s. In 1977, following the lead of congressional inquiries into American intelligence activities, Carter Administration Defense Secretary Harold Brown requested an internal review of CIA projects that had involved the Department of Defense. One of the activities revealed in the examination was project MKNAOMI; that project had begun in the early 1950s and was "intended to stockpile severely incapacitating and lethal materials and to develop gadgetry for dissemination of these materials."

A CIA memorandum dated June 29, 1975, also documents the SOD–CIA relationship and confirms that no written records were kept; management was by verbal instruction and "human continuity." The memo refers to "swarms of project requests" and cites examples of suicide pills, chemicals to anesthetize occupants, lethal "L-pills," and aphrodisiacs for operational use. The memo notes that "some requests for support approved by the CIA had apparently involved assassination."[574] Statements and memoranda relating to projects such as MKNAOMI often refer to the threat posed by Soviet use of similar toxins. CIA records show instances of Soviet poison attacks in Europe. These include the apparent use of a mystery agent that created symptoms of multiple sclerosis in some seven Soviet defectors at two CIA safe houses in Berlin.[575]

Assassination has indeed been a constant in shadow warfare, even if only from an "accessory" standpoint. We have explored the CIA's regime-change activities in providing intelligence and working with its surrogates in the construction of so-called blacklists in Guatemala, Cuba, and Nicaragua. Those lists included individuals ranging from regime leaders to political cadres. Surrogate fighters were trained in techniques of assassination and even provided with manuals on tactics and techniques. In the Dominican Republic, in Cuba, and in Chile, CIA officers worked with opposition groups targeting specific regime figures for assassination. And in Latin America, the CIA and military assistance teams worked in building large counterinsurgency databases. In both instances literally thousands of individuals were targeted and either captured or killed in what can only be called targeted warfare. The broad-based attacks associated with those operations resulted in tens of thousands of collateral deaths.

The twenty-first century and the War on Terror have brought the practice of American personnel targeting specific individuals (designated as high-value targets) for capture/kill operations. There have been a number of ethical and legal objections to that practice. Yet terrorists who choose to shield themselves by operating from nations that are either hostile to the United States or at best themselves chaotic—with weak central governments, and little in the way of their own security forces—present an exceptional challenge. Going after them in remote regions, with no cooperation and sometimes active regime military opposition, is very risky business from a tactical sense as well as regarding the personnel involved. Capture attempts are much more dangerous and often less successful than direct attacks on the terrorists. The fact that the capture of such targets is virtually impossible in many instances generates both legal and political issues as well as the risks of civilian casualties in targeted attacks.

Detailed legal guidelines for America's clandestine services are not in the public record and remain somewhat nebulous as compared to those in place for the American military. Military personnel and those in related service are given legal responsibility and protection under the Uniform Code of Military Justice (UCMJ). The code was established by Congress and serves as the foundation of American military law. It authorizes the president to set rules and procedures for its implementation, which was done in an executive order that established the Manual for Courts-Martial (MCM), implementing the military justice system. This code and legal process governs the actions of all members of the United States uniformed services, including National Oceanic and Atmospheric Administration commissioned personnel. It also covers Public Health Service commissioned personnel when detailed to a military unit or militarized by executive order. Retired members of the uniformed services who are entitled to retirement pay are also subject to the code. A series of "Punitive Articles" within the code details offenses, and the code also contains provisions for dealing with orders that may be considered illegal.

In concept the articles create some interesting questions in regard to active-duty military personnel detailed to nominally illegal CIA activities. They raise other questions for retired military who either volunteer for clandestine operations or go to work for commercial companies involved in them. We will examine instances in which clandestine service officers have on occasion been granted a degree of legal immunity in certain secret agreements between the CIA and the Justice Department. The question of whether those agreements would protect detailed or retired military personnel seems to remain open.

Failure to obey a lawful order is a serious offense, under some circumstances punishable by death. On the other hand, obedience of an unlawful order can lead to legal prosecution as well. Military courts have ruled that personnel are accountable for their own actions and that includes obedience to illegal orders. Personnel under the code cannot offer "I was only following orders" as a legal defense—even if under presidential order. That is a long-standing American tradition.

Historically the issue of illegal orders has existed from the earliest days of the United States. The first U.S. military incident involving obedience to an illegal order took place in 1799 when President John Adams ordered the American Navy to seize any vessel traveling to or from a French port. The problem was that Congress had passed legislation specifically authorizing the seizure of only vessels bound for French ports. The president's decision to exceed the limits of the legislation resulted in an order—obeyed by a Navy captain—that resulted in the captain's being convicted of an illegal act. The U.S. Supreme Court upheld the action, advising that individuals "act at their own peril" when presidential orders are illegal. Several incidents pertaining to individuals obeying orders occurred during American combat in Vietnam. In one instance, a soldier was convicted of shooting and killing a Vietnamese citizen. In *United States v. Keenan*, the accused was found guilty and the Court of Military Appeals ruled that "the justification for acts done pursuant to orders does not exist if the order was of such a nature that a man of ordinary sense and understanding would know it to be illegal."

Although CIA clandestine service officers are not listed as serving under the UCMJ, it seems possible that American legal tradition and prior court precedent places them in a conflicted position. They are certainly subject to being directed, in the routine performance of their assignments, to perform acts that are nominally illegal (or more accurately illegal under standard United States civil statutes). Yet those actions are authorized under separate legal code relating to covert operations under the National Security Act of 1947. That is the nature of covert and clandestine warfare. Personnel accepting orders in such a situation act in compliance with directions not only from their superiors but in a chain of command leading to the president and commander in chief, who carries the ultimate authority for their orders.

It is unclear exactly what written guidelines and rules of authorization exist inside the CIA to protect clandestine personnel. One current benchmark available to us comes from relatively recent remarks by the general counsel of the CIA, given during a 2012 presentation at Harvard Law School.[576] In that speech, Stephen W. Preston summarized the CIA's three basic areas of work, including covert action. He then pointed out that the Agency operates under the rule of law in that all activities must be "properly authorized pursuant to the full body of national security law." There must be legal authority to act—delineated under the National Security Act of 1947 and the Central Intelligence Agency Act of 1949—and the Agency must operate within the constraints of executive orders and under a variety of oversight. In describing that oversight Preston specifically mentioned the Department of Justice, to which the CIA "is required to report all possible violations of federal criminal laws by employees, agents, liaison, or anyone else." We will come back to that point to note certain exceptions for that stated requirement, including secret agreements and "understandings" between the Department of Justice and the Agency. In outlining certain examples of activities, Preston noted that they must be authorized by the president in accordance with the covert action procedures of the National Security Act of 1947. Congress must be properly notified of the action by a presidential finding and actions should comply by the terms dictated in the applicable finding.

Preston's remarks on the legal criteria for covert action all sound reasonable and quite concrete until referenced against actual historical examples such as the finding for the Angolan intervention, which was so general that it mentioned only the continent of Africa. The findings on Nicaragua were even more interesting. One of those was characterized by the administration involved as "retroactive" (after the fact) and one as simply as "mental" (unwritten and uncommunicated).[577] More recently, we find indications that certain—even relatively current—CIA activities also may not pass the test of congressional notification. In 2009, the House Intelligence Committee announced the termination of an unnamed CIA covert operation that it said was not only "very serious" but also had been kept from Congress for some eight years.[578] *The Wall Street Journal* reported that the program in question related to a directive from the president, in 2001, to find and kill Al-Qaeda operatives.[579] According to the chairman of the House Intelligence Committee, the operation had been intentionally buried—it had no oversight—and a series of CIA directors had consciously decided to go along with the operation, taking it upon themselves not to report their activities to Congress just as President George W. Bush appears not to have advised the appropriate congressional committees.[580]

Such failures to inform Congress would seem to constitute a violation of the "full body of national security law," and would have placed the president and the CIA directors at legal risk. Such a violation could conceivably have also exposed any CIA or servicemembers involved in the operations under the presidential directive. The report triggered a series of inquiries including an investigation by CIA Director Leon Panetta. Reportedly Panetta advised that Vice President Dick Cheney had ordered that Congress would not be briefed on the project.[581] Details of the operation, including information from the man assigned to manage the project, began to become available only in 2012. Certainly the overall conceptual framework described in Preston's Harvard Law speech appears impressive, but actual compliance remains its acid test. Beyond that, at a personnel level, it seems that any individuals receiving orders have little choice other than to assume that the president has authorized the project—in other words, that the tasks assigned have been itemized and approved by Congress, and that the order is itself legal. In reality it appears that to a large extent CIA personnel are essentially protected by presidential caveat. But even that assumption has issues. In his 2012 book *The Art of Intelligence: Lessons from a Life in the CIA's Clandestine Service*, career CIA officer Henry A. Crumpton expressed sincere dissatisfaction with the fact that CIA officers ordered to conduct detention and "enhanced interrogation" under directives from President George W. Bush were later exposed to investigation for possible legal violations by the attorney general under Bush's successor, President Barack Obama.[582]

Crumpton's concern illustrates another area of CIA employee risk. As we have pointed out, American legal tradition has consistently held that individuals act at their own risk in following an illegal order, even one issued by the president. In the incident Crumpton notes, the legality of the presidential directive appears to have been based strictly on advice from Bush Administration legal counsel, advice that was essentially an opinion and that continues to be challenged by legal scholars. As it happened, the Obama Administration chose not to pursue legal inquiries into the Bush Administration activities, so the CIA personnel involved were not charged or indicted. However, the risk remains that even presidential orders may be found to be unlawful, with secondary consequences for those following them. One solution to the quandary would be more congressional action in actually passing declarations of war or resolutions authorizing the commander in chief to conduct lethal action. We will return to that point.

We noted that one of the assurances given in the CIA counsel's Harvard Law speech was oversight by the Department of Justice, under which the CIA "is required to report all possible violations of federal laws by employees, agents, liaison, or anyone else." The problem with that assurance is that we now know of multiple instances in which "understandings" between the CIA and Justice negated such oversight. We also know that such agreements were routinely kept secret, so in essence we have no idea whether or not there might be similar understandings still in effect. The first example of such an agreement is a very early one, dating back to 1954. It developed from the understanding that clandestine personnel would be involved in normally illegal acts in the line of duty, but that they might also commit personally illegal acts while engaged in national security activities. Reporting such illegal acts to the Department of Justice and having them handled as a standard criminal investigation posed a very real threat of exposing information pertaining to CIA methods, assets, and actual operations.

The clandestine agencies involved, in particular the CIA, recognized the reality of that exposure and acted accordingly—if secretly. As early as 1954 the CIA sought and achieved a general "understanding" with the Department of Justice. That agreement, which remained confidential for decades, was made in talks between CIA

General Counsel Lawrence Houston and Deputy Attorney General William Rogers. Houston stated that there simply was no way in which such cases could be prosecuted without revealing highly classified information. Given the security implications, the deputy attorney general responded that it would serve no purpose to refer the case to Justice since no legal measures could proceed without full disclosure of all information pertinent to the crime. Therefore it would be left to the CIA to investigate and evaluate the possibilities of prosecution, informing Justice only if prosecution was possible without revealing secure information. The deputy attorney general also took the position that such practices could continue without any formal documentation. On February 23, 1954, Lawrence Houston prepared a memorandum for CIA Director Allen Dulles, documenting the agreement with the Justice Department. The memorandum makes it clear that in instances of "apparent criminal activities involved within highly classified and complex covert operations," outside agencies would be "unable to prosecute the case without revealing highly classified matters to public scrutiny." He concluded that in the case of covert operations, "there appears to be a balancing of interest in enforcing the law which is in the proper jurisdiction of the Department of Justice and the Director's [CIA] responsibility for protecting intelligence sources and methods."

This memorandum and the agreement between Justice and the CIA established a high-level precedent that allowed senior CIA officers to place national security ahead of criminal violations of Agency personnel. Former CIA Counsel Houston provided an extended discussion of this agreement, including testimony before a congressional subcommittee in 1975. Apparently the understanding was following some two decades with no notification of at least two subsequent attorney generals who served during following years.[583] In testimony Houston was forced to admit that the agreement could and did, "in certain cases," have the effect of allowing CIA officers the authority to give immunity to individuals for crimes up to and including murder. This was done in the face of federal statutes that ordered the reporting of criminal violations. In addition, the

CIA practice was carried out through subsequent administrations in which attorney generals were not notified of the memorandum of understanding. Houston's position was simply that the CIA director's statutory duty to protect intelligence sources and methods was considered to override normal standards or legal obligations. As one of the congressmen on the committee noted for the record, this interpretation allowed the Agency to "put the rule of law under suspension."[584]

A second example of an "understanding" between Justice and the CIA is much more recent, revealed only in 1998 during testimony by the CIA inspector general, but dating back to activities over the period of 1982 to 1995.[585] Inspector General Frederick Hitz stated that during the 1980s—when there was widely reported suspicion that both individuals and companies involved in support for the Contras were also associated with drug smuggling—there was actually a secret agreement in place between the Justice Department and the CIA. That agreement allowed the CIA to ignore any drug associations as long as those involved were indeed supporting the secret war against the Sandinista regime. The agreement, a memorandum of understanding (MOU), did not extend to CIA staff but rather covered "agents, assets, and non-staff employees." The memorandum also covered pilots, accountants, and military trainers. In its simplest terms, "There was no official requirement to report on allegations of drug trafficking with respect to non-employees of the agency."

Hitz did note that the memorandum of understanding was modified in 1986, directing that individuals "suspected" of drug dealing were not actually to be paid by the CIA but that they could continue to be used as assets as long as they were not paid. It is virtually impossible to relate such a qualification without also remarking on the tremendous naivety involved in a qualification that deals with not paying drug smugglers! The agreement remained in place throughout the entire Nicaraguan effort, rescinded by Attorney General Janet Reno only in 1995.

Although the actual documentation detailing the agreement is still withheld, reportedly the agreement originated in a direct request from CIA Director William Casey to Attorney General William French Smith. Smith's letter of response is on record and notes that "no formal requirement regarding the reporting of narcotics violations has been included in these procedures."[586] It appears this understanding with the Justice Department simply left the CIA free to verbally report any incidents or leads that might be deemed not to compromise its operations or security.[587] As in the preceding example, reporting would be discretionary and left up to the Agency, even though statutes in place during that period specified mandatory reporting of drug violations. While convenient for operational purposes, such as not turning in individuals or companies being relied on for covert activities, such memorandums of understanding add considerable confusion and risk for clandestine staff on several levels. First, it is unclear exactly who within the CIA would be briefed on the agreement and who would make the decisions. Such tacit understandings could create the impression among CIA personnel in the field that the use of drug-related assets was simply standard, approved practice. This could (and appears to have) meant that there would be little concern about such activities and also little reason to report them.[588] Certainly there would be confusion. If the use of drug-associated assets was accepted in the Contra effort, does that mean it was also approved throughout Latin America or, equally important, in Afghanistan? Certainly several of the CIA personnel involved in the Contra effort worked other operations as well during the period in question.

On another level of concern, the drug-related memorandum of understanding was put in place during a period of dramatically escalating drug use in the United States, sometimes referred to as the crack cocaine epidemic of the early 1980s. Drug use received considerable media attention, and accusations rose that the CIA was aiding and abetting it by working with drug smugglers. Obviously the revelation of the agreement does suggest that CIA officers were indeed using individuals connected to drug smuggling, otherwise there would have been no need for it. Of course that does not imply involvement of the CIA officers themselves, only that they were legally free to employ assets that were involved in drug activities. And if CIA personnel did become aware of the drug connections, their legal mandate to report them had been waived, essentially offering a degree of protection to the drug traffickers. While the revelation of the CIA–Justice mutual understanding agreement in 1998 received only modest media attention, it very likely would have created a political explosion if publicly known in the 1980s.

There is now absolutely no doubt that a number of individuals and companies used in the Contra support effort were involved with drugs. Those connections extended throughout the effort, not only in the first phase under CIA operational control but later when the initial CIA management had been secretly handed off to the second phase NSC–North effort. Later documents suggest that North should have been aware of the probable drug connections of certain assets being used by the Enterprise. A number of those individuals and companies would be investigated by both the DEA and a congressional committee in regard to drug activities. And as it turns out, the risks of "entanglement" are another area that became particularly noticeable beginning in the 1980s.

As detailed in previous chapters on the secret Nicaraguan war, many individuals who would play roles in the Enterprise were retired CIA officers, former CIA assets, or military personnel who had frequently been detailed to CIA covert warfare operations. Several of them had become associated with, and even investigated for dealings with, yet another former CIA employee, Ed Wilson. Apparently Wilson became convinced that he could make a lot more money than he was drawing from the CIA; and after committing a number of minor transgressions, including using a proprietary company as collateral in his personal business, he was released from employment. Of course that release was not circulated in any memorandum and Wilson continued his contacts with a host of individuals, who knew him strictly in the context of his former CIA employment. Wilson had been considered a master at his craft, creating and running an "operational" proprietary, a company that conducted legitimate business, had everyday employees, and even made money—all while being accessible and available for covert activities as necessary. Wilson specialized in transportation and logistics and his proprietary, Maritime Consulting Associates, required only a minor monthly subsidiary from the Agency, operating close to breaking even on its own business.[589] In his position as a contract employee Wilson operated as a private businessman, free to cover his own expense account and circulate among business and political circles while also becoming socially close to several senior CIA officers including Ted Shackley and Thomas Clines.

Wilson's contacts and his expertise would prove highly valuable in his business deals during the following years. They would be enhanced by the fact that he actually secured another intelligence job after the termination of his CIA employment. Wilson convinced a Navy captain that the right sort of business proprietary would be invaluable in collecting information on port activities and shipping around the world. The captain commanded an Office of Naval Intelligence group designated TF-157, which had been given a very similar mission in 1968. The group had only some one hundred personnel, a limited budget, and a notable gap in its coverage of activities in the Middle East. That area had become a hot spot and additional contract help seemed very attractive.[590] To that end, Wilson was hired, and he assembled a largely notional (nonexistent) company named Consultants International. Although various business deals cut by Wilson would be very real, the amount of intelligence actually provided to the Navy would be somewhat questionable. The full story of Consultants International and all the individuals who crossed Wilson's path and became entangled with his increasingly shadowy activities is told in Joseph Goulden's *The Death Merchant*. In 1976, Wilson actually ended up at a business luncheon with a very powerful senator who just happened to sit on an appropriations committee for the Navy. The senator invited to lunch a friend of his, Rear Admiral Bobby Inman, the head of Naval Intelligence. During the lunch, in which several business topics were discussed, Wilson chose to tell Inman that he actually worked for one of his intelligence units. Inman was taken aback and in the end Wilson's remarks would result in his very shortly being terminated from employment in TF-157; the comments would also bring some unwelcome attention to that group from the admiral.[591]

While that might appear to have been a bad result for Wilson, as it happened his separation was of course confidential and he was allowed to continue running Consultants International. He would effectively broker the aura of both his CIA and military intelligence connections throughout the rest of his endeavors. One point that stands out throughout Wilson's activities is the extent to which people with whom he connected—and even people who worked for him—assumed that he was somehow involved in government-sanctioned intelligence work, even long after his termination by both the CIA and the Navy. Wilson would continue to meet with his friends and associates, involving them in various business deals when possible and implying their involvement in other instances. His saga demonstrates that a network of retired and separated covert operators had come into existence by the end of the 1970s; within a few years it was becoming very difficult to tell when their activities and their businesses were in some fashion official, sanctioned, or otherwise covered by national security statute protection. That sort of confusion would continue for decades to follow, around the globe from Laos and Australia to Central America, from Southwest Asia to the new Central Asian republics that emerged after the fall of the Soviet Union. Familiar names appeared in unfamiliar places and with them a level of uncertainty in regard to whether the CIA or some other American intelligence group was somewhere in the shadows.

In 1980 the Australian bank Nugan Hand Ltd., with branches around the world, dissolved upon the death of one of its founders, Frank Nugan. The bank had been founded by Nugan and his partner Michael Hand in 1973. Nugan was an Australian lawyer. Hand had reportedly worked with Hmong tribal forces in Laos, either as an employee or a contractor (with neither position confirmed by the CIA). Inquiries revealed that the bank had been active in the movement of monies around the world, in activities including shielded funding for arms deals, mercenary contracts, and very likely the laundering of drug money coming out of Southeast Asia. In conjunction with those activities, individuals associated with the bank may also have provided intelligence information to a variety of agencies including both the CIA and DEA, receiving certain "protection" in the process. As it happened, Nugan Hand had opened a branch in Chiang Mai, Thailand, in 1983. Chiang Mai is located in northwestern Thailand, along major age-old trading routes out of Burma and Laos. Chiang Mai is also known as a conduit for the equally age-old drug traffic out of the Golden Triangle. Given its remote location and the extent of the local narcotics trade, financial transactions in and around Chiang Mai can truly be thought of as having a high potential for "risky business." It would seem to have been an unusual branch location for a financial institution representing itself as a "global merchant bank." [592]

On the other hand, it appears that Nugan Hand's office in Chiang Mai was rather well connected to the United States. There was a DEA presence in that same remote city, with its office on the same floor, in the same suite, and with the same receptionist answering calls for both the DEA and Nugan Hand. The individual recruited to run the Nugan Hand office there has gone on record as that he was specifically hired by Michael Hand to solicit drug money deposits. In doing so he was able to use influential contacts that Hand himself had made in covert supply operations during the Vietnam War. Hand's involvement in such supply activities has been verified.[593] The employee has also described carrying funds around the globe for CIA purposes, or at least being told they were for CIA purposes. Things had seemingly reached the point where the mere mention of the CIA would be accepted as an explanation for all sorts of shadowy activities.

Even following extensive investigations, exceptional mystery remains around the formation and operation of the Nugan Hand bank, including speculation that it was used by American agencies for covert activities and collection of intelligence regarding drug dealing. That speculation is fueled by the fact that a business card from William Colby (retired and with a personal legal practice), former Saigon station chief and later CIA director, was found in Hand's wallet at the time of his death. The notes on the card were for dates and locations in Singapore and Hong Kong—locations where Colby had traveled on the dates indicated.[594] There are other reports that Colby had actually served Nugan Hand in a legal capacity. Familiar names reportedly doing business with Nugan Hand included Thomas Clines, business partner of Ed Wilson and Enterprise weapons buyer. A good number of Nugan Hand associates were retired or separated from U.S. government service.

It seems that by the 1980s and 1990s the tightly managed and controlled covert warfare infrastructure of the 1960s had evolved into something very different. It had developed into a social and business network, linking individuals with their own agendas—both financial and political. It very probably was used, on occasion, by American agencies, certainly for intelligence, possibly for covert activities. That story has yet to fully emerge. But to a large extent, covert warfare was becoming increasingly privatized. And the actions of the individuals in that associated network were raising serious questions about who was doing what for whom.

Those questions would arise for both apparently legal activities and obviously illegal ones. Ramon Milian Rodriguez, indicted and convicted for activities including money laundering for a Colombian drug cartel, related the story of being solicited for $1 million in contributions for the Contra effort. The person he named as making the request was Cuban exile Felix Rodriguez. Milian Rodriguez was very much in touch with the Contra events of the time, and made it clear that he viewed the request for funds as being from the CIA itself. He stated that he might not have trusted the request or might have been skeptical if it were made by someone like Oliver North (who had no reputation as a CIA covert/clandestine officer), but Felix Rodriguez was very well-known for his CIA connections and service. Milian Rodriguez implied that he was given to understand the request for funds was being endorsed by none other than former CIA director and then–Vice President George H.W. Bush, a person known to be in contact with Felix Rodriguez. We have seen that Felix Rodriguez was indeed in contact with the vice president's office, specifically regarding Contra activities and problems with North's Enterprise operations. Felix Rodriguez himself denies the entire story of soliciting money from Milian Rodriguez. Regardless, one particular comment from Milian Rodriguez does seem to sum up a great many of the risks related to entanglement: "You know, everyone says he's ex-CIA."[595]

Assumptions about who is really working for the CIA at a given point, regardless of what they may say or imply, are truly risky on a number of levels. So are assumptions about whether particular projects, operations, or activities are sanctioned within the CIA or by the White House, or whether they are really someone's private business or agenda. Tangled webs have entrapped more than one clandestine operative and more than one staff officer.

CHAPTER 21

It Happens

In the spring of 2012, both CNN and *The Wall Street Journal* reported on allegations of drug and weapons smuggling within the Afghan air force. Officers in the Afghan air force were accused of smuggling and dealing in both drugs and weapons.[596, 597] By now the basic story is a familiar one, involving military officers using government aircraft to move both drugs and weapons, with the weapons sales to private groups. The Afghan air force had been trained, equipped, and funded at great expense by America. As is not unusual in such cases, little further information became available other than that the investigation had been initiated by both the American military and the Drug Enforcement Agency. Once again American-equipped and -funded surrogates were involved in drug and weapons trafficking and once again the United States was in the headlines, with its aircraft suspected of having been used for criminal activities.

In the previous chapter we reviewed certain of the legal and career risks involved in carrying out covert assignments, missions that go beyond civil or military legal codes. But shadow warfare has often involved a very specific type of legal risk: that of entangling covert operations with drug smuggling. Over and over again CIA connections to drug traffickers have hit the media, and on more than one occasion the subject has been internally investigated by the CIA and even by Congress. At this point in time, with the information now public, it would be woefully naive or verging on denial to assert that drug smuggling does not occur when surrogate warfare goes on in areas that are major regions of drug production, use, and trade. Early on we noted that the drug trade was going on in the Burmese–Thai area before the CIA became involved with Republic of China units there. The trails that were used to ship weapons into those forces were the same trails that were already in use in drug smuggling. The Thai police units that assisted in enabling the weapons movements were the same units that routinely either carried out or guarded drug shipments. The Taiwanese allied forces involved were the same units that maintained themselves off the drug trade both before and after becoming involved with the short-lived Operation Paper incursions into Yunnan province.

Those units continued the drug traffic for decades, moving from point to point as military or security pressures forced them from one location to another. After Burma we encountered them again in the Laotian border region, still making a living off the drug trade. The Republic of China units in the Golden Triangle region have been most accurately described as an army that "never fought" but instead "began a drug producing operation."[598] We also pointed out that one of the early CIA commercial assets, SEA Supply, which was used to supply the forces of Operation Paper, reportedly became so entangled in drug smuggling that it eventually was forced to end its activities in Thailand. By that point, other transportation options were becoming available, with supply activities by semiprivate Taiwanese air transport companies. Small commercial aircraft, flown into jungle airfields in remote border areas, provided further opportunity for illegal drug shipments and related graft. As we noted, when the supplies go in—whether by animal or jeep in the Golden Triangle or Toyota pickup in Afghanistan—it is very unlikely that nothing comes back on the return trip. It may not be in crates; it may be in personal baggage—but someone will bring drugs and money out.

Even with increased air access, the main drug routes out of the Golden Triangle and across Thailand remained on the ground, with security provided by Republic of China–affiliated paramilitary groups. In 1967, one of the major smugglers determined that he would move a shipment out through Thailand without paying the required protection fee. He sent a large mule caravan, escorted by some eight hundred fighters and armed "muleteers." Over a mile in length, its cargo was opium. ROC troops were sent to intercept the caravan inside Burma but ended up trailing it down the Mekong River. Both groups ended up inside the Lao border area, were confronted by Lao troops, and were ordered to surrender. Ultimately Lao T-28s were ordered to strafe and bomb both groups. Taking heavy casualties, the military group managed to make off with the opium cache and head back towards Burma, only to be surrounded by Lao troops demanding the drugs. After extended negotiations the Lao force was paid off, and the troops once again were off with the opium, this time towards Thailand.[599] Drug smuggling happens; the money is simply too good. As the covert warfare supply operations proceed, the drug shipments escalate along with improved transportation and logistics. That generally is not the primary concern of field officers in charge of a covert warfare mission. Their surrogates tend to have their own priorities, especially since they have extremely limited sources of income, and things seldom get better for them as combat escalates. When the covert warfare ceases and the outsiders leave, the smuggling continues.

We spent a great deal of time in discussion of the Hmong in Laos, and their struggles to defend their homeland against both the communist Pathet Lao and eventually the North Vietnamese Army units deployed to secure Ho Chi Minh Trail supply routes into South Vietnam. When the United States determined to support the Hmong as a surrogate army against the communists in Laos, it was engaging with a people whose primary cash crop was opium. That was a well-known fact. It had been that way for generations. Dealing with the Hmong meant dealing with a drug economy. Without doubt the U.S. and its aid mission worked to establish alternative crops and alternative trades, which is a matter of record. But as the fighting continued and as the Hmong irregulars were forced back and forth over their lands, ultimately far back, that opportunity faded away. Reality asserted itself and they were forced back to what had always been their trade staple: opium.

Initially, most supply of the Hmong was done via airdrops, but as matters progressed airstrips became more common, as did helicopter supply. Much of that supply was flown on CIA-contracted air carriers such as Air America. Obviously any effort to stop smuggling was left up to the pilots of such aircraft. Personal carry-on baggage was certainly never searched in the early years. In fact Air America had no Security Inspection Service until 1972, and then only at its major air terminals.[600] Beyond that, the Royal Lao Air Force conducted ongoing supply flights, and it is well documented that its senior officers were personally involved in drug smuggling.

A decade later, in 1988, PBS *Frontline* interviewed several individuals with firsthand experience in Laos.[601] Their stories were simple and straightforward. Former Air America pilot Neil Hansen described seeing "sticky bricks" (opium) brought on board his aircraft, and no challenge was made because it was regarded as personal property. He noted that that was mainly done on smaller aircraft flying in and out of the remote fields, and the bricks were carried by tribesmen. Ed Dearborn, another former Air America pilot, described flights from remote sites into Vang Pao's base, and photographer John Everingham observed one of Vang Pao's officers supervising the preparation of sticky black bamboo tubes filled with raw opium. Everingham casually asked what was going to be done with the opium tubes. The matter-of-fact answer was that the opium would be flown back to Long Tieng by contract helicopters, along with everything else that went to and from Vang Pao's headquarters. It was done as a service to the locals by Vang Pao's officers, who made money off the trade. Air transport also offered an outlet for the product as ground transportation became more and more difficult due to constant combat. Legendary CIA officer Tony Poe was also interviewed during the program, describing how Vang Pao had actually obtained control over a couple of planes for his own use, transported drugs on flights refueled at Pakse in the Laotian panhandle, and then flown on to Da Nang, South Vietnam, where the

Vietnamese would put the drugs into the lucrative American military market in that country.

As time passed, that sort of activity became fairly common knowledge and it resulted in a yet another form of distancing. In 1972, under continual media pressure, the CIA station in the Laotian capital conducted an investigation of the drug situation. Its report, "Investigation of the Drug Situation in SE Asia," contained extensive evidence of an active drug trade with Laotian generals participating, along with photographs of drug laboratories and even shipping schedules of military aircraft going to South Vietnam. Yet the report minimized the production of drugs by the Hmong and concentrated on the fact that no evidence was found that the trade was either encouraged or authorized as a matter of actual policy among senior CIA officers.[602]

Perhaps the most fundamental issue expressed in the report was that that "agents and local officials with whom we are in contact have been or may be still involved in one way or another with the drug business." In particular, the report noted that the CIA did not interfere with "tribals" who raised opium, due to fear that such interference might lead them to be "uncooperative." And in summary it stated, "The war has clearly been our overriding priority in Southeast Asia and other issues have taken second place in the scheme of things. It would be foolish to deny this and we see no reason to do so."[603]

The mission comes first. That has been a prevailing attitude from the very beginning of the Cold War and has continued for decades regardless of the type of warfare, covert or overt. That is even acknowledged by drug enforcement figures: "They [the CIA] have a tough job to do. They are not necessarily dealing with the angels of the world, and we really can't object when they end up rubbing elbows with some of the dregs of the world."[604] Many CIA officers were simply not inclined to compromise their mission and the security of their operations by exposing their assets, regardless of any illegal dealings. Examples of that attitude come out of Southeast Asia in the DEA investigation of a top Golden Triangle heroin trader, Lu Hsu-shui. One of the individuals involved in trafficking with Lu

Hsu-shui was known to the DEA and could have been used in prosecuting the case. However the CIA refused to involve the man because it considered him one of its key informants, stating that he had been used "in a high-level, sensitive national security operation."[605]

An instance in 1973 led to the arrest of a Republic of China drug network–affiliated smuggler in the United States. Reportedly the individual, Thai national Puttaporn Khramkhruan, had served as an intelligence source on many subjects, including drug smuggling. He maintained that his CIA contacts were perfectly aware of his drug activities and had raised no issues in that regard. The CIA, however, refused to cooperate with the Justice Department in prosecution of the case and advised in writing that it could not provide information on him as "it would prove embarrassing because of Mr. Khramkhruan's activities in Thailand, Burma, and elsewhere." The Agency did admit to Senator Charles Percy, who had protested the situation, that he had been a CIA source on the narcotics trade who was paid $144.58 a month while participating in a large-scale opium-smuggling operation.

Still, the Agency refused to provide documents or information, and in the end the case was dismissed and the overall Department of Justice effort targeting the drug ring aborted.[606] The incident in question occurred under Ted Shackley's oversight. Eventually the CIA itself would be legally tasked (officially) with providing intelligence about drugs to the DEA and the Department of Justice. That regulation was in place as Shackley appeared in a new Latin America assignment. His new Latin American command would become widely noted for a decided lack of enthusiasm for any CIA drug intelligence role. Indeed the drug enforcement people routinely complained that Shackley requested their informant lists and then converted the individuals into strictly CIA sources, without any notification. Lists provided by the CIA were said to be "brief."[607]

The drug entanglements of the Nicaraguan secret war were of a different nature than those in Southeast Asia, primarily because the American surrogate fighters, the Contras, were not themselves producing the drugs as were the Hmong in Laos. The drugs in question were coming largely out of the Colombian drug cartel, which became familiar to America in the 1980s and 1990s. To increase its business and pump huge amounts of drugs into the U.S. market, the cartel needed more and more transportation resources and especially a cover for those shipments, a way to get them past U.S. customs.

The situation was well summarized by John Mattes, a Miami public defender who had represented several Cuban Americans and "soldiers of fortune" who had been called before the Kerry Committee in its investigations of Contra-era drug smuggling. (The Senate Foreign Relations Subcommittee on Narcotics, Terrorism, and International Operations was more commonly referred to as the Kerry Committee, in reference to its chairman, John Kerry.) Mattes's point was that the traffickers were looking for protection. They had cash, planes, and pilots, and what they needed was access to airstrips and the ability to transship their product onto planes or boats being used in the Contra supply effort. The scenario was simply to use return trips to get drugs into the U.S. In return, it was easy enough to share the profits with Contra leaders who were either desperate for funding for their own efforts—especially as U.S. lethal funding was officially cut off—or simply interested in making money for themselves while in exile.

Just how the Contra effort became entangled in cartel drug traffic was initially very shadowy and mysterious. To a large extent it remained so even during some two and a half years of the Kerry congressional committee investigations, which grew out of the Iran–Contra scandal. In retrospect it appears that a number of CIA officers may have kept information from that inquiry, but to what extent they were simply operating under the protection provided by the Casey–Justice Department "understanding" remains unclear. It certainly illustrates the confusion such secret agreements generate and further explains why Congressional oversight becomes so difficult. The Kerry Committee report was issued in 1989 and in some four hundred pages (plus a six-hundred-page appendix) it presented more than enough information to support its overall conclusion: "It is clear that individuals who provided support for the Contras were involved in drug trafficking . . . and elements of the Contras themselves knowingly received financial and material assistance from drug traffickers."[608]

The committee also concluded that congressionally authorized money for humanitarian aid had been paid by the State Department to individuals and companies with prior drug indictments, in an amount estimated to be at least $800,000.[609] Some of the companies were even being paid at the same time they were targets of active and ongoing criminal investigation by federal law enforcement agencies. Fortunately, by combining the Kerry Committee work, documents now available from DEA investigations, and CIA information released following the testimony of CIA General Counsel Hitz in 1998, it's becoming possible to sketch a high-level picture of the elements and progression of the Contra–drug entanglement. That picture clearly illustrates the risks involved in privatizing deniable warfare and presents yet another dramatic illustration of the changes in covert practice that developed under the Reagan Administration.

In the earliest days following the Sandinista seizure of power in Nicaragua, their opponents were desperate for money: money for equipment and arms, money to sustain themselves, and, in the case of certain of the emerging leaders, money to remain outside Nicaragua and organize a rebellion against the Sandinistas. In the days before the U.S. committed itself to supporting them, the loose affiliation of regime opponents that became known as the Contras found their options limited. It now appears that from the earliest days of the Contra movement, in 1981, drug trafficking was one of their options. The information provided by CIA General Counsel Hitz lists some fifty Contra individuals who had been associated with CIA activities and whose businesses eventually became linked to drug traffic.

Once the U.S. and the CIA became involved with Sandinista opponents, the Agency immediately began receiving warnings and reports that a number of Contra figures had been and were involved in financing their efforts through drug traffic.[610] The Agency also received reports that one of the earliest Contra groups (ADREN) was using drugs for financing, and that one of its leaders, Enrique Bermudez, was involved in drug shipments to Miami in July 1981. Bermudez would later be appointed to command the leading American-supported northern Contra force, the FDN.[611] In turn the CIA would repeatedly be forced to deal with reports of Bermudez's drug connections. Knowledge that he and other of the Agency's Contra associates were routinely being reported for drug trafficking certainly could have undermined the use of these assets. We can only speculate that that was the concern behind CIA Director Casey's request for a memorandum of understanding with the Justice Department freeing the CIA from legally reporting drug involvement suspicions about its assets.

The Hitz releases document similar concerns being raised about the senior Contra leader on the southern front in Costa Rica, Eden Pastora. Suspicions of Pastora had been long-standing but the new information relates that an admitted drug trafficker, associated with money laundering for the Colombian cartels, had been placed in a liaison position to Pastora.[612] Officially the individual's connections were not confirmed until a follow-up CIA security review in 1987, when the Agency became reinvolved in Contra support. At that time the individual stated that beginning in 1982 he had helped family members who were engaged in drug traffic, aware that what he was doing was illegal. His brothers operated in Miami, running a money-laundering center for drug cash and also importing cocaine from Bolivia.

Details are uncertain, but apparently because of his connections and experience, the individual was used as a conduit for money sent from Contra contacts in Miami to the southern Contra front in Costa Rica. What is even more uncertain is to what extent it might have been legitimate support money or mixed with money skimmed from the drug trade to sustain Contra protection of drug shipments through remote airfields in Costa Rica and out through its ports, on fishing and shrimp boats working out of Miami.

Volumes I and II of the 1998 CIA report detail extensive reports of Contra drug activity as well as CIA responses to those reports.

In reviewing them it would be fair to say that the CIA had more than sufficient reason for concern that a number of its Contra associates were involved in drugs but also that no CIA personnel were themselves directly involved. It was acknowledged that it would be virtually impossible to work in contact with the Contra leadership network without some risk of drug contamination in the effort. Such a situation reveals the CIA's problem and need for an early request for an understanding with the Justice Department. That agreement allowed the CIA to proceed with its directive for covert action about the Sandinista regime—but it certainly would have reduced potential information available to the Drug Enforcement Agency in its own efforts against the cocaine epidemic of the same period.

DEA documents indicate that there had been rumors in regard to drugs in the early years of the Contra program but that the issue came to a head only in 1986, apparently because of various legal actions, press coverage, and the 1986 investigation by the Kerry Committee.[613] In April of that year, in something of a preemptive strike against the potential findings of any congressional investigation, the State Department had issued a report in conjunction with the Justice Department and CIA on "Allegations of Misconduct by the Nicaraguan Democratic Resistance."

The report confirmed that "drug traffickers were attempting to exploit the desperate conditions" faced by the Contras. It concluded by blaming any Contra drug-related problems on individuals, without any formal leadership approval or policy. "[T]he available evidence points to involvement with drug traffickers by a limited number of persons having various kinds of affiliations with, or political sympathies for, the resistance groups." It maintained there was simply not sufficient information to confirm allegations and stated that if the Contra groups had received drug revenues, "it probably would reflect a personal decision by the trafficker or an individual Contra member, not a systematic organizational effort." Besides that, any of those individuals were not believed to be true Contra political members but rather "contrabandistas" already involved in such things and taking advantage of the situation.

As with virtually all such reports, the wording was quite precise, obscuring the fundamental risk of escalating drug traffic associated with the cartel's taking advantage of the Contra opportunity. In reality the drug traffic appears to have become endemic to the entire Contra support effort and this time the consequences were going to be hitting home, in the United States. A handful of reporters were beginning to produce stories about the increasing inflow of cocaine, especially to the West Coast.[614] The thrust of their work was that a connection had developed between major drug suppliers and elements of the Contra leadership, especially among the FDN. In a 1986 San Francisco trial involving $100 million in drugs, two of the defendants stated that the drugs had come to them from Costa Rica and that proceeds from the sales were to go back to the Contras. One defendant stated that he had personally carried $500,000 to two Contra groups in Costa Rica and that the majority of the money had come from cocaine sales.[615] In addition, a well-documented Contra supporter was also suspected of doing over $1 million a month in drug traffic. He had hosted Contra/FDN fund-raisers in California and was reported by informants to have met with Contra leaders in Honduras. The dealer was Norwin Meneses and his drug involvement would eventually be confirmed in DEA documents. Meneses employed several FDN members, one of whom had been convicted of cocaine possession in 1985.

One of the scenarios proposed in the media reporting on the Contra–California drug connections was that the CIA itself might somehow be assisting (or at least covering up) Contra drug activities in an effort to replace the congressional lethal aid money that had been discontinued. Of course at that point in time any knowledge of major foreign funding for the Contras and of the transfer of lethal support from the CIA to the Enterprise was extremely secret. The CIA, the Reagan Administration, and virtually anyone and everyone involved with the Contras denied any involvement in such a thing, as did the DEA. However, information released in the following years reveals that while DEA inquiries failed to expose any firm connections, the DEA was actually forced to acknowledge that Renato

Pena, arrested and convicted on other drug charges, had served as a volunteer worker and fund-raiser for the Contra FDN. In addition the DEA knew that drug traffickers had made a number of calls to the FDN office in San Francisco, and it had informants who were offering information about Contra supporters in Los Angeles being involved in drug trafficking. The DEA also reported that it had informant information that Costa Rican drug traffickers were continuing to do business with individuals in the Contra movement's Democratic Revolutionary Alliance (ARDE). A pilot known to be close to ARDE leader Pastora was being prosecuted in Miami on drug charges and another individual closely associated with ARDE was a suspect in the seizure of some 414 kilograms of cocaine, which been concealed in a frozen-food shipment coming out of Costa Rica.

The DEA also acknowledged having ongoing information that certain drug traffickers in Costa Rica were working with individuals in the Contra movement. A number of examples of such entanglement are on record. In one instance a pilot was arrested with a full kilogram of cocaine; he was later reported to be a member of ARDE. The pilot was arrested by Costa Rican authorities. In another instance Jorge Morales was prosecuted in Miami on drug charges. Morales was alleged to be good friends and former business partners with Pastora. In retrospect, it seems rather clear that the DEA was receiving solid leads that Contra-associated individuals had established links into U.S. drug traffic and were using those links to bring in drugs and obtain funding. If the DEA had also been receiving the stream of ongoing reports that the CIA was getting, perhaps it might have been able to connect the dots and move against the new traffic effectively but the Casey–Justice Department understanding effectively precluded that possibility.

Networking between drug types and Contra supporters in L.A. and San Francisco; cooperation in "fund-raising" in return for a few favors in Costa Rica or Honduras or Miami or New Orleans—neither reflects the full story. The Contra drug entanglement had grown significantly by 1986 and a great deal of that had to do with the second phase of the Contra effort, orchestrated by the Enterprise. Oliver

North himself protested that while he ultimately managed to set up a system that did get money and weapons into the secret war, he did so without all the normal resources that the CIA routinely had available. His concern was well placed.

One fundamental Enterprise-era exposure lies in the fact that money was being deposited directly to individual Contra leaders, into private bank accounts. From those accounts it was circulated through a host of small cutout business in Florida, Panama, and Costa Rica. That process began in 1985 with President Reagan signing an executive order creating the Nicaraguan Humanitarian Assistance Office (NHAO). Some $27 million was allocated to humanitarian relief and approximately 60 percent of the money was distributed through individual bank accounts in Miami, the Cayman Islands, Panama, and Central America. Efforts by the Government Accounting Office (GAO) to monitor invoices and payments were stonewalled by the Assistance Office, which also refused to allow monitoring of field activities of the relief organization.[616] Only after subpoenas were issued in 1986 were bank records and brokers' records made available. At that point the GAO determined that of $14 million issued in humanitarian aid, some $4 million appeared to have gone missing. In addition, it reported that some $6.6 million had been placed in the Miami account of an individual who owned a small grocery store, and that his business was reported as the main *humanitarian aid* supplier to the Contras. Upon examination the GAO found that two checks for a total of $1.2 million had been written out to the Honduran Military Command.[617] There were a number of similar issues including a payment of some $3.3 million to one Contra leader, of which only $150,000 had been paid to "suppliers" in Central America. The remainder simply stayed in the account, drawing significant interest for the individual in question.

In following the humanitarian relief story, CBS News discovered that blank invoices were routinely filled out and sent back to Washington for payment and that many of the small Costa Rican pharmacies and grocery stores that had been named as suppliers had done little business for the Contras. In later years, a memo from

Oliver North's chief liaison to the Contra effort advised North that one of the main Contra leaders was trading NHAO dollars on the black market, for a 37 percent markup.[618] The level of corruption apparently going on with humanitarian aid suggests that a number of individuals were more than willing to break a few laws to make money from Contra support. With so much untraceable cash in play, it was almost inevitable that drug dealing would become part of the picture. We've discussed the opportunities for that in the small boat and aircraft traffic going into the remote border regions surrounding Nicaragua. But there were other options. One obvious opportunity was the main Enterprise air supply system itself, not little planes or boats but multiengine transports—airplanes with plenty of room to stow away limited but very profitable amounts of refined drugs. A few people just needed to look the other way, and it was also helpful if the Customs folks in Miami and New Orleans simply treated the Enterprise flights as they had the CIA covert air shipments.

In its Contra drug investigations the Kerry Committee had come across considerable evidence that certain of the commercial carriers used in the humanitarian Contra support effort had owner and/or employee connections to the drug traffic. The CIA had not been involved in vetting the carriers although under its newly limited role (as of 1986–1987) it was allowed to offer advice on the delivery and receipt of the humanitarian aid. The CIA was also not involved in those occasions when the Enterprise subcontracted aircraft used in aid deliveries to Honduras or El Salvador, picking up privately funded shipments of more lethal supplies and carrying them on distribution flights to Contra staging areas. Air and sea transportation companies appear to have been selected or approved by members of the team North had assembled to support the Enterprise. A brief exploration of the most suspect of those companies will establish context for the potential drug smuggling exposure they represented. The following commentary on companies is excerpted from a Department of Justice report on Contra air contractors and their personnel.[619]

Ocean Hunter and Frigorificos De Puntarenas were both involved in Contra support activities. The Kerry Report indicated that Ocean Hunter was linked to both drug trafficking and money laundering. Ocean Hunter was a Miami-based seafood company that Milian Rodriguez had established to enable Luis Rodriguez to "launder drug money." Ocean Hunter imported seafood from Frigorificos De Puntarenas and, according to witness testimony including that of Milian Rodriguez, intra-fund transfers were used to launder drug profits. Luis Rodriguez was indicted on drug trafficking charges by the U.S. Government in September 1987 and on tax evasion charges in April 1988 in connection with money laundering through Ocean Hunter. Milian Rodriguez was eventually convicted of money laundering. Moises Nunez was the General Manager of Frigorificos, which was reportedly provided some $261,000 to pass to the Contras in 1986. The funds came from Milian Rodriguez, who signed money orders for transfer to the Contras. On January 29, 1986, a cable reported to Headquarters that DEA had seized over four hundred pounds of cocaine concealed in a container of yucca on January 23. The container was leased to David Mayorg, a close advisor to Southern Front Contra commander Eden Pastora. In September, it was reported that the container in question had been destined for Ocean Hunter. **Ramon Milian Rodriguez was** arrested by United States Customs in May 1983 as he was preparing to leave the United States with $5.6 million aboard his Lear jet.

SETCO Aviation Corporation was formed by American operators doing business with Juan Matta-Ballesteros. The individuals involved with SETCO were known to the DEA to have been involved with smuggling narcotics into the United States. Beginning in 1984, SETCO became the primary company used for shipment of supplies and personnel to the Contra FDN groups in Honduras. In addition SETCO was used for supply drops to the Contra combatants inside Nicaragua.

SETCO was paid by Contra leaders out of the private funds set up to receive monies from Oliver North at the NSC. Yet U.S.

law enforcement records cited in the Kerry Report show that Matta-Ballesteros was classified as a "class 1 DEA violator." The same records show that he was a major figure in the Colombian drug cartel and that he was involved in the murder of a DEA agent. He was extradited to the U.S. in 1988 and convicted on drug trafficking charges. Confirmation of his drug involvement is found in a 1987 memorandum from the Los Angeles Chief, Assistant Secretary of State for International Organization Affairs. In that communication the CIA was requested to assist in bringing Matta-Ballesteros to the U.S. "to face charges." In handling the request, the CIA itself confirmed that Matta-Ballesteros had purchased a small air transport company—but did not provide the name of the company. An April 1989 DOJ communication confirms that the company in question was indeed SETCO. As late as 1992, a Department of Defense counternarcotics cable indicated that SETCO was being used in the Honduran Bay Islands by drug traffickers, who concealed narcotics under dried fish in transport through Honduras.

DIACSA was an aircraft dealership and parts company, headed by Alfredo Caballero. During 1984 and 1985 the Contra FDN selected DIASCA to handle "intra-account" transfer monies sent to them by Oliver North. A 1985 cable describes it as an "ARDE cover company" used to purchase aircraft in other activities. Caballero was investigated and confirmed as being associated in cocaine traffic with Manuel Noriega of Panama. Caballero and five others "were indicted for bringing 900 pounds of cocaine into the United States and laundering $26 million."[620]

Hondu Carib was formed by one of the pilots who had also flown Contra supply missions for SETCO, Frank Moss. Moss had been under investigation for drug trafficking since 1979 but had never been formally indicted or charged. In 1985 Moss formed Hondu Carib and entered into a commercial relationship with Mario Calero, the Contra FDN's chief supply officer. Under the legal agreement, Calero received an ownership interest in the company. In 1988 one of the Moss Contra supply aircraft was chased

> by Customs off the west coast of Florida and observed to dump a considerable quantity of material into the ocean. Upon landing it was inspected and significant marijuana residue was detected. The plane was found to have previously been seized by the DEA in March 1987. Earlier, in 1984, Moss was among a group suspected of using a Hondu Carib plane to smuggle both weapons and drugs through Merida, Mexico—with a cover of flying in fish from Honduras for export to Tampa, Florida. All the individuals connected with the plane and the flight had previous drug smuggling records. At the time of the search, Moss and the others claimed that they were either working for or at least with the CIA. Moss's record was extensive and involved other small airlines.

It is virtually impossible not to conclude that a number of the transportation companies working with Contra supply represented a serious risk in terms of drug traffic into the United States. The question that remains is whether or not North and the Enterprise people were aware of that risk. We have some insight to that subject, directly from North's own documents. North's diary summarized a meeting with Robert Owen in August 1985; Owen was one of North's chief staff members in the Contra effort. The two men discussed a plane being used by the brother of Contra leader Adolfo Calero, head of the Contra FDN. The plane was to be used in transporting supplies to Contras in Honduras. North wrote that the "Honduran DC-6, which is being used for runs out of New Orleans is probably being used for drug runs into U.S."[621] To date no documents have been found indicating that North reported the matter to the DEA or other agencies.

Separately, in 1985 Owen had advised North in regard to Contra activities on the southern front in Costa Rica and reported that Contra leader Calero had selected a new commander for that front—an officer who had been paid to defect to the Contras. Owen noted that several of the southern front people were "questionable" and that at least two of the senior people were believed to have "potential involvement with drug running" or to be connected to individuals "now involved in drug running out of Panama." In 1986, Owen sent North a memo in regard to a plane being used to carry humanitarian aid to the Contras; the plane had been previously used to carry drugs and belonged to the Miami-based company operated by Michael Palmer of Vortex, another company documented in the Department of Justice report on Contra air contractors having drug associations. In the memo to North, Owen expressed a fairly lighthearted concern over the backgrounds of some of the contractors selected for the humanitarian assistance shipments.

Certainly it seems that a great many of the people involved with the Contra effort were very much aware of their potential entanglement in drug accusations. Yet the mission clearly came first, as it normally does, and the risks were considered acceptable. President Reagan was personally committed to the Contra "freedom fighters" and to the goal of pushing back against perceived communist territorial expansion—just as other presidents had been in Southeast Asia. The collateral damage of using surrogates connected to drug dealing was not part of the decision-making process. In fact after surveying several decades of presidential decisions on covert action, there is little sign that such collateral damage has ever been a major point of discussion.

As to risk, generally the risks being considered were most frequently those of international or domestic politics. Certainly little thought seems to have been given to the legal and career risk of the mission participants themselves. As noted earlier, CIA personnel did pay a price following the Iran–Contra scandals. CIA Director William Casey died before the scandal erupted but his apparent successor, Robert Gates, endured extensive congressional questioning when nominated as CIA director. Gates admitted that a number of rules had been broken, that laws such as the Arms Export Control Act had been violated, and that he himself should have strongly objected to certain things that were occurring. Although he was found not to have been personally involved in any illegal acts, the political pressures and stress of the nominations review ultimately forced him to withdraw from the nomination. Other CIA officers did receive actual punishment. Dewey Clarridge—who had continually supported efforts of the Enterprise, even after the CIA had been ordered out of lethal Contra support—was reprimanded and dropped a grade. Alan Fiers, another CIA Enterprise supporter, was fired and other officers were reduced in grade, fired, or asked to resign.[622] Oliver North was indicted and convicted on three criminal counts, although North would continue to be heard from in public forums for many years.[623] As to President Reagan, he remained successfully distant from the legal backlash, effectively shielded by the practices of his direct subordinates. Matters had come a long way from the era of President Truman's "the buck stops here" philosophy.[624]

Still, with all the congressional and media attention, it was becoming more difficult to go truly covert—much less deniable. President Reagan's decision to actually make a public cause of American intervention in Nicaragua, including his support for fund-raising campaigns for the Contra "freedom fighters," was something new. Up to that point presidents had conducted shadow warfare either totally covertly or at least under official positions of neutrality. The Iran–Contra scandals brought unprecedented attention to the entanglements and risks of covert warfare. It seems impossible to deny that such entanglement has happened and will happen in the future. Whether it can be controlled and whether the collateral damage it causes can be justified remain open questions.

CHAPTER 22

New Enemies

Contemporary dialogue and discussion often seem to present the War on Terror as if it started on 9/11—declared and launched by President George W. Bush and now being conducted by President Barack Obama. In reality, the War on Terror has been in progress for well over four decades, beginning with a series of terrorist attacks during the Nixon Administration—while the Cold War with the Soviet Union remained the country's national security priority. At first, the appearance of a new spectrum of enemies was obscured by the intermittent nature of the incidents and the tendency to focus on the nuclear face-off with the Soviets.

Presidents Nixon, Ford, Reagan, and Carter were all faced with terrorist attacks—bombings, hijackings, and hostage-taking. In the early years almost all the incidents revolved around Palestinian political issues and involved Middle Eastern groups such as Fatah, Black September, the Abu Nidal Organization, the Palestine Liberation Front, and other Palestine Liberation Organization (PLO) affiliates and supporters. As early as 1969, TWA Flight 840 had been hijacked out of Rome and forced to land in Syria. In 1970, the U.S. Embassy in Beirut, Lebanon, came under rocket attack and in a single incident that year, four airliners were hijacked, including a TWA flight out of Frankfurt, Germany. Later in the year another TWA flight out of Zurich, Switzerland, was hijacked to Jordan. During the infamous

1972 Munich Olympics hostage massacre, one of those killed was an American citizen.

Hijackings had become even more common by the mid-1980s. In December 1984 Kuwait Airways Flight 221 was hijacked flying out of Kuwait and forced down in Pakistan. The hijackers demanded the release of seventeen Kuwaitis and when their demands were not met, they murdered two American passengers working for the U.S. Agency for International Development (USAID). In June 1985, TWA Flight 847 out of Athens, Greece, and destined for Rome was hijacked and forced to land in Beirut, Lebanon. When the terrorist demands for the South Lebanon Army's release of some seven hundred Shiite Muslim prisoners were not met, they cold-bloodedly murdered a U.S. citizen who was one of the plane's passengers, and dumped his body out onto the airport runway. It was becoming clear that Americans were likely to be priority targets in such terrorist attacks, but up to that point American reactions had been limited and largely reactive.

President Reagan set the stage for a series of more aggressive responses to such incidents in reaction to the October 1985 hijacking of the Italian cruise ship *Achille Lauro* and the murder of an American citizen being held hostage by the terrorists. Four Palestine Liberation Front members had seized control of the liner off Egypt, demanding the release of fifty Palestinians in Israeli prisons. Many of the passengers on the ship were American citizens and they received special attention from the terrorists. When denied permission to dock in Syria, the terrorists responded by shooting a wheelchair-bound American Jewish businessman, and dumping his body and wheelchair overboard. Eventually the hijackers were forced to surrender the ship in Egypt and were taken prisoner. President Reagan ordered military intervention and the effort was organized at the National Security Council level by Lieutenant Colonel Oliver North. American fighters were sent to intercept the Egyptian aircraft and it was forced to land at a NATO air base in Sicily. After an American confrontation with Italian authorities, the hijackers were taken into Italian custody.

Reagan further responded to the cruise liner hijacking by issuing a 1986 covert action finding to Congress, informing them that he was directing a number of intelligence activities to address the escalating terror incidents. In response the CIA established a separate organization within the Central Intelligence Agency, the Counterterrorism Center, headed by Duane "Dewey" Clarridge. He had been the CIA officer assigned to lead CIA activities in the first phase of the secret war against Nicaragua. He was known to be exceptionally "forward-leaning" and in that position he had conceived the plan to mine Nicaraguan harbors, which had turned into a major international embarrassment for the U.S. and the Reagan Administration.

Still, Reagan and CIA Director Casey clearly liked his initiative and his willingness to operate outside the box; apparently they expected Clarridge to bring his forward-leaning style into counterterror operations. And it appears Clarridge was prepared to do just that. Following his transfer to the new center, he reportedly began developing special action teams of foreign nationals, primarily Middle Eastern contract employees. Little is known about that recruiting process or his selection criteria but logically we would have to assume the foreign nationals would be from factions hostile to the various Palestinian militant groups. Years of Palestinian terror attacks throughout the Middle East had created a bitter hatred, especially within communities inside both Lebanon and Israel.

Clarridge planned to establish the new counterterror teams overseas, where they could be deployed to provide protection for CIA field officers attached to Middle Eastern stations or operating totally covertly inside nations in the region. The teams were also to be available for totally deniable rendition (apprehension of suspects and extrajudicial transfer to secret locations for intense interrogation). The suspects would be targeted through intelligence activities of the new Counterterrorism Center. However, deniable teams would be needed to actually seize the targets overseas and transport them to prearranged interrogation facilities—a practice that would surface on a large scale following the 9/11 attacks on America.

Apparently Clarridge's deniable action team project raised considerable organizational concern within the Agency, especially since the teams would have acted independently of any direct CIA field supervision.[625] One CIA officer expressed the issue in forthright terms: "What? We're going to arm some foreigners, with their own hates and axes to grind, and send them to kidnap people they are hostile to, in a foreign country, beyond the control of any CIA officer?!"[626] As far as is known, the foreign action team project never became operational during the Reagan Administration. However, in a frantic response to abort further terror attacks, secret rendition operations would become standard practice for the George W. Bush Administration following 9/11.

The terror attacks coming from the Middle Eastern groups were America's first real experience with stateless or nonstate enemies, attackers not tied to a particular country, with little in the way of fixed bases or facilities and continuously mobile, operating in and around several states in the Middle East, North Africa, and even southern Europe. The groups and their fighters became visible only intermittently as they engaged in actual bombings and hijackings. Locating and combating them was going to prove orders of magnitude more difficult than conventional or even covert warfare against targeted states and regimes. In the 1980s, the Reagan Administration faced the same type of stateless enemy challenge that President George W. Bush would following the attacks of September 11, 2001. In addition to responding with the establishment of a counterterror center within the CIA, Reagan targeted a very visible regime that was indeed providing aid and support to a variety of Middle Eastern terrorist groups. That regime was involved in launching its own overt attacks against neighboring states as well as covert attacks against the West, including Americans overseas.

That state was Libya, and its leader was Muammar Gadhafi. Gadhafi appeared to be eager to gain status by confronting the U.S. whenever possible, and the Reagan Administration was not one to take provocations lightly. In 1981, a Libyan challenge to the U.S. over access to the Gulf of Sidra in the Mediterranean led to the deployment of a carrier task group. Next, Gadhafi dispatched Libyan jets towards the task group; two of the aircraft were shot down by U.S. Navy aircraft. Gadhafi was to remain on President Reagan's mind for a number of reasons. In addition to his vocal support for the Palestinian militants, Gadhafi had begun to receive extensive military assistance from the Soviet Union, had a proven history of assassinating his own political opponents, and had sent thousands of troops into Chad, his southern neighbor in North Africa, essentially occupying that country. Gadhafi claimed to be acting in a peacekeeping role in Chad, which at the time was in the midst of what amounted to a civil war, with fighting among various factions—some of whom had already been receiving Libyan support. Once Gadhafi decided to directly intervene, Libyan artillery, along with Soviet tanks (and possibly Soviet advisors), proved much more than a match for any of the armed factions that attempted to oppose them.

Gadhafi's use of heavy airlift planes and tank transporters allowed the Libyans to move some thousand kilometers from their main bases, all the way to N'Djamena, the Chadian capital. However, in the months following the Libyan invasion, Gadhafi's forces actually antagonized all of the nationalist Chadian political factions, including those who might have been expected to support them. With popular opposition to the Libyans widespread, increased attacks on the Libyan forces, and no sign of any faction willing to act as a surrogate government, Gadhafi's personal ego seems to have come into play. While Libya was essentially occupying Chad, Gadhafi was also seeking the presidency of the Organization of African Unity (OAU). While playing host to an OAU meeting, Gadhafi agreed to a Libyan withdrawal from Chad, to be followed by the deployment of a replacement peacekeeping force from the OAU. While that solution ended that particular Libyan incursion into Chad, Gadhafi was not one to give up on expanding his influence so easily; there would be additional military incursions over the period of 1983 to 1987.

An early Reagan-era CIA report on Libya focused on the repeated Libyan military interventions in Chad. The report pointed out that the ongoing major sales of Soviet weapons and aircraft to Libya were essentially turning it into a client military ally of the Soviets and noted the expectation of further Gadhafi "adventurism" across Africa.[627] It also contained the comment that Gadhafi might well have "overextended" himself in Chad, given the fact that he had been unable to establish a surrogate regime in the country despite years of intervention. Given the Reagan Administration's overall agenda of pushing back against the Soviets as well as Gadhafi's history of support for Mideastern terrorist groups, Secretary of State Alexander Haig directed the State Department to develop a plan for undercutting Gadhafi's growing power.

Haig's position was that Gadhafi needed to "have his nose bloodied" and the way to do that was to "increase the flow of pine boxes back to Libya."[628] President Reagan responded with a presidential finding to Congress, authorizing a covert project against Libya and funding to work with a new Chadian surrogate insurgent force led by former Chadian Defense Minister Hissène Habré. Habré took advantage of the Libyan withdrawal and the relative weakness of the OAU peacekeeping force. With no Chadian faction in real control and an extremely weak central government in place, Habré's small force moved aggressively to establish military control over the country and in June 1982, some two thousand of Habré's fighters seized control of the capital. He immediately established a provisional government friendly to the Western bloc and was quickly granted recognition and aid by the United States and France—the former colonial power that had long been economically involved in the country. Habré's rule in Chad was initially chaotic: In a rapid series of events, he was ousted from power in a popular election, only to then remove the elected president in a new coup. A new secret police force, the Documentation and Security Directorate (DSD), was established and began a reign of brutally aggressive action against suspected opponents of the regime, especially opposition tribal groups. Human Rights Watch has estimated that the Habré regime carried out some forty thousand political murders and more than two hundred thousand instances of torture. Habré himself has been described as "Africa's Pinochet," a comparison to the brutal Chilean dictator.[629] There were ongoing human rights complaints about the regime but Habré was outspokenly anticommunist and that position led him to be viewed favorably by the White House. A U.S. military assistance program was established and Chadian security forces were retained under the International Military Education and Training program (IMET). The basic mission of the Chadian military assistance was quite similar to virtually all the American military assistance missions of the period:

> The objectives of the proposed IMET program are: to help the Chadian military develop the systems and operational and maintenance expertise needed for effective management, to encourage an indigenous training capability, and to promote a better understanding of the U.S. and demonstrate our commitment to democratic principles and human rights.

A decade later, documents provided to Congress would reveal that $25 million in emergency military equipment and services had been sent to Chad under section 506(a)(1) of the Foreign Assistance Act of 1961, as amended in 1987. Between $4 and $6 million in American military assistance funds had been spent each year from 1983 to 1986.[630] Equipment sent to Chad under the program included three C-130A aircraft, ammunition, Redeye man-portable surface-to-air missiles, grenade launchers, rifles, and four-wheel-drive vehicles.

America was far from being alone in attempting to bring down the Libyan ruler, widely viewed as aggressive and totally unpredictable. Beyond assisting Chad, the U.S. opposed Gadhafi with propaganda, political action, and outreach to Gadhafi opposition groups. Libyan anti-Gadhafi groups themselves had been active. In 1984 the Gadhafi residence was unsuccessfully attacked by some fifteen fighters associated with a Sudan-based group. Reportedly the group was being financed by Saudi Arabia, Egypt, Morocco, and Iraq. In turn Gadhafi continued on his own path, apparently driven by his ego and a desire to be seen as a power broker in regional politics. He never seems to have hesitated in moving against his opponents both inside and outside the country. He remained very much interested in establishing himself as a covert action force, organizing and supporting foreign assassination and terror attacks as he had back in the 1970s, when he had contracted such activities with former CIA officer Ed Wilson. His foreign policy would increasingly turn to terror bombings, using his own agents and surrogates. He would also claim association with and sponsorship of a variety of terrorist groups, using this as a type of misdirection to cover his own activities. Gadhafi, never known to give up easily, also continued to repeatedly invade Chad, only to be driven back out of the country. In one of the incursions, several hundred of his troops were captured. The U.S. recruited some six hundred of them, kept them out of prison camps, and began to organize them as a potential action force in support of a new anti-Gadhafi political front. The effort never reached fruition, largely because of Gadhafi's success in eliminating his opponents; but the project was kept in play, especially following a series of terror attacks in which Libya was suspected as the sponsor. Years later, in 1990, the former Gadhafi fighters, equipped with large supplies of U.S. weapons including Stinger portable surface-to-air missiles and dune buggies, became involved in an internal Chadian conflict, exposing ties between the fighters and the CIA.[631]

As previously noted, Libya's leader was not known for restraint (or good sense) and in April 1986, Libyan agents working out of their embassy in West Berlin bombed a nightclub in that city, killing 3 people and injuring another 229. The club was a favorite of American service personnel in West Berlin. President Reagan responded with an order for a full-scale air strike on Libya, conducted by strike aircraft from three U.S. carriers in the Gulf and supported by eighteen long-range F-11A fighters operating out of a Royal Air Force base in England. The aircraft flying out of England were refueled multiple times as France, Spain, and Italy had all denied overflight rights in support of the attack. The strikes were officially declared to have the goal of eliminating Libya's ability to train terrorists, but more fundamentally they were an all-out effort to intimidate Gadhafi.

From that perspective, the first major use of conventional American military force since Vietnam had limited effect, as Gadhafi certainly continued to act as a sponsor of terrorism. That same year, Libya was involved in the hijacking of Pam Am Flight 73 in Pakistan, with twenty people killed in the incident (although Libyan sponsorship was not fully confirmed until an investigation by a British newspaper in 2004). Libya also continued its funding and training of terrorist groups ranging from elements of the PLO to the Abu Nidal Organization. And in 1988, Pam Am Flight 103 was blown out of the sky over Lockerbie, Scotland, killing all 259 people aboard the aircraft. Libyans were charged and eventually convicted in the attack. In 2002, Gadhafi and the Libyan government finally accepted responsibility for the aircraft bombing and offered some $2.7 billion in compensation to the families of those killed in the terrorist attack.

The Reagan Administration and the George H.W. Bush Administration that followed it were both focused on global geopolitical issues, on the Soviet Union, and on asserting America's role as a conventional military force in the world. To a large extent, the George H.W. Bush era was a story not of covert action but of overt and conventional warfare. First it would be a major military operation to defend Saudi Arabian oil fields (Operation Desert Shield) and then another to push Saddam Hussein's Iraqi forces out of Kuwait (Operation Desert Storm). The Gulf War was a return to full-scale, multiservice conventional warfare, conducted in conjunction with a well-organized multinational coalition and with large numbers of American "boots on the ground." It was the sort of coalition that President Eisenhower had hoped to build for intervention in Indochina but that John Foster Dulles had failed to assemble. President Bush and his team were far more successful and the Gulf War (as with Vietnam, the term war is commonly used but technically incorrect) achieved the sort of congressional and public support not seen since World War II.

Covert warfare of any sort, even against terrorism, was not a major element of the George H.W. Bush Administration. In fact, Bush issued no official policy or directive on terrorism.[632] According to Richard Clarke—a major figure in counterterrorism (CT) activities under three separate presidential administrations—after taking office in 1989, Bush had actually asked his national security advisor, Brent Scowcroft, to tone down some of the more aggressive counterterrorism activities initiated by the NSC and Oliver North during the Reagan Administration.[633] The NSC, with North assigned to counterterrorism activities, had previously responded to a number of actual and potential attacks, primarily having to do with airline and ship hijacking/hostage situations. Given the political fallout from a variety of covert operations by North and Clarridge during the Reagan Administration, President Bush seems to have preferred a more moderate, lower-key counterterrorism approach. As an example of that moderation, when follow-up investigations revealed the connections between the Pan Am Flight 103 attack and Libya, there was no military response, and thc Bush Administration moved no further than calls for UN sanctions against Libya.

Of course covert action remained an option, and President Bush also appeared interested in preserving that option and in retaining executive flexibility, as had the presidents preceding him. He declined to support new legislation requiring forty-eight hours' congressional notice of covert action, preferring language calling simply for "timely" notification. He also let it be known that while he would "usually" provide notification within a few days, he would rely primarily on his authority as commander in chief in such matters.[634] Perhaps it wasn't going to matter anyway; covert action was a relatively unused option for the first Bush Administration. Within the CIA, the Operations Directorate remained a major force, consuming over half the CIA's budget of something over $3 billion a year. But covert action in general slowed, representing only about 5 percent of operations expenditures.[635]

Globally, in 1989, as the Reagan era was ending and the first term of George H.W. Bush beginning, the Cubans were withdrawing their forces from Angola, and the Russians had pulled out of Afghanistan after suffering their own Vietnam-style bloodletting. Against all expectations, in Nicaragua, the Sandinistas had held open elections and in doing so lost much of their political power. But it had been the internal political dynamic that had led to the fall of the regime rather than Contra military action. By the spring of 1990, the remaining six-thousand-man Contra force had begun to disbanded; estimates are that they had suffered more than nine thousand casualties during the period of their combat.

In 1991, the Soviet Union came apart at the seams. The USSR was dissolved in December of that year and the decades-long strategy of Cold War "pushback" against communist territorial expansion became something of a moot point—especially given the mutual acceleration of peaceful trade relations between the U.S. and China, and the dramatic reduction in funding for the Russian military. The Marxist regime in Kabul had continued to defend itself as best it could and the CIA continued its assistance, albeit somewhat more selectively, to rebel Afghan groups. Kabul fell in 1992, leaving the country in a state of ongoing civil warfare between the fundamentalist Taliban, supported by the Pakistani ISI, and a number of groups opposed to its domination.

In 1993, President Bill Clinton faced the first jihadi terror attack on American soil when the World Trade Center in New York City was bombed—which produced neither an overt or a covert military response. The reason for inaction was shockingly simple. At the time of the first World Trade Center bombing, the American intelligence system, as a whole, was not yet able to associate the attack's participants with any specific sponsor state or group. Indeed there was no conventional "state sponsor," as with previous attacks supported by Libya. Instead, the sponsorship had come from within a newly formed network, one organized by Osama bin Laden when he had been a key figure in moving large Saudi financial donations through Pakistan to select Afghan commanders.

Much of that new infrastructure involved financial fronts such as the Afghan Services Bureau, affiliated with charities declared to be supporting Arab combatants in the Afghan warfare.[636] Over time, bin Laden and his nascent Al-Qaeda organization would display a great deal of proficiency in operating globally within both charitable and commercial covers. Several ostensibly charitable and humanitarian Saudi citizen–funded entities—referred to as NGOs (nongovernment entities)—such as Al-Haramain were used by bin Laden and his followers for very compartmentalized dissemination of money and personnel for new jihadi operations far beyond Afghanistan.[637]

In contrast to the lack of any major American response to the first World Trade Center attack, President Clinton did order direct military response to what was perceived as an act of state-sponsored terrorism: a plot to assassinate former President George H.W. Bush during a visit to Kuwait. The plot had apparently been ordered by Iraqi leader Saddam Hussein as personal revenge against President Bush for Hussein's defeat in his attempt to invade and control Kuwait. The investigation that followed clearly showed that the effort had been organized by Iraqi agents and personally ordered by Saddam Hussein. The American reaction was overt, although more limited than that proposed by the Pentagon, which had called for strikes on multiple Iraqi targets. Instead, a number of cruise missiles were launched in a nighttime strike on the Iraqi intelligence complex in Baghdad. The attack was quite public, being announced to the international media by President Clinton. As an overt military action, it was conducted by an order from the president to the Joint Chiefs with no finding or apparently no advance congressional briefings. Clinton's position on the use of force in the response seemed quite definitive: "Well, this may teach him [Hussein] a lesson, but if it doesn't we'll have to do more."[638] In contrast to the much more massive Reagan Administration military strike on Libya, the Clinton action against Saddam Hussein seems to have been quite effective. Saddam had clearly gotten the message and no further Iraqi plots would be verified.

The Clinton Administration would come to know jihadi terrorism, Al-Qaeda, and Osama Bin Laden far too well, although it took time to appreciate the extent to which bin Laden and his various fronts—charitable, commercial, and financial—were actually recruiting and directing a multinational force. At first he was viewed simply as "a radicalized rich kid, playing at terrorism by sending checks to terrorist groups." Even the CIA initially opposed the idea that there was such an organization as Al-Qaeda.[639] Yet during the period from 1995 to 2000, both the CIA and national counterterrorism groups received constant increases in funding and became highly focused on tracking and understanding the escalation of global terror attacks.

One of the first signs that a networked, multinational jihadi organization was in operation appeared well before the wave of actual attacks at the turn of the century, during the war between Bosnia and Serbia. In 1992, significant numbers of Arabs, many former Afghan mujahedin, began to show up in Bosnia. They didn't just come as individual volunteers; they appeared as already organized brigades, officially attached to the Bosnian army but operating almost solely on their own. They were highly experienced, highly aggressive, and agonizingly brutal. And they came with a support organization of financial, commercial, and charity groups—the exact infrastructure that had developed in Pakistan to support Arab fighters introduced into the Afghan war against the Soviets.

In *Against All Enemies*, Richard Clarke, who headed the National Security Council counterterrorism effort under both the Clinton and George W. Bush administrations, describes the growing sophistication of the Al-Qaeda organization, tracking the funding for the Bosnian Arab brigades back to Sudan, and eventually to bin Laden. At the time and without full appreciation of what was happening or that it was indeed Al-Qaeda, the Clinton Administration moved politically against the growing jihadist force in Bosnia. The U.S demanded their expulsion as part of the Dayton Accords peace agreement. The Bosnian leadership agreed, but covertly allowed terror cells to evolve and act from its territories. Despite ongoing American protests, the jihadi elements were still operational in Bosnia as late as 2002. Only then, with information from the U.S., did Bosnian police begin raiding jihadi cells in that country.[640]

Following his forays into Pakistan and Afghanistan, Osama bin Laden and Al-Qaeda had become well established in the Sudan.

He purchased a very large farm but also spent a good deal of time connecting with former Afghan fighters and attempting to establish links into Yemen. Reportedly he even looked to a tribe he could marry into to build an allegiance. He also began introducing jihadi fighters into Yemen.[641] Beyond Yemen, he expanded Al-Qaeda by sending groups of jihadi fighters, arms smugglers, and organizers to Somalia, Kenya, Egypt, Libya, and Tajikistan. Al-Qaeda was very real but it was still primarily in "seeding" mode.[642]

As the U.S. began to obtain confirmation that bin Laden was operating from the Sudan, the issue of "sanctuary" or "haven" states became increasingly worrying. Sudan itself was not ordering international terror attacks; bin Laden was doing that. Instead, a friendly fundamentalist religious environment and an equally friendly Sudanese intelligence service were enabling bin Laden. He was using the Sudan and elements of its military and intelligence in the same way he would later use thc Taliban in Afghanistan.

In a first step against bin Laden in the Sudan, the U.S. and other regional countries obtained UN sanctions against the country—similar to earlier George H.W. Bush–era sanctions against Libya. The White House requested the Pentagon to prepare plans for a surgical military strike against bin Laden in Yemen. The Pentagon responded with a full plan for a Special Forces attack against both organizational and financial targets supporting bin Laden and Al-Qaeda. President Clinton had apparently hoped for something more covert, something less intense. Clarke described the military briefer's succinct response to concern over the scale of the planned attack: "That's what we do, sir. If you want covert, that's the CIA."[643] It would be two more decades before joint military–CIA "kinetic strikes" against high-value terrorist targets in denied areas would become accepted practice.

The literal truth was that at that point the CIA had no infrastructure, assets, or capabilities for a successful covert operation in the Sudan, so the Clinton initiative was abandoned. The Sudan affair demonstrated the extent to which the classic Cold War covert-action paradigm was becoming dated. For decades the CIA had used country station resources in Southeast Asia, Latin America, and Africa as platforms for covert action. In other instances, military assistance missions—first in Asia and then in Latin America—had served a similar purpose. With a new type of war emerging—a global effort against jihadist networks—the U.S. and the CIA simply lacked the reach to act on all the emerging fronts. That was about to change, but in the meantime bin Laden was forced out of the Sudan not by American action but through Egyptian retaliation for his sponsorship of an assassination attempt on Egyptian president Hosni Mubarak.

While the Clinton Administration had passed on conducting either overt military action or covert operations in the Sudan, President Clinton had approved five separate directives (memorandum of notification or MON) related to counterterror activities. A special bin Laden counterterrorism unit was established and focused on developing an operational picture of his network. And Clinton authorized broad-based covert action against both bin Laden and Al-Qaeda. That authorization included something quite dramatic, something not seen since the Eisenhower Administration and the instruction to eliminate Patrice Lumumba. Clinton had not just directed another covert operation but had effectively given the CIA the authority to capture and/or kill Osama bin Laden.[644]

In 1996 President Clinton directed the CIA to increase its focus on bin Laden; the CIA was also ordered to produce sufficient intelligence for a comprehensive plan of attack on Al-Qaeda. That initiative was stimulated by bin Laden's issuance of the first general jihadi fatwa, a "declaration of war." In that edict, bin Laden called for "fast moving light forces" to wage ongoing attacks against Americans and Israelis anywhere in the Muslim holy lands.[645] The CIA's "virtual" domestic station—the bin Laden Issue Station—began working with personnel from agencies throughout the U.S. intelligence community, but it was starting from scratch. As an example, in 1998 the FBI had no central file on Al-Qaeda, bin Laden, or the bin Laden family. The CIA task force liaison to the FBI was informed that the Bureau might be given a handful of leads, but that it would be necessary to visit each field office to initiate inquiries. The explanation for the lack of information was simple. The FBI investigates crimes and as of 1998, Al-Qaeda was not known to have committed any crime in the United States.[646]

Then bin Laden followed with a second declaration—specifically a call for war on America. That second declaration, issued in February 1998, was actually issued by a multinational alliance of jihadi militants, including Al-Qaeda group leaders from Egypt, Pakistan, and Bangladesh. Bin Laden was acting as spokesman for the entire group. The declaration called for open war on America and its allies, both civilians and military personnel. Muslims were called to kill Americans in every country where they could reach them.[647]

In retrospect, after reading the Al-Qaeda declarations of war and the explicit call for murder of Americans anywhere on the globe, it seems strange that they produced such a limited response. In 1941, America had declared war against Germany prior to any declaration of hostilities by the German government. America had engaged in massive conventional warfare in Korea, Vietnam, and Kuwait without any threat to its citizens or even a declaration of hostile intent against them. Yet Congress showed no indication of officially responding to Al-Qaeda with a counter-declaration of war; there was not even a congressional resolution on the threat. Congress was once again leaving a fundamental ideological conflict strictly in the president's lap. And there was no covert, clandestine, or overt military action against either bin Laden or Al-Qaeda until Al-Qaeda launched its first attacks on American targets.

On August 7, 1998, Al-Qaeda did just what bin Laden had announced in his declaration of war: it attacked Americans where it could get to them, in Africa. The American embassies in Dar es Salaam, Tanzania, and Nairobi, Kenya, were struck by suicide bombers. Over two hundred people were killed, over four thousand wounded. Twelve Americans died in the attacks. There was no doubt that Americans were now at risk and that Al-Qaeda definitely had no concern for civilians or collateral damage.

President Clinton did order a military response to those attacks; no doubt he hoped the response might eliminate bin Laden—his kill order was still in effect. In August of 1998, seventy-seven cruise missiles were launched against six presumed Al-Qaeda camps in Afghanistan and a suspected chemical warfare facility in the Sudan. Due to concerns over Pakistani connections to Al-Qaeda, the Pakistanis were given no notice and were quite upset when they detected the mass missile launch coming across their territory. President Clinton was clearly willing to commit to military action in some fashion, and to take the international political fallout it would bring. As to Congress, even after the coordinated attacks against the American embassies in multiple foreign countries, it made no response, once again leaving any national security response to the president.

The reality of the situation remained the same as it had earlier with bin Laden in his Sudan retreat. America did not have the military capability or the bases required to stage an effective response—whether overt or covert military action.[648] Bin Laden himself was effectively hidden by the Taliban sanctuary regime in power in Afghanistan. To ensure that sanctuary and enhance his value to the Taliban, bin Laden was paying some $20 million a year for camps, weapons, salaries, and subsidies for volunteers. Jihadi efforts beyond Afghanistan were costing another $10 million annually.[649]

New enemies had surfaced and actually declared war against the United States and its citizens anywhere in the world. They were non-state, virtual enemies—enemies who operated individually and in small groups, were highly mobile, and struck "soft" targets around the world. They had few fixed bases and a shadowy logistics and support system. When they could be located they were found in remote locations, in unfriendly and denied territory. Intelligence and military tools would evolve to deal with such enemies but that was a slow process, starting largely from scratch. The problem wasn't technology; it was in changing mind-sets and worldviews. We will trace the evolution of that new form of warfare in following chapters, beginning with the development of a new military structure focused on highly targeted missions in denied territories—and the weapons that emerged to serve that type of warfare. The evolution of both the military element and the weaponry will take us back to their roots in Vietnam.

CHAPTER 23

New Weapons

Going after "stateless" enemies demanded new military organizations and new weapons systems, capable of quickly striking small, mobile targets—the "fast-moving light forces" bin Laden himself had mentioned in his 1996 and 1998 fatwas. And it would mean operating at extreme distances, in denied territories in Southwest Asia, the Middle East, and Africa. It would also involve a heavy element of operational security and clandestine operations doctrine, since America would be going after bin Laden and Al-Qaeda in unfriendly if not openly denied territories; the Taliban had taken control of most of Afghanistan by 1996, declaring it an Islamic republic.

We'll detail specific efforts against bin Laden both before and after 9/11 in the following chapters. But first we need to examine how the military organization and weapons that would ultimately be effective in an expanded war on terror came into being. Both the concept of a new military force structure and the weapons it would need for low-intensity but highly targeted military action had origins in the 1960s in Southeast Asia. How that concept was tested, shelved, and reinvigorated is fundamental to following the evolution of both clandestine and covert warfare into the twenty-first century. Somewhat surprisingly, it would turn out to be a development more driven by the White House and Congress than one originating with the Joint Chiefs of Staff or command levels within the uniformed military services. But, harkening back to our discussion of conventional warfare in Southeast Asia, perhaps that is not totally surprising in light of our earlier discussion of President Kennedy's Green Beret and Special Forces initiative. It also recalls the point that senior echelons of the Army and the Joint Chiefs had never exactly been enthusiastic about special operations or low-intensity warfare—a position we first examined during Kennedy's push to move low-intensity and covert operations under the military.

Military Assistance Command, Vietnam (MACV) was a joint-service command of the Department of Defense. The Studies and Observations Group (SOG), operating under MACV, was a classified, multiservice command with access to resources and personnel from the U.S. Army, Navy, Air Force, and Marine Corps. The Studies and Observations Group was created for and dedicated to covert, highly targeted warfare. Under OPLAN34A, MACV and in particular the Studies and Observations Group coordinated with and received intelligence support from the CIA, with CIA officers assigned to support the black/covert operations against North Vietnam.

At one level MACV carried the overall military assistance mission to preserve a friendly regime. At another level it carried a great deal of authority and was given sufficient autonomy (and deniability) to conduct military operations beyond the borders of South Vietnam. Initially the Studies and Observations Group was assigned responsibility for clandestine military operations into denied areas of North Vietnam, aimed against high-value targets.[650] As the war broadened and North Vietnamese involvement escalated, SOG would also conduct covert cross-border missions into both Laos and Cambodia.

The Studies and Observations Group had access to Special Forces and units from multiple services; there was no question of the combat skills, bravery, or endurance of its personnel. However, the group's military commanders and personnel, unlike the Green Beret civil action and military assistance teams of the earliest days in Vietnam, were neither trained nor experienced specifically in unconventional warfare or covert operations.[651] Classic Special Forces units had been trained to perform high-risk missions as an operational complement to conventional warfare. They normally relied on the larger military commands for support and logistics.

In Vietnam SOG had to build its own air element for denied area operations.[652] The aircraft initially assigned were slow and had limited range. They had to be heavily modified for electronic countermeasures, intelligence collection, and Doppler navigation, but even then six of the aircraft assigned were lost in operations. Given that the planes had highly valued electronics collection capability, they were also tasked with "loitering" after personnel or supply drops to gather information on North Vietnamese antiaircraft, radar, and artillery installations—not an assignment popular with their crews.[653]

The Studies and Observations Group had initially been given two major covert assignments, not involving combat but primarily insertion of indigenous agents into North Vietnam. The second mission was very much combat intensive and it was executed under considerable political constraint. In 1965, some two years after it was created, SOG was tasked with deniable operations against the Ho Chi Minh Trail in Laos. According to those involved, those operations were significantly handicapped by the demand for total deniability and the limitations imposed on combat flexibility by micromanagement ranging all the way up to the White House.[654]

SOG ground activity, using South Vietnamese Special Forces and indigenous tribal teams, continued from the earliest Shining Brass and Daniel Boone operations into a pattern of sustained reconnaissance and disruption missions against the Ho Chi Minh Trail. In 1966, 137 teams launched against the trail, and by 1968 SOG was operating in both Laos and Cambodia, launching over four hundred missions. By that point it had begun facing huge North Vietnamese manpower deployments and it began to be a contest of Special Forces unconventional warfare on one side against aggressive conventional army formations on the other. SOG routinely had to move long distances into not just denied but into massively defended territory.

In retrospect the Studies and Observations Group suffered from a combination of political caution, strongly demanded deniability, and essentially always being sent late to the battle. Overall the use of SOG in Vietnam reflects poorly on the tendency of President Johnson, Defense Secretary McNamara, and Secretary of State Dean Rusk towards micromanagement of combat operations. It also strayed far from President Kennedy's original low-intensity, surgical Special Forces concept—but then Kennedy's concept was to have them involved in cooperative defense efforts that would have precluded the massive conventional warfare that came to Vietnam.

Pitting small Studies and Observations Group teams against the large-scale forces that North Vietnam deployed to defend its supply corridors down the Laotian side of the Vietnamese border was ultimately an impossible mission rather than a failure of the organization or its personnel. The imbalance only worsened during the final Nixon–Kissinger era in Vietnam. Ultimately the North Vietnamese always seemed to be one or more steps ahead of the White House.

The Vietnam experience had demonstrated that the Army command and the Pentagon were neither structured nor eager for low-intensity, unconventional warfare. It was a type of military action designed specifically for counterinsurgency operations, which up to that point had never been a primary focus of conventional military doctrine. Colonel Clyde Russell, the first chief of SOG in Vietnam, offered succinct remarks on the career potential of Special Forces in the Cold War Army:

> *In the early 1950's . . . Special Forces Groups were not a recognized part of the Army. They were seen as outsiders . . . great warriors . . . but they could not live comfortably within the peacetime regimental system . . . when I got to the 10th Special Forces Group in 1957 . . . I did not want to go . . . I was detailed to go.*[655]

In general, Army leadership had been uninterested in and on occasion disdainful of President Kennedy's Special Forces initiative. The head of the Joint Chiefs thought the administration had been oversold on the concept. Following a presidential address to the Joint Chiefs, Army Chief of Staff George Decker dismissed Special Forces and the tactics of counterinsurgency as a specialization, declaring that "any good soldier can handle guerrillas." Even General Maxwell Taylor, much admired by President Kennedy, dismissed counterinsurgency as "just a form of small war" and declared that it should not be receiving special attention.[656]

There is little doubt that those attitudes significantly constrained the potential of the Studies and Observations Group in Southeast Asia. It could be seen even in the details, such as assigning a chief with only the rank of colonel. At that level of rank SOG had no real access to senior MACV command and certainly none to the Joint Chiefs, much less the president. When MACV commander William Westmoreland planned his massive escalation of the war in 1964, the SOG commander's input was not only not considered; he was not even invited to the discussions or in any way included in the process.[657]

Following the withdrawal from Vietnam, America's military largely returned to the conventional worldview that had made special operations and unconventional warfare so challenging in Southeast Asia. While each service maintained its own special operations groups, they were redirected to the types of conventional combat support roles previously discussed.

Post-Vietnam-era special operations groups had been forced back into their pre-Vietnam role as complements to conventional warfare doctrine. It would be the hostage-taking and terror attacks of the late 1970s and 1980s that brought Special Forces units back to the attention of the White House and into a counterterrorism role. The first step in that process was a brutal lesson involving the attempted rescue of American hostages in Iran in a daring Special Forces operation, Eagle Claw, ordered by President Carter.

The details of Eagle Claw's failure have been covered in great detail elsewhere, as have its shortcomings. Fundamentally it demonstrated the consequences of an impromptu effort to combine units from different services who had never trained with each other, were unfamiliar with the capabilities of each other's equipment, and were not even practiced in the same communications procedures. It also demonstrated that the services had maintained some of the Special

Forces tools developed for Vietnam, but had also either neglected or totally discarded other key tools that would be needed for the new enemies and challenges that had developed.

The first response to the Iranian hostage mission failure came from President Carter, who immediately ordered planning for a second mission, authorized as Operation Honey Badger. Carter ordered that the mission have anything it needed to succeed. And, as we have seen in such agonizing failures, Carter also ordered Harold Brown, his secretary of defense, to conduct an inquiry into the reasons for the failure of Eagle Claw. The result of that inquiry was the creation of a standing joint Special Forces task force, which was to be treated as a national-security-level capability and assigned its own headquarters. It would also have the ability to call on Special Forces units from the various services and assume command authority for designated missions.[658] Activated in 1980, the new organization was designated Joint Special Operations Command (JSOC). The inquiry also identified several problems with the weapons systems utilized in the Iranian missions; building an enhanced American capability was going to involve new forces, new training, and new equipment.

The Joint Special Operations Command continued in place through the early years of the Reagan Administration as well as the administrations that followed. JSOC became the place to turn to for special White House needs such as hostage rescue. Later it would become a key counterterror resource for both the George W. Bush and the Obama administrations. It was not only charged with the study of special operations requirements and techniques but was given the mission to "ensure interoperability and equipment standardization," plan and conduct special operations exercises and training, and develop joint special operations tactics.

Another entity created during the planning for a second Iranian hostage rescue mission directed by President Carter was the Field Operations Group (FOG). Even though political events precluded a second rescue attempt, the group continued in place within the Army during the Carter–Reagan transition period. It was tasked specifically with the collection of mission-specific intelligence in support of special operations missions, in particular counterterrorism missions. Circa 1981 it was redesignated the Intelligence Support Activity, generally referred to simply as "the Activity."

The Activity performed various types of field intelligence, one of the most important being field signals and communications intelligence collection, monitoring all forms of electronic communications associated with selected targets. That specialty would become increasingly complex and much in demand as time passed, ultimately providing real-time targeting to combat forces. In 1989, apparently in the interest of operational security, the Activity began to use a variety of code names, changed approximately every two years. In 2003, the Activity was moved into a subcommand position under the Joint Special Operations Command as part of the large-scale buildup of JSOC in response to the 9/11 attacks.

In regard to the Joint Special Operations Command's own evolution, in 1985 a JSOC task force participated in the U.S. intervention in Grenada, focused on rescuing and evacuating American students on the island. The Grenada operation revealed numerous problems in coordination, communications, and practices, as well as an ongoing lack of usable field intelligence from the CIA.[659] It also exposed a lack of understanding and integration of new-era Special Forces by the conventional military. The JSOC task force commander documented and later gave congressional testimony on how poorly his unit had been used by the conventional forces commander, resulting in excessive Special Forces casualties.

On a more positive note, events in Grenada fully confirmed the absolute necessity of close air support by the AC-130 gunships that initially had been fielded in Vietnam and were made available to JSOC. In 1979, four AC-130H gunships had been deployed to Guam in response to the Iranian Embassy hostage crisis, and were later assigned to the abortive Eagle Claw hostage rescue mission. Midair refueling for the gunships had become standard practice, using propeller-driven MC-130J tanker aircraft. The gunships had been one of the few Vietnam-era weapons systems successfully retained within the special operations units—but not without a great deal of internal conflict within the U.S. Air Force.

One of the biggest problems of the Southeast Asia era had been the availability of effective air support for low-intensity operations. Earlier we detailed the efforts of Heinie Aderholt and Air Commando One to bring in the right mix of resources for effective transport, logistics, and attack in covert Laotian operations. Aderholt faced the same sort of conventional Cold War mind-set within the Air Force that the early Special Forces officers encountered in the Army. Covert warfare in Laos was often on the short end of the priority list, receiving air support when it could be diverted from missions into North Vietnam, and suffering from the limited "loiter" time (flying time over target) of the jet aircraft carrying the brunt of the Southeast Asian air war.

Aderholt related that propeller-driven A-26 aircraft proved exceptionally effective in missions against the Ho Chi Minh Trail. They were well armed, capable of night operations, and had superior loiter capability. However, the 7th Air Force took the conventional view that jets were superior in all things and opposed the deployment of propeller-type aircraft, including more of the AC-47 "Spooky" gunships that had begun to be deployed in Laos in 1967.[660] When his commander in Laos sent Aderholt to present his case to 7th Air Force, its commander barred him from their conferences.[661]

Upon his return from Southeast Asia, Aderholt was required to give a mandatory debriefing to Pentagon air staff. He began in his usual straightforward fashion by condemning the practice of consolidating all strike reports, essentially leaving the Air Force lying to itself about the effectiveness of jet aircraft attacks on certain types of targets. He then outlined the actual statistics, showing that the 56th Air Commando Wing's vintage propeller aircraft had been the predominant "truck killers" on the Ho Chi Minh Trail—although they had been only a small percentage of the total 7th Air Force missions. Aderholt noted that his remarks were not well received at the Pentagon and that considerable resentment was expressed.[662]

Aderholt clashed with his former 7th Air Force commander again when he supported further development on the propeller-driven AC-130 Spectre gunship (the replacement for the AC-47 Spooky) in the face of the superior officer's opposition to spending any further time or money on it. Aderholt described the AC-130 gunship as "without question the finest close air support system employed in Southeast Asia."[663] Time would prove Aderholt to be correct; the gunship and its derivatives would, along with special-purpose transport aircraft and helicopters, become a key element of both the services' Special Operations Forces (SOF) and the counterterror task forces of the tweny-first century.

Another positive finding from the Special Forces operation in Grenada had been the early use of a vitally important new technology—satellite communications. Portable satellite telephones would become invaluable for command and control in the chaos of special operations, providing a platform to resolve the sorts of field support problems that had plagued previous endeavors in Southeast Asia. When the first CIA special action team organized to go into Afghanistan after 9/11, a combination of satellite telephone systems was considered invaluable to the mission. One unit was briefcase sized, and capable of transmissions through very high-altitude geosynchronous satellites. Others were commercial phones using lower-orbit satellite networks.[664]

The Special Forces experience in Grenada had been mixed. It was clear that all the lessons learned from Eagle Claw in Iran had not been effectively implemented and in this instance Congress did insert itself into the issue.[665] Both the House and Senate passed Special Forces reform bills and after extended political compromise, in 1987 an independent command—U.S. Special Operations Command—was created. It was referred to as either USSOCOM or SOCOM. Special Operations Command was chartered with oversight over covert and clandestine missions of all types, ranging from reconnaissance and direct military action to psychological warfare. Each of the military services continued to maintain its own Special Forces groups, including the Army's Delta Force (Airborne) and the Navy's

SEALs. The Army's Rangers, Marine Special Forces, and a number of Air Force special operations units are on call for missions by SOCOM.[666] Individual joint operations missions are planned and executed with special mission units under operational control of JSOC, which itself operates as a component command of SOCOM. A key element of SOCOM's command-level status was having its own budget. That allowed the command not only to conduct planning and actual training exercises but also to engage in the acquisition of special equipment, weapons, supplies, and services specifically for the Special Operations Forces.

Early Special Operations Command activities included the protection of commercial shipping lanes in the Persian Gulf during the Iran–Iraq War (Operation Earnest Will in September 1987), relief efforts for Kurdish refugees and relief operations in Somalia, support of Desert Shield/Desert Storm in the Gulf War, and security operations in Haiti and Bosnia. During the 1990s, demand for Special Forces missions escalated dramatically, with actual operations more than doubling: by 1996 special operations personnel would be deployed to some 142 countries in counter-drug missions, training efforts, and joint exercises with other nations.[667]

One of the primary Special Forces needs—concentrated firepower deployed over long distances—had been answered with the AC-130 gunships in new and improved versions (Spooky was joined by the AC-130H Spectre, the AC-130J Ghostrider, and the AC-130W Stinger),[668] along with C-130 tanker and transport aircraft in the Combat Talon series.[669] With midair refueling, forces could be deployed far beyond land support bases.

In addition, one of the key problems with the Iranian hostage rescue mission had also been addressed. The inquiry into that failed mission determined that a key problem lay in the helicopters used: they simply were not up to the task of long-distance covert operations. There was an obvious need for superior helicopters with much greater reliability. The immediate answer was to turn to Sikorsky Black Hawk helicopters. The Black Hawk had entered Army field operations only in 1979 but quickly proved itself. Black Hawk variants, including those that could be refueled by the propeller-driven C-130 tankers, proved to be the solution to the long-range, covert mission helicopter challenge. The Black Hawks were so effective and reliable that an improved version would not go into operational service until 2007. Special operations had gunships and effective helicopters and the midair refueling capabilities for both—which could support long-distance strikes. It only needed a couple of additional tools, which had actually been developed as far back as Vietnam but discarded afterward.

Helicopter insertion had been a key element of conventional operations in Vietnam. However, the CIA's Special Operations Division Air Branch had been intrigued by the idea of a virtually silent helicopter to use in agent infiltration and intelligence collection. The product of that interest was a highly modified version of the OH-6A light observation helicopter from Hughes Aircraft.[670] Two of those helicopters were redesigned not only to reduce rotor noise but also to introduce a forward-looking infrared camera and infrared nose floodlight for night operations. With the addition of special fuel tanks, the small helicopter was ready for long-range operations.

The modified craft, known as "the quiet ones," were flown on missions into North Vietnam by Air America contractors in 1972. The goal was to tap into key communications lines used for North Vietnamese command and control. The mission was quite successful and the relative stealth of the helicopters impressed all those involved. But, as with other high-tech, low-intensity tools developed during the period, the quiet helicopters were simply discarded by the CIA following the withdrawal from Vietnam. Later, in the 1980s, Special Operations Command began developing new stealth helicopter designs. It initiated a project with Lockheed to apply designs used in the F-117 stealth aircraft. The existence of an actual stealthy Black Hawk operational variant was revealed in 2011, when one of the new craft was damaged in the successful mission against Osama bin Laden inside Pakistan.[671]

Despite improvements in training, coordination, communications, and weapons, the JSOC special operations teams of the 1980s and 1990s still faced ongoing problems with obtaining current field intelligence—and so did the CIA. Human intelligence in remote areas always had been a problem. With an increasing demand for totally real-time response to terrorist situations in very remote combat venues, the problem had only worsened. Whether it was intelligence for hostage rescues in foreign countries or targeting Osama bin Laden in the mountains of Afghanistan, the lack of real-time information caused missions to abort, fail, or take casualties that might have been avoided. And once again the technology for the solution to the problem of collecting remote intelligence had initially been fielded in Southeast Asian combat. In fact, the basic concept first had been tested even earlier, during World War II—the answer to real-time remote intelligence would lie in Remotely Piloted Vehicles (RPVs, eventually referred to as drones). Much contemporary writing on drones seems to consider that both unarmed surveillance and weaponized or armed drones—remotely targeted in real time—are something quite new. In reality they were in combat use decades ago.

The Germans deployed a variety of radio-controlled glide bombs during the Second World War, but the Allies quickly countered them with a suite of jamming techniques. In response, German scientists equipped a variant of the Henschel Hs 294 glide bomb with a television transmitter. The bomb could be remotely guided towards its target by visual imaging. Problems with overcontrolling (causing the image to jump all over the TV screen) immediately surfaced and the television version reportedly never was used in combat. During the 1960s the U.S. successfully deployed a television-controlled glide bomb: the Martin Marietta "Walleye." The Walleye became the first of a series of precision guided munitions ("smart bombs"). In May 1967, Navy pilots began using the television guided bombs and in one attack scored a direct hit on Hanoi's main power station. A second raid knocked the plant out of operation. But more important to our focus, Vietnam saw the introduction of a series of unmanned, highly capable spy planes built and supported in operations by the Ryan Aeronautical Company.

Along with the emergence of the new Special Forces military commands (JSOC and SOCOM), the development of drones has been so significant that it deserves to be explored in some detail. Over time the term remotely piloted vehicle (RPV) would evolve first into remotely piloted aircraft (RPA), then unmanned aerial vehicle (UAV), then unmanned combat air vehicle (UCAV)—with all of them ultimately becoming generically referred to as drones. The evolution of the drone occurred over some five decades, beginning with the awarding, in 1960, of a USAF contract of $200,000 to Ryan Aeronautical for the adaptation of its Firebee target drones for "unmanned, remotely guided photographic surveillance" missions.[672]

The modest project, known as Red Wagon, immediately ran into tough sledding at the Pentagon. Future Defense Secretary Harold Brown, at the time the Pentagon's chief weapons consultant, delayed the project by a full year and a half; ironically, years later it would be Brown who would frequently discuss how cruise missiles would revolutionize warfare. The assistant secretary of the Air Force verbally ordered the project canceled, but never issued a written order to that effect. So the project proceeded, sustained by the obvious challenges highlighted in both low-level and high-altitude photo reconnaissance over Cuba during the Cuban Missile Crisis in 1962.[673]

During eight years of Southeast Asian combat, the Ryan Aeronautical Company fielded a family of craft with over twenty-five variants for special tasks including both photographic and electronic intelligence collection.[674] It was a new technology: many flights produced useless photographs; others were shot down or simply failed to return for pickup. The first twenty-seven-foot "big wing" version became operational in 1965, used for high-altitude daylight photography. Nighttime photography began in 1967 and low-altitude photographic work began in 1967 and 1968. Versions with real-time television feeds were launched in 1972 and real-time data transmission began in 1974 and 1975.[675] Eventually the H and T versions would obtain a high-altitude capability of up to seventy-five thousand feet, carry fuel for over four hours of flight, and be able to photograph a strip twenty-two miles wide over some eight hundred miles. Real-time video through nose cameras would be added along with real-time data streaming of electronic and signals intelligence collection data.[676]

The success of Ryan's craft under actual combat conditions, their technological progress, and the number of models fielded in a short time were nothing short of amazing. The capabilities of those variants were equally impressive. The first model had a range of some twelve hundred miles, a photo capability from fifty-five thousand feet, and imaging resolution of two feet from that altitude. New variants provided continuous low-level, high-quality photography of denied areas and moved into offensive armed combat mode by launching both Maverick and Hobo "smart bombs."[677]

Ryan also developed the capability for its jet engine craft to be carried and launched from C-130 Hercules aircraft. That air deployment potential greatly extended their range and mission flexibility. In one mission, a Ryan RPV was carried by aircraft out of Kadena, Japan, was launched near Hainan Island off the South China coast, completed its mission over China, and was recovered in Taiwan. Ultimately a C-130 aircraft was configured to carry four RPVs for operational missions. The RPVs could be removed on land or even in midair at the end of a mission.[678] Ryan even developed the capability for ship-based launch of the craft.

The RPVs were strikingly successful, scoring firsts in many areas of photography, electronic and signals intelligence, and unmanned aerial attacks. Some three thousand missions were flown over not only North Vietnam but covertly over Laos and China. And after the war was over—much like anything not related to large-scale, conventional warfare—the whole technology was virtually forgotten. In his comprehensive book *Lightning Bugs and other Reconnaissance Drones*, William Wagner wrote that as of 1982, not a single RPV was operational, although the original Ryan Firebee target drones were still flying. Of course it had been Strategic Air Command that had benefited most from the classified "Lightning Bug" operation.

SAC's interest had been in reconnaissance, bombing missions, and saving pilot lives. Some five thousand airmen had been killed and over a thousand were missing in action during the Vietnam conflict. In contrast, 3,435 RPV missions had been flown, with some 554 of them lost in action and no lives lost.

The Vietnam War ended and the remotely piloted vehicles were scrapped. National security returned to a Cold War posture and by 1981, the U.S. military just wasn't thinking about RPVs. It was thinking about improved ICBMs, neutron weapons, and a much bigger Navy. Still, a few individuals were a bit more foresighted, if not immediately influential. Dr. Edward Teller, most often referred to as the father of atomic weapons, was one of those individuals. In 1981 he provided testimony to the General Accounting Office review of the potential of RPVs. Teller was once again on the money with his prediction, "The unmanned vehicle today is a technology akin to the importance of radars and computers in 1935."[679]

Actually Dr. Teller was only a bit ahead of real-world events. By the end of that same decade at least a few unmanned air vehicles were again in action with the military in the Gulf War. They were a far cry from what Ryan had flown in Southeast Asia. The Gulf War remotely piloted vehicles were largely derivative of small battlefield camera systems first flown successfully by the Israeli army. The U.S. Navy, Marines, and Army operated two types in the Gulf. The more sophisticated—Pioneer, an Israeli development—was some fourteen feet long and powered by a twenty-six-horsepower snowmobile engine. It had a range of approximately one hundred miles and a flight time of five hours. It was launched by catapult and carried a video camera that could take high-quality pictures from two thousand feet and transmit them some hundred miles. The Navy flew about one hundred RPV missions during the Gulf War, primarily for target spotting and damage assessment of its long-range battleship gun bombardments. The Marines flew ninety-four and the Army forty-eight.[680] The Gulf War RPVs were in support of conventional combat on well-defined battlefields and were flown under the shield of total air superiority. They were useful but their limited range and flying times prevented them from being a true solution for real-time, flexible combat intelligence in remote areas—much less a flexible attack system capable of remaining on station over hours or even days.

The CIA continued to be interested in an "endurance-class" aerial platform and followed a Defense Department project (Teal Rain) that was initially conducted with Leading Systems, Inc. The craft under consideration used a four-cylinder engine with a pusher propeller; it was nicknamed Amber. Amber was being developed for reconnaissance, electronic intelligence collection, and potential use as a low-cost cruise missile. The basic Amber platform was flown in 1986. It was especially interesting to the CIA because it offered an extended loiter time of some thirty-eight hours, and had a range of approximately twelve hundred miles. It was also equipped with a two-way data link and a nose-mounted television camera, which added a real-time control capability. That sort of true remote control meant that not only could information be passed back to an intelligence center but be an Amber-type craft could have weapons capability added and be used to actually carry out an attack after its intelligence had been analyzed and targets identified.

Amber was able to fly for almost forty hours and continued to be studied as a type of low-cost cruise missile platform. Some seven Amber craft were built, and by 1989 the Army had conducted field trials with three of them. Seven were delivered to the government but in 1990 the whole program was canceled, reportedly due to budget constraints. The original company that had developed Amber went into serious financial difficulties at that time and was acquired by General Atomics. General Atomics continued the unmanned aerial vehicle (by then simply known as UAV) project on its own, building a refined version of Amber designated the GNAT.[681]

In 1993, the Joint Chiefs needed a short-term solution for surveillance in the Bosnian UN peacekeeping operation and turned to the GNAT. Because military procurement was so slow, the program was turned over to the CIA, and in 1994 the Agency flew GNAT missions in Bosnia from a base in Albania. In the meantime, General

Atomics continued development and produced the next generation of UAVs—the Predator and the Global Hawk. There seems to be a bit of confusion over whether the craft flown in Bosnia was an upgraded variant of the GNAT or actually the first generation of its follow-up, the Predator; very possibly both craft were used.

According to CIA officer Henry Crumpton—who was personally involved in pre-9/11 CIA activities in Afghanistan—the CIA's Special Activities Division had been enthused over an early unmanned aerial vehicle of more limited capabilities and with no satellite data link. It was certainly an improvement for remote intelligence collection, but never could have been turned into a truly interactive weapon under remote control. But in 2000, marching orders came from CIA Director George Tenet to go after Al-Qaeda and bin Laden. A deadline of nine months was set to put a remote intelligence operation in Afghanistan and a budget of $5 million was allocated to a UAV. The CIA turned to General Atomics and a Predator reportedly left over from use in Bosnia.[682]

In the meantime, the Air Force had begun tests of arming the Predator—using the "Big Safari" rapid procurement program discussed previously. The armed variant had to have reinforced wings, weapons pylons, and a laser designator as well as remote video imaging and firing control. As early as February 2001, supersonic Hellfire missiles had been successfully fired. The CIA wanted armed Predators for Afghanistan and its bin Laden hunt.[683] Even with a rush program in place, the armed versions were not available in the fall of 2001, but some sixty Predators were used in the post-9/11 Afghan military campaign against the Taliban and Al-Qaeda.

From that point on, the Predator and its variants, first the Predator B (redesignated as the MQ-9 Reaper), would become synonymous with antiterrorist, clandestine operations. Reaper versions of the Predator have a much more powerful turboprop engine, which allows them to carry about fifteen times more weaponry and cruise at over three times the speed of the initial MQ-1 Predator. Some thirty-six feet long, with a wingspan of sixty-five feet and a payload of almost four thousand pounds, the Reaper can cruise at around two hundred miles per hour for some fourteen hours, with a range of over eleven hundred miles, and a service ceiling of fifty thousand feet.

Using hard points on the Reaper's wings, Hellfire missiles as well as Paveway II and joint direct attack munitions (JDAM) bombs are carried for air launch.[684] As of 2014, the next generation of extended-range Predator B drones is anticipated to have both a significantly improved mission radius of some twenty-nine hundred nautical miles and a potential of staying airborne for two to three times longer, possibly over forty hours. While the Predator drones do have attack capability, their primary use is in surveillance, reconnaissance, and intelligence collection. It is the MQ-9 Reaper that ultimately became the JSOC's primary "hunter/killer" tool. Over time the Reaper was used extensively during the Iraq War. Only six were in service as of 2006, but some fifty-four were in action by 2010; that year also represented the peak inventory of Predators, with 174 available.

The Predator is ideal for use in regions that do not have interceptor aircraft or extensive antiaircraft weapons, yet neither the Predator nor the Reaper is truly comparable to the Vietnam-era Ryan RPVs in terms of range and intelligence-collection options. Currently the U.S. Air Force operates the Global Hawk family of craft for the types of high-altitude, extended-range missions that were first conducted in Southeast Asia. Such missions are much more ambitious and demanding in terms of overall intelligence, surveillance, and reconnaissance (ISR) equipment suites. The Global Hawk craft have a wingspan of 130 feet, turbofan jet engines, a ceiling of some sixty-five thousand feet, and a range of over fifteen thousand miles. They carry extensive real-time sensor suites and represent the currently operational successor to the host of innovative firsts flown by Ryan Aeronautical. Global Hawks are expensive to operate though, and in 2013, the Air Force proposed to decrease their inventory and return to manned U-2 aircraft for a number of missions being performed by Global Hawks.

The need for an enhanced Special Forces capability emerged from the PLO terror attacks of the 1980s, primarily their seizures of commercial aircraft and cruise ships. Those incidents had all involved hostage taking and suggested the need for crack specially trained and rapid-response hostage rescue teams. The painful failure of the Eagle Claw Iranian hostage rescue mission brutally highlighted the hard reality that Special Forces had become neglected following the Vietnam War era. That mission also demonstrated the fact that it was foolhardy to expect to assemble impromptu forces from the different services—who had never trained with each other, shared equipment, or even used standard communications protocols—and expect anything other than potential disaster. That failure triggered a reappraisal and a move to preserve and improve the tools at hand.

It had taken decades, from the joint services command operations in Vietnam to the formation of an independent Joint Special Operations Command; from the disaster of Eagle Claw in Iran to ongoing joint training, common communications equipment, and weapons of truly integrated Special Operations Forces. The military organization had come into place, evolved, and been equipped with weapons specifically tailored to its needs.

In 1996, Osama bin Laden and Al-Qaeda formally declared war on America and Americans around the globe. America had dedicated and deadly new enemies; initially it underestimated them but ultimately a brand-new form of warfare emerged to address the terrorist threat. It was going to be a combination of covert and conventional practices—it would evolve in the hunt for bin Laden and come to its full potential in Afghanistan in 2001.

CHAPTER 24

A Turn to "Gray Warfare"

In 1998 Osama bin Laden and Al-Qaeda formally declared war on the West, America, and Americans around the globe. Rather than overtly responding, the U.S. covertly accelerated its targeted assassination campaign against Osama bin Laden. A presidential kill order was in effect, but to act on it the CIA was going to have to go after him, in Afghanistan. Their initial mission was highly focused, beginning with intelligence collection intended to lay the groundwork for lethal action against bin Laden. The effort was led by the CIA; there would be no intermediaries this time—CIA officers only would go into the field to establish personal relations with certain contacts within the anti-Taliban trial alliance. And the effort succeeded, to a point. The CIA established a network of some thirty paid Afghan assets dedicated to locating and tracking bin Laden down. The group was paid $10,000 a month; operating in Afghanistan always involved cash payments. The Afghan assets, designated as the GE/SENIORS, trailed and monitored bin Laden. On occasion they reported his exact whereabouts, but even then there was the fundamental problem of how to respond once he was located.[685]

Cruise missile attacks were not the answer to attacking him: there was simply too much lag time, on the order of hours, for a strike to be approved, missiles to be fired, and missiles to arrive at a target hundreds of miles away. The alternative was to get enough human intelligence to support sending in American Special Forces for a night attack on bin Laden. Such a mission would have required multiple helicopters and some forty personnel. It also would have been highly risky, flying some nine hundred miles to the target, with no combat recovery capability and no operating bases on the Afghan borders.[686] Despite the emergence of a Special Operations Command and the evolution of integrated joint Special Operations Forces under JSOC, there was still considerable angst over the disastrous Eagle Claw Iranian hostage mission during the Carter Administration.

In January 2000, the National Security Council issued a qualifying directive to the CIA: it was going to have to locate and positively identify bin Laden as a target—and then it would have to provide NSC-level decision makers with that information in real time in order for them to actually approve an executive kill order that had been in place for over three years. The new 2000 NSC order was given with the assumption that no American military would operate on the ground inside Afghanistan; there would be no American "boots on the ground." There was no American declaration of war in place and the elimination of bin Laden was to be done at a distance; the target was simply too remote to risk the capture or death of American personnel. That issue would arise again and again in regard to attacking terrorists in remote areas. And it would also be highlighted as one of the key concerns with conventional American military doctrine.

Standard military practice required that troops were deployed on the ground only when there were provisions to provide rescue and/or medical support during combat. No such capability existed for Afghanistan operations. Later, following the attacks of 9/11, that same issue would delay deployment of Special Operations Forces into Afghanistan, leaving the initial CIA paramilitary teams on the ground and on their own. And to set the bar even higher for the CIA's initial mission against bin Laden, its counterterrorism unit was also advised that setting up an actual CIA paramilitary base in-country to support the operation was simply "too dangerous and too expensive."[687]

The CIA's Counterterrorism Center (CTC) had been formed in early 1986; it had taken time and increasing budgets to establish its influence within the CIA, not only with the National Clandestine Service (NCS) but out to the geographic regions and CIA stations.[688] As the CTC's efforts in tracking bin Laden advanced, it became increasingly involved with other agencies—in particular the Joint Chiefs intelligence and operations staff. Taking the initiative onto themselves, a joint working group consisting of members of CTC, NSC (Counterterrorism Security Group), and the Joint Chiefs/DOD began to explore a technical solution—the use of unmanned aircraft for surveillance and intelligence collection. There had previously been joint interest in the use of an unmanned aerial vehicle (UAV), but the initial technology involved craft that did not have satellite link communications capability for real-time command and control, something that was going to be needed for action against bin Laden in Afghanistan.

CIA counterterror team leader Henry Crumpton describes the acquisition of a military UAV that was "collecting dust" in a DOD warehouse after being used over Bosnia in 1995. He also discusses the extensive effort required to create a team capable of not only operating the craft, but conducting the mapping and building of the technical targeting system needed to create an advanced, real-time intelligence network covering Taliban and Al-Qaeda targets in Afghanistan.[689] Before the arrival of the UAV in Afghanistan (launched and controlled from a secret base in Uzbekistan), targeting bin Laden had been quite frustrating to CIA operations officers and field personnel. Some of them had harsh words about the apparent timidity of senior Clinton Administration figures in regard to kill strikes on bin Laden. Others have described CIA Director George Tenet as politically "risk-averse," and it appears that it was Tenet himself who hesitated to push the president to order a strike in more than one instance.[690]

Still, senior CIA officers pushing the president to covert action do assume their own level of political risk, personally and for the Agency; a similar reluctance to push occurred during the Kennedy

Administration when CIA officers declined to lobby President Kennedy for air attacks during the Bay of Pigs landings. In defense of Tenet's caution, NSC counterterrorism head Richard Clarke, a participant in the decisions and someone not known for timidity, notes that on at least two occasions Tenet had to inform the president that the source who had located bin Laden's whereabouts was a single human informant. Tenet could offer the president no absolute confirmation of the bin Laden identification. In one incident the Agency would later confirm it had not been bin Laden, and the target itself was directly adjacent to a hospital.[691]

The deployment and operation of unmanned aerial vehicles quickly showed itself to be a major advance in intelligence collection, very possibly comparable to the CIA's development of the U-2 or its advanced reconnaissance satellites. Even in terms of the hunt for bin Laden, the craft proved successful. In one instance, a combination of human intelligence and real-time video surveillance indeed produced real-time imaging of bin Laden. Yet the fundamental problem remained that even with a positive identification, the time required to pull together the NSC principals, to receive authority to strike, and to launch against the target from a Navy submarine in the Indian Ocean was some six hours. CIA counterterrorism officers could see bin Laden in real time, but they could not guarantee bin Laden would remain at the target site for an additional six hours. Therefore the attack was not approved.[692] In pursuit of the mission, one obvious but technically challenging solution involved equipping the UAV with Hellfire missiles, under remote firing control. But such armed craft were still not available.

Following George W. Bush's election in November 2000, CIA Director Tenet and his deputy had given the new president a two-hour-plus briefing on the Al-Qaeda threat. It was considered "immediate" and described as "tremendous." Tenet placed bin Laden as among the top three threats to the United States. In October 2000, towards the end of the Clinton Administration, an Al-Qaeda cell in Yemen successfully attacked the U.S. Navy destroyer *Cole*, killing seventeen American sailors. Al-Qaeda had abortively tried to attack another

Navy vessel at the turn of the century, in a series of Al-Qaeda "millennium plots." That initial attack had escaped notice at the time because the group had exploded and sunk its own boat. The *Cole* attack was investigated by the FBI and the CIA, both of which were unable to conclusively identify the terrorist group as Al-Qaeda at the time. Senior administration principals were unwilling to retaliate without a firm identification and the Pentagon did not press the issue. There was no covert or overt response to the *Cole* attack. It appears that even with the focus on bin Laden and his elimination, Al-Qaeda as a network was not a presidential-level national security priority at the end of the Clinton Administration and during the first months of the George W. Bush era.

There is confirmation that the Al-Qaeda network was not at the top of the threat list for senior members of the new Bush Administration. Following the 2001 attacks on America, the National Commission on Terrorist Attacks Upon the United States (the 9/11 Commission) investigated the question of prior warnings about a possible Al-Qaeda attack. Records collected by the 9/11 Commission documented that on some forty occasions, CIA Director Tenet's presidential daily briefing had generally mentioned Al-Qaeda and its threat potential. However, the commission located virtually no related emails or other correspondence from National Security Advisor Condoleezza Rice on the subject of terrorism or Al-Qaeda. There were also no presidential findings, directives, or memoranda of notifications on the subject. The commission also found a host of correspondence from National Security Council counterterrorism advisor Richard Clarke, pushing warnings throughout 2001 about an upcoming and catastrophic attack by Al-Qaeda. Clarke had vehemently requested a personal briefing with President Bush on the subject; he had routinely conducted such briefings for President Clinton. Rice had allowed Clarke to brief Bush on cyberterrorism but not on Al-Qaeda. The records also showed that during the Clinton Administration, Clarke had called a de facto meeting of the White House Principals Committee to discuss terrorist threats; that access ceased when he began to report to Rice during the George W. Bush Administration.[693]

In April 2001, the Deputies Committee of the NSC approved a policy request asking that President Bush issue a directive to arm and support the United Front (Northern Alliance) in Afghanistan. They felt that with enough military pressure, Al-Qaeda's focus could be diverted to Afghanistan. The CIA efforts at intelligence collection inside Afghanistan were already sending several million dollars a year to anti-Taliban forces. In July the deputies proposed that the NSC pursue a full-scale effort to support the tribal insurgencies in a military offensive against Al-Qaeda and the Taliban—essentially anything to divert bin Laden from his global terror plans.[694] By early September the Deputies Committee was recommending up to $200 million to arm and support the offensive. But as we have seen, such things can take considerable time when the president or at least the national security advisor is not personally driving the process. The draft, recommending a new initiative involving the Afghan tribes against Al-Qaeda, did not make it to President George W. Bush prior to September 11, 2001.

On that date, Al-Qaeda did strike America, hijacking commercial aircraft in four multiple suicide attacks on New York and Washington, D.C. There were 246 casualties on the four hijacked airliners, with no survivors. The attacks immediately brought about 2,996 deaths, with over three thousand additional injuries. A significant number of casualties were taken by first-responder, fire, police, and medical personnel responding to the attacks. Citizens from ninety different countries were killed in the indiscriminate terror attacks. Following September 11, 2001, there was no doubt that America was going to massively escalate its efforts against bin Laden and Al-Qaeda in Afghanistan. In retrospect the only additional question seems to have been whether or not the American response was going to immediately involve Iraq as well.

An immediate effort certainly was made by George W. Bush Administration principals to connect the 9/11 attacks to Iraq state sponsorship. That effort is reflected in a very early conversation between President Bush and counterterrorism specialist Richard Clarke. The conversation occurred on the evening of September 12, 2001, outside the Situation Room in the White House:[695]

> PRESIDENT BUSH: I know you have a lot to do and all . . . but I want you, as soon as you can, to go back over everything. See if Saddam did this. See if he's linked in any way.
>
> CLARKE: But, Mr. President, Al-Qaeda did this!
>
> BUSH: I know, I know, but . . . see if Saddam was involved, just look. I want to know if any shred . . .
>
> CLARKE: Absolutely, we will look . . . again . . . but you know we have looked several times for state sponsorship of Al-Qaeda and not found any real linkage to Iraq. Iran plays a little, as does Pakistan, and Saudi Arabia, Yemen.
>
> BUSH: Look into Iraq, Saddam.

However, it soon became apparent that any agenda involving military action against Iraq was going to require a different justification than 9/11; in the interim, planning and preparations against Iraq were initiated. President Bush has confirmed that as early as November 2001, he instructed Defense Secretary Donald Rumsfeld to update the Pentagon's war plan for Iraq. Still, the first priority and the immediate response was to move against bin Laden and Al-Qaeda in Afghanistan.

The CIA took the lead in that new campaign, in a very traditional role—a combination of intelligence work and covert paramilitary action orchestrating tribal military action against the Taliban and its foreign fighters. In supporting the indigenous fighters, as in the earliest days of Laos and Vietnam, a mix of CIA operations (Special Activities Division, or SAD) officers, CIA military contractors, and eventually a small number of Special Forces teams would go on the ground inside Afghanistan. The result would be one of the CIA's most dramatically successful operations. The operation would also begin a transition to a new era of shadow warfare. No one ever doubted that America was going after bin Laden and Al-Qaeda, yet amazingly, there was still no declaration of war in place. Yet the CIA field teams continued to operate under standard covert warfare practices. It could hardly be called deniable, but it was done with as much distance as possible. The CIA was going to Afghanistan but the rules of engagement would be very, very strange.[696]

CIA officers had already begun going into Afghanistan, covertly organizing efforts to attack bin Laden during the Clinton Administration. They flew in surplus Russian military helicopters, purchased after having been abandoned at the end of the Soviet combat. Before September 2001, CIA officers had established contact with a number of insurgent tribal leaders and expanded their development of a new human intelligence network, with over a hundred sources. Days after the attacks of 9/11, CIA Director Tenet went to President Bush with a comprehensive plan for covert action in Afghanistan, including lethal action. He advised the president the cost would be major, some $1 billion for starters. Bush responded that there was no problem with that and there was no need to take the proposal to the NSC, much less to Congress.[697]

The first mission objective was simple: "Destroy the Al-Qaeda leadership" in Afghanistan. The second, much broader: "Remove their safe havens." Over a period of only months, CIA and Special Forces teams came together in a manner very similar to their predecessors in the Office of Special Services during World War II. It was one of the most demanding of all CIA paramilitary operations, involving very small numbers of American personnel working with large groups of Afghanistan tribal fighters. There had been no similar joint field combat operations between the CIA and U.S. Special Forces since the early days in Laos and later in South Vietnam under MACVSOG. It was a rapid learning experience for all parties and served as a prelude to a working relationship that would continue for over a decade in what would turn out to be a global campaign against radical religious terrorists and insurgents.

CIA operations teams led the way into Afghanistan. Although CIA officers had been going into the country again for some two years, the first post-9/11 team would be on its way to a transit airfield in Uzbekistan, the independent republic on the northern border of Afghanistan, by September 19. The team, led by Gary Schroen, was small and select, only a handful of highly experienced officers, including a communications officer, operations officers, and special action officers. Jawbreaker and the teams that followed were drawn from the Operations Directorate and its Special Activities Division. And the active-duty CIA military manpower pool was going to fall short of the demands that would be increasingly made of it, especially once the CIA came to understand that the administration was not going to deploy the regular American military into Afghanistan. The only commitment was going to be a very limited number of Special Forces personnel.

The Jawbreaker team went into Afghanistan covertly, first on an Air Force C-5 transport to Germany, and then on a chartered L-100 (the civilian version of the C-130 transport) to Tashkent in Uzbekistan. From there they proceeded across denied, Taliban-controlled airspace using a modified war-surplus Russian military helicopter. An earlier Russian helicopter, used in previous CIA flights into Afghanistan, had crashed after its last use by the CIA mission.[698] Team Jawbreaker had only ten men. That included Schroen, a deputy, one case officer, a communications officer, a medic, a combination of former special operations and paramilitary personnel, two pilots, and a mechanic.[699] As part of the Jawbreaker effort, Schroen carried $3 million in cash to gain the cooperation of the Afghans. Everyone was well aware that any effort in Afghanistan was going to be a pay-as-you-go operation. The Afghans had seen too many "visitors" and "friends" come and go to risk their forces on promises.

Schroen's team continued on its own for some weeks until Special Forces A-teams were inserted to back them up. Schroen had been in CIA operations for thirty-two years, a veteran of the "old school" field operations the Agency had done in past decades. With service in Iran, Turkey, Saudi Arabia, and Dubai, he had also been chief of the Kabul station until events had led to its closure. As deputy chief of the Near East and South Asia Division of the Directorate of Operations, he was almost out the door to retirement when the 9/11 attacks occurred. He volunteered for the Afghanistan effort and personally led one of the most successful, high-risk CIA field units ever to go into a combat environment.

Team Jawbreaker's first priorities inside Afghanistan involved working with Northern Alliance commanders, convincing them of the new American determination to actively assist them against the Taliban and Al-Qaeda units they were fighting. Along with that, within days of arriving near the Northern Alliance front lines with the Taliban, the team began intelligence collection, laying the groundwork for going after Osama bin Laden and his leadership. Eliminating bin Laden was certainly a priority but it would have to come in time. Field intelligence was critical, with detailed GPS coordinates being essential for targeting the Taliban front lines.

Jawbreaker operated on the ground in a mountainous area some seventy miles north of the Afghan capital of Kabul. By September 27, Schroen was personally communicating with senior Northern Alliance commanders, and members of the team were working with the Afghan general who commanded some ten thousand fighters facing the Taliban lines on the plains stretching towards Kabul. The tribal fighters were experienced and had held back Taliban advances for years (even as the Taliban had been strengthened by large numbers of Arab jihadi volunteers). However, they lacked the numbers to advance against the heavily entrenched and fortified Taliban lines.

The Kabul battle front looked like classic trench warfare, with Northern Alliance troops facing a conventional battle line. The Taliban units were emplaced and dug into well-fortified positions. On top of that, independent brigades of well-trained and very well-equipped Arab jihadi fighters were in place at key points on the line. Platoons (40 fighters) and companies (140 fighters) of Arab jihadis were located across the front lines. CIA sources estimated that as many as five hundred a day were crossing the border from Pakistan.[700] After investigation and intelligence collection, Schroen's opinion was that with a massive American precision air bombardment, such as it had never experienced, the Taliban might simply collapse. He also argued that the collapse of the Kabul front and the loss of the capital at Kabul would have a major psychological effect on Taliban forces throughout the country.[701]

As the senior officer on the ground, Schroen expressed his estimate of the situation in a series of personal appraisals to CIA headquarters, and the appraisals were circulated for high-level review. The problem seems to have been that at the senior staff levels, there simply was no strategy consensus.[702] United States Central Command (CENTCOM)—responsible for countries in the Middle East, North Africa, and Central Asia—was taking a very measured, conventional approach to the situation and had not defined any initial role for its Special Forces. America was not in a declared war and the administration had issued no directives for conventional military engagement. In essence, the CIA had responded far more quickly than the strategy coming from the Bush Administration or the directions coming from the secretary of defense and the Joint Chiefs.

In fact, the overall situation was so vague and the lack of direction so significant that CIA headquarters informed Schroen that Special Operations Command had suggested that Schroen actually invite Special Operations Forces to join his team. At one point he was even chewed out by CIA headquarters for not resolving the issue of Special Forces deployment himself—a problem clearly one for the military leadership and not for a CIA field team deployed in the Afghan mountains. The only clear executive direction was that a bombing campaign against the Taliban was scheduled to begin in October. However, it was going to be a very conventional "infrastructure" effort, directed largely towards the southern part of the country and not against the large, massed Taliban formations in the North.

In the interim, Jawbreaker proceeded with constructing a detailed map of the Taliban front line area, built using GPS coordinates. The mapping would include GPS references for the Northern Alliance positions, protecting them from friendly fire in any attack, and a considerable number of Taliban targets were identified with specific GPS locations.[703] GPS target maps were going to be a prerequisite for precision attacks from B-52 and B-1 bombers, dropping five-hundred-pound to two thousand-pound conventional bombs (joint direct attack munitions, or JDAMs). The GPS intelligence effort was a risky one, but it was aided by the relatively "loose" nature of Afghan warfare. It had long been a practice that on certain occasions, combatants from both sides crossed the lines to visit friends and family when no engagements were in progress. That allowed opportunities for tribal fighters to actually carry GPS devices and record the coordinates of Taliban lines and installations during their crossings.

In *The Art of Intelligence,* Henry Crumpton describes not only the work and coordination that went into the collection of minutely detailed intelligence from multiple sources in Afghanistan, but also its consolidation with targeting information inside a system he describes as the "magic box." To quote Crumpton, the magic box eventually could and did, in real time, answer questions such as:

> *Was the enemy in a particular valley? What was their order of battle? Their weapons? Where are the known minefields? The status of tribal alliances with local Afghan tribes? Which Afghan tribal leaders, allied with the Taliban out of existential necessity or political convenience, would switch to our side? What were the plans and intentions of our Afghan allies . . . where were mosques, schools, hospitals and other potential no-strike structures. . . . What impact would specific UAV Hellfire shots have on the enemy.*[704]

And the "magic box" eventually dealt with a host of other related questions, not just for the planners at headquarters, but for the field paramilitary officers. As more intelligence was accumulated, it was capable of supporting surgical military actions against the Taliban that were totally unlike the brute-force sweeps and search-and-destroy efforts in Vietnam, and also totally unlike the Phoenix computer-supported counterinsurgency operations. Within the first year, Afghanistan would become a very different battlefield environment, and the CIA and Special Forces teams would have full claim on aircraft and missile strikes. When combined with satellite topographic mapping, the new computerized real-time mapping and imaging tool—the magic box—could even display video images of target zones, with real-time visualization of attacks. The multiagency team had managed not only to put that resource in play quickly but also to coordinate and provide it to both CENTCOM and SOCOM by the time they began major combat operations—with real-time computer feed of magic box information.

Afghanistan was both a diplomatic and a logistics challenge for conventional American military action. There were few American bases in the region and each of the nations housing them had its own internal politics and international relations to consider. Beyond that, America never formally declared war on the Taliban government of Afghanistan. Both diplomatic concerns and logistics issues seem to have ruled against the George W. Bush Administration committing to putting American army units on the ground in Afghanistan. Even something as fundamental as the provision of basic search and rescue for American air crews was a major initial problem.

The net result was that other than a very limited number of instances in which American Special Forces conducted helicopter-borne attacks against very specific high-value targets, there were initially no acknowledged Americans on the ground in Afghanistan. The CIA teams were operating covertly and the Special Forces that would eventually back them up were deployed for very low-profile action, for technical intelligence collection and targeting of American air strikes.

Sufficient support for the first series of long-range air strikes against the Taliban and Al-Qaeda was not available until October 8. Even then, initial air strikes were limited to some thirty-one targets, including air defenses and known Al-Qaeda training camps. After those targets were hit, many of the tactical aircraft were left to simply loiter, looking for new targets in the south. What was not happening was a major bombing effort in the north of the country, specifically against the Taliban lines outside the capital. The lack of strikes in the north was extremely frustrating to the Northern Alliance and to the CIA teams that were by then working with several northern commanders. Schroen described being informed by CIA headquarters that Central Command (CENTCOM) was attacking targets elsewhere because "they can't find the high value targets in the Kabul area." This was after Jawbreaker had just spent the previous two weeks sending back geo-coordinates for literally hundreds of high-value targets in precisely that area.[705]

By that point additional CIA teams had been covertly inserted and connected with Northern Alliance field commanders; they found them eager, but with different needs. Some were leading mobile forces against a mix of Taliban positions and were happy simply to accept money and supplies, allowing the CIA special action teams to join in their fights—in one instance the CIA team joined a mounted group and observed a dramatic cavalry charge against Taliban positions. Others found CIA cash to be equally effective, quickly causing tribal groups to switch allegiance.

But the Kabul front was a different matter: it would require massive and precision targeted air attack to break the stalemate there, something that was just not happening. Jawbreaker waited for weeks as October progressed, watching massed Taliban forces on the ground, while all the air strikes were directed towards infrastructure in the south. It was not until late October that the first Special Forces group (ODA-555, better known as Triple Nickel) arrived, bringing the capability for laser targeting of smart weapons.

By the end of October, forward combat air controllers were also in place.[706] But their targeting requests were still receiving only sporadic response as all the daily "packages" of aircraft were going to other areas. In some ways it sounds reminiscent of covert combat in Laos, where repeated calls for air support often drew only stragglers from the air packages going against North Vietnam, planes with leftover bombs or whose targets had been unavailable due to weather:

> *"Just hit the front lines for me . . . I can take Kabul, I can take Kunduz if you break the line for me. My guys are ready."*
>
> —GENERAL FAHIM, Afghanistan Northern Alliance commander, October 2001[707]

How's it going? Same as usual . . . more targets than a hound dog has fleas, and we'll be lucky to get two or three aircraft to respond to our requests for strikes . . . the target deck for today is sixty-five aircraft . . . high priority tank repair depots and warehouses down south . . . secondary targets include a troop barracks and supply depot south of Kabul . . . we'll get the leftovers if any are available.

—Special Forces Master Sergeant,
Triple Nickel, late October, 2001[708]

The fundamental issue was simply that traditions and habits are hard to break. Conventional warfare, state against state, has always involved destruction of defenses, command and control, and fixed-site targets. Even with Special Forces in place, the Afghan air attack remained targeted on fixed sites; the CIA/SOF teams were getting the "leftovers." If a target wasn't found or if munitions were left, only then would planes become available to them.[709] It was an ingrained Pentagon practice to focus on fixed targets but now they were attacking a basically undeveloped country with little infrastructure and a very limited number of strategic targets. The CIA teams on the ground could see the difference. Jawbreaker and Schroen kept sending cables to CIA Director Tenet. By the end of October, Tenet was pressing the issue with the White House and the principals. In doing so he faced both political and personal issues.

First, the Bush Administration principals continuously circled around not only the political issue of supporting the Northern Alliance in an attack on Kabul but also the possibility that they might actually succeed and take the capital. President George W. Bush and his senior advisors appear to have been extremely conflicted in regard to the political sensitivities of anti-Taliban groups in the south and also to the sensitivities of Pakistan, long opposed to the Northern Alliance (and with strong ties to the Taliban regime itself). The United States had made a huge investment in Pakistan during the struggle to oust the Soviets and had strong ties to the Pakistani establishment. It also appears, at least at that stage of the War on

Terror, that not many senior officers were willing to admit the extent to which the earlier Pakistani cooperation had been one-sided.

Secondly, General Tommy Franks, the military commander of CENTCOM, was not particularly impressed with the Northern Alliance commanders. Franks had already been lobbied on a number of occasions to focus air support in the north of Afghanistan; the lobbying had not worked.[710] When directly questioned by the principals about the forces opposing the Taliban, Franks replied, "I don't place any confidence in the opposition." Franks would not even admit that they could be trained.[711] The DIA (Defense Intelligence Agency) had also come in with a very negative estimate of Northern Alliance success. Overall, at the end of October, the president's advisors were generally subdued, expressing little or no confidence in the Afghans the CIA was working with—there was even talk of needing to put up to fifty-five thousand U.S. troops into combat.[712] As November began there was a growing concern that the whole effort might stall in place over the winter; President George W. Bush had clearly become frustrated by the situation. And as of November 4, Gary Schroen was in the process of being succeeded by a new CIA team leader, Gary Berntsen.

What Washington was discussing over and over again seemed to have very little to do with what the CIA was reporting from its people on the ground. Berntsen had his own special moments of frustration on the Kabul front. He described waiting on November 8, having organized a major two-pronged Northern Alliance attack against the lines north of Kabul. Thousands of troops were waiting for the massive air support they had been promised. As the day passed, the two B-52 formations, supposedly coming from the U.S. and from Diego Garcia in the Indian Ocean, were nowhere to be seen. Only two F-16 jets appeared over the front. The Northern Alliance commanders were less than pleased and only later did Berntsen find out the bombers had been rerouted to other targets, with no notice given to him.[713] Still, after much further lobbying, and with the increasing lack of targets elsewhere, air strikes began to shift north early in November, with immediate and devastating effect on the Taliban. The Taliban simply had no idea of what modern, precision bombing could be like—they had laughed at the limited strikes they had received to that point. But when the B-52s and B-1s moved north in strength, the Taliban began losing hundreds of men in each strike. The effect was exactly what Gary Schroen had predicted to headquarters in his messages of September and October.

The end result was also just as Schroen had earlier anticipated, and the speed with which the Taliban had been routed from the capital and much of the country was totally unanticipated (by Washington at least). By the middle of November, CENTCOM had definitely gotten the message and quantities of aircraft were on call to bomb fleeing Taliban forces; AC-130 gunships were also in action, dispatched by the Joint Force Air Component Command (JFACC), established in Saudi Arabia.[714] Berntsen was able to operate without the constant frustrations faced by Schroen, and the pace of combat escalated dramatically.

By the end of November 2001, some 90 percent of the air attacks had become tactical, hitting troop concentrations and emplacements on the Taliban front lines. More CIA and Special Forces teams were going on the ground, with different Afghan groups across the country. The Special Forces teams included intelligence and weapons NCOs (noncommissioned officers), medical and demolitions specialists, and Air Force combat controllers equipped with satellite radios and SOFLAM (Special Operations Forces laser acquisition markers). Once a target was "lighted" with the laser, the combat controller called in laser-guided ordnance, normally from jet attack aircraft. The combat controllers also provided directions for attacks using radar and infrared targeted munitions.

The close air support SOF units began to call in very heavy bombing, destroying hundreds of vehicles and bunkers and decimating thousands of Taliban. The Taliban defenses had no ability to withstand fifteen-thousand-pound BLU-82 "daisy cutter" bombs and U.S. air, and they offered no opposition at all. Berntsen described the total decimation created by the daisy cutters dropped out of the back of MC-130 aircraft as "profound in terms of casualties and psychological impact."[715] The weapons had originally been devised to clear landing areas in Vietnam. Once the air assault began, the Taliban literally collapsed before the tribal forces, advancing behind the air attacks. Almost immediately, large-scale warlord defections began and thousands of Taliban and Al-Qaeda fighters were reportedly fleeing south, towards the mountains across the Pakistan border.

The overall effect of total air control and precision-guided weapons was comparable to that seen in the Iraqi flight out of Kuwait at the end of the Gulf War—only magnified by much more deadly weapons and precision targeting from both the air and ground. Events in actual combat had proved Schroen correct in the assessments he had submitted in his earliest advisory notices from Jawbreaker. At the beginning of October 2001, the Northern Alliance had held perhaps 15 percent of the country; by late November it held approximately half. By December it was in charge of most of the country, with the exception of the eastern and Pakistani border regions.

Of course, that border region was exactly where bin Laden had fled. The CIA followed, despite the fact that it had very few connections to tribal commanders in the region and only limited intelligence. And its personnel were going to be dramatically outnumbered if the team was detected by the substantial Al-Qaeda bands that had retreated to the east. The CIA team's only comfort was a verbal agreement with the Special Forces commander that if they made it in and found their targets, Special Forces Command would join them.[716]

In December, Berntsen and a group of some twenty CIA Special Activities Division paramilitary and soldiers from the 5th Special Forces Group were inserted by helicopter into the foothills of the mountain area where bin Laden was suspected to be staying. The area was defended by a large force of Al-Qaeda fighters. The Americans moved into the mountains and directed very close-in air attacks, including B-52 saturation bombing. Within a week Berntsen's group was joined by an additional seventy Army, Navy, and Air Force Special Forces personnel, who had come overland to support the bombing campaign. Several hundred Al-Qaeda fighters were either killed or captured in the effort, eventually accepting a truce. It is thought that bin Laden may have used the truce period to make his way out of the region and into Pakistan.

Berntsen himself notes that the relatively impromptu "shotgun marriage" of CIA and Special Forces had worked well overall, but he also expressed his extreme dissatisfaction with the fact that his repeated requests to CENTCOM for American troops to close the mountain passes—passes bin Laden would ultimately use for his escape—were ignored. Despite the urgent CIA requests, CENTCOM declined to send in the some eight hundred airborne Rangers that would have been needed to seal off the area.[717] Ultimately the CIA was forced to organize a ground operation involving paid local tribal militias as well CIA SAD and Special Forces personnel. By December 17, 2003, that operation had overrun the Tora Bora bunkers in the mountains but found no sign of bin Laden. In his book on the Afghanistan operations, Berntsen wrote that he was convinced they had isolated bin Laden's location within Tora Bora and that Al-Qaeda detainees had confirmed that for them—stating that bin Laden had escaped eastward into Pakistan. Gary Schroen corroborates Berntsen's assessment, as do certain references in Pentagon documents.[718] In contrast, CENTCOM commander Tommy Franks remained unconvinced that bin Laden was ever at Tora Bora or could have been captured there:

> *We don't know to this day whether Mr. bin Laden was at Tora Bora in December, 2001. Some intelligence sources said he was; others indicated he was in Pakistan at the time. . . .Tora Bora was teeming with Taliban and al Qaeda operatives . . . but Mr. bin Laden was never within our grasp.*[719]

General Franks eventually testified to the 9/11 Commission that he was satisfied with the decision process by which Afghan tribal forces were left to stop bin Laden. Based on the remarks in his own book, CIA Jawbreaker team leader Berntsen most definitely was not.[720]

America had not declared war against Al-Qaeda or the Taliban. Yet Congress had passed a resolution authorizing the president to conduct all necessary acts of both overt and covert warfare. And the George W. Bush Administration had done both, simultaneously. The CIA had covertly gone into Afghanistan to work with the anti-Taliban tribal leaders. American Special Forces had gone in to support them, but no large military formations had put boots on the ground. At the same time, massive amounts of American air power and selected strikes by armed CIA drones had driven the Taliban out of power and brought about regime change in the country. In the end, the amazingly quick ouster of the Taliban had been accomplished with some 110 CIA and 316 Special Forces personnel on the ground—supporting the Afghan indigenous forces and in turn supported by American air power.

The combination of covert and overt warfare in Afghanistan created a new paradigm for military action: no deniability, covert CIA activities, and a very overt air campaign. Indeed, deniability, the benchmark for traditional covert action, would never be a real option in the long War on Terror that followed. The legal underpinnings that had separated covert operations were still in place, but future actions would see joint CIA and Special Forces teams deployed on clandestine but certainly not deniable missions. And the CIA and the Air Force would significantly expand their use of drone attacks on terrorist targets—and the drone strikes could hardly be considered deniable. The move into gray areas of merged covert and clandestine activity was escalating and it would produce a whole new set of issues, especially in the continued absence of any formal declarations of war.

And beyond Afghanistan, there was Iraq. Senior figures in the Bush Administration continued to approach the global terrorist threat in terms of state sponsorship, adopting the strategy of "preemptive warfare" against regimes viewed as potential sponsors. The first public leak of the Bush Administration Iraq agenda and the fact that specific military planning was actually in progress came in September 2002. It revealed itself in remarks by the administration's chief economic advisor, Larry Lindsey, to the media. Lindsey offered an opinion that the cost of a war with Iraq would have only a minor effect on the U.S. economy, something between $100 and $200 billion, only 1 to 2 percent of the U.S. economy.[721] When the press remarks were reported to President Bush, he was clearly not happy: "It's unacceptable . . . he shouldn't be talking about that."[722]

Potential terrorist affiliations and access to weapons of mass destruction became the centerpiece in the Bush case for mandatory action against Saddam Hussein. Ultimately it led to a full-scale conventional military invasion and to regime change in Iraq. According to sources close to President Bush, he may well have held his own deeper ideological motivation for the effort, one involving the potential value of spreading democracy in the Middle East, viewing democracy as a stabilizing force against escalating radicalism.[723] In that sense, Bush's Iraqi decision seems to have been a mix of concern over terrorism and an older worldview of America, harkening back to earlier presidential beliefs in a national duty to blunt and push back against the global expansion of communism.

The Bush Administration's public campaign against Saddam Hussein and Iraq was reminiscent of President Nixon's highly visible public relations effort against the Sandinistas and Nicaragua. In the case of the Bush Administration, the effort was more comprehensive, and sophisticated, and ultimately much more successful. That campaign is described by Scott McClellan, traveling press secretary for the Bush campaign, who served as principal deputy White House secretary and, from 2003 to 2006, as White House press secretary. He provides an insider view of the Bush campaigns, first to present the case for the Iraq invasion, then for dealing with damage control ranging from the lack of the promised weapons of mass destruction to what eventually became a virtual civil war inside Iraq. We dealt with the selling of the Nicaraguan campaign in considerable detail; in regard to Iraq we are fortunate to be able to refer the reader to a primary source, McClellan's book *What Happened: Inside the Bush White House and Washington's Culture of Deception.*

At first it seemed that President Bush might have relied strictly on covert action against Iraq rather than turning to overt military force. During 2002 he had signed a new finding directing a covert effort against Saddam Hussein and Iraq. More than $100 million was allocated to the new Iraq operations, more than the $70 million the CIA had authorized for bin Laden and Al-Qaeda in Afghanistan. The CIA began a major new intelligence collections effort inside Iraq in preparation for the insertion of joint CIA–Special Forces teams. Such teams were already being used in Afghanistan.[724] Tens of millions of covert funding dollars were spent in recruiting and training a surrogate paramilitary force of exiled Iraqis, known as the Scorpions. It was anticipated that they would incite popular uprisings in conjunction with U.S. military intervention. In the end the teams played no role in the eventual American invasion of Iraq and were given duties as translators and guards.[725]

Ultimately, Bush turned to conventional warfare in Iraq and despite his early remarks about not playing a "police role" in Afghanistan—"U.S. forces will not stay, we don't do police work"[726]—America became not only involved in police and security work in Afghanistan and Iraq, but also deeply immersed in expensive nation-building in both countries. Bush's remarks would evolve into massive troop surges into both countries for security purposes, and huge expenditures for infrastructure and development work.

The priorities of the George W. Bush Administration have been addressed by others, in great detail. Our purpose in raising the topic is that those priorities appear to represent the first phase of a tipping point, a transition in which targeting of both overt and covert warfare began to shift from the more classic ideological, state-oriented focus to a more pragmatic effort, focused on individuals. Early in the White House discussions about a response to the Al-Qaeda attacks, Defense Secretary Rumsfeld raised the question, "Why shouldn't we go after Iraq, not just Al-Qaeda?" Vice President Cheney also continued to raise the issue of state sponsorship for the terror attacks.[727] Of course, in one very real sense, sponsor states were easier targets, especially for a massive response by the U.S. military. As Rumsfeld himself later commented, after the first round of air attacks in Afghanistan, if there were not enough obvious targets there, there were plenty in Iraq.[728] There were indeed more targets, but undeclared warfare in Iraq was going to get a great deal more complex than the CIA's dramatic ninety-day campaign in Afghanistan.

CHAPTER 25

Other Boots on the Ground

The initial post-9/11 campaign in Afghanistan has to be considered as one of the most successful CIA military efforts ever conducted—matching operations conducted by the British Special Operations Executive (SOE), Operation Jedburgh in Europe, or the OSS in Burma during the Second World War. Lessons learned from the early joint operations in Afghanistan eventually helped transform American military practices, especially in counterterrorism operations. Long-range, precise, close air support and special operations teams would join with the escalating use of both unarmed and armed Predator drones for kill or capture operations—especially in remote and denied areas where inserting large bodies of conventional forces would be virtually impossible. As the first decade of the new century advanced, it was becoming clear that America's special military forces were assuming a major role in both individual clandestine missions against terrorist targets and regime-building activities in Iraq and Afghanistan as the security situation grew dramatically worse in each country. U.S. Special Forces grew at a rapid pace to support the increasing security demand. Estimates as of 2010 put the number of SOF deployed overseas at some nine thousand combatants, virtually all in Afghanistan and Iraq.[729]

As their missions expanded it also became evident that distance, if not classic deniability, was still needed for many missions. Nobody would doubt that it was actually America going after Al-Qaeda and its supporters but certain of the actions were questionable in terms of international law, and objectionable to the countries involved as violations of their sovereignty. Certainly, operations against the Taliban and Al-Qaeda in eastern Afghanistan and across the border into Pakistan, or the pursuit of Al-Qaeda-affiliated rebels in Iraq operating across the Iranian border, posed obvious sovereignty challenges.

As we have seen over the decades, the solution for legal distance often involved the use of independent paramilitary operators. When independents working for the CIA in Indonesia were exposed in the 1950s, President Eisenhower tried to evade the issue by describing them as "soldiers of fortune." Later, CIA contract employees in Africa during the 1960s and 1970s were described as "mercenaries." In Afghanistan, in the period immediately following the attacks of 9/11, a new term appeared: "contractor."

In broad terms there are two types of CIA military employees. There are those more permanently on the rolls, who pass a comprehensive screening process, including polygraph testing and background checks for advanced security clearances. Such employees are currently referred to as blue badgers, apparently based on the color of identification cards they are issued for access to secure facilities. Another category is that of more temporary employees, individuals who pass a lesser level of security screening or background requirements, but who are kept on call for special missions or to bolster the rolls when a sudden demand occurs—as it did in Afghanistan. These personnel are referred to as green badgers.

Both types of CIA military employees eventually appeared in Afghanistan, and both types are often referred to as contractors. That is not an entirely accurate usage, especially as compared to other types of non-CIA security personnel we are going to discuss, but the term has been widely used. Long-term CIA paramilitary personnel have extensive military backgrounds, normally with special operations skills and considerable expertise in intelligence tradecraft and security—they know how to operate covertly. Rip Robertson might well serve as a benchmark for this type of shadow warrior. Another individual who defines the class is Billy Waugh.

One of the best-known of the CIA military employees going into Afghanistan—and one of the earliest to go—was Billy Waugh, alumnus of the Army Airborne as far back as 1948. After service in Korea he moved into Army Special Forces, eventually serving under MACVSOG in Special Forces A-teams in Vietnam, and in Laos in the 1960s. He retired from the Army in 1972 after a series of extremely dangerous missions in Southeast Asia, including insertion into denied North Vietnamese Army territory. During that period, Waugh was assigned to the CIA's Special Activities Division. After retirement Waugh, along with a number of other Special Forces veterans, worked in Ed Wilson's activities in Libya.[730] However, Waugh was approached covertly and informed that although the activities were not CIA-directed, he was to remain in place and collect photographic and other intelligence information during his work in Libya. Waugh relates that when things went bad in Libya and he managed to get out with nothing but the clothes he was wearing, he also carried a dozen rolls of undeveloped film.[731]

Waugh was called by the CIA to go "black" inside the Sudan during the Clinton era, tracking a variety of suspected terrorists—including bin Laden. And after 9/11, at the age of seventy-one and as possibly the oldest active CIA paramilitary officer, he was again called back to recruit contract employees to bulk up the CIA's move into Afghanistan. He would take his team into perhaps the most high-risk area of the country—the south, beyond the reach of the tribal alliance the CIA had already connected to in northern Afghanistan. Jawbreaker leader Berntsen describes Waugh's arrival in Kabul, sent along with a Special Forces colonel detailed to the CIA's Special Activities Division. He describes their mission as that of "training indigenous terrorist pursuit teams."[732] Based on later remarks from Waugh himself, as might have been expected, he did a good bit more than just train the teams and send them off to hunt Al-Qaeda.

Men like Waugh operated in the dangerous border regions of eastern Afghanistan in the first years of the American presence there, hunting Taliban and Al-Qaeda leaders. The long-term American effort in Afghanistan, lasting over a decade and eventually involving large numbers of conventional American military, is not our subject. However, shadow warfare in Afghanistan did continue for some time after Tora Bora and the failed capture of bin Laden. We have relatively few official details on those efforts. What wc do have is largely anecdotal, with no supporting documents. Much of it seems to have been done based on verbal instructions, with authorization based on presidential findings authorizing the elimination of both bin Laden and Al-Qaeda leadership in general. In the years immediately following 9/11, there was little concern about any American activity directed towards that goal and to a large extent many of the standard rules of CIA operations had gone by the board. Commander in Chief George W. Bush had made that quite clear:

> *I want you to understand that we are at war and we will stay at war until this is done. Nothing else matters. Everything is available for the support of this war. Any barriers in your way, they're gone. Any money you need, you have it. This is our only agenda. . . . I don't care what the international lawyers say; we are going to kick some ass.*[733]

A new chief of station was in place in Afghanistan in early 2002, facing a regrouping of Taliban and Al-Qaeda forces in the east-central mountains. The plains around the mountains and the mountains themselves were relatively unpopulated and provided an ideal refuge—as well as a rallying point to begin sending fighters back down into the occupied Afghan villages, often at night. In 2002, a team with elements of CIA and Special Forces organized itself into units to gather intelligence, perform surveillance, and, as possible, attack the remnant groups.[734]

Eventually, these eastern approaches came to contain a series of "fire bases" something similar to those of decades earlier in Southeast

Asia. The bases served to maintain a "border watch," manned by Army Rangers, who provided backbone firepower and ran night patrols. Special Forces teams operated from the bases on secret, targeted missions, as did a task group charged with looking for bin Laden and other key Taliban leaders. Reportedly—and certainly not acknowledged by the CIA or by Washington—deniable CIA paramilitary teams would operate well beyond the Afghan border, into Pakistan. Those contractors would be detached from the Special Activities Division and operate under total deniability, with no retrieval options. They got in and out by themselves, using totally local transportation. The border watch and the deniable penetration missions would continue for several years; what we know of its covert aspects is largely from on-the-ground investigative journalism by reporters such as Robert Young Pelton. In his book *Licensed to Kill: Hired Guns in the War on Terror*, Pelton details his own visits into the border area between Pakistan and Afghanistan and his conversations with CIA military contractors who were not officially there.[735] Pelton's reports make for interesting reading, but for our purposes it leads us into another subject: the expanding role of CIA military contract employees.

In the first and second decades of the twenty-first century, we continue to find former military service people acting in the War on Terror—not officially associated with the American military but directed by the CIA or the Pentagon. If asked about their employers, they would simply describe themselves as "other government agencies" (OGA) contractors. That proved to be a very useful term, especially when the individuals were obviously embedded with military/Special Forces teams or task forces.

However, it was (and likely still is) a practice that leads to the appearance of foreigners, dressed much like American military but with no military unit designations or insignia, circulating among the indigenous populations. Those populations have a difficult time making fine distinctions of who is military, who is CIA, who is with what U.S. government agency, or perhaps with what other government agencies—who is working for whom becomes very unclear.

Even within American forces and agencies it resurfaces the familiar problem of just who sanctioned what activities and . . . it all sounds quite familiar.

We've discussed how small the CIA's own Special Activities staff was at the time of the 9/11 attacks, which created the immediate need to bring experienced military employees in to supplement the teams rushed into Afghanistan. At the time, the Agency's security division, with the task of protecting overseas installations and staff, was also significantly understaffed for the rash of new demands for its services. In particular, the CIA Global Response Staff suddenly found itself needing to provide new levels of security, especially in Iraq and Afghanistan, as what was first presented as preventive warfare turned into nation-building—with all the security responsibilities that came with the task. The first major challenge of that situation was simply to provide security for the new Kabul CIA station itself, with no American military in-country at the time. At that point the Agency took a new step into relatively large-scale outsourcing.

The State Department had already been faced with the issue of upgrading its own security without significantly increased American military assets; their solution was to bring in private security companies and they contracted with one of the largest of the time, DynCorp. Actually, the move to private contractors for security was not a new one. State and federal government agencies had used security services from the Wackenhut Corporation over a number of years, including for security at U.S. nuclear installations.

Following the State Department's lead, the CIA also turned to a private security company and concluded a contract on a limited, noncompetitive-bid basis, citing "urgent and compelling" needs. That contract was with a relative newcomer to the field, a company that had done subcontracting work for DynCorp but would shortly come into its own as an industry leader. The company was named Blackwater and the contract was relatively small, involving two commanders and eighteen security personnel, and extending for only for six months. Still, the amount was $5.4 million, demonstrating the lucrative financial potential of private military security.[736] Over time

Global Response Staff (GRS) would come from a variety of sources, and assume an ongoing if covert role. GRS security work might be clandestine and extremely low profile; it was far from safe and the risk was ongoing.

In 2009, three CIA security employees were killed when a Jordanian double agent suicide-bombed a CIA compound in Khost, Afghanistan. Attacks on the American Embassy in Benghazi, Libya, in 2012 brought the diplomatic staff under the protection of Global Response team members, and two CIA contractors were killed in defending embassy personnel. The incidents in Khost and Benghazi both produced significant American domestic political controversy, but another incident in Pakistan developed into a major international incident. There, two GRS contractors were imprisoned following a shooting incident in Lahore. While the incident was apparently an armed robbery, the two were serving as security for a CIA counterterrorism case officer at the time. GRS employees have become a new factor in the CIA's covert paramilitary structure, and clearly it is dangerous employment. Due to the nature of their assignments, at least fourteen CIA/GRS contractors—all contract employees have died since 2009.[737]

To further complicate matters, new types of contractor positions appeared in Afghanistan and in much larger numbers in Iraq—and those contractors were not associated with the CIA in any fashion. Initially the men hired for those positions might have had the same background (former military, Special Forces, covert-action professionals) as the CIA military employees. But these contract slots were with other U.S. government agencies, including the State Department and American aid agencies working on construction and regime-building. In many instances the same individual would rotate between being a green badge CIA military contractor and being a security contractor for another government agency. His dress changed little, he was still obviously a foreigner, he was obviously armed, and as far as the locals were concerned, anybody and everybody might be from the CIA. Not surprisingly, such a situation also bred a few independents claiming to be working for or with the CIA, but with their own private agendas.

And then the security situation in Iraq imploded, just as a number of American aid organizations and commercial firms appeared in the American effort to rebuild that country. Given that the U.S. was not officially an occupying force, given that the American military had not been grown to wartime size (no declared war, no draft), the American military certainly was in no position to move in massive forces to stabilize the country—and certainly that would have looked a lot like an occupation.

In addition to the security requirements of the State Department and the Coalition Provisional Authority, commercial contracting in Iraq brought a virtual explosion in security contracting by private corporations. The reconstruction program and its huge budget (with an initial pledge of some $200 billion) brought a number of major corporate entities into Iraq—and into an increasingly questionable security environment. In order to minimize the deployment of American military, the authority required all contractors to subcontract for security but allowed them to wrap that into their cost-plus contracts. In many cases that added a good 30 to 40 percent to their work. Although private companies had worked in declared war zones before, with Vietnam as an example, they had generally been either remote from the combat or protected by allied or American military forces. In Iraq, virtually the entire country, including the capital, became a potential or actual combat zone.

The dramatic escalation in security contracting, and the growth of a major new set of businesses, began with security for State Department needs. In Afghanistan, the State Department determined that the new Afghan president, Hamid Karzai, would not be able to receive reliable security from an internal Afghan security force (a determination that spoke volumes about the fragility of the new central government).[738] In the short term Karzai's security was provided by a detail from SEAL Team 6, operating under the Joint Special Operations Command. The SEALs went in during the summer of 2002 and provided effective security for the new Afghan president. However, later that summer, during an attack on Karzai, the SEALs' standard protective response resulted in the deaths of three Afghan civilians who themselves had been trying to protect Karzai. That incident, along with concern that an American military security detail (even if covert) presented the appearance of Karzai being an American figurehead, led the State Department to a private security option. State had already been using private security services in Jerusalem and in Bosnia; they decided to work Karzai's protection into the existing DynCorp contract. The DynCorp security detail eventually involved forty-six paramilitary contractors, a mix of former military and law enforcement personnel. But as events progressed and nation-building began, DynCorp would eventually end up with contracts for at least $43 million in Afghanistan.[739]

Security contractors such as DynCorp and Blackwater would see their businesses explode in the post-9/11 era. The boom in security carried over to longtime industry titans such as the Wackenhut Corporation. Wackenhut was founded in 1954 (under the name Special Agent Investigators, Inc.) by four former FBI agents, including George Wackenhut. By 2002 the company was acquired by a Danish security-business holding company named Group 4 Falck. The Wackenhut name was retained until 2010, when it was changed to G4S Secure Solutions, Inc. G4S claims some fifty thousand employees servicing a broad number of government and private sectors.[740]

The 2010 name change for Wackenhut certainly seems to have been a response to problems and PR issues not uncommon to the security contractors working in Afghanistan and Iraq. In 2009 Blackwater Worldwide abandoned its well-known name, changing it to Xe in response to various legal and public relations issues it had encountered in Iraq.[741] Wackenhut's major public relations issues arose out of the behavior of its contracting staff in Kabul, where the American Embassy was forced to fire some eight Wackenhut guards in a sensational and broadly covered sex scandal.[742]

In the longer term, security contracting revenues in Afghanistan would pale in significance compared to State Department spending in Iraq. Many of those contracts would continue to be no-bid, to the tune of billions of dollars. It is not our focus to delve into the details or issues of security-related outsourcing; however, two examples will provide a feeling for the scope of the Iraq effort. The first was quite straightforward: the provision of personal security for Paul Bremer III, head of the Coalition Provisional Authority, charged with rebuilding Iraq. In the 1970s Bremer had been an assistant to Secretary of State Kissinger and had served as executive secretary to Defense Secretary Haig in the Reagan Administration. During the Reagan-era activities in Latin America, Bremer had served as the administration's ambassador-at-large for counterterrorism. Bremer's tenure in Iraq would see massive American private-sector involvement in the Iraq reconstruction effort as well as the evolution of a huge need for private security contractors. On a smaller scale, just protection for Bremer and other U.S. officials in Iraq would bring in a massive Blackwater contract. Bremer's own protective detail, put in place in 2003, would be a sole source, no-bid agreement for almost $28 million; it included two helicopters.[743]

The second security-related outsourcing example involved an ambitious project to train a new Iraqi national police force. Some $8 billion was spent in overall efforts to develop the force between 2004 and 2012. Details on the contracting are not readily available, but very early on, DynCorp was awarded a contract estimated at $50 million to conduct a security assessment and begin training for the installation of a new law enforcement, penal, and judicial system. Some one thousand personnel were to be hired as part of that early contract.[744] The police training program itself suffered significantly from the lack of general security within the country from 2003 to 2008; it literally became impossible or extremely risky for those involved to conduct the planned travel necessary to work with local police units. Reportedly the Iraqi response to the training and foreign police "advisors" was also generally negative, possibly due to cultural differences but also because the Iraqis felt that they were already law enforcement professionals and needed no training from foreigners. In 2012, the special inspector general for Iraq reconstruction (SIGIR) released an assessment concluding that at least $200 million spent on the police development program had been essentially wasted.[745] And at the end of 2012, in December, a DynCorp contractor was killed by an Iraqi police officer. The contractor had been acting as an advisor in the Afghan national police development program and had served repeated tours in the country for over a decade. His last tour had begun in 2011.[746]

In an associated example of U.S. government contracting, the rise of an Iraqi insurgent movement stimulated the same type of military assistance counterinsurgency response we have seen in venues such as Vietnam and Latin America. In Iraq the effort appears not to have been organized by the CIA as in Vietnam, but rather by military "consultants" brought in by the Department of Defense, under Secretary Rumsfeld's direction. Details of the effort emerged only in 2013 due to new reporting, but it appears that operations began in 2004 and were conducted under the auspices of the Iraqi Special Police Commandos. The Special Police Commando effort is now known to have received American funding in excess of $8 billion.[747] The Iraqi Special Police units were reportedly organized and advised by Department of Defense military consultants/contractors; they were largely staffed with recruits from militia groups violently opposed to the factions against which they were deployed. Their activities included intelligence collection, sweeps, and operating an extensive series of detention and interrogation centers. Among those named as organizing and directing the counterinsurgency initiative was a retired Army colonel formerly involved in 1980s-era counterinsurgency programs in El Salvador and Nicaragua.

Without being repetitive, it seems enough to say that the widespread reports of human rights violations and torture in the Iraqi Special Police detention centers seem virtually identical to what we saw in the Phoenix program in Vietnam and in El Salvador, and in Condor operations across the Southern Cone. Once again the situation seems to have been that American "advisors" may well not have ordered or participated in the brutality, but they effectively enabled it by developing an infrastructure that had no effective legal oversight or checks-and-balances system. In such a situation, especially one in which the forces involved have a long and bloody history with their targets, torture, political murder, and widespread humanitarian violence are almost certain to occur.

There is no doubt that security and nation-building in Iraq and Afghanistan led to dramatic increases in government agency and corporate contracting. A new type of surrogate paramilitary force came into play in Iraq and to a lesser extent in Afghanistan.[748] And in direct contrast to prior practices, that surrogate force was not indigenous to the country. The much later appearance of anti-Al-Qaeda tribal associations such as the Sunni Awakening Movement was a totally different matter, with tribal groups acting in their own security interests, which simply proved to be compatible with the multinational military efforts against an escalating Iraqi insurgency.[749]

Western security contractors quite obviously were not natives; they were widely viewed as acting in support of foreign interests and they were armed. Given the growing insurgency after 2004, they used their weapons both to preempt attacks and to respond to them. Robert Young Pelton describes in his book *Licensed to Kill* a drive from the Baghdad airport into the "secure" Green Zone of Baghdad, in a chapter titled "Running the Gauntlet."[750] He paints a picture of a heavily armed mobile contractor unit faced with the constant threat of attack, effectively warning off potential suicide car bombers with bursts of gunfire and being forced to maneuver in and around routine civilian Iraqi traffic. The contractors acted defensively but clearly were posing a hazard to those same civilians. A week after his own ride through the "gauntlet," the team he was with had one of its vehicles blown up by an improvised explosive device (IED); one contractor was killed, two seriously injured. In a 2004 incident, a Blackwater airport run with U.S. and Polish contractors came under attack (on the four-lane highway) by insurgents in four to five vehicles. All the attackers had automatic weapons and rocket-propelled grenade launchers. One Blackwater vehicle exploded after taking an RPG round in the middle of an intense firefight. Four of the contractors were killed in the mobile ambush.[751]

Rules of engagement required that private paramilitary contractors respond with concentrated fire only to break off and escape from attacks; however, in several instances groups of contractors did come under intense, long-duration attacks. Such combat occurred while the contractors were performing routine escort duty for corporate construction projects and even routine Coalition Provisional Authority aid and supply shipments. Combat also occurred when insurgents launched concentrated attacks on Coalition Provisional Authority sites where security contractors were located. In one incident, Blackwater security contractors and even Blackwater helicopters provided extended combat support for a sustained insurgent attack on CPA headquarters in Najaf, while a coalition army unit from the Ukraine remained bottled up inside its own base in the city. As time progressed, it became clear that the armed foreign contractors were coming to be viewed by much of the Iraqi public as simply an extension of the coalition military presence in the country—something that looked to them very much like an occupation. That view was no doubt supported by the fact that based on a directive, Order 17, issued by Paul Bremer, the contractors were also immune from any legal action by the Iraqi authorities. The Iraqi legal system was literally unable to prosecute a contractor for any crime committed while he was on duty, up to and including murder.

Pragmatically, the contractors were needed; there was simply not enough American military to bring security to Iraq. But clearly the contractors, to protect themselves and their missions, had to present an image of being armed, aggressive in force, and dangerous to anyone considering attacking the agencies or companies that were employing them. To project that image, Blackwater convoys actively ran civilian vehicles off the road and fired rounds to warn them away.

> *They made enemies everywhere. I would ride around with Iraqis in beat-up Iraqi trucks, they were running me off the road. We were threatened and intimidated. . . .[but] they were doing their job, exactly what they were paid to do in the way they were paid*

to do it, and they were making enemies on every single pass in and out of town . . . it broke the first rule of fighting any insurgency . . . .you don't make any more enemies.[752]

—COLONEL THOMAS X. HAMMES (Ret.),
U.S. Army, chief of Iraq reconstruction

The American and international effort in Iraq brought in a huge foreign presence—not only military forces but a host of State Department personnel and their contracted security, Bremer's Coalition Provisional Authority and its security personnel, and a number of major international corporations and their private security forces. All in all it looked very much like an occupation and was easily pictured as such by a number of anti-American factions. Beyond that image problem, which without doubt fueled the efforts of native insurgents and fundamentalist religious leaders, the large collection of foreigners drew growing numbers of jihadi fighters from around the region, all eager to repel the Western "crusaders" who appeared to have taken over the country.

If the populations of Iraq and Afghanistan had problems telling the difference between different types of private security contractors, it was understandable. After all, they dressed and armed themselves pretty much the same, sometimes wearing civilian clothing with body armor and weapons; but other times wearing American military-style helmets, body armor, and fatigues. It was equally difficult to differentiate coalition and reconstruction personnel (including other government agencies, CIA, and military intelligence officers) who routinely operated in civilian clothing. It was, at best, a somewhat chaotic environment. And once again there were people claiming to work with or work for the CIA. In his book *Licensed to Kill*, Robert Young Pelton tells the story of one such individual, a man who managed to fool a host of people in and around the world of clandestine and security activities—over some four years from 2001 to 2004.[753] The list of people entangled in his efforts ranged from individuals in the film industry to those in the national media and those running both humanitarian and even military activities in Afghanistan.

Since the real CIA officers and their real contractors were operating covertly, they were not going to be giving out any stories. Everyone dressed in the same fashion, and drove dusty SUVs; the only difference was that the real operators weren't talking—which meant that the media were left with those who were. In the instance Pelton describes, the individual talking obtained a paid, if temporary, position as a Fox network news consultant. Many in the media had become aware that he was questionable, but he was one of the few that would talk to them and at times any news is simply news. In January 2002 he managed to sell the rights to air purported Al-Qaeda training base videos to CBS News. That drama added significantly to the overall media confusion and chaos of the period. It would be some two and a half years before he become the subject of an investigation by U.S. authorities in Kabul, and some three months longer before he was actually taken into custody. It appears that initial American operations in Afghanistan were so low profile that even those in charge were having trouble telling who was real and who wasn't.

In chapter 20, "Risky Business," we noted that some individuals just keep turning up over and over again. As an illustration of how such things seem to go on and on, as recently as 2011, the press was covering Duane R. Clarridge, a figure familiar to us from the initial Contra operations. It seems that during the Afghanistan era, Clarridge had established his own private intelligence company and sent his own operatives into remote regions of Afghanistan on intelligence collection missions.[754] His effort was not a small one: a 2011 internal communication from his company, the Eclipse Group, sent following the termination of his Army contract, references "approximately 200 local personnel." Eclipse employed American, Afghan, and Pakistani contract employees. And while the contract cancellation may have curtailed certain of his operations, other activities indicated that he and his organization remained very active in Afghanistan. The contract with the Army had been arranged in 2009, and ultimately the officer involved was placed under investigation for violating Defense Department rules in awarding it. The result of that investigation and the charges is unknown as of this writing. Clarridge was also associated with the American International Security Corporation. That contracting firm won a $6 million contract with the Department of Defense; the exact nature of the contract is not known but the contracting officer was with the "information warfare" command in San Antonio. Clarridge's companies reportedly produced "an amalgam of fact, rumor, analysis and uncorroborated reports." The reports were apparently paid for by the U.S. Army and were provided to conservative television and radio commentators including Oliver North and author Brad Thor, a regular guest of Glenn Beck's radio show. Since government regulations ban hiring contractors as "spies," the contract work was described as relating to "atmospheric information" rather than intelligence. That contracting firm was later the subject of a criminal investigation by the Pentagon's inspector general.

As of this writing, there is little doubt that American experiences in Afghanistan and Iraq have created a great political and popular distaste for nation-building—or for that matter even for involvement in regime change. As far back as 1954, Kermit Roosevelt Jr. had offered advice based on his firsthand experience in regime change and nation-building. That advice was based in one of the very first CIA successes in changing regimes: Iran. Roosevelt's advice was quite simple: in a White House debriefing he stated that if the U.S. and in particular the CIA was ever going to do that sort of thing again, both the people and the Army in the country in question had to want what the United States set out to accomplish. If they did not, the job of regime change had best be given to the Marines. Time and events seem to have validated Kermit Roosevelt's observations—it remains good advice, not often taken.

In both Afghanistan and Iraq, the George W. Bush Administration attempted nation-building that clearly was not supported by an indigenous military force (which it immediately disbanded) or by major segments of the population. When that created a security nightmare, it turned to putting other types of boots on the ground, not the Marines and not the Army. Perhaps that could be considered a first step in the sort of "gray warfare" we have begun exploring. If so, it proved to be a major misstep. But even as the U.S. gradually withdrew from both those countries, it still faced a global jihadi threat and ongoing terror plots. The War on Terror was very much in play, and both the Bush and Obama administrations would try to preempt that threat. The tactics used in that effort would lead to a very different type of undeclared warfare.

CHAPTER 26

Merging Covert and Conventional

From the earliest days of the Cold War, America's leaders took the position that it was necessary to act preemptively—and often covertly—against the dramatic expansion of Soviet influence, viewed as a global communist threat to the nation's national security. The National Security Act of 1947 defined the context for covert action and authorized the activities required to implement it. A number of those activities would have been considered illegal under previously existing civil and military legal codes.

We've traced covert warfare though the decades of the Cold War, in operations aimed both at regime change and regime preservation. On the whole, covert operations targeted either regimes or regime leaders that were viewed as threats. No wars were officially declared against those targets; the presidents directing the operations acted on their authority as commanders in chief of the country's military. In later decades, following passage of the War Powers Act, presidents were required to provide notifications and briefings to Congress in conjunction with such operations. In all those interventions, one factor was supposed to be a constant—the covert intervention was to be deniable.

During later decades, as global terror attacks escalated, the focus on America's enemies shifted from communist and communist-leaning regimes, first to state sponsors of terrorism and ultimately to specific jihadi leaders and groups that had declared war on America, Americans overseas, and often Western culture in general. During that transitional period, rather than responding to the declarations of war by Al-Qaeda with a counter-declaration of war, or even a congressional resolution authorizing military action, the United States responded with a continuing series of covert actions, primarily targeting bin Laden personally. While there were incidents of overt action, including cruise missile attacks, overall the American effort remained operationally covert.

Following the Al-Qaeda attacks on New York City and Washington, D.C., in 2001, the country was enraged. America was facing what clearly amounted to war; still Congress once again made no formal declaration of war.[755] In this instance the enemy was "stateless." The combatants had no territory or even infrastructure of their own but operated internally throughout a series of foreign nations, some of whom were hostile, some neutral, and some officially American allies. At President George W. Bush's request, Congress did pass a joint resolution, the Authorization for Use of Military Force (AUMF). The AUMF granted permission for the president to take whatever military action was deemed appropriate against those who had committed, directed, authorized, or aided the 9/11 attacks.

Further, the authorization stipulated that the president's actions would be justified by the nation's right to self-defense and the government's obligation to protect its citizens both at home and abroad.[756] Fundamentally the resolution had established a legal basis for an ongoing return to preemptive tactics, through either covert or overt action, and it cites the authority of the War Powers Act in delegating military prerogatives to the president as commander in chief. That congressional Authorization for Use of Military Force continued for over a decade under both the George W. Bush and Obama administrations; it remains in force as of this writing and is the authority for ongoing intelligence and military actions designed to preempt further attacks on America or its citizens overseas.

President Bush immediately began to refer to his execution of the congressional resolution and to America's overall actions as a "global War on Terror." He told American military personnel that they should be prepared to go into action at an instant's notice. And it quickly became clear that an ongoing terrorist threat did exist. Within months, in December 2001, an attempt to blow up American Airlines Flight 63 from Paris to Miami failed only due to problems with triggering the explosives. In the following months and years, additional plots against the United States were discovered. Efforts to attack the Brooklyn Bridge, the New York Stock Exchange, and the New York subway system were thwarted in 2002, 2003, and 2004, respectively.

Internationally, other major terror attacks continued, with the Madrid train system bombings of 2004, which involved ten separate, coordinated explosions killing 191 people. The fatalities included 142 Spanish citizens as well as victims from seventeen other countries, and the attackers were shown to be connected to an Al-Qaeda–influenced terror cell. The following year, in July 2005, jihadi radicals launched another coordinated attack in Europe, this time on the London subway system. Four bombs were detonated across the city, three on separate trains and one on a double-decker bus. The victims included fifty-two killed and over seven hundred more injured.

Plots and attempts continued through the Bush Administration and into the Obama era. Targets included New York airports and transit tunnels, U.S. military bases including Fort Dix, New Jersey, and the Sears Tower in Chicago. Only the intervention of passengers prevented the triggering of a bomb on an airliner over Detroit in 2009. In 2010 a Pakistani American was taken into custody in Dubai and confessed to a bombing effort in Times Square, New York. Additional attacks against Americans were either carried out or thwarted overseas.[757] An ongoing war of terror was being waged by Al-Qaeda and its affiliates, and the war was targeting civilians around the globe.

With the 2001 attacks on New York and Washington, D.C., it was obvious to the world that America was to attack Al-Qaeda and bin Laden and anyone who was allied with them—that fact was simply undeniable. Following 9/11 there would be no more talk of deniability in the War on Terror. It would be only weeks before American air strikes began in Afghanistan. Yet one of President Bush's first actions in taking America to war against Al-Qaeda was to issue a finding authorizing the CIA to conduct covert action against its leadership. That finding provided the CIA with the legal authority to hunt and, if capture was not feasible, kill figures from Al-Qaeda and its associated groups and organizations. During 2002 a target list was prepared; those on the list were referred to as high-value targets and the Bush finding gave the CIA blanket authority to act without obtaining specific presidential approval for each individual action.[758] With that finding, President Bush had ordered the integration of covert intelligence and paramilitary operations with overt and undeniable military action. Covert and conventional practices began to merge into a hybrid, something we call gray warfare.

There were a variety of factors underlying the merger of traditionally covert intelligence practices with conventional military capabilities—one being the nature of the new enemy. In strictly conventional warfare, combat involves known and limited geographies: there are borders and hard targets such as bases, airfields, transportation infrastructure, enemy military formations, and enemy command and control systems. The Al-Qaeda global terrorist network was stateless; it consisted of mobile enemies who used satellite and cell phone networks as well as the Internet for their command and control system, used commercial airlines for global travel, and recruited volunteers in over a dozen countries to launch suicide bombing attacks not just locally but anywhere in the world. Combating such an enemy was going to demand a breadth of intelligence work, technical data collection, and real-time communications with American fighting units that had simply not been seen before the early days in Afghanistan. That learning curve had been a steep one, in only one country. The new hybrid force was going to have to operate not just in one country but on multiple continents at the same time.

The CIA and various counterintelligence units provided the intelligence to launch and drive this new, undeniable warfare on Al-Qaeda. And the Joint Special Operations Command provided the actual military power to carry out that warfare. During the Bush Administration, Defense Secretary Rumsfeld was a prime mover in authorizing and initiating gray warfare operations, directing them through the JSOC. In September 2003, Rumsfeld issued an order establishing the JSOC as the principal American counterterrorism force. In addition, he drafted the Al Qaeda Network Exord (execute order), which contained a preauthorized list of some fifteen countries where actions could be conducted.[759]

As we first saw in Afghanistan the new integration of covert and overt, merging intelligence with military ordinance, proved extremely effective. However, as it continued as a standard practice over an extended period of time, issues emerged for those military personnel assigned to operations declared to be covert. In a previous chapter we explored some of the risks associated with placing military personnel in CIA operations that involved them in illegal activities, as defined by the Uniform Code of Military Justice. The new practice of hybrid CIA–military activities had begun to raise other concerns about the legal exposure of military personnel.

Military personnel normally serve under the legal authority and constraints of the federal codes that pertain to military operations of the uniformed services and the Department of Defense (U.S. Code Title 10).[760] Intelligence and related covert activities are covered under a separate section of the code (U.S. Code Title 50).[761] As the War on Terror moved to mixing CIA and military personnel in joint operations and assigning them to missions that were clearly not deniable, the legal issues for those operations also moved into something of a gray area.[762]

Legal experts seem to be of the opinion that counterterrorism attacks are more easily and quickly authorized if the primary authority is that of the CIA rather than a conventional military operation.[763] One authority suggests that a Judge Advocate General legal advisor accompanying a joint task force is more likely to advise that a drone strike is legal if the drone is "owned" operationally by the CIA rather than launched as part of a purely military operation.[764] Since contemporary counterterrorism operations almost always involve members from both the military and the CIA, this new era of warfare may be legally authorized as "covert," but its complexity and the use of conventional military weaponry—not to mention the lack of any semblance of deniability—seem to define what has emerged as ongoing, global gray warfare.[765]

As of this writing, even within the military the question is being raised as to whether the new practice of assigning military personnel to missions conducted under CIA authority but carried out as at most simply clandestine military actions takes away the combat immunity and protections normally given to military service personnel.[766] It is becoming a concern that the merger of covert and conventional, which has become an ongoing part of counterterrorism, may have moved outside the established legislation and legal codes that pertain to its participants. Consolidated counterterror task forces and joint intelligence–military operations have become increasingly effective. However, there remains considerable debate about the legal gray areas involved in the merger of Title 10 and Title 50 operations.[767]

Organizing and operating hybrid forces became a critical element in effectively waging attacks against the global jihadi terror network. Still, there was a very fundamental presidential and administration decision to be made in regard to using the new integrated counterterrorism forces: whether to use them to launch preventive attacks or in retaliation after terrorist attacks occurred. In the earlier days of Cold War covert warfare, presidents consistently decided to act preemptively, and presidential decisions in regard to the global War on Terror were the same. And just as with Cold War covert operations, preemptive attacks in the undeclared War on Terror would raise their own legal and moral issues.

In addition to merging covert and conventional assets into a new type of hybrid striking force, President George W. Bush specified that a defense against terrorism was necessarily "preemptive." He outlined that position in a speech made at West Point. In his remarks he pointed out that the classic Cold War doctrine of "deterrence and containment," with its promise of massive retaliation, has no meaning to stateless terrorists.

> *If we wait for threats to materialize, we will have waited too long . . . the war on terror will not be won on the defensive. We must take the battle to the enemy, disrupt his plans, and confront the worst threats before they emerge. In the world we have entered, the only path to safety is the path of action.*[768]

Following his first election and during both of his terms, President Obama openly stated that he was serving as commander in chief during a national security emergency—initially declared by President George W. Bush. President Obama continued to issue similar declarations to extend that state of emergency. In 2009, Obama reiterated that America was a nation at war, against a far-reaching network of enemies. Even though the White House directed that the wording used in conjunction with terrorist-related military activities be changed from "global War on Terror" to "overseas contingency operations," it was clear that America remained in a state of preemptive military action against global terror networks.

Indeed, the ongoing threat of terrorist attacks has given rise to a certain similarity in preemptive action by both Presidents George W. Bush and Barack Obama, individuals that otherwise positioned themselves as being very different from their domestic political opponents. As an example, while running in his first campaign Barack Obama challenged the Bush Administration for not acting "aggressively enough" against Al-Qaeda's leadership and clearly stated that if Pakistan could not or would not take action against them he would act "to protect the American people." He also declared that there could be no safe haven for terrorists who had killed thousands of Americans and continued to threaten the American homeland.

The Obama Administration has retained the concept of preemption as tactical doctrine in its ongoing warfare against jihadi terrorism and insurgency, not targeting nation-states but rather individuals and groups operating globally, across borders. The strategy of preemption and the tactics of clandestine strikes, largely with combat drones, were strongly advocated by John Brennan, the Obama Administration's deputy national security advisor for homeland security and counterterrorism. Brennan had also been a primary counterterrorism advisor to the president in his first term. Brennan's twenty-five years in the CIA and a specialization in both the Mideast and counterterrorism contributed to his influence on both Presidents George W. Bush and Obama. His experience had begun as CIA chief of station in Saudi Arabia in 1996, during the Khobar Towers terror attack that killed nineteen American servicemen. He then served as the daily CIA briefer for President Clinton, and as chief of staff for CIA Director George Tenet. Following the attacks of 9/11, Tenet assigned Brennan as director of the National Counterterrorism Center.[769]

Brennan's approach to directly and preemptively attacking known terrorists is well-known and he has consistently championed the use of both drones and surgical special operations teams. As an advocate for preemptive targeting, he himself became the focus of drone program critics and civil liberties advocates objecting to what they define as "extrajudicial killings." His response to such criticism remains succinct and unapologetic: "We conduct targeted strikes because they are necessary to mitigate an actual ongoing threat—to stop plots, prevent future attacks, and save American lives."[770] In May 2012, Brennan offered further public remarks that acknowledged the ongoing preemptive attack program being conducted during President Obama's second term in office: "The United States Government conducts targeted strikes against specific Al-Qaeda terrorists, sometimes using remotely piloted aircraft, often referred to publicly as drones."[771]

Brennan also offered the Obama Administration's view as to its legal justifications of such attacks and provided some detail on the process for generating target lists. He provided no operational details and did not identify specific agencies involved in producing the lists. The legal justification offered for the continued covert strikes is that Al-Qaeda, certain of its affiliates and individual jihadi leaders, has openly declared war against the United States. Those groups and individuals had called for attacks on Americans, supported those attacks, and in doing so inserted themselves into "declared" warfare against the United States.

Under the UN Charter, any nation is allowed to act in its own self-defense. As might be expected, that justification, maintained by both Bush and Obama as a justification for preemptive attacks on suspected terrorists, is not wholeheartedly accepted by many human rights and legal activists. Still, as we referenced in a previous chapter, preemptive defense without declaration of war has a long tradition in America. When President Jefferson was faced with attacks on American shipping by Barbary pirates, Alexander Hamilton pointed out to his fellow congressmen that it was necessary that they declare war if the need arose to challenge a foreign nation. However, if America was attacked, the president had every right to unilaterally respond with military action in the role of commander in chief. Congress was apparently receptive to Hamilton's point and Jefferson ordered the American Navy into action against the pirate nation.

In regard to the War on Terror, the justification of a preemptive defense deals strictly with American action against "targeted" terrorist individuals or groups. It does not address the use of combat drones or JSOC resources in surrogate military action, for example in support of military assistance provided to nations engaged with jihadi insurgencies. While not receiving as much attention as the targeted strikes, the justification for such military support also seems to fall under the authority of the president as commander in chief in conjunction with support for various American military assistance agreements—which are themselves often classified.

Targeted attacks on individuals with American citizenship have also become a major issue and concern both politically and for civil libertarians. The seminal incident to date has been the drone killing of American-born Anwar al-Awlaki, who was an outspoken and vehement spokesperson for jihadi recruiting and action. Details of his exact operational relationships remain classified, but in testimony, Brennan linked him to Umar Farouk Abdulmutallab, convicted in the plot to blow up an American airliner flying into Detroit on Christmas Day 2009.

What is on record is the fact that al-Awlaki had openly praised terrorist attacks on the United States and called for Muslims in America to join the jihad against the United States.[772] In one video interview conducted inside Yemen, he called upon all Muslims and especially those in the Horn of Africa region to "participate in the jihad against America."[773] In another instance, he described himself as a "traitor to America," because his religion demanded it. It was necessary for he and his fellow believers to wage jihad for the rest of their lives, to "implant Islam all over the world."[774]

Legal issues in an American attack on Anwar al-Awlaki—who was neither charged with nor convicted of treason, sedition, or any actual crime, nor brought into the American legal system—are obvious. However, it should also be noted that the Supreme Court has issued an opinion that the U.S. military may indeed use force against an American citizen who is part of an "enemy force." If Congress had moved to issue a formal declaration of war against Al-Qaeda, its leaders, and its affiliates, matters of defining enemy forces, enemy combatants, and even individuals considered to have committed treason or sedition might have been legally simplified. Congress had not done so, leaving such decisions, and any resultant political fallout, strictly in the lap of the commander in chief.

In terms of the actual conduct of covert, preemptive operations, the Obama Administration has reportedly dealt with several of the most egregious issues that surfaced during the initial post-9/11 War on Terror. Currently covert action is authorized and overseen in a much more rigorous fashion than during virtually any of the administrations since the Kennedy era. Current oversight practices also continue to address a number of congressional concerns that were raised during the Nixon and Reagan administrations. Of course current covert actions are just that—covert. It would be unrealistic to claim knowledge of exactly how consistent legal oversight is today, but we do have a relatively clear picture of what is supposed to happen.

Proposals for covert action related to counterterrorism can come from the NSC staff, the National Counterterrorism Center (NCTC), the CIA, or even JSOC and its task forces. Orders from JSOC would be most likely if the action is in regard to a known terrorist target, very possibly one being activity tracked by JSOC units or even by NCTC "pursuit" group analysts. In the case of other types of covert actions, in particular any action that would involve nation-state-level action, the director of national intelligence would normally propose them, although the State Department has also been a source for such proposals. It will most likely take another thirty to fifty years before we will have further detail on the actual operations proposed and either approved or declined, including those related to covert cyber warfare.

All covert-action proposals are vetted by the director of national intelligence and his legal staff. The proposal then goes to the Deputies Committee of the NSC, where it is evaluated by lawyers from Defense, State, and the Department of Justice. If the deputies—and their lawyers—concur, the request is bumped up to the Principals Committee, which involves the heads of the administration's major departments plus the national security advisor and the attorney general—not unlike President Kennedy's EXCOMM group. If the principals and their legal staff concur, the proposal is submitted to the president for approval.

One of the most obvious changes to the Obama-era process is the number of staff—especially of legal staff—involved in the layers of review. Estimates are that some one hundred executive branch staff and ten or more lawyers would be involved in the passage of any particular proposal.[775] That is in addition to any JSOC legal staff or JAG (Judge Advocate General) staff attached at the regional military command level. Clearly it is a cumbersome process, with a great more legal oversight involved than in prior administrations, including that of Obama's predecessor, George W. Bush. Given our understanding of history, we can imagine Presidents Truman,

Eisenhower, and Kennedy endorsing such a process, but it's hard to imagine it always being fully honored under all circumstances.

Jack Goldsmith, Harvard Law School professor and head of the Office of Legal Counsel for George W. Bush, provides a detailed exploration of the transition in covert practice between the two administrations in his 2012 book *Power and Constraint: The Accountable Presidency After 9/11*. He points out that many of the legal and legislative restrictions on the president that emerged during the 1970s are still very much in place. It was purely a matter of presidential choice that, in response to the attacks of 9/11, President Bush chose to disregard those restrictions. In reality, Bush responded as presidents dealing with imminent attacks frequently have and likely always will—choosing to do whatever it takes to counter an imminent threat, acting unilaterally, and choosing to deal with criticism and legal issues after the fact.

In addition, Goldsmith details the extent to which the Bush Administration received extensive pushback by both military and CIA officers involved in certain of the practices outside covert action.[776] The story of that pushback is emerging as more personal stories come out of the early days of the global War on Terror. One CIA officer assigned to an Al-Qaeda interrogation project relates his immediate concerns about the briefing he was receiving. He was going to be working with a third-party country, one with a reputation for torture in interrogation. The following exchange between that officer and his supervisor in regard to interrogation and possible torture of prisoners inside third-party countries (generally known as rendition) reflects his concern that the legalities and rules he had been sworn to uphold had seemingly been tossed out the window:

> *Suppose our partners do something to _____ that I consider unacceptable? Well you just walk out of the room if you feel you should. Then you won't have seen anything will you? You will not have been a party to anything. We don't do that sort of thing. We do now.* [777]

The CIA officer was shocked. Given that we have seen repeated instances of similar distancing from Vietnam to Latin America, we may be less so. Certainly under the Phoenix and Condor counterinsurgency projects, torture was routinely conducted, and CIA officers and even State Department personnel had been forced (and ordered) to simply ignore it. But the contemporary-era CIA officer had been well trained in the legal requirements of presidential findings and congressional authorization.

He raised the legal issues to his supervisor and was told that there was no need to worry; they had authorization: "We have a letter from the president. We can do whatever we need to do. We're covered." He was shown the letter before departing on his assignment, and his interpretation was that President Bush's legal counsel had given the opinion that the CIA could "do what you want; what the President says is legal is legal."[778]

We spent a good deal of time on that particular issue in earlier chapters, one example being the similar acceptance of unilateral presidential command authority by Oliver North and National Security Advisor John Poindexter. In that instance we also discussed several CIA officers who were judged to have exceeded their own authorizations—and the congressional limitations in effect at the time. Several officers received disciplinary action or chose early retirement. In a similar vein, several figures would also be investigated in regard to their actions under the George W. Bush Administration. Some were cleared, but at least two remained under further criminal investigation. Any sanctions given to individuals as a result of the inquiries were not public at the time of this writing.[779]

By 2004, many of the initial Bush Administration War on Terror–related practices had either been modified or abandoned, including certain of those related directly to our study of covert action. In addition, the congressional reporting practices that had come into play due to the scandals and investigations of the 1970s appear to have been reimplemented during the Obama Administration. Presidentially approved covert actions are routinely being briefed to members of the Senate and House intelligence committees; actions of extreme sensitivity are communicated only to the top four congressional leaders plus two senior members of the Senate and House intelligence committees. In the period of 2009–2011 some four hundred formal "notifications" were sent to Congress and an additional seventeen hundred briefings, meetings, and hearings occurred.[780]

Another practice that has raised extensive discussion of both legality and morality relates to the use of drones in attacks on terrorist targets. The use of drones in preemptive attacks has proved tactically successful, killing Al-Qaeda and affiliated commanders, leaders, and fighters. It has also caused the deaths of civilians, including children, in the proximity of the targets being attacked. Drone warfare raises both the Title 10–Title 50 issues previously discussed and additional questions related to the strategy of preemption. The Obama Administration's legal structure and protocols for using unmanned weapons in preemptive strikes on terrorists, as well as for the oversight of such operations, were reportedly still not fully codified and fully classified as of the fall of 2012—possibly because of the extended multiagency and multilawyered legal opinion participation in the counterterrorism effort. The operations themselves were and remain fully classified at the time of this writing. It does seem clear, from disclosures on drone attacks, that there has been something of a shift in the second Obama term, from targeted leadership attacks (sometimes referred to as personality attacks) to military attacks on jihadi insurgent groups (referred to as signature attacks).[781]

While such groups do not routinely attack Americans as part of their localized combat they do frequently talk about their desire to attack Westerners, Americans, or America itself. And individual members of the groups do engage in such attacks. The argument put forth denying the legality of attacks on members of such groups is that they cannot be declared an imminent threat to national security or combatants against America. The counter to that argument is that the jihadi fighters have declared war on the West and on Americans and would attack either if presented with the opportunity, whether locally, overseas, or on American shores. There seems to be no imminent reconciliation of those two views; nor is it likely that the Obama Administration will totally abandon the tactic of targeted military action.

The argument that such individuals do pose a threat to Americans, even if not within the continental United States, was validated to some extent by a jihadi attack in January 2013. That incident, at a Norwegian-owned gas production and pipeline facility in Algeria, resulted in hostage-taking and subsequent larger-scale murders including the deaths of three Americans.[782] Investigation of the attack determined that it had been well planned and intricately organized, with intelligence collected from inside the facility. The attack specifically targeted Westerners, with the clear intent of killing as many foreign nationals as possible. Witnesses related that the attackers clearly stated they wished to kill only Christians and non-Muslims. Japanese and Filipino workers were hunted down and executed. French workers survived only by hiding and then fleeing. Thirty-seven foreign workers, including three Americans, were killed in the attack and hostage-taking. Several of the dead had been shot by single bullets to the head, execution style.

However, it was the composition of the attackers, self-described as linked to Al-Qaeda, that may have been most telling for the larger arguments in support of ongoing preemptive defense. Of the thirty-two terrorists, there were individuals from at least six countries: not only from Algeria and Mali next door, but also from Egypt, Niger, Mauritania, and Tunisia. Two of the terrorists were reportedly Canadian citizens. The news drew a quick response from the White House. David Plouffe, a senior presidential advisor appearing on Fox News, reemphasized the Obama Administration position that Al-Qaeda–affiliated groups remain a danger not only in North Africa but in other parts of the world. He also stated that the U.S. is adamant about continuing its efforts to assist other countries in destroying such networks, stating that the tragedy in Algeria shows once again that "all across the globe countries are threatened by terrorists who will use civilians to try and advance their twisted and sick agenda."[783]

The issue of using drones against American citizens remained a major topic of discussion when President Obama nominated John Brennan to be CIA director for his second administration. In 2013 congressional nomination hearings, Brennan gave a consistent message on drone strike targeting, with additional elaboration. He told the committee that targeted killing of suspected terrorists is not used as "punishment for past transgressions." Rather it is used only as a last resort for individuals who are considered to pose an active threat, in instigating, planning, and conducting actual attacks.[784] Brennan acknowledged that targeting can extend to American citizens abroad if they are considered to be senior operational leaders of Al-Qaeda or its affiliates.

In March 2013, Congress confirmed Brennan as the new CIA director, but only after additional concerns were expressed over using drone strikes against American citizens, in particular the concern that drones might be used in attacks inside the United States. In responding to those concerns, the Obama Administration's attorney general provided a legal opinion that the president does not have the authority to use a "weaponized drone" against Americans on American soil unless the individuals in question are engaged in actual combat.

A more recent exchange on the subject, following Brennan's confirmation hearings, has been a tentative proposal from some members of Congress to create a federal court to review and issue rulings on target lists, especially on any American citizens to be targeted. Immediate commentary from legal scholars raised a host of issues with such a concept, especially since it would most certainly "immerse the court deeper and deeper in national security judgments." University of Texas law professor Robert Chesney commented on several of the issues, pointing out that "Judges famously tend to defer to the executive branch when it comes to factual judgments on matters of military or national security significance . . . Especially when the stakes are as high as they will be represented to be in such cases."[785] It seems unlikely that the federal judiciary will be any more eager to share responsibility for such decisions than Congress itself has been.

In more practical terms, the Obama Administration appears to be moving towards consolidating command and control of all drone strikes within the military, leaving the CIA in an intelligence and advisory role, while the U.S. military operates the drones and conducts the actual strike operations.[786] Yet as we previously discussed, without legislation and modification of the U.S. legal code, gray warfare such as this would still leave a number of outstanding legal questions and disputable areas in regard to American servicemembers involved in such operations. It also needs to be noted that even in his strategic remarks in regard to the global War on Terror, Obama continues to strongly maintain the right for preemptive use of drones and other forces against evolving terror threats. He described them as a "necessary evil" but one that cannot be avoided given the nature of the terror threat. He also pushed back against more layers of oversight on covert attacks, stating that Congress is now being briefed on all major strikes.

President Obama's remarks also noted, but did not expand on, a particular point that is certainly relevant to the nature and level of ongoing counterterrorism to be conducted by the United States. While maintaining that the principle of self-defense justifies the legality of such actions, he specifically stated that "to say a military tactic is legal, or even effective, is not to say it is wise or moral in every instance."[787] In fact, the issues of the effectiveness and the wisdom of both drone strikes and expanding military assistance to regimes fighting jihadi insurgencies cannot be ignored in any discussion of contemporary gray warfare.

Given that a combination of covert and conventional military action has now been going on around the globe for over a decade and that hundreds of Al-Qaeda and affiliated leaders and fighters have been targeted and killed, it appears that Congress seems content with gray warfare, with preemptive strikes, and generally with the use of drones. Certainly the practices in place continue to provide Congress with its own form of distance, as its members are briefed but not required to officially approve or disapprove covert counterterrorism operations. As Professor Goldsmith points out, that situation leaves them with no responsibility, but several options.

They can choose to simply leak the action to the media—that would certainly bring pressure against any presidential operation to which they object. Media leaks would also be an option for political action against a president from a different party than his own. A second choice would be to take their issues with the matter to the full Congress, over any protest by the president. They could develop that into legislation to deny funding (as in Angola) or to put limits on the operation (as in Nicaragua). Given that a decade of military combat in Southeast Asia was driven by a single congressional resolution, and that a decade of military action against global terror is still being authorized by a single resolution of 2001, the possibility of any major change in congressional oversight in the near future seems improbable. It appears that Congress simply prefers to retain its options in regard to the ongoing global War on Terror rather than take the course of direct involvement with a broader action such as a declaration of war or even legislation for expanded oversight.

CHAPTER 27

The Evolving War on Terror

The Joint Special Operations Command serves as the primary vehicle for waging the ongoing War on Terror; it operates in several regions ("fronts") around the globe. The existence of the JSOC has never been a true secret, it had already been in existence for decades before it began to draw significant media attention. Still, it had maintained a low profile and its missions were generally subject to both operational security and classification. Media coverage of its operations was not encouraged, and in the early days of the War on Terror, Defense Secretary Rumsfeld maintained extremely tight control over Joint Operations missions; and to a large extent even President George W. Bush appears to have been insulated from actual JSOC operations. Bush talked with Secretary Rumsfeld and the Joint Chiefs but not routinely further down the chain of command. Rumsfeld and Vice President Dick Cheney generally assumed the covert operational oversight formerly conducted by the various oversight groups we described in preceding chapters. Under Rumsfeld, JSOC operated with extreme autonomy, independent of theater military commands in Iraq and Afghanistan, often not coordinating or even communicating its activities to either the CIA or the State Department.[788]

One of the most dramatic differences of the Obama Administration has been the degree of JSOC and Special Operations Forces access to National Command Authority, in particular to President

Obama. As described by *The Washington Post* in 2010, special operations commanders now routinely appear at the White House, far more routinely than during the second Bush Administration.[789] Then, the defense and the Pentagon structure was rigidly observed, and dialogues on operations were the province of the secretary of defense and the Joint Chiefs of Staff. The *Post* quoted an unnamed military officer:

> *"We have a lot more access," a second military official said. "They are talking publicly much less but they are acting more. They are willing to get aggressive much more quickly." The White House, he said, is "asking for ideas and plans . . . calling us in and saying, 'Tell me what you can do. Tell me how you do these things.'"*

The *Post* article noted that Defense Secretary Rumsfeld saw special operations as independent and extremely secret. In some instances he refused to advise the country's ambassadors of special operations activities—a practice very much in the classic Cold War CIA operational tradition. Reportedly the close relationship between Defense Secretary Gates and Secretary of State Hillary Rodham Clinton during the first Obama Administration ended the Rumsfeld practice. "In some places, we are quite obvious in our presence," Admiral Eric T. Olson, head of Special Operations Command, said in a speech. "In some places, in deference to host-country sensitivities, we are lower in profile. In every place, Special Operations forces activities are coordinated with the U.S. ambassador and are under the operational control of the four-star regional commander."[790] Such remarks suggest at least a recognition of a previous problem and a desire for coordination of special operations with State Department personnel. Even with its emergence as the preeminent player in the global War on Terror, it took over a decade for JSOC to become the subject of general media attention and political dialogue. Attention focused on it due to the 2011 mission against Osama bin Laden inside Pakistan, and contemporary debate over targeted killing and drone strikes. JSOC and CIA officers planned the bin Laden mission, which was ordered by President Obama and authorized under

Title 50 covert-action legal provisions. Originally, mission options included use of an Air Force B-2 bomber strike—using deep-penetration explosive JDAM. That option was driven by the possibility of a bunker beneath the bin Laden compound. Another option was the use of a CIA drone-launched tactical missile. In the end a helicopter-borne SOF raid was chosen.[791] The B-2 and drone strikes were tabled due to concerns over collateral damage, as well as the issue of proving that it was indeed bin Laden. Ultimately a capture or kill raid was authorized by President Obama. The bin Laden mission in Pakistan illustrated the exceptional degree to which covert and conventional warfare had been merged into a dramatically effective force.

In addition to specific missions such as the one against bin Laden, the Joint Special Operations Command organizes and coordinates the creation of longer-term task forces. Those task forces are assigned to regional operations ("fronts") in the War on Terror, and evolve along with changing circumstances and missions. JSOC has reportedly made considerable progress in coordinating with other commands, including the military theater commands, as well as with the State Department. Overall, intelligence collection and command and control have dramatically improved for Special Forces since the MACVSOG experience in Vietnam. The first major step towards a new and imminently more flexible counterterrorism force had been the integration of dedicated Special Forces units from within the various armed services. That integration forged land/sea/air units that could respond to extremely challenging missions, especially missions in remote and even hostile regions. The next step involved the integration of those joint Special Forces units with intelligence service assets. That effort led to the joint task forces of the post-9/11 War on Terror.

As the military reorganized its Special Forces efforts under the high-level command of JSOC, the CIA's paramilitary element was also changing, based in the intelligence community restructuring following 9/11. That restructuring further tightened its connections with the military special operations community. In 2005, the CIA paramilitary element, the Special Activities Division (SAD), began reporting to a new directorate-level function designated the

National Clandestine Service (NCS). SAD staffing procedures were also changing. Its elite military section, the Special Operations Group (SOG), would begin to take recruits solely from the military special operations commands. That would formalize the general recruiting practices we first saw as far back as 1954, with paramilitary CIA officers such as David Morales, Rip Robertson, and Carl Jenkins entering the CIA from either the Army or the Marines.[792]

This broad integration of forces, breaking down at least some of the barriers between services and agencies, was key to the effectiveness of the joint task forces that would become the primary weapon against Al-Qaeda affiliates around the globe. And as the first decade of the new century advanced, joint teams and Special Forces units assumed a much larger role in overall military operations. The size of the new forces grew substantially: estimates as of 2010 placed the number of special operations forces deployed overseas at some nine thousand combatants, virtually all in Iraq and Afghanistan.[793]

The first known post-9/11 JSOC regional force was Combined Joint Task Force 180, headquartered at Bagram Air Force Base in Afghanistan. In a previous chapter, we described some of its activities, primarily those targeting bin Laden and the Taliban leadership. It was later joined by Task Force 20 in Iraq, operating first in support of the American invasion and then independently targeting the Iraqi leadership. Task Force 20 also conducted classic Special Forces work such as identifying targets for air strikes and searching for missiles and weapons of mass destruction. Ultimately the task forces in Afghanistan and Iraq were consolidated into Task Force 121, with the dual mission of capturing and killing both Osama bin Laden and Saddam Hussein.

Things get fairly murky at that point, and it will be a long time before we see actual documents to clear up the details. Clearly, considerable effort has been made to shield the identities and specific missions of JSOC task forces. Reportedly Iraq also hosted Task Force 88, which involved elements of the Army's Delta Force and Rangers, along with Navy Special Forces and the Air Force 24 Special Tactics Squadron. Those same units and some of the same personnel had been involved in various deployments and missions, including work under Task Force 121. One of the reasons for such secrecy over Task Force 88 is that it reportedly conducted covert operations against Al-Qaeda in Syria, considered a hostile regime. A spin-off, Task Force 17, was directed against Iranian covert activities in Iraq.

Task Force 88 also became involved with early covert actions in the Horn of Africa.[794] Task Force 88 was believed to still have been operating as of 2008, albeit with its latest designations undisclosed. All that simply illustrates that task force designations evolve as missions change, and keeping current with them is supposed to be a challenge for anyone not directly involved—an aspect of operational security. The details of each task force's activities will provide the grist for numerous books and histories that will emerge within the next few years. It took twenty to thirty years to see the material now in print about combat in Vietnam and Laos; indications are that the time scale will be considerably compressed for at least some of the War on Terror actions.

One of the earliest, least-covered counterterrorism team missions was in the Philippines—targeting the Al-Qaeda–affiliated Abu Sayyaf ("Bearer of the Sword") group. The group had been founded by Osama bin Laden's brother-in-law and other veterans of combat against the Russian-backed regime in Afghanistan. It also had extensive ties to other very senior, very militant Al-Qaeda leaders, some of whom had been linked to the 1993 bombing of the World Trade Center in New York. Those leaders had also developed detailed plans for the concurrent bombing (Operation Bojinka) of some eleven airliners flying out of the Philippines on trans-Pacific routes in 1995. Due to intelligence work and some quick preemptive actions, the airliner plot had been not succeeded. In common with most jihadi militants, the group's stated goal was to establish an independent religious state in the southern islands and ultimately across Indonesia. It gained much media attention from its hostage-taking and ransom efforts, which generally targeted foreign tourists. The group was well networked to other Al-Qaeda affiliates in the region including

Jemaah Islamiyah—prominent because of its tourist bombings in Bali—and the Moro Islamic Liberation Front.[795]

A JSOC team was overtly deployed under military cover as a standard military assistance training/advisory mission, and arrived in the Philippines in 2002. Elements of the U.S. force were later acknowledged to have conducted field operations with Philippines security forces. Extensive intelligence-sharing was also performed as part of the mission, and intelligence assets made available to the mission included Predator intelligence, surveillance, and reconnaissance (ISR) drones and a manned P-3 Orion intelligence collection aircraft. Between 2002 and 2007, Philippines Armed Forces (AFP) operations against the rebel group killed its leader and two of its major commanders. Its fighting force declined from two thousand to approximately two hundred.[796] The AFP, clearly bearing the lead in operations and serving as the public face of the antiterrorist campaign, also conducted an aggressive public outreach program with the local populations, which was reportedly highly effective.

A peace agreement was reached with one Philippine group, the Moro Islamic Liberation Front, in 2008, but as background to the agreement, the government made it clear that American Special Operations Forces would remain in the country, continuing training and logistical support.[797] As of 2012, progress in the effort had continued to the point that the Philippine government announced that it planned to turn over all operations to the national police within four years. Along with the progress, the American troop presence had declined from some six hundred at its peak to approximately four hundred. The remaining task force members maintain a very low profile and keep largely to their own compounds, interacting only with their AFP counterparts.[798]

Apart from the Afghanistan and the Taliban regime, the Horn of Africa and specifically the states of Sudan, Yemen, and Somalia represented one of the most significant havens for jihadi terrorists prior to the attacks of 9/11. The Sudan had been an early haven for bin Laden, Somalia was essentially a nonstate with no central control or security apparatus, and Yemen had been one of the primary recruiting grounds for jihadi fighters going to Afghanistan to join the fight against the Soviets. The government of Yemen had coordinated and funded the recruitment and dispatch of thousands of jihadi fighters, afterward allowing their return and actually using them as surrogates against insurgencies in both the southern and northern regions of the country.[799] Yemen had been viewed as the base of the terrorists who had attacked the American destroyer *Cole*—a major propaganda victory that fueled the growth of the Al-Qaeda network. The Yemeni government had stonewalled American efforts to investigate that crime, publicly denying assistance to the FBI investigation into that attack, and the agents sent had been greeted by Yemeni security pointing machine guns at them; ultimately they simply had to withdraw under continued threats against them and against American embassy personnel.[800]

Realizing that Yemen could be an immediate target of American military action following the attacks on America, Yemeni ruler Ali Abdullah Saleh moved into an ongoing game of accepting American military assistance while redirecting much of it against the widespread insurgencies against his own government. He gave permission for drone flights over Yemen, acquiesced to targeted strikes against jihadi figures, and even claimed credit for attacks covertly conducted by American forces. By now the thought of a regime taking advantage of American military assistance for its own agenda should be no great surprise, but Saleh seems to have been exceptionally adroit at playing the game and leveraging the jihadi threat to maintain himself in power in the face of widespread and growing opposition.

One of the first major JSOC strikes inside Yemen provides an excellent illustration of the practices in this new era of gray warfare against the Al-Qaeda network. In 2002 JSOC teams, using extensive signals intelligence and drone flights, located the individual suspected of being the major Al-Qaeda figure operating in Yemen. SOF put his compound under observation and were preparing to assault it, and at that time the man and a number of his aides and fighters departed in a group of SUVs. An armed drone was quickly launched from the JSOC–CIA base in Djibouti and a high-speed chase followed.[801] Quick coordination with the Yemeni ruler produced an agreement that the strike would be made but the Yemeni cover story would be that the SUV had hit a land mine. A Hellfire missile strike destroyed the targeted SUV, killing all inside, including one American citizen from Buffalo, New York. Investigations would later connect him to a Buffalo cell organized to collect monies and recruit personnel for jihadi operations in Yemen.[802] Eventually several individuals from the Buffalo area—referred to as the Lackawanna Six—who had confessed to their involvement with camps in Yemen would be convicted and serve seven to ten years in prison for their activities.[803]

The Combined Joint Task Force–Horn of Africa (CJTF–HOA) is assigned oversight over some dozen nations in the Horn of Africa region. Initial force deployment was from Camp Lejeune, North Carolina, to a camp near Djibouti City in Djibouti. By 2004 task force elements included support, medical, and administrative staff from the Marines, Navy, Army, and Air Force, along with a helicopter detachment of four Sikorsky Super Stallions, a U.S. Army infantry company, a U.S. Army Reserve civil affairs company, military engineers, and a Special Forces operations unit (Task Force 150).[804] In addition, those operations have been supported by the Navy, with the USS *Mount Whitney* cruising in Horn of Africa and Gulf of Aden waters. The *Mount Whitney* is a command and control ship with capabilities for signals intelligence and the deployment of Marine combat units.

Yemen continued to see ongoing fundamentalist jihadi activity, beginning with the 2002 murder of three U.S. aid workers. Al-Qaeda's influence remained clear: in 2007 Al-Qaeda issued a warning to Jewish residents that if they did not leave, they would be abducted and murdered. Such threats and attacks have been broad-based. Eight Spanish tourists were killed in a suicide bombing in 2007, two Belgian tourists were killed in 2008, and four Korean tourists were killed in 2009. In addition, Al-Qaeda fighters attacked the American Embassy in Yemen in 2008; one American and eighteen others died in the attack.[805]

In response to the attack on the U.S. Embassy in 2008, American covert action in Yemen escalated dramatically. JSOC covertly conducted attacks on insurgent camps, targets, and leadership—including veterans of the USS *Cole* attack who continued to operate within the country.[806] One such individual, killed in a drone attack, was Fahd al-Quso, on the FBI's wanted list with a $5 million reward for information leading to him. He had been indicted in the *Cole* bombing and served five years in a Yemeni prison for the attack.

The covert-action story in Yemen seems to be a mixed one. The U.S. has been officially involved in military assistance and combat support to that nation's government and military in combating a jihadi insurgency. That, as with the actions in Somalia, illustrates the continuation of the Obama Administration policy of supporting nations threatened by fundamentalist insurgency, denying the evolution of new Afghanistan/Taliban–like terrorist sanctuary regimes. At a more clandestine level, JSOC continued its own effort to attack Al-Qaeda and affiliate group target lists developed by American law enforcement and the National Counterterrorism Center. The Obama Administration continued American support for the Yemeni regime, in the face of ongoing insurgencies and a worsening Yemeni political situation. Military assistance continued at significant levels, and the Yemeni military received ongoing training from the JSOC task force.

A major new American counterterror initiative began in Yemen in 2009, with three specific Al-Qaeda leadership targets. Once JSOC located the individuals, it requested what have become known as kinetic strikes within twenty-four hours. A kinetic terror attack is generally described as one in which massive destruction is highly focused—as compared to the intentionally wide-scale destruction of the terrorist airliner attacks on 9/11.[807] American kinetic military strikes involve the use of highly explosive munitions, delivered by high-speed weapons such as drone-launched Hellfire missiles or cruise missiles onto a very specific target—with devastating effects inside a small area. The munitions are in the five hundred to two thousand-pound range and are normally laser-guided or launched with very precise GPS coordinates.[808]

Such kinetic attacks have been described as "surgical" or "low-intensity." In comparison to the sorts of search-and-destroy missions seen in Vietnam, Afghanistan, or Iraq, that might be true—bombs and warheads are more focused than gunship attacks or B-52 saturation bombing. But in reality there is no such thing as a totally surgical strike in long-distance, denied-area warfare. One such kinetic attack in the new Yemen initiative used sea-launched Tomahawk cruise missiles to hit the location of an Al-Qaeda leader in a small, remote Aulaq tribal village in a mountainous area of Yemen. The cover story for the attack was that Yemeni air force planes had attacked an insurgent group that was hostile to the central government. Despite considerable obfuscation from all those involved, the reality seems to be that one Al-Qaeda leader may indeed have been killed in the strike, but that the warheads devastated the entire village, killing dozens of men, women, and children—even most of the tribe's sheep, goats, and cows.[809]

In contrast with such violent kinetic attacks, the general work of the Horn of Africa Task Force has been increasingly supplemented by a dramatically increased American commitment to economic development and social work. The Obama Administration increased American aid (USAID) to Yemen from $14 million to $110 million in 2010. Reportedly the CIA and State Department have become much more involved following the disastrous Tomahawk attack of 2009, and there is a major contemporary focus on civil development by the JSOC mission itself.[810] That involves an emphasis on contacts with schools and medical services in its region of operations, as well as military assistance activities with forces of the nations within its region.

Still, Yemen remains a haven for some numbers of jihadi network members and poses a direct concern to U.S. national security. In 2010, explosive packages were shipped out of Yemen in two separate air transport flights: one destined for the United States, the other for Dubai. Investigations revealed that the devices (inserted into printer cartridges) were in packages addressed to Jewish synagogues in the Chicago area. Later, Al-Qaeda itself claimed responsibility for the bombing attempts as well as for the crash of an air transport (UPS Airlines Flight 6) flying out of Dubai. Crash investigation of the UPS flight determined the primary cause as being smoke in the cockpit, apparently from a fire that had started in the cargo section of the plane.[811]

In terms of military action in Yemen, air attacks and drone strikes continued. An attack in May 2010 mistakenly killed a Yemeni provincial deputy governor conducting mediation efforts at the target location. Another on June 11, 2011, killed several known jihadi commanders and fighters as well as civilians in the area. In July 2011, an air attack was conducted against a police station that had been occupied by insurgent fighters. Other air and drone attacks continued throughout 2011, with some thirty-five attacks reported over a two-month period.[812] Ongoing air attacks by both American covert strikes and Yemeni aircraft were made throughout 2011. During 2012, both air attacks and drone strikes were conducted, with at least one attack against a Yemeni military base that had been overrun; estimates reported at least seventy-five insurgents were killed in the various 2012 attacks.

It is often difficult to determine which attacks are being made by Yemeni forces as opposed to the JSOC; however, it also seems to indicate a pattern we will discuss further. That pattern is a turn from specific global War on Terror strikes against Al-Qaeda leadership—which had in fact been considerably decimated—to something that looks a great deal more like the military assistance counterinsurgency activity with which we have become familiar. Preventing jihadi insurgencies from establishing new havens instead of fighting them directly is a definite direction in the emerging ideological conflicts of the twenty-first century—much as preemptive action to block communist insurgencies had been the model for the covert warfare of the second half of the twentieth century.

One of the most dramatic examples of that trend has been the evolution of American gray warfare in another Horn of Africa country, Somalia. Somalia had been a counterterrorism focus since a number of individuals involved with attacks on American embassies in Kenya and Tanzania had been tracked there. Somalia-based terrorists had bombed the American Embassy in Kenya in 1998, leaving 258 people dead and some 2,000 injured. In 2002, Somalia-based jihadi terrorists bombed a Kenyan vacation resort near Mombasa, killing thirteen people and wounding eighty others. Terrorists also fired two surface-to-air missiles at a departing Israeli airliner.

Given the lack of a functional central government in Somalia, military assistance was not an immediate option. Author Jeremy Scahill writes about an evolving effort that first had the CIA essentially contracting with a series of Somali warlords to locate, kidnap, or kill targeted terrorists.[813] Broad-brush targeting of that nature has virtually no precedent in CIA covert warfare, even though it was practiced by American allies during the Phoenix and Condor eras. Its conduct in Somalia seems to have reflected the direction to act extremely aggressively against Al-Qaeda in immediate post-9/11 operations and the chaos of operating inside a failed state. In terms of results, the operation undoubtedly killed some Al-Qaeda associates but it also led to kidnappings and attacks on a number of fundamentalists who were simply part of the Somalia political scene, worsening the general security situation in the country and creating more militant fighters on all sides. Scahill describes a bad situation growing far worse with American support first for an Ethiopian military intervention and later an African Union Mission in Somalia (AMISOM) force composed primarily of troops from Uganda and Burundi.[814] Both foreign incursions were seen as surrogate actions by America and simply strengthened fundamentalist calls inside the country for jihadi warfare against all invaders. They had also dramatically escalated the growth and influence of a homegrown fundamentalist group, Al-Shabab, which had declared itself an arm of Al-Qaeda. JSOC appears not to have been involved in the early Somalia activities beyond signals intelligence work and the fact that the JSOC naval element moved to interdict jihadi movements in and out of the country, especially across the Gulf of Aden in Yemen.

By the period of 2007–2009, Somalia had become a haven for terrorist targets; the possibility existed of a successful jihadi insurgency placing Al-Shabab military forces in control of the country, resulting in a terrorist haven on the scale of the Taliban in Afghanistan. Concern over that threat was fueled by an increasing number of Somali American citizens who were becoming active in fund-raising and recruiting in the U.S. for factions inside Somalia. Some of the American recruits would go on to suicide terror bombings inside Somalia, and there was growing traffic in activists traveling between the U.S. and Somalia. In 2009, some twenty men from the Minneapolis area were charged with raising funds, recruiting, and traveling to Somalia to train with Al-Qaeda–associated forces—including combat against African Union forces.[815] The Minnesota–Somalia connection became especially troubling, producing a lengthy investigation and additional charges. As late as 2013, several individuals were convicted and sentenced for conspiracy, including two women who had participated in door-to-door fund-raising for Al-Shabab as part of a pipeline providing money and recruits to jihadi combat in Somalia.[816]

Somalia had moved from being strictly a terrorist hunting ground to becoming a full-scale covert military operation by JSOC, targeting Al-Shabab not just with specific leadership strikes but with a broader range of Special Operations Command weapons. JSOC operated assets out of a base at Manda Bay in Kenya, and secretly flew AC-130 gunships out of an air base in Ethiopia. A combination of drone reconnaissance and gunship deployment provided for devastating attacks on Al-Shabab convoys and bases. During the same period of time, Ethiopian air strikes were attacking similar locations and it became difficult to distinguish JSOC attacks from those of other forces. Civilian casualties were reported in several of the strikes. There appear to have been a number of joint operations involving JSOC attack helicopters and gunships along with Ethiopian aircraft. Al-Qaeda leaders were indeed killed in the attacks, but the use of gunships also increased the collateral casualties.[817] As in Yemen, events in Somalia evolved from targeted attacks on Al-Qaeda network leadership to providing support for a chosen central government and aggressive active counterinsurgency against jihadi forces.

The Obama Administration formally acknowledged the change in direction in an April 2009 statement that there would be no purely military solution in Somalia, and that the U.S. would instead be moving towards a broader counterterrorism involvement with a number of African states. That did not mean that targeted strikes against terrorist network leaders ceased, and in September 2009 a JSOC helicopter attack team attacked a convoy of suspected foreign fighters inside Somalia. The U.S. officially had no comment on the attack but Al-Qaeda itself announced that several of its fighters—including three Al-Shabab leaders—had been killed, including the highest leadership figure in the Horn of Africa region.[818]

The Horn of Africa Task Force concentration on training for regional military forces is also beginning to mature. During the summer of 2012, a Kenyan ranger battalion that had been trained by Army Green Berets joined a U.S.-trained Kenyan special boat group for exercises at the Manda Bay facility in Kenya. Backed by American air intelligence and reconnaissance, the Kenyan force launched an amphibious assault on the last Al-Shabab–occupied urban area in Somalia. The Kenyans drove out the jihadi insurgent force and regained control over the port city of Kismayo—a key victory in denying support coming into Al-Shabab from the Arabian peninsula.[819] And in the fall of 2012, a U.S. Navy SEAL mission conducted a classified but successful rescue of two aid workers being held hostage by Al-Shabab. The hostages included one American and one Danish aid worker. Reportedly the attack was supported by ongoing drone reconnaissance and surveillance of Al-Shabab bases, and at least nine Al-Shabab fighters were killed in the attack. Other African countries including both Kenya and Uganda have suffered the brunt of Al-Shabab attacks, not just on police and military personnel but in dramatic kidnapping and hostage-taking as well as terror strikes.[820] Reportedly some $45 million in American military aid has been provided to Kenya, Uganda, and other African countries engaged in combat or security actions against Al-Shabab fighters. There also remain vague reports of foreign contract military personnel continuing to operate inside Somalia itself.[821] Continued military action weakened Al-Shabab in Somalia. It was driven out of the capital city and had its territorial influence considerably reduced. However, the country remained a major concern for its use as a haven and for conducting ongoing attacks into neighboring Kenya and across Africa. The Obama Administration made it clear that Al-Shabab was a legitimate terrorist target, specifically since its leaders continually call for attacks on Americans and America itself. Late in 2011, the senior U.S. military commander for Africa warned of the danger of Al-Shabab and the emergence of an alliance involving Al-Qaeda, Al-Shabab, and Boko Haram in northern Nigeria. His warning about the continued threat from Al-Shabab proved to be more than justified when a group operating out of Somalia conducted a highly organized and extremely deadly attack on Westgate, a major shopping mall in Kenya in September 2013. The mall was frequented by Westerners and tourists as well as by Kenyans. At least sixty-one civilians and six Kenyan security personnel were killed in the raid on the mall. The attackers used personal weapons rather than bombs, and the casualties were especially high as they showed no interest in taking hostages. A senior Kenyan government official noted that "They were not interested in hostage taking. . . . They only wanted to kill."[822]

The Joint Task Force effort has also focused on the trans-Sahara region of central and western Africa and has focused on military assistance programs and supporting policing actions against weapons and drug trafficking. Congress initially approved $500 million for these activities with the focus on Al-Qaeda operations in Algeria, Chad, Mali, Mauritania, Niger, Senegal, Nigeria, and Morocco. A variety of government agencies have been involved with the task force and its actual military activities have remained limited (or effectively covert). Military training and advisory activities with the nations involved began in 2005 with Exercise Flintlock.[823]

Flintlock training and exercises were held just to the south of the Sahara Desert, and were described as the largest American military activities in Africa since World War II. Some thousand U.S. forces participated in the effort, which focused on tracking and combating mobile terrorist groups in transborder movement. Just days before the exercise began, jihadists operating from the border between Algeria and Mali attacked and killed fifteen Mauritanian soldiers at an army base. The group had declared an insurgency against all nonfundamentalist Muslim regimes in the area and carried out attacks in Algeria, Mauritania, and Mali.[824]

While there was an initial amount of skepticism about the terrorist dangers in the region and the actual influence of Al-Qaeda, recent events have demonstrated the reality of terror attacks. Suicide bombings began in Mauritania in 2009, with responsibility claimed by a new group, Al-Qaeda in the Islamic Maghreb (AQIM). In a pattern similar to Somalia and Yemen, embassies were attacked, tourists were abducted and killed, and a pattern of anti-regime insurgency came into full play. Mauritanian police and military began aggressive counterterrorism strikes, joined by special operations forces of the French military—especially when the terror attacks involved kidnapping or murder of French citizens.[825]

By 2012, similar fundamentalist insurgencies, jihadi movements, and terror attacks had escalated across the region. The American Embassy in Benghazi, Libya, was attacked in the fall of 2012. The coordinated assault on both the embassy and an annex operated by the CIA resulted in the deaths of American Ambassador Chris Stevens, and GRS contractors. In December 2012, the Nigerian fundamentalist insurgent group Boko Haram, affiliated with both Al-Qaeda and Al-Qaeda in the Islamic Maghreb, carried out suicide attacks on Christian churches, killing dozens in an attempt to provoke full-scale religious warfare and fragment the country. In previous attacks during 2011, many on Christian churches and villages, the group, whose name literally translates as "Western education is sinful," had killed some six hundred people. Its most recent attacks have included suicide bombings of Nigerian police stations and foreign embassies.[826] The Obama Administration has taken the escalating African jihadi violence very seriously. General Carter Ham, the American military commander for Africa, is on record as stating that a jihadi trans-African network exists from Somalia on the Indian Ocean to Mauritania on the Atlantic.

As we noted, as of 2012, reports of actual American covert action in the trans-Sahara region have been virtually nonexistent and task force activities seem to have been much more on the order of military assistance training, civic action, and intelligence-sharing. To some extent that may be due to the fact that the French military has played a much more active military role with governments in the region. It is important to France not only because of business connections but also because of significant resident populations of French citizens. In 2013, military involvement by American forces in the region became more visible, largely because of a major jihadi move to actually take full control of the nation of Mali. In January 2013, insurgents began a major drive on the nation's capital at Bamako. The United Nations had previously voted for the intervention of an African military force in Mali, in part because of the brutality and repression going on in territory controlled by its jihadi insurgents.

The new insurgent push began as various African nations were assembling their contingents to move into the country. In an immediate response, Malian army units, supported by French strike aircraft, helicopters, and some two thousand French troops, began a counterattack. The Obama Administration committed American military support to prevent the takeover of Mali. Separately, nations of the West African regional bloc (Economic Community of West African States, or ECOWAS) began discussion of their own military response. Nigeria informed CNN that its first contingent would arrive in Mali within twenty-four hours and it planned to deploy some nine hundred troops, in battalion strength at the very least. Niger, Burkina Faso, Togo, Senegal, and Benin pledged troops to the UN-authorized force. Morocco and Algeria authorized French military overflights to Mali, and Britain began providing military transport aircraft to the French. Within a week the French and Malian forces had retaken cities overrun in the insurgent push, and by the end of January, the two forces had pushed the insurgents out of virtually all strongholds, which they had been holding in the north of the country for the better part of a year.[827]

The U.S. Air Force conducted airlift support for French and

African troops during the early months of 2013, as well as ongoing refueling missions for French aircraft engaged in Mali operations. In a further sign of increased American operational involvement in the region, in late February the Pentagon announced that a team of some one hundred U.S. military personnel had begun operating remotely piloted aircraft out of Niamey, Niger. The announced mission was intelligence, surveillance, and reconnaissance, using unarmed drone aircraft. The deployment was in support of a new military assistance agreement with Niger. The deployment had been communicated to congressional leaders prior to its announcement, and Congress was informed of its completion as of the end of February.[828] By March 2013, some four thousand troops from France, supported by a military force from Chad, had largely routed the jihadi forces from north-central Mali, capturing some fifty weapons caches as well as ten weapons workshops.[829] Nations including the United States, Germany, Belgium, and Canada supplied transport planes, and within a few days the U.S. Air Force had flown five C-17 transport missions with additional French troops and 124 tons of supplies and equipment. The U.S. provided tanker aircraft for refueling French air force operations.[830]

While military assistance and contingency operations seem to be the future of counterterrorist operations at the time of this writing, much more media attention has been given to the subject of drone warfare and its future role in the global War on Terror. While the contemporary gray warfare against terrorism that we have been describing has been characterized as "low-intensity" and almost surgical in terms of the actual geographic scale of the attacks, it can be exceptionally violent in terms of the weapons and technology used. To date the great majority of drone strikes have been in Afghanistan and Iraq, in support of conventional warfare and regime security efforts in those countries.

But beyond Afghanistan and Iraq, some 369 drone attacks have been conducted in Pakistan, with some 317 of those launched during the Obama Administration. The armed drones, used against denied western-border regions of Pakistan, have produced a significant percentage of civilian casualties. The most recent available studies estimate between twenty-five hundred and thirty-five hundred people killed there since 2004. Somewhere between 1,487 and 2,595 were reported as militants, leaving a civilian casualty rate of 20 to 25 percent for the total period. The year 2006 saw the highest percentage of nonmilitant casualties, over 60 percent. The attacks in Pakistan have declined significantly since 2011, when there were some 272 strikes. There were forty-eight in 2012. The nonmilitant casualties reportedly dropped to approximately 10 percent in 2012.[831] As combat shifted to Africa, 2010 saw some eleven attacks in Yemen, and eleven and forty-six in 2011 and 2012, respectively. As discussed earlier, the attacks in Yemen are a mix of Yemeni air attacks, U.S. drone attacks, and possibly attacks by American aircraft (details of all such strikes are classified).[832] The increasing number of Yemeni attacks of all types in 2012 was more likely a result of escalating military activity of the Yemeni regime against its insurgencies than of terror network strikes.

The attacks in Pakistan and Yemen have definitely produced civilian casualties and created broad and vocal protest, especially in Pakistan.[833] There is little doubt that the civilian deaths do radicalize local populations and generate recruits for the same militants who are being targeted in the attacks. Beginning in 2012 and continuing into 2013, media and political attention focused heavily on the effect of drone strikes in Pakistan as the source of radicalization. Media reporting from the Swat Valley of Pakistan dealt with the Pakistani government's effort to deal with large numbers of boys, from eight to eighteen, who had been recruited as fighters or suicide bombers; the government has established special schools in an attempt to deradicalize those taken into custody.[834]

Yet while media attention focused on drones in regard to the issue of radicalization in the Swat Valley, it must be noted that beginning in the 1990s, Taliban leaders had effectively seized the area from the Pakistani government, enforcing their own laws and converting government schools and facilities into radical religious training centers. Their control over the area lasted for almost twenty years, weakening only after senior Taliban leaders were killed or driven out in 2009–2010. Taliban attacks in Swat continued through 2011 and 2012. From a historical perspective, the growth of the radically religious Taliban had been encouraged by the establishment of a string of radical religious training centers along the Pakistan–Afghan border; the schools operated through the 1980s and beyond.

There is little doubt that the ongoing drone strikes, night raids, and kinetic strikes in Afghanistan, the Pakistan border regions, and Yemen during 2011 and 2012 were radicalizing individuals far beyond the areas of the strikes themselves. The perception of an ongoing ideological or culture war was beginning to emerge as the images of the attacks on America in 2001 had faded. With today's media and global Internet access, images are an increasingly powerful force. Contemporary coverage of the War on Terror in many instances includes images from devastated small villages. There are pictures of women and children being killed and wounded by drone strikes in Muslim countries. And those images are having their own radicalizing effects, even inside the United States and other Western nations. The 2013 Boston Marathon bombing was carried out by what appear to have been self-radicalized young Muslim men. Their declared motive was revenge for American attacks on Muslims worldwide. The horrific cleaver attack in London in the spring of 2013 is being attributed to men who quickly defended their actions as a response to the terrible war that the West was carrying out against their fellow Muslims.[835]

There are signs that the global War on Terror has become a permanent state, just as the Cold War existed for decades. Military assistance in Africa and elsewhere had come to involve even America's National Guard. Eight international guard partnerships were already in place by the spring of 2012 and a major push was under way to establish similar relationships in East African nations. Existing partnerships between African nations and state guard units included Botswana and North Carolina, Ghana and North Dakota, Liberia and Michigan, Morocco and Utah, Nigeria and California,

Senegal and Vermont, South Africa and New York, and Tunisia and Wyoming. The partnerships are vetted by state guard adjutant generals, who select individual guard units to become involved.

In March 2013, the head of the U.S. Africa Command—headquartered in Germany—proposed that Congress should grant strike authorities for Africa that would be similar to those previously issued for Afghanistan. The authorizations would allow contingency operations not strictly tied to Al-Qaeda but instead against a growing number of violent extremist organizations. General Carter Ham stressed the emergence of dangerous and violent threats to American interests and emphasized the value of preemptive action. He also pointed out that such a partnership approach would remove the need for any large commitment of American forces.[836] Ham's briefing paper for the House Armed Services Committee provides one of the most comprehensive and current overviews of America's new strategic approach to overseas military assistance and preemptive action.[837] Most recently a new study on "The Future of U.S. Special Operations" predicts the need for more indirect activities, and more military-to-military engagement with allies and partners, moving away from "persistent engagement" and updating authorities for preventive action.[838]

In the ongoing War on Terror, deniability is arguably no longer a practice unto itself as it was in the Cold War. Still, both covert and clandestine practices continue and have been thoroughly integrated into the operations of the Counterterrorism Center, the joint task forces, and the Joint Special Operations Command. In this work we detailed numerous examples of Cold War operations in which the CIA played primarily a logistics role, obtaining weapons and supplies through third parties and using individuals in friendly regimes to route the materials to surrogate fighters. Those surrogates were either insurgents, rebels, or military factions engaged in attempting to overthrow regimes considered unfriendly to the United States. In all those operations, the U.S. administrations involved denied lethal support for the surrogates—although on many occasions they were openly involved in nonlethal, humanitarian aid efforts to rebel forces. The need for such deniable surrogates has passed, but in the War on Terror they have been replaced with a broadly expanded military assistance effort throughout the regions containing jihadi networks and challenged by fundamentalist insurgencies. In broad terms it seems that the practices of shadow warfare, as well as the practice of the presidents, have remained constant—with one exception. The Reagan Administration's radical moves "outside the box," its turn to foreign governments for financing to provide weapons and supplies for secret warfare, and its allowing foreign intelligence services to control the funds and essentially take over the operations produced drastic long-term consequences. Of course those practices did seem to work well—until later events proved the strategy to be dramatically flawed, regardless of tactical success. Hopefully the lesson has been well learned.

In the spring of 2013, as a second-term president, Barack Obama described America as being at a "crossroads." His administration had moved to disengage the United States from conventional combat in both Iraq and Afghanistan. He had also begun an effort to shift strategic focus, declaring that the War on Terror no longer needed to be "boundless," that it was "self-defeating" to pursue it in terms of a perpetual fight. It too needed to end at some point, "like all wars."[839] In May 2013, in remarks delivered to the National Defense University in Washington, D.C., President Obama declared that the extensive Al-Qaeda terror network that had developed to conduct the sophisticated attacks seen both before and on 9/11 had been largely destroyed. Osama bin Laden was dead, as was the terror network's senior and even mid-level leadership. The network's safe havens in Afghanistan, Yemen, and Somalia had either been eliminated or significantly disrupted.

In light of the history we have reviewed in this work, it was not surprising to find Obama's remarks producing an immediate reaction from his political opponents—expressing concern that any phase-down in the War on Terror would increase American vulnerability and expose it to ongoing threats. Press headlines presented remarks from numerous Republican politicians who were "worried," "disturbed," or "troubled" that Obama might return the nation to a "dangerous level of unpreparedness." Other congressional leaders expressed concern that such remarks would embolden the Iranians or the North Koreans, indicating that America was going soft on national security, especially at a time when "tremendous threats are building not declining."[840] That sort of political national security counterpoint certainly sounds quite familiar. Overall it seems that America has come full circle, with the global War on Terror simply replacing the global Cold War against communism.

That reality reflects an ongoing War on Terror that seems to have been confirmed in President Obama's September 24, 2013, address to the United Nations, in which he cited the fact that Al-Qaeda had split into "regional networks and militias" and remains a "serious threat to governments, diplomats, businesses, and civilians around the globe." The president concluded that portion of his address with a commitment to dismantling terrorist networks, and declared that when it was necessary for the United States to act directly to defend against a terrorist attack, he would do so.[841] We can only conclude that the patterns of some seventy years will remain constant, and the first priority for any president will remain national security—both as an extension of the president's oath to preserve and protect not only the Constitution but the nation's people, and as a political reality of the office.

EPILOGUE

Benghazi

The State Department officially established a special mission and fa-cility in Benghazi, Libya, in November 2011, several months after the beginning of the civil war that ultimately ousted Muammar Gadhafi from power.[842] U.S. Ambassador Christopher Stevens had served as the initial American liaison with the Libyan insurgency, beginning in March 2011. Stevens was stationed at the American Embassy in the capital of Tripoli but routinely traveled to the major eastern city of Benghazi. By the end of 2011 the CIA had also established a significant covert presence in Benghazi, operating out of a compound designated as a State Department annex, with the ostensible mission of preventing weapons trafficking to insurgent and terrorist groups in the region. Given the huge stockpiles of weaponry accumulated by Gadhafi over decades, and "liberated" during the civil war, weapons traffic to a variety of insurgencies and military groups was a major Western and American concern. The CIA compound, located about one and a half miles from the American Embassy, was generally referred to as the the annex, reflecting its overt connection to the State Department. State Department personnel in Libya were themselves very much aware of the weapons trafficking going on in Libya, including the shipment of man-portable antiaircraft and anti-tank weapons.[843] Reportedly less than ten of the Americans in Benghazi were State Department employees, while over thirty were CIA personnel associated with the activities of the annex. Neither the embassy staff nor its own security, provided by five diplomatic security contractors, was as large as the CIA facility at the annex—which had its own ten-man security force. The new Libyan government seems not to have been aware of the CIA mission in Benghazi, very likely because so many of its staff carried "light cover" U.S. diplomatic passports. While the State Department was very much aware of the CIA presence, the relationship was compartmentalized and an investigation of the September 2012 attack on both the American facilities revealed a clear lack of understanding about mutual security responsibilities and communications between the State Department and the CIA.[844]

One particular reason for a major CIA mission in Benghazi, and Libya as a whole, was almost certainly an interest in the quantity of Russian-supplied antiaircraft and antitank weapons that had been in the country's arsenal during the Gadhafi era. As we have repeatedly seen, deniable weapons are the stock in trade of CIA covert operations. If deniability is a goal, then the weapons provided to the surrogates have to be foreign, and if at all possible must match the weapons used by the regime they are fighting—allowing them to be explained as captured in fighting or from defectors. It also means that the surrogates can easily integrate them and may well be familiar with those exact types of weapons. Taking control of Soviet weapons would have kept them out of a variety of jihadi insurgencies across Africa and the Southwest Asia; it would also have given the CIA a new set of advanced but deniable Soviet weapons.

Perhaps not coincidentally, the anti-regime protests in Syria were moving towards a full-scale insurgency in the fall of 2011. The Syrian army had begun to deploy into rebellious areas and Syrian aircraft were beginning overflights of cities where protests were occurring. Projections of a possible civil war were becoming more and more frequent. Clearly in such a conflict, all the insurgent factions, both nationalist and jihadi, would be looking for weapons—and in particular antiarmor and antiaircraft weapons to combat the extremely well-equipped Syrian military. To what extent the Obama

Administration might have been interested in the removal of the Assad regime in Syria will remain a matter of speculation for some time. Certainly Syria had opposed American efforts in the Middle East for decades—in particular efforts for a Middle Eastern peace process involving an Israeli–Palestinian settlement. Syria was also held to be a major supporter of a variety of terrorist groups.

In addition to a potential civil war in Syria, in North Africa there were intelligence indications of a pending jihadi effort against several regional nations—perhaps the most likely to be targeted being Mali. And in January 2012 the first such attacks did take place, with the government of Mali fighting for several towns in the north. Fighting would continue throughout the spring, with the rebels showing themselves to be exceptionally well armed and supplied. Clearly the huge amounts of Gadhafi-era weaponry in Libya would have had a number of parties interested in weapons traffic out of the country.

As of this writing there is no certain proof that what seemed a relatively large Libyan CIA mission, operating under State Department cover and working out of an embassy annex, was either attempting to prevent Libyan weapons from going to African jihadi insurgents, or possibly even working to acquire them for potential covert shipment to preferred Syrian rebel groups. The CIA would certainly not be expected to go on record about such activities, but reports indicate that it did conduct a major internal security effort with its own personnel following attacks on the embassy and annex in September 2012. In turn, the State Department officially maintained that its activities in Libya involved only damaged, aged, or unsafe weaponry. It was also careful to comment that it had no knowledge of weapons-related work in Libya by any other U.S. agency. It's highly unlikely that we will see any actual CIA records on its activities in Benghazi for many years. However, what we do have are a series of reports that such arms shipments out of Libya, destined for Syria, were indeed beginning in in the fall of 2012, shortly before the attack on the American facilities in Benghazi. The shipments were being organized by an individual friendly to the United States, and personally friendly to American State Department representatives including Ambassador Stevens. Following the Benghazi attacks of September 11, 2012, and the murder of Ambassador Stevens, such shipments out of Libya went into abeyance.

It is known that CIA field personnel were reported on the ground in Turkey and Syria in June 2012, contacting rebel groups and establishing plans for weapons distribution. Later reports discussed shipments coming from Libya, and described the Americans as simply facilitating the shipments, which would not be from the United States itself.[845] From the beginning of the Syrian conflict, the Obama Administration had criticized the Russians for their ongoing arms shipments to the Syrian regime, maintaining that the only American aid was nonlethal. In turn the Russians accused the U.S. of coordinating shipments of heavy weapons to the rebels; the American response was that the only heavy weapons in Syria were of "Soviet vintage."[846] Of course that statement would be equally true for weapons shipped to the regime or weapons moved out of Libya to the Syrian rebels.

Overall the reports describe limited shipments of weapons to the Syrian insurgents beginning in early 2012, peaking with a major boat shipment out of Libya in September and tapering off significantly for a time following the attacks at Benghazi. On September 6, 2012, a freighter docked in southern Turkey, with a weapons shipment organized by Tripoli Military Council head Abdelhakim Belhadj, who had worked closely with the Americans—including American Ambassador Stevens—during the Libyan revolution. The shipment reportedly contained SA-7 antiaircraft weapons and was directed across the Turkish border at Syrian rebel forces. On October 17, 2012, the first Syrian regime aircraft, a military helicopter, was downed; videos show that it appears to have been hit by a surface-to-air missile. In November 2012, an Assad regime jet fighter bomber was downed, and additional aircraft would be downed in following months. There are no further reports of weapons shipments in the months immediately following the Benghazi attacks.

However shipments began to resume in the spring of 2013, in the form of a series of air deliveries, primarily through Turkey.

The new airlift began with a single Qatar Emiri Air Force C-130 touching down in Istanbul, Turkey. Air traffic date records show that by the middle of spring a regular air bridge was coming into play, with six landings in Turkey. By August the Qataris had brought in fourteen more cargo flights. Aircraft spotters and transponder records show the flights to have originated at Al Udeid Air Base in Qatar, a major U.S. military logistics center in the Middle East.[847] Qatar itself denied shipping any arms to the rebels, stating that it sends only humanitarian, nonlethal aid. Qatar's full role, whether it involved actual purchase of arms or simply shipping them in mixed with humanitarian aid with funding by parties such as Saudi Arabia, will likely remain unknown. It should be noted that this supply chain, though Turkey, would feed into the north of Syria, where jihadi insurgent groups became increasingly strong during 2012.

Officially the Obama Administration did not authorize shipment of any sort of weaponry to Syria before the summer of 2013. However, the flow of weapons had obviously begun covertly much earlier than that. It is important to note that following the attack on the American facilities in Benghazi, escalating shipments did not come directly out of Libya to Turkey. Instead they were carried into Turkey by Jordanian, Saudi, and Qatari military-style cargo planes. Reports suggest that the CIA was involved in the shipments strictly in a "consultative" role, assisting Arab regimes to source the weapons in a variety of locations, including Croatia.[848] What role the administration and the CIA are currently playing in weapons shipments into Syria is unknown; by all appearances the Arab nations have become the primary funding sources for the purchases and have carried out the increasing shipments themselves. At the end of August 2013, the media was reporting a four-hundred-ton weapons shipment from Arab sources, going through Turkey and into Syria.[849] The tactical question of whether the Arab nations, have taken over field distribution to their favored rebel groups, as they did in Afghanistan, remains to be seen. Obviously the risk for the United States would be that if the distribution has been preempted, the Arab nations would have the ability to direct shipments to preferred jihadi groups, just as they did in the insurgency against the Soviets in Afghanistan.

Circumstantial evidence seems to suggest that in late 2011 the Obama Administration may well have been in the first phase of a covert operation to support nationalist Syrian insurgents against the Assad regime and to ensure that it controlled the sourcing, the supply chain, and the distribution of the weapons. It had officers on the ground, identifying groups, contacting leaders, and charting delivery logistics to bring arms into the north through Turkey. It may very well have been doing something similar in the south, based on its military assistance relationship with Jordan; that is unclear. In terms of sourcing, it was going to rely on the friendships with the new Libyan regime, built on its support of the successful revolution there. If the lessons of Afghanistan truly have been learned in Washington, it would seem quite possible that the Obama Administration may have tried to preempt a jihadi "seizure" of the Syrian insurgency by ensuring that nationalist and democratic forces were the ones receiving superior weapons.

The first small air shipments appear to have begun in 2012, followed by a major boat shipment from Libya to Turkey. Then the jihadi radicals attacked the State Department and CIA facilities in Benghazi. In the following media blitz, security scandal dialogue, and congressional inquiries, the American strategy for taking control of weapons delivered to nonradical groups in Syria may have been aborted. We know that the weapons shipments did resume within a few months; what we don't know is the extent to which the CIA remained integral in the chain of supply, or whether it was forced into the sort of high-risk intermediary role that it ended up playing in Afghanistan.

What seems increasingly certain is that the jihadi forces in Syria received superior support and became increasingly dominant. Access to weapons became the metric for success in the Syrian opposition movement, and the fundamentalist Islamist elements seemed to be the ones with superior funding and a more productive supply chain:

> *They also turned to more hardcore Islamist elements, who—with their superior funding, supplies, and discipline—have been pivotal in securing many rebel victories. This contributed to a vicious circle: the United States has long expressed fears that any weapons it might send to Syria's rebels will end up in the hands of extremists; the lack of weapons shipments has made the extremists stronger.*[850]

By the fall of 2013 eleven jihadi groups were sufficiently strong—especially in the north of Syria—to openly break with the umbrella insurgent alliance, declare common cause with an Al-Qaeda affiliate, and openly assert their goal of an Islamic republic in Syria under total sharia law.[851]

Another point that has become more firmly established is that the attack in Benghazi was very likely assisted and possibly incited by the larger Al-Qaeda–affiliated network. It does appear that assistance in the attack came from Al Qaeda in the Islamic Maghreb (AQIM), Al-Qaeda's affiliate in North Africa. A number of the individuals arrested after the attack were either from Mali or Algeria. More importantly, American intelligence later determined that at least three or four members of Al-Qaeda in the Arabian Peninsula (AQAP) had taken part in the Benghazi attack. The individuals spent the following night in Benghazi and were eventually traced to northern Mali, where they were reported fighting in the jihadi campaign.[852]

The nature of the Benghazi attacks themselves seems to suggest the type of extensive planning and coordination for which Al-Qaeda has become known. The initial attacks on the American embassy grounds included the use of rocket-propelled grenades, automatic weapons, mortars, and truck-mounted machine guns; and the attackers came equipped with diesel containers used to set fire to the compound, particularly the well-secured residency area. It is also clear that the American ambassador was personally targeted and that the attackers were very likely aware of his presence in Benghazi and had been very focused on his quarters. The annex was not attacked until early morning. However, the attackers not only besieged it but employed mortar, rocket, and machine gun fire. There is little doubt that their intent was to destroy both the ambassador and the CIA mission's activity in the country.[853]

If the Benghazi attack was indeed part of a larger Al-Qaeda strategy, it could have had two motives. The first would have been to abort American preemption of Libyan weapons moving within North Africa. That seems of particular importance, since a major territorial offensive was coming into play in Mali and reports are that much of the success of that offensive was fueled by new weapons coming out of Libya. We discussed the Mali insurgency in some detail in an earlier chapter. The events surrounding the fast-paced jihadi success there—overrunning much of the country and moving on the capital, only to be blocked by French and American intervention on the side of the Mali central government forces—do seem to suggest a general level of coordination and support between the jihadi groups in North Africa and those on the Arabian peninsula. The involvement of AQAP members in the Benghazi attack and their subsequent move to the Mali jihadi campaign would seem to support that motive.

Even more speculative is that the Benghazi attack represented an effort to disrupt the American strategy of controlling weapons shipments to ensure that they went to only non-jihadi groups inside Syria. It is suggestive that by the spring and summer of 2013, news sources consistently reported the jihadi-associated insurgent groups as having the best arms, rapidly enhancing their reputations and gaining them influence over the larger Syrian insurgency. If true, it could well be that the Benghazi attacks effectively undermined early American efforts at controlling the weapons channels. That could also suggest that the CIA has moved into a contest to see if it can resume its influence, even in the face of widespread popular and congressional opposition to involvement with either side in the Syrian civil war.

In any event, the attack in Benghazi illustrates the point that covert operations and the necessity of denial in the interest of national security continue; obviously the political risks for the president continue as well.

Endnotes

INTRODUCTION

1 Secretary of State John Foster Dulles provided an overview of the military strategy that would come to be described as Mutual Assured Destruction in a speech to the Council on Foreign Relations on January 12, 1954. The speech was titled "Evolution of Foreign Policy" and focused to a considerable extent on the economics of the strategy. Dulles pointed out that one of the basic maneuvers of world communism was forcing its opponents to overextend themselves—in essence, bankrupting them. A very similar strategy would actually be stated decades later by Osama bin Laden, in declaring that jihadi strategy was to force the Western nations to overextend and bankrupt themselves in their response to continual Al-Qaeda attacks.

2 The average citizen also didn't realize that each year, beginning under President Eisenhower, a special subcommittee of the National Security Council (the Net Evaluation Subcommittee) briefed senior government officials on "integrated evaluations of the net capabilities of the USSR, in the event of general war, to inflict direct injury upon the continental U.S. and key U.S. installations overseas, and to provide a continual watch for changes which would significantly alter those net capabilities." The evaluation was also to include assessments of a potential preemptive atomic strike by the Soviets. On occasion the Net Evaluation Subcommittee reports also led to discussion of the possibility and desirability of a preemptive first strike on the Soviets. National Security Council Directive 5511, Directive on a Net Evaluation Subcommittee, February 14, 1955, *Foreign Relations of the United States, 1950–1955, The Intelligence Community* 1950–1955, Document 207, U.S. Department of State, Office of the Historian; James Galbraith, "Did the U.S. Military Plan a Nuclear First Strike for 1963?" *The American Prospect*, December 19, 2001.
http://history.state.gov/historicaldocuments/frus1950-55Intel/d207
http://prospect.org/article/did-us-military-plan-nuclear-first-strike-1963

3 Richard G. Hubler, *SAC: The Strategic Air Command* (New York: Duell, Sloan and Pearce, 1958); Norman Polmar, ed., *Strategic Air Command: People, Aircraft, and Missiles*, Office of the Historian of the Strategic Air Command under the direction of John T. Bohn (Annapolis: Nautical and Aviation Publishing Company of America, 1979).

4 Ibid., 123, 149.
5 In 1981 NORAD was designated as the North American Aerospace Defense Command.
6 Marian Talmadge and Iris Gilmore, *NORAD: The North American Air Defense Command* (New York: Dodd, Mead and Company, 1967); *Guarding What You Value Most: North American Aerospace Defense Command, Celebrating 50 Years* (U.S. Department of Defense, U.S. Air Force, 2008).
7 James Oskins and Michael Maggelet, *Broken Arrow—The Declassified History of U.S. Nuclear Weapons Accidents* (Lulu.com, 2008).
8 William E. Burrows, *By Any Means Necessary: America's Secret Air War in the Cold War* (New York: Farrar, Straus and Giroux, 2001), 181–186, 201–202; Curtis Peebles, *Shadow Flights: America's Secret Air War against the Soviet Union* (Novato, CA: Presidio, 2001), 53–54.
9 Peebles, *Shadow Flights*, 127.
10 These secret Air Force intelligence missions reflected a surveillance commitment far beyond the more publicly known but numerically limited U-2 flights; they also produced a far greater number of incidents in which American aircraft were shot down, with the loss of entire crews ranging from three to sixteen or more servicemen. The full scope of the missions and the individual stories of a great number of the crews are described in *By Any Means Necessary* by William Burrows, *Shadow Flights* by Curtis Peebles, and *The Price of Vigilance: Attacks on American Surveillance Flights* by Larry Tart and Robert Keefe. *The Price of Vigilance* documents more than a dozen such incidents from 1950 through 1965 and records the number of American airmen killed or missing in each accident. Thanks to these authors and others such as Sherry Sontag and Christopher Drew, who addressed the Navy's secret submarine war in *Blind Man's Bluff: The Untold Story of American Submarine Espionage*, we have also begun to truly understand the secret side of the Cold War and the military casualties it produced.
11 The concept of mutual U.S.–Soviet aerial inspections was initially proposed in 1955, rejected by the Soviet Union, and eventually reintroduced by President George H.W. Bush in 1989. An actual treaty on aerial inspections was negotiated between NATO and the Warsaw Pact and signed in 1992. Flights began in 2002 and since then some thirty-four parties have joined the pact. As of September 3, 2013, one thousand inspection missions had been flown.
12 Richard Secord with Jay Wurts, *Honored and Betrayed: Irangate, Covert Affairs, and the Secret War in Laos* (New York: John Wiley & Sons, 1992), 48.

CHAPTER 1

13 Alexander Hamilton, Federalist Paper #70. http://www.constitution.org/fed/federa70.htm
14 James Madison, Federalist Paper #41. http://www.constitution.org/fed/federa41.htm
15 "DOD 101: An Introductory Overview of the Department of Defense," U.S. Department of Defense. http://www.defense.gov/about/dod101.aspx
16 The National Security Act of 1947, July 26, 1947, Public Law 253, 80th Congress; Chapter 343, 1st Session; S. 758. http://www.oup.com/us/companion.websites/9780195385168/resources/chapter10/nsa/nsa.pdf
17 The National Security Act of 1947 specified the statutory members of the National Security Council; other members designated by each president are regarded as nonstatutory. President Truman and most other presidents have included the national security advisor; others have included the secretary of the treasury or the attorney general. In 2009 President Obama consolidated the NSC with the White House staff supporting Homeland Security into a designated National Security Staff.

18 "Note on U.S. Covert Action Programs," *Foreign Relations of the United States, 1969-1976*, Volume E-10. http://history.state.gov/historicaldocuments/frus1969-76ve10/actionsstatement#fnref16

19 John Prados, *Keepers of the Keys: A History of the National Security Council from Truman to Bush* (New York: William Morrow and Company, 1991), 30.

20 Ibid., 83.

21 Ibid.

22 *Church Committee, Interim Report*, "Alleged Assassination Plots Involving Foreign Leaders," 1975, 52. http://history-matters.com/archive/church/reports/ir/html/ChurchIR_0033b.htm

23 John Stockwell, *In Search of Enemies: A CIA Story* (New York, W.W. Norton and Company, 1978), 45–46.

24 Ibid., pp. 46–47.

25 Congressional Record, House, 29 June 1954, 9176–9177, quotations from Lyndon Johnson and Republican leader William Knowland, 8922–8926; David M. Barrett, "Congress, the CIA, and Guatemala, 1954—Sterilizing a 'Red Infection.'" https://www.cia.gov/library/center -for-the-study-of-intelligence/kent-csi/vol44no5/html/v44i5a03p.htm

CHAPTER 2

26 James David Barber, *The Presidential Character: Predicting Performance in the White House* (Englewood Cliffs, NJ: Prentice Hall, 1992).

27 Robert Dallek, "Lyndon B. Johnson," excerpted essay. http://www.pbs.org/newshour/character/essays/johnson.html

28 John T. Correll, quoting Assistant Secretary of State William P. Bundy, "Encounters in the Tonkin Gulf," *Air Force Magazine*, January 2012.

29 Joint resolution of Congress (H.J. RES 1145), August 7, 1964. http://www.ourdocuments.gov/doc.php?flash=true&doc=98

30 Edwin E. Moise, *Tonkin Gulf and the Escalation of the Vietnam War* (Chapel Hill: University of North Carolina Press, 2004). The most current academic study of the Tonkin Gulf incidents may be found in Moise's work; he presents a strong case that the second purported destroyer attack indeed did not occur. The first incident was a North Vietnamese response to clandestine sabotage and a coastal attack missions by CIA-directed force. Even more troubling is a report in the NSA Journal, *Cryptologic Quarterly*, by Robert Hanyok. His 2001 article "Skunks, Bogies, Silent Hounds, and the Flying Fish: The Gulf of Tonkin Mystery" uses texts from key signals of North Vietnamese intercepts. Hanyok concludes that certain summary reports were deliberately skewed, using only selections that fit the "official scenario." No actual intercepts from the second night confirm an attack on the U.S. destroyer.

31 David Atlee Phillips, *The Night Watch* (New York: Atheneum, 1977), 147–150. David Phillips was assigned as the new chief of station for the Dominican Republic; he provides several personal and interesting remarks on Raborn's initial involvement with the crisis—and the admiral's total lack of knowledge or understanding of CIA operations.

32 Lawrence A. Yates, *Power Pack: U.S. Intervention in the Dominican Republic, 1965–1966* (Leavenworth, KS: Leavenworth Papers, Combat Studies Institute, U.S. Army Command and General Staff College, 1988), 173.

33 John Prados, *Keepers of the Keys: A History of the National Security Council from Truman to Bush* (New York: William Morrow and Company, 1991), 144–145.

34 Phillips, *The Night Watch*, 150, 155.

35 Prados, *Keepers of the Keys*, 147.
36 Yates, *Power Pack*, 173, 177, 178.
37 Don Bohning, *The Castro Obsession: U.S. Covert Operations Against Cuba, 1959–1965* (Dulles, VA: Potomac Books, 2006), 261.
38 *Foreign Relations of the United States/FRUS*, Volume X, Document no. 271, 668–672.
39 Barber, *The Presidential Character*, 346–364.
40 Material for this section on Kennedy back-channel contacts with Fidel Castro is largely based on the article "JFK and Castro: The Secret Quest for Accommodation," *Cigar Aficionado* (September/October 1999) by National Security Archive senior analyst Peter Kornbluh. Additional information, discussion, notes, and documents are contained in a separate study on the National Security Archive website, entitled "Kennedy Sought Dialogue with Cuba," posted November 24, 2003:
http://www.gwu.edu/~nsarchiv/NSAEBB/NSAEBB103/index.htm
http://www.cigaraficionado.com/webfeatures/show/id/JFK-and-Castro _7300
41 Jefferson Morley, *Our Man in Mexico: Winston Scott and the Hidden History of the CIA* (Lawrence, KS: University Press of Kansas, 2008), 165.
42 Bohning, *The Castro Obsession*, 170.
43 Ibid., 171.
44 John Prados, *The Sky Would Fall: Operation Vulture—The Secret U.S. Bombing Mission in Indochina, 1954* (New York: Dial Press, 1983), 145–148.
45 Prados, *Keepers of the Keys*, 149.
46 Ibid., 148–150.

CHAPTER 3

47 An "unvouchered expenditure" is any expenditure accounted for solely on the approval, authorization, or certification by the president or an official of an executive agency. http://clinton1.nara.gov/White_House/EOP/OMB/html/circulars/a034/partx.txt
48 "Note on U.S. Covert Action Programs," *Foreign Relations of the United States, 1969–1976,* Volume E-10, *Documents on American Republics, 1969–1972.* http://history.state.gov/historicaldocuments/frus1969-76ve10/actionsstatement#fnref16
49 "Note on U.S. Covert Actions," *Foreign Relations of the United States 1964–1968,* Volume XII, *Western Europe,* U.S. Department of State, Office of the Historian. http://history.state.gov/historicaldocuments/frus1964-68v12/actionsstatement
50 Ibid., XXXI–XXXV.
ww.fas.org/sgp/advisory/state/covert.html
51 Richard H. Shultz Jr., *The Secret War Against Hanoi: The Untold Story of Spies, Saboteurs, and Covert Warriors in North Vietnam* (New York: Harper Perennial, 2000), 19–22. NSAM 55 "eliminated exclusive CIA authority over planning and executing covert, paramilitary operations," while NSAM 57 stated that covert or deniable operations be assigned to the CIA only if "within the normal capabilities of the Agency." Specifically, any operation requiring significant numbers of military personnel and military equipment would become the primary responsibility of the Department of Defense. In accordance with Kennedy's movement of covert operations to the military, NSAM 124 (January 1962) created the Special Group for Counterinsurgency, which was to serve under both Special Group 5412 and Johnson's 303 Committee. In addition, the Joint Chiefs established the Office of the Special Assistant for Counterinsurgency and Special Activities (SACSA) to provide

staff to carry out counterinsurgency projects as directed by the Special Groups. The first SACSA chief, appointed in February 1962, was Marine Corps Major General Victor "Brute" Krulak. SACSA became a key element of deniable warfare during the Nixon and Reagan administrations, and would eventually receive service from many of the paramilitary officers who first served with the CIA.

52 Ibid.

53 *Staff Report of the Select Committee to Study Governmental Operations with Respect to Intelligence Activities* (commonly known as the Church Committee Report), "Covert Action in Chile 1963–1973." https://www.fas.org/irp/ops/policy/church-chile.htm

54 John Prados, *Keepers of the Keys: A History of the National Security Council from Truman to Bush* (New York: William Morrow and Company, 1991), 261.

55 Ibid., 228.

56 David Atlee Phillips, *The Night Watch: Twenty-five Years of Peculiar Service* (New York: Atheneum, 1977), 221.

57 The proposal selected had originated with the NSC staff. An alternative proposal (from staff member Oliver North) had been simply to mine Libyan harbors, but North's earlier proposal and the actual operation in which the Navy mined Nicaraguan harbors had been such a complete fiasco that this time his idea had little traction with the NSC.

58 Prados, *Keepers of the Keys*, 507–512.

59 Blanche Wiesen Cook, *The Declassified Eisenhower* (New York: Penguin Books, 1984), preface, xv–xvi.

60 Joseph Bunkhouser Smith, *Portrait of a Cold Warrior: Second Thoughts of a Top CIA Agent* (New York: Ballantine Books, 1981), 102.

61 House Select Committee on Intelligence, "Performance of the Intelligence Community," 813. For details on the Pike Committee and its inquiry, see "The Pike Committee Investigations and the CIA: Looking for a Rogue Elephant," Gerald K. Haines, April 14, 2007. https://www.cia.gov/library/center-for-the-study-of-intelligence/csi -publications/csi-studies/studies/winter98_99/art07.html

62 Bob Woodward, *Bush at War* (New York: Simon & Schuster, 2003), 46. At the risk of being too hard on Congress, Bob Woodward writes that Senator Robert Byrd, in remarks before Congress, stated that President George W. Bush actually told him he did not want a declaration of war—that would represent a blank check he did not desire. Of course such a statement must be taken in combination with Bush's often-expressed remarks in the early days about not occupying foreign countries, performing police and security functions, or regime building. The failure of Congress to do more than pass a resolution, more than a decade later, seems reminiscent of the warfare in Southeast Asia, conducted for a similar period of time with nothing more than an initial Gulf of Tonkin Resolution based on reports of attacks on American destroyers.

63 Ibid., 41.

64 Ibid., 21.

65 Alan Armstrong, *Preeemptive Strike: The Secret Plan That Would Have Prevented the Attack on Pearl Harbor* (Guilford, CT: Lyons Press, 2006), chapters 2–4.

66 Richard Secord and Jay Wurts, *Honored and Betrayed: Irangate, Covert Affairs, and the Secret War in Laos* (New York: John Wiley & Sons, 1992), 353–354.

CHAPTER 4

67 Alan Armstrong, *Preemptive Strike: The Secret Plan That Would Have Prevented the Attack on Pearl Harbor* (Guilford, CT: Lyons Press, 2006), 36, 56, 59, 96, 103.

68 John T. Correll, "The Air Force on the Eve of World War II," *Air Force Magazine*, October 2007. http://www.airforce-magazine.com/Magazine Archive/Pages/2007/October%202007/1007WWII.aspx

69 Alan Armstrong, *Preemptive Strike*, 26–28.

70 Ibid., 25–27.

71 Ibid., 169–171.

72 Ibid., 64, 110–111. Both Morgenthau and Claire Chennault (nominally an employee of the Bank of China but serving as air defense advisor to the Chinese Aeronautical Affairs Commission) felt that approach would have a massive psychological impact on the Japanese population and might lead them to restrain their military's aggressive ambitions. Exactly that strategy, massive firebombing of the Japanese cities (by B-29 bombers rather than B-17s), was eventually adopted by U.S. Army Air Corps General LeMay in 1944. The firebombing campaign was initiated with the specific goal of forcing a Japanese surrender.

73 Ibid., 6, 87–89.

74 Ibid., 92.

75 In regard to the financing of the Special Air Unit in China, it appears that loans and loan guarantees were the primary funding mechanism, rather than any direct American payments or donations from third parties. It is not clear to what extent any of the loans were repaid, or if the U.S. government was forced to assume fiscal responsibility for them. In terms of scale it was a truly major financial effort, but it would not be for three more decades—in Afghanistan and then in Nicaragua—that the U.S. would actually start soliciting third-party donations in support of surrogate forces.

76 Ibid.

77 Ibid.

78 Ibid.

79 James H. Doolittle, *Report on the Covert Activities of the Central Intelligence Agency*, Washington, D.C., July 26, 1954. https://docs.google.com/viewer?a=v&q=cache:TFz1prqQ6NsJ:www.foia.cia.gov/helms/pdf/doolittle_report.pdf+&hl=en&gl=us&pid=bl&srcid=ADGEESgGUVEdReoO2XsyRPZ_i0qYexDzo2SacjgOvnTYN 4vFx_WdNEBx-YSAXtAq4C7uB2ii9oGy6mnJkivsCKOzjgualrL81Tk WeYpeXDOaPgVyTWPUWn4tT9oxfF2YMmJb2XwFXAqkJ&sig=AHIEtbSXI69AsoUYL3q028QNiSxg8KJ32w

80 Pawley's mission to Batista, *Official History of the Bay of Pigs Operation*, Vol. III, 20–21. http://www.foia.cia.gov/sites/default/files/document _conversions/4186/bop-vol3.pdf

81 *CIA Memorandum for the Record*, conversation with Mr. Thomas Corcoran, signed by Stuart Hedden, April 16, 1952. http://www.foia.cia.gov/sites/default/files/document_conversions/89801/DOC_0000924155.pdf

82 *Memorandum of Conversation with Mr. Joe Montgomery and Mr. Thomas Corcoran of T* [sic], created July 22, 1954. http://www.faqs.org/cia/docs/106/0000920234/memorandum-of-conversation-with-mr.-joe-montgomery-and-mr.-thomas-corcoran-OF-T.html

83 *CIA Memorandum to Deputy Director of Plans*, July 22, 1954, *Foreign Relations of the United States, 1952–1954, Retrospective Volume, Guatemala, Document 279*, meeting between Mr. Joe Montgomery and Mr. Corcoran and Col. J.C. King, Chief CIA Western Hemisphere. http://history.state.gov/historicaldocuments/frus1952-54Guat/d279

84 Interview with E. Howard Hunt, National Security Archives, Cold War Interviews. http://www.gwu.edu/~nsarchiv/coldwar/interviews/episode-18/hunt1.html

85 John Prados, *Presidents' Secret Wars: CIA and Pentagon Covert Operations from World War II through the Persian Gulf War* (Chicago: Ivan R. Dee, 1996), 62.

86 Ibid., 65–66.
87 Ibid., 69–70.
88 Readers interested in the detailed history of CAT/Air America should take advantage of CIA/Air America archival collections—including CIA historical documents and studies available online.
http://www.air-america.org/ArchiveGuide/ArchiveGuide.shtml
89 Prados, *Presidents' Secret Wars,* 63–64.
90 Allen Cates, *Honor Denied: The Truth about Air America and the CIA* (iUniverse, 2012), 126–129.
91 Pacific Corporation held a series of companies including CAT Inc., Air Asia Company Limited (Air Asia Taiwan), Air America Inc., Civil Air Transport Inc., Southern Air Transport, Intermountain Airlines, Bird and Sons (BirdAir), and Robinson Brothers. An effort was made at that time to change the name CAT to Air America but legal issues delayed that for a further two years.

CHAPTER 5

92 David Atlee Phillips, *Secret Wars Diary: My Adventures in Combat, Espionage Operations and Covert Action* (Bethesda, MD: Stone Trail Press, 1989), 169.
93 United States Department of State, *Foreign Relations of the United States, 1951. Korea and China (in two parts), "The China Area"* (1951), 1475–1476. http://digicoll.library.wisc.edu/cgi-bin/FRUS/FRUS-idx?type=turn&entity=FRUS.FRUS1951v07p2.p0017&id=FRUS.FRUS1951v07p2&isize=M
94 When referring to presidential security directives in the general sense we will use the generic term NSAM. However, when discussing specific directives in which the full designation is available, we will give it for the benefit of readers who may wish to research it in more detail.
95 Richard Michael Gibson and Wen H. Chen, *The Secret Army: Chiang Kai-shek and the Drug Warlords of the Golden Triangle* (Singapore: John Wiley & Sons, 2011), 50.
96 Kenneth Conboy and James Morrison, *The CIA's Secret War in Tibet* (Lawrence, KS: University Press of Kansas, 2002), 37.
97 John Prados, *Presidents' Secret Wars: CIA and Pentagon Covert Operations from World War II through the Persian Gulf War* (Chicago: Ivan R. Dee, 1996), 70–71.
98 Partick Brogan and Albert Zarca, *Deadly Business: Sam Cummings, Interarms & the Arms Trade* (New York: W.W. Norton & Company, 1983), 46–50.
99 George Thayer, *The War Business: The International Trade in Armaments* (New York: Simon & Schuster, 1969), 48–49.
100 Gibson and Chen, *The Secret Army*, 10–11. By late March 1950, some eighteen hundred regulars and militia from the Chinese 8th and 26th armies had moved to the Burmese frontier along the tri-border (Golden Triangle) area of Burma, Thailand, and Laos.
101 W.R. Peers, *Intelligence Operations of OSS Detachment 101*, CIA Historical Reviews Program, September 23, 1993. https://www.cia.gov/library/center-for-the-study-of-intelligence/kent-csi/vol4no3/html/v04i 3a11p_0001.htm. Also, full background including photographs and oral histories is available online at the OSS Detachment 101 Association. website: http://www.oss-101.com/
102 Gibson and Chen, *The Secret Army*, 52–53.
103 Joseph B. Smith, *Portrait of a Cold Warrior: Second Thoughts of a Top CIA Agent* (New York: Ballantine, 1976), 105–106. Terminology often becomes a bit confusing when discussing such commercial companies. Generally speaking,

companies largely funded by the CIA and under direct management/operation of Agency personnel are referred to as proprietaries. Such companies provide "cover for status" (giving individuals an overt/business identification for travel and residency) and "cover for action" (a credible story to explain the places they go and the people in whose company they may be observed). Since such companies are largely funded by Agency money, they generally come under the oversight of the CIA's Commercial Division, which evaluates their expense versus their usefulness in terms of operational results.

The original Civil Air Transport would be an example of such a company. On the other hand, companies such as SEA Supply, involved in a broad range of commercial business and largely autonomous, are on call for Agency operations and not under day-to-day operational control. The Agency also used dummy companies as covers—those companies were nothing more than shells used to conceal CIA operations and had no actual business operations, few expenses, and few employees. Zenith Technical Services was the shell that provided a business cover for the CIA's huge domestic field office in Miami, charged with waging deniable warfare against Cuba.

Matters are further complicated (intentionally) by the Agency practice of using vetted companies and professionals that are cleared by security and trusted with limited activities that must be kept confidential. Vetted personnel included medical, psychological, and legal professionals as well as private security and investigative contractors who accept on-demand assignments.

Finally, the Agency has a long history of social and business networking with owners and managers of international companies operating both domestically and overseas. Such relationships are strictly on a voluntary basis but were viewed as highly patriotic during the Cold War. In certain instances the support went far beyond simply providing information or introductions. In the earliest days of the CIA's secret war against Cuba, a former American businessman who had worked in Cuba was used as an intermediary to obtain financial support for the purchase of a ship (the *Tejana*) to be used for covert missions into Cuba. The Klebergs of the King Ranch in Texas put up half the money for the purchase while Cuban exiles produced the remainder. The CIA encouraged the effort, provided advice on funding and tax write-offs, and paid to arm and supply the boat, without actually owning it. The CIA also organized and security-checked the crew for the vessel, and took over its operational tasking for Cuban missions. Document references: RIF 104-10172-10088 (CIA memorandum on AM/PARTIN and AM/DENIM), 104-10172-10438 (*Tejana* Returned Key West), and 104-10172-10067 (JM WAVE memorandum requesting crypts for *Tejana* crew).

104 Brogan and Zarca, *Deadly Business*, 214.

105 Gibson and Chen, *The Secret Army*, 61–62.

106 Ibid., 61–63.

107 Ibid., 105–106.

108 Ibid., 104–105.

109 Ibid., 106–108.

110 Ibid., 176.

CHAPTER 6

111 John Prados, *Presidents' Secret Wars: CIA and Pentagon Covert Operations from World War II through the Persian Gulf War* (Chicago: Ivan R. Dee, 1996), 317.

112 Ibid., 100–101. Historian John Prados describes an internal conflict in the early days of the Guatemala project, one in which certain officers argued that the CIA team should be working directly through Corcoran and United Fruit, even to

the point of utilizing the business's aircraft and available weapons. That option was rejected, but Corcoran kept United Fruit advised on the progress of Agency efforts.

113 *CIA Memorandum for the Record*, conversation with Mr. Thomas Corcoran, signed by Stuart Hedden, April 16, 1952. http://www.foia.cia.gov/sites/default/files/document_conversions/89801/DOC_0000924155.pdf

114 *Memorandum of Conversation with Mr. Joe Montgomery and Mr. Thomas Corcoran of T* [sic], created July 22, 1954. http://www.faqs.org/cia/docs/106/0000920234/MEMORANDUM-OF-CONVERSATION-WITH-MR.-JOE-MONTGOMERY-AND-MR.-THOMAS-CORCORAN-OF-T.html

115 *CIA Memorandum to Deputy Director of Plans*, July 22, 1954, *Foreign Relations of the United States, 1952–1954, Retrospective Volume, Guatemala,* Document 279, Meeting between Mr. Joe Montgomery and Mr. Corcoran and Col. J.C. King, Chief CIA Western Hemisphere. http://history.state.gov/historicaldocuments/frus1952-54Guat/d279

116 Interview with E. Howard Hunt, National Security Archives, Cold War Interviews. http://www.gwu.edu/~nsarchiv/coldwar/interviews/episode-18/hunt1.html

117 Louis J. Halle, Memorandum of the Policy Planning Staff to the Director of the Policy Planning Staff (Bowie), Washington, May 28, 1954. http://www.princeton.edu/~bsimpson/2010%20Hist%20380/Memo randum%20by%20Louis%20J.%20Halle,%20Jr.%20of%20the%20Policy%20Planning%20Staff,%20Washington,%20May%2028,%201954,%20OUR%20GUATEMALAN%20POLICY

118 Gerald K. Haines, *CIA and Guatemala Assassination Proposals: 1952–1953*, CIA history staff analysis, June 1995. Key sources for the CIA historical study are referenced as noted in the text. http://en.wikisource.org/wiki/CIA_and_Guatemala_Assassination_Proposals:_CIA_History_Staff_Analysis

119 Ibid.

120 *Foreign Relations of the United States,* "Guatemalan Communist Personnel to be Disposed of During Military Operations of Calligeris" (Armas), September 18, 1952, Box 134 (S).

121 Memo, "Conferences," December 1, 1952, Box 134 (S); memo, "Current Planning of Calligeris Organization," December 12, 1952, Box 134 (S). See also, *Acting Chief, [ ] Branch, Western Hemisphere Division*, which reported in November 1952 that Armas was studying PW use of liquidation lists. Memorandum for the Record, "PW Conferences," November 5, 1952, Box 151 (S). The case officer also reported that the Árbenz government had targeted Armas for assassination. March 10, 1953, Box 15D (S).

122 *Foreign Relations of the United States*, Report #3 *to* [ ], "Liaison between Calligeris and General Trujillo of Santo Domingo," September 18, 1952, Box 134 (S). The CIA study noted that "assignation a nasty but frequent tool of Guatemalan politics. Árbenz himself benefited from the killing of his archrival for the presidency Francisco Arans in 1949."

123 Murr notes that the COATHANGER designation appears to have been released only as a combination of clerical error and a missed redaction. The term is used only some four times in some fourteen thousand pages of project documents. References include the first of a series of memoranda to chief of staff, Department of Army pertaining to the shipment of foreign weapons and ammunition; the memorandum is dated August 6, 1952, Letter Order No. 02-00500 and carries a secret classification with ASTRAL notation. Follow-up letters in the same series are dated August 25 and October 2, 1952. http://www.foia.cia.gov/collection/guatemala

124 Memorandum dated July 28, 1952 to the Deputy Director of Plans (CIA); Subject: Packaging and Transportation of Materials—Classified "Secret" Security Information.

125 *Foreign Relations, Guatemala, 1952–1954, Memorandum for the Record*, July 28, 1952, "Outline of events for initial hardware shipment DTROBALO—FTZ NY—Puerto Cabezas." http://2001-2009.state.gov/ r/pa/ho/frus/ike/guat/20176.htm

126 Unnumbered report issued September 1, 1952, titled *Intermediate Report on Military Plans for Guatemala*, 2003 release under CIA Historical Review Program, 5.

127 Nicholas Cullather, *Operation PBSUCCESS: The United States and Guatemala, 1952–1954,* History Staff, Center for the Study of Intelligence, Central Intelligence Agency, 19.

128 *Congressional Record, House, 29 June 1954, 9176–9177,* quotations from Lyndon Johnson and Republican leader William Knowland, 8922–8926; David M. Barrett, "Congress, the CIA, and Guatemala, 1954: Sterilizing a 'Red Infection,'" Center for the Study of Intelligence, Central Intelligence Agency. https://www.cia.gov/library/center-for-the-study-of-intelligence/kent-csi/vol44no5/html/v44i-5a03p.htm

129 Richard Immerman, *The CIA in Guatemala: The Foreign Policy of Intervention* (Austin, TX: University of Texas Press, 1982), 103, 115, 156; Smathers, *Congressional Record, Senate, 28* May 1954, 7336–8.

130 George Thayer, *The War Business: The International Trade in Armaments* (New York: Simon & Schuster, 1969), 52. Reportedly the CIA learned of the purchases through a key connection to the world weapons trade, former CIA employee turned independent weapons dealer Sam Cummings. The Agency admitted only that it had gotten the information from "arms dealing circles." However, Cummings had only recently left the Agency and documents indicate that he continued to be an informant and key source of weapons trade intelligence.

131 Burton Hersh, *The Old Boys: The American Elite and the Origins of the CIA* (Tree Farm Books, 2001), 344–346.

132 Barrett, "Congress, the CIA, and Guatemala, 1954: Sterilizing a 'Red Infection.'"

133 "Log-PBFORTUNE Meetings," with handwritten notation "PBSUCCESS File—6 November, 1953," released in sanitized form in 2003, CIA Historical Review Board. The Grace National Bank, a holding of the W.R. Grace and Company focused specifically on business ventures in Latin America, was extremely profitable in the 1950s. In August 1965, approval was given for it to merge with Marine Midland, and the existing company is known as HSBC Bank USA. Standard Oil was active in Latin America and specifically in Guatemala, holding the ability to further pressure the Árbenz government financially. These corporate briefings were conducted in the Dolly Madison House, later known as the Wilkins Building. The building officially housed the National Advisory Council on Aeronautics but also served certain CIA technical staff, being referred to as the I Building.

134 Eyes Only Security Information Memorandum, August 17, 1953, sanitized and released by CIA Historical Review Board, 2003.

135 Cummings's association with weapons shipments for Armas put him in a key position to grow his new business. After Armas assumed power in Guatemala, Cummings found himself "in on the ground floor." The new government suddenly decided to scrap its entire inventory of Czech weaponry and replace it with American-compatible. 30-caliber arms. Since the U.S. was still working to maintain deniability in regard to intervention in Guatemalan internal affairs, arrangements were made to purchase the replacement inventory through Cummings. Over the next five years, Cummings purchased some eighty thousand pieces of surplus Guatemalan army weaponry and replenished the weapons with WWII surplus weapons purchased from Britain. That deal and similar swaps were key steps to Interarms's rise to a premier position in the world's independent weapons trade by the 1960s.

136 "Log-PBFORTUNE Meetings," with handwritten notation "PBSUCCESS File—6 November, 1953," released in sanitized form 2003, CIA Historical Review Board.

137 Gerald K. Haines, *CIA and Guatemala Assassination Proposals: 1952–1953*, CIA History Staff Analysis, June 1995.

CHAPTER 7

138 David Atlee Phillips, *The Night Watch: Twenty-five Years of Peculiar Service* (New York: Atheneum, 1977), 36.

139 The term *cadre* was used by James Angleton to describe the tightly knit and bonded first generation of senior CIA officers, individuals extremely loyal to the Agency and trusted by each other.

140 John Prados, *Safe for Democracy: The Secret Wars of the CIA* (Chicago, IL: Ivan R. Dee, 2006), 121.

141 John Prados, *Presidents' Secret Wars: CIA and Pentagon Covert Operations from World War II through the Persian Gulf* (Chicago, IL: Ivan R. Dee, 1996), 100–103.

142 *Foreign Relations of the United States*, "Chief's Calligeris Briefing Notes," J [ ] "Cost of Support for PBSUCCESS," September 17, 1954, Box 43 (S). He listed the twenty silencers present. See also [ ] to Headquarters, January 6, 1954, Box 75 (S) and [ ] 2 to Headquarters, January 21, 1954, Box 1 (S). See also report #5. [ ] . September 18, 1952, Box 73 (S) and [ ] Chief, memo for the record, "Pbt conference Held at [ ]" February 13, 1954, Box 74 (S). See also [ ] to Headquarters, January 4, 1954, Box 1 (S). The Headquarters Registry copy of the pouch manifest for January 8, 1954, Box 97 (S) lists the manual "A Study of Assassinations." A handwritten note of the original manifest says the pouch was carried to [ ] by [ ]. The serial assassination study is in Box 145 (S).

143 H.P. Albarelli Jr, *A Terrible Mistake: The Murder of Frank Olson and the CIA's Secret Cold War Experiments* (Trine Day, 2009); *A Study of Assassinations*, Appendix 2, 720–729.

144 *Foreign Relations of the United States,* "Dispatch to [ ], 'Training,' 6 June 1954, Box 75 (Secret, PBSUCCESS, Rybat) [ ]"; "Memorandum to LINCOLN Station, 16 May 1954, 'Tactical Instructions (part II)' (S)"; and "Specific Instruction: 'Nerve War Against Individuals,'" June 9, 1954, Box 50 (S).

145 *Foreign Relations of the United States*, "COS Guatemala City, to Western Hemisphere Division, undated, Box #6, (C) and Guatemala City 553 to LINCOLN, 14 May 1954"; "COS Guatemala City to LINCOLN, 14 May 1954, Box 145 (S). [ ]"; Memorandum for the record, "Weekly PBSUCCESS Meeting with [ ] 9 March 1954, Box 154 (TS)." Even before this meeting, [ ] suggested that the top Guatemalan leadership needed to be assassinated during the first hours of the revolution. They had to be "pulled out by the roots." If we waited, [ ] argued, "If too many of these birds get out they will be back in about three years." See [ ] Tape 17, Box 209 (S). [ ] Sec [ ] "Administrative Details." 15 April 1954, Box 70 (S); [ ] Memorandum for the record, "Meeting 2 March 1954, Box 70 (S)."

146 *Foreign Relations of the United States*, Chief, Economic Warfare, [ ] memo to All Staff Officers, "Selection of individuals for Disposal by Junta Group." 31 March 1954, Box 145 (S). We know [ ] visited [ ] on this date from the [ ] visitors' logbook. He signed into [ ] on 31 March and [ ] Log Book for 31 March 1954, Box 138 (S) also Memo, Box 145 (S).

147 *Foreign Relations of the United States*, "Disposal List Home Addresses," copied from an attachment to dispatch, [ ] to [ ] 1 June 1954. Box 145, (S). It contained 15 names, also [ ] routing slip for the attachment (Dispatch dated 25 May

1954), Box 145 (Secret, Rybat, [ ] draft memo, "Present Status and Possible Future Course of PBSUCCESS," 1 June 1954, Box 145 (also see "Contact Report," 2 June 1954, Box 146 (Secret, PBSUCCESS, Rybat). See also [ ] memo for the record, "Points Covered in H/W Discussion of June 1 and 2," 3 June 1954 and [ ] note for the file, "Disposal List Prepared by C/EW," 1 June 1954, Box 145 (S).)

148 Prados, *Safe for Democracy,* 119.

149 Phillips, *The Night Watch*, 42–48; Kate Doyle, *Guatemala—1954: Behind the CIA's Coup,* Consortiumnews.com, 1997. http://www.consortium news.com/archive/story38.html

CHAPTER 8

150 John T. Correll, "Over the Hump to China," *Air Force Magazine*, Vol. 92, No. 10, October 2009. http://www.airforcemag.com/Magazine Archive/Pages/2009/October%202009/1009hump.aspx

151 *Foreign Relations of the United States, 1958–1960, China,* Volume XIX, Document 373, "U.S. Response to the Rebellion in Tibet." http://history.state.gov/historicaldocuments/frus1958-60v19/ch5

152 *Lands and Peoples*, Vol. 4 (New York: Grolier. Inc., 1961), 119.

153 Kenneth Conboy and James Morrison, *The CIA's Secret War in Tibet* (Lawrence: University of Kansas Press, 2002), 7–8.

154 John Powers, *History as Propaganda: Tibetan Exiles versus the People's Republic of China* (New York: Oxford University Press, 2004), 113–116.

155 Conboy and Morrison, *The CIA's Secret War in Tibet*, 25.

156 Ibid., 26.

157 *Foreign Relations of the United States, 1964–1968,* Volume XXX, *China*, Document 342. http://history.state.gov/historicaldocuments/frus1964-68v30/comp2

158 Jeffrey T. Richelson, *The U.S. Intelligence Community* (Boulder, CO: Westview Press, 1999), 17.

159 Hamid Hussain, "Tale of a Love Affair That Never Was: United States–Pakistan Defence Relations," *Defence Journal*, June 2002. http://www.defencejournal.com/2002/june/loveaffair.htm

160 *Foreign Relations of the United States, 1958–1960, China,* Volume XIX, Document 367. http://history.state.gov/historicaldocuments/frus1958-60v19/ch5

161 Ibid., Document 371. http://history.state.gov/historicaldocuments/frus 1958-60v19/ch5

162 John T. Correll, "The Moon Squadrons," *Air Force Magazine*, July 2012. During WWII, the British had been amazingly effective in using light aircraft and operating in concert with a very organized French Resistance movement to fly agents into and out of German-occupied France. Carried out by the British SOE (Special Operation Executive) and unofficially referred to as the Moon Squadrons, the operations, while quite hazardous, had been quite successful. Agents were met by resistance members and moved through a structured covert network in-country; agents going out were handled in the same fashion and resistance groups provided at least some level of security in the areas designated for drops and pickups.

In a stark contrast, the use of blind drops in Tibet reflected a total lack of options; the CIA was well aware of the weakness of such insertions, based on its own dramatically unsuccessful Eastern European efforts in the early post-WWII years. In those efforts, hundreds of agents were inserted blindly, virtually all were captured, and a good number were "turned" to broadcast messages, drawing in yet more. Yet the method continued to be used, with similar negative results, in relatively large blind drop efforts into both North Vietnam and Cuba in the early

1960s. Such blind drop tactics actually led to the exposure and destruction of a very active and potentially successful resistance within Cuba in the early days of CIA activity there.

163 Warren Trest, *Air Commando One: Heinie Aderholt and America's Secret Air Wars* (Washington, DC: Smithsonian Institution Press, 2000), 37.

164 Ibid., 38.

165 Conboy and Morrison, *The CIA's Secret War in Tibet,* 44–45.

166 Trest, *Air Commando One*, 58–59. During training at "the Farm," Aderholt's pilots were also asked to participate in a series of missions against strategic targets on the East Coast to test the air defense system; SAC commander General LeMay also requested such missions to test his unit's detection capabilities. According to Aderholt neither Air Defense Command nor General LeMay was at all pleased with the results of the low-level, simulated nighttime attacks—all of which were either undetected or, if detected, unsuccessfully intercepted.

167 Conboy and Morrison, *The CIA's Secret War in Tibet,* 55–56.

168 Ibid., 58–61. During the Korean War, U.S. military crews had flown CAT aircraft over mainland China in intelligence and agent drop missions, but after one such flight was shot down in 1952, military crews were banned from flying on deniable covert operations.

169 John Prados, *Presidents' Secret Wars: CIA and Pentagon Covert Operations from World War II through the Persian Gulf War* (Chicago: Ivan R. Dee, 1996), 130–142.

170 Ibid., 40.

171 Ibid., 143.

172 *Foreign Relations of the United States, 1964–1968,* Volume XXX, *China,* Document 337. http://history.state.gov/historicaldocuments/frus 1964-68v30/comp2

173 *Foreign Relations of the United States, 1958–1960, China,* Volume XIX, Document 388. http://history.state.gov/historicaldocuments/frus1958 -60v19/ch5

174 Conboy and Morrison, *The CIA's Secret War in Tibet,* 170–172.

175 Ibid., 184–186.

176 Ibid., 187.

177 *Foreign Relations of the United States, 1964–1968,* Volume XXX, *China*, Document 337. http://history.state.gov/historicaldocuments/frus 1964-68v30/comp2

178 *Foreign Relations of the United States, 1964–1968,* Volume XXX, *China*, Document 342. http://history.state.gov/historicaldocuments/frus 1964-68v30/comp2

The following text is excerpted from the 303 Committee report to provide the reader with a feel for the language used in such assessments:

> 1. Summary—The CIA Tibetan program, parts of which were initiated in 1956 with the cognizance of the Committee, is based on U.S. Government commitments made to the Dalai Lama in 1951 and 1956. The program consists of political action, propaganda, paramilitary and intelligence operations, appropriately coordinated with and supported by [less than one line of source text not declassified]. This program was last reviewed and endorsed by the Committee on 20 February 1964. Current activities have been coordinated with and have the approval of [one line of source text not declassified], Mr. William Bundy, Assistant Secretary of State for East Asian and Pacific Affairs, and Mr. Lucius Battle, Assistant Secretary of State for Near East and South Asian Affairs.
>
> 2. Program Objectives—In the political action and propaganda field, Tibetan program objectives are aimed toward lessening the influence and capabilities of the Chinese regime through support, among Tibetans and among foreign nations, of the concept of an autonomous Tibet under the leadership of the Dalai Lama; toward the creation of a

capability for resistance against possible political developments inside Tibet; and the containment of Chinese Communist expansion—in pursuance of U.S. policy objectives stated initially in NSC 5913/1. [six lines of source text not declassified]

3. Appraisal of Current Programs—The cultural revolution in China expanded into Tibet bringing with it tremendous disturbances including the disruption of internal transportation, communication, travel and, to a significant extent, peace and order. Unfortunately there are no apparent signs that the Tibetan people are capitalizing upon this internal chaos to seek further autonomy. Chinese security has shown no signs of deterioration and their control over Tibet, both political and military, remains as pervasive as ever. Tibetan leadership has been purged, leaving the Chinese in direct control of the local administration, and a large number of underground assets have been uncovered and neutralized.

* * *

a. At present there are no radio teams remaining inside Tibet. Radio teams continue to function [less than one line of source text not declassified] although much of their information comes from the debriefing of traders and refugees. Singleton resident agent operations in Tibet, regarded as being the long-range replacement of the black radio teams, have not progressed as planned due to continued tightening of Chinese security in the border areas. Intelligence reporting from all sources deals primarily with military, political and construction activities along the Tibetan border.

b. The Tibetan paramilitary unit, a remnant of the 1959 resistance force, is dispersed in 15 camps [less than one line of source text not declassified]. The Tibetan leadership views the force as the paramilitary arm of its "government-in-exile" [two lines of source text not declassified]. Because of the diplomatic sensitivity occasioned by the presence of the Tibetan force [less than one line of source text not declassified] it has been enjoined from offensive action which might invite Chinese [less than one line of source text not declassified] retaliation. Joint efforts to disperse the force to other uninhabited areas [less than one line of source text not declassified] have not been successful because of Chinese [less than one line of source text not declassified] reaction or of difficulties in resupply.

179 The full story of the Tibetan personnel, from the CIA and American military's participants, to the Tibetan leaders and fighters, is told in the highly detailed historical work by Conboy and Morrison, *The CIA's Secret War in Tibet.* It traces the Tibetans through not only CIA involvement but also their longer-term association with Indian intelligence and military organizations.

CHAPTER 9

180 Stanley Karnow, *Vietnam: A History* (New York: Penguin Books, 1997), 138–139.

181 Ibid., 5.

182 Ibid., 175.

183 Ibid.

184 John Prados, *The Sky Would Fall—Operation Vulture: The Secret American Bombing Mission to Vietnam, 1954* (New York: The Dial Press, 1983), 7–8.

185 Ibid., 8–9.

186 Department of State, *Foreign Relations of the United States, 1952–1954*, Volume 23, Part 1, 969.
187 Prados, *The Sky Would Fall,* 49–50.
188 Ibid., 82.
189 Eisenhower's presidential personality has been characterized quite differently than his predecessors Roosevelt and Truman. Political science specialist James Barber described him as "passive-negative," naturally adverse to politics but motivated by a sense of duty. He would do what was necessary for the nation's interests, but in doing so he would rely on rules and procedures.
190 Ibid., 119–120.
191 Readers interested in the details of Eisenhower's requirements and the extended process by which his administration, particularly Secretary Dulles, struggled to meet them, are referred John Prados, *The Sky Would Fall.* Particular attention should be given to chapters 7 and 8.
192 Ibid., Hagerty Diary, entry for April 19, 144.
193 Prados, *The Sky Would Fall*, 185. Prados notes that an administration poll on Capitol Hill could find only five Congressmen who gave unequivocal support to intervention. *The Christian Science Monitor*, reported in the Congressional Record, listed three declarations in favor of intervention, fifteen that opposed it being done unilaterally, and seventeen that opposed the whole idea.
194 Telephone notes, Nixon–Dulles, April 19, 1954, as quoted in Prados, *The Sky Would Fall,* 144.
195 Evan Thomas, *The Very Best Men: Four Who Dared: The Early Years of the CIA* (New York: Simon & Schuster, 1996), 192.
196 "Message from the Director: 'Justice Done' Statement to Employees by Director of the Central Intelligence Agency Leon E. Panetta on the Death of Usama Bin Ladin," May 2, 2011. https://www.cia.gov/news-information/ press-releases-statements/press-release-2011/justice-done.html
197 Thomas Powers, *The Man Who Kept the Secrets: Richard Helms and the CIA* (New York: Alfred A. Knopf, 1979), 98.
198 Richard Michael Gibson and Wen H. Chen, *The Secret Army: Chiang Kai-shek and the Drug Warlords of the Golden Triangle* (Singapore: John Wiley & Sons, 2011), 181–185.
199 Ibid., 187–189.
200 John Prados, *Presidents' Secret Wars: CIA and Pentagon Covert Operations from World War II through the Persian Gulf War* (Chicago: Ivan R. Dee, 1996), 264. American support for Phoumi Nosavan was ensured at the highest levels when a member of President Eisenhower's 5412 covert operations review group (John Irwin, assistant secretary of defense for international security affairs) traveled to southern Laos for personal talks with Phoumi. From that point on all American military aid and assistance was sent directly to his forces rather than through the central Laotian government in Vientiane.
201 Richard H. Shultz Jr., *The Secret War against Hanoi: The Untold Story of Spies, Saboteurs, and Covert Warriors in North Vietnam* (New York: Harper Perennial, 2000), 11.
202 John Prados, *William Colby and the CIA: The Secret Wars of a Controversial Spymaster* (Lawrence: University Press of Kansas, 2009), 64.
203 Karnow, *Vietnam: A History*, 221–222.
204 Richard Secord with Jay Wurts, *Honored and Betrayed: Irangate, Covert Affairs, and the Secret War in Laos* (New York: John Wiley & Sons, 1992), 30–41.
205 Thomas L. Ahern Jr., *The Way We Do Things: Black Entry Operations into North Vietnam, 1961–64*, Washington, DC: Center for Intelligence Studies, 2005), 57.
206 Ibid.,7.
207 Prados, *William Colby and the CIA*, 74–75.

208 Shultz, *The Secret War against Hanoi,* 4–6.
209 Ibid., 28–29.
210 Ahern, *The Way We Do Things,* 13–27.
211 Prados, *William Colby and the CIA*, 80.
212 Ibid., 44–45.
213 Ahern, *The Way We Do Things*, 41.
214 Shultz, *The Secret War against Hanoi*, 37–40.
215 Robert M. Gillespie, *Black Ops, Vietnam: The Operational History of MACV-SOG* (Annapolis, MD: Naval Institute Press, 2011).
216 Shultz, *The Secret War against Hanoi*, 41–42.
217 Ibid., 37–38. Shultz also points out that army doctrine and training were oriented strictly towards the use of guerrilla operations in support of conventional warfare and that even the Special Forces personnel assigned to MACVSOG were trained for counterinsurgency as part of maintaining "friendly" regimes, not clandestine warfare to undermine hostile regimes in denied territories.
218 Ibid., chapter 2, 40–65.
219 Ibid., 58.
220 Ahern, *The Way We Do Things,* 61.
221 Shultz, *The Secret War Against Hanoi*, 312.

CHAPTER 10

222 Robert M. Gillespie, *Black Ops, Vietnam: The Operational History of MACV-SOG* (Annapolis, MD: Naval Institute Press, 2011), 39.
223 John Prados, *William Colby and the CIA: The Secret Wars of a Controversial Spymaster* (Lawrence: University Press of Kansas, 2009), 171–172.
224 Richard Secord and Jay Wurts, *Honored and Betrayed: Irangate, Covert Affairs, and the Secret War in Laos* (New York: Wiley & Sons, 1992), 59.
225 For further details on American military activities in Laos, readers are referred to the definitive work on special military operations in Vietnam and Laos, *Black Ops, Vietnam* by Robert Gillespie, and *Honor Denied: The Truth about Air America and the CIA,* by Allen Cates (Bloomington, IN: iUniverse, 2011).
226 Thomas L. Ahern Jr., *Undercover Armies: CIA and Surrogate Warfare in Laos 1961–1973* (Center for the Study of Intelligence, CIA History Staff, 2006), 23.
227 Ibid., 184.
228 Ibid., 117.
229 Ibid., 45.
230 Ibid., 100.
231 Ibid., 56–57. As early as 1961, American journalists were investigating U.S. support to the Hmong. There were rumors that it was some sort of local, rogue CIA action and that local Agency personnel were making an end run around Washington. During 1962 the same sort of speculation would be made about certain events in Vietnam. As noted previously, when Washington is overtly taking one stance—neutrality in Laos, noncombat advisory role in Vietnam—while conducting a variety of actual deniable military and combat operations, such things are to be expected. The official U.S. response was that Vang Pao was a regional FAR commander (true), that he was conducting operations coordinated with the central government (somewhat true, since the U.S. was driving the Laotian central government to be more aggressive), and that the context for the whole matter was Hmong support for the Laotian government against subversive forces and groups (the arming and training of Hmong irregulars was to be minimized while PEO aid efforts for the Hmong were to be highlighted).
232 John Prados, *Presidents' Secret Wars: CIA and Pentagon Covert Operations*

from *World War II through the Persian Gulf War* (Chicago: Ivan R. Dee, 1996), 273–274.

233 Ibid., 282.

234 Ibid., 281.

235 Ahern, *Undercover Armies*, 252.

236 Ibid., 144–145.

237 David Corn, *Blond Ghost: Ted Shackley and the CIA's Crusades* (New York: Simon & Schuster, 1994), 153–155.

238 Cates, *Honor Denied*, 94–107. Due to the practice of deniability, the losses of Air America personnel were never acknowledged; a listing of actual losses has only recently become fully available and is documented in Cates's writings on Air America.

239 Ahern, *Undercover Armies*, 217.

240 Ibid., 300.

241 Prados, *Presidents' Secret Wars*, 165.

242 Corn, *Blond Ghost*, 165–167.

243 Prados, *Presidents' Secret Wars*, 290–291.

244 Ahern, *Undercover Armies*, 431.

245 Ibid., 408–409.

246 Ibid., 349–351.

247 Ibid., 428. A CIA headquarters memorandum of 1972 notes that many in the State Department had been saying for some six years that "the North Vietnamese military moves in North Laos [have] been strictly reactive."

248 Ibid., 461–462.

249 Thomas L. Briggs, *Cash on Delivery: CIA Special Operations during the Secret War in Laos* (Rosebank Press, 2009), 47.

250 Ibid., 75.

251 Ahern, *Undercover Armies*, 511–515.

252 Ibid., 516–517.

253 Prados, *Presidents' Secret Wars*, 296.

254 Corn, *Blond Ghost*, 130.

255 Ibid., 169.

256 John Prados, *Safe for Democracy: The Secret Wars of the CIA* (Chicago: Ivan R. Dee, 2009), 206–207.

CHAPTER 11

257 Ibid., 208.

258 Ibid., 209.

259 Don Bohning, *The Castro Obsession: U.S. Covert Operations against Cuba, 1959–1965* (Washington, DC: Potomac Books, 2006), 195; Larry Hancock and Debra Conway, *Someone Would Have Talked* (Dallas: Lancer Publications and Productions, 2010), 20–21.

260 Salvador Diaz-Verson, "When Castro Became a Communist: The Impact on U.S.–Cuba Policy," Institute for U.S.–Cuba Relations, Occasional Paper Series, Vol. 1. No. 1, November 3, 1997. http://www.latinamericanstudies.org/diaz-verson.htm

261 Ibid., 54, 339–340.

262 The Cuba project went through a series of starts, resets, restarts, and designation changes between 1959 and 1964. Phase 1 is the author's designation for the earliest phase, begun under the Eisenhower Administration and continued by the Kennedy Administration until the eventual landings at the Bay of Pigs. In the first phase of the project, President Eisenhower was certainly influenced by Vice

President Nixon in regard to the necessity of the effort; later, President Kennedy's brother Robert became a major influence on the phases of the project developed following the Bay of Pigs. Kennedy's reaction to that disaster was a major factor in his move to a multiagency clandestine project (Phase 2, Mongoose) with the CIA in support but not playing a controlling role. That effort was led by General Lansdale, seconded to the effort from his staff position in the newly formed Office of Special Operations, a branch of the Special Operations Division under the Joint Chiefs of Staff.

263 Bohning, *The Castro Obsession*, 20.

264 David Atlee Phillips, *The Night Watch: Twenty-five Years of Peculiar Service* (New York: Atheneum, 1977), 86.

265 Ibid., 21.

266 Bohning, *The Castro Obsession*, 24–26.

267 Richard Bissell, *Reflections of a Cold Warrior: From Yalta to the Bay of Pigs* (New Haven, CT: Yale University Press, 1996), 155–157.

268 Taylor Branch and George Crile III, *Harper's Magazine*, "The Kennedy Vendetta," *Harper's* 251 (August 1975), 49–63.

269 David Phillips, *The Night Watch*. Phillips's book was published in 1977; the Taylor Report, which evaluated the Bay of Pigs disaster, was over a decade old at that point and it had clearly established that the Trinidad plan had morphed from a guerrilla project to something much different many months in advance; the only element that had changed was the choice of a landing site. In his book, Phillips blamed Dean Rusk for forcing the selection of an alternative landing site at the last minute.

270 Hancock and Conway, *Someone Would Have Talked*, appendix D, "The Way of Wave." Accordingly, UNIDAD—composed of some twenty-seven different groups—was not informed of the Bay of Pigs landing, and Castro's militia, alerted by rumors of an impending military invasion, conducted extensive searches and operations and managed to take the majority of the UNIDAD leadership into custody, breaking the back of the movement within Cuba. After the Bay of Pigs, the remaining UNIDAD leader, Alberto Fernandez, complained bitterly to the CIA about not being briefed and having their warnings disregarded in favor of the Agency's trust in Manuel Artime, one of the actual leaders of the invasion brigade.

271 Prados, *Safe For Democracy*, 256.

272 Bohning, *The Castro Obsession*, 23–24.

273 Ibid., 29, 44.

274 Ibid., 29, 63.

275 Peter Maas, *Manhunt: The Incredible Pursuit of a CIA Agent Turned Terrorist* (I Books, 2002), 65.

276 Bohning, *The Castro Obsession*, 48.

277 Ibid., 31–34, 48.

278 Ibid., 48.

279 Grayston Lynch, *Decision for Disaster: Betrayal at the Bay of Pigs* (Washington, DC: Potomac Books, 2000), 29–30.

280 Ibid., 159; Bohning, *The Castro Obsession*, 46. Allen Dulles presented the issue of disbanding the brigade, reporting that Hawkins and Esterline did not consider it a serious problem. He also discussed the subject with selected exile leaders, who made it clear to him that indeed it would have been—they might simply have decided to take over Guatemala and they had the manpower, weapons, and airpower to do so. In fact, one of the exile commanders told Bohning that it would indeed have been a "very big problem," and Kennedy had made the right decision.

281 Hurwitch, unpublished memoirs, 130, cited by Bohning in *The Castro Obsession*; Schlesinger in response to a question by Bohning, 79–80.

CHAPTER 12

282 Don Bohning, *The Castro Obsession: U.S. Covert Operations Against Cuba, 1959–1965*, (Washington, DC: Potomac Books, 2006), 153–154.

283 National Archives and Records Administration, RIF 104-10241-10174, Meeting with Ambiddy/1, on May 3, 1963. http://www.maryferrell.org/mffweb/archive/naraSearch.do

284 Ibid.

285 RIF 104-10241-10139, Meeting Between Chief, SAS and Ambiddy-1 on 1 July, 1963. www.maryferrell.org/mffweb/archive/viewer/showDoc.do?mode=searchResult&absPageId=499497

286 Ibid.

287 Ibid.

288 RIF 104-10241-10131, Notes for your meeting with Ambiddy-1 during week from July 1, 1963.

289 David Corn, *Blond Ghost: Ted Shackley and the CIA's Crusades* (New York: Simon & Schuster, 1994), 112. From January to November 1963, JM WAVE planned some eighty-eight Cuban missions of all types, including supply, intelligence, and cache placement; fifteen were canceled, and of the remainder only four involved actual sabotage attempts.

290 RIF 104-10315-1004, Dispatch AMWORLD, Background of Program, Operational Support, Requirements and Procedural Rules, from Chief of Western Hemisphere, Oliver Galbond, June 28, 1963. Galbond was the internal CIA pseudonym for J.C. King.

291 Bohning, *The Castro Obsession*, 122.

292 RIF 104-10308-10094, Ambiddy-1's Operational Philosophy and Concepts, by Jenkins. www.maryferrell.org/mffweb/archive/viewer/show Doc.do?mode=searchResult&absPageId=387743

293 RIF 145-10001-10121 and 145-1001-1022, Operational Plan Submitted to CIA by Quintero.

294 RIF 104-10308-10098, Second Meeting between Ambiddy-1 and Amlash-1, in Madrid on 30 December 1964.

295 RIF 104-10308-10096, Report on AMJAVA-4 Visit to Europe by Jenkins. http://www.maryferrell.org/mffweb/archive/viewer/showDoc.do?mode=searchResult&absPageId=387751

296 *Memorandum for the Record*, Richard Cates, Chief, Image Exploitation Group, National Photographic Interpretation Center, March 12, 1975. Document provided by NARA researcher Malcolm Blunt.

297 Felix Rodriguez, *Shadow Warrior: The CIA Hero of a Hundred Unknown Battles* (New York: Simon & Schuster, 1989), 65–66.

298 The *Tejana* had made several missions into Cuba during March and April 1961. In four missions, it had carried in sixty tons of war materiel, carried in twenty-seven agents, and carried out seventeen people in exfiltration. Logs record that Felix Rodriguez was carried in on a mission in March. On April 7, only eight days before the first air attacks preceding the landing of April 17, the *Tejana* suffered major engine problems and was forced to return to base, aborting the mission.

299 Bohning, *The Castro Obsession*, 189–190.

300 Rodriguez, *Shadow Warrior*, 116–118.

301 RIF 104-10241-10170, Cable: Ambiddy/1, Arr ZRMETAL NAT FLT, 224, May 9, 1963.

302 RIF 104-10241-10148, Agency file number 80T01357A, Memorandum telephone conversation between Ambiddy-1 and Raul Hernandez, 21 November, 1963; RIF 104-10241-10148, Classified Message SECRET; To Director from

JMWAVE. http://www.maryferrell.org/mffweb/archive/viewer/showDoc.do?mode=searchResult&absPageId=407336

303 Ibid.

304 RIF 104-10241-10136, Maritime Assets. http://www.maryferrell.org/mffweb/archive/viewer/showDoc.do?mode=searchResult&absPageId=494731

305 Ibid.

306 RIF 104-10241-10122, Telephone conversation between Ambiddy-1 and R. Hernandez, December 12, 1963. The *Joanne* appears to have been rented from a company named Baum by Maritime BAM on a monthly basis. The first month's rental was for November 1963, and the ship sailed from Baltimore in December.

307 RIF 104-104-10077-10204, MV *Joanne* left Baltimore Port 1 DEC AM.

308 Ibid.

309 RIF 104-10240-10440, Director Cable Re Delivery Subject Cooper-McDonald. http://www.maryferrell.org/mffweb/archive/viewer/showDoc.do? mode=searchResult&absPageId=407316

310 RIF 202-10001-10028, CIA Cuban Operations and Planning. http://www.maryferrell.org/mffweb/archive/viewer/showDoc.do?mode=searchResult&absPageId=325608

311 RIF 104-10275-10051, Contact Report #15; Pass Instructions Re Procurement of Material. It is interesting to note that in at least one document, Interarmco is referred to as a CIA proprietary company although clearly by 1963 it was quite a successful international business. http://www.maryferrell.org/mffweb/archive/viewer/showDoc.do?mode=searchResult&absPageId=808871

312 RIF 104-10241-10109, Memo: Telephone conversation between Ambiddy-1 and R. Hernandez, 18 Dec. 1963.

313 RIF 104-10241-10118, Memo conversation between Ambiddy-1 and Raul Hernandez, Dec. 1, 1963.

314 Corn, *Blond Ghost*, 114.

315 Bohning, *The Castro Obsession*, 192.

316 Rodriguez, *Shadow Warrior*, 119.

CHAPTER 13

317 Madeleine G. Kalb, *The Congo Cables: The Cold War in Africa—From Eisenhower to Kennedy* (New York: Macmillan Publishing, 1982), xii.

318 Ibid., 14–16, 27–39.

319 Richard D. Mahoney, *JFK: Ordeal in Africa* (New York: Oxford University Press, 1983), 40.

320 *Senate Intelligence Committee Report*, Section III: "Assassination Planning and the Plots, Congo," 14.

321 Kalb, *The Congo Cables*, 54–55.

322 George Lardner Jr., "Did Ike Authorize a Murder?" *Washington Post*, August 8, 2000, A23.

323 Bayard Stockton, *Flawed Patriot: The Rise and Fall of CIA Legend Bill Harvey* (Dulles, VA: Potomac Books, 2006), 160–161.

324 Kalb, *The Congo Cables*, 240–241; Thomas P. Odom, *Dragon Operations: Hostage Rescues in the Congo, 1964–1965* (Fort Leavenworth, KS: Combat Studies Institute, U.S. Army Command and General Staff College, 1988), 12. Timberlake's successor, Ambassador George Godley, an action-oriented former Marine nicknamed Cinccongo by certain of his staff, was equally assertive. In 1964, during the capture of Stanleyville and a number of related hostage crises, Godley developed his own rescue plan, requesting naval assets to support it. After

approval from the State Department, he organized Operation Flagpole, under command of the chief of the American military mission, using embassy Marine security personnel and with support from Cuban exile–flown fighters and extraction by helicopter. The mission was practiced but aborted at the last moment due to reports of rebel forces near the consulate.

325 Kalb, *The Congo Cables,* 372–373.

326 Stephen R. Weissman, "Why is U.S. withholding old documents on covert ops in Congo, Iran?" *Christian Science Monitor*, March 25, 2011. The lack of clarity is largely due to the fact that significant State Department foreign relations material on Africa for the period 1960–1968, which is required by law to be published, is still being withheld—even though the State Department Historical Advisory Committee called for its release in 2003. The same 1991 records-access law that initially provided us with so much detailed insight into events in Guatemala appears to have been successfully compromised by CIA objections over the Africa material. An exceptionally protracted Agency review and re-review process also blocked release of the material.
http://www.csmonitor.com/Commentary/Opinion/2011/0325/Why-is-US-withholding-old-documents-on-covert-ops-in-Congo-Iran

327 Frank R. Villafaña, *Cold War in the Congo: The Confrontation of Cuban Military Forces, 1960–1967* (New Brunswick, NJ: Transaction Publishers, 2009), 37–38.

328 Ibid., 68.

329 George Lardner Jr., "Cuban Surrogates in Africa: An Old Issue," *Washington Post*, June 6, 1978, A14.

330 Ibid., 70.

331 Villafaña, *Cold War in the Congo*, 81.

332 Ibid., 6.

333 Mike Hoare, *Congo Mercenary* (Boulder, CO: Paladin Press, 2008), 27.

334 Odom, *Dragon Operations*, 22.

335 Ibid., 33.

336 Ibid., 1.

337 Ibid., 91, 103, 131.

338 Ibid., 108.

339 Piero Gleijeses, *Conflicting Missions: Havana, Washington, and Africa, 1959–1960* (Chapel Hill: University of North Carolina Press, 2002), 127–129.

340 Hoare, *Congo Mercenary,* 253.

341 Villafaña, *Cold War in the Congo*, 40–411.

342 Ibid., 41.

343 Ibid., 144–145.

344 Considerable detail of combat operations (including several fierce battles) between Hoare's commandos, the Cuban exile volunteers, and the Castro detachment may be found in *Cold War in the Congo*.

345 Ibid., 162.

346 Kalb, *The Congo Cables*, 381–382.

CHAPTER 14

347 John Prados, *The Sky Would Fall: Operation Vulture: The Secret U.S. Bombing Mission to Vietnam, 1954* (New York: Dial Press, 1983), 90.

348 John Prados, *William Colby and the CIA: The Secret Wars of a Controversial Spymaster* (Lawrence: Kansas University Press, 2009), 95.

349 Dwight D. Eisenhower, Public Papers of the Presidents, Dwight D. Eisenhower, 1961, 1035–1040.

350 John Prados, *Presidents' Secret Wars: CIA and Pentagon Covert Operations from World War II through the Persian Gulf War* (Chicago: Ivan R. Dee, 1996), 81, 230–232.
351 Ibid., 230.
352 Hugh Wilford, *The Mighty Wurlitzer: How the CIA Played America* (Cambridge, MA: Harvard University Press, 2009), 225–226.
353 Ibid., 226.
354 Ibid., 226–227.
355 Don Bohning, *The Castro Obsession: U.S. Covert Operations against Cuba, 1959–1965* (Dulles, VA: Potomac Books, 2006), 192–193.
356 Ibid.
357 Hal Hendrix, *The Miami News*, "Backstage with Bobby," July 14, 1963.
358 David Corn, *Blond Ghost: Ted Shackley and the CIA's Crusades* (New York: Simon & Schuster, 1994), 113.
359 Ibid., 114.
360 Jim Hougan's conversations with Frank Terpil, *Probe*, March–April 1986, 21; Jim Hougan, *Secret Agenda: Watergate, Deep Throat, and the CIA* (New York: Random House, 1984).
361 Once again, Hecksher was operating independently of the U.S. ambassador, who protested the CIA activities to the State Department. In Chile, instead of the CIA coming to his rescue, Secretary of State Henry Kissinger overruled the U.S. ambassador, supporting Hecksher and directing the contacts to continue.
362 Peter Kornbluh, *The Pinochet File: A Declassified Dossier on Atrocity and Accountability* (New York: New Press, 2003), 20.
363 Corn, *Blond Ghost*, 243–247.
364 Interestingly, one of JM WAVE's first media assets (the original AMCARBON) has commented that he certainly could not have been a true "propaganda outlet" since he himself had written exposés of Artime's project and the government connection to it—which of course would be true, since such stories were not at all what RFK or the Special Group Augmented wanted to see.
365 Larry Hancock and Debra Conway, *Someone Would Have Talked* (Dallas, TX: Lancer Publications and Productions, 2010), 19–22.
366 Documents are available on the Mary Ferrell website: http://www.mary fer rell.org/mffweb/archive/viewer/showDoc.do?docId=28964&relPageId=2
367 Later in 1963 the *Leda*'s sister ship, the *Rex*, would be compromised in a Cuba mission; both boats would be exposed and it would turn into a considerable public relations problem for all concerned.
368 Miguel Acoca and Robert K. Brown, "The Bayo–Pawley Affair: A Plot to Destroy JFK and Invade Cuba," *Soldier of Fortune* 1, no. 2 (1975). The magazine article contains an extensive description of the Bayo–Pawley mission as well as a number of photographs taken by the *Life* magazine photographer allowed to join the mission. http://www.maryferrell.org/mffweb/archive/viewer/showDoc.do?docId=28888&relPageId=2
369 RIF 1993.08.04.16:25:36:340007, Folder Reviewed by HSCA re the "Bayo–Pawley affair." http://www.maryferrell.org/mffweb/archive/viewer/show Doc.do?docId=105573&relPageId=208
370 William Turner, *Rearview Mirror: Looking Back at the FBI, the CIA and Other Tails* (Roseville CA: Penmarin Books, 2001), 194.
371 RIF 1993.08.04.16:25:36:340007, Folder Reviewed by HSCA re the "Bayo–Pawley affair." http://www.maryferrell.org/mffweb/archive/viewer/ showDoc.do?docId=105573&relPageId=228
372 RIF **104-10312-10177**, JMWAVE dispatch to C/SAS, Dispatch: Maritime After Action Report—Tilt Operation, 29 June, 1963.http://www.maryferrell.org/mffweb/archive/viewer/showDoc.do?docId=105573&relPageId=223

373 Bayard Stockton, *Flawed Patriot: The Rise and Fall of CIA Legend Bill Harvey* (Dulles, VA: Potomac Books, 2006) 146–147.

374 Arthur Krock, "The Intra-Administration War in Vietnam," *New York Times*, October, 3, 1963. www.jfklancer.com/Krock.html

375 Prados, *Presidents' Secret Wars*, 96–97.

376 Harry S. Truman, "Limit CIA Role to Intelligence," *The Washington Post*, December 22, 1963, A1.

INDEPENDENCE, MO., Dec. 21—I think it has become necessary to take another look at the purpose and operations of our Central Intelligence Agency—CIA. At least, I would like to submit here the original reason why I thought it necessary to organize this Agency during my Administration, what I expected it to do and how it was to operate as an arm of the President. I think it is fairly obvious that by and large a President's performance in office is as effective as the information he has and the information he gets. That is to say, that assuming the President himself possesses a knowledge of our history, a sensitive understanding of our institutions, and an insight into the needs and aspirations of the people, he needs to have available to him the most accurate and up-to-the-minute information on what is going on everywhere in the world, and particularly of the trends and developments in all the danger spots in the contest between East and West. This is an immense task and requires a special kind of an intelligence facility. Of course, every President has available to him all the information gathered by the many intelligence agencies already in existence. The Departments of State, Defense, Commerce, Interior and others are constantly engaged in extensive information gathering and have done excellent work. But their collective information reached the President all too frequently in conflicting conclusions. At times, the intelligence reports tended to be slanted to conform to established positions of a given department. This becomes confusing and what's worse, such intelligence is of little use to a President in reaching the right decisions. Therefore, I decided to set up a special organization charged with the collection of all intelligence reports from every available source, and to have those reports reach me as President without department "treatment" or interpretations. I wanted and needed the information in its "natural raw" state and in as comprehensive a volume as it was practical for me to make full use of it. But the most important thing about this move was to guard against the chance of intelligence being used to influence or to lead the President into unwise decisions—and I thought it was necessary that the President do his own thinking and evaluating. Since the responsibility for decision making was his—then he had to be sure that no information is kept from him for whatever reason at the discretion of any one department or agency, or that unpleasant facts be kept from him. There are always those who would want to shield a President from bad news or misjudgments to spare him from being "upset." For some time I have been disturbed by the way CIA has been diverted from its original assignment. It has become an operational and at times a policy-making arm of the Government. This has led to trouble and may have compounded our difficulties in several explosive areas. I never had any thought that when I set up the CIA that it would be injected into peacetime cloak and dagger operations. Some of the complications and embarrassment I think we have experienced are in part attributable to the fact that this quiet intelligence arm of the President has been so removed from its intended role that it is being interpreted as a symbol of sinister and mysterious foreign intrigue—and a subject for cold war enemy propaganda. With all the nonsense put out by Communist propaganda about "Yankee imperialism," "exploitive capitalism," "war-mongering," "monopolists," in their name-calling assault on the West, the last thing we needed was for the CIA to be seized upon as something akin to a subverting influence in the affairs of other people. I well knew the first temporary director of the CIA, Adm. Souers, and the later permanent directors of the CIA, Gen. Hoyt Vandenberg and Allen Dulles. These were men of the highest character, patriotism and integrity—and I assume this is true of all those who continue in charge. But there are now some searching questions that need to be answered. I, therefore, would like to see the CIA be restored to its original assignment as the intelligence arm of the President, and that whatever else it can properly perform in that special field—and that its operational duties be terminated or properly used elsewhere. We have grown up as a nation, respected for our free institutions and for our ability to maintain a free and open society. There is something about the way the CIA has been functioning that is casting a shadow over our historic position and I feel that we need to correct it.

377 David Cort, *The Sin of Henry Luce: An Anatomy of Journalism* (Secaucus, NJ: Lyle Stuart, 1974).

378 RIF 104-10170-10145. Subject: Ramparts, John Garrett Underhill Jr., Samuel George Cummings, and Interarmco, July, 19, 1967. http://www.maryferrell.org/mffweb/archive/viewer/showDoc.do?mode=searchResult&absPageId=427279

379 Ibid.

380 May 1966 letter from Asher Brynes.

381 Copies of May and June 1966 correspondence, Charlene and Robert Fitzsimmons. http://jfk.hood.edu/Collection/Weisberg%20Subject%20Index%20Files/U%20Disk/Underhill%20Gary/Item%2011.pdf

CHAPTER 15

382 The Tonkin Gulf Resolution/Southeast Asia Resolution, Public Law 88-408.

383 Eugene G. Windchy, *Tonkin Gulf: A Documentary of the Incidents in the Tonkin Gulf and Their Consequences* (New York: Doubleday and Company, 1971).

384 *Foreign Relations of the United States*, 1969–1976, Volume E-10, *Documents on American Republics*, 1969–1972, "Note on U.S. Covert Action Programs." http://history.state.gov/historicaldocuments/frus1969-76 ve10actionsstatement#fnref16

385 War Powers Resolution, Public Law 93-148, 87 Stat. 555. The War Powers Resolution is sometimes referred to as the War Powers Act, its title in the version passed by the Senate. This joint resolution is codified in the United States Code (USC) in Title 50, Chapter 33, sections 1541–48. Full analysis of the law is available online at the Library of Congress website. http://www.loc.gov/law/help/war-powers.php

386 Title 50 deals with CIA intelligence activities including covert warfare, while Title 10 addresses military action under control of the uniformed armed forces. The president, acting as commander in chief, has authority to initiate operations in compliance with either title. However, the chain of command guidelines and oversight vary as to the titles related to each. Debate over presidential decisions in regard to the use of Title 50 versus Title 10 authority remains a matter of ongoing contention of this writing. For further discussion see Robert Chesney, "Further Thoughts on Congressional Oversight, the UBL Operation and the Title 10/Title 50 Issue," *Lawfare: Hard National Security Choices*, May 3, 2011. http://www.lawfareblog.com/2011/05/further-thoughts-on-congressional-oversight-the-ubl-operation-and-the-title-10title-50-issue/

Also see Andru E. Wall, "Demystifying the Title 10–Title 50 Debate: Distinguishing Military Operations, Intelligence Activities & Covert Action," 2011. http://harvardnsj.org/wp-content/uploads/2012/01/Vol.-3_Wall1.pdf

387 Richard Mahoney, *JFK: Ordeal in Africa* (New York: Oxford University Press, 1983), 35.

388 Ibid., 187.

389 Ibid., 196.

390 William Blum, "Angola 1975 to 1980s: The Great Powers Poker Game," Common Courage Press, 2008. http://www.thirdworldtraveler.com/Blum/ Angola_KH.html

391 Mahoney, *JFK: Ordeal in Africa*, 204.

392 Ibid., 218.

393 Henry Kissinger initially held the position of national security advisor in the Nixon Administration; in 1973 he was also appointed secretary of state—serving Nixon in both functions. Kissinger continued only as Secretary of State in the Ford Administration.

394 Piero Gleijeses, *Conflicting Missions: Havana, Washington, and Africa, 1959–1976* (Chapel Hill: University of North Carolina Press, 2002), 230–232.

395 *Foreign Relations of the United States*, 1969–1976, Volume E–6, *Documents on Africa, 1973–1976*, Document 17, "National Security Study Memorandum 201," Washington, April 25, 1974. http://history.state.gov/historicaldocuments/frus1969-76ve06/d17

396 *Foreign Relations of the United States*, 1969–1976, Volume E–6, Documents on Africa, 1973–1976, Document 21, "Response to National Security Study Memorandum 201," Washington, October 8, 1974. http://history.state.gov/historicaldocuments/frus1969-76ve06/d21

397 John Stockwell, *In Search of Enemies: a CIA Story* (New York: W.W. Norton & Company, 1978), 67.

398 *Foreign Relations of the United States*, 1969–1976, Volume E–6, *Documents on Africa, 1973–1976*, Document 22, "Minutes of the Secretary of State's Staff Meeting," Washington, December 23, 1974. http://history.state.gov/historical documents/frus1969-76ve06/d22

399 John Prados, *William Colby and the CIA: The Secret Wars of a Controversial Spymaster* (Lawrence: Kansas University Press, 2009), 317.

400 National Security Council meeting transcript, June 27, 1975. http://www.gwu.edu/~nsarchiv/NSAEBB/NSAEBB67/gleijeses6.pdf

401 Office of the Historian, United States Department of State, "Milestones: 1969–1976, The Angola Crisis 1974–1975." http://history.state.gov/milestones/1969-1976/Angola

Material from documents previously available on the State Department website, including the above document, is still being used in support of our study of Angola in lieu of its being returned to public access.

402 Stockwell, *In Search of Enemies*, 53.

403 Walter Isaacson, *Kissinger: A Biography* (New York: Simon & Schuster, 1992), 675.

404 John Prados, *Keepers of the Keys: A History of the National Security Council from Truman to Bush* (New York: William Morrow and Company, 1991), 318.

405 Ibid., 55.

406 Gleijeses, *Conflicting Missions*, 250–252.

407 Isaacson, *Kissinger*, 676.

408 Stockwell, *In Search of Enemies*.

409 Ibid., 268–269.

410 Ibid., 177–179.

411 Ibid., 169.
412 Ibid., 179.
413 Ibid., 188.
414 Ibid., 189.
415 Gleijeses, *Conflicting Missions*, 261.
416 *Interagency Intelligence Memorandum*, "Soviet and Cuban Military Aid to the MPLA in Angola During February, 1976." http://www.faqs.org/cia/docs/48/0000681967/SOVIET-AND-CUBAN-AID-TO-THE-MPLA-IN-ANGOLA-DURING-FEBRUARY-1976-%28NIO-IIM-76-013.html
417 The Nixon Administration in general had little confidence in the nationalist independence movements and leaned towards supporting the stability of existing African governments. In 1969, NSSM 39 had concluded that insurgent movements were ineffectual and neither "realistic nor supportable" alternatives when compared to the continuation of colonial rule. That report was based on an interdepartmental review and Kissinger himself had expressed doubt in "the depth and permanence of black resolve" and the chances of any black nationalist movement succeeding. The 1969 finding seems to have been an extension of the assessment in the National Intelligence Estimate Number 70-1-67, The Liberation Movements of Southern Africa. That estimate concluded that "the liberation movements stand little chance of significant progress toward deposing any of the White Regimes of Southern Africa through 1970 and probably for some significant time thereafter." The estimate was however quite accurate in projecting that only a civil revolt within Portugal, ejecting the existing leadership, could lead to Angolan independence.
418 Records of the Department of State, Policy Planning Staff, Director's Files (Winston Lord), 1969–1977, "White House Memorandum of Conversation with Chinese Officials, re The Soviet Union; Europe; the Middle East; South Asia; Angola." George Washington University National Security Archive, National Archives Record Group 59, Box 373. http://www2.gwu.edu/~nsarchiv/NSAEBB/NSAEBB67/gleijeses4.pdf
419 Gleijeses, *Conflicting Missions*, 319–321.
420 *Foreign Relations of the United States, 1969–1976*, Volume E–6, *Documents on Africa*, 1973–1976, Document 33, "Intelligence Appraisal DIAIAPPR 4-76 Prepared by the Defense Intelligence Agency," Washington, January 9, 1976. http://history.state.gov/historicaldocuments/frus1969-76ve06/d33
421 "Clark Amendment article," City University of New York. http://academic.brooklyn.cuny.edu/history/johnson/clark.htm
422 Isaacson, *Kissinger*, 678–679.

CHAPTER 16

423 White House Audio Tape, "Brazil Marks 40th Anniversary of Military Coup: Declassified Documents Shed Light on U.S. Role." http://www.gwu.edu/~nsarchiv/NSAEBB/NSAEBB118/index.htm
424 Ibid.
425 David Atlee Phillips, *The Night Watch: Twenty-five Years of Peculiar Service* (New York: Atheneum, 1977), 220–223.
426 David Corn, *Blond Ghost: Ted Shackley and the CIA's Crusades* (New York: Simon & Schuster, 1994), 261.
427 National Security Archive, New Declassified Details on Repression and U.S. Support for Military Dictatorship, March 23, 2006. http://www.gwu.edu/~nsarchiv/NSAEBB/NSAEBB185/index.htm

428 National Security Archive, Secretary of State Henry Kissinger, Staff Meeting Transcripts regarding Argentina, March 26, 1976, 1, 19–23. http://www.gwu.edu/~nsarchiv/NSAEBB/NSAEBB185/19760326%20Secretary%20of%20Stet%20Kissinger%20Chariman%20apgesl%201-39%20-%20full.pdf

429 National Security Archive, Secretary Kissinger's Meeting with Argentine Foreign Minister Guzzetti, October 6, 1976. http://www.gwu.edu/~nsarchiv/NSAEBB/NSAEBB104/Doc5%20761006.pdf

430 National Security Archive, Other aspects of September 17 conversation with Foreign Minister, September 20, 1976. http://www.gwu.edu/~nsarchiv/NSAEBB/NSAEBB104/Doc1%20760920.pdf

431 National Security Archive, Communiqué regarding Argentina affairs. http://www.gwu.edu/~nsarchiv/NSAEBB/NSAEBB185/index.htm #19780715

432 The name Military Assistance Advisory Group (MAAG) has been succeeded to a large extent by United States Military Group (USMILGP) and in more recent years the number of such groups has declined considerably. Groups do continue to function in several Latin American countries—with a smaller but growing number in areas of emerging jihadi terror and insurgency, especially in the Horn of Africa and the trans-Sahara region.

433 Cindy Cannizzo, *The Gun Merchants: Politics and Policies of the Major Arms Suppliers* (New York: Pergamon Press, 1980), 3.

434 Records of Interservice Agencies, Record Group 334; details of the individual MAAG agreements, as conducted by the Joint Chiefs of Staff. Brief histories of each group are available online.

435 Felix Rodriguez, *Shadow Warrior: The CIA Hero of a Hundred Unknown Battles* (New York: Simon & Schuster, 1989), 100–112.

436 Ibid., 128.

437 State Department Memorandum of Understanding Concerning the Activation, Organization and Training of the 2d Ranger Battalion—Bolivian Army, National Security Archive. http://www.gwu.edu/~nsarchiv/NSAEBB/NSAEBB5/che14_1.htm

438 National Security Archive, "CIA Debriefing of Felix Rodriguez [aka Benton Mizones], June 3, 1975." http://www.gwu.edu/~nsarchiv/NSAEBB/NSAEBB232/19750603.pdf

439 Ibid.

440 *Memorandum for the President*, "Death of 'Che' Guevara, October 17, 1967." http://www.gwu.edu/~nsarchiv/NSAEBB/NSAEBB232/19671011.pdf

441 Rodriguez, *Shadow Warrior*, 173–174.

442 Ibid., 178.

443 JMARC Intelligence Plan, Counter Intelligence Plan for an FRD Security Service, attachments to a CIA memo for the record prepared by R.D. Shea, June 2, 1962. See also the debriefing interview with David Morales, GS-14, Chief of Counter Intelligence Section, Miami Base. It should be noted that Shea gave Morales high marks for initiative and efficiency and that the Morales AMOT organization, first headed by Luis Sanjenis and later by Tony Sforza, became the core of the JM WAVE–connected Cuban Intelligence Service, which also provided the majority of intelligence during the JMATE program that followed JMARC. The majority of key Cuban exile and Cuban domestic intelligence reports now available have come from AMOT sources.

444 Grayston Lynch, *Decision for Disaster: Betrayal at the Bay of Pigs* (Washington, DC: Potomac Books, 1998), 34.

445 John Prados, *William Colby and the CIA: The Secret Wars of a Controversial Spymaster* (Lawrence: University Press of Kansas, 2009), 185–186.

446 Ibid., 187. Before 1970 the PRUs were supervised by CIA officers, who in turn were supported by military advisors from the Army Special Forces or Navy SEAL

teams. During 1970, the PRUs were transferred to Vietnamese national police control, with U.S. military advisors assuming the primary field support role.

447 John Prados, *William Colby and the CIA*, 197.

448 The PRUs earned a reputation for not taking prisoners or detainees, especially when attempts to snatch targeted VCI personnel degenerated into a firefight. Since many VCI leaders had their own bodyguards on call, such firefights were common occurrences. They could lead to widespread casualties in entire villages. Additionally, the PRUs had no legal standing and over time the Vietnamese themselves insisted that PRU units be pulled back under national police control. In the final year of their independent operations, the PRUs ran some fifty thousand-plus missions, captured over seven thousand VCI, and killed almost forty-five hundred.

449 Office of the Special Assistant for Counterinsurgency and Special Activities, *Memorandum for the Record*, Meeting at the State Department, 1100, 31 August 1963; Subject: Vietnam, 31 August 1963. https://www.mtholyoke.edu/acad/intrel/pentagon2/doc135.htm

450 Terminology for such missions and practices changes with the territory; in Vietnam it was "search and destroy." Decades later, in Afghanistan and Iraq, we will see the practice described as "night raids." The concept of both would be the same: use intelligence to target insurgency supporters, whether Viet Cong, Taliban, or Al-Qaeda; then assault, capture, or destroy that base to destroy the insurgency. Sometimes described as "low intensity" in comparison to full-scale conventional warfare, the individual assaults become extremely focused and very intense for those involved.

451 Robert M. Gillespie, *Black Ops Vietnam: The Operational History of MACVSOG* (Annapolis, MD: Naval Institute Press, 2011), 83–87. Also see SACSA Memorandum on ICEX. http://www.thememoryhole.org/phoenix/icex-briefing.pdf

452 Review and discussion of the various CIA and Vietnamese government efforts (including CIA circulars issued to Phoenix participants) to address charges against the Phoenix program.
http://www.american-buddha.com/phoenixprog20.htm

453 Prados, *William Colby and the CIA*, 213.

454 Ibid., 209.

455 Rodriguez, *Shadow Warrior*, 186–187.

456 Corn, *Blond Ghost*, 216.

457 Prados, *William Colby and the CIA*, 194–201.

458 Ibid., 217. SEAL team leader Mike Walsh noted that his group would have to hide their agent lists and intelligence particulars when CIA officers performed oversight visits.

459 We will see that such conflicts certainly are not unique to the CIA. Decades later, the Joint Special Operations Command would assume an autonomous role in Afghanistan and Iraq, targeting terrorist and insurgent infrastructures with many of the same tactics as Phoenix. And in those countries JSOC task forces would come into operational conflict with regular military commands assigned to those countries.

460 Ibid., 185. Orrin DeForest, Region III CIA chief of interrogation.

461 Ibid., 186.

462 John Stockwell, *The Praetorian Guard: The U.S. Role in the New World Order* (Boston: South End Press, 1999), 47–48.

463 Prados, *William Colby and the CIA*, 236.

CHAPTER 17

464 David Pion-Berlin, "Military Dictatorships of Brazil and the Southern Cone," *World Scholar, Latin America and the Caribbean* (Stamford, CT: Cengage Learning,

2012). http://www.academia.edu/2900228/Military_Dictatorships_of_Brazil_and_the_Southern_Cone

465 John Dinges, *The Condor Years: How Pinochet and His Allies Brought Terrorism to Three Continents* (New York: New Press, 2005), 18.

466 Ibid., 43–44.

467 Ibid., 50–51.

468 Ibid., 51–53.

469 Steve J. Stern, *Remembering Pinochet's Chile: On the Eve of London 1998* (Durham, NC: Duke University Press, 2006), 22.

470 John Prados, *Presidents' Secret Wars: CIA and Pentagon Covert Operations from World War II through the Persian Gulf War* (Chicago: Ivan R. Dee, 1996), 321.

471 Dinges, *The Condor Years*, 57–58.

472 Peter Kornbluh, *The Pinochet File: A Declassified Dossier on Atrocity and Accountability* (New York: New Press, 2003), 20–21.

473 Ibid., 24–25.

474 Ibid., 26.

475 Ibid., 27–35; supporting documents, 36–78.

476 RIF 104-10121-10285, Morales, David Sanchez (Agreement with AID). http://www.maryferrell.org/mffweb/archive/naraSearch.do

477 David Morales CIA personnel file, National Archive. All assignments and postings as well as Morales's separation résumé are in the author's personal files. Additional information on Morales from Reuban Carbajal is from his personal conversations with Gaeton Fonzi (HSCA investigator) and Robert Dorff and from the author's own conversations with Carbajal.

478 Felix Rodriguez, *Shadow Warrior: The CIA Hero of a Hundred Unknown Battles* (New York: Simon & Schuster, 1989), 203–206.

479 Ibid., 64–65. DINA's "national intelligence" unit is acknowledged as having organized one of the most far-reaching and practically effective services in the Southern Cone nations. It involved itself in every aspect of social, economic, and political activities in a search for anything resembling an antigovernment view, which was considered to be subversive. Anyone identified as subversive was imprisoned or deported; in fact, the head of DINA prided himself on the fact that only some three thousand subversives had been killed in Chile. He felt that number was nothing at all compared to over a hundred thousand deaths in El Salvador and Peru or tens of thousands in Argentina. U.S military intelligence confirmed the dramatic reach and effectiveness of DINA, comparing it to the German Gestapo and the Soviet KGB.

480 David Atlee Phillips, *The Night Watch: Twenty-five Years of Peculiar Service* (New York: Atheneum, 1977), 258, 261.

481 Dinges, *The Condor Years*, 71.

482 Ibid., 120–123.

483 National Security Archive, Memorandum to the Secretary from Shlaudeman, August, 30, 1976. http://www.gwu.edu/~nsarchiv/NSAEBB/NSAEBB312/1_19760830_Operation_Condor.PDF

484 Ibid.

485 National Security Archive, Kissinger cable to Shlaudeman, September 16, 1976. http://www.gwu.edu/~nsarchiv/NSAEBB/NSAEBB312/3 _19760920_Operation_Condor.PDF

486 Peter Kornbluh, ed., "Kissinger Blocked Demarche on International Assassinations to Condor States," National Security Archive Electronic Briefing Book No. 312. http://www.gwu.edu/~nsarchiv/NSAEBB/NSAEBB312/index.htm

487 Dinges, *The Condor Years*, 169–172.

CHAPTER 18

488 William M. LeoGrande, *Our Own Backyard: The United States in Central America, 1977–1992* (Chapel Hill: University of North Carolina Press, 2000), 11–13.
489 *Foreign Relations of the United States, 1969–1976,* Volume E–10, *Documents on American Republics, 1969–1972,* Document 497, "Telegram 1696 From the Embassy in Nicaragua to the Department of State, September 28, 1970." http://history.state.gov/historicaldocuments/frus 1969-76ve10/d497
490 *Foreign Relations of the United States,* 1969–1976, Volume E–10, *Documents on American Republics, 1969–1972,* Document 492, "Telegram 645 From the Embassy in Nicaragua to the Department of State, April 17, 1970." http://history.state.gov/historicaldocuments/frus1969-76ve10/d492
491 *Foreign Relations of the United States, 1969–1976,* Volume E–10, *Documents on American Republics, 1969–1972,* Document 488, "Airgram A-5 From the Embassy in Nicaragua to the Department of State, January 18, 1970." http://history.state.gov/historicaldocuments/frus1969-76ve10/d488
492 LeoGrande, *Our Own Backyard,* 15.
493 *Foreign Relations of the United States,* 1969–1976, Volume E-10, *Documents on American Republics, 1969–1972,* Document 489, "Memorandum of Conversation, Managua, January 20, 1970." http://history.state.gov/historicaldocuments/frus1969-76ve10/d489
494 *Foreign Relations of the United States, 1969–1976,* Volume E–10, *Documents on American Republics, 1969–1972,* Document 513, "Telegram 446 From the Embassy in Nicaragua to the Department of State, February 23, 1972." http://history.state.gov/historicaldocuments/frus1969-76ve10/d513
495 LeoGrande, *Our Own Backyard,* 30–31.
496 Ibid., 43–45.
497 Cyrus Vance, *Hard Choices: Critical Years in America's Foreign Policy* (New York: Simon & Schuster, 1983), 384.
498 Steve Coll, *Ghost Wars: The Secret History of the CIA, Afghanistan, and Bin Laden, from the Soviet Invasion to September 10, 2001* (New York: Penguin Books, 2004), 39.
499 Peter Dale Scott, *The Road to 9/11: Wealth, Empire, and the Future of America* (Berkeley, CA: University of California Press, 2008), 78.
500 Ibid., 41.
501 John Prados, *Safe for Democracy: The Secret Wars of the CIA* (Chicago: Ivan R. Dee, 2009), 469.
502 Coll, *Ghost Wars,* 51.
503 Ibid., 55.
504 Ibid., 57.
505 Ibid., 66–67.
506 Prados, *Safe for Democracy*, 482.
507 Readers are referred to *Ghost Wars* by Steve Coll for a much broader discussion of the religious elements in the warfare in and around Afghanistan. Coll delves into the personalities and motives of many of the key figures and also explores the belief system that united the fundamentalist Muslims with the intensely religious director of the CIA during this period, William Casey. Coll's insight into how Casey's personal beliefs reinforced the broader American relationship with the two countries is fascinating. However, the personal relationship also produced a level of reliance on Pakistani and Saudi intelligence structures and operatives that had a major impact long beyond Casey's tenure.
508 Ibid., 480.
509 Prados, *Safe for Democracy*, 494–495.

510 Ibid., 89.
511 NSDD-17.
512 John Prados, *The Presidents' Secret Wars: CIA and Pentagon Covert Operations from World War II Through the Persian Gulf War* (Chicago: Ivan R. Dee, 1996), 379.
513 Ibid., 385.
514 Peter Kornbluh, *The Price of Intervention in Nicaragua: Reagan's Wars against the Sandinistas* (Washington, DC: Institute for Policy Studies, 1987), 19–20.
515 Prados, *The Presidents' Secret Wars*, 386–386.
516 In reality there were three separate Boland amendments offered between 1982 and 1984. Each was aimed at limiting funding to the Contras. The first was attached as a rider to the Defense Appropriations Act of 1983. In December 1983, for fiscal year 1984, a second Boland Amendment limited the amount spent in Nicaragua for military aid. In December 1984, a third Boland Amendment prohibited covert assistance for military operations in Nicaragua.
517 Kornbluh, *The Price of Intervention in Nicaragua*, 56.
518 Ibid., 46.
519 Prados, *The Presidents' Secret Wars*, 389.
520 Leslie Cockburn, *Out of Control* (New York: Atlantic Monthly Press, 1987), 12.
521 Prados, *The Presidents' Secret Wars*, 390–391.
522 Kornbluh, *The Price of Intervention in Nicaragua*, 47–48.
523 Ibid., 50.
524 Prados, *Safe for Democracy*, 509. Clarridge was viewed by CIA Director Casey as a real go-getter, extremely action-oriented and not one to brook obstacles. After a short brief on the situation at the time of his assignment, Casey asked him to come back with ideas on how to improve the secret war. According to Clarridge himself, he came back in a week and gave his plan to Casey: "My plan was simple: 1) Take the war to Nicaragua and 2) Start killing Cubans." Casey reportedly loved the response. However, a significant problem in actually executing the Clarridge plan was that Clarridge, the CIA, and the Contras were never able to locate Cubans actually involved in supplying the El Salvadorian rebels through Nicaragua once the secret war against Nicaragua had gotten under way.
525 LeoGrande, *Our Own Backyard*, 311.
526 Oliver L. North and William Novak, *Under Fire: An American Story* (New York: HarperCollins, 1991), 222.
527 LeoGrande, *Our Own Backyard*, 336. After extending his apology in committee, Casey told his own deputy, John McMahon, "I sure didn't want to do it; I gagged on it . . . I only apologized to save the Contras."
528 Martin Tolchin, "Senate, 84 to 12, Acts To Oppose Mining Nicaraguan Ports; Rebuke to Reagan," *New York Times*, April 11, 1984. http://www.nytimes.com/1984/04/11/world/senate-84-12-acts-to-oppose -mining-nicaragua-ports-rebuke-to-reagan.html
529 Kornbluh, *The Price of Intervention in Nicaragua*, 61.

CHAPTER 19

530 Oliver L. North with William Novak, *Under Fire: An American Story* (New York: HarperCollins, 1991), 140.
531 Richard Secord, *Honored and Betrayed: Irangate, Covert Affairs, and the Secret War in Laos* (New York: John Wiley & Sons, 1992), 204. It should be noted that Richard Secord, in his autobiography *Honored and Betrayed*, adamantly takes exception to the fact that the North project was an illegal end-run around congressional intentions and legislation. He refers to that view as a "myth," noting that

legislation left the door open for private fund-raising. It is certainly not possible to know what each member of Congress had in mind in voting for restrictions on Nicaraguan activities, but given the commentary in Director Casey's internal communications it appears that administration figures were quite conscious that they were setting their own course irrespective of congressional intent—the question of legality as argued by Secord being a separate issue entirely.

532 *Memorandum from CIA Director William Casey to Presidential National Security Advisor Robert McFarlane*, Subject: Supplemental Assistance to Nicaragua Program, March 27, 1984.

533 North and Novak, *Under Fire*, 251.

534 William M. LeoGrande, *Our Own Backyard: The United States in Central America, 1977–1992* (Chapel Hill: University of North Carolina Press, 2000), 401.

535 Leslie Gill, *The School of the Americas: Military Training and Political Violence in the Americas* (Durham, NC: Duke University Press, 2004), chapter 6. From a military perspective, clearly it is in the interest of continental defense for U.S. military services to have close ties to senior military officers and commanders in Latin American nations. It can also prove valuable for legitimate counterterrorism activities as well as for related missions such as drug interdiction. There has been a long history of establishing those relationships, going back before WWII. The issue is that in recent decades a number of Latin American officers and commanders became deeply involved in wide-scale political warfare within their own countries. Gill's *School of the Americas* provides insights and commentary from both the American offices involved in training and liaison work and the Latin American officers themselves, some of whom go into considerable detail on the justification for their own actions. The book is recommended as valuable background for the discussion of pros and cons of the military training and advisory relationships, a subject outside the focus of this work.

536 Peter Kornbluh, *Nicaragua: The Price of Intervention—Reagan's Wars against the Sandinistas* (Washington, DC: Institute for Policy Studies, 1987), 198–201.

537 LeoGrande, *Our Own Backyard*, 401–402.

538 Scott Anderson and Jon Lee Anderson, *Inside the League: The Shocking Expose of How Terrorists, Nazis, and Latin American Death Squads Have Infiltrated the World Anti-Communist League* (New York: Dodd, Mead and Company, 1986), 151–152.

539 Ibid., 260–261.

540 Ibid., 268–269.

541 North and Novak, *Under Fire*, 265.

542 Ibid., 407–408.

543 Kornbluh, *Nicaragua: The Price of Intervention*, 71.

544 LeoGrande, *Our Own Backyard*, 403.

545 Jonathan Kwitny, *The Crimes of Patriots* (New York: Simon & Schuster, 1987), 310–311.

546 David Corn, *Blond Ghost: Ted Shackley and the CIA's Crusades* (New York: Simon & Schuster, 1994), 252.

547 Ibid., 208.

548 Ibid., 231.

549 Ibid., 215–216.

550 LeoGrande, *Our Own Backyard*, 403–405.

551 Felix I. Rodriguez, *Shadow Warrior* (New York: Simon & Schuster, 1990), 244–245.

552 Ann Louise Bardach and Larry Rohter, "A Bomber's Tale: Taking Aim at Castro; Key Cuba Foe Claims Exiles' Backing," *New York Times*, July 12, 1998. In 1998, Posada admitted being behind a series of 1997 bombings at Cuban hotels, restaurants, and discothèques. In interviews Posada described receiving payments over several years from CANF, which funded his living expenses and certain of

his operations. He also claimed to have been close to its founder, Jorge Mas Canosa. While CANF officially denied the relationship, Posada was adamant about receiving support from the Miami exiles over a number of years.

553 National Archives and Records Administration, RIF 180-10096-10282 HSCA memorandum, CIA documents on Rolando Otero.

554 Gaeton Fonzi, *The Last Investigation: What Insiders Know about the Assassination of JFK* (New York: Thunder's Mouth Press, 1993), 341, 344. Officially Posada had left the CIA in 1967. Shortly afterward he was approached by an individual offering him a position with DSIP. By 1971 Posada was DSIP security chief, in charge of surveillance and counterintelligence. While Posada denied knowing David Phillips, Phillips was independently interviewed, not knowing of Posada's denial.

555 Rodriguez, *Shadow Warrior*, 238–239.

556 North and Novak, *Under Fire*, 272–275.

557 John Prados, *Safe for Democracy: The Secret Wars of the CIA* (Chicago: Ivan R. Dee, 2006), 562.

558 Ibid., 564–565.

559 Steve Coll, *Ghost Wars: The Secret History of the CIA, Afghanistan, and Bin Laden, from the Soviet Invasion to September 10, 2001* (New York: Penguin Books, 2004), 60–61.

560 Ibid., 62.

561 Steve Coll, *The Bin Ladens: An Arabian Family in the American Century* (New York: Penguin Press, 2008), 250.

562 Ibid., 253–254.

563 The detailed story of the fundamentalist seizure of influence, including an exploration of the personalities that enabled it, is addressed in Steve Coll's excellent book *Ghost Wars*. That story ranges into both religious and political aspects that are far beyond our focus. It carries through to the ultimate emergence of both the Taliban and the pan-Arabic fundamentalist movement that led to Al-Qaeda and 9/11.

564 Coll, *Ghost Wars*, 127–128.

565 Ibid., 132–133.

566 Ibid., 136.

567 Ibid., 155.

568 Ibid., 201.

569 Gary Schroen, *First In: An Insider's Account of How the CIA Spearheaded the War on Terror in Afghanistan* (New York: Ballantine Books, 2006), 52.

570 Henry A. Crumpton, *The Art of Intelligence: Lessons from a Life in the CIA's Clandestine Service* (New York: Penguin Press, 2012), 127.

571 Peter Dale Scott, *The Road to 9/11: Wealth, Empire, and the Future of America* (Berkeley: University of California Press, 2009), 73.

572 Khaled Ahmed, "Second Opinion: Some Generals Get Away with Corruption," *Daily Times of Pakistan*, July 16, 2004. http://www.dailytimes.com.pk/default.asp?page=story_16-7-2004_pg3_3

573 Schroen, *First In*, 56–57.

CHAPTER 20

574 Hank Albarelli Jr., *A Terrible Mistake: The Murder of Frank Olson and the CIA's Secret Cold War Experiments* (Walterville, OR: Trine Day Publishing, 2009), 65, 781 on 1975 memo, 531–533 in reference to the DOD internal inquiry. The initial agreement was later formalized in a 1952 memorandum of understanding between the CIA and the Army Chemical Corps officer.

Several senior CIA officers were privy to the work being done on both lethal chemicals (drugs, poisons, and diseases) and nonlethal drugs (including a number of LSD derivatives) for use in interrogation and temporary incapacitation. Those officers included the head of the Office of Security, the head of Counterintelligence, and the head of Operations. All three officers were members of a group reportedly (and likely unofficially) referred to as the Health Alteration Committee.

575 Ibid., 781–782.

576 Remarks by CIA General Counsel Stephen W. Preston as prepared for delivery at Harvard Law School, April 10, 2012. Text of speech available online. https://www.cia.gov/news-information/speeches-testimony/ 2012-speeches-testimony/cia-general-counsel-harvard.html

577 John Prados, *Safe for Democracy: The Secret Wars of the CIA* (Chicago: Ivan R. Dee, 2009), 567.

578 "Lawmaker: Panetta terminated secret program," MSNBC.com, July 10, 2009.

579 Siobhan Gorman, "CIA Had Secret Al Qaeda Plan," *Wall Street Journal*, July 13, 2009.

580 Associated Press, "Senators: CIA concealment may have broken law," *USA Today*, July 12, 2009.

581 "Cheney ordered intel withheld from Congress–Senator," Reuters, July 12, 2009.

582 Henry A. Crumpton, *The Art of Intelligence: Lessons from a Life in the CIA's Clandestine Service* (New York: Penguin Press, 2013), 125.

583 Memorandum for Director Central Intelligence from General Counsel Houston, Report of Criminal Violations to the Department of Justice, February 23, 1954, and Memorandum for Deputy Attorney General, Department of Justice from CIA General Counsel Houston, Washington D.C., March 1, 1954.

584 Albarelli Jr., *A Terrible Mistake*, 535.

585 Martha Honey, "Don't' Ask, Don't Tell," *In These Times*, May 1998.

586 Reply letter on MOU from Attorney General William French Smith to CIA Director William Casey, February 11, 1982. http://www.angelfire.com/id/ciadrugs/images/cia-doj-agreement.gif

587 Reply letter on MOU from CIA Director Casey to Attorney General Smith, reference communication of understanding to other government agencies, March 2, 1982. http://www.angelfire.com/id/ciadrugs/images/cia-doj-agreement2.gif

588 Richard B. Still, "Pilots, Companies and Other Individuals Working for Companies Used to Support the Contra Program," Central Intelligence Agency Report, October 8, 1998, paragraph 1072. Material in this report provides corroboration for suspicions of Contra involvement in drug traffic; the following comment is excerpted from that report: The DO [director of operations] assigned a low priority to collecting intelligence concerning the Contras alleged involvement in narcotics trafficking." As a result, Agency analysts had only a small number of reports on which to base their analysis. According to CIA records, only three DO reports regarding Contra drug trafficking were found to have been disseminated between October and December 1984. These were reports describing the alleged agreement between Eden Pastora's associates and a Miami-based drug trafficker involving material support for the Contras in return for the trafficker's access to the southern front's pilots and landing strips. https://www.cia.gov/library/reports/general-reports-1/cocaine/contra-story/pilots.html

589 Joseph C. Goulden, *The Death Merchant* (New York: Simon & Schuster, 1984), 39.

590 Ibid., 46–47.

591 Ibid., 83–86.

592 Jonathan Kwitny, *The Crimes of Patriots: A True Tale of Dope, Dirty Money and the CIA* (New York: W.W. Norton & Company, 1987), 207.

593 Ibid., 208.
594 Ibid., 21–22.
595 Leslie Cockburn, "Guns, Drugs and the CIA," PBS *Frontline* 613, original air date: May 17, 1988. http://www.pbs.org/wgbh/pages/frontline/shows/drugs/archive/gunsdrugscia.html

CHAPTER 21

596 "U.S. looks into Afghan air force drug allegations," CNN wire staff, March 8, 2012. http://www.cnn.com/2012/03/08/world/asia/afghanistan -air-drugs-investigation/index.html
597 "Afghan Air Force Probed in Gun Running," *Wall Street Journal*, March 10, 2012. http://online.wsj.com/article/SB10001424052970204276304577263032415519426.html
598 John Ranelagh, *The Agency: The Rise and the Decline of the CIA* (New York: Simon & Schuster, 1986), 221.
599 Richard Gibson with Wen H. Chen, *The Secret Army: Chiang Kai–shek and the Drug Warlords of the Golden Triangle* (New York: John Wiley & Sons, 2011), 254–256.
600 John Prados, *Safe for Democracy: The Secret Wars of the CIA* (Chicago: Ivan R. Dee, Inc., 2009), 358.
601 Leslie Cockburn, "Guns, Drugs and the CIA," PBS *Frontline* 613, original air date: May 17, 1988. http://www.pbs.org/wgbh/pages/frontline/shows/drugs/archive/gunsdrugscia.html
602 Prados, *Safe for Democracy*, 359.
603 Jonathan Marshall, *Drug Wars: Corruption, Counterinsurgency and Covert Operations in the Third World* (Forestville, CA: Cohen & Cohen Publishers, 1991), 39.
604 Ibid., 38.
605 Ibid., 40.
606 David Corn, *Blond Ghost: Ted Shackley and the CIA's Crusades* (New York: Simon & Schuster, 1994), 300.
607 Ibid., 258.
608 Selections from the Senate Committee Report on Drugs, Law Enforcement and Foreign Policy chaired by Senator John F. Kerry. http://www.pinknoiz.com/covert/contracoke.html#X
609 Ibid.
610 Robert Parry, "CIA's drug confession," Media Consortium, October 11, 1998. http://flag.blackened.net/revolt/mexico/usa/cia_drugs.html
611 Ibid.
612 Ibid.
613 U.S. Department of Justice, "Previous Investigations Concerning Allegations of Contra Drug Trafficking." http://www.justice.gov/oig/special/9712/ch01p2.htm
614 A decade later, in 1996, Pulitzer Prize–winning reporter Gary Webb would begin his "Dark Alliance" series of articles in the *San Jose Mercury News*. The focus of his work was that CIA-associated Contra figures had helped smuggle cocaine into the U.S., playing a part in triggering the crack cocaine epidemic of the 1980s. He maintained that the CIA was aware of drug-dealing by the Contras and that they were shielded from prosecution by the CIA and the Reagan Administration. Webb supported his views with FOIA documents, and in particular with excerpts from unclassified sections of 1988 reports released by CIA Inspector General Frederick Hitz.

Webb's story was hugely controversial, especially in terms of his linkage to the crack cocaine epidemic. It was officially denied and major pressure was brought on his newspaper, which abandoned him, leaving his career in ruins. Yet well-respected investigative journalists continued to defend and reinforce Webb's work and ultimately the Justice Department was forced to address it in detail. The DOJ investigative report on Contra drug associations is now public and section F specifically deals with Webb's work at the *San Jose Mercury News*.

The DOJ/OIG findings failed to confirm a number of Webb's specific allegations about individuals, especially in regard to government protection for them or official government interference with legal investigation of them. In other areas they merely commented on the difficulty and lack of cooperation in investigating some of his information. In terms of data the findings provide an interesting reference but simply present work on a list of named individuals.

In studying the findings and the other materials now available, the authors can only conclude, along with many others, that Webb's fundamental insights on CIA and Enterprise Contra assets and drugs were correct. Reagan Administration senior officers had had indeed "issued a pass" in the interest of conducting covert warfare against the Sandinistas. That is now documented. U.S. Department of Justice, "Previous Investigations Concerning Allegations of Contra Drug Trafficking," Section F. http://www.justice.gov/oig/special/9712/ch01p2.htm

615 Peter Kornbluh, *Nicaragua: The Price of Intervention—Reagan's Wars against the Sandinistas* (Washington, DC: Institute for Policy Studies, 1987), 202–203.

616 Ibid., 198–199.

617 Ibid., 199.

618 Ibid., 200.

619 U.S. Department of Justice, "Previous Investigations Concerning Allegations of Contra Drug Trafficking." http://www.justice.gov/oig/special/9712/ch01p2.htm

620 Ibid.

621 Peter Kornbluh, National Security Archive Electronic Briefing Book No. 113, "The Oliver North File: His Diaries, E-Mail, and Memos on the Kerry Report, Contras, and Drugs," February 26, 2004. http://www.gwu.edu/~nsarchiv/NSAEBB/NSAEBB113/index.htm

622 Prados, *Safe for Democracy*, 573–575.

623 Summary of Iran–Contra legal prosecutions:

After Independent Counsel Lawrence E. Walsh's appointment in December 1986, fourteen persons were charged with criminal offenses. Eleven persons were convicted, but two convictions were overturned on appeal. Two persons were pardoned before trial and one case was dismissed when the first Bush Administration declined to declassify information necessary for trial. On December 24, 1992, President Bush pardoned Caspar W. Weinberger, Duane R. Clarridge, Clair E. George, Elliott Abrams, Alan D. Fiers Jr., and Robert C. McFarlane.

Oliver L. North was indicted on March 16, 1988, on sixteen felony counts. After standing trial on twelve, North was convicted May 4, 1989, of three charges: accepting an illegal gratuity, aiding and abetting in the obstruction of a congressional inquiry, and destruction of documents. He was sentenced by U.S. District Judge Gerhard A. Gesell on July 5, 1989, to a three-year suspended prison term, two years' probation, $150,000 in fines, and twelve hundred hours of community service. A three-judge appeals panel on July 20, 1990, vacated North's conviction for further proceedings to determine whether his immunized testimony influenced witnesses in the trial. The Supreme Court declined to review the case. Judge Gesell dismissed the case on September 16, 1991, after hearings on the immunity issue, on the motion of independent counsel. http://www.fas.org/irp/offdocs/walsh/summpros.htm

624 In discussing the changes in the decades following Truman, Merle Miller succinctly described matters with a simple question: "Can you imagine a member of his [Truman's] Cabinet seriously telling a Congressional committee that he had 'shielded' Harry from the truth?" Merle Miller, *Plain Speaking: An Oral Biography of Harry S. Truman* (New York: Berkley Publishing Corporation, 1974), 19–20.

CHAPTER 22

625 Glenn L. Carle, *The Interrogator: An Education* (New York: Nation Books, 2012), 36.

626 Ibid.

627 Bob Woodward, *Veil: The Secret Wars of the CIA, 1981–1987* (New York: Simon & Schuster, 2005), 97–98.

628 Ibid., 90–91.

629 "Profile: Chad's Hissene Habre: Former Chad leader Hissene Habre is 'Africa's Pinochet' according to pressure group Human Rights Watch," *BBC News*, July 3, 2006. http://news.bbc.co.uk/2/hi/africa/5140818.stm

630 "Chad: The Habre Legacy," Amnesty International, October 15, 2001.

631 John Prados, *Safe for Democracy: The Secret Wars of the CIA* (Chicago: Ivan R. Dee, 2006), 580–581.

632 Richard A. Clarke, *Against All Enemies: Inside America's War on Terror* (New York: Free Press, 2004), 73.

633 Ibid., 75.

634 Prados, *Safe for Democracy*, 582.

635 Ibid., 595.

636 Clarke, *Against All Enemies*, 79.

637 Gary Berntsen and Ralph Pezzullo, *Jawbreaker: The Attack on bin Laden and Al-Qaeda: A Personal Account by the CIA's Key Field Commander* (New York: Crown Publishing, 2005), 18, 26. CIA officer Gary Berntsen writes that bin Laden experts were well aware of the potential of NGOs such as Al-Haramain as early as the massive terror bombings against multiple American embassies in Africa in 1998. It would not be until 2004 that the U.S. Department of the Treasury officially moved globally against Al-Haramain and certain of its senior figures (including two within its U.S. branch) on the basis of its documented links to bin Laden and Al-Qaeda. The United Nations also placed the organization on its list of Al-Qaeda and Taliban affiliates. In regard to the African embassy attacks, one of the principal figures involved (formerly a secretary to bin Laden) had been operating under the cover of yet another charitable NGO called Help Africa People.

638 Clarke, *Against All Enemies*, 83.

639 Ibid., 96.

640 Ibid., 137–138.

641 Steve Coll, *The Bin Ladens: An Arabian Family in the American Century* (New York: Penguin Press, 2008), 381.

642 Ibid., 409.

643 Clarke, *Against All Enemies*, 141.

644 Philip Shenon, *The Commission: The Uncensored History of the 9/11 Investigation* (New York: Twelve, 2008), 357.

645 "Bin Laden's Fatwa," *PBS NewsHour*, August 23, 1996. http://www.pbs.org/newshour/updates/military/july-dec96/fatwa_1996.html

646 Henry A. Crumpton, *The Art of Intelligence: Lessons from a Life in the CIA's Clandestine Service* (New York: Penguin Press, 2012), 111–113.

647 "Al Qaeda's Second Fatwa," *PBS NewsHour*, February 23, 1998. http://www.pbs.org/newshour/updates/military/jan-june98/fatwa_1998.html

648 In general the response to the embassy bombings was that of a criminal action, with the FBI directed to work overseas with the nations involved. At that point, even following the two Al-Qaeda declarations, domestically little had been done in regard to intelligence collection or proactive action. Readers interested in the initial domestic response are referred to Henry A. Crumpton's book, *The Art of Intelligence*, chapters 7 and 8.

649 Coll, *The Bin Ladens*, 495.

CHAPTER 23

650 Robert Gillespie, *Black Ops, Vietnam: An Operational History of MACVSOG* (Annapolis, MD: Naval Institute Press, 2011), 11–13.

651 Ibid.

652 Ibid., 18–19. The CIA had been using planes flown and crewed by extremely experienced Chinese Nationalist crews, many of who had flown covert missions for the Agency for years, including hundreds of missions over the People's Republic of China. New military demands on the Chinese crews reportedly soured relations, not only from the perspective of increased discipline but new operational demands that were more of an intelligence nature than insertion and supply drops—exposing the crews to far higher risks.

653 Ibid., 19.

654 Richard H. Shultz Jr., *The Secret War against Hanoi* (New York: HarperCollins Perennial, 1999), 50–51, 67.

655 Ibid., 51–53.

656 Ibid.

657 Ibid., 52.

658 Tom Clancy with General Carl Stiner and Tony Koltz, *Shadow Warriors: Inside the Special Forces* (New York: Putnam's Sons, 2002), 9.

659 Ibid., 12–13.

660 Chris Hobson, *Vietnam Air Losses: United States Air Force, Navy and Marine Corps Fixed-Wing Aircraft Losses in Southeast Asia, 1961–1973* (Midland Publishing, 2001), 268. AC-130s reportedly destroyed more than ten thousand trucks and provided ground force support in many crucial Cobalt operations in Vietnam. Six Spectres and fifty-two air crew were lost during the combat in Southeast Asia.

661 Warren A. Trest, *Air Commando One: Heinie Aderholt and America's Secret Air Wars* (Washington, DC: Smithsonian Institution Press, 2000), 192.

662 Ibid., 213–214.

663 Ibid., 220–221.

664 Gary C. Schroen, *First In: An Insider's Account of How the CIA Spearheaded the War on Terror in Afghanistan* (New York: Ballantine Books, 2005), 27.

665 *United States Special Operations Command*, 6th ed., March 31, 2008. http://www.socom.mil/Documents/history6thedition.pdf

666 In February 2013, the Air Force opened the Air Force Special Operations Air Warfare Center, headquartered at Hulburt Field in Florida, with satellite locations at Duke Field in Florida and Robins Air Force Base in Georgia. The new unit is modeled on Kennedy-era Special Air Warfare Center activities circa 1962; that unit stood down after the Vietnam War. Readers may recall that Hulburt Field

was used for training on WWII-type aircraft in the early 1960s and that the early covert air operation into South Vietnam staged personnel assigned from that unit. The activation of the new Special Operations Air Warfare center is a further indication of a return to a focus on special operations in the early twenty-first century.

667 Clancy with Stiner and Koltz, *Shadow Warriors*, Appendix I.

668 AC-130 H/U Air Force Fact Sheet, July 30, 2010. http://www.af.mil/AboutUs/FactSheets/Display/tabid/224/Article/104486/ac-130hu.aspx

669 MC-130E/H Combat Talon I/II, Air Force Fact Sheet, March 28, 2003. http://www.af.mil/AboutUs/FactSheets/Display/tabid/224/Article/ 104534/mc-130eh-combat-talon-iii.aspx

670 James R. Chiles, "Air America's Black Helicopter: The secret aircraft that helped the CIA tap phones in North Vietnam," *Smithsonian Air and Space* magazine, March 2008. http://www.airspacemag.com/military -aviation/the_quiet_one.html

671 Sean D. Naylor, "Mission helo was secret stealth Black Hawk," *Army Times*, May 4, 2011. http://www.armytimes.com/news/2011/05/army -mission-helocopter-was-secret-stealth-black-hawk-050411/

672 William Wagner, *Lightning Bugs and Other Reconnaissance Drones: The Can-Do Story of Ryan's Unmanned "Spy Planes"* (Armed Forces Journal International in conjunction with Aero Publishers, Inc., 1982), foreword.

673 Ibid.

674 Wagner, *Lightning Bugs and Other Reconnaissance Drones*, 23. The RPV program was run under the "Big Safari" expedited purchase program established in the early 1950s for reconnaissance projects. The concept was to make available a process for "instantaneous reaction capability" and with approval from a sufficiently high level and money from contingency funds, the process worked quite well, and extremely quickly.

675 Ibid., 212–213.

676 Ibid., chapter 25.

677 Ibid., 24–25.

678 Ibid., 57, 92, 108.

679 Report by the Controller General of the United States, "DoD's Use of Remotely Piloted Vehicle Technology Offers Opportunities for Saving Lives and Dollars," April 3, 1981.

680 "Intelligence Successes and Failures in Operations Desert Shield/Storm, Report of the Oversight and Investigations Subcommittee, Committee on Armed Services, U.S. House of Representatives, August 1993," available in PBS *Frontline* news report "Weapons: Drones, RPVs." http://www.pbs.org/wgbh/pages/frontline/gulf/weapons/drones.html

681 Andreas Parsch, *Directory of U.S. Military Rockets and Missiles*, Appendix 4, "Undesignated Vehicles: Gnat." http://www.designation-systems .net/dusrm/app4/gnat.html

682 Henry A. Crumpton, *The Art of Intelligence: Lessons from Life in the CIA's Clandestine Service* (New York: Penguin Press, 2012), 150–151.

683 Sue Baker, "Predator missile launch test totally successful," Aeronautical Systems Center Public Affairs, February, 27, 2001. http://www.fas.org/irp/program/collect/docs/man-ipc-predator-010228.htm

684 U.S. Air Force, MQ-9 Reaper Fact Sheet, August 18, 2010. http://www .af.mil/information/factsheets/factsheet.asp?id=6405

CHAPTER 24

685 Bob Woodward, *Bush at War* (New York: Simon & Schuster, 2002), 6.

686 Ibid., 5.

687 Henry A. Crumpton, *The Art of Intelligence: Lessons from a Life in the CIA's Clandestine Service* (New York: Penguin Press, 2012), 149–150.
688 Ibid., 122–124.
689 Ibid., 150–160.
690 John Prados, *Safe for Democracy: The Secret Wars of the CIA* (Chicago: Ivan R. Dee, 2006), 623–624.
691 Richard A. Clarke, *Against All Enemies: Inside America's War on Terror* (New York: Free Press, 2004), 200.
692 Prados, *Safe for Democracy*, 154.
693 Philip Shenon, *The Commission: The Uncensored History of the 9/11 Investigation* (New York: Twelve, 2008), 146–148.
694 Ibid., 34–35.
695 Clarke, *Against All Enemies*, 32.
696 Crumpton, *The Art of Intelligence*, 173.
697 Woodward, *Bush at War*, 41–42.
698 Gary C. Schroen, *First In: An Insider's Account of How the CIA Spearheaded the War on Terror* (New York: Ballantine Books, 2006), 25.
699 Woodward, *Bush at War*, 142.
700 Gary Berntsen and Ralph Pezzullo, *Jawbreaker: The Attack on Bin Laden and Al-Qaeda: A Personal Account by the CIA's Key Field Commander* (New York: Crown Publishing Group, 2005), 128.
701 Schroen, *First In*, 99.
702 Ibid., 146–147.
703 Ibid., 93; Woodward, *Bush at War*, 198–215.
704 Crumpton, *The Art of Intelligence*, 200–205.
705 Schroen, *First In*, 185.
706 Ibid., 199, 216. Afghanistan would lay the foundations for highly effective joint CIA–special operations teamwork. But it was rocky in the first weeks and months. The two groups had not routinely worked together for years and coordination was not all that it could have been. The first attempted insertion of a Special Forces A-team using American Pave Low military helicopters was totally uncoordinated with the CIA team (Jawbreaker) that would have to receive it. The Special Forces unit (Task Force Dagger) in Tashkent had dispatched the helicopters without Jawbreaker having been notified or confirmed. Weather forced the flight to abort but the Afghans, who had been rushed to receive it with no notice, were not impressed. They were also not impressed when the team finally did arrive and landed at the wrong coordinates. Jawbreaker team members quickly regretted bragging to the Afghans that the Special Forces would be able to land exactly on target, even in the dark.
707 Woodward, *Bush at War*, 239.
708 Schroen, *First In*, 290–291.
709 Crumpton, *The Art of Intelligence*, 217–218.
710 Schroen, *First In*, 304–305.
711 Woodward, *Bush at War*, 291–292.
712 Ibid., 290–291.
713 Ibid., 164–165.
714 Ibid., 157.
715 Berntsen and Pezzullo, *Jawbreaker*, 136–137.
716 Ibid., 214.
717 Woodward, *Bush at War*, 255–258.
718 Mike Mount, "Document suggests bin Laden escaped at Tora Bora," CNN, March 24, 2005. http://www.cnn.com/2005/US/03/24/pentagon.binladen/
719 Ibid.
720 Ibid., 305, 308, 315.

721 Scott McClellan, *What Happened: Inside the Bush White House and Washington's Culture of Deception* (New York: BBS Public Affairs, 2008), 121–125.
722 Ibid., 123.
723 McClellan, *What Happened*, 128–131. Bush's private ideological views regarding the expansion of democracy in the Middle East as essential to bringing about a more secure political environment are discussed by Bush Administration press secretary Scott McClellan. Bush felt a free Iraq would "embolden" democracy in Iran and that, basically, free countries are peaceful and don't start wars with each other. McClellan notes that these personal views were held in reserve in regard to the Bush Administration media and political initiative that targeted Saddam Hussein. That effort focused strictly on his pursuit of weapons of mass destruction, his use of such weapons on his own people, and the risk such weapons might be used again or end up with terrorists.
724 Woodward, *Bush at War*, 329.
725 Prados, *Safe for Democracy*, 625.
726 Woodward, *Bush at War*, 310.
727 Ibid., 48–49.
728 Clarke, *Against All Enemies*, 30–31.

CHAPTER 25

729 Karen DeYoung and Greg Jaffe, "U.S. 'secret war' expands globally as Special Operations forces take larger role," *Washington Post*, June 4, 2010. http://www.washingtonpost.com/wp-dyn/content/article /2010/06/03/AR2010060304965.html?nav=emailpage
730 In our earlier discussion of Wilson and his associates, we noted the complex world of retired and separated service personnel. In that regard, it is worth noting that Wilson himself long maintained that his work was CIA-sanctioned as a source of intelligence on the Libyans and their Soviet arms suppliers. That story initially did Wilson no good; he was convicted and imprisoned with a fifty-three-year sentence. However, in 2003 he was ordered released when a judge ruled that the CIA had knowingly withheld information from the original trial—not reporting some eighty contacts that it had with Wilson during the period of the Libyan project.
731 Robert Young Pelton, *Licensed to Kill: Hired Guns in the War on Terror* (New York: Crown Publishing Group, 2006), 25–26.
732 Gary Berntsen and Ralph Pezzullo, *Jawbreaker: The Attack on Bin Laden and Al-Qaeda: A Personal Account by the CIA's Key Field Commander* (New York: Crown Publishing Group, 2005), 191.
733 Richard A. Clarke, *Against All Enemies: Inside America's War on Terror* (New York: Free Press, 2004), 24.
734 Pelton, *Licensed to Kill,* 261–262.
735 Ibid., chapter 2. Robert Young Pelton was a CNN reporter in Afghanistan during the combat against the Taliban. Jawbreaker team leader Berntsen mentions him in his book *Jawbreaker*. Pelton conducted interviews with Al-Qaeda prisoners: Arabs, Chechens, Pakistanis, Uzbeks, and a few Europeans. The depth of hatred in the prisoners' remarks was extreme; the CIA edited out the section of Berntsen's book in which the prisoners were discussed.
736 Pelton, *Licensed to Kill*, 36.
737 Greg Miller and Julie Tate, "CIA's Global Response Staff emerging from shadows after incidents in Libya and Pakistan," *Washington Post*, December 26, 2012. http://www.washingtonpost.com/world/national-security/cias-global-response-staff-emerging-from-shadows-after-incidents-in-libya-and-pakistan/2012/12/26/27db2d1c-4b7f-11e2-b709-667035ff9029_story.html?hpid=z2

738 Pelton, *Licensed to Kill*, 71. The problem is not unknown in Saudi Arabia; the Saudi royal family hires former American Delta and other Special Forces personnel for their own security needs.
739 Ibid., 73, 83.
740 Government Security Services, internet business website and corporate brochure, available online. http://www.g4s.us/en-US/What%20we%20do/Sectors/Government/
741 Associated Press, "Blackwater Changes Its Name to Xe," *New York Times*, February 13, 2009. http://www.nytimes.com/2009/02/14/us/14 blackwater.html?_r=0
742 Richard Sisk, "U.S. Embassy fires 8 guards involved in sexual misconduct," *New York Daily News*, September 4, 2009. http://www.nydailynews.com/news/world/embassy-fires-8-guards-involved-sexual-misconduct-scandal-article-1.401751#ixzz2SLNJnpjW
743 Jeremy Scahill, *Blackwater: The Rise of the World's Most Powerful Mercenary Army* (New York: Nation Books, 2008), 69.
744 Pelton, *Licensed to Kill*, 104.
745 Jamie Crawford, "Report finds 'waste' in Iraqi police training," CNN, July 30, 2012. http://security.blogs.cnn.com/2012/07/30/report-finds-waste-in-iraqi-police-training/?hpt=hp_t2
746 Masoud Popalzai, "Afghan police officer kills American contractor," CNN, December 24, 2012. http://www.cnn.com/2012/12/24/world/asia/afghanistan-attack/index.html?hpt=hp_t1
747 Mona Mahmood, Maggie O'Kane, Chavala Madlena, Teresa Smith, Ben Ferguson, Patrick Farrelly, Guy Grandijean, Josh Strauss, Roisin Glynn, Irene Baque, Marcus Morgan, Jake Zervudachi, and Joshua Boswell, "From El Salvador to Iraq: Washington's man behind brutal police squads," *Guardian*, March 6, 2013. http://www.guardian.co.uk/world/2013/mar/06/el-salvador-iraq-police-squads-washington
748 Pelton, *Licensed to Kill*, 94. There were certainly distinctions between the State Department and other government agency contractors in Iraq, and those corporate paramilitary contractors hired for reconstruction security projects. Reportedly the State Department's Diplomatic Security Service held a dim view of the corporate contractors as "overpaid cowboys." In turn the corporate contractors viewed the DSS details as "bureaucratic losers." Both sets of contractors were simply one more responsibility that the U.S. military, and its own service personnel were being paid a good deal less than any of the contractors.
749 Kenneth Katzman, *Iraq: Politics, Governance and Human Rights* (Congressional Research Service, 2012), 18; Michael O'Hanlon and Jason H. Campbell, "Iraq Index: Tracking Variables of Reconstruction and Security in Post-Saddam Iraq" (Washington, DC: Brookings Institution, 2007). Beginning in 2005, certain Sunni tribes began to lose control of their territories to Al-Qaeda allies. That pressure led them to turn to the American military for arms and support. In 2006 various such groups affiliated with the Anbar Awakening Council committed to opposing Al-Qaeda and its allies. Their preeminent leader was assassinated by suicide bombing in 2007; his brother replaced him but failed to unite the various Awakening Movement militias. In 2008, the central Iraqi government took the position that it could not allow independent military groups and assumed the responsibility for paying the groups, pledging to take numbers of their fighters into the Iraqi military. Supporting the Awakening Movement was seen as a major success in the American military effort against the Iraqi insurgency. However as of 2010 there were widespread reports that thousands of Awakening Movement fighters had gone out of action for various reasons. Continued Sunni distrust of Shiite factions in the government is a major factor in the ongoing mistrust of the power center in Baghdad, and the parliamentary elections of 2010 proved a major disappointment to the fractured Sunni political movement. As

of 2011, estimates placed the number of Awakening Movement members taken into either the Iraqi military or other government positions at sixty to seventy thousand, with another thirty thousand still engaged in some level of security activities in Sunni tribal areas while being paid a monthly government salary.

750 Pelton, *Licensed to Kill*, chapter 8.

751 Scahill, *Blackwater*, 162–163.

752 Ibid., 71.

753 Pelton, *Licensed to Kill*, chapter 9.

754 Mark Mazzetti, "Former Spy with Agenda Operates a Private CIA," *New York Times*, January 22, 2011. http://www.nytimes.com/2011/01/23/world/23clarridge.html?pagewanted=all&_r=1&

755 Bob Woodward, *Bush At War* (New York: Simon & Schuster, Inc., 2002), 46. Author Bob Woodward notes that Senator Robert C. Byrd, the president pro tempore of the Senate, did address the full Congress—telling them that President Bush did not want a declaration of war, but that he would "be interested in a resolution endorsing force." Byrd went on to expound on the fact that Bush should not expect to receive the same sort of blank check Congress had given President Johnson with the Tonkin Gulf Resolution.

756 Richard F. Grimmett, *CRS Report for Congress,* "Authorization For Use of Military Force in Response to the 9/11 Attacks (P.L. 107-40)," Legislative History, January 4, 2006. http://www.law.umaryland.edu/marshall/crsreports/crsdocuments/RS22357_01042006.pdf

757 John Avlon, "9/11 in Memoriam: 45 Foiled Terror Plots since 9/11," The Daily Beast, September 8, 2011. http://www.thedailybeast.com/articles/2011/09/08/9-11-anniversary-45-terror-plots-foiled-in-last -10-years.html

758 James Risen and David Johnston, "Threats and Responses: Hunt for Al Qaeda; Bush Has Widened Authority of C.I.A. to Kill Terrorists," *New York Times*, December 15, 2002. http://www.nytimes.com/2002/12/15/world/threats-responses-hunt-for-al-qaeda-bush-has-widened-authority-cia-kill.html

759 Jeremy Scahill, *Dirty Wars: The World Is a Battlefield* (New York: Nation Books, 2013), 114.

760 Titles 10 and 50 codify federal laws of the United States; they are part of the overall federal code of laws referred to as Code of Laws of the United States, United States Code, U.S. Code, or simply USC. U.S. Code contains fifty-one titles and additional titles have been proposed. Supplements to the code are published annually. Title 10 outlines the role of the armed forces and provides the legal framework for the organization, roles, and missions of the individual services as well as the Department of Defense. It contains subtitles dealing with general military law including the Uniform Code of Military Justice and the Army, Navy/Marine Corps, Air Force, and reserve components of the services. Title 50 pertains to war and national defense. It contains chapters relating to national security, espionage, alien enemies, disclosure of classified information, nuclear and atomic weapons, foreign intelligence surveillance, intelligence community authorities, the Central Intelligence Agency, and the National Security Agency, as well as a number of other topics. A full listing of chapters is available online from Cornell University Law School. www.law.cornell.edu/uscode/text

761 Ibid.

762 Scahill, *Dirty Wars*, 10, figure C.

763 Legal experts note that even the operation to strike Osama bin Laden in Pakistan was assigned by President Obama as a covert task—even though the vast amount of those actually participating were from the uniformed military services.

764 Andru E. Wall, "Demystifying the Title 10–Title 50 Debate: Distinguishing Military Operations, Intelligence Activities & Covert Action," *Harvard Law School National Security Journal* 3 (2011).

765 The standard usage of several of the terms and practices discussed in much of this book began to change significantly following the end of the Cold War and the attacks of 9/11. The war against Al-Qaeda and its associates certainly has not been covert in the traditional sense of the U.S. denying or publicly acknowledging its involvement. At most, operations are either obfuscated or simply not acknowledged. The use of surrogates declined significantly, especially after the early days in Afghanistan, with U.S. military forces becoming primary combatants. The clandestine support role the military formerly played has become much less passive, and military personnel and units are directly assigned to operations with none of the classic detailing or covers we saw during the Cold War. And the expanded use of the military under Title 50 authority and overall CIA operational authority has raised a number of legal questions in a debate that is ongoing as of this writing. Gray warfare seemed like the most accurate characterization of the new operational and authority structure that evolved under the Bush and Obama administrations.

766 Ibid., 6–7.

767 Robert Chesney, "Military–Intelligence Convergence and the Law of the Title 10/Title 50 Debate," *Journal of National Security Law and Policy*, Vol. 5:539. http://jnslp.com/wp-content/uploads/2012/01/Military-Intelligence -Convergence-and-the-Law-of-the-Title-10Title-50-Debate.pdf

768 Ibid.

769 Pam Benson with John Berman, "Obama to name John Brennan to lead CIA," CNN Security Clearance, January 7, 2013. http://security.blogs.cnn.com/2013/01/07/obama-to-name-john-brennan-to-lead-cia/

770 Ibid.

771 Jack Goldsmith, "John Brennan's Speech and the ACLU FOIA Cases," *Lawfare*, Hard National Security Choices, May 1, 2012. http://www.lawfareblog.com/2012/05/john-brennans-speech-and-the-aclu-foia-cases/

772 Scahill, *Dirty Wars*, 361.

773 Ibid., 163.

774 Ibid., 181.

775 Jack Goldsmith, *Power and Constraint: The Accountable Presidency After 9/11* (New York: W.W. Norton & Company, 2012), 89.

776 Ibid., 37–39.

777 Glenn L. Carle, *The Interrogator: An Education* (New York: Nation Books, 2012), 20–22.

778 Ibid., 23–24.

779 Goldsmith, *Power and Constraint*, 238–239.

780 Ibid, 90.

781 Scott Shane, "Election Spurred a Move to Codify U.S. Drone Policy," *New York Times*, November 24, 2012. http://www.nytimes.com/2012/11/25/world/white-house-presses-for-drone-rule-book.html?pagewanted=all&_r=0

782 Julian Borger, "Algeria hostage crisis: survivors tell of cold-blooded killers," *Guardian*, January 21, 2013. http://www.guardian.co.uk/world/2013/jan/21/algeria-hostage-crisis-survivors-accounts

783 Aomar Ouali and Elaine Ganley, "37 Foreign Hostages, Including 3 Americans, Dead in Algeria Gas Plant Siege," NBC News, January 21, 2013. http://www.nbcbayarea.com/news/national-international/NATL-37-Foreign-Hostages-Dead-Algeria-Gas-Plant-Siege-Standoff-Islamist -Al-Qaida-Militants-187727421.html

784 Pam Benson, "Five things we learned from John Brennan's confirmation hearing," CNN Security Clearance, February 7, 2013. http://security.blogs.cnn.com/2013/02/07/five-things-we-learned-from-john-brennans -confirmation-hearing/?hpt=hp_t2

785 Pam Benson, "Drone court considered," CNN Security Clearance, February 9,

2013. http://security.blogs.cnn.com/2013/02/09/legislators-consider -new-court-to-oversee-drone-strike-decisions/?hpt=hp_t3

786 Daniel Klaidman, "No More Drones for CIA," Daily Beast, March 19, 2013. http://www.thedailybeast.com/articles/2013/03/19/exclusive-no-more-drones-for-cia.html

787 Eliott C. McLaughlin, Jamie Crawford, and Joe Sterling, "Obama: U.S. will keep deploying drones—when they are only option," CNN News, May 23, 2013. http://www.cnn.com/2013/05/23/politics/obama-terror-speech/index.html?hpt=hp_t3http:/

788 Scahill, *Dirty Wars,* 100.

789 Karen DeYoung and Greg Jaffe, "U.S. 'secret war' expands globally as Special Operations forces take larger role," *Washington Post*, June 4, 2010. http://www.washingtonpost.com/wp-dyn/content/article/ 2010/06 /03/AR2010060304965.html?nav=emailpage

790 Ibid.

791 Mark Mazzetti, Helene Cooper, and Peter Baker, "Behind the Hunt for Bin Laden," *New York Times*, May 2, 2011. http://www.nytimes.com/2011/05/03/world/asia/03intel.html?_r=0

792 Interestingly, the published organizational charts for the CIA, the most recent version online as of this writing being 2009, do show the National Clandestine Service, but neither the Special Activities Division nor the Special Operations Group is pictured underneath it. https://www.cia.gov/library/publications/additional-publications/the-work-of-a-nation/cia-director-and-principles/70040_BLU_SEPT_07_OPA.pdf

793 DeYoung and Jaffe, "U.S. 'secret war' expands globally."

794 Ibid.

795 Peter Brookes, "Flashpoint: No bungle in the jungle," *Armed Forces Journal*, September 2007. http://www.armedforcesjournal.com/2007/09/ 2926516

796 Ibid.

797 Carlo Muñoz, "US to keep counterterrorism outpost in Philippines, despite peace deal," The Hill, September 8, 2012. http://thehill.com/blogs/defcon-hill/operations/260837-us-to-keep-counterterrorism-outpost-in-philippines-despite-peace-deal-#ixzz2I0RwbGTB

798 Wyatt Olson, "US troops see terrorism threat diminish on Philippine island of Mindanao," *Stars and Stripes*, September 28, 2012. http://www.stripes.com/news/us-troops-see-terrorism-threat-diminish-on-philippine-island-of-mindanao-1.191126

799 Scahill, *Dirty Wars*, 62.

800 Ibid., 62–63.

801 James Kitfield, "US Airpower in Africa," *Air Force Magazine*, June 2013. The base in Djibouti joins a similar operation out of Arba Minch in Ethiopia and the Seychelles in the Indian Ocean as key support sites for JSOC activities in the Horn of Africa region. Reports have some sixteen Predators deployed to Djibouti, but the small airfield there also supports anti-pirate activities in the region's waters, especially off Somalia. U.S. operations are based at Camp Lemonier, a former French Foreign Legion post. The airstrip itself has been expanded and services C-130 transports, Predators, American and French fighters, and attack helicopters, as well as Japanese P-3 patrol aircraft. http://www.airforcemag.com/MagazineArchive/Pages/2013/June%202013/0613africa.aspx

802 Scahill, *Dirty Wars*, 75–76.

803 Mary Friona and Claudine Ewing, "Lackawanna Six: Ten Years Later," WZRG-TV, September 14, 2012.Three men involved with the group escaped arrest, two were reportedly recruiters, and another eventually was arrested in Yemen, later escaping prison there and remaining involved in jihadi activity. Some of the Lackawanna Six

had actually left the Yemeni camps before the 9/11 attacks, in reaction to a visit by Osama bin Laden. http://www.wgrz.com/news/article/181654/1/Lackawanna-Six-Ten -Years-Later

804 "CJTF–HOA Under New Command," CJTF–HOA Public Affairs Office, May 2, 2009.

805 Shane Bauer, "U.S. Embassy hit in Yemen, raising militancy concerns," *Christian Science Monitor*, September 18, 2008. http://www.csmonitor .com/World/Middle-East/2008/0918/p07s02-wome.html

806 Ahmed Al-Haj, "Airstrike kills senior al-Qaida leader in Yemen," Associated Press, May 6, 2012. http://news.yahoo.com/airstrike-kills-senior-al-qaida-leader-yemen-185236164.html

807 Robert K. Ackerman, "Future Threats Drive U.S. Intelligence," *AFCEA* magazine, April 2008. http://www.afcea.org/content/?q=node/1548

808 "Kinetic Strikes in Afghanistan," *Air Force Magazine*, May 29, 2008.http://www.airforcemag.com/DRArchive/Pages/2008/May%202008/May%2029%202008/KineticStrikesinAfghanistan.aspx

809 Scahill, *Dirty Wars*, 303–306.

810 Combined Joint Task Force Horn of Africa. http://www.hoa.africom.mil/.

811 CNN wire staff, "Yemen-based al Qaeda group claims responsibility for parcel bomb plot," November 6, 2010. http://edition.cnn.com/2010/WORLD/meast/11/05/yemen.security.concern/?hpt=T2

812 Mohammed Al-Qadhi, "Militants killed in air attacks in south Yemen," *Washington Post*, August 1, 2011. http://www.washingtonpost.com/ world/middle-east/militants-killed-in-air-attacks-in-south-yemen/2011/08/01/gIQArZmDoI_story.html

813 Scahill, *Dirty Wars*, 119–122.

814 Ibid., 206–209.

815 Chris Welch, "Minnesota men charged in Somali bombing," CNN News, July 16, 2009. http://www.cnn.com/2009/CRIME/07/13/somalia .americans.killed/index.html?iref=allsearch

816 Associated Press, "2 Minnesota women sentenced in Somali terror case," CBS News,May 16,2013.http://www.cbsnews.com/8301-201_162-57584972/2-minnesota-women-sentenced-in-somali-terror-case/

817 Scahill, *Dirty Wars*, 219–222.

818 Ibid., 294–295.

819 Kitfield, "US Airpower in Africa."

820 Greg Jaffe and Karen DeYoung, "U.S. drone targets two leaders of Somali group allied with al-Qaeda, official says," *Washington Post*, June 29, 2011. http://articles.washingtonpost.com/2011-06-29/national/35234554_1_qaeda-somalia-strike-drone-strike

821 "U.S. Warplanes Enter Somalia Warspace," *New York Times*, January 13, 2013. http://www.nytimes.com/2013/01/14/world/africa/us-warplanes-enter-somali-airspace.html?ref=alshabab

822 Michael Pearson and Zain Verjee, "Questions linger after Kenya mall attack," CNN, September 25, 2013. http://www.cnn.com/2013/09/25/world/africa/kenya-mall-attack-aftermath/

823 Donna Miles, "New Counterterrorism Initiative to Focus on Saharan Africa," American Forces Press Service, May 16, 2005. http://web.archive.org/web/20070115212856/http://www.defenselink.mil/news/May 2005/20050516_1126 .html

824 Catherine Fellows, "US targets Sahara 'terrorist haven,'" BBC News, August 8, 2005. http://news.bbc.co.uk/2/hi/africa/4749357.stm

825 Lt. Colonel Mohamed Taghioullah Ould Nema, "The Rise in Terrorist Attacks in the Western Sahara," *Journal of ERW and Mine Action*, Issue 15.1, Spring 2011. http://www.jmu.edu/cisr/journal/pdfs/151.pdf

826 Horand Knaup, translated from the German by Jan Liebelt, "Suicide Attacks in Nigeria: Islamist Terror Network Gains Strength in Africa," Spiegel Online International, January 4, 2012. http://www.spiegel.de/international/world/suicide-attacks-in-nigeria-islamist-terror-network-gains-strength-in-africa-a-806749.html

827 Ingrid Formanek and Dana Ford, "U.S. steps up involvement in Mali," CNN, January 28, 2013. http://www.cnn.com/2013/01/26/world/africa/mali-unrest/index.html

828 Jim Garamone, "Africa Command Deploys 100 Service Members to Niger," American Forces Press Service, U.S. Department of Defense, February 22, 2013. http://www.defense.gov/news/newsarticle.aspx?id=119361

829 Colin Freeze and Renata D'Aliesio, "Two al-Qaeda notables reported killed in Mali," *Globe and Mail,* March 3, 2013. http://www.theglobeandmail.com/news/world/two-al-qaeda-notables-reported-killed-in-mali/article9254570/

830 Laura Smith-Spark and Vlad Duthiers, "Rebels still hold key town in Mali, French defense minister says," CNN News, January 16, 2013. http://www.cnn.com/2013/01/15/world/africa/mali-military-offensive/index.html

831 "Drone Wars Pakistan: Analysis," New America Foundation, 2004–2013. http://counterterrorism.newamerica.net/drones

832 Chris Woods and Alice K. Ross, "Revealed: US and Britain launched 1,200 drone strikes in recent wars," Bureau of Investigative Journalism, December 4, 2012. http://www.thebureauinvestigates.com/ 2012/12/04/revealed-us-and-britain-launched-1200-drone-strikes-in-recent-wars/

833 Pam Benson with John Berman, "Obama to name John Brennan to lead CIA," CNN Security Clearance, January 7, 2013. http://security.blogs.cnn.com/2013/01/07/obama-to-name-john-brennan-to-lead-cia/

834 Nic Robertson, "In Swat Valley, U.S. drone strikes radicalizing a new generation," CNN News, April 15, 2013. http://www.cnn.com/2013/04/14/world/asia/pakistan-swat-valley-school/index.html?hpt=hp_c3

835 Frida Ghitis, "The real enemy in London hacking death," CNN Opinion, May 23, 2013. http://www.cnn.com/2013/05/23/opinion/ghitis-ideology-hacking-death/index.html?hpt=hp_t1

836 Amy McCullough, "Boosting State Partnerships in Africa, Europe," *Air Force Magazine*, March 18, 2013. http://www.airforcemag.com/DRArchive/Pages/2013/March%202013/March%2018%202013/BoostingStatePartnershipsinAfrica,Europe.aspx

837 General Carter Ham, United States Africa Command, Statement to House Armed Services Committee, March 15, 2013. http://docs.house.gov/meetings/AS/AS00/20130315/100396/HHRG-113-AS00-Wstate-HamUSAG-20130315.pdf

838 "Looking beyond Afghanistan for Special Operations," *Air Force Magazine* Daily Report eNewsletter, May 13, 2013. http://www.airforcemag.com/_layouts/AFA/DailyHtml.aspx?ReportDate=05%2f13%2f2013

839 Bryan Monroe, "Five things we learned from Obama's speech," CNN Politics, May 24, 2013. http://www.cnn.com/2013/05/23/politics/5-things-obama-terror/index.html?hpt=hp_t3

840 Kevin Liptak, "New terror stance worries Republicans," CNN Politics, May 26, 2013. http://politicalticker.blogs.cnn.com/2013/05/26/new-terror -stance-worries-republicans/

841 "Text of Obama's Speech at the U.N.," *New York Times*, September 24, 2013. http://www.nytimes.com/2013/09/25/us/politics/text-of-obamas-speech-at-the-un.html?pagewanted=all&_r=0

842 Unclassified Report, Accountability Review Board for Benghazi, United States Department of State. http://www.state.gov/documents/organization/ 202446.pdf

843 Michael Kelley, "There's a Reason Why All of the Reports About Benghazi Are

So Confusing," *Business Insider*, November 3, 2012. http://www.businessinsider.com/benghazi-stevens-cia-attack-libya-2012-11

844 Adam Entous, Siobhan Gorman, and Margaret Coker, "CIA Takes Heat for Role in Libya," November 1, 2012, *Wall Street Journal*. http://online.wsj.com/article/SB10001424052970204712904578092853621061838.html

845 Eric Schmitt, "CIA Said to Aid in Steering Arms to Syrian Opposition," *New York Times*, June 21, 2012. http://www.nytimes.com/2012/06/21/world/middleeast/cia-said-to-aid-in-steering-arms-to-syrian-rebels.html?pagewanted=all

846 Michael Kelley, "The CIA's Benghazi Operation May Have Violated International Law," *Business Insider*, November 5, 2012. http://www.businessinsider.com/us-sending-heavy-weapons-is-a-problem-2012-11

847 C.J. Chivers and Eric Schmitt, "Arms Airlift to Syria Rebels Expands, with Aid from C.I.A.," *New York Times*, March 24, 2013. http://www.nytimes.com/2013/03/25/world/middleeast/arms-airlift-to-syrian-rebels-expands-with-cia-aid.html?pagewanted=all

848 C.J. Chivers and Eric Schmitt, "Saudis Step Up Help for Rebels in Syria with Croatian Arms," *New York Times*, February 25, 2013. http://www.nytimes.com/2013/02/26/world/middleeast/in-shift-saudis-are-said-to-arm-rebels-in-syria.html

849 Khaled Yacoub Oweis, "Large arms shipment reaches Syrian rebels: opposition," Reuters News Service, August 25, 2013. http://www.reuters.com/article/2013/08/25/us-syria-crisis-arms-idUSBRE97 O04T20130825

850 Rania Abouzeid, "Syrian Opposition Groups Stop Pretending," News Desk, *New Yorker*, September 26, 2013. http://www.newyorker.com/online/blogs/newsdesk/2013/09/#slide_ss_0=1

851 Ben Hubbard and Michael R. Gordon, "Key Syrian Rebel Groups Abandon Exile Leaders," *New York Times*, September 25, 2013. http://www.nytimes.com/2013/09/26/world/middleeast/syria-crisis.html?_r=0

852 Paul Cruickshank, Tim Lister, Nic Robertson, and Fran Townsend, "Sources: three al Qaeda operatives took part in Benghazi attack," CNN, May 4, 2013. http://www.cnn.com/2013/05/02/world/africa/us-libya-benghazi-suspects

853 Erin Burnett, "Benghazi attack timeline," CNN Politics, August 7, 2013. http://www.cnn.com/2013/08/06/politics/benghazi-attack-timeline/index.html

Index

Q

R